TRADITION AND MODERNIZATION
IN JAPANESE CULTURE

This is the fifth in a series of six volumes to be published by Princeton University Press for the Conference on Modern Japan of the Association for Asian Studies, Inc. The others in the series are:

Changing Japanese Attitudes Toward Modernization, edited by Marius B. Jansen (1965)

The State and Economic Enterprise in Japan, edited by William W. Lockwood (1965)

Aspects of Social Change in Modern Japan, edited by R. P. Dore (1967)

Political Development in Modern Japan, edited by Robert E. Ward (1968)

Dilemmas of Growth in Prewar Japan, edited by James William Morley (1971)

Tradition
and Modernization
in Japanese Culture

Edited by

DONALD H. SHIVELY

CONTRIBUTORS

CARMEN BLACKER	ROY ANDREW MILLER
ROBERT H. BROWER	MICHIO NAGAI
TŌRU HAGA	BENITO ORTOLANI
HOWARD S. HIBBETT	JOHN M. ROSENFIELD
DONALD KEENE	EDWARD SEIDENSTICKER
WILLIAM P. MALM	DONALD H. SHIVELY
EDWIN McCLELLAN	EUGENE SOVIAK

VALDO HUMBERT VIGLIELMO

PRINCETON UNIVERSITY PRESS

PRINCETON, NEW JERSEY

This book has been composed in Linotype Granjon
Printed in the United States of America
by Princeton University Press, Princeton, New Jersey

First PRINCETON PAPERBACK Printing, 1976

Contents

Foreword—JOHN WHITNEY HALL   vii

Editor's Preface—DONALD H. SHIVELY   xi

PART ONE: STRATEGIES FOR MODERNIZING

I. On the Nature of Western Progress:
The Journal of the Iwakura Embassy—
EUGENE SOVIAK   7

II. Westernization and Japanization: The Early
Meiji Transformation of Education—
MICHIO NAGAI   35

III. The Japanization of the Middle Meiji—
DONALD H. SHIVELY   77

IV. The Sino-Japanese War of 1894-95 and Its
Cultural Effects in Japan—DONALD KEENE   121

PART TWO: THE ARTS IN THE MEIJI PERIOD

V. Western Style Painting in the Early Meiji
Period and Its Critics—JOHN M. ROSENFIELD   181

VI. The Formation of Realism in Meiji Painting:
The Artistic Career of Takahashi Yuichi—
TŌRU HAGA   221

VII. The Modern Music of Meiji Japan—
WILLIAM P. MALM   257

PART THREE: THE SEARCH FOR IDENTITY IN LITERATURE

VIII. Natsume Sōseki and the Psychological Novel—
HOWARD S. HIBBETT   305

IX. Tōson and the Autobiographical Novel—
EDWIN MC CLELLAN   347

CONTENTS

X. Masaoka Shiki and Tanka Reform—
ROBERT H. BROWER
379

XI. Kobayashi Hideo—EDWARD SEIDENSTICKER   419

XII. Fukuda Tsuneari: Modernization and
Shingeki—BENITO ORTOLANI   463

PART FOUR: PHILOSOPHY, RELIGION, AND LANGUAGE

XIII. Nishida Kitarō: The Early Years—
VALDO HUMBERT VIGLIELMO
507

XIV. Millenarian Aspects of the New Religions in
Japan—CARMEN BLACKER   563

XV. Levels of Speech (*keigo*) and the Japanese
Linguistic Response to Modernization—
ROY ANDREW MILLER   601

List of Contributors   669

Index   673

List of Illustrations

(following pages 206 and 238)

CHAPTER IV—DONALD KEENE

I. Migita Toshihide. "The Surrender of Wei-hai-wei by Ting Ju-ch'ang."

II. Bairin. "Astonishment of Li Hung-chang on hearing the report of the capture of Port Arthur by our troops."

III. Kobayashi Kiyochika. "Naval engagement off P'ung-do in Korea."

CHAPTER V—JOHN M. ROSENFIELD

I. Koyama Shōtarō. "Kawakami Tōgai."

II. Yokoyama Taikan. "Ch'ü Yüan."

III. Kawakami Tōgai. "Kayabemine District."

CHAPTER VI—TŌRU HAGA

I. Takahashi Yuichi. "Sake."

II. Takahashi Yuichi. "Oiran-zu."

CHAPTER VII—WILLIAM P. MALM

I. Cover of *Collection of Japanese Popular Music* (1892)

II. Illustration in *Tekukin Dokukeiko* (1894)

Foreword

SCHOLARLY studies of Japan have had a truly remarkable growth in the United States and other English-speaking countries in the years following World War II. To some extent this has been the natural result of the popular boom of interest in Japan stimulated by the war and its aftermath and by the increased opportunities which Westerners have had to associate with the Japanese people. But it is more directly the result of the spread of academic programs devoted to Japan and particularly the growing number of specialists trained to handle the Japanese language.

In the fall of 1958 a group of scholars gathered at the University of Michigan to seek some means of bringing together in more systematic fashion the results of the widely scattered studies of Japan which had begun to appear in the years since the end of the war. The Conference on Modern Japan which resulted from this meeting was dedicated both to the pooling of existing scholarly findings and to the possibility of stimulating new ideas and approaches to the study of modern Japan. Subsequently the Conference received a generous grant from the Ford Foundation for the support of a series of five annual seminars devoted to as many aspects of the history of Japan's modern development. Later the number of seminars was expanded to six.

The Conference on Modern Japan existed from 1959 to 1969 as a special project of the Association for Asian Studies. The Conference was guided by an executive committee consisting of Ronald P. Dore, Marius B. Jansen, William W. Lockwood, Donald H. Shively, Robert E. Ward, and John W. Hall (chairman). James W. Morley subsequently joined this group as the leader of the sixth seminar. Each member of the executive committee was made responsible for the organization of a separate seminar devoted to his particular field of specialization and for the publication of the proceedings of his seminar.

Although the subject of modernization *in the abstract* was not of primary concern to the Conference, conceptual problems were inevitably of interest to the entire series of seminars. Because of this, two less formal discussions on the theory of modernization were planned as part of the Conference's program. The first of these, organized by John Hall, was held in Japan during the summer of 1960. Now commonly known as the "Hakone Conference," it has been reported on as part of the first volume of published proceedings. A second informal meeting, held in Bermuda in January of 1967, was devoted to a review of the contributions to theory made by the five seminars which had been held up to that point. One outcome of this meeting was the establishment of the Social Science Research Council—American Council of Learned Societies Joint Committee on Japanese Studies and the drafting of plans for a new series of seminars which will place more emphasis upon the comparative dimensions of Japanese studies.

The present volume edited by Professor Donald Shively is the fifth in a series of six published for the Conference on Modern Japan by the Princeton University Press. The other volumes, of which the first four have already appeared, are: *Changing Japanese Attitudes Toward Modernization,* edited by Marius B. Jansen; *The State and Economic Enterprise in Japan,* edited by William W. Lockwood; *Aspects of Social Change in Modern Japan,* edited by Ronald P. Dore; *Political Development in Modern Japan,* edited by Robert E. Ward; and *Dilemmas of Growth in Prewar Japan,* edited by James W. Morley.

As their titles suggest, the annual seminars have adopted broad themes so as to include a wide variety of scholars working within each of several major fields of interest. Within these broad fields, however, the seminar chairmen have focused upon specific problems recommended either because they have received the greatest attention of Japanese specialists or because they have seemed most likely to contribute to a fuller understanding of the modernization of Japan. We trust, as a consequence, that the six volumes taken together will prove both representative of the current scholarship on Japan and comprehensive in their coverage of one of the most fascinating stories of national development in modern history.

The fifth seminar of the Conference on Modern Japan met in Puerto Rico in January of 1966 under the chairmanship of Professor Donald Shively. Assistance in organizing the seminar was given by Professors Howard S. Hibbett and Donald Keene. The subject of discussion was cultural change in modern Japan as revealed in the fields of thought, language, education, philosophy, literature, and the arts. In all, twenty-one scholars from Japan, the United States, England, and Italy participated in the conference. In addition to the authors of papers contained in this volume, the following individuals were present: Professors Nathan Glazer, Harvard University; John W. Hall, Yale University; Sei Itō, University of Tokyo; Marius B. Jansen, Princeton University; Richard N. McKinnon, University of Washington; and Robert E. Ward, University of Michigan. All contributed most usefully to the discussion, and the editor and authors would like to express their gratitude to them.

JOHN WHITNEY HALL

xi

Editor's Preface

IN 1868 the new Meiji government stated its intention to abandon benighted traditions and to borrow extensively from the West. This, of course, was not the beginning of the modernizing process. For some decades behind the facade of the shogun-daimyo political structure, knowledge and technology introduced from the West had increasingly been put to use. And prior to that, for a century or more of development largely unaffected by Western influence—in education, in intellectual life, in social organization, and in commerce—traditional culture was undergoing changes which were to have some bearing on the rapid pace of modernization after the Meiji Restoration.

The papers presented here, like those in the earlier volumes of this series, deal largely with changes that have taken place in the process of transforming Japan into a modern country in the century since the Meiji Restoration. On the surface Japan appears to have turned away from her past traditions to follow Western models. But a close examination of the individual cases dealt with here reveals that the general product owed more than might be suspected to the quality of Japanese tradition.

The preceding volumes were shaped to a large degree around disciplinary topics. Beginning with intellectual history, the conferences for which these papers were written went on to deal with economic growth, social change, and political development. There remain other areas of life which should be represented in any comprehensive survey of Japan's development. One is the "cultural" sphere, which is our assignment. Even such a broad term as "culture," however, may not suggest all that should be included. Besides the arts, which are clearly central to our concern, we have attempted to touch on subjects such as language, education, philosophy, and religion. All of these are in themselves very large fields which, in fact, include a variety of different activities that should be described individually. For example, literature, fine arts, and the performing arts each encompass several genres or media, and within almost every genre there are several styles or schools. The number of religious sects in Japan runs into the hundreds, and the philosophical styles typically defy categorization. It is obvious that an attempt to write surveys of such broad fields would result in chapters so general as to make little contribution to our present knowledge.

Instead, most of the papers in this volume are studies in some depth of individual people, styles, or phenomena. It is only when a subject is treated in detail that we can discern the fine texture created by the action of new forces on traditional ways. Among the papers in the volume are studies of two novelists, one poet, one critic, one playwright, one philosopher, and two oil painters. We would not wish to claim that they are particularly representative. Of all the professions there is none more concerned with developing individual viewpoint and style than the modern writer, artist, and philosopher. We would call them creative rather than representative, pioneers in the process of reshaping their fields at a time when their society was undergoing rapid transformation.

In a country embarking on a program of planned modernization of its government institutions, educational system, industry, and transport, it is of course inevitable that there will be changes in the social and economic life of the people. It follows that most forms of cultural activity will be affected sooner or later by the changes taking place in society. Extensive changes in cultural life could be anticipated in Japan, because there was remarkably little opposition to change in other areas. Within a few years after the Restoration there was nearly universal and generally enthusiastic acceptance of the concept of progress and the necessity to modernize. Differences of opinion were limited mainly to the question of what modernization meant in specific measures, that is, what were the things that needed to be reformed and according to which model or plan should they be changed.

Modernization progressed rapidly in the more technical sectors such as transportation and industry, where there was less necessity for delay to consider alternatives or to overcome resistance. The practical desirability of railways and the telegraph, the presumed need for a modern army and navy, placed the first priorities there and on other such unquestionably functional items. Straightforward steps led directly to impressive results. The government also gave high priority to the reorganization of political institutions and the educational system, and although the course of development in these areas was modified frequently in the early stages on the basis of experience or because of criticism and pressure from groups both inside and outside the government, they were carried forward purposefully to serve practical ends in the building of a modern nation.

Innovation in cultural areas came about quite differently. The arts had a far lower priority in government concern. The artist or writer was relatively free of suggestions from the government that he serve national needs, but he was also without government sponsorship or encouragement, and he proceeded very slowly in making his own way. His livelihood depended on a public which would accept and support his efforts. The emergence of such a public was a gradual process, the product of modern education and industrial and commercial development. It is to be expected, then, that the appearance of mature works in cultural fields would lag behind modernization in other areas.

Our concern in this volume is largely to develop empirical data in the form of case studies in a variety of cultural fields. It would divert us from our primarily humanistic interests to reopen problems of definition and theory in studies of modernization. But to attempt to relate cultural changes to modernization taking place in other sectors of a society is to venture into an area that has been investigated very little. And it is quite apparent that by getting into uncharted regions, we encounter rather new problems of definition and methodology. How does one measure modernization in the arts, in philosophy, or in religion? While it is not difficult to recognize Western influences in Japan, to what extent does their adoption constitute modernization? The change in Japan was not simply from a premodern to a modern society, but from a relatively isolated, extraordinarily homogeneous, native tradition in Asia to one extremely receptive to borrowing from the West.

In cultural subjects we see from a somewhat different perspective the distinctions between Westernization and modernization, and the interaction between these two trends and the contribution of native traditions, which in some instances play only a passive, residual role, but in others constitute a resurgent force.

Parts One and Two of this volume deal with the first decades of change after the Restoration, and the papers are concerned primarily with how the Japanese went about borrowing from the West once the decision to modernize became official policy. The emphasis in the first papers is on the formulation of the strategies for modernizing, and how they were put into practice. These are followed by accounts of the early Meiji experience in oil painting and music, where the purpose was to adopt and adapt Western models.

The latter two parts of the book deal mostly with the twentieth century. By this time the West itself has changed greatly. Japan has become a world power and is increasingly confident and sophisticated in its evaluation of the West. What it means to be modern changes constantly. The problems facing literary men at this time are considerably more complex than in earlier times as they search for their own identity and the position of modern Japanese society in the contemporary world. The adjustment of the individual to modernization (or his maladjustment) is a recurring theme in this volume, much more than in earlier volumes. It is illustrated with particular intensity in the experience of writers and, of course, in philosophy and religion. Here we begin to see more of the darker side, the pathology of modernization. The emphasis of the second half of the volume, therefore, shifts slightly from Western innovation in the earlier period, to the effects that progressive modernization had on culture in an increasingly complex society.

DONALD H. SHIVELY

Strategies for Modernizing

Introduction

THOSE ungainly words—Westernization, modernization, Japanization—give us some rough measure of successive shifts in Japan's course during the first three decades after the Meiji Restoration. Although all three tendencies are present continuously, sometimes reinforcing each other, sometimes working at cross purposes, the emphasis changes from one to another with the accumulation of knowledge and experience.

In the process of studying the West for its practical lessons, the Japanese became increasingly discriminating in their understanding of differences among the many Western countries. They became aware that the more advanced Western countries had become "modern" only a few decades earlier, and that there were European countries which could not yet be called modern. And if the West offered examples of institutions which were liberal and progressive, it also provided models of authoritarian institutions more in keeping with Japanese traditions—or at least with the objectives of the government leadership. As the distinction between Westernization and modernization became better understood, there was more concern in some quarters as to how Japan could modernize without losing, under the flood of headlong Westernization, the qualities that were uniquely Japanese. In reexamining Japan's history and traditional values, it was not always easy to agree upon what these qualities were, but there was no mistaking the upsurge of national consciousness. While this Japanization checked some trends in Westernization, it also helped to maintain national unity and consensus, and in this way it appears to have benefited modernization, at least in the short run.

The first three papers in this volume illustrate some of the complexities of the trends roughly categorized as Westernization, modernization, and Japanization. We find that the

3

ingredients under these labels—the policies and innovations that they refer to—change with the passing years, and that from one decade to the next they come to represent somewhat different phenomena.

The Iwakura Embassy of 1871 to 1873, described by Professor Soviak, made a systematic survey of Western countries and suggested some of the practical steps that should be taken to modernize Japan. There had been earlier surveys of the West, and numerous measures toward modernization had already been taken. But the effectiveness of the Embassy lies in the fact that many of its members, upon their return, occupied key positions in government and could set about at once implementing programs according to their findings. The first priorities went to innovations in Western technology, administrative institutions, and education, carried out with the help of foreign advisors in a spirit of apprenticeship to the West.

Professor Nagai is concerned with some of the complications that arose during the succeeding decade or two as a result of following too closely models of school systems found in the West. The new educational system announced by the government in 1872 met with criticism and resistance, which contributed to several changes in direction before its course was steadied. The new centralized school system was violently attacked for its foreign curriculum, which some feared would displace traditional values. On closer examination, this resistance was more than merely a native reaction to Westernization. The emotional issue of national consciousness masked other reasons for dissatisfaction, such as the problem of local financing for a new school system which was little understood and which was centrally controlled. These are the same kinds of issues that would arise in any country attempting to implement a radical reform program. Over the course of nearly two decades we see experimentation with a series of modified Western models, each tested against Japanese tradition and needs and against another factor, a non-cultural element—

the amount of economic investment in education that the nation can tolerate at a given time.

Donald Shively's paper on Japanization deals with the ground swell of nativist reaction in the years around 1890, which included a wide range of viewpoints, from reactionary old Confucianists educated before the Restoration to progressive young reformers whose education had been largely of the Western type. Alarmed by the relentless deluge of Westernizing measures, many Japanese were especially anxious to retain a knowledge of their traditions and to preserve a sense of national identity. The result was more than a culturally reactionary attitude, for it led to the strengthening of national self-consciousness, a distinguishing characteristic of modern nations. Their Japanization was not so much resistance to Western civilization as disaffection with many of the programs and procedures of the oligarchs, whose policy of heedless Westernization was one of the more conspicuous sources of irritation.

The new national self-consciousness and sense of national identity articulated in some quarters in the late eighties spread throughout the country as a result of the effort made by the entire nation in the Sino-Japanese War of 1894-95. It was Japan's first foreign war in three centuries. Her quick and decisive victory over a far larger foe astonished the world. Popular enthusiasm for the war and its great success fanned to a flame a modern nationalism of the type that existed in Western countries in the late nineteenth century. Moreover, the war was an international demonstration of how effective the process of Japan's modernization had been in the military and technological sector, including the mobilization of human and material resources. But the rapidity of Japan's modernization in this area stands in contrast to the slow pace of development in the cultural sphere. We find in Professor Keene's account of the cultural effects the war had in Japan that a war can provide the occasion and stimulus for modernizing developments in journalism and language, in newspapers and magazines, in illustrating and in song. Whatever the quality of the products, they represented the new stage of modernization that comes with the development of media which reach a far larger segment of the population.

CHAPTER I

On the Nature of Western Progress: The Journal of the Iwakura Embassy

EUGENE SOVIAK

WITH the Iwakura Mission, Japan made an important step toward joining the modern world. In November 1871, Iwakura Tomomi, Itō Hirobumi, Kido Takayoshi, and Ōkubo Toshimichi set out with nearly a hundred other Japanese to visit the United States and Europe in an attempt to begin preliminary discussions for revision of the unequal treaties and at the same time to find out as much as they could about their great adversary and model, the West. When they returned in September 1873, they had made little ostensible progress toward revising the treaties, which persisted until 1899, but they had learned about the West. They had learned enough to realize that drastic political, judicial, and social reforms along Western lines, in addition to technological innovation and knowledge of international law, were necessary before Japan could hope to negotiate on an equal footing with the West. And they had begun to realize the enormity of the task that faced them as they recognized the practical problems and the dangers involved in transplanting Western civilization to Japanese soil. They saw more clearly than ever before that Japan could not compete with the wealth and power of the West.

In the meantime, of course, the "caretaker" government left behind, including Saigō Takamori of Satsuma, Itagaki Taisuke of Tosa, and Ōkuma Shigenobu of Hizen, despite a pledge to make no major innovations while the embassy was away, had confidently proceeded with plans for the invasion of Korea. In the controversy that ensued upon the mission's return, the envoys' experiences during nearly two years abroad

7

had a decisive influence. In October 1873, after lengthy debates that shook the entire government, the plans for a Korean invasion were abandoned in favor of internal reform, and Saigō, Itagaki, and several others resigned their posts to organize opposition to the government.[1] A significant turn in Meiji government policy had occurred, largely as a result of what the embassy had learned abroad. Moreover, since members of the embassy were to wield great political power through the next decades of Meiji, it was largely they who determined the course of Japan's rapid modernization.

That the Iwakura Mission was one significant factor in the development of modern Japan is unquestionable. The Taishō and Shōwa statesman Makino Nobuaki (second son of Ōkubo), who went along on the mission as a student and was himself strongly influenced by the experience, remarked in his memoirs, "Together with the abolition of the *han*, dispatching the Iwakura Mission to America and Europe must be cited as the most important of the events that built the foundation of our state after the Restoration."[2] Even allowing for a certain measure of subjective bias in such a statement, it is nonetheless curious that an event thus appraised should have received so little attention from historians. The Iwakura Mission has been examined only rarely, except within the context of Japanese diplomatic history. This relative neglect is particularly surprising and regrettable since the embassy produced such a massive official report, the *Tokumei zenken taishi Bei-Ō kairan jikki* (Journal of the Envoy Extraordinary

[1] Saigō went back to Satsuma and rallied discontented conservatives from the old order, who were to break out in open rebellion in 1877. Itagaki took a progressive stand and left with Soejima Taneomi, Gotō Shōjirō, and Etō Shimpei to form the People's Rights Party (*Minkentō*). In January 1874 they presented a memorial demanding the immediate establishment of a popularly elected national assembly. Ōkuma stayed on in the government until 1881, when he too resigned in protest against his colleagues' gradualist policies and the long delay in instituting a parliamentary system.

[2] Makino Nobuaki, *Kaisō roku*, 1 (Tokyo, 1948), 44-45.

Ambassador Plenipotentiary's Travels through America and Europe) (five volumes, 1878), a minute record of impressions and reactions which amounts, in fact, to a thorough and systematic assessment of the West. Coming as it did at a crucial moment in Japanese history, this assessment was of considerable importance in setting the patterns of reform policy in early Meiji. The report is important, too, because it reflects the outlook of the embassy members, among whom were included so many of the very leaders of the Meiji state. If, as this writer feels, the *Jikki* provides significant insights into the nature of this all-important elite's experience abroad, their attitudes toward modernization, and their reassessment of their own tradition, then study of the work in terms of intellectual and cultural history is long overdue.[3]

Moreover, the work is significant in its own right, as an "enlightenment document" articulating the new preoccupations and expectations of the times. In this respect it is no less impressive than its more celebrated counterparts, Fukuzawa Yukichi's *Bummeiron no gairyaku* (An Outline of Civilization) (1876), and Taguchi Ukichi's *Nihon kaika shōshi* (A Short History of Japan's Enlightenment) (1877-82). In a sense, the *Jikki* is but one link, though a vital one, in a long tradition of learning from abroad. It is another specific illumination of the more positive phase of that acceptance-rejection pattern typical of Japan's cross-cultural relations.

The Iwakura Embassy was the first official diplomatic mission abroad since the Meiji Restoration. It was the first Japanese mission designed according to the principles of Western diplomacy. It was perhaps the first mission in world history to include such a large proportion of a country's leadership,

---

[3] Some sensitive essays on the *Jikki* have been done by Haga Tōru in his lengthy "Meiji shoki ichi chishikijin no seiyō taiken," *Shimada Kinji kyōju kanreki kinen rombunshū* (Tokyo, 1961); and his shorter work, "Kindai Nihon no sekkei: Iwakura shisetsudan no Bei-Ō kairan," *Jiyū* (Tokyo, Nov., 1964). Katō Shūichi devotes a section to the *Jikki* in his "Nihonjin no sekaizō," *Kindai Nihon shisōshi kōza*, viii (Tokyo, 1961), 234-43.

9

sent abroad for an extended period at a time of national crisis. But it was not an entirely new idea. Some of the Bakumatsu missions (in 1862 and 1867, for example) had engaged in cultural inquiry of a similar nature, although much more limited in scope. In contrast to the narrow perspectives of these earlier missions, the Iwakura Mission was planned in an atmosphere of flexibility and receptivity to change. There was now the firm intention of applying what they learned from the West to the problems of Japan. There was a pre-departure aura of confidence that this examination of the West would reveal the ultimate sources of Western power and wealth. There was, too, a sense of a final closing in on the West that would enable prompt achievement of equality in all areas.

The Meiji government had been committed from the outset to rational, deliberate reform in all spheres. Some administrative, legal, economic, and social reforms had been carried out by 1871, but most of what had been done since the Restoration had been haphazard, the result of policy based on stopgap solutions to daily problems. Guiding principles and a long-range program were needed, and these the Iwakura Mission was intended to provide—a philosophy and a blueprint for modernization, based on a definitive "empirical" exposure of the West's secrets of success.

The specific objectives of the mission, as set forth in a letter from Prime Minister Sanjō Sanetomi to Foreign Minister Iwakura in October 1871, were threefold.[4] First, it was to be a mission of friendship to the governments of the fifteen countries with which Japan had official diplomatic relations.

[4] The text of Sanjō's letter is quoted in *Iwakura Kō jikki* (Tokyo, 1906), II, 926-34. The genesis of the mission is expertly reconstructed by M. J. Mayo in "Rationality in the Meiji Restoration: The Iwakura Embassy," in Harootunian and Silberman, eds., *Modern Japanese Leadership* (Tucson, 1966), pp. 323-69. See also M. J. Mayo, "The Iwakura Mission to the United States and Europe, 1871-1873," in *Researches in the Social Sciences on Japan*, Columbia University East Asian Institute (New York, June 1959), 6: 28-47.

Second, the ambassadors were to begin treaty revision negotiations with the foreign heads of government themselves,
although just how far the Japanese envoys were authorized to
negotiate was a matter of considerable controversy. Third and
most important, the mission was to be a learning expedition.

The composition of the group was determined accordingly.
At the top were the ambassador and vice-ambassadors, all of
whom had experience in foreign affairs and some knowledge
of the West and were chosen from among the real leaders of
the government. Below them were commissioners, experts in
various fields and taken mainly from the ministries. Under
the commissioners were numerous assistants, secretaries, and
translators, the ablest young members of the bureaucracy.
Finally, about half the group was made up of students. The
mission was headed by Iwakura, Minister of Foreign Affairs,
who was promoted at the time to Minister of the Right. He
held the title Envoy Extraordinary Ambassador Plenipotentiary (*tokumei zenken taishi*), the highest in the series of
ranks created in 1871 to correspond with Western diplomatic
ranks. There were four vice-ambassadors (*fuku zenken
taishi*): Ōkubo, Minister of Finance; Kido, a member of the
Council of State; Itō, Vice-Minister of Industry; and Yamaguchi Naoyoshi, an Assistant Vice-Minister of Foreign
Affairs. The list of commissioners (*rijikan*) included Sasaki
Takamori, Vice-Minister of Justice; Tanaka Fujimaro, an
official in the Ministry of Education; Yamada Akiyoshi, Lieutenant General in the Imperial Army; and seven others.[5]

All members of the embassy, including the ambassadors,
were to take part in the study of Western institutions and culture, but it was the responsibility of the commissioners and
their assistants and secretaries to compile the official reports
to be submitted to the government upon the mission's return.
Vice-Ambassador Kido, for instance, took personal charge of

[5] The entire list of the embassy contingency is given in Charles
Lanman, *The Japanese in America* (Tokyo, 1872), pp. 8-9.

law and government, and he supervised the work of Tanaka Fujimaro and First Secretary Ga Noriyuki from the Ministry of Foreign Affairs, in a study of American legal and administrative procedures.

In addition to nine major cities in the United States, members of the embassy traveled to England and Scotland, France, Belgium, the Netherlands, Germany, Russia, Denmark, Sweden, Italy, Austria, and Switzerland. They had intended to go to Spain and Portugal, but were prevented from doing so by the Spanish Civil War. They did not all travel together but broke up into smaller groups according to interest and specialty, and the groups often went their own ways, some visiting iron mines, for example, while others investigated the public school systems. Some of them went to special exhibitions, notably the International Exhibition in Vienna, which Iwakura and Itō attended in 1873 to see the modern products and recent inventions displayed. It was the Iwakura Embassy, too, that made the first contacts with the eminent German scholars Rudolph von Gneist and Lorenz von Stein, whose political thought was later to be so influential with the Meiji government elite.

The results of the Iwakura Embassy's prodigious cooperative efforts are meticulously recorded in the mission's only published official report, the *Jikki* mentioned above. A superficial scanning of the *Jikki*'s approximately two thousand pages might suggest little more than a wearisome travelogue of America and Europe, with some hurried glances at Africa and Asia. Naturally, a substantial portion of the work consists of schedules, statistics, and descriptions of landmarks and industrial processes. The physical descriptions and the pictures, which abound, no doubt made the West come alive for those who had to content themselves with secondhand accounts. But the *Jikki* undertakes much more than a travelogue of Western exotica. It is actually a presentation on several levels. One of these, of course, is the day-by-day, almost hour-by-hour, account of the embassy's travels per se. Another is the seemingly endless recitation of facts and figures. Still another is the interpretive commentary woven throughout all five volumes, as reflective asides accompanying banal observations on bridge lengths or bread baking. This commentary is then expanded and more carefully organized and presented as reflective essays in the last volume. While this last level is obviously the most interesting, the statistics should not be neglected altogether, since they provide a sort of quantitative counterpoint, a valuable support for the generalizations.

The *Jikki* is the work of many minds though the product of a single brush. It was written by the embassy's diarist, Kume Kunitake, who served as Iwakura's chief secretary. Kume continued research and study after the embassy's return to Japan, and before completing the *Jikki*, which was not published until October 1878, he apparently consulted with many of the specialists assigned to specific topics abroad, several of whom had compiled their own reports. The *Jikki* is therefore the collective expression of various points of view, though it is doubtless imprinted with the stamp of the author's personality.

Kume Kunitake was particularly well suited to the task of compiling such a work. He was born in Saga in 1839, and his formative years were spent in the midst of the innovations and experiments in industrial enterprise, armaments, and shipbuilding for which that *han* was known. Saga, of course, was the home of Nagasaki, where there was a considerable European population, as well as a famous center for Western studies. Closely associated with the progressive daimyo of Saga, Kume was at the very center of the intellectually exciting *han* atmosphere. Later he was to study in Edo at the Shōheikō, the official Bakufu Confucian school which had its beginnings in the seventeenth century under Hayashi Razan. Thus he had a foothold in both the new Japan and the old. Shortly after the Restoration, he became a clerk in the Meiji government bureaucracy. His specialty was law, and while abroad he conducted a study of the French constitutional system in addition to preparing the *Jikki*.

In a sense, the *Jikki* is a kind of culmination of the in-process examination of Western civilization, examination which was formally concluded with the drafting of the Meiji Constitution in 1889 but continued on many other levels throughout the Meiji period. The work is, as Marius Jansen characterizes it, "the last and the greatest of the documents filed by Japanese learning missions."[6]

One basic theme pervades the *Jikki*: the implicit question, What is the nature of the West, and how are its wealth, power, and enlightenment to be accounted for? In other words, How did the West get that way? Most important of all was the complementary question, How could Japan get that way? It is the *Jikki*'s proposed answers to these questions, and some of the implications of the answers, which will concern me here. A detailed analysis of such an expansive work, however, is beyond the scope of this paper. I hope simply to give a general picture of what the *Jikki* is like and to indicate in broad terms its attitudes toward the West and modernization. I have relied heavily on direct quotation to convey the flavor of the work.

The *Jikki* sees all the nations of the West as engaged in a struggle for wealth and power. This struggle takes the form of a vast race for progress, with enormous expenditure of natural and human resources on all sides. It is true that there are variations in approach, and varying degrees of success, but the ends are always the same: to get ahead in the world. Any country that refuses to compete, or is too late in starting, will in the end be overwhelmed by its most powerful opponents. Thus all are forced into furious participation, and as history proceeds the present unevenness of development among West-

[6] Marius B. Jansen, "Changing Japanese Attitudes Toward Modernization," in Marius B. Jansen, ed., *Changing Japanese Attitudes Toward Modernization* (Princeton, 1963), pp. 68-69.

ern nations will level off somewhat. Even Africa and Asia are passively involved in the struggle. Lethargic and backward themselves, they are victims of Western colonialism. This constant competition is the West's "warfare of peacetime."[7]

The *Jikki* does not view "Euro-America" (*Bei-Ō*) indiscriminately as an undifferentiated whole. Much is made of regional and national differences. According to the *Jikki*, Europe can be divided into broad geographical areas based on relative enlightenment. "Setting out from Paris, the farther east one goes, the shallower civilization gradually becomes" (IV, 1-2). Russia is the farthest east and the least advanced, having begun her transformation into a modern state only some twenty years ago. Her resources are rich, but because of inadequate technology she has not yet been able to utilize them profitably, and she is still dominated commercially by the English and the Germans. When she develops sophisticated industrial techniques, she will become a nation to be feared. Hungary, only now beginning to emerge into the modern world, might offer instructive parallels for Japan.

In evaluating the contemporary condition of Hungary there are many things which should be considered carefully by Japan as she advances toward enlightenment. . . . In Hungary only agriculture is respected, and a mere subsistence level is maintained [among the people]. When one reflects on it, however, the great nations of the present who were in the same state before the nineteenth century are many. . . . The various nations who today are delayed in their enlightenment will be deeply impressed by studying the circumstances of Hungary. (IV, 460)

Similarly, Europe may be divided at the Alps into an industrious, prosperous north and an indolent, impoverished south. England, with her modern steam machinery, mining, railroads, and marine fleet, "swaggers fearlessly in the world"

---

[7] *Tokumei zenken taishi Bei-Ō kairan jikki*, V (Tokyo, 1878), 2. Hereafter cited by volume and page number inserted in text.

(II, 7). French manufacturing is highly developed, and France is the arbiter of artistic taste and luxury for all of Europe. Germany has the impressive Krupp armament works. Even the small nations such as Holland and Belgium are formidable in their industrial and commercial sophistication. The southern countries, in contrast, are backward. Italy still relies on handicraft industry for a large part of the national income, and in Spain and Portugal conditions are yet worse.

Going even farther south, Africa and tropical Asia, with their fertile soil and abundant natural resources, are industrially and commercially completely undeveloped.

> Such nations are weak in the spirit of competition for profits and encouragement of enterprise since they are rich in fertile land. To say that the actual profits of both their imports and their exports are held in the hands of the Europeans would not be a great exaggeration. (v, 262)

In accounting for such regional differences, the *Jikki* stresses the importance of "national character." The temperament of the people controls the fate of a nation. According to the *Jikki*, the most important quality for the people of a progressive nation is industriousness. England has colonies on every continent, and her navy encircles the globe. This is because the English people subscribe fanatically to the belief that time is money, and they never rest.

> If the will of a people is not strong, they cannot extend their power over great distances. The waxing and waning of nations is related to the will of their people. Skill and wealth are secondary considerations. (v, 306)

Climate, topography, and natural resources have a direct influence on national character. A warm climate and natural abundance provide no inducement to hard work. One learns to work only by having to overcome physical hardships. Thus natural obstacles are a stimulus to progress.

16

France and England, because of their infertile soil, rigorous climate, and [natural] deficiency in all things, have exerted strenuous efforts and produced the brilliance of civilization. (IV, 437)

The Prussians live in the frozen northern wastelands. Their [natural] poverty prods the people's spirit, and they increase their power of endurance. . . . In contrast, Austria has the placid spirit of a fertile land. . . . At present, Prussia is on the ascendant and Austria is gradually declining. (IV, 437)

In tropical climates,

There is nothing to produce the desire for knowledge, no need to endure hardships and undertake enterprises. The people go no further than preserving life. In the end the world merely passes them by. . . . Poverty is a grindstone which enriches people, and surfeit is the foundation of laziness. (V, 310)

National temperament is not, however, completely determined by environmental factors. There is something inherent in certain nationalities to account for their industry and ingenuity.

If people with the minds of the Dutch lived in the lands of China, one knows that hundreds of Hollands would be produced in the East. When we think about it, cannot the industrious efforts of Holland be compared to those of Japan? (III, 240)

Industry, of course, is one of the most important factors in Western wealth and power, and one of the most conspicuous. Everywhere resources and energies are poured into manufacturing. Everywhere, "during the day one hears the clanging of wheels and axles and at night one sees the heavens scorched with flame." (V, 1)

Originally, industries are developed to increase the productive power of the people by furnishing efficiently the necessities of life. Moreover, greatest industrial profits lie in the most widely distributed products. The emphasis, therefore, is on mass production of necessities rather than luxury items for a limited market. As a nation's wealth increases and her population begins to prosper, more and higher quality products are considered necessities. As the standard of living rises, the market increases, and industry flourishes all the more. Wool fabric is a case in point. In Europe even the middle and lower classes now buy ready-made clothing. Consequently, there are textile mills for mass production of cloth. Moreover, as manufacturing techniques are refined, the consumers' tastes become more fastidious, stimulating constant rivalry among manufacturers to produce articles of better and better quality. This rivalry, of course, is the basis for general industrial progress.

Commerce is as important as industry to Western prosperity and power. There is in the West a highly developed economic network through which raw materials and manufactured products are distributed and controlled. The market value of individual commodities is determined by this system, and the wealth of entire nations may depend on their internal and external commercial development and on their favorable inclusion in world trade.

The commodities which together make up the nation's wealth are scattered throughout the world; they have value when they have been collected. By then thoroughly distributing what others have gathered, middlemen further increase the value of these commodities. (I, 21-22)

The harbor of San Francisco has become a great link in the trade between Europe and the Orient. . . . This is very important to the present and future of our country. . . . One of the principles of trade is that when a land prospers in one area there is certain to be a land prospering in another area. When London prospers, so does Paris. When London and Paris prosper, so do New York and Philadelphia. When San Francisco prospers, the ports on the other side of the

Pacific that should prosper are Yokohama in our country and Shanghai in China. . . . If one side of the Pacific can attain such prosperity, why not our side, why not Yokohama and Nagasaki? (I, 77-80)

Western nations do not fail to realize the overwhelming importance of commerce. According to the *Jikki,* "the people throughout a country hope for the thriving of commerce in the same way as the Asian hopes for an abundant harvest." (v, 245)

Even when we had audiences with emperors, kings, and queens, when we were entertained by foreign ministers, these two words [commerce and industry] always appeared in their speeches. As we traveled, commercial and industrial companies in every city vied with each other to welcome us. There were banquets overflowing with delicacies. . . . Each time a speech was made to the crowds, when there was talk of friendly relations with our country and flourishing trade, all threw up their hats and stamped their feet. (v, 245)

Overseas colonies play an extremely important role in the commercial network. They are both the much contested preserves of the raw materials for Western industry and the markets for Western manufactured products. "Now all the countries of Europe develop markets in the Orient and seize the opportunity to compensate for their own inadequacy of raw materials for manufacturing." (III, 346) The colonial system is run according to the principles of mercantilism.

In general, countries that expand their maritime trade and possess colonies establish the technique of increasing their import levels by the principles of the "mercantile system." In this technique there is tyrannical, exclusive monopoly purchase of the colony's raw materials, and the suppression of its industrial production. (v, 245)

19

Efficiency in operating such a vast and complex system depends on sophistication in industrial techniques, banking and finance, management, and so forth. Highly developed methods of communication and land and sea transportation are also necessary. The perpetual extension of trade is accompanied not only by material enrichment through development of industry and the exchange of products, but also by intellectual enrichment through the exchange of knowledge and ideas. The vital points of the commercial network are ever-expanding cities, centers of commercial and industrial development and of cosmopolitan enlightenment.

The development of industry and commerce is a relatively recent phenomenon even in the West. Historically its origins are related to the end of feudalism and to the French Revolution.

> On the basis of the decline of feudal practices in Europe and the indulgence of freedom in business and industry, iron machinery appeared, and a taste for tools of convenience and beautiful things was created. There has been a catering to the taste of the people. The yearly increase in the number of luxuries is like a runaway horse. (III, 344-45)

With the emergence of constitutional governments, the productivity and the buying power of the people gradually increased. And as affluence spread, there were demands for the extension of popular rights. People left the land to congregate in the cities, and progressive urbanization took place as the cities became focal points of manufacturing and commerce, the distribution centers for both things and ideas.

One reason for the advancement of industry and commerce in the West is her expertise in "social technology," that is, organization and management. Her success in this area is due to a strong commitment to efficiency and careful planning on every level: the individual, the family, the company, and the national government. Westerners also show a surprising capacity for cooperation and large-scale coordination of efforts.

Productivity is optimized by skillful "social engineering" on the part of both company and government, to keep the people healthy, well-trained, and content with their jobs.

No task in the West is approached without careful forethought and meticulous planning, and the ultimate goal is always kept in mind.

> When the Westerner engages in a business venture, as he constructs his plans he concentrates intensely on his aims. His detailed consideration of every matter is the complete opposite of the Japanese tendency. . . . Based on strict accounting of profit and business volume, factory buildings and machinery are steadily increased, improved, and perfected. (III, 315)

The operation of any Western factory is so complex that it must be rigorously coordinated in every detail.

> The construction of a whole ship is decided in the blueprint room. Those in the office are familiar with the design of the entire ship, and they learn the logic of its construction. . . . Generally blueprints are essential in a factory; they are like the brain of a man. . . . Artists make the drawings, wheelwrights make the wheels. Dyers dye, painters paint. There is a fine division of labor, and the benefits are numerous. The various talents become increasingly specialized. The coordination of all this lies in pictures and patterns. (II, 144)

Such minute planning is continued on a larger scale, in remarkable cooperative efforts for regional and national profit.

> The calculations of the credits and debits of trade are always carefully scrutinized by each company. [Then the figures for] each city are calculated as a whole. These calculations are called statistics. Their essential feature is to call attention to the important products in the different regions of a country, and reference is made to such factors

as population size, productive capacity, and the circulation of commodities. . . . These calculations are clear evidence upon which national profits can be assessed. (v, 252)

If a company is to prosper, there must be smooth relations between management and labor. Indeed, the entrepreneur's profit depends on the workers, whose uncooperativeness can be ruinous. The workers are naturally foolish and lazy and in want of training. Therefore there is great company paternalism, which is supported by the government. The worker's physical well-being is provided for, he is given practical education, and he is inculcated with the value of thrift and hard work. Enticing fringe benefits—company housing, educational facilities, savings arrangements—keep the workers content with their lot, and strikes to a minimum.

It is the general practice for factory owners to give protection and assistance to the worker. Accordingly, the government establishes ways of encouraging and relieving the laboring commoner, and it has the responsibility of providing him protection. This protection is an all-important duty with respect to the wealth and poverty of a nation. Its main purpose is to encourage and patronize the labor and enterprise of every man. (III, 72)

Another recurrent theme in the *Jikki*'s analysis of Western progress is the ingenious development, utilization, and conservation of natural resources and human energies. Western technology permits exhaustive exploitation of raw materials. Even agriculture has been raised to the level of a science.

Because of agricultural societies throughout the country, agricultural schools have been established and flourish. There are also itinerant teachers, whose visits are eagerly anticipated. Experimental stations have been set up everywhere, and these have encouraged progress. The use of machinery by agriculture increases year by year. (III, 304-05)

Intense efforts are made to control the use of natural resources so that the supply will not diminish through time. In forestry, for example,

> In England, Greece, Spain, and France, great damage [from indiscriminate cutting] was incurred. Because of evils such as these, a system of forest control emerged. At present, contrary to the trend of increasing political freedom in Europe, . . . the control of forests has abolished the freedom of the past. Even government restrictions . . . have been introduced. In the end, these are really intended for the further benefit of the people. (III, 232-33)

Industry makes full use of raw materials. Even waste products are converted to useful by-products in seemingly infinite variety.

> Flax is drawn and then cut into long fibers. The residue then serves varied uses. When the flax has been drawn out and cut, even the short fibers are made use of. At the very end, the waste is sent to paper factories. Thus there is constant economizing, and it is possible to exhaust the virtues of the material. (III, 197)

In its determination to waste nothing, Western industry invents new products as well as new uses for old ones.

> Mineral and organic materials are transformed into the ingredients for manufacturing cosmetics. From coal tar aniline dyes are created. . . . In accordance with the progress of the Western textile industry, the dyes which have become necessities have increased year after year. . . . Thus refined use is made of the products of chemistry. (III, 311-12)

Human resources too are maximized in the West. With education and technology, human ingenuity and productivity are constantly expanding.

> Society advances daily, and there is no end to its vitality. Human knowledge rushes toward enlightenment. And no

longer relying on the strength of human limbs, they seek techniques for borrowing the strength of things. (III, 209)

Advances in knowledge and industry have been accompanied by increasing sophistication in human energy-saving devices. Coal, steam, and waterpower are used instead of manpower. No human labor is wasted on a job a machine could do.

> In accordance with the advance of knowledge, strength is economized, and great effort is made to emphasize responsibility. The people of Europe do not shoulder freight. . . . They use their splendidly maintained roads [and wheels] to carry their freight. The strength that would have been devoted to shouldering freight is used by the European man in repairing the roads. (v, 179)

A general characteristic of the West's progress is its cumulative nature. The *Jikki* emphasizes the recency of the phenomenon of Western power and productivity, which is so newly emerged, in fact, that many of the European nations are, like Japan, only beginning or still in the process of their basic transformation. Yet the *Jikki* stresses over and over that the present heights of Western civilization are the result of historical experience, the accumulation of ever more refined skills and knowledge. Indeed it is the West's veneration of the past and preservation of its artifacts which provide the basis for the new day. Thus the report underlines the importance of tradition and suggests that Japan may lack the proper tradition and historical background for modernization along Western lines. The *Jikki* recognizes moreover how difficult it would be to alter long-established political and social patterns in Japan in order to make way for the new.

It is then, in part, the West's conscious attention to the past, reflected in its museums, libraries, and archives, upon which contemporary progress is based. These museums and libraries document the West's continuous succession of technological advancements, proliferation of knowledge, and ever more ingenious utilization of natural resources and human skills and energies.

When one goes through a museum, the order of a country's enlightenment reveals itself spontaneously to the eye and heart. If one studies the basic reasons when a country flourishes, one learns that it is not a sudden thing. There is always an order. Those who learn first transmit their knowledge to those who learn later. Those who open their eyes first awaken those who wake later. By degrees there are advances. We give this phenomenon a name and call it progress. By progress we do not mean merely throwing away the old and planning the new. . . . There is nothing better than a museum to show that order. . . . As museums are built sensations are sharpened and practical benefits widened. When one enters a museum and sees the old things, one senses the hard work and toil of times past. . . . As one sees the order of progress, one feels obliged to work harder thereafter. Inspiration moves the heart. Ideas for learning spring up, and one cannot control them. Thus books are collected and schools built for the purpose of acquainting people with the practical arts. . . . There has been [in Japan] no historical record-keeping of past and present progress to cause people to learn these things. No museums have stimulated the sight. No exhibitions have encouraged the acquiring of new knowledge. (II, 111-12)

Thus, although the brilliance of modern Europe is a recent phenomenon, it is the result of a long process of development through history.

Even though England, France, and Germany are flourishing now, the basic factors responsible for their enlightenment are naturally traceable to ancient Rome. . . . It is said that those who discuss the civilization of Europe first of all invoke its Roman historical heritage. Ah! the culmination of a country's civilization is not achieved in a day. It is conceived several thousand years in advance; then afterwards it seems to burst into brilliance. When one thinks deeply about this, one is impressed anew. (IV, 319)

When one tours about the ancient city of Rome, [one realizes that] all the so-called enlightenment of the West draws from this city as its source. And one knows the great age of these origins. The knowledge acquired by the people who study these beginnings has the depth of accumulated learning. It covers great distances and does not disappear. (IV, 358)

While it is obviously necessary for backward nations such as Hungary, Russia, and Japan to work consciously toward achieving the heights of Western civilization if they are to compete in the modern world, doing so entails certain risks.

Since the Western theory of progress is being transmitted and planted in Japan, things are being carried out carelessly and without forethought. The old is abandoned and there is competition for what is new. These "new things" cannot always be obtained. What should be preserved of the old is destroyed, and in the end there is no trace of it. Ah! how indeed can this be spoken of as daily advancement? How can it be called progress? (III, 55)

Historical evidence suggests that there are dangers in sudden radical alterations of traditional patterns, and social dislocation and confusion are often the results.

Not only does the matter of suddenly changing to new things and abandoning the old produce extreme disquiet in the human heart, but all countries are characterized by a desire to retain old institutions and practices. . . . The benefits of forcing the people to abandon ancient practices are extremely few. The disadvantages of injuring their traditional sentiments and producing discontent are numerous. (IV, 217-18)

Thus, choosing to join the Western march of progress would require great caution, adaptation, and selectivity in adopting Western techniques and institutions, especially for Japan, whose historical experience is so different from that of the West. For instance,

> If one attempted to implement these techniques [legal counsel and juries], it would probably be a difficult matter. In the whole country there is no one who could be given an attorney's license and be seated in the courtroom. If a jury were assembled, they would be afraid of the officials and would do no more than agree meekly. And even if one chose strong-necked people who would dare to speak, they would be ignorant of the principles of law, and dissent based on moral arguments would be rank. . . . When it comes to witnesses, it is unlikely that they would express themselves truthfully. . . . The West has the Ten Commandments, just as Japan has the five relationships [of Confucianism]. One of those Ten Commandments says, "Thou shalt not bear false witness." . . . If the laws and systems of the West are adopted recklessly, without abandoning the outward form and taking the essence, there will be frequent instances of the cork not fitting the bottle. (III, 145-46)

In its search for the keys to Western dynamism and wealth and power, the *Jikki* emphasizes the importance of the basic values and the "racial temperament" of the Occidental peoples. The distinctive world view deriving from these basic values is unmistakably reflected in its government, law, education, religion, and international relations. The *Jikki* contrasts the Western world view with that of the East, with its corresponding basic temperament and institutional patterns. The differences between the two then contribute significantly to their disparate levels of wealth and power.

According to the *Jikki*, one of the important characteristics of Western peoples is a highly developed spirit of individual competition. The Occidental is acquisitive and assertive, in contrast to the self-denial and passivity of the Oriental. On a larger scale this competitiveness develops into the philosophy of nationalism and the unending struggle of countries to attain national independence and autonomy. Thus such a strong competitive spirit is one of the prime reasons for the rise of nations to power.

The standard Eastern and Western forms of government are natural outgrowths of their respective temperaments. The *Jikki* contrasts the family-style rule of the Orient, based on moral principles and the sovereign's benevolence and affection for the people, to Western governments designed to protect individual property and rights in a society of universal distrust.

> The white race are avid in their desires and zealous in their religion, and they lack the power of self control. . . . The yellow race have weaker desires and are strong in subduing their natures. . . . Consequently, the main purposes of their political institutions are also different. In the West there is protective [of self-interest] government; in the East there is benevolent government. (v, 148)

Similarly, Western legal systems are primarily concerned with protecting the life, liberty, and property of the individual. It is devotion to self-interest that has inspired constitutional restrictions on leaders, and the establishment of civil rights. In contrast, the people of China and Japan consider moral training the principal concern of government, and ethics the means of controlling the people. They attach little importance to personal property.

It is apparent that East and West have different views of the nature of man. The West sees man as basically corrupt. Religion consequently assumes the role of helping to restrain their evil natures and put their selfishness to constructive use.

> Now, for the people of the West, human nature is fundamentally bad. Their desires are avid, and they are avid in

their pursuit of wealth. The purpose of religion is primarily that of directing this nature. . . . Western peoples put faith in their religion to protect their property. (v, 157)

Religion may also place value on hard work and self-improvement, encouraging the Western spirit of competition. Accordingly, religion has come to exercise a powerful role in Western society, touching on every aspect of life.

In the administration of political affairs, in the stimulation of military preparations, in the encouragement of commercial enterprises, in the development of agriculture and husbandry, the influence of religion is significant. (iv, 62)

Sometimes, however, religious institutions can wield too much power over the people, deceiving them and working against their better interests.

If one speculates on the depth of religious convictions, religion can be seen as a tool for absorbing the spirit of the people and entangling them in proscriptions. . . . One sees that the foolish people are manipulated by means of this tool. (iv, 62)

In certain instances rampant religious power may actually obstruct national development. In Spain, for instance:

The extreme abuses of religion are indeed unbearable to behold. First, the government is crushed by the power of the clergy and is incapable of escaping from this oppressive control. Hundreds of reforms have been destroyed by the clergy. Second, the people are all misguided and bewildered by the clergy, who perpetuate the indolence of the nation. Beggars gather in front of the churches. If someone gives them a bit of small change, the beggars immediately turn and drop half of it into the offering box, in gratitude to God, keeping for themselves only the remaining half, without so much as a word of thanks to the donor. (v, 135-36)

Sharply contrasting, according to the *Jikki,* is the Oriental image of the fundamental goodness of man. Religion and religious institutions consequently assume a subordinate position in the total scheme of things. This is both good and bad. The religiously based work ethic is weak in Japan, but on the other hand such excesses of religious power as are found in the West are inconceivable "within the sphere of gentle Buddhism." (v, 158)

Similarly, basic differences are evident in the purposes and techniques of learning in East and West. Western education is utilitarian. Moreover, learning is made available to all, irrespective of sex or social status. Its practical value as preparation for one's occupation and for intelligent citizenship is enormous. On a larger scale, the relation of education to Western technology and progress is obvious. Eastern learning, however, is motivated by the moral preoccupations of Oriental benevolent government. In Confucian terms, education fosters wisdom and goodness, not practical skills, and it is a characteristic of the gentleman. The East is relatively indifferent to practical learning and technical training, concentrating instead on abstruse philosophy.

The learning of Asia derives from benevolent government, and the single subject of morality alone is supported. Amusement is found in esoteric writings and abstract philosophical studies. Practical matters of everyday life are regarded as vulgar and common. Consequently, admirable customs and excellent conduct have not extended to the general mass of the people. Women have been confined to the inner recesses of their homes. . . . Because the farmer, artisan, and merchant have been without leisure in their coarse lives, they have not been able to inquire into the way of human relations. The entire population is boxed in by illiteracy. Even gentlemen and lords, if they neglect their . . . livelihood, though they may elevate their spirits, will lose their original wealth. . . . As for the West, . . . great effort is expended in practical philosophies. The practical matters of business and mathematics are expounded. The principles of morality are left to the clergy. (v, 82)

The different temperaments of East and West are also reflected in the motivations of their international relations. The West is essentially an armed camp. It is the scene of incessant struggle between weak and strong nations for independence and wealth and power.

All the countries of Europe deal with a powerful enemy on every side, and the competition in military preparedness increases. In times of peace there is rivalry for advantages in training and weapons. When there is war, according to their experiences in victory or defeat, they study techniques for improvement. (III, 92)

Moreover,

Even though the diplomacy of all Western nations outwardly expresses friendliness, secretly there is mutual suspicion. Even though the foreign offices assume a position of neutrality when faced with a crisis, this is only on the surface. . . . The military maneuverings of Europe are full of deception. . . . The small countries of Belgium, Holland, Sweden, and Switzerland, like porcupines bristling their quills, shore up their defenses. . . . While they secure their nations they are not able to loosen the straps of their helmets. (III, 108-09)

The result is a hierarchy of international domination maintained by a balance of power among the most powerful nations, England, France, Germany, and Austria. Strong and weak alike are committed to constant maneuvering for power.

Is it to be said that Russia alone desires to annex the five continents? The expansion of English and French colonies clearly indicates those nations' ambitions to absorb the world. Germany still does not have power overseas. Yet can she be

31

said to be completely without such ambitions? If one suspects [any] foreign nations of being tigers and wolves, then
which nation is not a tiger or a wolf? (IV, 107)

Such are the main contours of the *Jikki*'s ambitious attempt
to put the West through the analytical sieve. The thoroughness of its presentation clearly indicates the embassy's dogged
determination to understand the outer forms of Western civilization and then go beyond them and come to grips with
the essence and inner workings of the West.

Naturally, a major concern of the *Jikki* is the gap in development between East and West, especially between Japan
and the West. The *Jikki* leaves no doubt that Japan's acquisition of Western industry, technology, and learning would
close the gap and admit her to the company of the civilized
and progressive nations of the world. But this conviction is
tempered by the realization that the Western phenomenon of
progress is extremely complex. The *Jikki* repeatedly shows
that the embassy was conscious of the breadth and depth of
the nonmaterial foundations of the West's opulence and
power. It was in large part the West's historical experience,
cultural values, social structuring, and so forth, that accounted
for the West's superior status, and the proper combination of
factors might be impossible to reproduce elsewhere. The
increased understanding of the West resulting from the
embassy's experience thus seemed to create as many new questions as answers. Their elaboration of the West's emphasis on
religion is one considerable advancement over the Bakumatsu simplistic slogans on Eastern spirituality and Western
materialism. But the price of this new sophistication was
surely to compound the uncertainties about how to proceed,
making the content, scope, and timing of "Westernization"
reforms much more difficult to decide. Japan's new leadership
had to realize the magnitude of the job that confronted them.
Was it possible to transplant Western industry and technology without adopting the whole socio-political structure and

value system of the West? And what then was the fate of the still lingering Japanese traditions? Could there be a workable synthesis of the two?

Beyond some indirect hints, the *Jikki* offers no answers to questions like these. If the experience of the embassy indicated anything, it was that there were no ready-made solutions. The *Jikki* after all is detailed testimony to the fact that while the ultimate goals of progress may be universal, the means of their realization vary. The West, then, clearly offered no master blueprint, but a collection of models for emulation or inspiration. Moreover, the *Jikki* frequently warns of the dangers of rapid, radical change. These would seem to be strong arguments for the greatest caution and gradualism in planning out Japan's course of development, and for painstaking re-evaluation of Japanese tradition and the part it was to play in a new Japan.

Obviously, then, the *Jikki* and the leadership for whom it spoke were not prepared to launch blithely into the ambitious social and political reconstruction advocated by the Meirokusha enthusiasts, still less the programs demanded by the Popular Rights supporters. In fact, the *Jikki* in a sense represents a kind of apologia, a justification of the moderate pace of Meiji reforms to date. It was a reassertion of the indisputable need for change if Japan hoped to overtake the West, but at the same time it was a reassurance to uneasy traditionalists that change would be slow, guarded, and dutifully respectful of tradition.

One should not lose sight of the fact, however, that despite their hesitations these leaders were absolutely committed to change. The *Jikki*'s emphasis on the small nations of the West and their impressive show of progress quite obviously reveals a sense that Japan might do the same thing. A territorially insignificant Japan might, after all, aspire to the wealth and eminence of a Holland or a Belgium. And if nations more closely approximating Japan's present state of development, such as Hungary, Italy, or Russia, were already striving for national advancement, why not Japan? Reinforcing such optimism was the insistence on the comparative recency of the West's ascendance.

In fact, those who compiled the *Jikki* often seem to have submitted to the hypnotic sway of progress. To be sure, this new perspective on history and change had begun to appear at the end of the Tokugawa period. And the Meiji government had already embarked on its *bummei kaika* "civilization and enlightenment" programs, soon after the embassy's return. But the *Jikki* made the case, perhaps, stronger than ever before. There is a powerful undercurrent of historical necessity running through the work, a sense of irresistible challenge. If history was progress, as the West seemed to demonstrate, then one might be confident that conscious, rational effort could produce all the exciting changes needed. Moreover, action had to come quickly. The rate of progress in the West was constantly accelerating, and the gap between advanced and backward nations increased accordingly. If Japan wanted to catch up with the West, she had better do it now, before it was too late. An implicit fear echoes throughout the *Jikki* that Japan will fail to join the ever faster march of progress as an active participant and thus will become one of its passive victims, consigned to historical oblivion.

In a sense the *Jikki* represents a coda to the long first movement of Japan's intercultural learning process. Knowledge gained from studies of the West already had been, and would continue to be, translated into creative action: with assurance and alacrity in the economic sphere, with almost tortured hesitation in the political sphere, with adaptive ingenuity in the traditional sphere. The *Jikki* had pried open the lid of the Pandora's box of modernization. How successfully the problems released were solved is something that still remains to be seen.

CHAPTER II

Westernization and Japanization:
The Early Meiji Transformation of Education

MICHIO NAGAI

Three Viewpoints

THE transformation of Meiji Japan which began in 1868
is the first and most striking example of Westernization in the non-Western world. In education this
transformation took place more conspicuously than in most
other fields. The introduction of a modern school system in
1872 (Meiji 5) and the successive changes which followed are
generally considered to have been carried out with a fairly
high degree of success. This seems particularly true in the light
of the difficulties encountered by similar attempts in other
parts of the non-Western world.

Westernization certainly played an important role in bringing about this transformation, but the modernization of
Japanese education cannot be explained in terms of Westernization alone. Efforts to Westernize education met with indigenous resistance, and the conflict between Westernization
and Japanization which ensued complicated the process of
change, altered the course of education first in one direction
and then another, and sorely tried the ingenuity of the Meiji
leaders. Moreover, the complicity of education in the course

INTRODUCTORY NOTE: In the preparation of this paper I have depended
heavily on: (1) Kaigo Tokiomi, *Kyōiku chokugo seiritsushi no kenkyū*
(Tokyo Daigaku Shuppankai, 1965); (2) Tsuchiya Tadao, *Meiji zenki
kyōiku seisakushi no kenkyū* (Kōdansha, 1962); and (3) Ogata Hiroyasu, *Gakusei jisshi keii no kenkyū* (Azekura Shobō, 1963). The specific points at which I have either quoted or adapted material from
these three works are noted in the text by references to the author's
name. I am grateful to Jerry K. Dusenbury for the translation of this
paper into English.

35

of events which led to Japan's destruction in World War II indicates that the rapid transformation of Meiji education cannot be considered an unqualified success.

Though a comprehensive treatment of the whole question of Westernization lies beyond the scope of this brief essay, I do hope, through empirical inquiry into early Meiji education, to make clear several of the issues involved in this process. For the time being I would like to point out that there are at least three important viewpoints from which the transformation of early Meiji education can be understood.

I. WESTERNIZATION AND JAPANIZATION

Judged by prevailing world standards, the Fundamental Code of Education (*Gakusei*),[1] established in 1872, was of high quality. The extensive plans for the new school system did not, however, achieve immediate results. No sooner were the new plans inaugurated than the government confronted a whole range of new problems which required it to change the system again and again. The extent of these problems was such that stabilization of the Japanese educational system, in terms of basic objectives and organization, was not finally achieved until the promulgation of the Imperial Rescript on Education in 1890 (Meiji 23).

The nearly twenty years between 1872 and 1890 was a period of trial and error during which various educational systems and modes of thought were successively tried and discarded. The Fundamental Code of 1872 represented a positive response to Westernization—that is, to external stimulus and pressure from the West. But in Japan, as in other non-Western societies, efforts aimed at total Westernization faced serious difficulties. The non-Western world consisted historically of pre-industrial societies characterized by a "backwardness" which made them different from the modern West. Moreover, non-Western societies have their own traditions

---

[1] The law of 1872, known in Japan simply as *Gakusei* (literally, "School System"), is best known in English as the Fundamental Code of Education.

and history. Thus no matter how strong the external pressure, the non-Western world cannot be transformed into a perfect facsimile of the West. When these societies come under strong pressure from the West, their cultural traditions resist rapid change, and yet they are forced, for their own survival, to seek to develop their own approach to modernization through rapid self-transformation. Thus after 1872 resistance to Westernization was coupled in complex ways with a search for a distinctively Japanese approach to modernization. After nearly twenty years of trial and error, the promulgation of the Imperial Rescript in 1890 put an end to this search and modern Japanese education entered a period of stability through the temporary completion of Japanization. Thereafter Japan moved along its own peculiar road to modernization.

2. WESTERN PILGRIMAGE

It should not be supposed that Westernization and Japanization were sharply antagonistic historical processes. The diversity embraced by the "Western world" meant that it was possible to find, within the West, elements which were not necessarily in conflict with Japanese tradition. Today, when many newly emerging nations are seeking in the name of Westernization to introduce American-type liberalism or Soviet-type socialism, it is interesting to note that nationalism is often united with one in their rejection of the other. When a non-Western society sets out to discover its own path to modernization it faces a situation in which the choices are not simply between West and non-West but are complicated by the dissonance between heterogeneous elements within the West itself. It soon finds itself on a long, uncharted journey— a pilgrimage to the West.

The West to which Japanese education looked for a model after 1872 was by no means a monolith. France, Germany, Holland, England, America, and Russia all had different educational systems and traditions of educational thought. Japan's task lay in combining elements from these different traditions and shaping them into a system which corresponded to the needs of the Japanese situation. She was aided in this task by the absence of explicit ideological divisions in the nineteenth-century world—a fact which made it relatively easy for her to incorporate portions of several educational systems simultaneously. Nevertheless, a close look at the changes which occurred between 1872 and 1890 reveals that at any given time, one Western country provided the model which exercised major influence.

At the time of the establishment of the 1872 school system, French influence was dominant. In part this can be attributed to the fact that French education was the most systematized in the West and was therefore the easiest to understand and assimilate. Its extremely centralized character made it appropriate for an underdeveloped Japan which sought to carry out reform from the top down under the pressure to change from outside.

The Fundamental Code as planned and designed by the government, however, was too progressive, and its very progressiveness proved to be its undoing. First of all, the financial requirements of such a system were too heavy a burden for the Japanese economy. Second, its stress on the acquisition of Western intellectual knowledge provoked dissatisfaction among that portion of the populace which had been nurtured for generations in the moralistic Confucian tradition. As a result the system collapsed and the government, in the Education Ordinance of 1879 (Meiji 12), boldly introduced a system which favored the American rather than the French pattern.

This shift to the American system with its emphasis on decentralization and local autonomy is not difficult to understand. The government had failed in its efforts to force change from the top down and now hoped for spontaneous development from the bottom up. But the American system did not function in Japan in the same way that it did in the United States. When local communities were permitted to exercise more freedom, school attendance declined. The percentage of children attending school had been increasing steadily since the beginning of the Meiji period. The few years immediately after the promulgation of the Education Ordinance of 1879 represented the sole exception to this trend. In some areas the permissiveness of the law was reflected in the content of education as well, traditional elements being reintroduced into the curriculum in the name of freedom.

Confronted with this situation the government abandoned the American-type educational system. The Education Ordinance was partially revised in 1880 (Meiji 13), and in 1885 (Meiji 18) sweeping changes were made. Now the government sought to build its system along Prussian lines. Like the French, the Prussian system was centralized, thereby facilitating reform from the top down. But the idea that compulsory education was subordinate to the political objectives of the State was much stronger in the Prussian system, and this recommended it to the Meiji leaders who considered it well adapted to the immediate needs of Japan.

In tracing the course of the Westernization of Japanese education from the French type to the American and then to the Prussian, one notes that Westernization and Japanization were not always in conflict with one another. Rather, Japanization, or the search for a Japanese type of modernization, and Westernization were at least partially overlapping processes. Change did not occur in a neat movement-countermovement pattern. The movement was instead from Westernization of a type quite foreign to Japan to a Westernization which had more affinity with the Japanese situation. Thus the meaning of Westernization itself underwent a qualitative change.

3. LATENT DIFFICULTIES IN JAPANIZATION

What were the forces which brought about these changes in the Japanese understanding of Westernization and led society and culture in the direction of Japanization?

First there was the elemental discord with traditional Japanese culture. Four years after the new French-influenced school system was promulgated, Fukuzawa Yukichi, a leading advocate of Modernization, wrote in 1875 as follows concerning the difficulties involved in the process of Westernization:

> In civilizations one can distinguish two types of elements—those things which are externally visible and those of the spirit which dwell within. External civilization is easy to adopt but to seek internal civilization is difficult. In promoting the civilization of our own country let us take up what is difficult first and put aside the easy until later.[2]

When Fukuzawa speaks of "external civilization" and "internal civilization" he is making a distinction between material objects and objective social realities on the one hand and those things which do not fit into these categories on the other. If this interpretation be permitted, then the former—the legal system, systems of knowledge, machines, tools, etc.—were easy to adopt, but the latter—the process of industrialization, moral values, the spirit of learning, ethos, social climate, etc.—were not easily assimilated.

The implication of Fukuzawa's analysis is that the external aspects of Japanese culture were readily Westernized, but the internal elements were not easily transformed. The internal dimension of culture, as the repository of tradition, resists change, for tradition is tradition precisely because it is rooted deeply in a fixed historical past. Any serious attempt to build a new Japan had to deal with the continuing strength of tradition as an obstacle to the assimilation of the "internal civilization" of the West.

With the breakdown of the first educational system, awareness of this problem intensified. The *Kyōgaku taishi*[3] (The

---

[2] Fukuzawa Yukichi, "Bummeiron no gairyaku," *Fukuzawa Yukichi zenshū*, IV (Iwanami Shoten, 1959), 14.

[3] The *Kyōgaku taishi* is sometimes referred to as the *Kyōgaku seishi*, for it bore the characters *seishi* to emphasize that it was the Emperor's "sacred will."

Great Principles of Education) of 1879 (Meiji 12) represented the Emperor's approach to this question. This document attributed the confusion and degeneration of Japanese society and culture to Westernization and asserted that only a revival of tradition could rehabilitate education and bring about proper development of the nation.

Yet the problem was not simple. Pre-Restoration Japan lacked the historically established facilities necessary to modernize by itself. It was precisely this lack which made Westernization a necessity. Thus, even if tradition were to be revived, one had to decide which elements should be incorporated in the new and which elements were to be thrown away. Prior to the issuing of the *Kyōgaku taishi*, there were among the oligarchs men like Itō Hirobumi whose opinions on Westernization differed from those of the Emperor. But the basic position represented in this document gradually gained strength and emerged triumphant eleven years later in the Imperial Rescript on Education.

The results were far-reaching. Japan now embarked on a path of development fundamentally different from that of England, France, or the United States. The most important difference lay in the relationship between politics and education. Whereas in these Western countries education preserved its independence of and freedom from political control, government and education in Japan were understood in accordance with the Confucian tradition as being fundamentally of the same order. Government control of education was thereby legitimized, and an educational system based on the principle *seikyō itchi*, "unity of government and education," was adopted.[4]

A second problem in the Japanization process was that of "backwardness." The principle standard applied when speak-

[4] *Seikyō itchi* refers literally to the "unity" of *sei* (government or politics) and *kyō* (education, religion, teaching, philosophy, etc.). This concept is fundamental to Confucian thought and implies that one of the functions of government is the establishment of the true teaching or orthodox doctrine.

ing of one society as more "backward" than another society is the stage of economic growth which it has reached. Yet in order for a backward society to develop rapidly, changes must occur not only in the field of economics but also in politics, education, science, technology, etc. It is not easy to determine what kind of changes are required and at what speed they should be undertaken.

The Fundamental Code of 1872 was clearly progressive, even when compared with Western systems, but it proved to be an excessive burden for Japan's economy. On the other hand, the Education Ordinance of 1879 lacked the positive government initiative which was required to stimulate national development. Through a series of advances and retreats the government continued its search for an educational system which could function as a powerful force for social development within the limits imposed by the contemporary economy. Did the Meiji government finally arrive at the most "appropriate" system? The answer to this question must await the historical judgment of future generations. It can be said, however, that this search for an appropriate Western model was an important part of the process of Japanization.

The impact of the West and the pressure of Westernization on underdeveloped societies brings about an initial break with the past and a leap into the future, but unless a system appropriate to the particular underdeveloped society is found, sustained growth cannot be assured.

In summary, there are at least three aspects of the Westernization of Japanese education which should be noted. First, while Westernization induced the transformation of Japan, it was strongly resisted by Japanization and by the search for a distinctively Japanese pattern of development. Secondly, in the process of interaction between these two forces, a qualitative change took place in the meaning of Westernization itself. Gradually a Western model more desirable from the point of view of Japanization was selected. Thirdly, the immediate causes of the Japanization which brought about this changed understanding of Westernization were the problems of cultural tradition and of the stage of economic growth.

These three observations do not provide a comprehensive description of all the problems involved in Westernization. They are simply keys which may serve to facilitate our understanding of some of the issues involved.

Imperial Leadership

Though I have thus far considered the development of Meiji Japan primarily in terms of the Western impact and the Japanese response, rapid change was taking place, of course, prior to the onset of Westernization. While these changes alone did not constitute a sufficient impetus to modernization, they did contribute significantly to the way in which Japan responded to the external challenge. By the time of the Restoration, Japanese society had already reached a fairly high degree of maturity in the crucial areas of politics, economics, and education. The very existence of these internal conditions enabled the Japanese to understand the meaning of the Western challenge and to meet it with a sense of crisis. This sense of crisis reached a climax in the Restoration; a break was made with the past and the Japanese leapt boldly into the future.

Not all Japanese, however, were prepared for such an immediate break with the past. It was partially due to this situation that the Restoration took the form of a reformation from above carried out by a group of leaders who responded sensitively to the Western impact. Nevertheless, this link between forces from the outside and forces from above was not clearly forged at the outset. In the history of early Meiji education one finds a diverse group of men, grounded in the teachings of Kokugaku (Japanese Learning) and Kangaku (Chinese Learning), who thought that the key to social development lay not in Westernization but in the reconstruction of tradition. These men sought to strengthen education by combining leadership from above with tradition from within.

Their position remained dominant in government circles only during the first years of the Meiji period. After 1870, the leading point of view changed to a combination of outside impact and leadership from above. It was this concept which gave impetus to the reform of the school system and proved to be a distinguishing mark of Japanese education thereafter.[5] In spite of the many shifts in policy which took place during the next twenty years, the government never lost its pre-eminent position in the field of education. In contrast to the West, and particularly to England and the United States, guidance and control from above remained an important and basic characteristic of Japanese education.

Before elaborating on the activities of the government, however, we should have in mind that the Emperor himself played an extremely important and positive role in the continuing debate on education which characterized the twenty years of trial and error. His efforts were, in fact, by no means inferior to those of the oligarchy. The Imperial Rescript of 1890 which led to the stabilization of education was not restricted by the Meiji Constitution which had been promulgated in 1889. As an independent expression of the Emperor's personal views on education it stood parallel to the Constitution and, with respect to education, it carried absolute authority.

But I have proceeded too quickly. During the period in which educational policy was still in flux, that is, during the period prior to the promulgation of the Meiji Constitution and the Imperial Rescript, the question of constitutional restrictions was not even at issue and the Emperor was relatively free to demonstrate his strong powers of leadership. Moreover, this was a period in which the young Emperor,

[5] See Nagai Michio, *Kindaika to kyōiku* (Tōdai Shuppankai, 1969), pp. 15-22.

44

who had come to the throne at the age of sixteen, was a youthful, vigorous ruler in his twenties and thirties. Kaigo Tokiomi's recent book on the Imperial Rescript on Education (see Introductory Note) has given us the fruit of several decades of research and made a notable contribution to our knowledge of the Emperor's activities during this period.

The Emperor was not averse to making frank statements about specific individuals, even in his official writings. In an official letter addressed to the Imperial Household Minister in 1885, the Emperor criticized the appointment of Tani Kanjō, President of the Peers' School for boys and an accomplished military man, as President of the newly created Peers' School for Girls.

> Though it would be premature to pass judgment on the appointment of Tani as President, women's education is not the same as men's. The position of President of the Girls' School would have been more appropriately filled by a person of calm, rather than active disposition. Women's education has heretofore been conducted in a vigorous manner but the bad effects of this are numerous. Therefore, a person of greater composure should have been selected to direct the education of girls. (Kaigo, pp. 123-26)

The Emperor kept in touch with education by frequent visits to local schools. These inspection tours were not merely formal gestures but occasions for the Emperor to raise questions about what he saw. After his return from these tours, the Imperial Lecturer, Motoda Nagazane, records that the Emperor advised him of particular areas which required further study. In 1878, on one of these tours, the Emperor found that some students engaged in "English conversation" were unable to translate into Japanese the English they were speaking. On another occasion when he asked students what contribution the Western ideas and theories they were discussing could make to the betterment of Japanese life, the students were unable to reply (Kaigo, pp. 70-75).

If these reports of the Emperor's activities indicate his keen interest in education, his official statements made prior to the promulgation of the Imperial Rescript of 1890 reveal that the Emperor himself was, like concerned leaders of the period, in search of a course suitable for the modernization of his country. He became increasingly critical of the consequences which followed the process of Westernization in the latter half of this period. However, in the former half he was so much in favor of Westernization of education as to be inclined to neglect the value of the traditional education.

His first public statement on education was embodied in the Imperial message to the nobility of October 1871. The message began by pointing to the fact that the contemporary world was dominated by the Western powers whose enlightened civilizations competed with one another for supremacy. This state of affairs the Emperor attributed to the diligence of the peoples of these nations. In such a world, what should Japan do in order to grow into an independent, modern state? The message argued that Japan could "compete in the race with the powers" only through a "reformation of the old system." As Japan sought to enter this race the nobility bore a particularly heavy responsibility, for the "nobility were in a key position; it was to them that the expectant eyes of the people were turned." This required them to be "all the more diligent, taking the initiative in encouraging the people."

The Imperial message did not end with abstract principles. The Emperor went on to deal with the meaning of Westernization in intellectual and practical terms. "Diligence," the message continued, "is nothing less than opening the doors of wisdom and sharpening our abilities. . . . Nothing is more important than opening our eyes to the whole enlightened world, mastering its achievements, and sending students abroad to study the means by which those things useful to us can be carried out."

The Emperor's insistence on Westernization is clear. Diligence was not merely a moral teaching. It was born from intelligence, and intelligence was cultivated by study abroad.

The message also revealed the Emperor's positive attitude toward "civilization and enlightenment" (*bummei kaika*) for women: "Due to the inadequate provisions for the education of women in our country, most of them are not able to understand the meaning of civilization." To remedy this situation, men who went abroad should be accompanied, when possible, by women. Specifically he suggested: "It is obviously desirable for men who go abroad to take their wives and sisters with them." This would give them an opportunity to learn the "essentials of civilization and methods of child rearing" from Western women. The arguments for the education of women and the suggestion that women too should learn from the West in order to improve their intellectual ability, were consistent with the general Westernizing position of the message.

The young Emperor was fully conscious of the importance of learning from the West and was himself a strong advocate of Westernization. He sought to be a model for the people by wearing Western dress. But as suggested earlier, even the Emperor reexamined his views during the years of trial and error. Behind the attempt to build a new educational system through outside stimulus and leadership and control from above lay this serious concern of the Emperor. It was in this setting that the new school system was introduced.

The New School System and French-type Education

Let us now turn to a description of the main features of the *Gakusei*, the Fundamental Code of 1872. Ogata Hiroyasu has provided us with an interesting comparison of the influence of various Western educational systems on the new system. The following chart, taken from his well-documented study of the *Gakusei* (see Introductory Note), is based on an investigation of contemporary works designed to acquaint the Japanese with Western systems of education (Ogata, pp. 130-32).

47

CHART I

Elements of the New School System Drawn from Western Systems

Country	Provisions included in the New School System	Percent
France	64	43.5
Germany	39	26.5
Netherlands	17	11.6
England	11	7.5
America	9	6.1
Russia	1	0.7
Other	6	4.1
Total	147	100.0

The above figures serve to point out two characteristics of the *Gakusei*. It was not exclusively modeled on any one particular Western educational system but rather incorporated features from several different countries. At the same time, French influence was by far the strongest. This is particularly true with respect to the general organization of the system. It was modeled so closely after the French pattern that it can legitimately be called a French-type system.

The new system divided the country into eight university districts and provided for the establishment of one university in each district. These eight districts were further subdivided into 32 middle school districts which were in turn broken down into 210 elementary school districts. Each of these districts was to have its own elementary school split into upper and lower elementary schools of four years each. There were detailed regulations governing the age, qualifications, and compensation of teachers at all three levels. Since on all the above matters the *Gakusei* copied the French code (Ogata, pp. 132-33), the fact that the whole system was not an exact reproduction of the French is of considerable interest.

Tsuchiya Tadao, in another excellent study on the Meiji school system (see Introductory Note), has pointed out some ways in which the Meiji system did differ from the French. In the latter, the traditional European dual system was employed beginning with the latter half of elementary school.

In Japan, however, a single unified system was adopted—a fact which suggests the influence of American egalitarianism. In including spelling, penmanship, vocabulary, conversation, and reading in the lower elementary curriculum, the Meiji system was also following the American and English pattern of language education (Tsuchiya, p. 65). Nevertheless, in comparing the Meiji school system as described by Tsuchiya with that of France, one finds only two or three differences.

The foundations of French education had been laid by the Napoleonic reforms of 1806. Freed from the control of the Church by the Revolution in 1789, the schools acquired autonomy for the first time. Napoleon consolidated these gains through the creation of a national system called the University of France. Subdivided into university and middle school regions, the University of France provided the institutional framework for a modern school system independent of religion. But Napoleon's reforms did not extend to elementary schools which remained under the control of the Church until the Guizot Law of 1833. This law also contained a full-scale plan for the training of teachers. The implementation of these reforms was interrupted, however, by the wave of reaction which set in under Napoleon III. Thus it was not until 1881 that elementary education became entirely tuition-free.

Nevertheless Napoleon had laid the foundations and Guizot had completed the blueprint for an educational system conspicuous in its thoroughness and centralism, a system which was to endure without major changes until the outbreak of World War II. Thus it is that the French system of 1939 (Fig. II) strongly resembles the new Meiji school system (Fig. I).[6]

The Meiji government, while under the influence of French education, made every effort to learn about objective conditions in other countries. One manifestation of their industry in this regard was the Iwakura Mission which set sail from Yokohama at the end of 1871 (Meiji 4) to observe conditions

[6] Meyer, Adolph E., *The Development of Education in the Twentieth Century* (New York, 1949), pp. 203-05.

49

FIGURE I

The School System (*Gakusei*) of 1872

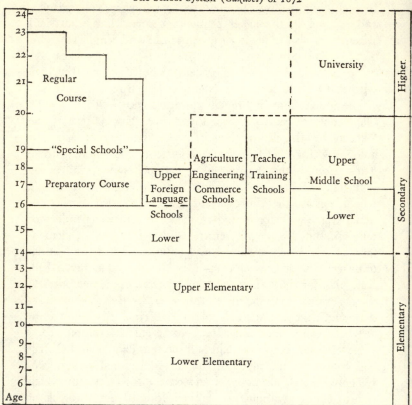

From Tsuchiya, p. 64.

in Europe and America. Tanaka Fujimarō, who was later to play a central role in the formation of educational policy, was assigned to the group to study education. Tanaka himself spent more time studying the American and German systems than he did the French, but his report was not made until after the *Gakusei* had already been established.

FIGURE II

The Schools of France

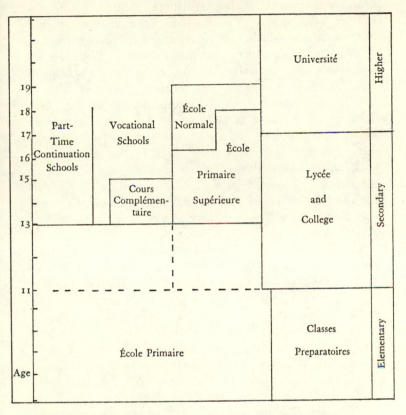

From Alonzo F. Myers and Clarence O. Williams, *Education in a Democracy* (New York: Prentice-Hall, 1937), p. 63.

In Tanaka's absence, preparations for the new educational system continued at the Ministry of Education. Work on the new system was carried out by an eleven-man committee composed of a group of "experts" on the West who had newly emerged (men like Mitsukuri Rinshō, Iwasa Jun, and Uchida Masao) to which were added a few Kokugaku and Kangaku scholars. In planning the new system the committee's chief guide seems to have been a translation of a book on the French educational system. This translation, entitled *Futsukoku gakusei*, was made by Sazawa Tarō, a retainer of the old Fukuyama *han* which had already carried out two reforms of the *han* school system, the first in 1868 and the second, which was little more than a copy of the French system, in 1870. Ōki Takatō, the head of the Ministry of Education at this time and the man who bore responsibility for the establishment of the new school system, was himself strongly influenced by Western education. As a product of the Saga *han*, where the American missionary G. F. Verbeck had exercised considerable influence as a *han*-employed teacher since his arrival in Nagasaki in 1859, Ōki availed himself of Verbeck's advice. We may surmise that the Dutch-born Verbeck was able to provide information about European as well as American education.[7]

The French system thus recommended itself on several counts. The Japanese had already gained a certain familiarity with it through the experience of the Fukuyama *han*. Furthermore it was readily intelligible as a system, all aspects of education being drawn together under centralized authority. It is not surprising then, that the Meiji government, whose goal was the creation of a completely new modern educational system, should have found the French system a more relevant model than such pluralistic systems as those of America or England. This preference for the French model led to the development of a national plan. This plan was even more progressive in its attitude toward education than the French system. There was to be no distinction of class or status in the elementary schools. Article 21 of the *Gakusei* stated explicitly the intention of the government that "Every man should learn," and the law included a bold plan for eight years of

[7] My discussion of the period prior to the establishment of the *Gakusei* is based on Tsuchiya, Chaps. 1-2, and Ogata, Chap. 3.

compulsory education (four years lower and four years upper elementary) (Tsuchiya, p. 52).

The Proclamation of the Dajōkan issued at the time of the announcement of the *Gakusei* is well known for its progressive tone. It is not possible to quote the entire document but the main points are worth noting.

The Proclamation rejected the Japanese educational tradition:

> Centuries have elapsed since schools were first established, but man has gone astray through misguidance. Learning being viewed as the exclusive privilege of the *Samurai* and his superiors, farmers, artisans, merchants, and women have neglected it altogether and know not even its meaning. Even those few among the *Samurai* and his superiors who did pursue learning were apt to claim it to be for the state, not knowing that it was the very foundation of success in life. They indulged in poetry, empty reasoning, and idle discussions, and their dissertations, while not lacking in elegance, were seldom applicable to life.

In other words traditional education had been the privilege of a special class, the samurai. In terms of content, this education had given priority to state ends and was divorced from daily life. It was this which had to be rejected. True education was precisely the opposite. "Every man should pursue learning . . . there shall, in the future, be no community with an illiterate family, nor family with an illiterate person. Every guardian, acting in accordance with this, shall bring up his children with tender care, never failing to have them attend school."[8]

The Preamble was an explicit declaration of the importance

[8] Tsuchiya, p. 79. The translation of the Proclamation is excerpted from Kumaji Yoshida, "European and American Influences in Japanese Education," in Inazo Nitobe et al., *Western Influences in Modern Japan* (Chicago, 1931), pp. 34-35.

of both compulsory education and equality of educational opportunity. It stressed the betterment of the daily life of the individual rather than the needs of the State. "Learning," it continued, "is the key to success in life, and no man can afford to neglect it. It is ignorance that leads man astray, makes him destitute, disrupts his family, and in the end destroys his life."

The ideals of the government as expressed in the Preamble reflected both its utilitarian bent and its concern for equality. There was in fact little difference between the views of the government and those of Fukuzawa Yukichi, generally considered to be the most progessive thinker of the day. Taking a position which was more progressive than the majority of the people, the government sought to put its ideals into effect in one stroke by means of a French-type, centralized system.

Underdeveloped societies in a hurry to modernize cannot wait for spontaneous development from the bottom up. They must rely upon the power of a few leaders who have felt the impact of the West to instigate reform from the top. This was the position of the Meiji government and it was a position which was supported by the young Emperor. Thus, at the outset of the modernization process, Japan was inevitably involved in a contradiction between means and ends. Education could be democratized only under central government leadership.

The Breakdown of the New School System

In terms of ideals and organization the *Gakusei* was an extremely progressive system which aimed at the improvement of national life. It did not, however, meet with complete acceptance among the people. Some ignored it; others resisted, sometimes to the point of overt violence.

In 1873, the year following the creation of the new system, riots began to break out across the country. In Tsuruga followers of Shinshū Sect of Buddhism rioted, demanding restoration of the "True Law," rejection of Christianity, and discontinuation of the use of Western texts in the schools. In

Okayama Prefecture, farmers rioted against the conscription law and school education and destroyed almost all of the Prefecture's 46 elementary schools. Ten thousand farmers in Tottori Prefecture rose up in opposition to the schools, conscription, and the Gregorian calendar (also introduced in 1873). In Kagawa Prefecture 34 elementary schools were razed and in Fukuoka Prefecture 29 elementary schools were burned down or otherwise destroyed (Ogata, pp. 258 ff; Tsuchiya, pp. 158 ff).

The opposition movement continued unabated for several years. In 1876, 29 schools in Mie Prefecture were burned to the ground and another 29 destroyed. These incidents are frequently overlooked in accounts of education during the early Meiji period and the reputed Japanese fondness for education, but they should serve to remind us that Meiji Japan experienced the same difficulties that accompany the dissemination of education in any underdeveloped country.

These difficulties are clearly reflected in the statistics of the period. During the seven years after the creation of the new system, the increase in school attendance was only 13%. The increase in attendance by girls was a mere 8% and in some areas authorities had almost given up hope of getting girls to attend school. In Akita Prefecture, for instance, school attendance of girls stood at only 3.1% in 1875 (Meiji 8) (Tsuchiya, pp. 111-13). (See Chart 2.)

The government was of course concerned about these difficulties. When the new system was put into effect it had sought to raise attendance levels through the creation of a system of school inspectors. To this local areas added their own devices. The regulations of Saitama Prefecture required police to admonish any child found out of school during school hours. In Kyoto, children who attended school regularly were given a round, minted badge with the name of the school inscribed on the front and their own name on the back. Schools in Ishikawa Prefecture with attendance records of 70% or above were allowed to display a crimson flag with

CHART 2

Fluctuations in School Attendance

Year	School Attendance		
	Boys	Girls	Average
1873	39.90%	15.14%	28.13%
1874	46.17	17.22	32.30
1875	50.49	18.58	35.19
1876	54.16	21.03	38.32
1877	55.97	22.48	39.88
1878	57.59	23.51	41.26
1879	58.21	22.59	41.16
1880	58.72	21.91	41.06
1881	59.95	24.67	42.98
1882	64.65	30.98	48.51
1883	67.16	33.64	51.03
1884	66.95	33.29	50.76
1885	65.80	32.07	49.62
1886	61.99	29.01	46.33
1887	60.31	28.26	45.00
1888	63.00	30.21	47.36
1889	64.28	30.45	48.18
1890	65.14	31.13	48.93

From *Japan's Growth and Educati.u.* (Tokyo: Ministry of Education, 1965), p. 180.

the character *shō* (for elementary school) in white, while those with less than 70% attendance were forced to fly flags of a white background with the character *shō* in crimson. Textbooks were also used to preach the value of education and to stress the importance of going to school. Volume One of the first elementary readers published by the Ministry of Education in 1873 contained the following: "Without study, one will not be successful in any endeavor. Therefore, all persons when they become seven years of age should enter elementary school and apply themselves to ordinary studies. The school is the place where everyone—samurai, farmers, artisans and merchants alike—should study and be taught."[9]

Despite these efforts to expound the importance of school education, the government continued to meet with resistance.

[9] For a discussion of various means used to encourage school attendance, see Tsuchiya, Chap. 5.

Why did the establishment of universal education prove to be such a difficult task?

First of all the government's educational policy lacked the necessary financial backing. The government had succeeded in devising an educational system after the French model but the Japanese economy was still too weak and backward to make the implementation of such a grand plan feasible. In some underdeveloped countries the prior growth of education has stimulated economic development and quickened the pace of social change, but in Meiji Japan, education was too far ahead of economics. On paper the system was more democratic and more ambitious than the French system of seventy years hence. Thus the chief cause of the breakdown of the *Gakusei* can be found in the great lag which existed between the educational system itself and the economic power available to support it.

This economic weakness was reflected in the government's fiscal policy, the first principle of which was that the cost of the schools should be borne by the people. Of the 1,940,000 yen expended for public schools in 1873, government assistance amounted to only 12%; the remainder represented a direct burden on the people. This meant that the implementation of the new system was pitted against poverty. Though in some cases contributions were made by former daimyo and wealthy families, the greater part of the necessary funds was collected from the common people according to rates fixed by local government authorities, very much in the same way as local taxes. Of course some consideration was given to the size of the income and property holdings of each household, families being divided into several categories for this purpose. In addition almost half the schools waived tuition for the children of families unable to pay. According to statistics for 1876, 10,996 schools had such provisions while 11,587 schools did not.

Nevertheless, the education costs which fell directly on the people were for the majority too heavy a burden. The income of farmers differed, of course, depending on whether they were landlords, independent farmers, or tenants, but the average annual income per household during this period was only 30 to 40 yen. Educational costs for the average household (these figures are for 1873) amounted to 2 yen 29 sen, or slightly less than 10% of income. Faced with other taxes and tenancy payments, farmers were steadily impoverished. It is hardly surprising that many of them sought to burn and destroy the schools (Ogata, pp. 252-55).

Many government leaders were well aware of these difficulties and anxious lest they have serious consequences. Kido Kōin, who together with Ōkubo and Saigō stood at the head of the Meiji oligarchy, pleaded strongly, upon becoming Minister of Education in 1874, that the meager budget which he was given made it impossible for him to bear responsibility for the execution of the government's educational policy. He clashed sharply with those who were urging foreign expeditions to Korea and Taiwan on the grounds that Japan had no excess funds for such overseas endeavors and that all national energies should be devoted to domestic development. When the government finally decided to send troops to Taiwan, Kido resigned as Minister of Education. In his letter of resignation he wrote: "The Court's conduct of education is in some respects inferior to that of feudal days. Herein lies the reason for the people's continued distrust of the new government."

In the year in which the *Gakusei* went into effect the government, after considerable struggle, was able to find only two-thirds of the necessary budget. In the following year the estimated budget had to be cut in half, and it was several years before the government was free of constant financial worries. The situation was made even worse by the outbreak of the Satsuma Rebellion in 1877 (Meiji 10). The suppression of the Rebellion cost the government 41,560,000 yen. During the same year, only a little more than 1% of this amount, or 560,000 yen, was expended in assistance to elementary schools. In a situation in which the people were financially unable to support education and government assistance was so meager, the grand plan for the new school system inevitably collapsed.

The second difficulty which confronted the new system was cultural. In terms of both structure and content it was a direct import from the West. This made it difficult for the common people to understand and contributed to popular antagonism toward the schools. The Fundamental Code went into considerable detail in its plans for the content of education. The four-year lower and upper elementary schools were each divided into eight semesters. One semester was defined as a six-month period of instruction, five hours per day, thirty hours per week. To insure that instruction was actually carried out in proper fashion, the curriculum for each semester and the textbooks to be used were clearly specified.

Regulations such as these made the *Gakusei* an overly uniform system which disregarded local peculiarities. Moreover, the thoroughly Western system was too foreign to the Japanese educational tradition. This fact, coupled with an almost total disregard of the problems posed by the juxtaposition of two heterogeneous cultures, proved to be a major obstacle to the successful implementation of the system.

The type of situation which resulted is described in considerable detail by Tsuchiya (Chapter 6). The elementary school curriculum, in addition to the standard reading, writing and arithmetic, incorporated instruction in the new knowledge prerequisite to the creation of a modern culture—geography, natural history, chemistry, etc. The latter would have been difficult for the pupils to grasp in any case, but the situation was complicated by the fact that there was only a limited number of teachers who could teach these subjects. One can imagine that most teachers were as baffled by the translation of Adam Smith (used as an economics text) as were their pupils. Many teachers were also unable to grasp the significance of two other modern elements in the curriculum—physical education and singing. The result was that the teaching of physical education was often neglected and the time allotted for singing was sometimes spent in reading the *Hyakunin isshu*, an anthology of classical Japanese poetry. First graders struggled with such abstract sentences as the following which appeared in a first grade textbook: "God is the ruler of the universe; man is the soul of creation."

The government, for its part, looked upon teacher training as the key to the strengthening of elementary education. But such training takes time, and the *Gakusei* was launched before a sufficient number of teachers could be trained. The situation which resulted is reflected in the frank criticism leveled at the system by Nishimura Shigeki and Kuki Ryūichi. After observing education in rural schools they concluded that the content was too difficult for the average person and pointed out that, in spite of the government's progressive and pragmatic ideals, education in the schools had in fact fallen into a formalism and standardization which made it quite impractical.

The state of government schools being what it was, it was possible to argue that the old *terakoya* (commoners' schools) and *juku* (private schools) of the Tokugawa period actually provided a more useful education. New private schools in Yamaguchi, Akita, and many other parts of the country sought to revive Confucian education. Those who favored separate education for girls (there were already many separate institutions in existence) also took advantage of the situation to strengthen their position. Opposition to the schools was not confined to the rural masses but included many ex-samurai who resisted the Western character of the new education. Their opposition to the new schools found political expression in the Saigō-led movement against the government bureaucracy (Tsuchiya, Chapter 6).

These opposition movements, to the extent that they represented stirrings from below against government leadership and control, were democratic movements. In fact, the People's Rights Movement which developed in the years which followed included many ex-samurai who had been excluded from the new government. But these same movements sought a revival of native tradition—a tradition which was by no means free of reactionary elements.

The Fundamental Code of Education of 1872, after a splendid take-off, soon broke down amidst intellectual chaos and cultural conflict. One can see in the series of events which led to its replacement by the Education Ordinance the first steps toward Japanization, although at this stage it was not always clear what this Japanization meant. It did not, as I noted at the beginning, mean that Westernization was simply discarded.

The Education Ordinance and American-Type Education

The short-lived Fundamental Code was replaced in 1879 (Meiji 12) by the Education Ordinance (*Kyōiku-rei*). The product of strong American influence, the new ordinance reflected the American emphasis on local autonomy, pluralism, and freedom as contrasted to central government planning. One might be tempted to assume that the new stress on local peculiarities and freedom reflected an attempt by the government to overcome popular opposition to its educational policy while continuing to press Westernization. But a closer look at the pattern of events which led up to the adoption of the Education Ordinance reveals that a more complex set of factors was at work.

The complex nature of the situation becomes clearer when we recall that the *Kyōgaku taishi* and the Education Ordinance were issued simultaneously. The former, as shall be detailed later, pointed to the negative effects of Westernization and emphasized the importance of Japanization (Kaigo, Part I, Chapter 3).

When these two documents are placed side by side, the contradiction in the educational policies pursued by the Meiji leaders as of September, 1879, is quite apparent. These policies lacked logical consistency. The American system was more progressive than the French in that it sought to embody more thoroughly the traditional Western ideals of equality and freedom. Thus, it is possible to see in the adoption of the American model an increasing tendency toward Westernization. But the *Kyōgaku taishi*, with its critical attitude toward the negative effects of Westernization and its emphasis on Japanization seems to point in the opposite direction.

The different approaches represented by these two documents can be explained by the fact that the Court (which issued the *Kyōgaku taishi*) and the government (which was responsible for the Education Ordinance) differed in their opinion on education. This interpretation is correct, but a question still remains: why did these, the two highest organs of the State, make their differences public?

I have previously stated the two main reasons for the failure of the *Gakusei*—lack of economic power and resistance against Western culture. Both the government and the people failed to perceive the nature of these two problems clearly or to deal with them in a systematic fashion. Both accepted the state of confusion as it was, and the continuing chaos gave rise to political conflict and disorder. Two major sources of disruption were the People's Rights Movement, and the shifts in relative influence which occurred among the Meiji leaders. While the limits of this paper prohibit a detailed discussion of either of these movements, in order to understand the complex interrelationship between Westernization and Japanization, it will be helpful to trace the main forces at work among both the leaders and the people.

The People's Rights Movement began in 1874 (Meiji 7) with the formation of the Aikoku-kōtō (Party of Patriots) led by Itagaki Taisuke of Tosa. As the name of the movement suggests, its professed aims were freedom and people's rights. The actual composition of the movement, however, suggests a more complex set of demands. Farmers who had suffered increasing impoverishment as a result of the Meiji reforms sought economic stability. Former samurai and mid-

dle and small landlords joined the movement out of dissatisfaction with their exclusion from the new government and
opposition to the government policy of protecting newly arisen
capitalists. Thus, at the time of the Saigō Rebellion in 1877,
the most powerful element in the People's Rights Movement,
the Tosa group, sought to aid Saigō in his attempt to over-
throw the government. Though the situation was brought
under control before the Tosa group could take effective
action, the movement continued to gain momentum after
Saigō's destruction. By March 1879 when their second national
meeting was held in Osaka, it had expanded to include
twenty-one groups from eighteen prefectures.

In addition to being anti-government, the movement was
intensely nationalistic. In this sense it was an anti-Western
movement which sought to preserve the samurai tradition. It
may be doubted that the majority of those who participated
in the movement really understood the meaning of freedom
and popular rights. The annual report of the Ministry of Education for 1879 attributed the disruption of education in
Yamanashi Prefecture to the prevalence of an understanding
of freedom as "doing what one pleases," or "freedom from
restraint."

In short, the demands of the People's Rights Movement
were a miscellaneous array of mutually contradictory elements—the demand for freedom and rights per se, the demand
for economic stability, the desire "to do what one pleases,"
and finally, the revival of tradition.

At the very time when the spreading confusion called for
positive leadership, the Meiji oligarchy lost its ability to lead.
The inability of the oligarchy to take the initiative was due
first to the growing dissension among the three pillars of the
early Restoration government, Saigō, Ōkubo, and Kido, and
finally to the passing of these three men from the scene. Saigō
Takamori, as the general who led in the destruction of the
Tokugawa Bakufu, had been the first hero of the Restoration
government. But after the new government was established

and Japan entered a period of construction, Ōkubo increasingly played the central role and a subtle shift took place in the relative positions of these two men. Saigō's passion for the invasion of Korea and Ōkubo's and Kido's insistence on the priority of domestic concerns finally led to an open conflict in the Satsuma Rebellion. The war dealt a hard blow to government finances, but the conflict among the three heroes of the Restoration itself was to have more serious consequences for the government. Saigō died in battle in his native Kagoshima in September 1877. The war greatly upset Kido and he died in May, four months before Saigō. Of the three, only Ōkubo was left to rebuild the government. In the following May, however, he was assassinated by a group of Saigō's supporters, former samurai from Ishikawa Prefecture led by Shimada Ichirō. Thus in one year the government lost its three top leaders.

The passing of these three leaders was a serious blow to the young Emperor who had, with their cooperation, come to play a leading role in the building of the new state. Motoda Nagazane and others close to the Emperor, however, saw an opportunity in the crisis which developed to strengthen the Emperor's link with politics through invoking the principle of Imperial decision on all matters (*banki goshinsai*) (Kaigo, p. 76). The personal relationship between the old oligarchs and the Court had disappeared and it was up to their successor, Itō, to rebuild it. While Itō was an able leader he had not yet acquired the power or the ability of the three Restoration heroes to unite various factions. Well-versed in Western civilization, he sought to continue the process of Westernization and to maintain the progressive character of the Restoration. This brought him into conflict with the Confucianist Motoda who proposed to overcome the crisis through the revival of tradition. (I shall deal with the differences between these two men later.) The growing influence of the People's Rights Movement posed a more immediate problem. Shaken by the transfer of power within its ranks, faced by the revival of tradition at the Court, and challenged by the rising People's Rights Movement, the government was forced to undertake the reconstruction of the education system from a position of weakness.

The Education Ordinance was prepared by Tanaka Fuji-marō, who had been the leading figure in the Ministry of Education since the promulgation of the Fundamental Code, and David Murray, whom Tanaka had brought from the United States as his advisor (Murray's official position was Education Inspector). In its final stages the draft was studied by Itō. While all three men endeavored to rebuild the educational system in such a way as to bring under control the confusion which had resulted from the failure of the *Gakusei*, each had a somewhat different understanding of how best to cope with the situation.

Murray's plan was the most moderate of the three. While attempting to correct the weak points of the *Gakusei*, he proceeded on the assumption that the system was not beyond redemption and that it could be gradually strengthened through making the most of its strong points. Murray's first suggestion was that an eight-year elementary school was unrealistic. Compulsory education should be limited to the four years of lower elementary school, and the four-year upper elementary school should be divided into two two-year stages to be developed gradually as resources permitted. Only in unavoidable cases, however, should exceptions be made to the four-year compulsory education requirement and even then the minimum requirement should be four months per year for four years. Murray felt that the Ministry of Education should continue to supervise the content of education and his plan contained detailed regulations governing the curriculum, entrance qualifications, the length of the course of study, etc., in middle and teacher-training schools as well as elementary schools.

While accepting some of Murray's suggestions, Tanaka's draft proposal was a much more laissez-faire document which

65

gave greater scope to local authorities. It continued the eight-year elementary school but left the question of the development of the upper four years to local authorities to be determined in accordance with their needs. Compulsory education was fixed at sixteen months in eight years (instead of four years as Murray suggested). Furthermore, Tanaka's draft recognized private schools: "Those who are not enrolled in public schools but who are otherwise receiving ordinary instruction shall be considered in attendance (for the purposes of the compulsory education requirement)." For those communities too poor to maintain an adequate staff, Tanaka approved a rotation system whereby teachers would teach at more than one school. The laissez-faire character of the draft proposal was also evident in its lack of regulations concerning middle schools and teacher-training institutions. Here too wide latitude was given to local areas. Finally, a unique feature of Tanaka's proposal was a plan for Educational Assemblies on the national and regional levels aimed at improving education through debate.

Tanaka's draft of the Education Ordinance first passed through the hands of Sanjō Sanetomi and then was given to Itō, who, after studying it carefully, submitted it to the Genrō for formal approval. At this stage the document was abbreviated still further and its laissez-faire character firmly fixed. From a document containing 19 sections and 718 chapters it was shortened to 419 articles. Of the eight articles dealing with the rights and responsibilities of the Minister of Education, six were omitted. In addition an article urging teachers and students to devote themselves to moral education was crossed out. In return, corporal punishment of pupils was prohibited and an article was added, exempting land belonging to public schools from taxation. In short, the final document was even more laissez-faire in character than Tanaka's Draft Proposal (not to mention Murray's). After the Genrō had finished with it, almost no trace of the *Gakusei* remained.

Educational policy, Tanaka wrote, must ultimately be based on "popular sentiment" (*minshin*). Can the differences of opinion among these three men be adequately interpreted as a reflection of their relative commitment to "popular sentiment" and "freedom" in education? The facts suggest otherwise.

Tsuchiya Tadao has dealt with these differences in terms of the degree to which they were immediately involved in and directly affected by the political turmoil of the day—that is, in terms of their relation to the problems posed by the spread of the People's Rights Movement and the shake up within the oligarchy. Of the three, Murray was the furthest removed from, and thus the least affected by, the immediate political situation. This allowed him to take a gradualist position. The relatively laissez-faire character of the Ministry of Education proposal drafted by Tanaka on the other hand, aimed at a compromise with political realities. In particular it took into consideration popular dissatisfaction with the *Gakusei* and the demands of the People's Rights Movement.

Itō was in an even more vulnerable position than Tanaka. Ōkubo had been assassinated on the day on which Tanaka presented his draft proposal to Sanjō Sanetomi, leaving Itō to deal with this problem alone. It is not surprising that he was even more willing to compromise with the movement for popular rights than Tanaka. Itō was in fact caught between the demand for popular rights on the one hand and the steady revival of traditional Confucian thought at Court on the other. In this situation the problem of moral education posed particular difficulties. In his final draft Itō attempted to avoid a head-on collision by eliminating as much of the discussion of moral education as possible and strengthening the laissez-faire character of the document.

These are the main points of Tsuchiya's argument (Tsuchiya, Chapter 9). Given the circumstances under which it was produced it is only natural that the Education Ordinance had an even shorter life than the *Gakusei*. According to the new law, attendance at public schools was no longer mandatory inasmuch as private elementary schools were also deemed acceptable. The number of private elementary schools increased rapidly, and the year following the promulgation of the Education Ordinance there were three and one-half times as many private schools as public in Tokyo. In the name of freedom, education in these private schools was often quite informal. Frequently they represented little more than revivals of the old *terakoya*. In the three-year period between 1878 and 1880, girls' attendance decreased 1.5% and the average (including boys) also showed a slight decline (see Chart 2) (Tsuchiya, Chapter 10).

The Education Ordinance was stillborn. Though some specialists were seriously engaged in the study of American education at the time and Murray himself was the first of many Americans to give unsparingly of his energies, the shift from French to American education did not grow out of a popular understanding of the spirit of American education. It was undertaken because it seemed to fit the political situation of 1879 (Meiji 12).

Historically speaking, the qualitative change in the content of Westernization which can be seen in the process of the formation of the Education Ordinance was rooted in a movement for Japanization. Compared to the time when the new school system was established, the movement from below against leadership from above was much stronger. But in underdeveloped societies, movements from below are not infrequently linked with the conventions of tradition. Even though the movement was in name a movement for freedom and popular rights, the majority of the people did not understand that these concepts implied an autonomous, well-developed system of national education. In the name of freedom, the modernization of Japanese education took a step backward.

Prussian Influence and the Completion
of the Meiji Educational System

The Education Ordinance was not the only attempt to deal with the situation created by the failure of the *Gakusei*. While the government's search for a new system led it to the American model, the Court turned to the revival of tradition as the basis for the reconstruction of education. As pointed out earlier, the thinking of the Court was expressed in the *Kyōgaku taishi*, issued in the same year and (it is supposed) in the same month as the Education Ordinance.

The *Kyōgaku taishi* had three main points. First, the introduction of Western civilization (*bummei kaika*) had resulted in a situation in which "many ignore the standards of good conduct and violate customs and manners." Second, this situation the *Kyōgaku taishi* traced to the loss of Japanese tradition which was occurring in the course of "vain attempt to emulate Western manners." Third, the way to reconstruction was "Confucian-centered moral learning based on the ancestral teachings. . . . Hereafter, we should devote ourselves to a clarification of humanity, righteousness, loyalty and filial piety on the basis of the classic teachings of our ancestors. . . . If the teachings of the Sages are spread throughout the nation, in our independence of spirit we shall be inferior to none."

The Court, in sharp contrast to the Government, was clearly calling for Japanization (Kaigo, Part I, Chapter 3).

This difference of opinion between the government and the Court soon became explicit in the dispute between Itō Hirobumi and Motoda Nagazane. Following the publication of the *Kyōgaku taishi*, Itō, at the Emperor's request, submitted his views on education in the form of a *Kyōiku-gi* (*Opinion on Education*). These views immediately drew sharp criticism from Motoda, who replied with his own opinion paper. The substance of their debate was as follows: Itō admitted that the disruption evident in Japanese society had led to a state of affairs in which irresponsible theories were rampant. He also acknowledged the importance of strengthening education in order to cope with this problem. But this alone, he felt, would not bring the situation under control. Why? Because confusion inevitably accompanied social change. Moreover, insofar as this social change was destroying the feudal system and giving liberty to the people, Itō thought that it was desirable. The strengthening of education was necessary but misguided "revival of the evil customs of the past" should be avoided. The creation of a state orthodoxy (*kokkyō*) and state interference in education was retrogressive. A union between government and education (*seikyō no itchi*) could be achieved only when the ruler was a sage. In ordinary times it was impossible. But Itō was not a mere Westernizer. He recognized "history, literature, customs, and language as elements fundamental to the organization of national polity," and saw the importance of the formation of national character. He attached particular importance to the separation of government and education (*seikyō bunri*). To Itō, scientific learning would not develop in Japan until the Confucian idea of the oneness of government and education was abandoned. Many people still clung to this Kangaku teaching and thus, even though they studied Western science, they immediately turned to political discussions. The true spirit of scientific inquiry which Itō felt to be so necessary could only be developed, "through long years of careful study and singular devotion to pragmatic inquiry."

Motoda disagreed with Itō at almost every point. While he did not advocate abolition of all Western thought, he attributed the contemporary social confusion and laxity in public morals to excessive dependence on Westernization and neglect of Japan's traditional morality. For Motoda, a national orthodoxy (*kokkyō*) had existed from olden times and thus it made no sense to speak as Itō did as if it were a matter of creating one. Itō had said that a sage-ruler could not easily be found, but Motoda argued that the Japanese were already blessed with such a philosopher-king. "The Emperor," he insisted, "had a heavenly calling (*tenshoku*) as both ruler (*kun*) and teacher (*shi*)." Motoda also opposed Itō's idea of the separation of government and education and his advocation of the scientific approach to learning. The goals of education were not scientific but moral, for it was through moral training that the state could develop promising men of talent. Finally, Motoda did not feel that his position was retrogressive. He argued rather that the revival of tradition would return Japan from the extreme Westernization of the post-Restoration period to the Middle Way (Kaigo, Part I, Chapter 5).

The outcome of the dispute was clear from the beginning. Motoda had the absolute authority of the Emperor behind him. Moreover, the revival of traditional culture had a nostalgic attraction for the large segment of the population which was dissatisfied with the almost totally Western character of the *Gakusei*. An emphasis on tradition might also be expected to appeal to the strong nationalism which lay just beneath the surface of the People's Rights Movement. Itō, on the other hand, had little in his favor. Having been thrust into a major position of leadership by the sudden death of Ōkubo, Saigō and Kido, he was still a new and thus a weak leader. His position was further weakened by his association with the abortive Education Ordinance.

With the end of this dispute, the course of Japanese education was all but fixed. Though it was ten years before the Imperial Rescript on Education was promulgated, subsequent changes in the educational system reflected the growing strength of the traditionalist position represented by Motoda.

Elementary education is a case in point. Attached to the *Kyōgaku taishi* was a paragraph on elementary education which contained more concrete provisions for elementary education than did the main text. This document was thorough in its insistence on a return to the Confucian virtues of benevolence, justice, loyalty, and filial piety. It rejected the teaching

71

of "abstract theories" which would obstruct the functioning of government. Finally, it argued for the necessity of vocational education related directly to daily life (Tsuchiya, pp. 262-63).

The changes in education policy which followed the failure of the Education Ordinance approximated the course which this document had outlined. The first major revision of the Education Ordinance took place under Minister of Education Kōno in December 1880, less than two years after it had gone into effect. Kōno moved the course of moral training from the end to the head of the curriculum, strengthened the compulsory nature of education, established new vocational schools, and emphasized the importance of bureaucratic control over the management and content of education.

At the same time, this revision abolished the system of aid to elementary and teacher-training schools and did little to strengthen school finance.[10] The result was that after two years in which school attendance showed an increase, the percentage of both boys and girls attending school began to drop again in 1883. In the five years between 1883 (Meiji 16) and 1887 (Meiji 20) school attendance declined about six percent from 51.03% to 45%.[11] In order to reverse this trend further changes were made in the Education Ordinance in 1885. (This was the year of the formation of the first Itō Cabinet with Mori Arinori as Minister of Education. Under Mori's leadership the educational system was finally consolidated.)[12]

This brings me to the final portion of my argument. Even though I have said that the course of Japan's education was largely determined by the *Kyōgaku taishi* of 1879, it should not be supposed that the revival of tradition urged by this document led to Japanization at the expense of the total rejec-

[10] Tsuchiya, Chaps. 1 and 12. These two chapters contain a detailed discussion of the two revisions of the Educational Ordinance.

[11] Ministry of Education, *Japan's Growth and Education* (Tokyo, 1965), p. 180.

[12] Nagai Michio, *Kindaika to kyōiku*, pp. 102-51.

tion of Westernization. The Western pilgrimage continued. In 1882, Itō, accompanied by several others, set out for Europe on another observation mission. The chief purpose of this mission was the study of Western political systems in preparation for the drafting of the Japanese constitution, but Itō did not forget to study education as well. Itō was looking for a model for monarchial government and his search took him first to Rudolf von Gneist in Berlin and then to the University of Vienna where he studied with Lorenz von Stein. Von Stein taught that supreme legislative and administrative power resided in the monarch and that the monarch and the state were synonymous. In describing the impression which these two men made upon him, Itō records that those who followed the teachings of the extreme liberals of England, America, and France were erroneously leading Japan down the wrong path, but that through his encounter with these two men he had gained the confidence which would enable him to secure the Imperial foundations and to structure the state in accordance with the Imperial principle. Having found in Prussia a model for the building of Japan he wrote: "I feel that I can die a contented man" (Tsuchiya, Chapter 15).

German culture and the German educational tradition were not devoid of respect for local autonomy and for the autonomy of learning and the arts, but the Germany which Itō observed was a country in the midst of the process of centralization. Under Prussian leadership, political unification had been accomplished in 1871, and strong control by the central government was proceeding apace. Local autonomy had not been completely destroyed, but government control over elementary education had been consolidated under the principle, "as the state, so the school." During the late eighteenth century, the "benevolent despot" Frederick the Great devoted his energies to education, not so much out of humanitarian respect for his people, but because he believed that education ensured the prosperity and power of the state. While he strove to wipe out illiteracy and to raise up a more efficient people, he also expected obedient and law-abiding subjects. In keeping with these aims he developed a dual system of education in which elite and mass were separated from the beginning. The former received a relatively liberal education and were expected to continue their studies through the university, but the latter received only minimal education designed to make them able and obedient servants of the state.[13]

Insofar as the centralization of authority is concerned, the Prussian system resembled the French. The purpose of central leadership in the French system was, however, to educate men in the progressive principles of liberty, equality, and fraternity. The Prussian system, on the other hand, was aimed at strengthening the power and prosperity of the state and in training men who would serve this cause. Negatively, government control represented a precaution against the possible disruptive effects of local autonomy and liberal intellectuals. The politically oriented, conservative German system seemed definitely more appropriate for Japan than the French-type centralized system. After all, the latter was tinged with some of the same liberal values that characterized the already discredited Education Ordinance.

On his way home from Germany, Itō summoned the Ambassador to London, Mori Arinori, to Paris, where the two discussed the future of Japanese education. Mori's concept of education was similar to the Prussian system in envisaging a dual system which distinguished between elite and mass education. It is probable that the foundations of the educational system which Mori as Minister of Education was later to complete were laid during these talks in Paris.[14]

With the reconstruction of the system under Mori the attendance figures (which, as we have previously noted, decreased steadily until 1887) took an upward turn. From 45% in 1887 (Meiji 20) attendance figures rose to 91.57% in 1902 (Meiji 35).[15] Three years after this upward trend began

[13] Meyer, pp. 226-28.   [14] Nagai, pp. 102-51.
[15] Ministry of Education, *Japan's Growth and Education*, p. 180.

the Imperial Rescript was promulgated, and the revival of tradition which had first been advocated by the *Kyōgaku taishi* became the keystone of modern education.

I shall not attempt to evaluate the Imperial Rescript. Suffice it here to say that after its promulgation there were no major changes in Japanese education (in terms of either principles or system) until the end of World War II. The proclamation of the Rescript brought to a halt the changes which had been going on during the first twenty years of the Meiji period and established the basic principles of education for the next sixty years.

In concluding this discussion of the early Meiji transformation of education I would particularly like to underline two points. While it is possible to say, as I did at the outset, that the twenty-year period between 1872 and 1890 witnessed a general shift away from Westernization and towards Japanization, this statement carries with it the limitations which accompany any generalization. Though economic and cultural factors did lead to recurring demands for Japanization, this drive was paralleled by the search for a new Western model. Following Motoda's triumph over Itō, the revival of tradition became the keystone of educational policy. But even at this stage, it was not possible to build a modern educational system with the resources of tradition alone. Motoda's plans for the Japanization of education were strengthened by Itō's study in Prussia and by the adoption of the Prussian model. In this sense the process of Japanization was accompanied at each stage by a Westernizing process based upon the type of Westernization thought to be most desirable at that point in time. One may suspect that this historical process cannot be lightly regarded in any consideration of the development of non-Western countries.

Second, the process of Westernization did not mean the importation of Western models in toto. The *Gakusei* though patterned after the French system was on paper at least more progressive. The Education Ordinance reflected the influence of American education but, in the context of Meiji Japan, American ideas were used as a means of compromise with the People's Rights Movement and with general popular opposition to the *Gakusei*. In the adoption of the Prussian system as well, its iron-like political control and cold efficiency were employed to reinforce the Confucian idea of the family state. Seen in this way the basic forces behind the historical changes during this period were internal. Westernization, as impact and model, functioned as a means.

The case of Meiji Japan as described above is not directly applicable to the transformation of other non-Western, developing countries. Nevertheless, I feel that the questions raised here about the historical relationship between the processes of Westernization and indigenization in Japan may be suggestive for any appraisal of other developing societies.

CHAPTER III

The Japanization of the Middle Meiji

DONALD H. SHIVELY

Evil customs of the past shall be broken off and everything based on the just laws of Nature.
Knowledge shall be sought throughout the world so as to strengthen the foundations of Imperial Rule.

Oath of Five Articles, April 6, 1868

The Way here set forth is indeed the teaching bequeathed by Our Imperial Ancestors, to be observed alike by Their Descendants and the subjects, infallible for all ages and true in all places.

Imperial Rescript on Education, October 30, 1890

THE contrast between these passages from two of the fundamental statements issued by the Meiji Emperor illustrates what is often spoken of as the "nationalistic reaction" to Westernization in the Meiji twenties. The eagerness with which the Japanese sought knowledge throughout the world and introduced Western technology, ideas, and institutions, was accompanied by enthusiastic experimentation with foreign customs and costumes. The rage for Westernization, which led at times to indiscriminate borrowing, seemed to sweep over and submerge traditional elements during the first two decades of the Meiji period. Then about 1887, a riptide of reaction broke the surface. This was the response of conservative thinkers and also of young progressives to those innovations which they found too extreme and too rapid, which they feared would effect such a thorough transformation

The author wishes to thank the colleagues who have read this paper and offered suggestions for revision, beginning with the participants of the Conference, members of the Colloquium on Modern Japan at Harvard, and also Miss Kakegawa Tomiko of Tokyo University and Professor Motoyama Yukihiko of Kyoto University.

of the Japanese people that they would lose those unique qualities which set them apart from the peoples of other countries.

Examples of the reaction are to be found in the resurrection of Confucian ethics as the basis for moral education and
in attacks in the late eighties on the corrupting influence of
Western thought and customs. There was a revival of interest
in traditional Japanese art, literature, and history, which had
been largely neglected for two decades. And it might be considered that some of the measures taken by the Meiji oligarchs
to increase the authority and sanctity of the Emperor and to
develop authoritarian institutions within the government were
a utilization, at least, of traditional values.

A nativistic reaction is to be expected at some stage in a
process of cultural borrowing. There is a suggestion of this
pattern in the Japanese reaction to Chinese cultural influences
in the ninth century. The picture is of a gourmand who, after
a rich and exotic feast, has an attack of indigestion before
the foreign matter is digested and his internal equilibrium
reestablished. It suggests a swing of the pendulum of the sort
that used to delight historians.

Below the smooth surface of the generalization, however,
there is a confused series of cross currents. There is the calculated introduction of German ideas, for example, to counteract the use of a French or English import in order better to
perpetuate the traditional qualities of a native institution. This
is a kind of "native" reaction in the sense that the objective
is conservative-traditional even though the means is Western.
Examples of this kind bring to our attention the role played
by political motivation. The government was attacked by its
critics for favoring Westernization at the expense of native
tradition and hence weakening the country. Nationalist and
anti-foreign sentiment was used as a weapon in the political
struggle in a way that is reminiscent of the use, twenty years
earlier, of the slogan "Expel the Barbarians" (*jōi*) in order to
embarrass the Tokugawa regime. At the same time, the government accused some of these same critics of advocating radi-

cal Western political ideas which would undermine the national polity of Japan.

However cynical or pragmatic the use of appeals to native traditions in political maneuvers, the fact that this device was extremely effective in the late eighties is indicative of the ground swell of national self-consciousness which was at the basis of the "native reaction."

It is not possible to confine our discussion entirely to the intellectual and cultural world, because even there the reaction was to a large degree in the form of a protest against the administration's Westernization policies and thus became entwined with criticism of domestic and foreign affairs. The public outburst came most strongly from a number of journals founded in the years 1888 to 1890. The philosophers, educators, and critics-at-large clamored for a reversal of the oligarchs' "Europeanization" policy of the eighties, which ranged from the Germanization of political institutions to sponsoring ballroom dancing. These became symbols of the accelerated and overwhelming pace of cultural change. A tide of foreign influences was inundating the country, and they were struggling desperately to regain some footing on native soil before they were swept away into an alien sea.

This was the first time the Japanese had paused, in their headlong rush into the modern world, to consider what it meant to be Japanese: what was it about the Japanese that made them distinct from other peoples? At the rate things were going, they would become so Westernized that they would lose those distinctive qualities, whatever they were. Would they then become second-rate Westerners? They came to the realization that it was not enough to take in and understand Western civilization. It was also necessary to know Japan. They began to discuss those features of Japan which set her off from other traditions: the unbroken succession in the Imperial line and the sacred land unsullied by foreign invasions. These were records, they said, without parallel in the world. Others preferred not to mention the Emperor or the national polity, but instead saw in art or in literature, in ethics or in family relations, qualities of unrivalled beauty. The uniqueness of Japan must mean that Japan had a special role, a special mission to perform in the world. If she were to become so Westernized that she lost her special qualities, Japan would be nothing.

This general point of view was widely expressed, although with a variety of opinion as to whether the role would be moral or military, commercial or cultural.

Westernization and Reaction in the Seventies

Several decades earlier, when Japan began to borrow from the West, few Japanese would have suspected that this step could lead to Westernization. For those who advocated the importation of some elements from the West, the aphorism was "Western science, Eastern morality." The borrowing was a desperate move, in the face of encroachment by Western powers, to acquire the weapons and military organization to stave off the diplomatic and military threat. But it soon became evident that military strength was dependent for support upon a base in industry and trade. Such a program could advance systematically only after the Meiji Restoration brought to power a vigorous, young leadership which could marshal the resources of a unified nation. The new government began at once to introduce the obvious conveniences of the contemporary civilization of the West—the telegraph, railroads, steamships, gas lights, improved streets and sanitation. These in themselves would not seem to pose a threat to traditional society and values.

The innovations could not function, however, without modern governmental machinery and an educated citizenry. The Restoration had, as the word implies, brought back into active service the offices of the ancient Imperial Court, but within a few years these began to be modified or supplemented with new agencies, and there was some experimentation with deliberative bodies. The education law of 1872 was an unusually radical departure from the past, outlining an ambitious program of compulsory education for all classes. It accepted the French and American notion that the purpose of education was the advancement of the individual, materially as much as intellectually. American school readers were translated to replace the primers of Confucian maxims.

These changes caused considerable bewilderment, and there was some resistance. However, the slogan *bummei kaika* ("Civilization and Enlightenment") was efficacious in silencing objection to innovations, especially after 1873 with the return of the Iwakura Mission from its tour of the Occident. In the same year, the Meirokusha was founded, a society of scholars dedicated to bringing the light of Western civilization to dispel the darkness of Japan's "feudal" isolation. English and American theories of representative government and women's rights were heady stuff. During this flush of admiration the saying was "America our mother, France our father."

Erwin Baelz (1849-1913), a German doctor who went to Tokyo in 1876 to teach in the medical school, was struck by Japanese repudiation of their own traditions, at least when talking to foreigners: "In the 1870's at the outset of the modern era, Japan went through a strange period in which she felt a contempt for her own native achievements. Their own history, their own religions, their own art, did not seem to the Japanese worth talking about, and were even regarded as matters to be ashamed of."[1]

While it was the Westerners who were the barbarians before 1868, the Japanese leaders now became extremely sensitive to the fact that their own society appeared backward and barbaric to the West. As numbers of foreign residents came into the principal cities, the authorities attempted to effect reforms, in 1871 ordering ricksha men and day laborers not to strip to their loincloths but to keep decently covered, with the admonition, "You must not be laughed at by foreigners." Steps were

---

[1] *Awakening Japan: The Diary of a German Doctor: Erwin Baelz*, ed. Toku Baelz, tr. Eden and Cedar Paul (New York, 1932), p. 72.

taken to segregate the sexes in public bath houses and to suppress the sale of erotic prints. In 1872 there was an abortive attempt to free indentured prostitutes, geisha, and men and women servants.[2] It is evidently a cultural characteristic of the Japanese to be unusually self-conscious and anxious not to appear ridiculous in the eyes of foreigners. A factor which perhaps contributed to the defensive attitude of these times was a realization of the cultural implications of the unequal treaties—the realization that it was because the Westerners considered Japan to be uncivilized that they insisted on extraterritorial provisions for the trial of their nationals in consular courts. Perhaps more important was the frank admiration of the technological and scientific achievements of the West, which made fashionable the adoption of Western ways.

The rage for Western clothing is described in an early issue of the *Tokio Times*:

> . . . in the 2nd and 3rd years of Meiji, the demand for foreign goods remarkably increased. Those who formerly looked upon them with contempt changed their minds and even dressed in foreign clothes. Our males adopted the European style. They put on fine tall hats instead of wearing large cues on their heads, and took to carrying sticks after discarding their swords. They dressed in coats of the English fashion and trowsers of the American. They would only eat from tables and nothing would satisfy them but French cookery.[3]

Western haircuts replaced the topknot about 1870, and were de rigueur by 1872. Gold watches, diamond rings, and Western-style black umbrellas were the mode. Officials sported mustaches and beards according to the style of Western diplomats, and in 1872 Western dress was prescribed for men at official functions. The Emperor appeared in military uniform in the fashion of European royalty.

[2] G. B. Sansom, *The Western World and Japan* (New York, 1950), pp. 385-86.

[3] *Tokio Times*, Jan. 27, 1877, p. 46, giving as its source, "Kinji Hioran—Translation of Japan Gazette."

These are examples of cultural borrowing which are not essential features of modernization in the same sense as gunboats. Nor in fact did these innovations strengthen the defenses of Japan in any way except, supposedly, by improving her image abroad.

If we are to take stock at the end of the first decade of the Meiji period of the reaction to the changes, we find that there has been some objection, but not general criticism, of the borrowing of these superficial as well as more utilitarian offerings of the West. The oligarchs were under heavy fire for their modernization program, but not primarily because it was too Western. The Saigō faction from Satsuma, unable to have its way within the inner circle, withdrew in protest against the precipitousness of the modernization measures, and it blundered into armed revolt in 1877. Although this faction objected to unnecessary innovations, its protest was motivated less by ideology than by the loss of privilege of the samurai class at large and the conservative Satsuma clique in particular.

Other factions, from Tosa and elsewhere, disappointed at their exclusion from participation in high office, demanded a representative assembly and used Western liberal political doctrine to attack the government. Mounting pressure from this quarter, and Ōkuma's split with the other oligarchs in 1881, wrested from the government the promise of a national assembly to be established in 1890. In the face of the clamor for an English-style parliamentary system of responsible cabinets and the appearance of political parties agitating in their newspapers for radical programs, the oligarchs, who by now included more of the Satsuma-Chōshū clique than at any other time, counterattacked ferociously. They dissolved the parties, prohibited political agitation, and imposed repressive controls over publications so that they could proceed without harassment with the construction of governmental institutions during the nine years of time they had bought with the promise of a Diet. During this period they developed a set of institutions and laws which were designed to limit the actual power of the Diet, and they placed beyond its control the ministers and officials appointed by the Emperor. These measures all seem intended to keep political initiative in the hands of the oligarchs. There was an ingenious blending of authoritative traditions from Japan with techniques adapted from Central European states, notably Prussia, where institutions were found that seemed best suited to perpetuate the level of authoritarianism which the Japanese oligarchs wished to maintain within a constitutional system.

The Authoritarian Structure

In order to gain information and advice on constitutional and other matters, Itō Hirobumi was dispatched to Europe in February 1882. He spent almost all his time in Austria and Germany, from where he telegraphed a request for the appointment of three advisors, recommended by Bismarck, to come to Japan to aid in drafting political reforms. Some of the palace officials and the Great Minister Sanjō Sanetomi believed that Itō's brains had been Germanized, and that his advisors would turn Japan into a German state. The Minister of the Right, Iwakura Tomomi, the power in the government, approved the appointments. However, at the same time (February 2, 1883) he wrote to Sanjō asking him to have a book compiled for the guidance of the German advisors which would make clear "the basis of the national polity, the Imperial line unbroken for ages eternal, and the customs which date from antiquity. Use a historical approach throughout, and set forth all essential general principles in a simple way. Have it translated into German, and present it courteously to the three appointees. Once they have thoroughly understood that these things are basic and fundamental, let there be a division of legislative, administrative, and judicial powers."[4]

Upon his return to Japan, Itō took the leadership in the

[4] Watanabe Ikujirō, *Kyōiku chokugo no hongi to kampatsu no yurai* (1931), pp. 232-34.

government reorganization which culminated in the Constitution of 1889. Among the measures he instituted were a number designed to elevate the position of the Emperor. The Imperial Household Ministry was moved outside the cabinet. The ancient court title Naidaijin (Lord Keeper of the Privy Seal) was revived (1885). The Imperial Household's private holdings of forest lands and mines, already extensive, were greatly increased to make less effective any budgetary pressures the future Diet might attempt to exert. The Imperial House Law was also drawn up.

A particularly interesting example of the blending of traditional and German elements to construct an authoritarian institution was the creation in 1884 of a peerage. The new peerage was explicitly a bulwark of the throne, a nucleus of conservative membership for the House of Peers which would convene in 1890. The original roster of 508 was made up almost entirely of former daimyo and court nobles, but thirty-two statesmen of samurai family background were unobtrusively insinuated. The scheme of five hierarchical titles and the legal framework were German, but the titles themselves, since similar ones had never existed in Japan, were taken from Chou China.

Rehabilitating a peerage with titles was proposed by Kido Takayoshi (Kōin) in 1876, and following his death the next year, Itō worked out the plan. It was eight years, however, before he found sufficient support in the government to put it into effect. A letter he wrote to Itō Miyoji in 1881 set forth quite baldly the arbitrariness of the scheme:

The creation of titles of peerage is an indispensable device for fortifying the position of the Imperial House. . . . We have both been concerned about the recent tendency of all classes to slip unknowingly into the spirit of republicanism. If nothing is done about it now, the situation will become irremediable. . . . Although today it would to some extent be contrary to the trend of the times and would go against people's sentiments, I should like very much to try this means of recovering the situation and take advantage of the fact that the last glow of feudal reverence for the Emperor has not died out. Concerning the names of the titles, although there is nothing to which we are forced to adhere, I am distressed that it seems unavoidable that we shall have to bring out the Chinese system. . . . However, if you have some other good idea, please let me have it.[5]

Among other steps taken by Itō was the establishment of the Privy Council (Sūmitsu-in) as another conservative body (1888). He discarded the Council of State (Dajōkan), a restored court institution, in favor of a strong executive cabinet on the German model. The system of appointments to the bureaucracy was also modernized (1885), civil service examinations were established (1887), and the bureaucracy was brought under the close control of the executive branch. The Constitution of 1889, largely an amalgam of articles from European constitutions of the preceding decades, placed few restraints on the ruler or his ministers. These borrowed elements were prefaced by an expression of the unique qualities of the national polity of Japan:

Article I. The Empire of Japan shall be reigned over and governed by a line of Emperors unbroken for ages eternal.
Article III. The Emperor is sacred and inviolable.

In the field of education, the reforms of the early Meiji government had been particularly revolutionary. Placing the reason for the establishment of schools squarely on the cultivation of the individual, the proclamation of the Council of State of 1872 said: "The means by which men establish their positions, manage their property well, prosper in their enterprises, and thereby attain full lives are none other than the following. These accomplishments are dependent upon developing their character, enlarging their intellect, and increasing

[5] *Itō Hirobumi den*, II (1940), 218.

their abilities. But men cannot develop their character, enlarge their intellect, and increase their abilities without study. This is the reason for establishing schools. . . ."[6]

To achieve the highly utilitarian objectives of such schooling, the traditional texts were replaced, for the most part, with translated material from the American Wilson readers, and even English and American ethics texts were used. In many schools European history was taught but not Japanese history.

Motoda Eifu (1818-91), Confucian tutor to the Meiji Emperor, criticized the new school system, predicting that the products of the Westernized education would be "deficient in the spirit and soul of our country and shallow in their foundation in morals and in courage for righteous causes. One would try in vain to make pillars of the nation out of them. . . . Efforts are being made to convert Japanese into facsimiles of Europeans and Americans."[7]

In 1879 he criticized the Western-style ethics texts as being responsible for the decline in morals. The Japanese family system and loyalty to the state were being destroyed; students were being taught high-sounding academic theories and empty arguments which would make them useless as government officials and troublemakers as citizens. Disaster could be averted only if education were "founded upon the Imperial ancestral precepts, benevolence, duty, loyalty, and filial piety, and Confucius were made the cornerstone of our teaching of ethics."[8] Two years later Motoda's views were accepted by a new Minister of Education, Fukuoka Takachika (1835-1919), who declared that the guiding principles of the education system would henceforth be loyalty, filial piety, and

---

[6] Fujiwara Kiyozō *(Meiji, Taishō, Shōwa) Kyōiku shisō gakusetsu jimbutsu shi*, 1 (1943), 118-19.

[7] Tokutomi Iichirō, *Motoda Sensei shinkō roku* (Tokyo, 1910), Lecture 6 (ca. 1878), pp. 93-94; D. H. Shively, "Motoda Eifu: Confucian Lecturer to the Meiji Emperor," in *Confucianism in Action*, ed. D. S. Nivison and A. F. Wright (Stanford, 1959), pp. 327-28.

[8] "Kyōgaku taishi," in *Kyōiku ni kansuru chokugo kampatsu gojūnen kinen shiryō tenran zuroku* (Tokyo, 1941), p. 4a.

patriotism. Western ethics texts were banned. The ardent Westernizer Fukuzawa Yukichi (1835-1901) was most indignant about this change of policy: "[The Ministry of Education] brought together old-fashioned Confucianists to compile readers, and otherwise staged the farce of trying to restore past customs in a civilized world. The books written and translated by me were adjudged to be harmful and without value as school texts; ridiculously enough, not one passed the inspection."[9]

This policy was reversed by Mori Arinori (1847-89) when he became Minister of Education in 1885. As a member of Itō's Germanizing cabinet, he rejected Confucian teachings as too old-fashioned, too unscientific to use as a basis for building a really strong authoritarian state. In line with Itō's policy of building institutions that emphasized the supremacy of the state over the individual, the purpose of education was directed toward service to the state. Changing the name of Tokyo University to The Imperial University in 1886 and the adoption of school uniforms were symbolic of the new orientation which was to remain essentially unaltered until 1945. Mori was in the midst of his program of inculcating his unique brand of modern nationalism through education in the schools when, in 1889, he was assassinated by an old-style nationalist because of his ostensible disrespect for Shinto traditions.

With Mori removed from the scene and the nativist reaction in full swing, and with Yamagata now Prime Minister, Motoda was able at last to achieve his goal; he had the Emperor issue an Imperial Rescript establishing "the precepts of the Imperial Ancestors" as the basis for Japanese education. Precedent for an Imperial pronouncement on ethics was found in the "Sacred Edict" of the K'ang-hsi and Yung-cheng Emperors.[10] The Imperial Rescript on Education, announced on October 30, 1890, was the crowning touch that brought the

[9] "Fukuzawa zenshū shogen," in *Fukuzawa Yukichi zenshū*, 1 (1958), 61; cited in Watanabe, p. 209.
[10] Shively, "Motoda Eifu," p. 329.

authoritarian edifice to completion less than a month before the convocation of the Diet.

Europeanization and Treaty Revision

Of the many problems which beset the administration during the eighties, one of the most vexing and most urgent was how to gain the agreement of the Western powers to the revision of the unequal treaties in order to abolish extraterritoriality and achieve tariff autonomy. These treaties were one of the dominant influences on Japanese politics for a period of over forty years, from the time of their inception in 1858 until they finally expired in 1899. When the Tokugawa negotiated the treaties, there seemed to be advantages in not having to dispense justice to the troublesome foreigners. But criticism of the treaties proved to be one of the most effective ways of harassing the Tokugawa regime and giving substance to the cry "Expel the Barbarians."

The Meiji regime began its attempt in 1870 to secure revision because of economic and political problems which the treaties aggravated. Import and export duties fixed at five percent were small defense against the importation of manufactured goods that disrupted native industries, or the exportation of gold and silver bullion. The government looked to higher duties as a source of revenue for financing the modernization program. One of the principal objectives of the Iwakura Mission was to seek changes in the treaties, but the reception to their overtures, both in the United States and in Europe, was extremely cold.

Because of the urgency of the economic problem during the following years, the government decided to propose the return of tariff powers first, and to deal later with the problem of consular jurisdiction. The Foreign Minister, Terashima Munenori, negotiated a treaty with the United States in 1878 which would have restored complete tariff autonomy, but it did not go into effect because of the refusal of the other powers to follow suit. The Japanese press attacked Terashima for not taking up the question of extraterritoriality, and he was forced to resign.

The next Foreign Minister, Inoue Kaoru, completed a draft treaty in 1880, but it was disapproved by the British Minister. During the next year Inoue held a long series of conferences with foreign representatives, but without significant results. In 1884, the Japanese were informed that the treaties would be discarded only when law codes were put into effect which met standards accepted in the West.

In earlier attempts to draft various types of new legal codes, there had been an inclination to ignore Japanese customary practice and Chinese codes. Difficulties with the civil code were particularly complex. The draft of 1878 was rejected as too close an imitation of the French civil code. As a result of many drafts and revisions and innumerable postponements over the next two decades, a code was finally agreed upon which not only contained English and German elements as well as French, but also showed a reassertion of ideas concerning the Japanese family system. The household was placed under the control of the family head, and although the code provided for inheritance of property by any children, women were placed at a disadvantage in inheritance, as they were in marriage and divorce.

Inoue resumed conferences with the foreign representatives from May 1, 1886, and his latest treaty draft as modified in the meetings, was nearing the point of acceptance in April 1887.

Legal modernization was the most important, but it was only one of the measures taken to convince the foreign powers that Japan had made sufficient progress into the modern world. A more picturesque government program directed to the same end was the attempt to bring Japanese and foreigners into social contact, emulating in Tokyo the gay social life of a European capital. Not only to gain treaty revision but also for Japan to make her way in the competition with Western powers, it was necessary, Inoue believed, to undertake thorough

Westernization. In a document he prepared for the Cabinet, he defended his solution to the problem of treaty revision:

> ... it is my opinion that what we must do is to transform our Empire and our people, make the Empire like the countries of Europe and our people like the peoples of Europe. To put it differently, we have to establish a new European-style Empire on the Eastern Sea. . . . The Japanese must achieve a system of self-government and a vigor of conduct sufficient to assure the creation of a strong people and a powerful and effective government. . . . How can we impress upon the minds of our thirty-eight million people this daring spirit and attitude of independence and self-government? In my opinion, the only course is to have them clash with Europeans, so that they will personally feel inconvenienced, realize their disadvantage, and absorb an awareness of Western vigorousness. . . . I consider that the way to do this is to provide for truly free intercourse between Japanese and foreigners. . . . Let us change our Empire into a European-style Empire. Let us change our people into European-style people. Let us create a new European-style Empire on the Eastern Sea. Only thus can our Empire achieve a position equal to that of the Western countries with respect to treaties. Only thus can our Empire be independent, prosperous, and powerful.[11]

Before describing the implementation of Inoue's social program, we might note some illustrations of the fever for Westernization which raged through much of society. Toyama Shōichi, a professor at Tokyo University, argued in 1884 for adopting more of Western ethics and culture: "In dealing with the kind of people who believe in Sakyamuni, Confu-

---

[11] *Segai Inoue Kō den*, III (1934), 913-20; the first part of the passage is quoted in M. B. Jansen, "Modernization and Foreign Policy in Meiji Japan," in *Political Development in Modern Japan*, ed. R. E. Ward (Princeton, 1968), p. 175.

cius, Nichiren, Suitengū, and Kompira, it will not do to use reason alone. There is, after all, no other means than to bring forth some figure to be worshipped such as Jesus or Mohammed." He said that people who advocate Christianity fall into two groups: those who maintain that Christianity is the only true religion and those who hold that although Christianity does not differ particularly from other religions, it would be extremely convenient to adopt it in order to have better relations with Westerners. Toyama suggested further advantages: "Christianity ought to be adopted for, first, the benefit of progress in music, second, the development of compassion for fellow men and harmonious cooperation, and third, social relations between men and women."[12]

Mutsu Munemitsu (1844-97), who later became Ambassador to the United States and Foreign Minister, remarked during a speech in Wakayama in 1886:

> Customs and usages differ from one European country to another . . . but throughout Europe there is a single culture and a common element. The adoption of this element as a means of reforming the life of the people, to make it the same as that of the people of Europe, is the most important consideration for the survival of the Japanese people. For that purpose we must reform everything, from such intangibles as education and morals to the concrete things of everyday life such as clothing, food, and houses.[13]

A similar viewpoint was expressed in 1874 by Nishi Amane (1826-94), who had been a member of the Meirokusha and subsequently occupied minor posts in the War Ministry and the Imperial Household Ministry:

> At the present time an immense number of European customs are pouring in upon us; it is as though a bottle has

[12] "Shakai kairyō to Yasukyō to no kankei," in *Sanzan sonkō*, ɪɪ (1909), 142, 144; cited in Watanabe, p. 205.
[13] Watanabe, p. 206.

been overturned. Clothing, food and drink, houses, laws, government, customs, even all kinds of crafts and scholarly pursuits—there is nothing which we are not taking from the West. Moreover, the advent of mixed residence and Western religion is only a matter of time. . . . Since this trend is pressing rapidly on us, and since we cannot take seven-tenths and discard three-tenths, I would say that it would be better to adopt the alphabet also. Our form of writing was taken from China by the early sovereigns. At that time, all literature was taken from China. Now, with changing conditions, we have already borrowed the literature of the West. Why argue only against taking the alphabet?[14]

The next year the Romaji-kai was founded, advocating the replacement of writing in characters and *kana* with a romanized script. Mori Arinori, one of the founders of the Meirokusha, had advocated in his earlier days, before he had to be so nationalistic, that Japan should adopt the English language.

The middle eighties broke into a rash of improvement societies (*kairyōkai*) almost all of which were dedicated to the Westernization of some aspect of life and culture. Among these societies were those devoted to drama, speech making, singing, dancing, music, novel writing, fine arts, foreign hairstyles for ladies, housing, manners and customs, and social intercourse between young men and women.

A satirist tells us that some ladies crimped their hair with curling irons in the attempt to look like Westerners, and lamented they could not dye their eyes blue or whiten their skins.[15] It was actually proposed that Japanese clothing be prohibited. Countess Itō was a leader in the Ladies Costume Society, which promoted the wearing of Western dress and required it of its members. The craze for foreign styles reached

---

[14] "Yōji o motte kokugo o sho suru no ron," in *Meirokusha zasshi*, No. 1 (Mar. 1874), reprinted in *Meiji bunka zenshū*, XVIII (1928), 52; cited in Watanabe, p. 204.

[15] Watanabe, p. 207.

the court ladies, who, in 1886, ordered gowns, corsets, and shoes from Berlin. The Western residents were appalled by the results, and tried to persuade them to return to the native costume. Mrs. Cleveland even wrote a letter to this effect. The pioneer Japanologue, Basil Hall Chamberlain (1850-1935), who was then Professor of Japanese Philology at The Imperial University, records the scene: "No caricature could do justice to the bad figures, the ill-fitting garments, the screeching colors that ran riot between 1886 and 1889."[16] Dr. Baelz noted in his diary after a formal reception in April 1889: "The Empress, who has gradually got used to wearing European dress, made a very good appearance. She has a graceful figure, and delicately moulded features with a moderately aquiline nose." In the same passage he also gives indication of a reaction, or at least of a response: "I am glad to say that many of the Japanese ladies were wearing native dress. Happily this seems to be coming into its own once more."[17]

One of the more seminal improvement programs was that set forth by Takahashi Yoshio in 1884 in his book on the improvement of the Japanese race. The Japanese "with their weak minds and bodies" could not hope to compete with Caucasians, he asserted, and would only become exhausted in the attempt and thus be further weakened. The only remedy would be to strengthen the race through intermarriage with superior Caucasians.[18] This possibility seems to have been seriously argued for some years by leading statesmen and scholars. They even sought Herbert Spencer's opinion in 1892. He advised against it as a general practice.[19]

The symbol of these years was the Rokumeikan (Hall of the Baying Stag), an elaborate structure in Renaissance style designed by an English architect and completed in 1883, at a

[16] Basil Hall Chamberlain, *Things Japanese* (Kobe, 6th edn., 1935), pp. 141-42.

[17] *Awakening Japan*, pp. 87-88.

[18] *Jinshu kairyō ron*, quoted in Watanabe, p. 206.

[19] Herbert Spencer's letter to Kaneko Kentarō, London *Times*, Jan. 18, 1904.

cost of 140,000 yen, after nearly three years of construction. This building and the Tokyo Club were designed to provide an appropriate setting for social intercourse between Japanese and foreigners, for dining, playing cards, and balls. Dances were held on Sunday evenings, and there were frequent musicales and bazaars. The opening was attended by over 1,100 people—Imperial princes and nobility, the diplomatic corps, and the leading officials. Dance studios mushroomed throughout the capital.

The most notorious affair was a fancy-dress ball (*fuanshi bōru*), held at the official residence of Prime Minister Itō on April 20, 1887. The four hundred guests were greeted by the host, dressed as a Venetian nobleman, and the hostess, in a Spanish gown of yellow silk and wearing a mantilla. Miss Itō was dressed as an Italian peasant girl. Prince Arisugawa came as a European knight and Prince Kitashirakawa in the scarlet robes of a Southern European nobleman. Yamagata, then Home Minister, wore, appropriately enough, the uniform of a leader of a Chōshū *kiheitai* unit of twenty years before, with black body armor, two swords crossed, and a whistle. The Governor of Tokyo Prefecture was dressed as Benkei at Gojō bridge and his wife as the young Yoshitsune. Shibusawa Eiichi was a *yamabushi* and his wife a dancer in the costume of "Kochō." Watanabe, President of The Imperial University, was dressed in the grey robe and hood of the monk Saigyō on his travels. Nabeshima Katsuratarō and Suematsu Kenchō were the Soga brothers. Ōkura Kihachirō was dressed as Urashima, and the jewelled box he carried was lighted by means of batteries.[20] "The wives and daughters of these high officials appeared as romantic or poetic characters in Japanese legend and were much sought after as partners by foreign gentlemen, many of whom appeared in Japanese dress."[21] The *Japan Weekly Mail* reported that this was indeed "a gay

[20] Tsuji Zennosuke, *Nihon bunka shi*, VII (1953), 64-66: *Japan Weekly Mail*, Apr. 30, 1887.
[21] Sansom, pp. 370-71.

and motley throng of warriors and peasants, gods and devils, kings and nobles."[22] The dancing lasted until four in the morning. As one participant expressed it later, he had "danced for the sake of the country."

It is not surprising that at this spectacle of the great men of the country dressed like actors and dancing with their arms around foreign women, there were Japanese who took fright, thinking that the fate of their country had fallen into the hands of madmen.

Another gala event was held the next week, when Inoue entertained at his residence on four successive nights. Having erected on his grounds a theatre which would seat three hundred, and was lighted by electricity (available in Tokyo only that year), he presented an evening of *kabuki*. For some of the Japanese officials as well as the Western diplomats, it was the first time that they had seen this plebeian form of drama. The Emperor attended the first night, the Empress the second, and the Empress Dowager the last evening.[23]

Unprecedented as was this social whirl, it would probably have caused no furor had it not been for the revelation, only a few weeks later, of the terms under negotiation for treaty revision. Foreign Minister Inoue, after five years of hard work, was at the point of achieving agreement with the powers. Discussions had proceeded in the greatest secrecy for fear of the sort of public reaction which had embarrassed earlier attempts. Because of the increasingly nationalistic tone of the political opposition and the press, the government was anxious to get this issue settled before the opening of the Diet provided a troublesome public forum.

Among the terms which became known was that Western judges would be appointed to cases involving foreigners, that import duties, although increased, would still be determined by treaty, and that the residence of foreigners would no longer be restricted to a few of the principal cities and the entire

[22] *Japan Weekly Mail*, Apr. 30, 1887.
[23] *Japan Weekly Mail*, May 7, 1887.

country would be opened up to them. There was strong protest from all sides, including government officials in the Ministry of Justice, the Genrō-in, and the palace circle. Even the French legal advisor Gustave Émile Boissonade was opposed to the use of foreign judges and the provision that the Western powers were to approve the new law codes. The most telling criticism came from within the cabinet. Tani Kanjō (1837-1911), Minister of Agriculture and Commerce, who had been touring the United States and Europe, reached Japan in June, and the next month he submitted a fiery denunciation of the treaty terms. The greater part of his statement, however, was a broad attack on the Sat-Chō clique—he was one of only two members of the cabinet not from those domains—for its monopolization of power and for its Germanization of the government.[24] The document, published and circulated privately, inflamed the public. When Tani resigned from the Cabinet he became a hero, and public demonstrations were held in his support. The popular rightists also joined in the attack. Itagaki and other politicians submitted long statements complaining of the abuses of the times. These denunciations stressed the excesses of Europeanization, and did not fail to deplore the extravagant and dissolute social activities sponsored by the Cabinet.

Public indignation over the treaties was linked to a number of international and domestic issues. Resentment toward foreigners was aggravated by an incident in October 1886. In the wreck of the English freighter "Normanton," the crew of twenty-six made off in lifeboats while the twenty-three Japanese passengers were lost with the ship. The British consular court at Kobe exonerated the captain, but after vociferous pub-

---

[24] Tani had been trained in French military science, had been in France, and had become a Francophile. He viewed France as a country where the people were strong and the government weak, and regarded the situation in Germany as the reverse. He considered himself a spokesman for the people in protesting the growth of a German type of statism in Japan. Motoyama Yukihiko, "Tani Kanjō no seiji shisō," in *Jimbun kagaku*, VI (1956), 104-09.

lic protest, the case was reviewed and he was given a three-month sentence. This affair exemplified the high-handedness of the Westerner and the helplessness of the Japanese in an international legal case. Japanese were becoming increasingly sensitive to the attitude of superiority of the foreign residents, the monopoly of much of the trade by the Western merchants, the Japanese dependence upon high-salaried foreign advisors and teachers, and the activities of missionaries, which were regarded as a slur on Buddhism and Shinto. There still remained some of the old fear of Christianity, a survival of habit from two centuries of indoctrination by the Tokugawa regime that this was the most pernicious of all religions. But only at this late date did many of the Japanese, who had been resentful of the "inequalities" of the treaties, realize the implications of equality, which would open up to foreigners the hinterland, the pure and unspoiled rural areas of the country, not only for economic exploitation but for the spread of foreign religions and social teachings.

Anti-foreignism mounted during the eighties, with the involvement of increasing numbers of people in the discussion of political issues and the growing role of the press. Dr. Baelz, from his experience of thirteen years in Japan, remarked on the atmosphere early in 1889: "On the whole, Japanese sentiment is anti-foreign, and especially adverse to foreigners as individuals. The reaction we have long been anticipating has at length set in."[25] Anti-foreign sentiment became such a problem as the convocation of the Diet approached in 1890 that the government discussed whether there should be an Imperial Rescript to check the "*jōi* enthusiasm."[26]

Despite these manifestations, it would be misleading to take

[25] Baelz, p. 81.

[26] Jansen, "Modernization and Foreign Policy," p. 186, citing Usui Katsumi, "Jōyaku kaisei to Chōsen mondai," in *Iwanami kōza Nihon rekishi*, XVII (Kindai, IV) (Tokyo, 1962), 116-17.

such anti-foreignism at full face value. It reflects a new stage in the people's attempt to establish Japan's position in relation to Western countries. Japan felt the lack of weapons to be thwarting her ambition to achieve equality with the West. She did not yet possess the military power to impress the West. She was not yet accepted into the family of nations. That would be accomplished only a decade or two later as a result of military victories. Lacking military power now, the Japanese looked to national cultural integrity to give them security. The people feared giving away too much to gain revision of the treaties, and they mistrusted the Cabinet, which appeared to be doing just that. The political outsiders wanted to delay treaty negotiations until the Diet was at last convened, in order to use that body to supervise and review the negotiations and to safeguard against Cabinet ministers who were "too anxious to please foreigners." Expressions of anti-foreignism, therefore, were also expressions of opposition to the oligarchs' policies and their monopoly of political power.

Resentment against the government in 1887 was not only for its relations with foreigners but also for its domestic policies. The government was *gaijū naikō* ("soft outside, hard inside"). It coddled foreigners with concessions and dances while it oppressed its own people. Two domestic grievances of long standing were the high land tax and the repression of freedom of speech and assembly. These two and treaty revision were the three issues that made up the program of Gotō Shōjirō's Great Coalition (Daidō Danketsu), which began to take form from October 1887, bringing together the leaders of over seventy political groups to work in opposition to the government. Students and other demonstrators flocked to Tokyo from all over Japan to petition the Emperor and demand confrontations with ministers to urge them either to change their policies or to resign. They argued that if the ministers knew their own people better they would change foreign policy to benefit Japan instead of foreigners. The government countered with the Peace Preservation Law of December 25, 1887, arresting 570 of the opposition leaders in the middle of the night and banishing them from Tokyo.

Inoue had been forced to resign in August. Itō persuaded Ōkuma, who had been out of the government since 1881, to take on the post of Foreign Minister in order to continue the work of treaty revision. In April 1889 the terms of the new proposal, which had also been kept secret, were published in the London *Times*, revealing that the Japanese government still intended to agree to foreign judges. The Great Coalition sprang into action again, and the government was peppered with 300 memoranda bearing 57,000 signatures, calling for the abandonment of the new draft. The cabinet itself was split, and on October 18, 1889, before it could reach a decision, a bomb was thrown into Ōkuma's carriage, resulting in the loss of his leg. (The would-be assassin, a member of the chauvinistic Gen'yōsha, was wearing a frock coat.) The Cabinet resigned. It was another five years before a satisfactory treaty was signed, to go into effect in 1899.

The Intellectual Protest

This excursion into the political realm provides the background against which we must view the "native" reaction of scholars and critics of various sorts. They were not merely responding to Westernization; they were also reflecting the anti-foreignism which surrounded the treaty-reform question and the anti-Cabinet sentiment.

While it is possible to catalog a number of writings in the decade before 1887 which deplored the harmful effects of Westernization, these were essentially an attenuation of the *jōi* sentiment and Shintoistic chauvinism of the middle sixties, and were therefore of negligible influence in the age of "Civilization and Enlightenment." We are concerned with those who began their protest against Westernization about 1887. One individual who began protesting a decade earlier is of interest, however, because he suddenly gained a considerable following in 1887 with the change in the tenor of the times, a change which he may have had some part in bringing about.

Nishimura Shigeki (1828-1902), an original member of the Meirokusha, never progressed very far beyond the viewpoint he held before the Restoration, that borrowing should be highly selective and adaptive so that the Japanese people would not lose those moral and social qualities of the Tokugawa heritage which were admirable. He had been setting forth in articles for some years his concerns about the measures taken by the oligarchs, but it was too much for him when European dress was adopted by the Empress and when the Peers School for Girls required Western garb. In December 1886, less than half a year before Itō's fancy-dress ball, Nishimura delivered a series of public lectures at The Imperial University on three successive days, which he shortly published under the title *Nihon dōtoku ron* (On Japanese Morality). The Japanese, he said, "regard whatever is their own as inferior to the others', i.e., the West, whether it is good or evil, beautiful or ugly, and do not in the least regret abandoning the traditions and teachings of their ancestors."[27]

As Nishimura remarked, years later, on the situation at this time:

. . . the new administration of the Itō Cabinet imitated Europe and America in every detail in the legal system, customs, and ceremonial, and decked itself completely with foreign civilization. It gave special hospitality to foreigners, presenting such foreign amusements as balls, masquerades, and tableaux vivants, assiduously sought to win their favor, and seemed to disregard and abandon the spirit of loyalty, filial piety, honor, duty, valor, and shame, which had been the traditional foundation of our country since ancient

[27] *Hakuō sōsho*, I (1909), 11-12; D. H. Shively, "Nishimura Shigeki: A Confucian View of Modernization," in *Changing Japanese Attitudes Towards Modernization*, ed. M. B. Jansen (Princeton, 1965), pp. 193-241.

times. The officials who were appointed were largely men of cleverness and flattery, and those who were simple and sturdy were always rejected. . . . After carrying on for one year, the people became increasingly rash and flippant and frivolous in their manners and customs.[28]

Encouraged by the reception of his lectures, Nishimura revived the ethical society which he had founded years before. The sudden growth of his organization after 1887 is an index of the change in public interest in the problem of Japanese morality. The original Tokyo Shūshin Gakusha (Tokyo Society for Moral Training) was founded in 1876 and after four years had a membership of 32. He reorganized it in 1884 as the Nihon Kōdōkai (Japanese Society for Investigation of the Way), at which time it had 328 members. In September 1887 he made a homophonic change of the character *kō* in the title of the Society, making it the Japanese Society for Expansion of the Way, with 6,000 members in 1895 and 10,000 by 1902, an unusually large number for a private society at this time. It grew to 130 local chapters, complete with a women's auxiliary, and it published a magazine, the *Kōdōkai zasshi*.

This will serve as a representative example of the five or six societies of a generally conservative stripe which were formed between 1887 and 1890, each with its own publication. In each instance the stated objective is to counteract the deplorable trends of the times, of which the Europeanization policy of the government appears to be the principal concern.

A new type of group was the Seikyōsha, founded in 1888 by Miyake Setsurei (Yūjirō, 1860-1945), Shiga Shigetaka (1863-1927), Inoue Enryō (1859-1919), Sugiura Jūgō (1855-1924), and seven others. Beginning in April, it published the bi-monthly *Nihonjin*, dedicated to "the preservation of the national essence" (*kokusui hozon*). The prospectus stated:

The Japan of today is the same Japan which was founded originally. Accordingly, despite the fact that our activities

[28] *Ōjiroku*, in *Hakuō zensho*, ii (1905), 193-94.

have become increasingly complex, the major problem confronting us today is still to select systems of religion, education, art, politics, and production appropriate to the ideas and skills of the Japanese people and to the countless external and environmental factors present in the land of Japan.[29]

The objectives of the group appear to have been to stress the merits of Japan's past, and to resist unnecessary innovations, such as some measures of the Europeanization policy which would adversely affect the national essence. The articles in *Nihonjin* attacked the government's politics with such vigor that the magazine was frequently suspended.

In his articles and in his booklet, *Shinzembi Nihonjin* (The Japanese: the True, the Good, the Beautiful, 1891), Setsurei emphasized the importance of maintaining the independence and integrity of the different national cultures rather than encouraging them to merge together. Maintaining their separateness would lead to mutual appreciation and respect. It was essential that the Japanese develop a deep understanding of both Japanese and Western cultures. For Japanese culture to be good and strong, the people must be prosperous and independent, and not subservient to the government. He proposed that the Imperial Museum in Tokyo, at that time a general art museum, should confine itself to Oriental art, a change in policy which actually took place some years later. Only through a knowledge of Japan's heritage and special abilities could the nation perform its mission in the world:

Nature exerts her influence in hidden and unfathomable ways. Today the countries of Asia are following one after another into destruction, while far across the sea to the east there stands a tiny island, towering and independent, called the Japanese Empire. This cannot be without reason. . . . There is no doubt that the Japanese are burdened with the great responsibility of exerting their special talents, making up for the imperfections of the white races, and advancing

[29] Watanabe, p. 235.

the world to a state of perfect happiness, of total truth, goodness, and beauty.[30]

The university education of the four leaders of the *Nihonjin* group was in Western philosophy or science. Setsurei's field
of study was English philosophy and political thought, especially that of Carlyle and Spencer. After graduating he studied
the history of Japanese religions for a time, and then turned
to problems of Japanese social and political life as viewed by
a person of philosophic interests. Shiga was a geographer
trained by American teachers at the Sapporo Agricultural
School. Inoue Enryō was raised in a Buddhist temple, but left
Buddhism for the study of Confucianism. In 1873 he discarded
that also and devoted himself enthusiastically to Western
philosophy. Stimulated by his study of English Neo-Hegelian-
ism, and provoked by the stir created by Christian thought in
Japan, he began to reexamine Buddhism in the attempt to
find truths there which could be the basis for revitalizing it
for use in contemporary life. The survival of the unique spirit
of East Asians and their very independence could be guaranteed, he said, only by invigorating Buddhism and reforming
it into a popular religion for the laity. In his many books and
articles, beginning in 1886, he attacked Christianity and pro-
pounded patriotic Buddhism.

The fourth of this group, Sugiura Jūgō, studied chemistry
in England for four years, but, upon his return to Japan in
1880, he moved from a specialization in science to interest in
educational questions. His articles emphasized that Japanese
education should provide a thorough knowledge of Japan
before dealing with Western studies. It should take into
account the unique traditions of Japanese history: the unity
of government and religion in ancient Japan and the special
relationship between the Imperial family and the people.

[30] *Miyake Setsurei shū*, in *Meiji bungaku zensho*, xxx (1967), 203-
04; from Henry D. Smith II, " 'The True, the Good, and the Beautiful': Miyake Setsurei's Conception of the Japanese People" (unpubl.
paper, 1965), p. 28.

Because of this heritage, the moral training provided in schools should be based not on Christianity or any other religion, but on principles of natural science.[31] (How this was to be done is not made clear.)

These views were expressed a year before the formulation of the "national essence" movement. Sugiura voiced similar views in his "Nihon kyōiku genron," published in February 1887. In that essay he also said:

Everyone knows that each of the countries of the world which maintains its honor has its own special style. The style of course exists spontaneously, but it is an indisputable fact that all the people will put great effort into cultivating and preserving it. . . . I think the basis for Japanese education, or the element of education necessary for being Japanese, lies in the preservation of the spirit peculiar to Japanese from ancient times. Someone composed the following poem:

Shikishima no	With the spirit
Yamato gokoro o	of old Japan
tane to shite	as the seed
yomeya hitobito	Read, people,
kotokuni no fumi	foreign writings.

Although not of an elegant tone, this poem appeals to me exceedingly. There might be various ways to cultivate the Japanese spirit, but one cannot rely on reason alone but must depend a great deal on sentiment. Therefore, children should be thoroughly acquainted from an early age with the history and geography and literature of our country. The most vital point for Japanese education is that the aforementioned element [Japanese spirit] should always be included in maxims . . . elementary school readers, and other textbooks used in elementary schools. For having said this, I

[31] "Nihon kyōiku genron," in *Tendai Dōshi chosaku shū* (1915), pp. 45-46; Watanabe, p. 216.

might be taken for a commonplace *kokugakusha* type. I am nothing of the kind. The more one is acquainted with the customs, civilization, and political systems of foreign countries, the more one feels the need [for knowing the Japanese spirit].[32]

In criticism of the education policy of the government, he wrote the same year:

Current education is a matter of plastering Western civilization on one's person—and not merely plastering, either, for they are not satisfied until the body itself changes into that of a Westerner. Moreover, we have reached the point where some people advocate not only changing the body into that of a Westerner, but also changing the spirit into that of a Westerner, so that in the end all human races will change into Western races.[33]

The same month that *Nihonjin* began publication, Kuga Katsunan (1857-1907), a man of similar views, resigned his position as a minor official in order to do what he could to oppose the Europeanization policy. The paper he started, the *Tokyo dempō*, was renamed *Nihon* and a few months later, in February 1889, he received financial backing from Tani Kanjō. His paper was so effective in its criticism of the government that it was suspended thirty-three times during the next seven years. Kuga coined the term *kokumin shugi*, "people's nationalism," to distinguish his own viewpoint from the nationalism of more reactionary and chauvinistic groups and from the state-centered nationalism of the Sat-Chō regime. He explained that "people's nationalism" meant externally the independence of the people and domestically the unity of the people. Setsurei and Sugiura of *Nihonjin* worked closely with Katsunan, and when his guidance of the *Nihon* came to an

[32] *Tendai Dōshi chosaku shū*, pp. 44-45.
[33] "Nihon kyōiku no hōkō," in *Kyōiku jiron*, No. 57 (ca. 1887), reprinted in *Tendai Dōshi chosaku shū*, p. 173.

end with his death in 1907, they renamed their magazine
Nihon oyobi Nihonjin (Japan and the Japanese).

A more conservative type of nationalism was expounded by
the Nihon Kokkyō Daidōsha (The Society of the Great Way
of Japanese National Teachings), formed in January 1888 by
Torio Koyata (1847-1905), a former General from Chōshū,
with Kawai Kiyomaru, Yamaoka Tetsutarō, and others. Its
publication, *Daidō sōshi*, explained that the "National Teachings" consisted of Shinto, Confucianism, and Buddhism as
they were brought into harmony by the early Japanese emperors. In recent years, however, their teachings were in peril:

There are people who, by destroying the work of the early
rulers, throw the national spirit into confusion, damage the
organization of society, undermine the foundations of morality, injure the spirit of loyalty and patriotism, and, worst
of all, seek to replace the spirit of our country with the
teachings of foreign nations. The national teachings are the
spirit of our nation. Upon them depend the ancestral temples and national altars, the Imperial line and the national
polity, morals and ethics—the very life of the nation. . . . If
the great Japanese empire, which has existed in independence on the Eastern Sea for three thousand years without
bowing its head for an instant or losing an inch of its soil,
is to be maintained for all eternity, we must respectfully
acquiesce to the work of the early rulers and thereby develop
a cohesive national spirit, bringing order into the social
structure, cultivating the foundations of morality, and rous-
ing the spirit of loyalty and patriotism.[34]

A year later Torio organized a political party, the Hoshu
Chūsei Tō (Conservative Imperial Party), with the *Hoshu
shinron* as its organ. Its purpose was to oppose the government's Europeanization policy and the programs of the political parties, the Jiyūtō and the Kaishintō.
In May 1890, adherents of a Shinto group formed the Kan-

[34] Watanabe, pp. 236-37.

nagara Gakkai, which published the magazine *Kannagara*, devoted to expounding the Imperial Way of Shinto. It criticized the adherents of Europeanization, saying that although they were registered as Japanese, their minds had undergone a change and they could no longer be considered pure men of the Land of the Gods.[35]

Nose Sakae, an official of the Ministry of Education, issued a periodical called *Futsū kyōiku*, beginning in 1889, and the following year he published his views on moral education under the title *Tokuiku chinteiron*. This book, published only a few weeks before the Imperial Rescript on Education was issued, said that the principles of moral education should not be prescribed by the Minister of Education, nor was a prescription necessary in Japan. "The ethics arising from the ordinary consciousness peculiar to Japan consist of loyalty to the sovereign, piety toward parents, high regard for honor, concern for reputation, minimization of desire, and the chastity of women. . . . Japan's loyalty and filial piety are virtues unique to our country."[36] Japan should therefore follow these national virtues, which exist apart from Confucianism and Buddhism. Japan must not rely entirely on Western things to the exclusion of all else, as the advocates of Westernization would have it, or it would become impossible to protect the independence of Japan and preserve her national polity.[37]

This dreary enumeration serves to illustrate the range of societies and publications dedicated to the preservation of some aspect of native values. It was not merely in conservative quarters that there was a resurgence of national spirit. Even among the young Christian converts, who came from the Kumamoto Band at Dōshisha or Clark's group at the Sapporo School, there is ample evidence of national spirit. The desire to naturalize Christianity is seen in Ebina Danjō's attempt to harmonize Christianity, Shinto, and Japanese ethical morality, and in the "No Church" movement of Uchimura Kanzō, who,

---

[35] Watanabe, p. 237.　　　　[36] Watanabe, p. 238.
[37] Watanabe, pp. 238-40.

after his return to Japan in 1888, worked to establish a Japanese Christian movement independent of Western missionaries and sectarianism.

A graduate of the Dōshisha group, Tokutomi Soho (Iichirō) (1863-1957) formed the Min'yūsha (Society of Friends of the People) in 1887 and began publication of *Kokumin no tomo* (English title: *The Nation's Friend*). This magazine, in its campaign for social reform and its call for a moral rebirth, was one of the most popular publications of its day.

Soho was, at least at that time, an advocate of Westernization, and there is in his interest in English political movements and Fabian socialism a latter-day version of the spirit of enlightenment that began in the *Meiroku zasshi* in 1873. He was opposed, however, to the superficial aspects of the government's Europeanization program. At the same time he disapproved of the anti-Europeanization stance of the other critics of this program—the Daidō Danketsu for its political motivations, and the other magazines for the retrospectiveness of their nationalism. *Kokumin no tomo* urged the common people, especially the youth, to lead the way. Soho's mystique of the common people, suggested by the name of the society and its publication, and his appeal to youth (he was all of twenty-four) to lead Japan's "resurrection," as he called it, were also set forth in his *Shin Nihon no seinen* (The Youth of New Japan, 1885, to use the title of a later revision) and *Shōrai no Nihon* (The Future Japan).

He said that it was necessary to have a second Meiji reform, because of the urgency of the problem forced upon Japan by the situation in Asia. The Western powers, having swallowed India, were encroaching further, upon Annam and Burma, and also upon China and Korea. Even Japan was not safe, and should quickly rise to her mission of serving as a "breakwater" to save the rest of Asia. This point of view made some common ground with Kuga Katsunan, editor of *Nihon*, and led to cooperation between the two with the approach of the

Sino-Japanese War, as Soho's interests shifted from social reform toward a more extreme nationalism.[38]

Fukuzawa Yukichi (1835-1901), the original and greatest advocate of the English style of "Civilization and Enlightenment" in the opening years of the Meiji period, was displeased with the Europeanization of the middle eighties, both because of the authoritarian product under the Itō program and because of its dances and other social frivolities. Are these necessary adjuncts of civilization? he asked. In adopting the good things that the West has to offer, is it necessary to take what is extraneous and superficial?[39]

Like other Japanese, Fukuzawa was much concerned for the safety of Japan in a world of predatory powers, and more aware than he had been earlier of the importance of developing a national consciousness in the people. While he had previously been concerned with fostering independence in the individual, by 1882 he placed emphasis on the importance of a spirit of independence in the people and in the nation as a whole:

> . . our desire is to make our scholarship independent, not merely tasting the dregs left by Westerners; to make our commerce independent, not subservient to their restraints; to make the laws of our country independent, not subject to their contempt; and to make our religion independent, not to be trampled down by them. In short, we value the independence of Japan, and our life-aim is focussed on national autonomy. . . .[40]

Japan needed a core of strength which would give unity to the nation and maintain a spirit of independence. Perhaps Fukuzawa had cherished hopes that representative govern-

---

[38] Kenneth B. Pyle, *The New Generation in Meiji Japan: Problems of Cultural Identity, 1885-1895* (Stanford, 1969), pp. 25-52.

[39] *Japan Weekly Mail*, May 21, 1887.

[40] In the first issue of *Jiji shimpō*, March 1, 1882, reprinted in *Fukuzawa Yukichi zenshū*, VIII (1960), 7-8.

ment would provide such strength, but the irresponsibility of the popular rights movement and power struggles between the political parties convinced him that reliance could not be placed there, at least in the near future.[41] He emphasized that the steadying force must be the Imperial House, which he described in the most glowing terms:

> Our Imperial Household is a precious gem unflawed for a myriad generations, a great rallying point bringing together men's hearts. Bathed in the bright radiance of this gem and assembled within its rays, our Japanese people must preserve social order at home and extend national prestige abroad. This gem must not be infringed upon; this rallying point must not be disturbed.[42]

In this essay, "Teishitsu ron" (On the Imperial House, 1882), and in "Sonnō ron" (On Revering the Emperor, 1888) in which he expressed essentially the same views, he seems to have looked upon the Imperial institution as playing a role similar to that of the Throne in England.[43] He starts in the following passage to describe a function which might pass for English, only to slide into a more native view:

> The Imperial Household acts as a rallying point bringing together men's hearts, mitigates the friction arising from the political debates of subjects, controls the spirit of army and navy personnel and teaches them their aims, rewards filial sons, virtuous wives, and meritorious persons, brings sincerity to the moral education of the entire nation, sets the example of honoring letters and esteeming scholars, makes Japanese learning independent, rescues the arts from their abandonment, and promotes the prosperity of civiliza-

[41] A. M. Craig, "Fukuzawa Yukichi: The Philosophical Foundations of Meiji Nationalism," in *Political Development in Modern Japan*, pp. 132-35.

[42] "Teishitsu ron," in *Fukuzawa Yukichi zenshū*, v, 279.

[43] Carmen Blacker, *The Japanese Enlightenment: A Study of the Writings of Fukuzawa Yukichi* (Cambridge Univ., 1964), p. 119.

tion. It is impossible to express the infinite greatness and importance of its virtuous deeds.[44]

A different type of national spirit and aspiration is found in the political novels popular from 1885 to 1890. These were essentially protests against the tyranny of the oligarchs by popular rightists, spinning out day dreams of the new Japan that would be brought into being by representative government after the granting of the Constitution.

Tōkai Sanshi (Shiba Shirō, 1852-1922) studied in a commercial school in San Francisco and at the University of Pennsylvania. Directly upon his return to Japan, he wrote *Kajin no kigū* (Strange Encounters with Elegant Females, 1885). In this novel the Spanish beauty, Yūran, tells our Japanese hero:

"Now that your country has reformed its government and, by taking from America what is useful and rejecting what is only superficial, is increasing month by month in wealth and strength, the eyes and ears of the world are astonished by your success. As the sun climbs in the eastern skies, so is your country rising in the Orient. . . . Then will the occasion arise for doing great things in the Far East. Your country will take the lead and preside over a confederation of Asia. The peoples of the East will no longer be in danger. In the West you will restrain the rampancy of England and France. In the South you will check the corruption of China. In the North you will thwart the designs of Russia. You will resist the policy of European states, which is to treat Far Eastern peoples with contempt and to interfere in their domestic affairs, so leading them into servitude. Thus it is your government and no other that can bring the taste of self-government and independence into the life of millions for the first time, and so spread the light of civilization."[45]

Another prominent writer of political novels, Suehiro Tet-

[44] "Teishitsu ron," in *Fukuzawa Yukichi zenshū*, v, 289.
[45] Sansom, p. 414.

chō (1849-96), was not so satisfied, however, that the superficial aspects of Western civilization had been discarded. In a speech in October 1887 he criticized the government's policy as being more concerned with what foreigners thought of Japan than with Japan itself. As an active politician, later to serve in the Diet, he took the line of the popular rights leaders. He criticized the government restrictions on ricksha men and horse-cart drivers, the adoption of Western clothes for women, the extravagances of the ministers' residences and government offices, the Rokumeikan, and the dance parties, which necessitated higher taxes. He also decried the fact that the only literature published was translated novels.

He glows with national pride in *Setchūbai* (Plum Blossoms in the Snow, 1886) as he has a vision of Tokyo in A.D. 2040, more prosperous than London and Paris, a Japan where learning and literature flourish as in no other country and thanks, presumably, to the strong army and navy, "there is no place where the Rising Sun Flag does not fly."[46]

> Until a hundred years ago our country was said to be the weakest and poorest in Asia and we were despised by Europe and America. The great increase in our national strength that has taken place in so short a time is due to the virtue of our wise sovereign, who at an early date decreed a constitutional form of government and opened our Parliament this day one hundred and fifty years ago. Truly it behooves us and our descendants to serve the Imperial house with fullest loyalty.[47]

The Revival of Interest in Traditional Culture

The scramble toward Westernization during the seventies seems to have had a numbing effect on creativity in literature. Translations of European novels were in great demand, but more as sources of information about the life and customs of the West than for their merits (any that may have survived

[46] Sansom, p. 416.   [47] Sansom, pp. 416-17.

translation) as literary works. The novels of Disraeli and Bulwer-Lytton were extremely popular because of their applicability to the popular rights movement in Japan. These translations led directly to efforts to write Japanese political novels during the middle eighties, with the results that we have already sampled. In spite of certain nationalistic sentiments expressed in these works, from the standpoint of technique they are, like the translated novels, examples of the Westernization of literature in a particularly crude form.

Literature of quality does not begin until 1885, when Tsubouchi Shōyō introduced the criteria of Realism in his *Shōsetsu shinzui* (Essence of the Novel). Although this essay had a strong Westernizing effect on Japanese literature, the principles it advocated were considerably naturalized when they were applied in Tsubouchi's own *Tōsei shosei katagi* (1885-86) and Futabatei Shimei's *Ukigumo* (1887-89).

Also from 1885, the students at the University who formed the Ken'yūsha group began to experiment in their stories circulated in the *Garakuta bunko*, with the style of Tokugawa writers. Within a few years this revival of interest in the Edo period bore fruit in *Ninin bikuni iro zange* (1889), *Kyara makura* (1890), and other writings by Ozaki Kōyō which were heavily influenced in style, as in title, by Saikaku. During the same period, Yamada Bimyō, a member of the same group who had decided to go his own way, received recognition for his historical novels *Musashino* (1887) and *Kochō* (1888). Saikaku's sharp insights into human behavior exert a strong influence on writings of Kōda Rohan such as *Issetsuna* (1889). The idealization of the native craftsman's passion for his art is the dominant theme in Rohan's *Furyū-butsu* (1889) and *Gojū no tō* (1891). All of these writers showed an absorption in Japanese tradition which contrasted sharply with the dominance of the translated novel and the political novel in the previous decade.

The analogy in poetry to the translated novel was the anthology *Shintai shishō* (1882), which contained translations of English poems and original poems in the style imposed on the translator by the English models. A reawakening of interest in *waka* was sparked by Hagino Yoshiyuki's articles in 1887, and led to important developments in the composition and study of this classical form. New departures in haiku did not become significant until about 1890, when a number of haiku societies were formed. Masaoka Shiki, who first had become devoted to haiku in 1885, began a few years later to write a *haikai* column for the newspaper *Nihon*.

In the heat of enthusiasm for Westernization in the educational system, the Meiji government adopted a policy of teaching mainly Western-style pencil drawing in art classes in elementary schools. The first government art school, the Kōbu Bijutsu Gakkō (Industrial Art School) opened in 1876, with its leading faculty imported directly from Italy—Edoardo Chiossone and Antonio Fontanesi teaching painting, and Vincenzo Ragusa offering instruction in sculpture.

The decline of interest in Japanese art after the Restoration, with the changing fortunes of the daimyo families, temples, and other owners of old paintings, had resulted in the scattering of collections, the sale of objects to foreign collectors, and neglect in the protection of masterpieces of the artistic heritage. In 1878 a private group was formed (taking the name Ryūchikai the next year) with the purpose of promoting the preservation and encouragement of Japanese art. It published a serial (*Ryūchikai-hō*), and it agitated for exhibitions of old and new painting. It finally gained government support with the first national exhibit restricted to Japanese painting (Naikoku Kaiga Kyōshinkai, 1882) and the exhibition of Japanese art in Paris (1884). Ernest Fenollosa (1853-1908), a recent graduate of Harvard, was appointed to lecture on philosophy at Tokyo University in 1878, and before long he was decrying the neglect of Japanese painting. In particular, his lecture before the Ryūchikai in 1882 had a great impact in reviving interest in Japanese art. Two years later, Fenollosa, his associate Okakura Kakuzō (Tenshin) (1862-1913),

Kawase Hideharu of the Ryūchikai, and others formed the Kangakai (Society for the Appreciation of Painting), which played a major part in the revival of painting in traditional styles. Kanō Hōgai (1828-88) and Hashimoto Gahō (1835-1908), two painters of the Kanō school who had fallen into obscurity during the decade after the Restoration, became leading painters of the revived Japanese style. Fenollosa and Okakura were sent abroad in 1886 to investigate art schools in preparation for the opening in 1889 of the Tokyo School of Fine Arts (Tokyo Bijutsu Gakkō, later the Tokyo Geijutsu Daigaku). Okakura was appointed Principal in 1890, with Hashimoto Gahō as the main teacher. Initially Okakura would permit only the teaching of Japanese-style painting, but later he was impelled to add a Western section.[48] Further evidence of the revival of interest in Japanese art was the founding of the scholarly art magazine *Kokka* (1889). In 1885 the Ministry of Education reversed its earlier policy concerning art classes in elementary education, replacing pencil drawing with brush-and-ink painting in the Japanese style.[49]

The new attention to Japanese art contributed to the revival during the nineties of activity in schools of tea ceremony, flower arrangement, and *nō* drama.

The scholarly study of Japanese literature was encouraged in 1882 by the establishment of a curriculum in classical Japanese and Chinese texts at Tokyo University. In 1890, graduates of this program, Ochiai Naobumi, Hagino Yoshiyuki, and others, began the publication of ancient Japanese texts in modern editions with the series *Nihon bungaku zensho*. Such publications became extremely numerous from that decade on. Kokugakuin was founded in 1889 as a school specializing in ancient Japanese literature, history, and Shinto studies, and began issuing the *Kokugakuin zasshi* in 1895. In 1891 *Waseda bungaku* began publication, *Teikoku bunko* in 1895, and the

[48] See the paper in this volume by John Rosenfield, pp. 201-19.
[49] Rosenfield, p. 211.

Shiryō Hensanjo was established at The Imperial University the same year, as the official historical compilation office.

The excitement of the students at this time as they discovered Edo literature may be seen in Shimazaki Tōson's (1872-1943) description of his own experience:

> As I recall my period as a student at Meiji Gakuin in Shirogane [1887-91], the revival just then of scholarship and the arts was rather remarkable, and I received a variety of stimuli as I grew from a boy into a young man. At just the time when I set my ambition on literature, Japanese classics, which had until then been buried, began to be published almost every month in collections of Japanese literature and poetry. It was also at this time that the literature of the Tokugawa period, and especially of the Genroku era [1688-1704], were dug out of the dust. Chikamatsu's collected *jōruri* were published, Saikaku's works were reprinted, and the surviving writings of Bashō and other poets of his school received attention at last. We young people were greatly stimulated by the rediscovery of these classics.[50]

Japanization as a Stage in Modernization

In the course of this paper I have cited a confluence of events and statements from the last years of the 1880's which support the thesis that there was a nativistic reaction to Japanese "Westernization." Although the neatness of the generalization is inevitably disturbed by a considerable amount of chaos in factual detail, in broad outline this interpretation appears to be useful.

Early in the paper I referred to circumstances which caution us that the phenomenon was more complex than a simple

---

[50] "Bungaku ni kokorozashita koro," in *Shimazaki Tōson zenshū,* XIV (1949), 318; cited in *Japanese Thought in the Meiji Era,* ed. Kōsaka Masaaki, tr. David Abosch, *Japanese Culture in the Meiji Era,* IX (Tokyo: Pan-Pacific Press, 1958), 188.

native reaction to Western elements. There was more than one brand of Westernization, and different groups had a variety of political motives in adopting, or criticizing, Westernizing programs. The anti-foreignism surrounding treaty revision problems was another factor that influenced events, but it had little to do with Westernization or Japanization as a concept. Nor should we deny that there were significant instances of native reaction in earlier years. Still, by comparison, on a relative scale, the reaction of the late eighties was massive and comprehensive.[51]

"Reaction" perhaps does not do justice to the phenomenon, as the connotations of the word are rather negative, in any case not progressive. While it is true that the movement had its reactionary side, this was probably a more obvious than important aspect, especially since the extreme position is generally most likely to attract attention. At the basis of the development was not "reaction" so much as a growth of self-consciousness and awareness of Japan's position, her past, and her future prospects. It was the search for an answer to the questions posed by the feeling that Japan was losing her identity in the flood of Westernization.

There can be no doubt that the movement brought great benefits in the cultural area, not only in the preservation and appreciation of works of the past, but also as a force in revitalizing—not simply reviving—the arts.

The effect is more difficult to argue in the intellectual and political spheres. Not merely national consciousness, but patriotism as well, were necessary conditions for modernization, at least in the nineteenth century. They were needed to achieve an efficient level of national unity, and they were

[51] An intriguing complexity is the role of the foreigner in urging the Japanese to have more regard for their own traditions in selecting or adapting imports from the West. Chiossone, Fenollosa, Murray, Baelz, Boissonade, even Mrs. Cleveland, to mention only the names which have appeared in this paper, gave advice. The interesting point is that the advice was followed only when the time was ripe.

needed to induce the people to undergo the sacrifices necessary in the modernization process. While selective Westernization was essential to the modernization of Japan, Westernization that was too rapid or too extreme could cause confusion and disunity and thus retard the rate of modernization itself. This was perhaps part of the problem of the late eighties. The growth of national consciousness appealed in one way or another to all factions in Japan, and helped to create the degree of unity that was needed. Through the schools, the government began a program to inculcate state-centered nationalism, and private societies advocated their own programs. The means varied but there was universal agreement on the ultimate aim—to strengthen Japan. Nationalism was a quick way to national unity and to modernization. So was the use of tradition, and so was authoritarianism. These had substantial short-term advantages in speeding the process of nation-building.

When we look beyond 1890, however, Japanese nationalism becomes considerably more sobering. The pendulum which had swung to "nativist reaction" in the late eighties did not seem to swing back. Fanned by the Sino-Japanese War, the nationalism of intellectuals became more stifling as illustrated by the magazine *Nihon shugi* of Inoue Tetsujirō and Takayama Chogyū. The Gen'yōsha spawned the Kokuryūkai. Reverence toward the Emperor was heightened in the school texts, in the ceremonial readings of the Imperial Rescript on Education, and in the enshrinement of the Emperor's portrait in schools. The cultivation of State Shinto and the infringement of historical inquiry gave evidence by the year 1900 that an ugly chauvinism was rampant.

CHAPTER IV

The Sino-Japanese War of 1894-95 and Its Cultural Effects in Japan

DONALD KEENE

THE Sino-Japanese War of 1894-95 is as remote and uncontroversial to most Japanese today as the Spanish-American War is to us. The leaders of Japanese thought are little interested in a half-forgotten conflict which, insofar as it is discussed, is usually dismissed as a stage in the development of Japanese capitalism. The grim volumes of the official history of the war certainly do not invite perusal except by a specialist in military campaigns, but the now forgotten deeds of bravery and violence inspired works of literature and art that may still intrigue us. This paper will not treat the causes of the Sino-Japanese War, nor its battles, nor its effects on Japanese industrialization; instead, I shall attempt to show in what ways the war affected Japanese literature, art and theatre.

Japan and China in the Early Meiji Period

The distinctive cultural feature of the war was provided by the enemy—China, the model or object of emulation of Japan throughout most of its history. From the eighteenth century, it is true, scholars of national learning had denigrated China, insisting on the mystical supremacy of the Land of the Gods; and the scholars of Dutch learning, in their enthusiasm for European civilization, frequently criticized the lack of a scientific spirit in China, contrasting the accuracy of Dutch medical books with the fantasies recorded by the Chinese anatomists, or the "spiritually" evoked scenes of the Chinese painters with the realism of European depictions. Nevertheless, Chinese cultural influences remained exceedingly strong in nineteenth-century Japan. The Meiji Restoration, though ushering in an era of uncritical imitation of Western things, did not fundamentally alter the prestige of Chinese culture. The visits of the Emperor Meiji to Shinto shrines were recorded in classical Chinese on stone monuments, and the Confucian philosophy of the Tokugawa rulers, though modified, was not displaced by either a "pure" Japanese or a Western system of thought.

Japanese feelings towards the country China, as contrasted with Chinese culture, were more ambivalent. As early as the eighteenth-century Hayashi Shihei had depicted China as a potential menace to Japanese security, and some advocates of national defense took this view seriously. The defeat of China in the Opium War naturally revealed to the Japanese how much weaker militarily China was than a European power like England, but the tradition of respect for Chinese military strength was not easily shattered. Most Japanese of 1890 believed China was a powerful country. The inconclusive war with France of 1883-85, carefully reported in Japan and even depicted in woodblock prints, had considerably restored Chinese prestige, and the reinforcement of the Chinese Navy with warships far superior to any possessed by the Japanese had even aroused consternation. The visit of the Chinese fleet in July of 1890 inspired the caption writer for the newspaper *Kokumin shimbun* to an ironic poem: "The Chinese have been showing off, and all the cowards are scared."[1] Toyama Masakazu (1848-1900) (Shōichi), a leading educator and writer, at one time President of Tokyo University, described his impressions on visiting the Chinese flagship *Ting-yüan*:

Not long ago, as a member of the House of Peers, I was invited by His Excellency Ting Ju-ch'ang, Commodore of the Chinese North Pacific Fleet [to inspect his flagship]. . . . The *Ting-yüan* is truly a splendid warship, reputed to be

[1] As reported by Kunikida Doppo, *Aitei Tsūshin* (Iwanami Bunko), p. 159.

virtually without peer within the various navies of the East. When I examined the guns I was struck by their large calibre and by the remarkable ease with which they could be maneuvered. The ship moreover is armored throughout with thick steel. The officers, from the Captain down, all appear exceedingly well trained. They are very polite to visitors, and most of them understand English. . . . I thought how truly fortunate it was that the East now boasts a fleet with a warship of this quality, manned by officers of such distinction. I did however regret somewhat that many sailors seemed rather listless, pale and undernourished. Otherwise, I was enormously impressed.

At the suggestion of a Japanese naval officer, Toyama also visited that day the Japanese flagship, *Takachiho*. He was assured that the smaller Japanese guns were more maneuverable than the heavier rifles of the *Ting-yüan*, but was not entirely convinced. What struck Toyama most aboard the *Takachiho* were the sailors:

Although the ship was to sail the following day and had already raised its sails and was getting up steam, the sailors were gathered in their quarters. Some were sewing their trousers, some writing letters back home, some reading. Our warships are manned by sailors who long for home, their families, their wives and children. Is it not sad that we force such sailors, such officers, to worry about winning a war with a foreign country? If war breaks out, our first line of defense against the enemy is our warships. Our officers and men, ceaselessly pondering day and night how to win naval engagements, are gentle men of Yamato who think of their parents, their families. It is our duty as citizens to see to it that they do not die like dogs. . . . Such were the feelings I had on visiting the Chinese warship and the *Takachiho*. Some people are given to comparing the Chinese and Japanese, but I dislike such comparisons. The Chinese and ourselves are like elder and younger brothers. We should definitely not make the Chinese our enemies.[2]

Even amidst their fears aroused by the visit of Admiral Ting's fleet, seemingly a show of strength to impress the Japanese, Toyama and others expressed their respect for Chinese culture. Admiral Ting and the other Chinese officers were honored at a banquet given at the Kōyōkan in Tokyo by the Asia Society (Ajia Kyōkai). The poems exchanged by guests and hosts, in Chinese of course, consist mainly of graceful compliments paid by the Chinese to the local scenery and to the entertainment they had been offered. This typically undistinguished poem is by Ch'en En-shou, second in command of the *Ting-yüan*:

> Japan has lovely scenery that delights on repeated viewing;
> In Kōyō Hall we listen to drums and strings.
> The three countries join in the pleasure of opening the feast:
> Assembled dignitaries bear witness to their common feelings.
> Although our costumes today are changed
> The Chinese characters are still the same as in olden days;
> We write short poems, we record past events,
> I regret only I have no fine verses worthy of such friendship.[3]

Katsu Kaishū (1823-99), the noted statesman, offered this verse to Admiral Ting:

> The iron-clad ship is several hundred feet long;
> It chases whales on the Great Eastern Sea.

---

[2] *Chuzan Sonkō*, II, 401-05. Toyama is so prolix that any translation inevitably involves drastic reduction.

[3] *Kaiyo Shōshū* in *Kaiyoroku*, XI, 22a.

We shake hands amidst mountain and river scenes
And anticipate the pleasures of good friendship.[4]

One can hardly escape the feeling that the members of the
Asia Society, no less than Japanese of a millennium earlier,
were desperately anxious to impress the Chinese. The various
Chinese emissaries who resided in Japan prior to the Sino-
Japanese War were entertained with a cordiality not apparent in the more lavish entertainments provided for European
or American dignitaries. Japanese visitors to China were
not always favored with such hospitality; despite Japanese
material progress, which by this time had outstripped that of
the Chinese, they remained "eastern barbarians" in the eyes
of many Chinese, who saw no need to win Japanese
approbation.[5] The Chinese literati in Japan, however, were
feted wherever they went, and they clearly fitted into the
Japanese scene in a way impossible for Europeans. The pleasure that Japanese literary men experienced in exchanging
poems with the scholar Wang T'ao or with the diplomat
Huang Tsun-hsien was possible in the world of *kanji*, the
Chinese characters which transcended national boundaries;
this was the world of gentlemen-scholars, an ideal common
to China and Japan.

For most Japanese, "the image of China imprinted on our
minds before the Sino-Japanese War was of a splendid, romantic and heroic country."[6] The Chinese classics were a basic
part of education, and these studies had the effect of glorify-
ing China. Treasured objects of art often depicted Chinese
personages in surroundings at once romanticized and easy for

[4] *Ibid.*, p. 22b.
[5] See Takeuchi Minoru, "Meiji Kangakusha no Chūkoku Kikō," in
Jimbun Gakuhō, No. 36, 1963, p. 92. Takeuchi quotes an article by
Sanetō Keishū, "Ōtō no Raiyū to Nihon Bunjin," contrasting the reception given to Wang T'ao in Japan with the cold treatment Oka Senjin
received at times in China.
[6] Tsurumi Shunsuke, *Nihon no Hyakunen*, VIII, 149.

a Japanese to appreciate, in contrast to many works of Western art. Japanese cultural dependence was so great that "nobody in Japan was sufficiently confident to claim that Japanese were better than Chinese. They undoubtedly would have been quite content not to be inferior." On another level, the Chinese pedlars in Yokohama were "extremely well-liked," though some Japanese feared that if the Chinese were permitted to live outside the concessions their superior business skills might overwhelm the Japanese merchants.[7] The Chinese in the concessions, it is true, on occasion showed themselves as arrogant as the Westerners,[8] but such instances were exceptional; China of all countries was closest to Japan. It is a melancholy fact that it took but a few months to destroy the tradition of respect built up over the centuries and turn the Japanese from friendship to contempt.[9]

Outbreak of War

The Japanese were prepared for the formal declaration of war with China on August 1, 1894 by a complicated series of events in Korea which had steadily embroiled the Japanese forces ever deeper. News of the outbreak of war was greeted everywhere with enthusiasm, and if the initial pitch of enthusiasm could not be maintained indefinitely, there was virtually no trace of anti-war feeling at any later stage. The only resistance to the war, if we may speak of such, came from the writers who chose not to concern themselves with the war in their writings. Among the works published during the war years the most famous—*Takekurabe* by Higuchi Ichiyō, *Kiri Hitoha* by Tsubouchi Shōyō, and *Takiguchi Nyūdō* by Taka-

[7] *Chuzan Sonkō*, II, 405.

[8] Recollections by Kishimoto Saisei in *Kamigata*, No. 81, p. 64.

[9] Some Japanese, especially men like Oka Senjin who had actually visited China, had long since been disillusioned, whether because of the Chinese addiction to opium or their hidebound attitude towards Confucian learning. (See Takeuchi, pp. 80-90.) But most Japanese still believed China to be a major power as well as the source of their own civilization.

yama Chogyū—were unrelated to the war. But those whose authors chose the war for their theme expressed themselves with unbounded enthusiasm. Yosano Hiroshi (Tekkan) (1873-1935), on hearing of the declaration of war against China wrote eight *tanka*, the last being:

inishie ni	What need we yield
nani ka yuzuran	to ancient glories?
mimizuka wo	The time is near
futatabi tsuku mo	when again we shall build
hodo chikaku shite[10]	a mound of ears.

Fukuzawa Yukichi (1835-1901), after warning against over-confidence, urged everyone to devote each word, action, and material good to the promotion of a Japanese victory. Fukuzawa saw a war with China as necessary in order that China might benefit by the enlightenment kept out by her obstinate Manchu rulers. He considered China's interference in Korea an intolerable attempt to prevent the spread of enlightenment, and the war itself not merely a struggle between two countries but a "battle for the sake of world culture."[11] Fukuzawa retained his fervor throughout the war, convinced not only of its necessity but its desirability.

Uchimura Kanzō (1861-1930) was initially no less convinced than Fukuzawa of Japan's mission in the war. He published in August, 1894, an article in English entitled "Justification of the Corean War." Though Uchimura was later known for a pacifism largely induced by disillusion with the Sino-Japanese War, in 1894 he was certain that the "Corean War now opened between Japan and China" was a "righteous war."[12] After citing numerous examples from classi-

---

[10] Reference is made to the Mound of Ears (*mimizuka*) raised by Hideyoshi in Kyoto from the ears and noses of Chinese soldiers killed in Korea. The poem is found in *Nisshin Sensō Jikki* (henceforth abbreviated *NSJ*), No. 2, p. 83.

[11] *Fukuzawa Yukichi Zenshū*, XIV, 500.

[12] *Uchimura Kanzō Zenshū*, XVI, 27.

cal, Biblical and European history to prove this contention, he went on:

> But leaving all legalities aside, (and we by no means disregard them), is not a decisive conflict between Japan and China an unavoidability,—we might almost say, a historical necessity? A smaller nation representing a newer civilization lying near a larger nation representing an older civilization,—was there ever such a situation in History without the two coming to life-and-death struggle with each other at last? . . . The Corean War is to decide whether Progress shall be the law in the East, as it has long been in the West, or whether Retrogression, fostered once by the Persian Empire; then by Carthage, and again by Spain, and now at last (last in world's history, we hope) by the Mantchurian Empire of China, shall possess the Orient forever. Japan's victory shall mean free government, free religion, free education, and free commerce for 600,000,000 souls that live on this side of the globe.

He issued a call to the nations of the world "to see and understand the cause we fight for." "Japan is the champion of Progress in the East, and who except her deadly foe,—China the incorrigible hater of Progress,—wishes not victory to Japan!"[13]

Mori Ōgai (1862-1922), as a professional soldier, was naturally first among the writers to go to Korea, arriving in Pusan on September 4, 1894. His extensive war diary,[14] though a model of his incisive style, is utterly devoid of interest, consisting mainly of dispatches on the deployment of medical personnel. Other writers and artists eagerly volunteered for duty as correspondents at the front. Kunikida Doppo (1871-1908) had some moments of fear and regret after he decided to serve as a naval correspondent,[15] but his articles for the *Kokumin Shimbun* were filled with delight over his experiences. These

---

[13] *Ibid.*, p. 35.
[14] *Ōgai Zenshū, bekkan* I, pp. 185-278.
[15] Itō Sei, *Meiji Bundan Shi*, III, 234.

articles, collected in the posthumously published *Aitei Tsūshin* ("Letters to My Beloved Brother," 1908), overflow with a childish enthusiasm and patriotism, as exemplified by an impromptu address given by Kunikida to the officers of the warship *Chiyoda*: "People of our great Japanese Empire are proud that they have military men brave and loyal as you! You too should always remember this. Above your heads is His Majesty, an Emperor endowed with supreme literary and military virtues. Behind you are your forty million compatriots, all but burning with emotion. You are fortunate. Where else in the entire world are there military men who can compare with you in the good fortune of having above you this Emperor and behind you this people? You are fortunate." Following this oration, there was a shout of *wan, tsū, surii* and all present burst into song.[16]

Masaoka Shiki (1867-1902) was another eager volunteer. He later recalled that "I felt that unless I could see service with the troops somehow, there would be no point in having been born a man."[17] He did not actually arrive in China until April, 1895, and his one-month stay produced little writing. The sight of Chinese corpses strewn around gun emplacements at Chin-chou sickened him into writing one of the few negative works inspired by the war:

nakihito no	Hide from sight
mukuro wo kakuse	the corpses of the dead,
haru no kusa[18]	grasses of spring.

[16] Kunikida, *Aitei Tsūshin*, pp. 62-63.

[17] Oka Yasuo, "Nisshin Sensō to Bundan," in *Kokubungaku*, ix, No. 12, p. 14.

[18] Takahama Kyoshi, *Shiki Kushū* (Iwanami Bunko edition), p. 114. The importance of this and other haiku written by Shiki about his war experiences in the formation of his distinctive *shasei* (sketches from nature) style is discussed in Matsui Toshihiko, *Kindai Hairon Shi*, p. 79. Shiki's poems, based on personal observation, confirmed his interest in the theory of *shasei* expounded to him earlier in 1895 by the painter Nakamura Fusetsu. Comparisons of the *haiku, tanka,* and

Aboard ship, returning to Japan, Shiki coughed blood, the first sign of the illness which would take his life. The bad treatment he received aboard ship at the hands of the military also colored his later remembrances of his wartime service.

The newspapers were filled with accounts from the front, illustrated by artists like Kubota Beisen (1852-1906), whose prints depicting fearless Japanese troops routing terrified Chinese set the tone for the descriptions. They also carried serialized novels or short stories about the war, some directly describing the conflict, others pretending (in the traditional manner) to treat historical events but spicing their accounts with obviously contemporary references. Tokutomi Roka began publishing *Nisshin Sensō Yumemonogatari* ("A Dream Tale of the Sino-Japanese War") in September, 1894. In the following month Izumi Kyōka (1873-1939) began serial publication of *Yobihei* ("Reserve Soldier") in the *Yomiuri Shimbun*. At the end of this story the hero, a medical lieutenant named Nogawa Kiyozumi, collapses of sunstroke during maneuvers after a forced march with full military gear under the broiling summer sun. As he lies on the ground his sweetheart Madoka, who has followed the troops disguised as a laborer in order to be close to Kiyozumi, rushes up and identifies herself. A medical corpsman, leaning over Kiyozumi, urges him to release his grip on his sword so that treatment may be administered, but Kiyozumi refuses: "My duty as a military man will not permit me to yield my sword and lose my combat effectiveness. Please let me die as I am. This is my heart's desire." Madoka wails aloud, and the sergeant, clenching his fists, lets fall tears like hail. "*Appare da. Appare da. Yo, yo, yoku osshatta: Rippa da. Ri, ri, rippa na mono da!*" The story ends as a general descends from his horse to kneel before Kiyozumi's body, assuring him (in classical Japanese) that his gallant action will inspire the entire army.[19]

kanshi composed by Shiki at Chin-chou are made by Kitazumi Toshio in *Shasei-ha Kajin no Kenkyū*, pp. 34-35.

[19] *Kyōka Zenshū*, I, 221-22.

The novelist to profit most by the war was Emi Suiin (1869-1934), whose stories, published in *Chūō Shimbun*, enjoyed such great popularity that he earned spectacular increases of salary. Suiin later recalled that he had desired to serve as a war correspondent, but so huge was the popularity of his stories that the owner of the newspaper refused to let him go. "To tell the truth," Suiin added, "I felt that I was giving my all for the nation, with a pen instead of a sword."[20] *Chūō Shimbun*, thanks in part to Emi Suiin's stories, came to be called "the war newspaper" (*sensō shimbun*).[21]

News of the war was even more exciting to readers than fictionalized accounts. The editors curtailed such normally popular newspaper features as the scandals and murders traditionally found on the third page to devote more space to the war. The poetry columns were taken over by works describing in Chinese or Japanese the poet's exultation. One poem beginning, "*Kai naru kana. Kai naru kana. Aa, kai naru kana*" ("How delightful! How delightful! Ah, how delightful!") concluded "*Aa kai naru kana. Kai naru kana.*"[22]

The book publishers were quick to take advantage of the aroused interest of the readers. Summer was normally a poor season for books because the Tokyo university students left the city, but after the outbreak of war in August, 1894, books sold well, especially non-fiction about China and Korea. The firm of Hakubunkan began publication of the tri-monthly *Nisshin Sensō Jikki* in September, followed by the rival *Nisshin Kōsenroku*, published by Shunyōdō. The latter company, long known as the bastion of the novel, postponed publication of fiction indefinitely.[23] The enormous popularity of *Nisshin*

---

[20] Emi Suiin, *Jiko Chūshin Meiji Bundan Shi*, p. 202.

[21] Takagi, "Shimbun ni arawareta Sensō Bungaku," in *Hon no Techō*, No. 46, p. 30.

[22] *Waseda Bungaku* (henceforth abbreviated *WB*), No. 69, p. 250. Pagination of the first series of this periodical is maddening. Anyone who does not find a reference the first time is respectfully urged to persist.

[23] *WB*, No. 70, p. 269.

Sensō Jikki later occasioned the publication of *Taiyō*, a general magazine aimed at mass readership.

The newspapers, magazines and fiction published at the opening of the war are marked by unmistakable exhilaration and confidence. The Sino-Japanese War, the first conflict with a foreign power in three hundred years, naturally aroused patriotic sentiments, but a consideration of the relative strengths of China and Japan should have induced greater anxiety about the possible outcome of the war. The foreign press was nearly unanimous in predicting eventual victory for China once Japan's initial advantages of discipline and preparedness had been dissipated. Even after Japan scored a number of victories foreign opinion remained divided. "I have no hesitation in expressing the conviction that China is certain in the end to triumph if both states are left to fight out to the bitter end a long and exhausting struggle," wrote one expert on the Far East.[24] *The Spectator*, insisting that China was "virtually invincible," decried the admiration aroused in England by Japanese successes. "It would be most unfortunate if, because the Japanese make pretty fire-screens, and seem to have been impressionists without knowing it . . . we should give our moral support to Japan. . . . China is the one Asiatic Power whose friendship is of supreme importance to us."[25] But all observers agreed that the Japanese people were united behind the war: "The enthusiasm in Japan continues, and the spectacle of this Eastern nation fighting and maneuvering and organizing with a *verve* and intelligence worthy of a first-class European war has sent a thrill of admiring wonder through the military world."[26] The Japanese, as many doubtlessly sensed, were proving by incontrovertible successes in the war, that their modernization, so often belittled abroad, had been genuine. This may be why the outbreak of war was greeted with enthusiasm even

[24] Demetrius C. Boulger, "The Corean Crisis," in *Nineteenth Century*, Nov. 1894, pp. 782-83.

[25] *The Spectator*, Aug. 4, 1894, pp. 132-33.

[26] *The Illustrated London News*, Oct. 20, 1894, p. 491.

by those who could not really understand why Japan, the long-time emulator of China, had now to crush her.

The Creation of Hostility

Hardly had the war begun than *Yomiuri Shimbun* announced a prize competition for war songs which "will arouse feelings of hatred against our national enemy." The Sino-Japanese War was to inspire more and better war songs than any other conflict in which the Japanese engaged. Virtually every event of the war was celebrated, often in songs distinguished both for their words and melody. At first the emphasis was on the justice of the Japanese cause:

> Our empire, rich in benevolence and chivalry,
> Has guided our neighboring country, Korea,
> And is devoting every effort to make it
> Worthy of the name of independent country,
> And to maintain peace in East Asia eternally:
> But China, overweening in its immense pride,
> Claims that Korea is a tributary. . . .[27]

The words, even in the original, can hardly be described as lilting or even singable, but these songs tended to be plaintive narrations rather than infectious ditties.

Before long the burden of the songs shifted from idealism to denigration of the Chinese weaklings or cowards. The song about the Chinese vessel *Ts'ao-chiang*, surrendered to the Japanese, was typical:

[27] Soeda Tomomichi, *Enka no Meiji Taishō Shi*, p. 62. It may be wondered what the Koreans thought of the high ideals expressed by the Japanese. One observer declared, "It is remarkable that the Coreans themselves appear to be unanimously on the side of the Chinese, whose wickedness in upholding the present regime is so loudly condemned." (R. S. Gundry, "Corea, China, and Japan," in *The Fortnightly Review*, No. cccxxxv. N.S. Nov. 1, 1894, p. 635). But Yi In-jik, whose story *Hyol ui nu* is considered to mark the beginning of modern Korean fiction, was clearly on the side of the Japanese. Undoubtedly, there were supporters of both sides among the Koreans.

Feckless China, behold the *Ts'ao-chiang*'s end . . .
Ts'ao-chiang, warship in name only,
Knowing not what to do, flounders,
"Raise the white flag and surrender!"
We investigate, to see if it is true,
They strike the Ch'ing naval flag,
And set fluttering aloft
Our own. . . .[28]

Other songs were directed specifically against Li Hung-chang:

ri, ri, Ri Kōshō no hanabecha,	Li, Li, flat-nosed Li Hung-chang,
cha, cha, chanchan bōzu no ikedori ya	chang, chang, Chinese prisoners of war,
ya, ya, Yamagata taishō ken nuite	war, war, General Yamagata draws his sword,
te, te, teikoku banzai daishōri,	sword, sword, hurrah for the Empire, victory,
ri, ri, Ri Kōshō. . . .[29]	*Ri, Ri, Ri Kōshō. . . .*

Others, like the many variants on the tune *Miya-sama, Miya-sama*, are rather brutal in their war-spirit. One example runs:

Mina-san, Mina-san	Ladies and gentlemen,
o-uma no mae ni	what is it rolling
korokoro suru no wa	before the prince's horse?
nan jai na	That is the pumpkin-head
are wa chanchan bōzu no	of a Chinaman, don't you know?
kabocha atama wo shiranai ka tokoton yare ton yare na.[30]	*Tokoton yare ton yare na.*

Toyama Masakazu, who proudly claimed to have written the lyrics of the first Japanese war song, *Battōtai* ("The Drawn

[28] In *Shōbō Gunka*, n.p.
[29] Hiraizumi Toyohiko, "Nisshin Senso no koro," in *Kamigata*, No. 81, p. 63.
[30] *WB*, No. 71, p. 282.

Sword Unit"), was pleased that at last the nation had come to recognize the importance of war songs. The Minister of Education directed that students be taught these songs at school.[31] A 149-page book of Army and Navy songs issued in 1897 included pieces by Sasaki Nobutsuna, Ochiai Naobumi, Ōwada Tateki, Yosano Tekkan, Toyama Masakazu, and a German named F. Schroeder. The effectiveness of war songs in preserving morale during the fighting was noted. On October 15, 1894, for example, two companies led by a Colonel Satō were faced by severe enemy fire. Satō ordered his men to sing; by the time they reached the words "trampling over the four hundred and more counties of China" in the long ballad *Rappashu wo tomurau* ("In Memoriam of the Bugler"), their morale was up a hundred times and they experienced no difficulty in breaking through the enemy defenses.[32]

More important even than the war songs in creating feelings of hostility toward the Chinese were the *nishikie*, colored woodblock prints. Lafcadio Hearn reported that, "The announcement of each victory resulted in an enormous manufacture and sale of colored prints, rudely and cheaply executed, and mostly depicting the fancy of the artist only, but well fitted to stimulate the popular love of glory."[33] Over three thousand war

---

[31] *Chuzan Sonkō*, II, 271. Toyama's song *Yuke Nihon Danji* contains some of the most sensational anti-Chinese sentiments. He calls the Chinese "evil monsters," "burglars," "wolves," "the enemy of our mothers, the enemy of our wives, the enemy of our sisters and daughters," and urges that "the pure blood of the divine land not be defiled by the beasts of the enemy country." (*Rikkai Gunka Zenshū*, pp. 24-25.) These are rather strong views for a man who four years earlier had considered the Chinese and Japanese to be "elder and younger brothers."

[32] *Nisshin Kōsenroku* (henceforth abbreviated *NK*), No. 13, p. 50. The extraordinary importance of the war songs at this time has been likened to the sung narrations of the *Heike Monogatari* or *Taiheiki* in medieval Japan. (Fukuchi Shigetaka, *Gunkoku Nihon no Keisei*, p. 172.) The songs swept the country, fostered perhaps by the advances in mass printing.

[33] Lafcadio Hearn, *Kokoro*, p. 91.

prints were published during the course of the war, which lasted less than a year.[34] Kobayashi Kiyochika (1847-1915), the finest printmaker of the Meiji period, alone produced at least eighty triptychs and another hundred or so cartoons. Other artists were even more prolific. The prints were enormously popular, as we know from a great variety of evidence. A report in the November 1894 issue of *Waseda Bungaku* states,

> The *nishikie*, formerly devoted chiefly to actor portraits and the depiction of mores, now treat almost nothing but the Sino-Japanese War or related persons and incidents. The actor portraits are derived from war plays, and the usual portraits and scenes are unavailable except at the largest shops. The *nishikie* come in two varieties. The inferior ones, intended for the pleasure of women and children, are drawn in extremely gaudy colors; the superior ones are rather artistic in comparison, both in design and execution. . . . The lithographs are of course more realistic in picturing the war, but are for the most part uninteresting, and seem likely to be overwhelmed by the *nishikie*.[35]

The newspapers printed many pictures of the war.

> Newspaper illustrations formerly consisted of portraits of deceased persons or occasionally of topical cartoons, or else of illustrations to the serialized novels published in the tabloids. Since the Sino-Japanese War, however, it has become an almost universal practice to add illustrations to reports of the news. Not a newspaper but has published two or three illustrated war supplements, notably the *Kokumin* which features frontline illustrated reports drawn by Beisen, Kinsen and other artists.[36]

Newspaper illustrations, however, did not satisfy the public demand for pictures of the war, whipped up with each successive victory. The most popular *nishikie* reputedly sold as many as one hundred thousand copies each, and so dense was the

---

[34] *WB*, No. 3 (2nd Ser.), p. 149. [35] *WB*, No. 75, pp. 54-55.
[36] *Ibid.*

press of crowds at the print stores that special warnings about pickpockets were issued. The bright colors of the *nishiki*, particularly the cruder ones, entranced the public. A passage from *Haru*, the novel by Shimazaki Tōson, describes the scene:

> When he reached Fujimi-chō, there was a crowd of men and women before a print shop, everybody struggling to get a better look at the blood-thirsty war pictures. "On to Peking! On to Peking!" the eyes of the passersby seemed to say.[37]

Tanizaki Junichirō recalled many years later seeing war prints for sale:

> The Shimizu-ya, a print shop at the corner of Ningyō-chō, had laid in a large stock of triptychs depicting the war, and had them hanging in the front of the shop. They were mostly by Mizuno Toshikata, Ogata Gekkō and Kobayashi Kiyochika. There was not one I didn't want, boy that I was, but I only rarely got to buy any. I would go almost every day and stand before the Shimizu-ya, staring at the pictures, my eyes sparkling . . . I was horribly envious of my uncle who would buy all the new triptychs as fast as they appeared.[38]

The *nishiki* played a major role in shaping the Japanese image of China. The best artists usually attempted to incorporate some artistic effect in their works; Kiyochika sometimes portrayed scenes only casually related to the war because he had been intrigued by their possibilities of artistic composition. But the *nishiki* by the mass of artists appealed to prospective buyers on a far more elementary level. They uniformly portray the Japanese soldiers in poses of heroic determination and show the Chinese as abject cowards, running pell-mell from combat. Unlike the Japanese, invariably attired in sombre blacks and grays, the Chinese are clad in screaming reds, blues, purples and greens. These were the same colors Japanese artists had

---

[37] Shimazaki Tōson, *Haru* (Shinchō Bunko, 1933), p. 233.
[38] Tanizaki Junichirō, *Yōshō Jidai*, pp. 97-98.

used fifteen years earlier for Japanese troops at the time of the Satsuma Rebellion, but by 1894 these crude aniline colors had fallen into disfavor, and were used to suggest primitive taste, if not barbarity. The Chinese are distinguishable from the Japanese not only by their costumes and grotesque grimaces of fear, but by their facial features. No two peoples ever seemed more strikingly dissimilar than the Japanese and Chinese of these prints. The Chinese have jutting cheekbones, broad noses, gaping mouths, slanting eyes and, of course, pigtails. The Japanese are dignified of mien and look distinctly European in their military moustaches and carefully trimmed haircuts. A print issued ten years later, at the time of the Russo-Japanese War, depicts the Japanese and Russians as virtually identical, except for the brownish tinge to the Russians' hair. Not only do the Japanese bear strong facial resemblances to the Europeans, but they stand as tall and maintain a similar dignity of demeanor, unlike the Chinese. The famous print (Plate I) by Migita Toshihide (1862-1925) of the surrender of the Chinese admiral Ting Ju-ch'ang after the battle of Wei-hai-wei shows the Japanese officers in black uniforms towering over three cringing Chinese clad in green, purple and blue. Two European advisers of the Chinese also bow in defeat, but with greater dignity; they also wear black. This picture is one of the least denigratory to the Chinese; prints by such hacks as Adachi Ginkō portray the Chinese with savage derision. The cartoons even by Kiyochika show hideous, sub-human creatures, quivering with terror.

The Chinese willingness to become prisoners in particular aroused the contempt of the Japanese. Numerous prints show the Chinese abjectly begging for their lives or allowing themselves to be bound by the Japanese troops. The first Chinese prisoners to reach Japan were greeted everywhere with derision. A crowd waited for them at the Shimbashi Station in October. A reporter noted that the prisoners seemed unconcerned even by the jeers of the surrounding thousands; some even ate as they walked along, making them look all the more undignified.

A woman in the crowd shouted at the prisoners, *"Chanchan no heitai wa anna mono ka?"* ("If that's what the Chinese soldiers are like, I could kill a couple of them myself.") The writer commented, "Indeed this is true. They would be no match even for the women of our country."[39]

The words *chanchan, chankoro* and the like, said to be derived from *Chung-kuo jen* (the Chinese words for "a Chinese") remained for many years epithets of contempt.[40] Another term in favor at the time, though since disappeared, was *tombi*, a literal translation of the English word "pigtail." The word inevitably gave rise to rumors that the Chinese smelled like pigs or acted like them. One reporter suggested that Japanese troops cut off the pigtails of the Chinese as a proof of the numbers they killed. This would not be cruel, like amputating the ears and noses (in the manner of Hideyoshi's forces in Korea), but would dispel the stubborn doubts of foreigners about the magnitude of Japanese victories. The pigtails eventually could be sold to wig-makers, though Japanese women might, of course, object to wearing wigs made from the hair of *tombikan*, smelling of pigs.[41]

Though the prisoners were subjected to harsh mockery, the Japanese felt it was essential that they distinguish themselves from the barbarous Chinese by their good treatment of prisoners, the mark of an advanced country. By the time the Japanese captured Pyongyang in Korea they had over six hundred Chinese prisoners.

If we had been like the obdurately ignorant Chinese army, these prisoners would have been cruelly tortured before finally being slaughtered. As a matter of fact, before the fall of Pyongyang, when soldiers of ours on patrol were captured by the Chinese, they were subjected to all kinds of humilia-

[39] *NK*, No. 13, p. 50.
[40] In 1896, when the first group of Chinese students arrived in Japan, the taunts of *chankoro* were so offensive that many cut short their stay. (See Saneto Keishu, *Chūkokujin Nihon Ryūgaku Shi.*)
[41] *NK*, No. 10, p. 50.

tion, cords were brutally passed through their nostrils, and they were paraded around, before finally the Chinese lopped off their limbs and murdered them. This is intolerable. But we whose warp consists of mercy and justice and whose woof is civilization (*bummei*) could never follow the Chinese in their barbarous practice and return savagery for savagery. That is why our army has given the prisoners the best possible treatment. The prisoners from the *Ts'ao-chiang* were sent to Sasebo, later transferred to Hiroshima, and are now lodged in temples in Matsuyama. Their daily rations are almost identical with those of our troops.

Japan, it was averred, would abide by the Geneva Convention on the treatment of prisoners, no matter how cruelly the Chinese behaved.[42] Indeed, many prisoners were so pleased with the treatment they had received that they showed not the least desire ever to return to China.[43] An occasional prisoner might suggest that there was "a lone crane among a flock of chickens"; one Chinese being led off into captivity with thirty or forty others, suddenly broke away and bashed out his brains against a stone wall. "Truly there must be a few such among four hundred millions," the Japanese commented.[44] Suicide was the most effective way the Chinese had of redeeming themselves in the eyes of the Japanese; Admiral Ting Ju-ch'ang, who killed himself after the defeat at Wei-hai-wei, enjoyed considerable esteem in Japan. Chinese atrocities against European missionaries were prominently reported as well as notices published by the Chinese Army offering rewards for heads cut from the Japanese dead. In contrasts to these examples of barbarity, the Japanese prided themselves on their chivalry in action.[45] Almost every printmaker and some oil painters

[42] *NSJ*, No. 6, pp. 50-54.

[43] *NK*, No. 15, p. 33. See also *NSJ*, No. 9, p. 79.

[44] *NSJ*, No. 9, p. 100.

[45] A dismally contradictory report on Japanese chivalry may be found in James Allan, *Under the Dragon Flag*, pp. 79-95, where the massacre of Chinese at Port Arthur is described in gory detail. Allan

depicted Captain Higuchi, a Chinese waif he has rescued under his left arm, brandishing a sword with his right. In some prints the child's grateful father kneels before the Captain, in others the mother hovers behind a rock, frightened by the hail of bullets which do not daunt Captain Higuchi.[46]

The anti-Chinese feeling was levied specifically at Li Hungchang. This statesman had formerly been highly esteemed in Japan, especially when General Grant reported in 1879 that Li was one of three great statesmen of the world. Li was sometimes even called the Bismarck of the East. But with the outbreak of war he became a figure of fun, fantastically garbed, generally depicted by the *nishikie* artists in attitudes of astonishment or terror. When confronted at the conference table by a Japanese resolutely laying down demands with a thump of the fist, or when presented with the news of a military disaster, Li looks comically incompetent. In a print (Plate II) depicting Li as he learns of the fall of Port Arthur, a wine glass is clenched in his right hand and an enormous peacock feather towers above his hat. Around the table sit advisers outlandishly costumed in greens, purples and reds, all listening with gaping mouths to some frantically gesticulating soldiers who report the defeat. In the background distracted waiting women pass around soup tureens.

---

also writes of "placards, in the sacred imperial yellow, inciting these atrocities" committed by the Chinese. "The bodies of the Japanese soldiers, killed in encounters with the enemy as they closed on the place, were often found minus the head or right hand, sometimes both, besides being ferociously gashed and slashed. Corpses were still hanging on the trees when the fortress fell, and it is not surprising that their former comrades should have been maddened by the sight, though of course the officers are greatly to blame for permitting the fearful retaliation which ensued to be carried to such lengths. The massacre seems to have been allowed to continue unchecked until no more victims could be found" (p. 67).

[46] Captain Higuchi was celebrated in song (see Horiuchi Keizō, *Ongaku Gojūnen Shi*, p. 159) and in poetry (see *Bungakkai*, No. 29). Eastlake and Yamada, in *Heroic Japan*, head their account of Higuchi's gallant gesture with the title THAT BABY! (pp. 333-34).

Li Hung-chang figured as the villain of the play *Nisshin Senso* staged by Kawakami Otojirō in Tokyo on the 31st of August, playing before huge crowds for forty days. The dramatic highlight occurred in the fifth act, when the Japanese reporter Hirata (played by Kawakami himself) is dragged before Li Hung-chang (played by Takada Minoru). Charged with being a spy, he defends himself by expounding the duties of a newspaper reporter and referring to the principles of international law. He concludes by denouncing the tyrant Li Hung-chang. Takada Minoru in a pigtail and "Confucius beard" made a great hit with the audience.[47]

Li Hung-chang's reputation in Japan would be restored only after the end of the war when, in Shimonoseki for the peace treaty, he was wounded by a superpatriot. Alarmed lest the reputation of Japan, so carefully nurtured during the war, should be damaged abroad by this act of terrorism, the Japanese were more generous than they had intended with the peace terms, and the Empress herself made bandages for the wounded Li. But generous gestures could not alter the new relationship between the Chinese and Japanese: the prints, songs and war plays had convinced the Japanese that the Chinese were backward, cowardly and even contemptible, unworthy heirs of a once-great tradition.

The belief that China, once a great country, now represented a menace to civilization found expression in the war songs, including the famous *Pekin made* ("On to Peking") by Yokoi Tadanao (1857-1928):

Shina mo mukashi wa	China long ago was the land
seiken no	Of the teachings of the sages,
oshie aritsuru kuni naredo	But as dynasties changed and
yo wo kae toshi wo furu	the years passed
mama ni	She gradually has fallen
shidai ni kaika no atojisari	behind in progress.

[47] *Engeki Hyakka Daijiten*, IV, 314-15.

kuchi ni wa chūka to	She prides herself on being
hokoredomo	Middle Flowery Land,
kokoro no yaban wa	In inverse proportion to the
hampirei	barbarity of her heart;
sono mōmai wo yaburazuba	Unless we destroy her
wa ga tōyō no yo wa akeji	ignorance,
	The night of the East will
	never dawn.

The lines were rendered by an English clergyman:

> China was wise of old
>   China is wise no more
> Back into darkness has rolled
>   For all her sages and lore.
>
> She may boast as the Kingdom of Heaven,
>   Her barbarous heart is of hell,
> What light to the East shall be given
>   Till wisdom her darkness dispel?[48]

It became an easy step to assert that Japan, not China, was the true heir to the ancient Chinese glories. Okakura Kakuzō became the most persuasive exponent of this view which may account for the respect still accorded traditional Chinese culture even after China itself had been discredited.

The Japanese Heroes

The counterpart to the denigrating of the Chinese was the creation of Japanese war heroes who were the embodiments of traditional virtues. The heroes of the Sino-Japanese War were almost all from the humblest ranks. The Russo-Japanese War brought world fame to General Nogi, Admiral Tōgō and to Commander Hirose; the Sino-Japanese War was remembered largely in terms of heroic first-class privates.[49] This emphasis

---

[48] *WB*, No. 89, pp. 278-79.
[49] Virtually every hero in *Yōchien Shina Seibatsu Tegarabanashi*

on the achievements of unknown farm recruits, rather than on trained officers, the descendants of samurai, may have been accidental, but it may have been intended to bring home the lesson that universal military conscription had been the basis of Japanese success. The fact that humble soldiers could perform deeds of gallantry normally associated with the samurai proved that their virtues were shared by the entire Japanese people and not the property of professional soldiers. In contrast to the Chinese, cowardly and ready to become prisoners, even the humblest Japanese was courageous and loyal to the death. The successful charge of some unarmed Japanese coolies against a battalion of Chinese troops was cited as proof of the superiority of any Japanese to any Chinese. A short story by Emi Suiin tells of a soldier with a broken arm who insists nevertheless on going to the front. The young man says "One arm—that's no problem! Even with two broken arms I could take on any number of Chinese soldiers! Stupid Chinese soldiers! They don't amount to anything."[50] Even the most ardent American zealot never spoke of fighting with *both* hands tied behind his back!

The first war hero of the Sino-Japanese War, as it happens, was an officer, Captain Matsuzaki Naoomi, honored as the first Japanese casualty of the war. Struck by a bullet in the leg he went on fighting until another bullet struck his head. "I'm done for!" (*yarareta*) was his last utterance. Matsuzaki was often depicted in *nishikie*. When the Emperor Meiji was presented with a collection of *nishikie*, his first question was, "Which is Matsuzaki?"[51] (*Matsuzaki wa dore ka*.) He also figured in the first war plays. Nakamura Ganjirō, known for his portrayal of the rather effeminate heroes of the Chikamatsu love-suicide plays, appeared as Captain Matsuzaki in Osaka.

("Stories for Kindergarten of Meritorious Deeds During the Conquest of China") is a private.

[50] *NK*, No. 32, pp. 27-28.

[51] *Shimbun Shūsei Meiji Hennen Shi* (henceforth abbreviated *MHS*), ix, 164.

In the great *mie* of the part, he grabbed two Chinese soldiers by their pigtails and cried, "*Tombikan, yokku kike! Ware koso wa Dainippon Rikugun Hohei Taii nani no nanigashi nari.*" ("Pigtails! Listen carefully! I am none other than the infantry captain of the Army of Great Japan, such-and-such by name.") At the close of the play Ganjirō charged onstage waving a sword. Hit by a bullet, he fell crying, "*Susume! susume! susume!*" ("Charge!") at the final curtain.[52]

Captain Matsuzaki's fame was soon eclipsed by that of an ordinary private who fell in action on the same day, July 29, 1894. Early reports told of a bugler who, though struck by a bullet, went on bugling to his last breath. When they found his corpse the bugle was still pressed to his lips. The incident caught the imagination of the Japanese. Before long a flood of artistic composition had been inspired by the heroic bugler, identified as Shirakami Genjirō. The print by Toshihide, showing the bugler lying on his back, trumpeting to the sky, is the most successful of the *nishikie*.[53] Shirakami's bravery, first celebrated in *Kokumin Shimbun*, was compared to the ideal bugler described by the German poet Mosen.[54] The existence of a European prototype may account for the remarkable attention attracted by the resolute bugler. On August 16, 1894 Yosano Tekkan published *Rappashu*, followed by *Rappasotsu* by Kosugi Tengai (1865-1952), which contains the immortal lines, "I blow my bugle with my soul; its voice is the voice of

[52] *Kamigata*, No. 81, pp. 40-44.

[53] Apparently based on the sketch by Kubota Beisen in *Nisshin Sensō Gahō*, II.

[54] The poem by Mosen is entitled *Der Trompeter an der Katzbach*, found in his *Sämmtliche Werke* (Leipzig, 1871), pp. 16-17. The poem begins:

> Von Wunden ganz bedecket
> Der Trompeter sterbend ruht,
> An der Katzbach hingestrecket,
> Der Brust enströmt das Blut.

The German bugler, however, puts down his bugle after sounding the charge.

Yamatodamashii."[55] Lengthy poems were composed in Chinese, despite the difficulty of fitting the name Shirakami Genjirō into the prescribed tonal patterns. One, by a man who used the penname of Koro Gyoin, began:

> The lingering moon was about to sink by Asan,
> The sky was full of stars, the woods bright,
> Ten thousand hearths seemed asleep, ten thousand
>   sounds dead;
> Suddenly swords rang with a clang of metal;
> Our troops shouted as they slashed the enemy
>   positions.
> The barbarian soldiers fled in all directions,
>   confused.
> A bugle sundered the clouds with its echoes
>   clear . . .

The poem ends:

> The bugle at his mouth, his call still unfinished,
> A cry of pain tells he is fatally wounded.
> The imperial forces owe their victory to your strength.
> Your name will pass into history for a thousand years.
> Ah, you are heroic, Shirakami Genjirō!
> Ah, you are mighty, Shirakami Genjirō![56]

Another song, *Rappa no hibiki* by Katō Yoshikiyo (1862-1941), contains these lines in Lafcadio Hearn's translation:

> Easy in other time than this
>   Were Anjo's stream to cross:
> But now, beneath the storm of shot,
>   Its waters seethe and toss. . . .
>
> Death-stricken, still the bugler stands!
>   He leans upon his gun,—
> Once more to sound the bugle-call
>   Before his life be done.

[55] Homma Hisao, *Meiji Bungaku Shi*, II, 429.
[56] *NSJ*, No. 5, p. 78. I have been unable to identify the poet.

What though the shattered body fall?
  The spirit rushes free
Through Heaven and Earth to sound anew
  That call to Victory![57]

The masterpiece among the poems on the bugler was "A
Japanese Soldier" by Sir Edwin Arnold, published in London
on November 14, 1894.

Shirakami Genjiro
  Bugler in the Line!
You shall let our Westerns know
  Why the kiku shine!
Why the Sun-flag, gleaming,
  Bright from field to field,
Drives the Dragon, screaming,
  Makes the Pig-tails yield.

Shirakami Genjiro
  (Okayama man)
Left his ripening rice to go
  Fighting for Japan;
Musket on his shoulder,
  Bugle on his breast,
Unto each beholder
  Linesman, like the rest.

[57] Hearn, pp. 92-93. There is a fine description in Horiuchi's *Ongaku
Gojūnen Shi* (pp. 155-56) of how Katō, on hearing the story of Shirakami Genjirō's bravery was immediately inspired to write this poem
and the accompanying music. After racing around the practice hall
three times he went inside, picked up a clarinet and started blowing a
tune, but his breath gave out. He next tried a baritone trumpet, but
again his breath failed. Finally he scribbled words on a blackboard.
Still in this breathless, white-hot fury of creativity, he got another
musician to help him. The music and words were completed in half
an hour. The Emperor Meiji was especially fond of this piece, and
generally had it played for him by a military band every evening after
dinner.

Sad for grey-haired husbandman,
    Fatherly—in years—
Sad for pretty Yoshi San,
    Proudly checking tears;
No one in the village,
    Only Genjiro,
Careless of the tillage,
    Glad to ship and go.

But the Emperor doth proclaim
    Soldiers must come forth!
Is there not despite and shame
    To Nippon, in the North?
Good at target practice
    And bugle-calls to blow,
Duty bids! The fact is
    Genjiro must go.

Ah, poor boy! the home-place
    Never fairer seemed;
Never out of Yoshi's face
    Softer sunshine beamed;
Yet his country calls him;
    Dai-Nippon hath need;
Whatso'er befalls him
    Genjiro will speed.

The last three verses of this immensely long poem run:

He blew the charge so loud
    It blared across the plain,
It rattled, large and proud,
    From mountain unto main:
He blew so clear and soft
    The Pig-tails made to fly,
Before the Sun-flags, borne aloft
    Could reach the enemy.

And, while he blows the boy's blood
    Fell, scarlet drop by drop,
The bugle's mouth—and his—imbrued,
    Nor from that wound would stop
The trickling trickling! Stoutly,
    He sounded *Susumé*,
The call that bids all soldiers
    Close in the deadly fray.

To tune of that brave clamour
    The Sông-hwan wall was won;
The fierce charge sped, the foeman fled,
    The day's great work stood done.
But when they turned, victorious,
    There! on the crimsoned ground,
Clasping his bugle, glorious,
    Young Genjiro was found.[58]

Toyama Masakazu contributed a lengthy poem, *Ware wa rappashu nari* ("I Am a Bugler"), one of his series on great deeds of the Sino-Japanese War. Toyama emphasized the lowly rank of Shirakami Genjirō with exquisite subtlety:

Okayama kenjin Shirakami Genjirō.
Kare wa mata ikko no rappashu narishi nari.

[58] Sir Edwin Arnold, *The Tenth Muse*, pp. 151-59. The poem bears the note, "Extract translated from letter of an officer in Marshal Yamagata's Corean Army: 'I send you the enclosed true account of the death of Shirakami Genjiro, a young soldier, who was the first man killed at our battle of Sông-hwan.'"

F. Schroeder also wrote a poem in English on Shirakami Genjirō entitled "The Bugler of Soeng-hwan." It is dated October 13, 1894. The fifth stanza is typical:

    Another rush, as again rings the signal:
    Advance, ad—! What is that, out of breath, little Gen?
    We look back, he totters, yet his lips to his bugle:
    Ad—vance!—Why, your bugle is red, little Gen!

                    (Schroeder, *Eastern World*, p. 75.)

Hito wa ieri. Kare wa tadatada rappafuki nari to.
Kare wa ieri. Ware wa tadatada rappafuki nari to.[59]

Shirakami Genjirō, Okayama man,
He too was a bugler.
People said, "He is just a bugle-blower."
He said, "I am just a bugle-blower."

and so on. The gallant Shirakami Genjirō was celebrated even in *kyōka*, though a comic verse form would seem inappropriate:

kuni no tame	For the sake of his country
waga mi no ue wo	He ignores his own fate,
shirakami ya	O Shirakami!
fuku ne to tomo ni	Together with the note he blows
kiyuru tama no o[60]	Fades away the thread of life.

Plays (now lost) were performed in memory of the glorious bugler, the action no doubt padded with references to such creations as Genjirō's sweetheart Yoshi (celebrated by Sir Edwin Arnold) and to his fatherly-in-years father.

Shirakami seemingly attained immortality when in November 1894 the official new eight-volume readers for elementary schools were issued. The seventh volume contains the bugler's story and a picture of Shirakami lying on his back, one knee raised, blowing the charge. The selection concluded, "The name of this bugler was Shirakami Genjirō, and he came from Okayama Prefecture."[61] This identification is of more than usual interest because Shirakami Genjirō, for all the immortality promised him, soon disappeared from textbooks, to be replaced by one Kiguchi Kohei, a first-class private of identical attributes. The authors of *Heroic Japan* explained the mystery: "Shirakami Genjirō was, however, quite another man.

[59] *Chuzan Sonkō*, ii, 309.
[60] Hirano Sanjirō in *Kamigata*, No. 81, p. 27.
[61] *Nihon Kyōkasho Taikei, Kindai Hen*, v, 769.

Not even a trumpeter, but a second-class private of the First Reserves, he was none the less a comrade of Kiguchi, and belonged to the Ninth Company, while Kiguchi was one of the Twelfth Company men. He also lost his life at Sŏnghwan, being similarly killed by a breast wound."[62] It is not clear why the authorities felt it necessary, many months after the incident occurred, to give credit to Kiguchi Kohei for the deed which had made Shirakami Genjirō famous.[63] Kiguchi's name soon replaced Shirakami's and acquired a legendary character; he became the symbol of the virtue of loyalty to duty (*chūgi*) preached in school textbooks. "Kiguchi Kohei died with the bugle pressed to his lips" came to be featured in second-year elementary schoolbooks as the perfect example of *chūgi*.[64] At times in the 1920's when liberal Japanese educators objected to the militaristic tendencies in textbooks, Kiguchi Kohei was a special target.[65] Others, however, praised the loyalty of Kiguchi Kohei as sharing with the selections on the emperor the distinction of being the most successful part of Japanese *shūshin* (moral) education. In the *shūshin* textbooks Kiguchi Kohei figured more frequently than any other soldier of modern times, tying with such figures as Columbus and Jimmu Tennō in total number of appearances.[66] Every Japanese over thirty has heard of Kiguchi Kohei, but it is hard to suppress the suspicion that he may never have existed; he may have been the most successful fictional creation of the war.

The second most famous hero was Harada Jūkichi, the heroic

---

[62] F. Warrington Eastlake and Yamada Yoshi-aki, *Heroic Japan*, p. 23.

[63] Muneta Hiroshi (in *Heitai Hyakunen*, pp. 73-74) describes how, even as the memorial to the gallant Shirakami was being erected in his native village the news came that Kiguchi, and not he, had been the loyal bugler. But Muneta offers no explanation of how it was finally ascertained which of two buglers, both from Okayama, and both killed on the same day in the same action, had kept bugling to the death.

[64] Karasawa Tomitarō, *Kyōkasho no Rekishi*, p. 259.

[65] *Ibid.*, pp. 342, 365.   [66] *Ibid.*, p. 673.

scaler of the Gembu Gate at Pyongyang who let the Japanese forces into the city. Harada Jūkichi too was a familiar figure in the *nishikie*, and his deed was commemorated in poetry and prose. One song bearing his name was especially famous. It includes the verses:

ame yori shigeki dangan no	Diving under bullets thicker than rain,
shita wo kugurite jōheki no	he scrambles up the castle wall,
mashira no gotoku yojinobori	like a monkey
hirari to tobikomu sono hito wa	and lightly jumps inside; this man
kore zo Harada no Jūkichi shi	is none other than Mr. Harada Jūkichi
tsuzuite Mimura shōtaichō[67]	following him, platoon commander Mimura

The emphasis is definitely on second-class private Harada rather than on Lieutenant Mimura. Eastlake and Yamada, less interested than the Japanese authorities in celebrating the glories of an anonymous son of Yamato, declared in *Heroic Japan* that "Harada Jūkichi had the distinction of being selected to open the gate because the Lieutenant desired in some measure to reward him for his intrepid obedience."[68] But Harada, not Mimura, received the Order of the Golden Kite, and his house was deluged with presents from well-wishers. Even before Mimura's platoon broke through the Gembu Gate, however, a suicide squad had already scaled the wall. A member of this squad named Matsumura Akitarō, at first supposed dead, survived and returned to Japan. The authorities, fearing that his story if known would lessen Harada's glory, forbade him to disclose it.[69] Matsumura Akitarō spent the rest of his life in the

[67] Soeda, p. 64.
[68] Eastlake and Yamada, pp. 54-55.
[69] The story of Matsumura Akitarō is told at some length, but with evident embellishments by Muneta, pp. 109-114. According to Muneta,

back of an antique shop, gloomily staring at old relics, a man of silence. Harada Jūkichi, for his part, found the role of the hero too demanding. He sold his Order of the Golden Kite and drank the proceeds. For a time he appeared on the stage, reenacting his epic deed; his last recorded performance was in 1900 in Osaka. When Harada's story was presented at the Kabuki-za in *Kairiku Renshō Asahi no Mihata* ("Successive Victories on Sea and Land, the Rising Sun Flag") his part (called Sawada Jūshichi) was performed by the great Kikugorō. Harada himself in the part struck people by the close resemblances of his poses to Kikugorō's.[70]

The third hero of the war remains anonymous to the end. He was the sailor who gallantly extinguished a fire aboard the *Matsushima* during the naval battle off Wei-hai-wei. Dying, he asked the second-in-command if the enemy flagship *Ting-yüan* still had not sunk. The sailor, assured that the *Ting-yüan* had been knocked out of action and that the *Chên-yüan* was now under fire, said with his dying breath, "Please strike the enemy."[71] His words became the theme of the most haunting song to come out of the war, *Mada shizumazu ya Teien wa* by Sasaki Nobutsuna. It concludes:

mada shizumazu ya Teien wa	"Hasn't the *Ting-yüan* sunk yet?"
kono koto no ha wa mijikaki mo	These words though brief
mikuni ni tsukusu kunitami no	Will long be engraved in the hearts
kokoro ni nagaku kizamaren	of loyal subjects who strive for Japan.
mada shizumazu ya Teien wa	"Hasn't the *Ting-yüan* sunk yet?"

Matsumura died in 1945 at the age of 78, revealing his story only to his children and grandchildren, with the warning they must never pass it on. See also Soeda, p. 65.

[70] *Kamigata*, No. 81, p. 41.   [71] *MHS*, IX, p. 149.

kono magokoro no koto no ha wa	These words of sincerity
mikuni wo omou kunitami no	will be recorded in the burning breasts of
moyuru mune ni zo shirusaren[72]	loyal subjects who love Japan.

The unknown sailor, like the bugler and the wall-climber, emerged as a symbol of the anonymous Japanese masses. The wave of exultation and self-confidence that foreign observers noted owed much to the conviction that it was the Japanese people who had vanquished China. Hearn wrote, "It is a race feeling, which repeated triumphs have served only to strengthen."[73] The combination of denigration of the Chinese and elevation of the Japanese, the implicit object of the war art, had succeeded in its object, though by literary or artistic standards it may seem foolish or even pathetic today. Disappointment in the war was felt only by those who expected it would result in artistic works of the highest aesthetic quality.

Literary and Artistic Importance of the War

Shortly after the war began an anonymous correspondent for *Waseda Bungaku* related his hopes for wartime writing:

What influence will this great event exert on our literary world? Will the results be good or bad? . . . For the information of readers I should like to describe in general the thoughts I have had on this subject.

1. The result of the hatred of the enemy felt by our people, imparting to them a clear consciousness of the nation, an awareness of what it means to be a Japanese, and a sense of the fairness and justice of our heroic undertaking in Korea, is likely to be beneficial in raising the cultural level of the thoughts and emotions of authors and readers.

2. The glorious victories of our forces, each report stirring the spirits of our people and lifting to the heights its national

---

[72] *Rikkai Gunka Zenshū*, p. 97.   [73] Hearn, p. 90.

pride, will stimulate the hot passions of the poets, the most sensitive of men, and should result in poetry and prose of such splendor and eternity as to move the demons and gods.

3. The war, by causing writers and readers to pay close attention to present realities and to turn their eyes to the future, will naturally result in lessening the habit of vainly reflecting on the dead past, of depicting dead matters simply because they are dead; it will make people realize the necessity of studying living societies and living people.

4. Literature will, in the nature of things, become concerned with this world; poetry will become subjective and depict for the most part emotions felt at a particular time. Novels and plays will also come to reflect more obviously matters of interest to the public. Probably too, novels and plays written to embody the particular views of an individual will be shown greater favor than at present.

5. The *shintaishi* (poetry in the new style) which at the moment seems moribund should now if ever, put forth sprouts again and reach its fulfillment.[74]

After the end of the war many critics expressed disappointment over what actually had been produced. Takayama Chogyū complained in June, 1897, that "with the exception of a small number of superficial war stories written by authors of the second rank or worse, not a single man celebrated patriotism or righteous courage."[75] Most of the poetry and fiction quickly disappeared from sight, as quickly as the immortal names of the triumphs and heroes were forgotten; the plays were never printed and survive today, if at all, in manuscript; the paintings are forgotten, and the numerous prints, the cheapest of all woodblock prints today, have never been studied and are rarely even collected. Yet, in a curious way, most of the prophecies made in *Waseda Bungaku* were fulfilled: excitement over the war increased the readership of newspapers and magazines markedly, an increase later channeled into maga-

[74] *WB*, No. 69, pp. 249-50.   [75] Oka, p. 13.

zines of a higher cultural level; no poetry or prose of "splendor and eternity" came out of the war, but this was too much to expect of so short a period—a longer war with a less monotonous string of victories might have produced better literature; the war did shift the attention of writers from the past to the present, though the results were not always what the *Waseda Bungaku* writer anticipated; individuality came to acquire greater importance in Japanese literature; and, finally, the *shintaishi* movement received an impetus which brought new life.

I. THE DRAMA

The drama perhaps provides the best example of the manner in which the Sino-Japanese War affected artistic production. It provided Shimpa ("the new school") with its first great successes and established the foundations for the modern Japanese theatre, even though the plays themselves were trivial.[76]

Shimpa had been founded late in 1888 in Osaka as a kind of educational arm for the *Jiyū Minken* (Freedom and People's Rights) movement. The plays performed, political in content, appealed to audiences through their lively presentation of recent political events. Once, when an actor playing the part of Itagaki Taisuke, the leader of the popular rights movement, accidentally was stabbed in a scene depicting an attempted assassination, he went on performing, the blood streaming from his face, to the delight of the audience.[77] Kawakami Otojirō, one of the founders of Shimpa, opened his first season in Tokyo in 1891, attracting publicity just before the theatre was opened to the public by galloping on a horse up and down before the place, accompanied by young members of the troupe. In his eagerness to attract attention, he was not above employing stage tricks of the crudest nature, or calling the plays by outlandish titles.

The outbreak of the Sino-Japanese War came as a godsend

[76] Akiba Tarō, *Nihon Shingeki Shi*, I, 303.
[77] *Ibid.*, p. 269.

to the hard-pressed Kawakami. On August 12th, not two weeks after the declaration of war, Kawakami announced he would present *Nisshin Sensō*, and on the 31st day the play opened at the Asakusa Theatre. As Kawakami promised in his first formal announcement, the naval battle in the sixth act was staged realistically, with electrical machinery and a liberal use of fireworks, in the manner of his earlier ventures. The text, by Fujisawa Asajirō (1866-1917), an actor of the troupe, though devoid of literary pretensions, supplied the actors with suitably patriotic or villainous speeches, as in this passage from the scene where the reporter Hirata first sees Li Hung-chang:

> HIRATA: Are you the General Li I have heard about? Ha-hah. I knew all along that the Chinese prided themselves on making mountains out of molehills, but to think that you are General Li, the man so renowned for possessing the learning of Confucius and Mencius, the sages who made China famous! A hundred hearings are not worth one look— it's just as they say. Hearing and seeing are two quite different things! Do the likes of you pass for a great statesman in China? *Uwahahahahahaa.*[78]

The musical accompaniment for the play, in keeping with the theme, was supplied by bugles instead of samisens, and war songs were liberally incorporated into the text. The enormous success of *Nisshin Sensō* naturally encouraged the production of similar works elsewhere. In Kyoto, the Fukui Mohei troupe put on *Nisshin Sensō Yamatodamashii* on September 7th, and Sudō Sadanori, another founder of Shimpa, staged *Nisshin Gekisen* in October in Yokohama. Osaka theatres were crowded for performances of such notable works as *Nissei Jiken Uwasa no Kachitoki* (September 16, 1894).

Kawakami did not choose to rest on his laurels after his triumph. He decided to see the front for himself in order to obtain new materials. He left on October 22nd for Korea and Manchuria. Prints show him in various heroic poses; in one,

---

[78] Manuscript in Engeki Hakubutsukan at Waseda University.

he stands with a pistol in his hand menacing a kneeling Chinese who begs for mercy; the legend states in part, "Seeking to arouse still further our people's hostility toward the enemy, he travelled at the risk of his life to the distant Manchu land, and standing amidst clouds of dust and rains of bullets, personally inspected conditions at the front." Kawakami's next play *Senchi Kembun Jikki*, based on his experiences, opened in Tokyo on December 3rd. It proved another hit. Soon afterwards, on the 11th, Kawakami and Takada Minoru gave a special private performance for the Crown Prince, the future Emperor Taishō. It had originally been planned to stage the scene from *Nisshin Senso* in which Hirata denounces Li Hung-chang, but it was feared that the scene, though stirring, might depress the Prince by its gloominess. Instead, livelier scenes from the current success *Senchi Kembun Jikki* were performed. "When it was over His Highness vouchsafed words of praise, saying that the play was unusual and interesting."[79] In May of 1895 Kawakami's troupe performed at the Kabuki Theatre in *Ikaiei Kanraku* ("The Fall of Wei-hai-wei"), a success that ran for thirty-five days. To have been permitted to perform at the Kabuki Theatre was a sign of the magnitude of the triumph of Shimpa in plays of a contemporary nature. It not only signalized the emergence of Shimpa as an important factor in the Japanese theatrical world but defined the future functions of Kabuki.

At the very beginning of the war, when Kawakami first announced his intention of staging a play describing recent events, *Yomiuri Shimbun* declared that Kabuki actors, for the most part uneducated, were incapable of representing the Sino-Japanese War; if they ventured to appear in the roles of officers it would be an affront to the dignity of the Imperial Army. Kawakami's actors, on the other hand, had some degree of education and would not be objectionable even performing as officers. If the Kabuki actors wished to stay abreast of the times by staging a war play, they should try *Kokusenya Kassen*

[79] *MHS*, IX, 174.

("The Battles of Coxinga"), which would foster national pride by showing how Watōnai denounced and slew the Pigtails.[80]

This statement on the functions of Kabuki was truly startling. The Kabuki actors were accustomed to appear as generals and nobles, even if under slightly disguised names, and ever since the beginnings of Kabuki current gossip had inspired many plays. Moreover, had not the ninth Ichikawa Danjūrō advocated *katsureki*—plays in which historical personages were called by their real names—in order to enhance the dignity of Kabuki by removing the foolish and fanciful elements? If Kabuki were to be condemned to keep the distance of *Kokusenya Kassen* from the war, the burning issue of the day, its whole character would be changed.

As a matter of fact, however, the Kabuki actors quickly responded to the challenge of the Shimpa war plays. On September 11th *Nippon Dai Shōri* was staged in Tokyo, and October 10th the Osaka Kabuki players performed *Waga Teikoku Bambanzai: Kachi uta Yamatodamashii* in three acts. In November the Tokyo Kabuki troupe made a massive attempt to recapture its lost audiences by presenting *Kairiku Renshō Asahi no Mihata* with a text by Fukuchi Ōchi, the leading playwright of the day. Danjūrō appeared as the heroic sailor who asked about the *Ting-yüan* and Kikugorō as Harada Jūkichi, but the play was a dismal failure. The aged Danjūrō was pronounced "more pathetic than dashing" in a sailor suit, and the attempts to imitate the tricks of Shimpa by setting off live gunpowder onstage did not make up for the inadequate plot and performance.[81] Kawatake sums up the results of this fiasco:

> It would seem that at this point Kabuki realized that new works of the *zangiri* style or realism of the *katsureki* variety should be left to the modern drama, and resigned itself to the fact they went beyond the limits of its own possibilities.

[80] *WB*, No. 70, pp. 268-69.
[81] Kawatake Shigetoshi, *Nihon Engeki Zenshi*, p. 856.

Of course, new works derived from modern life were presented any number of times in later years, but they represented experiments of a collateral nature or special entertainments, and not new developments in the main stream. . . . At this juncture Kabuki, though appreciated by the public of the time, seems to have lost its contemporary quality which was capable of closely reflecting the present-day, and to have become an increasingly classical and non-contemporary drama.[82]

The success of Danjūrō in the familiar old work *Datekurabe Onna Kabuki* in February 1895 confirmed the belief that the domain of the Kabuki actors was not that of Shimpa.

A similar pattern on a much smaller scale was traced by the Bunraku troupe. As early as August 1894, at the suggestion of the great samisen player Tsurusawa Dampei, the chanter Takemoto Tosadayū inserted in an existing play a scene relating the victories in Korea at Asan and Chemulpo.[83] After a few other attempts, some rather successful, at capturing public favor by up-to-date war plays, the company eventually was convinced that modern works were beyond its capacities, though Bunraku like Kabuki had originally developed as a mirror of contemporary gossip. The Western uniforms worn by the soldiers and sailors must have made manipulation of the puppets extremely difficult, for trousers conceal far less of the figures of the operators than a Japanese kimono. In any case, from this time onward Bunraku rarely presented plays treating contemporary life.

The Nō, of course, had never reflected contemporary life, but the outbreak of the war threatened its existence. Theatres were taken over as soldiers' billets. The public showed no interest in Nō plays about the war, though a few were apparently written.[84] Only by staging benefits for the troops (which also

[82] *Ibid.*, pp. 856-57.   [83] *Kamigata*, No. 82, p. 22.
[84] *WB*, No. 78, p. 257.

brought income to the actors, of course) did the Nō actors pull through the war.[85]

The effect of the Sino-Japanese War on the theatre, to resume, was to create on the one hand the foundations for a modern drama capable of representing realistically contemporary events, and to define as the particular functions of the traditional theatres the performance of works drawn from a classic repertory.

2. GRAPHIC ARTS

The popularity of *nishikie* during the war has already been described. Inevitably, the quality of most of these prints, produced in a great hurry by artists whose main concern was with pleasing an ill-educated public rather than with producing works of art, was low. The worst of the Japanese war prints bear a curious resemblance to the Chinese prints produced at the same time,[86] possibly because the cheaper varieties of Japanese prints were widely known in China.[87] These prints, brightly colored and light-hearted even when the scene depicted is a massacre, were never meant to be taken seriously as art. A few *nishikie* artists, however, took pains with their work, and even produced masterpieces which mark a fitting conclusion to the whole of the *ukiyoe* art. It is possible to date the end of *ukiyoe* art with some precision: a report in *Yomiuri Shimbun* published in the autumn of 1895 noted that sales of *nishikie* had dropped drastically; war prints, of course, were no longer in demand but even the usual actor prints barely sold two hundred copies.[88] The print never again met with wide

[85] Yanagisawa Hideki, *Hōshō Kurō Den*, p. 74.

[86] James Wheeler Davidson, *The Island of Formosa*, gives some examples. See also *Nisshin Sensō Gahō*, VI.

[87] *NK*, No. 36, pp. 65-66. A Japanese officer, describing things which surprised him most in China, mentions the large number of Japanese prints he found.

[88] Asakura Haruhiko and Imamura Tetsugen, *Meiji Sesō Hennen Jiten*, p. 373.

public demand. At the time of the Boxer Rebellion in 1900 the publishers hopefully commissioned prints, but they sold few copies. Again, during the Russo-Japanese War of 1904-05 many prints were executed, but sales were far smaller than for the Sino-Japanese War and the prints themselves of slight artistic importance. Cheap war prints continued to be produced on a small scale even during the 1930's, and an entirely different kind of print, expensive and aimed at connoisseurs of art rather than the general public, attracted attention, but the *nishikie* was gone. Its place was taken by the photograph. Already during the Sino-Japanese War photographs became a prominent feature of such magazines as *Nisshin Sensō Jikki*, and by the time of the Russo-Japanese War magazines consisting mainly of photographs were more popular than the prints.

Photographs played a behind-the-scenes role even in the *nishikie* of the Sino-Japanese War. A few artists like Kubota Beisen actually visited the front, but the rest had to choose between relying on their imagination or consulting photographs. In some instances one can see how a photograph has been translated directly into a print, sometimes with considerable skill; at other times the borrowings consist of architectural details or items of military equipment. None of the photographs I have seen has the least artistic interest; it is not surprising that the public found the *nishikie* provided a more exciting portrayal of the Sino-Japanese War.

The best artist of the period, Kobayashi Kiyochika, was in the doldrums when the war began. He had first gained fame during the years 1876-81 when he produced a great many prints depicting the Tokyo of his day: rickshaws drawn up before Western-style buildings lit by gaslight, figures under Japanese umbrellas passing a lighthouse on a rainy night, a huge fire ravaging a quarter of the city. His works, though clearly in the *ukiyoe* tradition, are influenced by Western perspective and shading. Kiyochika is believed to have been a pupil of the English artist Charles Wirgman (1832-91) who originally came to Japan in the late 1850's as a correspondent for *The Illustrated*

London News. In the 1860's, Wirgman began to publish *The Japan Punch*, starting a vogue for a kind of cartoon known in Japan as *"ponchi-e"* which Kiyochika himself would draw during the Sino-Japanese War. It is not certain that Kiyochika actually studied under Wirgman, though this has often been asserted; at any rate, it cannot have been for very long. Kiyochika also appears to have studied photography with Shimooka Renjō (1823-1914), a founder of the art in Japan, and *ukiyoe* techniques with Kawanabe Gyōsai (1831-89), a devoted follower of Hokusai. From each teacher Kiyochika acquired elements of his style, but the peculiar poetry of his landscapes of Meiji period Tokyo is his alone.

It has often been wondered why Kiyochika suddenly abandoned the landscapes which account for his fame today. Some have suggested that a nationalistic reaction to the uncritical mania for all things Western of the early Meiji period caused people to turn from Kiyochika's depictions of the Rokumeikan era,[89] but this theory does not square with the evident popularity of other *ukiyoe* artists who portrayed the *bummei kaika*. It has been suggested also that Kiyochika's prints, executed with far greater care and detail than others of the time, made them too expensive for the public,[90] but this fails to explain why Kiyochika did not choose to make simplified versions of his Tokyo scenes rather than the book and magazine illustrations which provided his livelihood in middle years. It seems more likely that Kiyochika suffered some kind of shock that affected his artistic production. We know of one such incident. In 1881 fire broke out in Kiyochika's neighborhood. Rushing outside, he began furiously sketching. His wife, not realizing where her husband had gone, waited in their house with their two small daughters, until finally the spreading fire reached their building and forced her to flee with the children. When Kiyochika returned the next morning, exhausted from the night's sketching, the house was in ashes. The wife, enraged

[89] Yoshida Susugu, *Kiyochika*, pp. 224-25.
[90] *Ibid.*, p. 229.

163

at his seeming callousness, left Kiyochika. He never again painted the landscapes which had made him famous,[91] but the sketches of the fire and the prints made from them rank among Kiyochika's masterpieces.

Kiyochika's fascination with fire was a part of his constant absorption with the problem of rendering light. He delighted in night scenes lit by the moon, gaslight, fireworks or flames, in the reflections of light in puddles, silhouettes against a brilliantly illuminated sky, the glow from a furnace on the iron-workers. It may be that after years of hackwork, performed with little love and not much display of talent, Kiyochika's imagination was stirred again by the thought of depicting the Sino-Japanese War—explosions at night, men huddled around campfires, searchlights directed out to sea, burning villages. Almost all his good prints of the war depend on his employment of the effects of light, a matter of no interest to his predecessors in *ukiyoe* or to any other artists of the Sino-Japanese War (except his own pupils). Many artists depicted fire in terms of colorful patches in the sky or landscape, but Kiyochika used light to evoke mood—loneliness, terror, intimacy. Even his failures generally have one beautiful panel of the three, suggesting that though he may have drawn by some publisher's order, Captain Asakawa's patrol, or a similar subject, his interest was not in the self-satisfied figure of the central panel but in the shadowy figures fighting in the foggy rain or in the Chinese corpses looming from the fog at the Captain's feet. He tried to convey with an impressionistic use of color the dazzling intensity of a shell-burst or of a ship exploding at night. (Plate III). Unlike Toshihide, whose figures are often effectively drawn portraits, Kiyochika clearly was uninterested in the faces of the various officers he was required to draw, usually with no knowledge of their actual features or of their personalities. In his best works lighting and atmosphere, appropriate

[91] *Ibid.*, p. 223. See also Higuchi Hiroshi, *Bakumatsu Meiji no Ukiyoe Shūsei*, p. 63.

to the war but not necessarily associated with a specific event, create much of the poetry of his early landscapes.

The prints of Kiyochika were the finest artistic works to come out of the Sino-Japanese War. Yoshida Susugu, the author of an important study of Kiyochika, wrote, "The works of Kiyochika depicting the Sino-Japanese War are the peak in the short history of the *ukiyoe* and *nishikie* art, and would seem to deserve a considerable place within the history of the Japanese print."[92] This is high praise, especially in view of the general indifference to these works—they are not mentioned in any Western book I know of—but it may be that a general prejudice against Meiji art has obscured judgment of these prints.

Artists of the Western style on the whole were not greatly affected by the war. In 1893, the year before the war began, Kuroda Seiki (1826-1924) the founder of the modern art movement in Japan, returned from France. Kuroda went to the front in Korea (as a correspondent of the French periodical *Le Monde Illustré*) and executed some sketches, but his main activities of the period lay in another direction.[93] In 1895 he exhibited a nude painting which caused an immense sensation; it was the first nude by a Japanese (except for those of pornographic intent). Some critics have traced to this event the beginnings of mature painting in the Western style.

The war certainly did not inspire the nude, but the free exhibition of such a work, obviously in a foreign style and deriving from foreign traditions, was notable, and Kuroda's repeated and open insistence that most Japanese paintings in the Western style were worthless because the artists did not understand the Western culture behind the style, tells us much about the nature of the war itself. Although it is frequently stated, with justice, that the Sino-Japanese War ushered in a period of strong nationalism, during the war itself the Japanese

[92] Yoshida, p. 262.
[93] Kumamoto Ken, *Kuroda Seiki Sakuhin Shū*, p. 28.

enjoyed a freedom of expression which contrasted markedly, say, with the situation prevailing during the Greater East Asia War. If no opposition was voiced to the war, doubtless this was because none was felt: casualties were light, victories unbroken, and rising prices or poor business conditions did not afflict people seriously enough to make them doubt "the great trust of a nation regenerated through war," described by Hearn.[94] But at a time when Japanese were rediscovering the glories of their heritage, and the magazine *Taiyō* was founded specifically to spread Japanese culture abroad (the reverse of a process of borrowing which had begun when Japan first came in contact with Chinese civilization two thousand years before), it is startling that Kuroda Seiki should have expressed so bluntly his disdain for the prevailing school of painting in Japan. In 1896 he founded the Hakubakai, a society which was to dominate Japanese painting in oils for many years. The critic for *Waseda Bungaku* who predicted that novels and plays, thanks to the war, "would embody the particular views of an individual" might well have included paintings.

3. LITERATURE

None of the prose or poetry stemming directly from the war is remembered today, save possibly for a few songs.[95] Even at the time, as we have seen, critical judgments were severe. Most writers refrained from treating the war, and the government exerted no pressure to make them support the war effort. Though *Waseda Bungaku* carried regular articles on the war and its literary products, *Bungakkai* hardly mentioned it. Hirata Tokuboku (1873-1943) in an article entitled "Seeing Off the Year 1894" went so far as to state:

At the present time, to mention war literature is the very quintessence of foolishness. . . . What the litterateurs now

[94] Hearn, p. 89.
[95] The war figures in a subordinate role in some more famous works of fiction, such as *Hototogisu* by Tokutomi Kenjirō.

call war literature or new-style military poetry is, as Rohan
has said, nothing but the uninteresting husk of poetry, the
abortive work of poets with rather dubious goals. Though
they may, thanks to mass hysteria, be popular for a time,
there is not one particle of eternal poetic values in their work.
For writers to divert their writing to war is the same as for
the masses to drop excitedly all enterprise for war. This time
is especially one demanding elevated thought.

Hirata concluded, "To speak of a war literature at the present
time is the height of shallowness. These are the words with
which I send off the year 1894."[96] It is hard to imagine a more
sweeping condemnation of literature written in support of the
war, but no one ostracized the author for these views. Individualism was accepted, even if it ran counter to general public
feelings, a rare situation in Japan.

It is possible to trace the development of the novel of ideas
and of the pessimistic novel, two varieties which emerged after
1895, to the greater concern with current problems of the time,
but perhaps more important was the controversy over the Japanese language which began during the war and eventually led
to the creation of a new medium of expression. The vicissitudes
of the *gembun itchi* (identity of speech and written word)
movement and the triumph of Futabatei Shimei's novel *Ukigumo* have often been chronicled, but it is significant that
hardly a single work in prose or poetry dealing with the war
was in the colloquial style. At most, as in Izumi Kyōka's stories,
the conversational passages are in the colloquial. Even in the

[96] Quoted from Kōsaka, *Japanese Thought in the Meiji Era*, translated by Abosch, pp. 266-67. The original may be found in *Bungakkai*, No. 24, Dec. 30, 1894, pp. 35-36. Hirata also states, "We cannot
but admire the deed of the brave man who opened the Gembu Gate,
and we cannot but think of the hardships encountered by our soldiers
on distant expeditions, who tread dangerous ground and brave many
difficulties, and there is no reason why literary men cannot turn their
thoughts to these heroes and express in writing their poetic emotions.
However, a new domain for poetry and literary prose cannot be
opened in a day."

elementary school textbooks prepared in 1894, almost every phrase is in the classical language. The first sentence in Book One which is recognizable as either classical or colloquial is in the classical *"ike ni hasu ari."* The deeds of Shirakami Genjirō and Harada Jūkichi, needless to say, were also recounted in the classical language. Clearly the *gembun itchi* movement had not yet swept all before it.

Far from being in the colloquial, the largest part of the war poetry was in classical Chinese. Throughout the war compositions in Chinese, often denouncing the Chinese as barbarians, flowed from the pens—or, rather, the brushes—of the Japanese scholars. Even in magazines of wide circulation like *Nisshin Sensō Jikki* it was not felt necessary to punctuate Chinese poems for Japanese reading, let alone to translate them. But the sentiments of nationalism inevitably aroused by a war could not easily be reconciled with the use of a foreign language, particularly one associated with the enemy, in expressing the thoughts closest to Japanese hearts. The war stirred not only a revival of interest in the Japanese classics (it might be mentioned that *Kokugakuin Zasshi* began publication in January, 1895) but in the proper manner of writing the Japanese language. Although some proposals made at this time were never adopted, and others were adopted only after some time had elapsed, the Sino-Japanese War provided the stimulus for a more fruitful consideration of the national language problem than the *gembun itchi* movement of the earlier period.[97]

[97] Summaries of some of the arguments on reform of the Japanese language published at the time may be found in Kikuzawa Sueo, *Kokuji Mondai no Kenkyū*, pp. 78-79. The necessity of language reform as the main task facing writers was the theme of many articles. Tsubouchi Shōyō declared that the two urgent questions facing literary men were: (1) what to do about Japanese grammar; and (2) what to do about the writing of Japanese. ("Shin Bundan no Ni Daimondai," in *Shōyō Senshū*, XI, 537-72.) The desirability of using modern language (*kōgo*) was urged by such men as Nakamura Akika ("Shokan Buntai wa Kyōsei sezaru bekarazu," in *Taiyō*, I, No. 10,

Certainly the Japanese language at the time of the war was unsuited to the marked increase in popular education during the period immediately following. The formal style was larded with Chinese allusions, and even when Japanese words were used they often were transcribed in perversely difficult characters, ostensibly to express slight shades of nuance. Letters were written exclusively in the *sōrōbun* style with its almost facetious use of Chinese characters to render Japanese sounds. At the opposite extreme, the language of speeches and formal addresses was prolix beyond belief. Any page from an address by Toyama Masakazu, for example, will yield such gems as "*hotondo nai to iu yō na raimei ga arimasuru yō de arimasu.*" The pompous *no de aru no de aru* style was especially popular in the Japanese Diet. No form for the copula had been established for the colloquial, and in the effort to avoid abruptness such meaningless locutions multiplied.

During the war itself a number of influential writers devoted themselves to problems of language reform. Okada Masayoshi (1871-1923), whose proposals for reform of the Japanese language were accepted by the Japanese Diet in 1900, leading to the formation of the Committee for Study of the National Language (Kokugo Chōsa Kai) in 1902, proposed in 1895 that the use of *kanji* be totally abolished. In a long article published in *Teikoku Bungaku* he advocated the exclusive use of a modified form of *kana* for all writing.[98] His later views were less drastic, but the sharp reduction in the number and variety of characters taught in the schools and used by writers after 1900 certainly owed much to Okada's initial rejection of the Chinese characters.

Other proposals made about the same time were even more dramatic. Miyake Setsurei published in *Taiyō* an article advo-

---

32-37), who objected particularly to *sōrōbun* as being like "using bows and arrows in present-day warfare."

[98] *WB*, Jan. 1896, p. 35.

cating that the Japanese adopt the Korean script. He argued that the *kana* was inadequate for representing Korean or Western words, complicated to form calligraphically, and unsuited to writing horizontally. The *kana* might be modified, he agreed, but if modifications were to be made, why not use Western script? Proposals for the use of roman letters were by no means new, but the revival of strong feelings about the national essence made it unlikely that the Japanese would adopt the script of the Western countries, for it would suggest that the nation had acknowledged their superiority. Adopting the Korean alphabet might then be the best solution. It is unattractive to look at, but capable of rendering sounds more exactly than the *kana*, and no one would imagine that Japan, in borrowing the Korean writing, was bowing before a stronger country.[99]

Saionji Kimmochi (1849-1940), who became Minister of Education in October 1894, proposed in August 1895 that English be made the central part of education, and that it might eventually be desirable to eliminate altogether the teaching of the Japanese language and literature in the schools.[100] This was not an unprecedented opinion. Toyama Masakazu had advocated as early as 1884 the urgent necessity of abolishing *kanji* and promoting the study of English, and Mori Arinori (1847-89), Minister of Education at the time of his death, had suggested as early as 1872 that English be made the language of Japan. What makes Saionji's proposal both curious and important is that it was made on the heels of Japanese victory in the war, at a time when nationalistic sentiment was supposedly at its peak. It reflects both Saionji's intransigence on educational matters and the flux of opinions concerning the Japanese language at the time.

The need for creating a unified Japanese language was strongly felt in 1895, both because of the renewed sense of the importance of Japanese literature and because of the increased conviction that classical Chinese or a classical Japanese heavily

[99] *WB*, No. 88, p. 260. [100] *MHS*, IX, 287.

influenced by Chinese was not an appropriate language for poetry and prose by Japanese. Ueda Kazutoshi (1867-1937), a scholar of Japanese language and sometime advocate of roman letters, urged in 1895 after the end of the war the necessity of establishing a standard language (*hyōjungo*) and of creating an artistic *gembun itchi* through the cooperation of writers.[101] Ozaki Kōyō published in September 1895 the story *Aobudō* ("Green Grapes") in *de aru* style, and in the following year began to publish serially his long novel *Tajō Takon* ("Many Feelings, Many Sorrows") in the same style; these works brought a fully effective modern-language style to fiction even though Ozaki himself at times reverted to the classical style. By the end of the century such writers as Uchimura Kanzō were publishing newspaper articles in the *gembun itchi* style, and the Hototogisu group of *haiku* writers led by Masaoka Shiki used it for their "sketches from nature." Of course, the use of classical Japanese did not cease immediately, but the years 1895-99 marked the turning point in the development of modern Japanese.[102]

At the same time, the period marked the beginning of a sharp decline of both Chinese and English studies. Yoshikawa Kōjirō has pointed out how the Confucian training among literary men went as far as Natsume Sōseki and Mori Ōgai, among military men as far as Yamagata Aritomo and Nogi Maresuke, and among politicians as far as Saionji Kimmochi and Hara Kei, all men educated before this time.[103] But though *kambun* remained a part of the curriculum, taught as a part of *kokugo* (national language), the private schools where Confucian scholars had taught Chinese composition gradually disappeared. Inoue Tetsujirō, an ardent nationalist though a student of Chinese philosophy, urged in 1895 that Chinese studies not be abandoned, even though China had

---

[101] Hisamatsu Sen'ichi and Yoshida Seiichi, *Kindai Nihon Bungaku Jiten*, p. 287.
[102] *Ibid.*
[103] Yoshikawa Kōjirō, *Jusha no Kotoba*, p. 90.

shown itself to be corrupt. The Chinese, he declared, lacked the scholarly ability to study their own writings of the past; the Japanese must do it.[104] Chinese studies developed henceforth as a special discipline, much as Inoue suggested, rather than as a basic part of education itself. Similarly, the increased emphasis given to the Japanese language meant that all subjects of a modern nature came to be taught in Japanese, though English had formerly been used in geography, science and like subjects. English continued to be stressed as the most important foreign language, but it was nothing more than that; as a result, the kind of English written by such men as Uchimura Kanzō, Okakura Kakuzō and Natsume Sōseki was not to be attained by later men, who may have been better trained in economics, the sciences and so on.

The effects on literature of the war, then, were chiefly in the urgency given to the creation of a true *gembun itchi* style, free of the pedantic Chinese flavor of the earlier writers.

Japanese Culture and the World

It was not surprising that the first war of recent times with a foreign country should have aroused Japanese awareness of themselves. We have seen how this awareness expressed itself with respect to the Chinese. Reactions in Europe and America to the war were closely followed, and the increasing admiration for the Japanese aroused by the victories was joyfully recorded.

It was reported in April, 1895:

> Ever since the Chicago Exposition foreigners have gradually acquired some knowledge of Japanese culture, but it has been limited to the fact that Japan produced beautiful pottery, tea and silk. Since the outbreak of the Sino-Japanese War last year, however, an attitude of respect for Japan may be felt everywhere, and there is talk of nothing but Japan this and Japan that. Resident Japanese have been invited in

[104] *WB*, No. 89, p. 284.

truly enormous numbers even to dinner parties and coffee gatherings. Most amusing is the craze for Japanese women's costumes. Many American women wear them to parties, though they are most unbecoming, and the praise they lavish on the Japanese victories sounds exactly as if they were boasting about their own country. It is said that women who fail to wear Japanese kimonos to parties are ostracized for not following the current modes. The popularity of the kimono seems also to have induced American women to perform in Japanese plays. At the end of February last a play was performed at one of the leading theatres on Broadway in New York. Everything from the props to the costumes was ordered from Japan, and the text of the play itself was exactly the same as when performed in Japan. Most of the plays have dealt with vengeance. It is rather amusing to see a samurai wear three swords, but the plays, being Japanese, enjoy such great popularity that they are now much in fashion.[105]

Other artistic results of the war were reported the following February: "Japanese painting has come in recent years to be widely appreciated in America, but ever since victory in the war the taste for Japanese art has increased all the more. At present there is a great fad for Japanese scenes on the walls of studies and so on, and Japanese artists resident in America are reputedly making large profits."[106]

In Europe, too, admiration for the Japanese mounted. In London a large peepshow showing the *Matsushima* sinking the *Chen-yüan* was popular, and a troupe which had been performing a play about the Sino-Japanese War at the Antwerp Exposition moved to London to give performances. The covers of *The Illustrated London News* were given over to scenes of Japanese war correspondents at work in the field. Sir Edwin Arnold, the doughty champion of Japan, declared that "in attacking China in Corea, she is guarding the civilized world." He saw two dangers overhanging the civilized world, the

[105] *NK*, No. 38, p. 70.   [106] *MHS*, IX, 369.

"Mongol" (represented by China) and the "Slav" (represented by Russia). He warned, "Those do well who dread the sullen and sombre weight of China, controlled, as it is, by the social system springing from that arch-opportunist Confucius, the most immoral of all moralists."[107]

The Sino-Japanese War undoubtedly produced a change of opinion about Japan in the West. Few experts predicted that Japan would win the war against the mighty continental power, and when the initial victories proved not to be flashes in the pan, it was grudgingly admitted that the much-decried "superficial modernization" was in fact genuine. Okakura Kakuzō wryly commented that as long as Japan indulged in the gentle arts of peace she had been regarded as barbarous, but victory in war had induced the foreigners to call Japan civilized.[108]

The rising nationalism after the Sino-Japanese War, so often commented on by historians, had the support of the outside world, confirming the Japanese in the peculiar sense of mission. Nationalism and imperialism and also an industrialization promoted by the indemnity received from China, changed Japan in many ways, but some Japanese critics insisted that basically Japanese culture would remain unchanged. Shimamura Hōgetsu, in reviewing Japanese literature after the war, predicted that its future progress would be based on the essential nature of the Japanese people:

> What is the lifeblood of the Japanese people? History replies: it is *bushidō*, it is *Yamato damashii*. Truly, the spirit of this one Way pervades all of Japanese history unchanged . . . what is there except for this which makes Japanese literature Japanese literature?[109]

Shimamura concluded his essay, "Will not the future Japanese literature come to be based, directly and indirectly, on the

[107] *The Spectator*, Sept. 1, 1894, p. 263.
[108] Okakura Kakuzō, *The Book of Tea*, p. 7.
[109] *Hōgetsu Zenshū*, ii, 301-02.

feelings of the Japanese people aroused by the conquest of China? When will our *Minna von Barhelm* be written?" As far as I know, these questions were never answered, but the national awareness evoked by the Sino-Japanese War certainly provided the impetus for many cultural developments in the years to come.

PART TWO

The Arts in the Meiji Period

Introduction

Two examples of the actual practice of the arts in the early Meiji period are Western-style oil painting and music. There are few art forms which differ as much from earlier Japanese tradition. The studies by Professors Rosenfield and Haga take us back in time to an exploration of Western models that parallels the experience of the Iwakura Embassy in observing and attempting to understand the functioning of things Western. The Japanese were apprentices to the West, and at this time to follow Western models was to modernize. These papers deal with two painters who, a few years before the Meiji Restoration, set out to learn the techniques of oil painting. We are moved by the dedication of these pioneers to their new calling as they proceed in a craftsmanlike manner to develop and master the materials and techniques of this foreign art. Continuing their work in the early Meiji period, when practical utility for nation-building set the priorities, they had to justify their art to others as well as to themselves. There was a decade of favorable recognition for Western-style painting, after which the oil painters lost ground for a time to Japanese painting in the traditional style, which enjoyed a resurgence during the period of cultural reaction. The conflicts and competition in the artistic world reflect the tension between Westernizing influences and native tradition that was seen in political and intellectual life.

Western music began to be studied actively in Japan from about the time of the Restoration. In spite of the fact that it must have seemed even more alien than oil painting, Professor Malm's paper shows that it found surprisingly quick acceptance, although only in the less sophisticated forms actively sponsored by the government for use as school music and as military band music, and those introduced by missionaries as church music. The full integration of Western music, that is to say, the development of appreciation for chamber and symphonic music and the composition of original works, proved to be a considerably slower process.

179

CHAPTER V

Western-Style Painting in the Early
Meiji Period and Its Critics

JOHN M. ROSENFIELD

THE two portraits reproduced here (Plates I and II) are important works of Meiji-period painting, and the differences between them reflect the artistic and cultural conflicts of their day. In the first, oil paints and varnish were applied to canvas; in the other, thin water-soluble pigments were painted on silk. In one, the face is dramatically lighted against a dark background, but is nonetheless shown in a detached, objective way; in the second, an even and shadowless light plays over the figure, while darkening clouds and the wind blowing through the garments suggest an atmosphere of tension and stress. The first subject is dressed in Western clothing, the second in ancient Chinese robes. These obvious differences should not blind us, however, to the many elements which the paintings share in common.

The first work, done in 1877, is one of the earliest examples of Western-style portraiture in oil colors painted by a Japanese in his homeland.[1] It depicts Kawakami Tōgai, a pioneer student and teacher of Western-style arts, and was done by his loyal disciple Koyama Shōtarō at a time when both men were virtually the official painters to the Meiji government.

The second is an allegorical portrait of Okakura Kakuzō, leader of the movement to retain classical Japanese and Chinese elements in the arts.[2] It was painted in 1898 by his follower

[1] "The Portrait of Kawakami Tōgai," by Koyama Shōtarō. Oil paints on canvas. 54 x 29¾ inches. Collection of the Tokyo Geijutsu Daigaku. Illustration from Itō Kiyoshi *et al., Kindai yōga,* Tokyo Geijutsu Daigaku Zōhin Zuroku (Tokyo, 1954), Pl. 18.

[2] "Kutsugen," by Yokoyama Taikan. Sumi and color on silk. 52¼ by 114 inches. Collection of the Itsukushima Shrine, Miyajima, to

181

Yokoyama Taikan, who was then a young man of 30 and who lived until 1958 as one of the outstanding masters of the traditional Nihon-ga style. The figure which Taikan painted is the Chinese poet Ch'ü Yüan (Kutsugen in Japanese), active in the fourth century B.C. and author of the wildly eccentric and imaginative "Li sao," familiar to most Japanese with a classical education.[3] This poem, whose title may be translated "On Encountering Trouble," describes the writer's life-long search for truth and virtue, his disappointments, the slander and vilification he suffered at the hands of a corrupt society, and his thoughts of suicide. Pervading the "Li sao" is an air of bitterness and resignation which Taikan clearly attempted to capture: "The age is disordered in a tumult of changing: How can I tarry much longer. . . ? Orchid and iris have lost all fragrance. . . ." There is no question that this painting is a disguised portrait of Okakura, who had recently been forced to resign as head of both the Tokyo School of Fine Arts and the Art Section of the Tokyo Imperial Museum, creating an imbroglio which rocked the Japanese art world.

Each of the four persons involved in these portraits—the two subjects and the two painters—were men of such prominence that they were subject to extreme pressures in the cultural crises of the Meiji era. These pressures accentuated the normal grouping of artists into schools which contend for prestige and commissions; they led to virulent controversies, emotional breakdowns, and possibly (in the case of Tōgai) even to suicide.

The relationship between artistic styles and national policy in Meiji Japan underlines the interactions between two realms of human experience: the private vision of the artist working quietly alone in his studio, and the artist as a man among men,

---

which it was given in 1934 as a votive offering by Shimada Zennosuke of Hiroshima. Illustration from Yoshizawa Chū, *Yokoyama Taikan* (Tokyo, 1962), Pl. 4.

[3] For a translation of the "Li sao" and accounts of Ch'ü Yüan, see David Hawkes, *Ch'u Tz'u* (Oxford, 1959), pp. 1-34; Lim Boon Keng, *The Li Sao* (Shanghai, 1929).

affected by the fate of his family, friends, city, and nation, and by the ideas which leap from mind to mind about him. To be sure, our interests are above all centered on the artist's works, on the delights and insights which these alone can give. The artist himself, taken as a social or economic phenomenon, is of interest chiefly to sociologists or economists; when we neglect the unique experiences offered by the work of art itself, we have denied the essential reason for the artist's existence.

On the other hand, it is a mistake to claim that in order to understand the uniqueness of artistic expression one should ignore the milieu of the artist, a viewpoint accepted today by many Western students of Asian painting. The questions which we must ask, actually, are not whether the conditions outside of his studio affect an artist's work, but rather to what degree they affect him and whether or not he is aware of them. There are many instances in history where the formation of the artist's style seems remarkably free from conditions other than his own will and taste, but they are probably a minority. To be sure, studying such conditions will never lead us to an understanding of how he attains excellence in his work; this comes from analysis of artistic material alone. But external circumstances help explain how a man, and what kind of a man, becomes an artist.

The history of early Meiji painting is a classical account of painters' direct, conscious involvement with social issues, of their realization that pictures themselves are powerfully creative forces in society. This involvement may actually have weakened Meiji art esthetically, drained it of some of the richness and intensity of formal effects which we admire, for example, in the painting and prints of the Edo period. Without question, Western collectors and museum men are less interested in Japanese arts from the hundred years after 1850 than from any other time in her history; that is until the rise of the Sōsaku Hanga movement in print making and the international non-figurative style which developed after World War II.

Our tolerance of these shortcomings is increased when we explore the conditions under which the Meiji artists worked. No less dedicated than men of the past, they faced unprecedented upheavals in Japanese learning, social structure, and economics. Scores of old-style artisans—lacquer makers, potters, weavers, wood carvers, bronze casters—were being absorbed into mechanized industries and given entirely new skills. For painters and sculptors, a totally new system of training was devised to replace the master-apprentice method of traditional workshops. A new apparatus of patronage was built to replace the one which had collapsed with the impoverishment of the Buddhist temples and many old samurai or aristocratic families. But above all, the Meiji painters were ushered into a world in which the religious and esthetic values which had guided the arts for centuries were obscured by the most severe doubts and criticisms. Ancient certainties lost their authority, and the struggle to establish new ones, or defend the old, placed a heavy burden upon men little accustomed to dealing with the theoretical basis of the arts.

Tōgai and Koyama

At the time Koyama made the portrait study of his teacher in 1877, both men were at a pinnacle of prestige.[4] Together they had been invited to join the party of distinguished leaders of the Restoration who had followed the Emperor Meiji in his first inspection trip of Hokkaidō and northern Honshū in August, 1876. They toured with such men as the Great Minister Sanjō Sanetomi, Itō Hirobumi, who was then Minister of

[4] Most of this account of Tōgai and Koyama is based upon Kumamoto Kenjirō, "Kawakami Tōgai to yōfūga," *Bijutsu kenkyū*, No. 79 (1938), and revised in his *Kindai Nihon bijutsu no kenkyū*, pp. 42-72; Takumi Hideo, *Kindai Nihon yōga no tenkai* (Tokyo, 1964); Moriguchi Tari, *Meiji Taishō no yōga* (Tokyo, 1941); Kawakita Michiaki, *Kindai bijutsu no nagare*, Heibonsha Nihon no Bijutsu series, xxiv (Tokyo, 1965); Uyeno Naoteru, *Japanese Arts and Crafts in the Meiji Era*. English adaptation by Richard Lane. Japanese Culture in the Meiji Era, viii (Tokyo, 1958).

Industry, and the War Minister Yamagata Aritomo. And the two artists stayed officially in Hokkaidō for nearly a month, sketching the scenery and natives of that once remote region whose development was a major economic project of the Restoration government.

Three weeks after their return to the capital, Tōgai presented to the War Minister three large oil paintings in a flat wooden box as a memorial of the journey.[5] Of the two pictures which have survived, one is a landscape of the Kayabemine district (Plate III), where the last resistance to the Restoration on the island had been suppressed only nine years earlier. At first glance, the painting seems to be simply a pleasant, genre-like view of a verdant forest trail with a group of peasants in the foreground. It was composed according to the principles of deep spacial recession in the Renaissance manner with an implied vanishing point in the middle of the picture plane, with a soft atmospheric treatment of the distant trees, and patches of dappled sunlight playing on the grass and branches below. However, overtones of a topical nature were injected by a small troop of uniformed horsemen, perhaps a cavalry patrol, in the middle ground and by a power line strung from trees and makeshift poles.

The other painting remaining from this set is a scene of the interior of a crude hut with three Ainu men lounging about a hearth set in the floor. Done in dark tones with only a single source of light in a small, overhead window, this is an essay in tenebrism, or "gloomy lighting" of the kind which European painters such as Caravaggio or Georges de la Tour or Rembrandt brought to a high degree of expressive power.

The paint has flaked away in many parts of these two pictures, and the portrait of Tōgai once suffered, apparently, from the neglect into which many early examples of Western-style painting fell before the Japanese realized their documentary as well as esthetic value. And the entire corpus of early Meiji

[5] The remaining works are illustrated in Kumamoto Kenjirō, Pls. VIII and IX (Pls. 12 and 14 in the revised version).

period oil painting has been sadly depleted because of the use of imperfect pigments and binders and paint grounds, and because the artists as yet had little experience with the specialized techniques of underpainting, glazing, overpainting, scumbling, and the like.

It is difficult today even to imagine the degree to which men like Tōgai or Koyama had been obliged to change their habits as artists. Just as their modes of diet and clothing, politics, and transportation were changing year by year, so also were their most mundane experiences as painters—the shape and stiffness of the brushes they handled, the acrid smells of oils and varnishes, the cumbersome task of stretching canvas cloth and coating it with glue and primers. While the materials of traditional Japanese arts and crafts were as highly sophisticated as any in the world—an array of fine papers, gold and silver leaf, delicate brushes of badger and rabbit hair, and colors of the greatest subtlety—they had been keyed to a distinct set of esthetic sensations and were of little use to Western-style artists. The materials of oil painting were intended to produce totally different effects which generally were based on the principles of illusionism, of recreating the effects of light falling on volumes in space.

By contemporary European standards, Koyama's portrait of Tōgai was an accomplished work—up to a certain point. The characterization, vivid and sympathetic, was done with an air of objective detachment. The painting master was dressed in a Western mode in a starched shirt and bow tie. He wore a stylish chesterfield with a fur collar, and sported a moustache and goatee. In his left hand was a pair of glasses on which Koyama lavished considerable effort even though they were not essential to the portrait. He managed with indifferent success to foreshorten the fingers (a formidable problem for a neophyte), and to reproduce the reflections of light on the surface of the glass and metal rims.

The face was modelled in a simple pattern of light and shade with little emphasis on the source of light. The feeling of solidity in Tōgai's head resulted rather from the contrast between the opacity of the light pigment in the face with the dark and semi-transparent glazes in the background. The chief failing in Koyama's illusionism, however, is to be seen in his treatment of the torso and arms. His lack of training in scientific anatomy was revealed by the imbalance of the shoulders, and the lack of organic relationship between the head, neck, and body. Regardless of this, Koyama's painting compares favorably with the photograph-like portraits of Restoration leaders made slightly later by imported Italian painters like Chiossone or San Giovanni.[6]

Prior to the time of this portrait, Koyama had received nearly all of his training in Western-style art from Tōgai. At the age of fifteen, he had entered Tōgai's private art school, the Chōkō-dokuga-kan, which had been founded in 1869 in Tokyo and had been among the first of a number of small private academies of Western-style painting. Another prominent one was the Tengai-rō, opened in the Nihombashi district in 1873 by Tōgai's long-time pupil and associate, Takahashi Yuichi. During the first decade of the Meiji era, the teaching of Western painting as well as languages and literature centered primarily in such informal institutes, so much so that this is often referred to as the Shijukujidai, the era of the private schools.

The manner by which Kawakami Tōgai amassed the skills which he taught to Koyama is an extraordinary story, for it is by no means clear why he should have been destined for such a career. He was born about 1827 in Shinano (Nagano Prefec-

[6] Edoardo Chiossone (1832-98) was an engraver brought to Japan in 1875 to serve in the Printing Bureau of the Treasury and to help inaugurate the manufacture of paper currency and stamps in Japan. Before this, Western-style currency had been printed in New York or Frankfort. For Chiossone's portraits of important political figures of the period, such as Saigō Takamori, Iwakura Tomomi, and Sanjō Sanetomi, see Kumamoto Kenjirō, *Kindai Nihon bijutsu no kenkyū*, Pls. 124-37.

ture) in a farming family of some wealth and position by the name of Yamagishi.[7] Rather little is known of him until his sixteenth year, when he moved to Tokyo. There, he received training from Ōnishi Chinnen (1792-1851), a painter of samurai origin who had worked in both the Nanga style of Tani Bunchō and the Maruyama-Shijō manner, but his reputation was built chiefly upon the latter. At the time of his death, he was the outstanding exponent of the realistic Shijō school in Edo.

It was the Bunjin style, however, which appealed to Tōgai, and he became a well-established member of the movement in Eastern Japan. At first glance, it seems unlikely that Western imagery would have appealed to a man steeped in this individualistic, Chinese mode of expression. In principle, the masters of Bunjin-ga (Chinese *Wenjen-hua*) were amateurs in the strict sense of the word, non-professionals who painted for their own enjoyment and philosophic stimulation; their artistic life was closely linked with poetry and scholarship aimed at personal cultivation. Although the Wenjen tradition was of great antiquity in China, it had been implanted systematically in Japan only in the eighteenth century, when it responded to the encouragement of Confucianism scholarship by the Tokugawa Shogunate. It appealed greatly to the Japanese, and flourished vigorously through the remainder of the Edo period and into the modern era, so much so that, ironically, many Bunjin painters became professionals who sold their works for high prices.

Actual examples of Tōgai's work in the Bunjin style are rare, but they show a very high level of skill.[8] One of them is

[7] The year of his birth is not precisely known. His full name, by which he is often referred to in contemporary documents, was Kawakami Kan; his *azana* was Shiritsu, and his familiar name was Mannojō. Tōgai was his *gō*. He took the name Kawakami when he was adopted by a samurai of that name in Edo, an official of the Bakufu. It has been suggested that he caused himself to be adopted in order to ease his entry into government service in the Bansho Shirabesho.

[8] Two Bunjin-ga paintings are reproduced in the *Nihon-ga taisei*,

a fan painting done in a fluid, loosely brushed manner depicting bamboo, rocks, narcissus, and chrysanthemums. According to its inscription, it was copied after a work of a celebrated Wenjen painter of the Ming period, Ch'en Shun (1482-1544), a student of Wen Cheng-ming. Another is a hanging scroll showing Field Poppies done in a boldly inventive style, and also copied from an older Chinese work. Tōgai was closely associated with the leading master of the Bunjin style in Edo, Yasuda Rōzan (1830-82), who had spent ten years in China in order to study Wenjen-hua at the source.

Tōgai continued to paint in the Bunjin manner even after his interests in Western art had been aroused, but the latter finally dominated his thought and career. To account for his interest, it would make a pleasant fable to claim that he had been moved to tears by the evocative powers of a copy of Rembrandt's "Hundred Guilder Print" secretly brought to Tokyo; but in fact, there is no record of Tōgai ever having seen masterpieces of European art. His prime motivation was pragmatic, much in the spirit of men of the Meirokusha group like Fukuzawa Yukichi and Mori Arinori, who believed that the chief fruits of Western civilization were the rational, practical, and scientific skills which would strengthen the nation and promote enterprise and prosperity. For Tōgai and later Koyama, the visual arts were seen very much in the light of *Jitsugaku*, as Koyama clearly demonstrated in his celebrated debate over calligraphy with Okakura described below.

Tōgai's attraction to Western arts must have been similar in motivation to that of a small number of Edo period painters who were convinced that Japanese art had reached an impasse from which it could advance no further, and that European arts were intellectually superior. Most articulate of these men was Shiba Kōkan (1748-1818). A painter and ukiyo-e print

---

xxi (Meiji-hen), Pls. 143, 144. The painting "Field Poppies" is very close in style to works of Tsubaki Chinzan (1801-54), who was one of Tōgai's associates until Chinzan's early death.

designer who had worked in the shadows of the master Harunobu, he studied Western botany and astronomy and also
experimented with a variety of Western pictorial techniques.
Gleaning through his biographical reminiscence *Shumparō
hikki* of 1811 and his treatise on Western art, *Seiyōga-dan*, one
finds him complaining of the corruption of Buddhism and of
traditional Chinese and Japanese learning. "We all have minds
like women"; "no one cares about the laws of the Universe."[9]
He praised Western painting for possessing the means by
which the real appearance of a thing can be depicted in terms
of darkness and light, concavity and convexity, nearness and
distance, depth and shallowness. He said that Western painting
is informative in the same way as is writing, whereas Eastern
painting is trivial, more of a plaything, incapable of showing
things as foreshortened, and often taking refuge in artificially
shaped contour lines.

Shiba Kōkan had studied with Hiraga Gennai (1728-79), a
linguist, botanist, popular writer, and painter in the Western
style as well. Gennai himself lived for a while in Nagasaki and
assembled at great cost a small library of Dutch scientific books;
he also taught in the Akita Han in the far northeast, and
trained a regional school of painters in the Western manner.
Known as *Akita Ranga* (Akita Dutch Painting), this school
included such men as Odano Naotake (1749-80), Satake Shozan (1748-85), and others, some of whom remained active in
the region and also in Edo as late as the 1830's.[10]

Most of the basic traits of European painting of which Shiba
Kōkan wrote were widely understood in Japan from the last
half of the eighteenth century onward: vanishing point perspective, depiction of light sources inside a picture, scientific
mastery of anatomical and botanical structures, and the spirit

[9] Arthur Waley, "Shiba Kōkan," *Ostasiatische Zeitschrift*, N.F. v
(1929), 60-75; Kawakita Michiaki, pp. 19-21; also the unpublished
dissertation by Calvin French on Kōkan, Columbia University, 1966.
[10] *Nihon yōga no akebono; Akita Ranga*. Catalogue, Yamato Bunka-
kan (Nara, 1967).

of careful illusionistic drawing. While Edo-period painters would customarily establish their identities as members of one or another of the accepted styles, they would freely explore and borrow from the others. The Western style was an acceptable option, but despite the efforts of Shiba Kōkan or Aōdō Denzen (1748-1822) and Gennai and his followers, it was not a fully recognized school with the same standing as the Kanō or ukiyo-e or Bunjin groups.

The influence of Western art was none the less ubiquitous. In the work of the Kyoto master Maruyama Ōkyo (1733-95) and his followers, for example, analytical and objective drawing of birds and animals went far beyond traditional Sino-Japanese realism. Ōkyo even drew a Kyoto street scene by showing the figures in the nude, giving careful attention to muscles and anatomy, and then adding the clothing in a manner much like that used by Jacques Louis David in his preparatory drawings for "The Tennis Court Oath" of 1789. Ōkyo made careful studies of different types of human heads and facial expressions; he sketched figures who were running or doing awkward gestures. He experimented with vanishing point perspective in his *Megane-e* (Spectacle Pictures), which were a great commercial success; painted with two distinct horizon lines, they were to be looked at through a mirror and a convex lens and gave a startling impression of a real scene.[11] As a rule, Ōkyo did not paint Western subject matter as did Shiba Kōkan; he was loyal to traditional themes, and his naturalism thus was a source of inspiration to Okakura Kakuzō and Fenollosa a century later, who were anxious for the Japanese to adapt Western techniques but not Western ideals.

Even in the works of the Bunjin painters Western elements are to be found. Ike no Taiga (1723-76) painted a panoramic view of Asama Mountain in 1750 with a strongly European

[11] *Ōkyo meiga-fu* (Kyoto, 1936), Pls. 21-27 for the *Megane-e*; Pl. 39 for the street scene based on anatomical studies; Pl. 35 for physiognomic studies; Pl. 27 for gesture drawings; Pl. 31 for an exceptional example of a Dutch-style drawing.

sense of spatial construction and care for observed detail.[12]
Such spatial effects appear throughout his work, even those
which are Confucian in subject matter and painted with Chinese style brush work. Yosa Buson (1716-83) and Tani Bunchō
(1763-1840) were accustomed to Western forms of spatial
organization, and the portraits done by Watanabe Kazan
(1793-1841) reveal his interest in European learning, for their
interpretation of character is Western in spirit.[13]

The ukiyo-e print designers and painters, although presumably more plebian in their interests, were also subject to the
same influences. Deep perspective compositions with a single
vanishing point appear in the works of Masanobu in the 1740's
and Toyonobu in the 1750's. Toyonobu delighted in painting
the illusion of the transparency of cloth to a degree far beyond
that of traditional Yamato-e designs. Utamaro was also
intrigued by this problem; and he too experimented with perspective and with depicting lamps glowing in the center of
compositions, causing shadows to be cast on floors and objects.[14]

Hokusai was unusually well informed about Western techniques, and was able to reconcile their greater power of realism
with the emotional appeal of Eastern painting. Among some
recently discovered material said to date from Hokusai's last
years are extraordinary pencil studies of the foetus of a deer, as
searchingly analytical as any drawing of Dürer or Pisanello.[15]
Also there is an oil painting of sea shells dating from around

[12] *Ike no Taiga sakuhinshū* (Tokyo, 1960), No. 51.

[13] For the tragic story of Kazan's death, see G. B. Sansom, *The Western World and Japan* (New York, 1951), pp. 261-66; Kazan's son, Watanabe Shōka (1835-87) was a close friend of Tōgai's, and the record of the father's oppression at the hands of the Bakufu and sui-cide was well known among the Rangaku-sha of Edo.

[14] One man who successfully adapted the woodblock print medium to the Western style was Kobayashi Kiyochika (see the account of Donald Keene, p. 162ff.). A detailed study of his training and back-ground in the Western style is Yoshida Susugu, *Kobayashi Kiyochika* (Tokyo, 1964).

[15] Ozaki Shūdō, *Katsushika Hokusai* (Tokyo, 1967), Fig. 181.

1842 which closely anticipates the still-life pictures of Taka-hashi Yuichi.[16] During his latter years, the aged Hokusai and his patron and student Takai Kōzan were even said to have dissected the corpse of a suicide.[17] Like the masters of the early Florentine Renaissance, they were seeking to know more about the underlying structures of the body.

Despite these many instances of interest in European meth-ods, it was not until the Meiji restoration that the Western style became a recognized and flourishing school of art. This was due of course to the efforts of Tōgai, Takahashi, Koyama, and the others, but it is also a classic example of the triumph of an idea whose time had finally come, a time when the most influential men throughout the social order had decided that Japan must master Western techniques in every aspect of life.

Whatever were the immediate causes of Tōgai's interests, his conventional biographies state only that well before the Resto-ration, he foresaw the great cultural changes that were destined to take place and decided that the Dutch language, still the key to Western learning, ought to be mastered. Secretly and diligently he taught himself this difficult tongue; then, wish-ing a place to study further, he was enlisted as a grammarian or linguist in the Bansho Shirabesho, the Institute for the Study of Western (read Barbarian) Documents set up by the Bakufu. This was in 1857, only a year or so after this remarkable estab-lishment had been founded in order to assemble and study Western documents of all sorts—political, economic, military, literary. The contents were made available in a restricted, con-trolled manner to the Shogunal government, which felt the need to understand the technology and thinking of the West in order to escape exploitation by it, to avoid the fate of China and India.

Tōgai's abilities were quickly recognized by the head of the Institute, and he was urged to do research into painting tech-niques. The Institute was enlarged in 1861 and a regular

[16] *Ibid.*, Pl. 30.   [17] *Ibid.*, pp. 52-56.

Painting Study Section was set up under Tōgai's direction. In the following year, he was given a number of assistants and began teaching Western techniques. In 1863, the Institute was renamed the Kaiseijo (a more appropriate name taken from ancient Chinese sources suggesting the opening of wisdom, the dispelling of ignorance), and three years later, Tōgai's staff was augmented by the appointment of additional men, including Takahashi Yuichi (1828-94). Takahashi was about the same age as Tōgai, but he was more gifted as a painter and was destined to become one of the most influential figures among the Western-style artists of the early Meiji period.[18]

At first, Tōgai's knowledge of European art was based on Dutch texts of considerable age, well removed from the esthetic issues which were affecting contemporary European art. This situation was not really changed even in the later 1860's when more up-to-date French and English books were imported. Among these was a drawing manual by Robert Scott Burn, a British writer who specialized in instructions for self-teaching of artistic and mechanical subjects.[19] Tōgai translated it under the title *Seiga shinan* (*Guide to Western Pictures*), and it was published in 1871. Tōgai also worked with *Coe's Drawing Cards for Schools*, a set of lessons reducing the basic techniques of illusionistic drawing to the simplest possible terms.

The level of insight conveyed by these texts was purely pragmatic. Tōgai had no urge, apparently, to explore matters more deeply, to reach the theoretical foundations of the Renaissance tradition, or to discover the true conditions of mid-nineteenth-

[18] See the account of Haga Tōru, pp. 221ff.

[19] Burn's *Illustrated London Drawing Book* (London, 1852), contains lessons in pencil sketching, figure and object drawing, perspective and isometric drawing, sketching in crayons, and engraving in metal and wood. His *Self-aid Cyclopaedia for Self-taught Students* (London, 1863) incorporates the above volume and adds to it essays on architectural, mechanical, and engineering drawing, ornamental drawing and design, mechanics, and steam engine design. In these volumes Burn is described as the author of such other texts as "The Lessons of my Farm," "Implements and Machinery," and "Practical Ventilation."

century European art. The first path would have involved a mountain of difficult texts, from Alberti's to those of Sir Joshua Reynolds, and a Japanese would have had scant interest in one essential part of the Renaissance tradition, the arts of ancient Greece and Rome with their emphasis upon the nude human figure and classical mythology. The second path would have led into a quagmire of conflict and instability, into the struggles between European Classicists (affirming the Renaissance tradition) and Romantics (denying it in many ways), and the rise of the social realist and naturalist schools. The Japanese had problems enough of their own and, in any event, historically they had hitherto shown little interest in the theory of art—that body of lore which coordinates artistic practice with philosophical principles. It was the next generation, that of Okakura Kakuzō (1862-1913), which realized the necessity of formulating theoretical systems. Okakura made art theory a major subject in the Tokyo School of Fine Arts (Tokyo Bijutsu Gakkō). The fact that Taikan as a student had done poorly in this subject caused Okakura to reject him as a regular faculty member for a while, despite his brilliance as a painter.

Not only did Tōgai and his followers depend on simple texts for their research, they also sought out foreigners who might have information on painting techniques. In 1863, for example, they learned that an accomplished painter was living in Yokohama, the wife of the American journalist Raphael Schoyer. He was the publisher of the *Japan Express*, an ephemeral English-language newspaper, one of the first of its kind in Japan. Takahashi Yuichi described in his diary how the group came to visit Mrs. Schoyer in Yokohama only to find her accidentally away from home, but they saw her paintings and were greatly impressed. Later, she brought some of her work to Tokyo, received a party of Tōgai's followers, answered their questions, and presented them with some sailcloth canvas, blue paint, and brushes.

Also living in Yokohama was the Englishman Charles Wirgman, a correspondent for *The Illustrated London News* and the publisher of an informal, satirical journal called *The Japan Punch* for the entertainment of the foreign community. He was an artist of distinctly limited gifts, but was sympathetic to the Japanese. Not only did he do many genre studies of local life, he also agreed to instruct young men and women eager to learn the secrets of Western art. Among his pupils were a number of men who made their mark in Western-style arts in Japan: Takahashi Yuichi, who was the close associate of Tōgai; Goseda Yoshimatsu and Yamamoto Hōsui, both of whom continued their training in Paris; Kobori Seigan, who adapted wood-block printing to the Western style; and Tamura Shuritsu, who returned with this style to Kyoto.

Through such fragmentary accounts and artistic relics, one can sense what must have been an exhilarating mood of discovery as these men, in the waning years of the Bakufu, explored one by one the complicated visual effects of European painting—perspective, anatomy, lighting effects—as well as its subject matter traditions and the purely mechanical side of the problem. At the Research Institute, Tōgai systematically practiced the techniques of oil painting, fresco (painting on wet plaster with dry pigments mixed into a medium such as egg-yolk), water color, crayons, and various print techniques: engraving in cooper or wood, and lithography.

However, certain very surprising deficiencies have been noted. Kumamoto states that easels were not used until the Meiji period proper; thus the painters had an additional problem in trying to create illusions of great pictorial depth while working on a horizontal surface. It was not until 1863 that foreign pigments and other materials began to be freely imported.[20] And Takahashi Yuichi described the great pains which Tōgai took in order to prepare a proper ground for oil painting. He took pieces of Mino paper which had been treated with alum and then pieced them together to form a large painting surface. Then he would sketch in his composition in *sumi*

[20] Kumamoto, *Kindai Nihon bijutsu no kenkyū*, pp. 47ff.

ink and color it with light traditional colors. The back would then be lined with heavy paper brushed with fish glue. Oxide of silver was placed in bean oil and left in the sun for a week to thicken and to make an oil medium into which dry pigments were dissolved. With these the composition was then painted as though with ordinary oil paints. The choice of paper instead of native linen cloth must have been dictated by a lack of proper paint grounds, such as gesso and glue, which prevent the oil in the paint from soaking into the cloth, leaving the surface dull and discolored.

The Establishment of the "Western Style"

Upon the successful creation of the Restoration government, the influence of the Western-style artists became more pervasive, their activities more open and varied. For Tōgai, the practical, scientific side of European arts became a dominant concern, whereas most of his followers explored the expressive possibilities of the new idiom.

Tōgai had once been directed by military authorities of the Bakufu to make some paintings to be used at the military school at Numazu. In 1872, he became a teacher in that school, and two years later he gave instruction in drawing and painting in the Military Academy. He also assisted foreign teachers there, particularly the Franco-Dutch draftsman Abel Guerineau, who accepted Koyama Shōtarō as a student for awhile. In the same year Tōgai compiled his own teaching manual of illusionistic drawing, the *Shakei hōhan*, containing fifty illustrations done with crayon and reproduced by lithography.

These are the oldest lithographs made in Japan, and to produce them, Tōgai had been obliged to teach himself the craft. The presses had been imported from Holland by the Kaiseijo and then set up at the Numazu Military School. They were inoperable, however, until Tōgai mastered the instructions which had come with them; and he also translated a Dutch text on the making of inks, which he adapted for use in lithography. When the Italian printmaker Edoardo Chiossone arrived in 1875, Tōgai consulted with him on various problems, but by then the *Shakei hōhan* had already been printed.

After this, Tōgai was attached to the General Staff, for whom he investigated the Western science of cartography—for obvious military purposes. He published short treatises, such as "On the coloring of maps," and seems to have been held in great esteem up to the time he was accused of having sold such maps to foreigners.

The Meiji government used Tōgai's skills also in the Ministry of Education, where he and Takahashi Yuichi conducted research into methods of art instruction. Tōgai's translation of Robert Scott Burn's teaching manual appeared in 1871, and the next year he and Takahashi promulgated lessons for elementary schools based on careful descriptive drawing of objects in a modified Western manner using pencils instead of inks and soft brushes. This system remained in effect until 1885, when Fenollosa, Okakura, and others forced the return to one based on traditional methods.

In 1877, about the time Koyama painted his portrait, the government called on Tōgai for yet another service. He was charged with heading the jury for the art section of the First National Industrial Exhibition, which was a major governmental effort to stimulate the arts through the salon system.

In Europe throughout the nineteenth century, national governments had been obliged to take up the support of the visual arts, replacing the Church and the educated aristocracy whose wealth and prestige had been steadily declining. The main instrument of government support was the Academy, usually a state-subsidized art school which also held periodic competitions (the Salons) for different categories of work. Not only were the prizes important sources of income to an artist, but the seal of approval helped him sell his works.[21]

In Japan, the cultural and economic dislocations of the new era had equally disturbed the old patterns of artistic patronage,

[21] For a detailed account of the system, see Nikolaus Pevsner, *Academies of Art, Past and Present* (Cambridge, Eng., 1940).

and there was great economic distress among the hereditary families of artists and craftsmen. The Japanese learned of Western forms of governmental support through the Iwakura Mission, for example, or the efforts of Dr. Gottfried Wagner, an Austrian adviser on arts and crafts, or through Japanese participation in international expositions, especially the one in Vienna in 1873.[22]

Thus the First National Industrial Exhibition was intended as one means of revitalizing the arts. Supported vigorously by Ōkubo Toshimichi, then the Minister of the Interior, it was held despite the outbreak of the Satsuma Rebellion. The Emperor Meiji attended the opening ceremonies; and from him came honorific presents to the judges of different sections. Tōgai received a length of damask cloth in honor of his patient efforts, which had consumed an entire month.

Another basic part of the scheme of state patronage was the founding in 1876 of the Kōbu Bijutsu Gakkō, the Technological (or Industrial) Art School. The government official most directly responsible for it seems to have been Itō Hirobumi, then Minister of Industry. It was set up along strictly Western lines and three Italians were brought to teach sculpture, painting, and basic studies. The painting master was Antonio Fontanesi, who had been trained as an academician in Turin and Paris but was essentially a romantic painter specializing in tranquil, pastoral landscapes at twilight. His soft, semi-impressionist style had caused him to be severely criticized in Italian academic circles which were more addicted to figure painting, and this seems to have prompted him to accept the invitation to come to Japan. He was a man of great personal warmth and dignity who struck a sympathetic chord in his students. The small, private painting schools such as Tōgai's willingly sent their pupils to Fontanesi, and Koyama attached himself to the Italian master with such zeal and worked so well that he was promoted to the rank of assistant instructor. Indeed, the por-

---

[22] See Eugene Soviak's account of the Mission's reports dealing with museums, pp. 12, 24-25; also Tōru Haga, pp. 245ff.

trait of Tōgai, Koyama's first master, was probably painted while he was under the tutelage of Fontanesi, and the few surviving examples of Koyama's landscapes seem little more than school pieces in Fontanesi's style.

Fontanesi returned to Italy in 1878 because of ill health, but despite the shortness of his stay in Japan, the force of his personality was a major factor in strengthening the development of Western-style painting there. Proof of this was the fact that his successor, an Italian named Feretti, displeased the Japanese students so greatly that Koyama and his fellow classmates withdrew from school and set up their own private group, the Jūichi-kai.[23]

The new art school seemed to be the culmination of the efforts to promote Western-style arts—with its skillful foreign teachers, enthusiastic students, proper teaching materials, and imported art supplies. Yet, not only did the school fail to flourish, its doors were closed in 1882 after only five years of activity. The closing was caused by many factors, but one which should be mentioned here was the wave of sentiment hostile to the Western style which had begun to undermine its prestige. In fact, one of the first signs of this was the decision rendered by the painting jury headed by Tōgai himself at the exhibition of 1877. The highest awards were given to men who worked in traditional ways: Kikuchi Yōsai, Shibata Zeshin, and Takamura Tōun. Lesser awards were given to the Western-style painters: Goseda Yoshimatsu, Tōgai's associate Takahashi Yuichi, and Yamamoto Hōsui, who had studied with Wirgman and Fontanesi. While it was claimed that this decision proved the fairness and generosity of Tōgai, the fact that the exhibition was an instrument of government policy suggests

[23] The Jūichi-kai, named after the month of November when the group quit school, included such men as Koyama, Asai Chū, and Matsuoka Hisashi, who later became leading figures of the second generation of Meiji Western-style artists. Also, when Okakura eliminated the Western style from the curriculum of the reopened government art school, the Jūichi-kai became the main center for instruction in the forbidden manner.

that the decision may not have been made solely on the basis of artistic quality. Indeed, in choosing between excellent works of radically different artistic intent, a judge can do nothing other than decide which style is ideologically the more valuable.

In May of 1881, Tōgai committed suicide at an inn in Atami. He had been accused of selling to foreigners secret maps belonging to the headquarters of the Army General Staff, and also of "transmitting rumors." While it is impossible at this distance to confirm or deny these charges, one can recognize in them an archetypal pattern.[24] In a time of growing violence from extreme rightists and the rise of the Kokusui Hōzon (Preservation of National Purity) movement, people with strong Western interests had come under attack. Whether or not this actually affected the death of Tōgai, artistic circles in Japan were violently torn by the resurgence of nationalistic sentiment.

Okakura and Taikan

The history of early Meiji painting seems to fit with deceptive clarity into a simple chronological scheme. From 1868 to 1877, Western styles were adopted with enthusiasm. The following decade was marked by growing resistance to foreign modes of culture, by the fear that native traditions, which both Japanese and foreigners recognized as possessing great merit, were in grave peril. A strongly conservative movement led by Ernest Fenollosa and Okakura Kakuzō was one aspect of this resistance. When the government art school was reopened in Tokyo in 1888 with Okakura as its leader, it offered no instruction in the Western style; and efforts were made even to forbid the import of Western art materials. By the last decade of the nineteenth century, however, the situation had become

[24] The circumstances of Tōgai's death are commonly ignored in most accounts of the man and his times. They are given, however, by Umezawa Waken, *Nihon Nanga-shi* (Tokyo, 1919), p. 945, who states that the source of this information was a recorded conversation with Koyama Senraku (*i.e.*, Shōtarō). See also the account of Tōgai in the *Dai jimmei jiten*, II (Tokyo: Heibonsha, 1953), 182.

stabilized. Western-style arts were too powerful and well-established to be eliminated. Government officials and many persons in the universities were sympathetic to it, and students returning from abroad came with a deeper knowledge than that of the pioneers of Tōgai's generation.[25] In 1896 Okakura agreed to offer training in Western methods in the School of Fine Arts: but a style which he and his associates had devised had become the preferred one in most government-sponsored activities. Functioning much like the official French Beaux-Arts style of the nineteenth century, it went under the simple name of Nihon-ga (Japanese painting).

Taikan's portrait of Ch'ü Yüan is a classic example of early Nihon-ga. Traditional Asian subject matter and materials predominate, as in the silk used as the painting surface, the *sumi* ink in the outlines and shading, and the opaque water-soluble pigments. Taikan painted no cast shadows on the body, a feature of Western notions of pictorial lighting, nor did he give the work a wooden frame. Instead it was mounted as a large hanging scroll, 114 inches in width. The spirit in which Taikan drew the hands, garment folds, and the underlying anatomy of the body was equally traditional, showing none of the searching, objective vision of Western illusionism present in the portrait of Tōgai. The entire figure was governed by a series of softly curving, harmonious linear movements, as idealized as any in a Fujiwara-period Buddhist painting.

The Western elements in this picture are less obvious. They are present even though Taikan had proclaimed at this stage of his career that he had no intention of incorporating them into his work. Chief among them is an overriding sense of

[25] Kuroda Seiki, for example, returned from France in 1893. Despite the moralistic furor caused the same year when he exhibited in Tokyo the painting of a nude which he had done in Paris, his essentially bland impressionistic style and respect for Japanese subjects did not arouse the same enmity in Okakura as did the earlier generation of Western-style painters. Thus Okakura accepted Kuroda as the teacher in charge of Western-style painting in the Tokyo School of Fine Arts even though this outraged the extreme traditionalists.

melodrama, of individualism, of theatrical self-consciousness in the face of Ch'ü Yüan and in the landscape setting. This trait is never found in the impassive, reserved visages of traditional portraiture in Japan, not even in the many paintings of Suga-wara no Michizane (Kitano Tenjin), a theme remarkably simi-lar in content to that of Ch'ü Yüan. Not only was the subject interpreted in a mood of romantic egoism, but Taikan himself was striving to establish a highly personal style of painting, one which would shock his audience. Okakura and Fenollosa had urged their students to attain freedom and individuality, to "keep the soul free through art," and Okakura's description of the painting recognizes this element: "Taikan brings into the field his wild imagery and tempestuous conceptions, as shown in his 'Kutsugen Wandering on the Barren Hills' amongst wind-blown narcissus—the flower of silent purity—feeling the raging storm that gathers in his soul."[26]

The story of Ch'ü Yüan was two thousand years old and familiar chiefly to those with a classical education, but Okakura had encouraged such a return to ". . . the ancient spirit of race-myths and historical chronicles."[27] Antiquarian themes are common in early Nihon-ga—Buddhist deities, Chinese court scenes, Japanese historical events—but many of them have as thinly disguised relevance to contemporary issues as did Jacques Louis David's "Oath of the Horatii" of 1785, which placed French revolutionary sentiment into a Roman republican guise. It is no accident, moreover, that in selecting the theme of Ch'ü Yüan to refer to events less than a year old, Taikan consulted with his friend Shimamura Hōgetsu (1871-1918), a novelist and playwright, a leading figure in the Shingeki movement and a major exponent of naturalism in the theater.

The modernity in the mood of emotional turmoil and intro-spection in this painting is complemented by certain formal traits. The ground plane recedes with radical foreshortening; it is not tilted upward in the traditional manner of Chinese

[26] Okakura Kakuzō, *The Ideals of the East* (London, 1903), p. 233.
[27] *Ibid.*, 231.

perspective. The sense of pictorial depth is also enhanced by the wildly twisting branches in the foreground, for they were done without outlines, their forms established simply by contrasts of light and dark. This was a part of the personal style being developed by Taikan and his friend Hishida Shunsō, the *mōrōtai* (or "dimness style") for which they were severely criticized by antiquarian purists.

Finally, an analysis of this painting should not fail to note its perfection of detail and finish, as though Taikan was consciously striving to create a masterpiece. He attempted a great project, like the giant *raigō* pictures of the Japanese Middle Ages or the wall paintings of Hōryū-ji; but his theme was essentially a personal one, an ephemeral political episode lacking the contact with deep spiritual values and a broad cultural consensus which gave those ancient works a sense of necessity. The contrived content of his painting was not equal to its scale or to Taikan's burning ambitions, and the result is a sense of rhetorical emptiness which this painting shares with dozens produced by French academicians or the British Pre-Raphaelites in the mid-nineteenth century, burdened by heavy literary symbolism and surface perfection of form.

Behind this painting, however, lay years of intense labor during which Okakura and his group tried to create a new basis for Japanese art in an amalgam of East and West, old and new, subjective and objective.[28] Their teaching program, broadly synthetic in nature, was influenced by the ideas of Ernest Fenollosa (1853-1908), the young Harvard University graduate student who had come to Japan in 1878 to teach philosophy at Tokyo University. He had also been trained in both art history and drawing, and found himself increasingly engrossed in collecting Japanese art and studying it systematically. Okakura had attended his philosophy classes, and the two men became closely associated. After graduation in 1880,

[28] Lawrence Chisolm, *Fenollosa: The Far East and American Culture* (New Haven, 1963); Miyagawa Torao, *Okakura Tenshin*, Nihon Bijutsu-shi Sōsho, viii (Tokyo, 1956).

Okakura joined the music research section of the Ministry of Education, but he continued to serve Fenollosa as a guide, translator, and companion.

From Harvard, Fenollosa had brought a rather bland mixture of Hegelianism, the evolutionary doctrines of Herbert Spencer, and a taste for metaphysics taken from Emerson and the New England Transcendentalists; when applied to the history and practice of art in Japan, they produced a potent ideology, a sacred cause. Fenollosa wrote in 1898, for example, that the modern age had brought an encounter of Asia and the West, of ancient spiritual goals and modern technical means, a division which went to the bottom of all values; but from this encounter (of thesis and antithesis) would come a new synthesis, one which would be world-wide and final and bring mankind to a new and higher cultural plane. Both East and West had exhausted their traditions, the East full, over-ripe and despairing of new expression, the West antiquated and bound in materialism. In a spirit of mutual sympathy and insight, however, artists and educators should select the best elements of the two and thus build an art of the future.[29]

As leaders of a cultural movement, Okakura and Fenollosa had personal powers bordering on charisma. The foreigner was articulate and sensitive, had gradually mastered some spoken and written Japanese, and was armed with an ideology of great appeal; in addition he affirmed the opinions of a growing number of Japanese concerning the worth of their national traditions. Okakura was skilled in English and a gifted poet in Chinese, and he possessed a fiery temperament and infectious enthusiasms. Also important to their success was the generous support given by persons from the Boston area who were either wealthy or intellectually influential: Dr. Edward Sylvester Morse, who came to Japan in 1877 and organized the Department of Zoology at Tokyo University, who was instrumental in bringing Fenollosa to the University, and who became a pio-

[29] "The Coming Fusion of East and West," *Harper's*, xcviii (1898), 115-22.

neer in the science of paleontology in Japan; Charles G. Weld, a wealthy Boston doctor and yachtsman who purchased much of Fenollosa's collection for the Museum of Fine Arts there; Dr. William Sturgis Bigelow, perhaps the most important of all, was the scion of a family of Boston doctors, an energetic collector of Japanese art, a convert like Fenollosa to Tendai Buddhism, and a frequent contributor of funds to Okakura's and Fenollosa's projects; the painter John LaFarge and Henry Adams, both of whom stayed with Fenollosa and his wife at Nikkō; Mrs. Isabella Stewart Gardner, who came to Japan in 1888 and later gave Okakura a role at the center of her artistic and social world at Fenway Court in Boston.[30] These were formidable allies to add to their supporters in Japan.

Among the early efforts of Okakura and Fenollosa was the encouragement they gave to two masters of the Kanō School, Kanō Hōgai (1828-88) and Hashimoto Gahō (1835-1908). Both painters had been impoverished and driven to work outside their profession during the first decade of the Meiji era. Hōgai was reduced to drawing designs in a pottery factory and even to tending silkworms; Gahō worked as a draftsman in a naval shipyard and also served in a stable for a while as a groom. By 1878, they had made their way back to Tokyo and begun to paint and exhibit again, and they seemed to offer an ideal link between the arts of the traditional past and the future which Okakura and Fenollosa envisaged.

Hōgai, who died after only four years of activity with the group, specialized in Buddhist deities painted in a traditional, hieratic manner modified by a tightly controlled realism and highly refined surface finish. Fenollosa could describe him as ". . . the great central genius of Meiji, [who is] striking a last note on the great instrument which Godōshi [Wu Tao-tzu] first sounded . . . ," but it was Gahō, appointed head of the painting department of the Tokyo School of Fine Arts, who played the crucial role in the new movement. An eclectic by

[30] See Van Wyck Brooks, *Fenollosa and His Circle* (New York, 1962), pp. 1-68

I. Migita Toshihide. "The Surrender of Wei-hai-wei by Ting
    Ju-ch'ang, Commodore of the Northern Fleet."

II. Bairin. "Astonishment of Li Hung-chang on hearing the report
    of the capture of Port Arthur by our troops."

III. Kobayashi Kiyochika. "Naval engagement off P'ung-do in
Korea. The Chinese warship 'Kuang-i' being pursued by the
Japanese fleet and severely damaged, the crew themselves set the
ship afire and flee for the land."

I. Koyama Shōtarō. "Kawakami Tōgai." Oil paint on canvas. Tokyo Geijutsu Daigaku.

II. Yokoyama Taikan. "Ch'ü Yüan," detail. Color and ink on silk. Miyajima, Itsukushima Shrine.

III. Kawakami Tōgai. "Kayabemine District." Oil paint on canvas.

nature, he was perhaps more responsible than any other single man for the synthesis of the early Nihon-ga style. Not only did he ransack the history of Sino-Japanese painting for appropriate subject matter, he blended together stylistic elements from the ink paintings of the Ashikaga and Southern Sung masters, the narrative scrolls of the Kamakura period, the works of Kōrin and the Tosa school colorists, and the naturalism of Ōkyo.

The hopes of Okakura and Fenollosa, however, were focused on the corps of young students training at the School of Fine Arts, of whom Taikan was outstanding, along with Hishida Shunsō (1874-1911) and Shimomura Kanzan (1873-1930).[31] Taikan had been born in the founding year of the Meiji era in Ibaragi Prefecture (and lived until well after World War II, until 1958); his father was a samurai whose affairs had been greatly disrupted by the changing social order, and when Taikan was ten, the family moved to Tokyo. While a student in an English-language school, he showed talent in pencil sketching and was persuaded by his friends to enter the Tokyo School of Fine Arts, then admitting its inaugural class in 1888. He thus came under the tutelage of Hashimoto Gahō in painting techniques, and Okakura in the history and theory of art. He graduated in 1893, but remained as a teacher in a preparatory art school. He then went to the Kyoto-Nara region to make hand-copied replicas of ancient paintings under a scheme devised by Fenollosa and Okakura. This provided him with intimate acquaintance with the finest works of the past, but he also earned considerable renown in competitive exhibitions there and in the capital. He served as a teacher in Kyoto, and in May of 1897 returned to Tokyo to become an Assistant Professor in the School of Fine Arts—just as the pressures which led to Okakura's resignation had begun to build up.

Okakura's resignation on March 28, 1898 was a bitter, stinging defeat which cost him his cachet as the official arbiter and

[31] Yoshizawa Chū, *Taikan*. English edition (Tokyo, 1962); Ibaragi Prefecture (ed.), *Yokoyama Taikan-den* (Ibaragi, 1959).

leading intellectual force in Japanese art circles. It was caused by a complex crisis of personalities and issues no longer entirely clear today. It is known that Okakura was criticized by extreme conservatives who regretted the modernist and Western elements in his thinking, restrained even as those elements were. Some of the faculty claimed that his methods of administration were despotic, and circulated a petition for his dismissal. Also, officials of the Ministry of Education in the Bijutsu Gyōsei Kanri (Bureau of Art Administration) resented Okakura's flagrant individualism and lack of bureaucratic skill. Less easy to estimate is the importance of a widely known and scandalous affair which Okakura had with the wife of one of his superiors in the Ministry of Education, Kuki Ryūichi; it could not, however, have strengthened his cause.[32]

Upon his departure, he was joined by seventeen sympathetic faculty members, including Gahō and Taikan, and by advanced students. Together, they sought to continue their careers and set up with optimistic energy and great personal expense a private institute called the Nihon Bijutsu-in, the Japan Art Academy. By pooling their resources, selling as many paintings as possible, and soliciting funds from Japanese and American friends, especially Sturgis Bigelow, they financed a new building constructed near Okakura's house in Yanaka, a suburb of Tokyo. By October of the same year, the members of the Nihon Bijutsu-in held their first exhibition, and Taikan's painting of Ch'ü Yüan was awarded a silver medal (First Prize). The mood of truculence and bitterness in the painting clearly expressed Okakura's feeling at the time, and presaged the anticlimactic quality of his later life.

Okakura and Western-style Painting

That extremists among the cultural conservatives became enemies of Okakura is understandable but ironical. Theoreti-

[32] See especially Horioka Yasuko, *The Life of Kakuzō* (Tokyo, 1963); Miyakawa Torao, "Meiji Nashiyonarizumu to Okakura Tenshin," in *Nihon Bunka-shi*, Chikubo Shoten series, VIII (Tokyo, 1966), 202ff.

cally, his intellectual position was in the middle of the road, between the liberal, utilitarian, and pro-Western circles on the one hand, and the xenophobic nationalists, Shinto revivalists, and authoritarian militarists on the other. In fact, however, he was closer to the right than the left for practical as well as ideological reasons.

He waged a long struggle against Koyama and his allies to control the government apparatus of art training and patronage, and he sincerely believed that these men were deluded. He wrote in 1903 that in their eagerness and profound admiration of Western knowledge, they had confounded beauty with science, and culture with industry; "The Japanese attempt at Western imitation . . . grovelled in darkness from its infancy and yet succeeded, even at its inception, in imposing that hard crust of mannerism which impedes its progress to the present day." He spoke of "the scorching drought of modern vulgarity," "the clouding of the mirror of Yamato by the perplexities of Western thought."[33]

An early skirmish in this battle came in 1882, when he published (at the tender age of 20 and with Fenollosa at his side) a rejoinder to an essay of Koyama Shōtarō, who had succeeded Tōgai as the leading spokesman for the Western style.[34] Koyama's essay was called "Sho wa bijutsu narazu" ("Calligraphy is not art"), and the gist of his argument is that written characters are symbols of spoken language just as the Western alphabet. This alphabet possesses beauty in its utility and makes no attempt to go beyond efficiency and clarity. Chinese and Japanese calligraphy, on the other hand, even though it tempts man's spirit to a special realm, does not expand learning. It should not be considered an art because it does not possess the range of resources of painting and sculpture, and the shape of the characters is standardized and not changed according to

[33] Okakura, *Ideals of the East*, pp. 226-27, 243, 244.
[34] The debate was printed in the pages of the *Tōyō gakugei zasshi*, 1882; quoted at length by Takumi Hideo, *Kindai Nihon yōga no tenkai*, pp. 31ff; Miyakawa Torao, *Okakura Tenshin* (Tokyo, 1956), pp. 31-35.

the ability of each writer. It cannot be exported abroad; it serves neither as a basis of progress in the crafts nor as an aid to enterprise and commerce; it is without profit or utility.

Koyama's argument seems almost a paraphrase of those of Fukuzawa Yukichi, criticizing Confucian learning in *Gakumon no susume* ten years earlier. Okakura's rebuttal was eloquent. He said that Koyama, in referring to commerce and profit, had injected a mercenary element, which misses the very reason for which the arts are created. Koyama sees the arts simply as an aid to public affairs and an adjunct to language and never venturing beyond those limits, but this is not the essence of the matter. In fact, said Okakura, calligraphy in the East has historically attained the level of the arts through long practice and study, and has been guided by the taste and likes of men of different ages. Okakura's argument rested primarily on the subjective, almost mystical experiences of one deeply absorbed in traditional art, but it was enough to reveal the theoretical weakness of the early Western-style painters and also how inappropriate are utilitarian arguments in the realms of taste.

The calligraphy debate was but one episode in the growing offensive against the Western style launched in 1882. On May 14th, Fenollosa delivered an impassioned speech attacking it along with Bunjin-ga before a small, private and aristocratic art club, the Ryūchi-kai (Dragon Lake Society). He extravagantly praised traditional Japanese arts, and urged the nation to return to them before taking anything further from the West. This was said to have an electric effect upon an audience that included the Minister of Education Fukuoka Takachika (1835-1919), and Sano Tsunetami (1822-1902), perhaps the most influential official in government art policies.[35] Under

---

[35] Fukuoka had helped draft the Charter Oath (*Seitaisho*) of the Meiji government in 1868; Sano had arranged the Japanese exhibits at the Vienna Exposition of 1873. See Shimomura Eiji, *Tenshin to sono shokan* (Tokyo, 1964), pp. 23ff. for a detailed account of these men and their relation to Okakura.

the auspices of the Ryūchi-kai, Fenollosa's address was quickly translated into Japanese under the title of *Bijutsu shinsetsu* (*A True Account of the Fine Arts*), printed, and widely distributed. And in October of the same year, Western-style works were excluded from the first of the government sponsored painting competitions called the Naikoku Kaiga Kyōshin-kai.

Small study groups like the Ryūchi-kai provided Okakura and Fenollosa a focus for their activities, where they could sharpen their arguments and win converts. In 1884, they organized their own Kanga-kai (Painting Appreciation Society) in order to hold both exhibitions and lectures on traditional arts, to learn to judge the authenticity of old works, and also to encourage contemporary artists. Sturgis Bigelow was a founder and supporter of this group, as was Kawase Hideharu (1839-1907).[36] It was about this time that Okakura and Fenollosa began actively campaigning for the reopening of the government art school along the lines of their art theories. In 1885, a preliminary planning office for the school was established and staffed primarily by members of the Kanga-kai.

In the same year, 1885, Okakura and Fenollosa clashed again with Koyama, this time over art education in the elementary schools. All three men belonged to the Pictorial Research Committee of the Ministry of Education and in a bitter debate lasting five months, Okakura and Fenollosa, who were joined by Kanō Hōgai, succeeded in eliminating the system of Western-style drawing with pencils established fifteen years earlier by Tōgai and Takahashi. When this was replaced with brush and ink painting, Koyama resigned from the Committee in protest. All parties here realized that in an apparently secondary issue, the materials with which a school child is taught to draw, his cultural orientation is given a powerful turn—whether he is initiated into the ancient ritual of grinding his ink stick on a

---

[36] Kawase was a government official active in the Treasury, Home Ministry, and the Ministry of Agriculture and Commerce. He was also a manager of a prosperous paper company, and an enthusiastic supporter of Kanō Hōgai and Okakura. Shimomura, pp. 25-26.

slate palette, dipping in a brush of soft and pliable hair, and stroking the silhouette of bamboo leaves on absorbent paper; or whether he takes a hard lead pencil and sketches, objectively and analytically, the shadows and highlights of a stuffed bird or a vase and some apples set in front of him. This was an issue worthy of a hard fight.

By 1886, the activities of Okakura and Fenollosa reached an amazing level of intensity and variety. In October, they joined with Hamao Arata (1849-1925), Okakura's superior and protector in the Ministry of Education, on an official trip abroad to survey art education, museum methods, and the preservation of monuments. After a year of travel in the United States, England, and Western Europe, and the purchase of many books and photographs, they returned, Okakura becoming the Kanji (Manager) of the projected School of Fine Arts and Fenollosa a Professor of Esthetics and the History of Art. In October of 1888, the two men joined the staff of the Tokyo Imperial Museum, and Okakura was appointed Head of the Art Section there the following May, Fenollosa remaining a member of the administrative board. In February of 1889, the School of Fine Arts opened its doors under the nominal direction of Hamao Arata; it was run chiefly by Okakura, who became the official head in October, 1890. In January of 1889, Okakura and a friend founded the art historical magazine *Kokka*, a monthly bound in a traditional format with beautifully printed wood-block color plates and fine gravure illustrations. The early issues carried articles by Fenollosa on ukiyo-e, by Okakura praising Maruyama Ōkyo and Kanō Hōgai, by Bigelow, Kawase, and other members of the Kanga-kai. Okakura and Fenollosa lectured regularly at their own school and at many others throughout Tokyo; two or three times a year they would travel to different parts of Japan making a survey and registry of antiquities for the National Treasures Research Bureau of the Ministry of Education.

In 1890, however, Fenollosa left Japan to become Curator of Chinese and Japanese Art at the Museum of Fine Arts in Boston. His leaving was prompted by many factors, among them the realization that he and Okakura had attained many of the goals they had set for themselves, and that foreign specialists were being eased out of teaching and administrative posts. Fenollosa was one of the last to hold a high office; so after twelve years in Japan and the receipt from the Emperor Meiji of the Order of the Sacred Mirror, his third such honor, he returned with his family to the United States. He and Okakura remained in contact however, while the latter continued his whirlwind pace, even leaving for a short, official survey trip to China in 1893. Okakura helped establish a Fine Arts Research Institute in Ueno Park as the main center for documentation and study of the nation's artistic heritage; and during this time, he was constantly serving on juries of art exhibitions, receiving visitors, advising painters, writing critical and art historical essays.

Equally impressive was the intellectual range of Okakura's and Fenollosa's minds. Their work in education and art criticism aimed at creating a coherent theoretical basis for the arts of the future along with a whole array of government institutions to support these activities. They were equally concerned with the arts of the past, which they considered the wellspring of vitality and sensibility for the future. They both became pioneer art historians in the modern sense, Fenollosa more so perhaps than Okakura, and their efforts to preserve and study traditional arts are probably their most enduring monuments. Their vision was also cosmopolitan, pointing as it did toward a world-wide synthesis of culture, and thus they travelled widely and wrote for international audiences.

Okakura's interests took on a political coloration as well. He supported the Chinese revolutionaries opposed to the Manchu dynasty; and while in India in 1901-02, he espoused the cause of that nation's independence from Great Britain so firmly that when Taikan and Shunsō followed him there to paint murals in a princely palace in 1903, they were harassed by the British authorities and forced to leave. Okakura established common cause between his group and that of Rabindranath Tagore at Santiniketan in Bengal, and their ideals of national regeneration were closely similar. Okakura's sympathy for anti-colonial and revolutionary movements abroad reached the point of his calling for guerrilla warfare against oppressors, but strangely, this attitude was not directed toward internal Japanese affairs. He played no role in the agitation for increased political or economic rights of the masses, nor did he resist the growing authoritarian nature of the government. He supported the Imperial Constitution of 1889, he praised the Education Rescript of 1890, and he saw in the Sino-Japanese War the fruition of a half-century of work and sacrifice by his nation.

Okakura's position was similar to that of a number of moderates among the cultural conservatives of the time. He had close ideological and personal ties with a group of poets, the Negishi Tanka-kai, who took their name from that of a Tokyo district close to one of Okakura's homes.[37] Like Okakura, they studied Western forms, but their greatest interest was in traditional Japanese poetry as embodied in the *Man'yō-shū* or the haiku of Bashō, and they would inject touches of realism into the traditional framework.

Similarly, an impressive delegation of Okakura's supporters appeared at the inaugural exhibition of the Nihon Bijutsu-in. One of them was Miyake Setsurei (1860-1945), a former student of Fenollosa's, a romantic and independent spirit like Okakura, and a serious reader of Western literature. Miyake founded in 1888 the Seikyō-sha (Society of Political Education), dedicated to the conservation of national culture, and he published the magazine *Nihonjin* to which Okakura contributed articles under a pseudonym. Also present was another of the founders of the magazine, Shiga Shigetaka (1863-1927), a

[37] These men included Morita Bunzō (Shiken) (1861-97) and Sudō Nansui (1858-1920) among the older generation of Meiji writers deeply interested in Western literature but hoping to maintain their own tradition. Among the younger men were Nagatsuka Takashi (1879-1915), a fervent poet-traveller through Japan in the spirit of Bashō.

leading force in the Kokusui Hōzon movement and a voluble critic of Itō Hirobumi's masquerade ball at the Rokumeikan.[38]

It would exceed the intention of this essay to explore further the careers of Fenollosa and Okakura other than to observe that for both men their later years were an anti-climax. Both died at a relatively early age, and both seem to have been thwarted in the sense that the scope of their vision and ambitions had been enormous, demanding the support of mighty institutions—governments and museums. Okakura never regained the official status and powers lost in 1898, and Fenollosa's position at the Museum of Fine Arts was forfeited even before that. Returning to the United States in 1890, he spent five busy years organizing exhibitions of Japanese art in Boston and at the Chicago World's Fair, spreading his doctrines in popular lectures and even in poetry, and developing his theories of art education. In 1895, however, he was divorced by his first wife, a Salem-born woman of high social standing, and he quickly married a handsome woman on the staff of the Boston Museum. This so violated the mores of the day that he was obliged to resign his postion and to sacrifice most of the support which he had enjoyed from sympathetic and wealthy Bostonians. Thereafter he lived as an independent scholar and never returned to that city. Instead, he went to Japan in 1896 and again in 1897, this time to settle. But as his strongest ally Okakura was retreating before extreme and xenophobic conservatives, there was little hope for an official position for him apart from teaching English. He lived quietly with his second wife chiefly in Tokyo, studying the *nō* drama, writing on art, and serving to some extent as an art dealer. In 1900 he returned to the United States primarily to lecture and write, and died in 1908 while on a visit to London. His monumental two-volume *Epochs of Chinese and Japanese Art* was unfinished at his death, but was completed and published by his wife in 1912.

As for Okakura, the relative poverty of the Nihon Bijutsu-in

[38] See the account of Donald Shively, pp. 94-95.

offered little scope for his ambitions. Although his disciples continued to work with semi-religious ardor, he tended to lose interest in the Academy, to leave its direction to Hashimoto Gahō or Yokoyama Taikan, and to travel more and more frequently. After his trip to India in 1901-02 he went to the United States accompanied by Taikan and Shunsō. There he lectured in Boston and at the St. Louis World's Fair. In 1906 he went to China. The Bijutsu-in was moved from Tokyo to a more remote and inexpensive site at Izura. In 1910, Okakura was appointed Curator of Chinese and Japanese Art at the Boston Museum and was responsible for many important acquisitions, but his tenure was interrupted by frequent travel and poor health, and he died in 1913 in Japan at the age of 51.

As early as 1903 Okakura had confessed that Japan, in the tangled skein of the Meiji period, was unable to find that single thread which will give her the clue to her own future.[39] He meant, in fact, that he had already lost confidence in the solutions which he had so confidently proclaimed. Doomed to failure in advance were his dreams of creating a new and viable national art, for his synthesis was an artificial one, not fully rooted in the realities of national life. It was unrealistic to promote handicrafts and medieval art techniques while ignoring the potentialities of scientific thought and industry in a nation which was becoming industrialized more rapidly than any other in history. To study ancient art treasures would make one aware of profound spiritual values, but most of those values had long ago evolved into newer forms and could not be revived on esthetic grounds alone. Without an iron dictatorship, moreover, it was futile to attempt to control the artistic life of a nation like Japan whose culture was so pluralistic, so divided by regional and economic and sectarian traditions, that it had sustained at least ten recognized, major styles of painting.[40] Moreover, some of the dictates of Okakura and

[39] Okakura, *The Ideals of the East*, p. 242.
[40] In the last half of the Edo period, outstanding nationwide schools of painting included the Bunjin, Kanō, Tosa, traditional Buddhist,

Fenollosa were clearly arbitrary, especially their violent opposition to Bunjin-ga, whose credentials as an ancient Chinese tradition were impeccable; but the taste of these two men had been molded by the Kanō school painters to whom they had turned for guidance, and enmity had flared between the Kanō and Bunjin painters throughout the Edo period.[41]

Strangely enough, Okakura and his circle, as well as Rabindranath Tagore and his, can be seen as Eastern examples of a world-wide phenomenon of the nineteenth century. In the West, artists and poets had organized themselves into confraternities to oppose the corruption of esthetic and spiritual values in many of the European academies. They also opposed the ugliness and inhumanity of industrial life, the shallow and mercenary values of capitalist commerce, and the withering of man's mythic and devotional powers in the hard light of rationalism. One of the first groups were the quasi-religious Nazarenes, formed by Austrian painters with strong Christian beliefs who went to Rome and attempted to revive the purity of early Renaissance religious art. In England the British Pre-Raphaelite movement had similar motives, but some of its members

---

Shijō-Maruyama, Ukiyo-e, and Rimpa; strong local traditions were represented by the Yokohama, Nara, Ōtsu, and Nagasaki schools; also individualism *per se* should be recognized as a virtually autonomous way of working in the case of men like Jakuchū or Shōhaku. Moreover, each of these schools, which had their own patterns of patronage and support, tended to break down into sub-groupings.

[41] Fenollosa described Chinese *Wenjen-hua* as a school of feeble landscape painting. No longer understanding anything about line, its drawing is a travesty. It has no mastery of spatial effects, it is literature and not art; it may have a certain prettiness of coloring in birds and flowers; on the other hand these pictures have a degenerating "mossiness" and wriggling "worminess." In Japan, the school has burned down national popular traditions, converting them into fields of cold ashes. It is an impudent hypothesis, an awkward joke. Only the samurai and the genius of Tan'yū and his Kanō followers stood out as a great promontory against the mad storm. And so on. *Epochs of Chinese and Japanese Art*, II (New York, 1913), 145-48, 153-54, 161-66.

were interested in the crafts and industrial arts as well. The French Barbizon painters were devoted more to an ideal of peasant simplicity and identification with nature similar to that of Jean Jacques Rousseau. In all such cases, whether in Europe or Asia, artists sought to re-establish an aura of spiritual integrity which would again nourish their profession and give it a goal. Of all these, Okakura's group resembles most closely the Pre-Raphaelites, especially in their concern for education and crafts and wide changes in society; Okakura himself seems analogous in many ways to both William Morris and John Ruskin.

With the benefit of decades of hindsight, it is instructive to see how these struggles to determine the character of the artistic life of Japan were solved not by the passions of the artists nor the fiats of the administrators but by the orientation of the entire social order. Whatever pressures were exerted to maintain the traditional Nihon-ga styles in the Taishō and Shōwa periods, it was the outcome of the Second World War which fixed the large outlines of Japan's cultural orientation, and the younger generation of Japanese artists has become almost entirely devoted to the international styles of non-figural imagery. Japan's conversion to an increasingly industrialized, modern state has almost automatically suppressed most of the ancient values which sustained her traditional arts; and so long as her current economic and political orientation remains unchanged, this is likely to continue. The tea ceremony and flower arrangement may also continue, perhaps for centuries, but the ability of such arts to move the younger generations emotionally will probably diminish.

The visual chaos of industrial cities in Japan is even more painful to us today than it must have been to Okakura. It is equally painful, moreover, in the West; and artists in both Japan and the West stand on virtually the same ground, facing the task of maintaining the heritage of visual beauty and its spiritual sources in an industrial, commercial world of growing spiritual anarchy. The sentimental, buoyant revivalism of

Fenollosa and Okakura was both an indispensable act of affirmation and a futile gesture of defiance—affirming the grandeur of past achievements while denying the Western-style artists their rights of expression. Unrealistic also were their attempts to revive ancient arts in a totally different order of society and technology. Okakura and Fenollosa could only deplore the mighty and corrosive forces of industrialism; their intellectual weapons were not adequate to the task of controlling them.

It was rather Kawakami Tōgai and his followers, naive and ineloquent as they may have been, who found the key to their country's artistic future. By accepting fully the challenge of Western arts, they expanded their powers of thought and expression; by freeing themselves from the narrow confines of nationalism, they recognized the universality of the arts and took the crucial first steps by which the resources of this most artistically gifted people could be joined to the mainstreams of art in the modern world.

CHAPTER VI

The Formation of Realism in Meiji Painting:
The Artistic Career of Takahashi Yuichi

TŌRU HAGA

IT SEEMS strange that no adequate account is given by Japanese art historians of the significance of Takahashi Yuichi (1828-94) in the development of oil painting in Japan from the end of the Tokugawa period until the early years of Meiji.[1] It is strange in view of his role as a pioneer in the field and the

[1] The author is deeply grateful to Mr. Takeyama Michio for his initial encouragement of this study, and to Professor Frank Hoff of Sophia University for his devoted help with the translation.

The most basic factual studies of Takahashi's life and work can be found in Kumamoto Kenjirō, "Takahashi Yuichi no shōgai to sakuhin," *Bijutsu kenkyū*, No. 59 (November, 1936) and "Takahashi Yuichi no fukeiga," *Bijutsu kenkyū*, No. 160 (March, 1951); both articles reproduced with minor revision in the same author's *Kindai Nippon bijutsu no kenkyū* (Kokuritsu Bunkazai Kenkyūjo, 1964), a monumental book. Short critical references to Takahashi and some interesting episodes on his life can be found in Fujioka Sakutarō, *Kinsei kaiga shi* (Kinkōdō, 1903, 1st ed.); Moriguchi Tari, *Meiji Taishō no yōga* (Tōkyōdō, 1941); Ishii Hakutei, *Nippon kaiga sandai shi* (Sōgensha, 1942); and Hijikata Teiichi, *Kindai Nippon yōga shi* (Hōunsha, 1947). Recently there has been a sudden increase of interest in the artist: Hijikata Teiichi, "Hajimete hirakareta Takahashi Yuichi no kaiko-ten," *Geijutsu shinchō* (June, 1964); Sasaki Seiichi, "Takahashi Yuichi no *Sake-zu* ni tsuite," *Bijutsushi kenkyū* (Waseda University), No. 3 (July, 1965); and Haga, "Takahashi Yuichi to Shiba Kōkan," *Rangaku shiryō kenkyūkai hōkoku*, No. 147 (July, 1963), "Bakumatsu no aru yōgaka—Takahashi Yuichi no bunkashi-teki ichi," *Jiyū* (Dec., 1963) and "Takahashi Yuichi to riarizumu," *Mizue*, No. 713 (July, 1964). Takumi Hideo, *Kindai Nihon yōga no tenkai* (Shōshinsha, 1964), and Hijikata Teiichi, *Nippon no kindai bijutsu* (Iwanami [Shinsho], 1966) are recent attempts at a synthesis in this delicate and troublesome field of modern Japanese history. Kotohira-gū Shamusho ed., *Kotohira-gū Yuichi gashū* (Kotohira, Kagawa-ken, 1940)

221

considerable level of achievement of his mature work. Two factors may account for the neglect. Until the Second World War the academicism stemming from the oil painting of Kuroda Seiki (1865-1924) was extremely influential. This taste prevented true appreciation of Takahashi, who could claim little relationship to the academic mainstream. The reestablishment of the Okakura Tenshin school during the war years had the same effect. The prominence of these two men obscured Takahashi's work, or indeed, caused it to be viewed as some outlandish curiosity lingering from the early days of Meiji. Even the postwar years brought no really fundamental reappraisal of his importance. Thus two of the pictures discussed in this paper, both good examples of his mature style, are not on permanent exhibition at the library of the College of Fine Arts at Ueno (Tokyo Geijutsu Daigaku), but are brought out of deep recess only upon request. A number of his important paintings are on exhibit, though not at Ueno—*Tōfu* (*Bean-curd*), *Namari* (*Half-dried Bonito*), *Tokuhon to sōshi* (*Reader and Notebook*), and several landscapes. But in what a remote place—the Museum attached to the Kotohira Shrine in Shikoku. To explore his work more broadly, to piece together its importance, one must travel to Sendai or to Yamagata Prefecture.

These difficulties account for the great impact of the exhibition of some seventy pieces and related documents in Takahashi's first large-scale showing, held at the Museum of Modern Art in Kamakura in May of 1964. It took seventy years

is still the only album of reproductions of Takahashi's works, although it is limited to those belonging to the collection of the Shrine. A catalogue of the Takahashi Yuichi Show at the Museum of Modern Art of Kamakura (April-May, 1964) gives titles, names of collectors, approximate dates and sizes of 60 paintings of the artist. Since the completion of this paper, an excellent article on Takahashi has appeared, with interesting remarks on the fertile conflict of tradition and innovation in his oil painting: Takashina Shūji, "Takahashi Yuichi, Nippon kindai bijutsushi nōto (1)," *Kikan geijutsu*, No. 1 (April, 1967).

from the time of his death until this one-man show. But what extraordinary effect! The show was a call to reinterpret, perhaps to reappraise, the importance of Takahashi's work, and to place it, as it belongs, in some wider perspective than that of modern Japanese art history. His passionate, single-minded experimentation in the techniques of his medium, a tentative, imperfect, but increasingly refined search, and the personal anguish and steadfastness of the man tell in a quiet way the story of the greater process of modernization at work during this period.

The clearest motive of the process—we see it both in the personal record of Takahashi and in the larger movement itself—is the creation of new ways of perceiving. The work of the innovators of oil painting in Japan first appears crude, childish, futile. But their efforts have enriched the sensibilities of modern Japanese. Created by men, like Takahashi, who labored despite the initial handicap of working in a medium which had been developed exclusively in the West, early oil painting turned away from conventional Japanese forms and began serious exploration of international techniques. The road the innovators took stretches back over the past hundred years. It widens before the creators of new Japanese painting. The first to point the way is not Kuroda Seiki or Asai Chū. It is Takahashi Yuichi.

Takahashi's First Adventures

The major oil paintings of Takahashi Yuichi can be ranked with the critical works of Fukuzawa Yukichi and Nakae Chōmin, the poetry of Masaoka Shiki, and the prose of Mori Ōgai as the major cultural monuments of the Meiji era. Takahashi was the oldest of the leading personalities. As he was already forty when the period began, his realism was forged within the cultural environment of the Tokugawa period. His achievement was largely a native one.

Before embarking on experiments in Western painting techniques, Takahashi had mastered traditional Japanese forms.

He notes in the Introduction to his autobiography, *Takahashi Yuichi rireki*,[2] "The only arts I learned were those of the samurai and the painter." Takahashi was the grandson of Takahashi Gengorō, a retainer of Hotta Masahira, the daimyo of Sano in Shimotsuke. Introduced to the fashionable painting of the period by teachers of the Kanō and Tani Bunchō schools, he was restrained by his grandfather: "Your interest in the arts is of secondary importance. What you inherit with my house is first and foremost the warrior's way." But being sickly he was forced to take up the brush.

Takahashi was sensitive by nature and demanding when it came to his own performance. Even before turning seriously to painting, he was quick to express dissatisfaction with his teachers, the last of a line of academicians. The nature of the artistic world of the time is suggested by the Kanō school. From the early eighteenth century it had enjoyed considerable status, but life had left it. Its masters were in the service of local daimyo. Reared within the conventionalized ways of the school, they accorded great respect to the school's copy book and taught a formalized brush technique. The school had already become the subject of criticism by Motoori Norinaga and Kikuchi Yōsai.[3]

Even the two art forms which had prospered toward the end of the Tokugawa, the painting of the literati (*bunjin-ga*) and the *ukiyo-e* of the townsmen, were in decline. What Watanabe Kazan (d.1841) had feared had in fact taken place. The painting of the *bunjin* had become an abstract pursuit of grace and the elegant resonance. In his words, "They've gone to pieces. They paint empty landscapes. It's bungling, but they have it in their heads that it is elegance. It's just a burst of movement,

---

[2] A pamphlet of about 30 pages, published in 1892 by his son, Yanagi Genkichi. Reproduced, with several regrettable misprints, in *Mizue* (July and Sept.-Dec., 1929).

[3] One chapter of Norinaga's *Tamakatsura* and *Yōsai gai* by Kikuchi Yōsai (1787-1878) are both reprinted in Sakazaki Shizuka, *Nippon garon taikan* (Arusu [Ars], 1927-29).

but they take it for the 'vital spirit.' That is what things have come to."[4] *Ukiyo-e* was, for the most part, bent on vulgarity and insignificance. Hokusai, Hiroshige, and Kuniyoshi had passed their zenith.

Thus the stage was set for Takahashi's discovery of Western lithographs, which came at about the time Perry was opening Japan to the West. "I discovered in them truthfulness to reality and, what is more, taste." We cannot be sure what type of European lithograph Takahashi saw—probably Dutch prints of no special distinction. Perhaps anonymous. The style of realistic beauty found in the Dutch print had already been discovered by Shiba Kōkan (1748-1818) and Aōdō Denzen (1744-1822) toward the end of the eighteenth century. The Japanese had even been able occasionally to outstrip the originals. Watanabe Kazan obtained examples of Western lithographs some time in the Tempō period (1830-43).[5] In time he too was producing work of remarkable excellence with Western methods. Yet not a single report of these accomplishments reached Takahashi, trapped as he was within the bounds of the Edo taste. The discovery of Western art was for Takahashi a completely personal, private one. It awakened him to a new way of thinking about painting and a new visual experience.

This twenty-year-old samurai from a small *han* of only 16,000 *koku* set himself resolutely to learning Western art forms. The process of copper lithography and the technique of Western painting that had once gained a certain popularity through the efforts of Kōkan and Kazan had almost disappeared in contemporary Japan. There may have been some traces left in Nagasaki, but none in Edo. In 1862 Takahashi was admitted to the newly opened Painting Section of the Bansho Shirabesho. During the decade or more from his discovery of the prints until that time he had had no choice but to educate

---

[4] "Kazan shokan," in Sakazaki.

[5] Miyake Tomonobu, "Kazan sensei ryakuden," in *Kazan zenshū* (Kazan-kai, 1940, 4th ed.), p. 319. See also Yoshizawa Tadashi, *Watanabe Kazan* (Tōdai Shuppan, 1956), p. 34.

himself while holding down his post in the *han* office. It was a period when, he recalls, "my labor and anxieties were constant night and day." His training at the Institute began with reading Dutch treatises such as the "Outline Treatise on Painting" and "Treatise on the Rules of Drawing." There was the inconvenience of a shortage of materials and implements.[6] And further, the main instructor at the Institute, Kawakami Tōgai, had little to impart other than his own reactions to similar reading.[7] Kawakami's style has been criticized as never rising above an uneasy compromise between *bunjin* and Western influences: "The skin is a Western one. The flesh Japanese."[8]

There is a self-portrait of Takahashi which probably belongs to this period.[9] Still with topknot, eyes glaring, mouth open, jutting chin, a strong nervous line running down the middle of the brow, it is quite different from the dour, severe face portrayed in his later years. For the young man of the portrait

[6] Copies from these textbooks are found in the *Takahashi Yuichi kankei shiryō* (Documents Related to Takahashi), hereafter referred to as Takahashi Documents: two boxes containing a number of volumes of sketch-books, scrapbooks, albums of letters, drafts and copies of illustrations, and a "Shanghai Diary." One of Takahashi's daughters, who was married to a rickshaman, is said to have sold these documents, together with some important paintings, to the College of Fine Arts (Bijutsu Gakkō, the present Tokyo Geijutsu Daigaku). The old, creaky, Western-style, wooden building of the Library of the College, where Mori Ōgai once held office as President of the Imperial Library, provides a most suitable environment for re-creating the life of the Meiji artist through these documents. I am deeply grateful to the staff of the Library for their generous help in my study.

In the *Takahashi Yuichi Sketchbook*, one of the Takahashi Documents, there is a picture of his colleagues at the Painting Section, sitting on benches facing their easels. Their brushes, canvases, and paints were made by their own hands with laborious care.

[7] See John Rosenfield's discussion of Tōgai, especially pp. 194-97. Also see Kumamoto Kenjirō, "Kawakami Tōgai to yōfūga," *Bijutsu kenkyū*, No. 79 (July, 1938), reprinted in his *Kindai Nippon bijutsu no kenkyū*, pp. 42-56.

[8] Fujioka, *Kinsei kaiga shi*, p. 355.

[9] Reproduced in Sawamura Sentarō, *Tōyō bijutsu shi no kenkyū* (Hoshino Shoten, 1932).

there must have been much cause for dissatisfaction and irritation with the general mood of the Institute and the attitude of his instructors. He was constantly demonstrating against it: reproving his fellow students and teachers, issuing "direct petitions" or "appeals" to the men in charge. There is one very interesting episode. "One day one of my seniors remonstrated with me. 'You're always arguing. There is nothing wrong with what you have to say. It is just that from time to time between your arguments it would be worth your while to study painting a little.' My answer was this: 'Painting is an activity of the spirit. When I'm arguing I'm removing what is corrupt and degenerate. Only then, cleansed, can I apply myself for the first time to genuine painting.'"[10] Takahashi trained himself in the techniques of Western painting to cut away from within himself whatever had gone bad in traditional aesthetics, to attempt a conscious, radical remaking of himself.

Encounter with Shiba Kōkan

It was probably while Takahashi was still working in the Painting Section of the Institute that Shiba Kōkan, representing the spirit of late eighteenth-century positivism, emerged as a significant influence in his career. Echoes of Kōkan's *Talk on Western Painting* (*Seiyō gadan*, 1799)[11] are discernible in the "Statement for the Painting Section" (*Yōga-kyoku tekigen*)[12]

---

[10] At about the same time, Mori Arinori, as a Satsuma student in London, wrote to his brother in Kagoshima: ". . . Since crossing the ocean I have experienced a profound change in spirit (*kompaku*). I myself am surprised. The thing I need to learn most about is the study of human beings. I must use all my powers to *cleanse my dirty spirit* (*okon o sentaku*)." From a letter dated 1865 (Keiō 1, 9th month, 1st day), in Ōkubo Toshiaki, *Mori Arinori* (Bunkyō Shoin, 1944), p. 18. (Translation taken from an unpublished essay by Minor L. Rogers.) This coincidence in expression is extremely interesting. The one was in London, the other at the Institute of Western Studies in Edo, and both were striving for "self-improvement."

[11] Nakai Sōtarō, *Shiba Kōkan* (Atoriesha, 1942), pp. 55-66.

[12] In the Takahashi Documents can be found a draft written on

which Takahashi posted upon the wall of the school in the early winter of 1865 in hope of "promoting the prosperity of our Section." Like Kōkan, Takahashi maintains that only in the Western style can a painting adequately fulfill its function as a medium of exact visual communication and "serve the government" as a means of public education. Traditional Japanese and Chinese painting remains but "a personal, a minor art in which to dabble." It was a conviction shared by Takahashi and Kōkan that the "representation of truth" (*shashin*), which is the essence of Western painting, consists in depicting "the unevenness of surface, the distance, the depth and the light and shade" of an object according to "the principles of three dimensions and chiaroscuro." Directed not merely by the impetuous flow of his brush, a Western-style painter strives to lay hold of "the substance" and "the logic" of things, so that his work appears "as if it were animated by real life." In this way painting can serve as an initiation into "the meaning of Creation" (Kōkan), into "the secrets of Creation" (Takahashi).

We may safely consider Kōkan's *Talk* to be the direct predecessor of Takahashi's "Statement," from the numerous close similarities in general perception and specific terms. This argument is strengthened by the fact that Kōkan's work was widely disseminated. In addition, Takahashi himself in his later years expressed sentiments of respect and affection for Shiba Kōkan as a venerable precursor in the formation of Western-style painting in Japan.

Around 1875 Takahashi executed in oil *Portrait of Shiba Kōkan* (61 x 45.5 cm.). He relied upon a self-portrait of the philosopher from his later years, one which Takahashi had borrowed from the Ema, a family of hereditary doctors in Gifu.[13]

---

the stationery of the Bansho Shirabesho. It is quoted in full in Takahashi's *Rireki* and also in Kumamoto, p. 59.

[13] See Haga, "Takahashi Yuichi to Shiba Kōkan." The self-portrait in profile of Kōkan (with a farewell poem) is reproduced in Fujioka,

Its faithful depiction of the outlandish facial features of old Kōkan conveys the unabated vigor of this *avant-garde* of the modern mind of Japan, what Muraoka Tsunetsugu once called "his unyielding spirit, his temper, cynicism, self-praise and self-scorn and unconventionalism."[14]

In 1893, one year before his death, Takahashi organized a retrospective show, "Development of Oil Painting (in Japan)." It was staged at Tsukiji, in Tokyo, in collaboration with his former disciples. Besides his own works and other documents representing his career from the early years in the Painting Section to the present, he exhibited in the same hall, a fairly wide range of works of what he considered the pioneers and fellow combatants who had shared the trials of establishing this new art in Japan. These included Kōkan and Aōdō Denzen, Hokusai, Kikuchi Yōsai, Tani Bunchō, Tachihara Kyōsho, Mori Tetsuzan, Kawakami Tōgai, two foreign teachers (Charles Wirgman and Antonio Fontanesi), and two confreres from early Meiji (Kunisawa Shinkurō and Yokoyama Matsusaburō). The selection of names is interesting itself in that it reflects Takahashi's own interpretation of the history of Western-style painting in Japan. This retrospective show was one of the first such attempts in the Meiji period. A contemporary review of the exhibit records that "Shiba Kōkan, Kawakami Tōgai, and Fontanesi were paid reverence by the sponsor in a special way: their portraits were hung at the front of the hall and bottles of *sake* were offered before them."[15] This virtual canonization of Kōkan, upon an altar raised to the two who had taught Takahashi oil-painting techniques, suggests how closely the artist felt himself bound up with the author of *Seiyō gadan*.

---

p. 318, and Takahashi's copy of it, dated August 1887, in Inoue Kazuo, *Ukiyo-e shi den* (Watanabe Hangaten, 1931). I owe this last information to Dr. Suzuki Jūzō of the National Diet Library.

[14] Muraoka Tsunetsugu, "Shisei no tetsujin Shiba Kōkan," in his *Zoku nihon shisōshi kenkyū* (Iwanami, 1939), p. 251.

[15] *Mainichi Shimbun*, Nov. 10, 1893.

In the latter half of the eighteenth century a movement which might well be called an "Enlightenment" took place in many areas of Japanese culture. It was carried on by various groups of intellectuals. They shared in common an anti-traditional attitude, although they differed in their personal abilities and orientations. Such ardent pioneers of Dutch learning as Maeno Ranka (1723-1803), Hiraga Gennai (1728-79), Sugita Gempaku (1733-1817), and Shitsuki Tadao (1760-1806) took great steps forward in empirical studies of nature. The discovery of Europe made by Hayashi Shihei (1738-93) or Honda Toshiaki (1744-1821) was generally contemporary with the rediscovery of the Japanese national mind by Motoori Norinaga (1730-1801) in his reappraisal of its *état primitif* through new philological exegesis of ancient Japanese literature. In the dialectic of cognition developed by Miura Baien (1723-89), in the wide range of flourishing pre-romantic literature—from the fantastic tales of Ueda Akinari (1734-1809), to the lyricism of the poet-painter Yosa Buson (1716-83), to the rebirth of Chinese poetry led by Kan Sazan (1748-1827)[16]—as well as in the Western-style painting attempted by Maruyama Ōkyo (1733-95), Shiba Kōkan, Aōdō Denzen, Odano Naotake (1749-80), and Satake Shozan (1748-85),[17] Japanese culture of the so-called Tanuma period (ca. 1760-90) manifested a new brilliance and a new tonality, a distinctly modern quality. It saw a significant change in the intellectual life and the psychological state of the Japanese. Generally, it was a movement toward a more rationalistic, realistic and, at the same time, romantic attitude toward nature and society. The impact of the West was still but half imagi-

[16] The realism of Kan Sazan is discussed by Tsuda Sōkichi with sympathy and affection in various places in his *Bungaku ni arawaretaru kokumin shisō no kenkyū*, IV, especially in Chaps. 10 and 13, *Tsuda Sōkichi zenshū*, VII (Iwanami, 1964). Fujikawa Hideo, "Shikyū-an shiwa," *Mugi* (1964-66), reprinted as a book: *Edo kōki no shijin-tachi* (Mugishobō, 1967), gives a lively description of the changing *kanshi* poetry of the period.

[17] See Haga, "Shiba Kōkan to sono jidai," *Mizue*, No. 721 (March, 1965).

nary; thus the trend seems essentially a product of internal change slowly nurtured after the early eighteenth century and brought to fruition in the favorable milieu of the less restraining rule of Tanuma Okitsugu.[18] Of those who led the movement, the Vagabond (Fūrai-sanjin) Gennai and his follower, Kōkan, were typical. They were typical in their restless pursuit of knowledge and in the breadth of their activities, from natural history to oil painting. Typical also was their discontent with the established social order and their constant malaise. Grieving over his tragic death, Sugita Gempaku called Gennai, his companion at arms, an "extraordinary man given to extraordinary acts." There were others also, including Gempaku himself, who lived a *crise de la conscience*, in many respects prefiguring the modern alienated intellectual.[19]

No doubt this movement in the late eighteenth century foreshadowed the Meiji Restoration. Needless to say it was not to develop continuously into the Meiji period. In the early and mid-nineteenth century it came under increasing restrictions. Dutch learning spread rapidly among the leading *han*, but even there it tended to be exploited by the domain administrations principally as a source of technological knowledge. It is remarkable that the transient cultural vigor of the Tanuma period was soon to recede into stagnation and swiftly pass from sight leaving little trace for the Bakumatsu generation. Even in the small circle of the Rangakusha, where continuity was relatively well maintained, Fukuzawa and his companions knew little of the famous *Rangaku kotohajime* (*The Beginning of Dutch Studies*) of Sugita Gempaku until 1865 or

[18] See John W. Hall, *Tanuma Okitsugu: Forerunner of Modern Japan* (Cambridge, Mass., 1955), and also Donald Keene, *The Japanese Discovery of Europe: Honda Toshiaki and Other Discoverers, 1720-1798* (New York, 1954). Hayashi Motoi, "Hōreki Temmei-ki no shakai jōsei," in *Kōza Nihon rekishi, Kinsei*, IV (Iwanami, 1962-64), is an exciting and challenging account of the gradually developing social unrest in late 18th-century Japan.

[19] See Haga, "Edo no zen'ei-tachi, Gennai, Gempaku, Kōkan," *Nippon* (Aug., 1965).

1866;[20] Watanabe Kazan had no occasion to study the Western-style painting of his eighteenth-century precursors, and, until 1865, when he discovered Kōkan's pamphlet, Takahashi had had no access to this half-developed tradition which he was now to develop further.

Although the Enlightenment of eighteenth-century Japan was short-lived, still it remained an undercurrent which refreshed the intellectuals of the Bakumatsu. Takahashi's "Statement for the Painting Section," although only a brief discussion, is one of those rare documents which make it possible to establish an historical perspective in an area where it had seemed negligible if not, in fact, nonexistent. The artistic realism of Gennai and Kōkan had not altogether vanished. As this student of Western painting of the Bakumatsu period came upon Western lithography, so, in his reading of Kōkan, he came to recognize his lost roots.

Stages of Takahashi's Development

Despite the great political confusion and public hysteria suggested by Fukuzawa's *Autobiography*, changes in Japan following the opening of the country brought about conditions which helped Takahashi in his anxious pursuit. Day was beginning to break upon his path.[21] It was in Yokohama in the summer of 1866, the year after his "Statement for the Painting Section," that Takahashi, through the good offices of Kishida Ginkō (1833-1905) and others, met Charles Wirgman (1832-

[20] Fukuzawa Yukichi, "Rangaku kotohajime saihan jo" (1890), quoted in the Notes by Ogata Tomio to the Iwanami Bunko edition (No. 5095, 1959) of the *Kotohajime*, pp. 120-22. See also Ogata Tomio, "Rangaku kotohajime no igi," *Rangaku shiryō kenkyūkai hōkoku*, No. 170 (May, 1965).

[21] A Bakufu mission to Europe, perhaps Ikeda Naganobu's party of 1864, brought back a trunkful of art supplies to "the great joy" of the Painting Section students. Takahashi, recalling this in his *Rireki*, says: "Looking back upon this event now, it seems as if it were a dream."

91), a correspondent and illustrator for *The Illustrated London News*. It is pleasant to imagine Takahashi, with his topknot, going to the home of a Westerner, "delightedly hurrying" along the streets of the newly opened port that Kuniyoshi had already begun to depict with the exact perspective of his prints.

Although Wirgman was in fact nothing more than an amateur with some skill in oil painting,[22] Takahashi recalls in his *Rireki*, "I was amazed by and so filled with admiration for his unusual artistic ability that I nearly got lost on my way back." From this British illustrator Takahashi learned the basic theory and technique of oil painting, and traces of Wirgman's influence remain in the landscape paintings of his later years. Moreover Takahashi continued to treat Wirgman with courtesy and respect long after his own proficiency in painting had surpassed that of his teacher.[23]

In 1867, taking advantage of an opportunity to join a small experimental commercial mission sent by his *han*, Takahashi made his first and only trip abroad: a three-month journey to Shanghai.[24] Takahashi seems to have made a traditional response toward China, viewing her as a senior partner in a "common culture," and paying his respects to her artists, men

[22] His skill in illustration can be appreciated in Rutherford Alcock, *The Capital of the Tycoon, a Narrative of a Three Years' Residence in Japan*, 2 vols. (London, 1863). See also the useful catalogue of the Wirgman Exhibition held at the Prefectural Library of Kanagawa in 1962 in commemoration of the centenary of his arrival in Yokohama.

[23] Besides Takahashi, many artists of the early Meiji period, like Goseda Yoshimatsu, Kunisawa Shinkurō, and Yamamoto Hōsui, entered Wirgman's school.

[24] On the same day in 1867 that Takahashi left for Shanghai (Keiō 3, 1st month, 11th day), a ship set sail from Yokohama with Tokugawa Akitake's party and also carrying works of art of the Painting Section students, destined for the Universal Exposition of Paris. Takahashi's contribution was an oil painting entitled "Two Japanese Boys Admiring a Portrait of Napoleon I."

of letters, and famous places.[25] His *Picture Diary of Shanghai*,[26] one of the most fascinating of the Takahashi Documents, reveals his vivid curiosity at work. It furthermore shows the extent of his own skill in the traditional art of rapid brush drawing. Yet the extent to which this trip contributed to the development of his Western-style painting remains doubtful. It may be presumed that some samples of European paintings brought back from Holland in the same year by Uchida Masao were more influential. Takahashi's *Gold Bream* (*Tai*) (44 x 59 cm.), a still life in the Kotohira Collection, seems to follow closely the Dutch pattern of decorative motifs, and even *Sake* (to be discussed later) is not far from Dutch still life.

Throughout the early stages of the Meiji Reforms, Takahashi suffered the common fate of the lower-class samurai. He was soon deprived of his stipend, small as it was, and of his status as a retainer of the *han*. At the same time, Western painting was still a new and financially unrewarding profession. Destitution was not limited to the legendary cases of the traditional-style painters Kanō Hōgai and Hashimoto Gahō. Faced with the need to feed his family in a period of rapid inflation, Takahashi bartered away his clothes and utensils and moved from house to house in the still-unsettled Tokyo.[27] Takahashi was a stoic samurai, exacting, proud, and stubborn in his self-imposed artistic mission. He could never condescend to follow the example of his colleague Goseda Hōryū, who earned his living by painting *Yokohama-e* (souvenir pictures

[25] According to one of Takahashi's later documents, he seems to have met with Western-style painters while in Shanghai. They asserted, says Takahashi, the importance of the Western way of sketching. He saw once again Kishida Ginkō, who had come to the Chinese port accompanying Hepburn.

[26] The main body of the text is reproduced in Sawamura, pp. 476-91.

[27] According to his family register of 1892, Takahashi had already three girls and one boy by 1872.

for foreigners) and setting up a "diorama" show in Asakusa under the patronage of the head of a street-gang.[28]

With the help of Kishida Ginkō, an enthusiastic patron of anything new, including Western painting, Takahashi was recommended to Itō Hirobumi and given a petty job in the Minbushō.[29] This job lasted only a few months during 1870-71 and was followed by the more respectable position of instructor in the South School (Nankō), which succeeded the Kaiseijo. After a brief term (1871-72) Takahashi left this job as well. The real reasons remain unknown, but he may well have been dissatisfied with the curriculum of the art course, begun by Kawakami Tōgai, which placed too much emphasis on mechanical drawing for the "pragmatic" Takahashi. In a document dated 1871 Takahashi declares himself "born to have a stronger liking for Western painting than for food and drink" and apologizes for his inability to bear the burdens of formal office. The artist, already forty-three, appealed to "gentlemen of noble mind" to provide financial assistance that might permit him to overcome his desperate poverty and thereby "achieve success" in his artistic career.[30]

Takahashi was not forgotten by friends, who provided moral and material support. "I've just come across a person interested in your works," writes Kishida Ginkō from Yokohama in March 1870. "Please send me one or two of your paintings if you have any recent ones on hand. I would like to show them to this person."[31] Other names which appear in Takahashi's

[28] Kumamoto Kenjirō, "Goseda Yoshimatsu ni tsuite," in his *Kindai Nippon bijutsu no kenkyū*, p. 86.

[29] In the Takahashi Documents are several drafts of projects, which he wrote while he was working in the Mimbushō, promoting the establishment of an art school. In these papers he recommends the appointment of Charles Wirgman as an instructor.

[30] A draft found in the Takahashi Documents.

[31] This letter (Takahashi Documents) and even the *Woosung Diary* (1867) of Kishida are written in an individual, colloquial style. He is one of the most charming of the slightly eccentric characters pro-

records for this period are mostly those of liberal intellectuals, themselves seriously concerned with Westernization, many of whom knew the painter from the days of the Bansho Shira-besho (Kaiseijo). Among these are Yanagawa Shunsan, Naka-hama Manjirō,[32] Katō Hiroyuki, Utsunomiya Saburō, Fukuchi Gen'ichirō,[33] Kawamoto Kōmin, and Shimooka Renjō.[34]

In the albums among Takahashi's documents there are a number of drawings that appear to be careful copies of illus-trations found in European children's books, travelogues, and textbooks of history and zoology. There are also copies of litho-graphs. Most of these seem to belong to the Bakumatsu and early Meiji periods. Mixed in are sketches of Tokyo, the Tōkaidō, and the Kansai area, later converted into a series of oil paintings and displayed at the various private and official "Industrial Expositions" frequently held after 1872 in accord-ance with a nation-wide "Promotion of Production."[35] Char-acteristic of this early group of landscape paintings (until 1877-78) is their conformity to the traditional, well-established con-ceptions of scenic beauty exemplified by the genre of *meisho-zue* (albums of noted places) and the *ukiyo* prints of the Toku-gawa period. Unlike the unconventional approach to nature found in the etchings of Aōdō Denzen, and the naive freshness of the woodblock prints of Kobayashi Kiyochika, Takahashi's work was somehow unable to break with the landscape tradi-tion. *Enoshima* (ca. 1874), *View of Mt. Fuji from Makigahara*

---

duced in the "Civilization and Enlightenment" period. His son is the artist Ryūsei, whose Dutch-style realism is closest to Takahashi's.

[32] Yamauchi Yōdō was one of the earliest persons to show interest in Takahashi's oil painting. Takahashi was introduced to him by Nakahama Manjirō and demonstrated his skill before him (*Rireki*).

[33] Fukuchi bought a landscape by Takahashi through the offices of Kishida. Fukuchi's letter of acknowledgement of September 23, 1876, is in the Takahashi Documents.

[34] Draft Portraits of Kawamoto and Shimooka in the Takahashi Documents.

[35] Takahashi contributed a *View of Mt. Fuji* to the Vienna Exposi-tion of 1873.

(ca. 1874), *Futamigaura Rocks* (ca. 1874-75), *Tago no Fuji* (ca. 1874-75), *View of the Shinagawa Coast from Atago Hill* (1874-76), *Shinobazu Lake* (ca. 1876), and *Honmoku Beach* (ca. 1877) represent little more than stereotyped *meisho-zue*.[36] Their titles alone suggest antiquated mannerism. The painter frequently attempts to depict in great detail tree trunks and branches, or grasses and rocks in the foreground, but his brush does not move freely; strokes are placed meticulously as if by Japanese ink brush. The effect is stiff and formal. Use of pinkish clouds and sun-bathed waves reflects the extent to which Takahashi learned all too carefully Wirgman's faults. Some of these pictures may even recall mural landscapes in the public baths of Tokyo today—awkward, stifling, somewhat "camp." That the original rough sketches in ink, aquarelle, or pencil, though conventional in perspective, appear far more tasteful and freer in execution indicates the difficulty Takahashi found in adjusting to new pigments.

Watanabe Kazan had earlier encountered a similar difficulty in his portraits. His finished works do not retain the vividness seen in ink drafts. The problem seems to center on the limitations imposed by the pigments of traditional Japanese painting. It soon became apparent that these were not suitable for "realistic" painting. Hence the search for new materials by artists of the Bakumatsu period. While some progress had been made in the area of pigments by the early Meiji years, Takahashi still found himself bound by conventional brush techniques and by the traditional conception of landscape. As a result he was unable to give full play to the potential of his new medium. While he had declared his opposition to the ancient régime of art, he was still tied to its vestiges. His landscapes betray a problem common to many early Meiji intellectuals—tradition and modernization were at war with one another. This struggle burst to the surface of Takahashi's canvases.

To break successfully with the past required not only new

---

[36] For dating I have relied upon Kumamoto and the catalogue of the Takahashi Yuichi Exhibition of Kamakura.

materials, but also emancipation from the old formulae of the *meisho-zue* and *ukiyo-e* tradition. The Japanese of the Tokugawa period tended to see and interpret nature as an episodic background to human existence.[37] The Japanese artist had yet to learn to confront nature directly, to admire manifestations of her independent life, and to discover what Takahashi called "the secrets of creation" in plants, mountains, water, and sky. It was only after years of trial and error under instruction by Antonio Fontanesi that Takahashi was able to achieve something of this in his landscapes of the 1880's.

The culmination of Takahashi's artistic career coincided with a broader commitment to the public promotion of Western painting in Japan. Since its opening in Hamachō in June 1873, his school, the Tenkairō, had become one of the chief centers for aspiring artists.[38] From 1875 the school gave a monthly exhibit of the work of its members. Takahashi encouraged both his students and the public to participate: "Oil painting does not merely depict the form of things; it reveals their implicit meanings. Hence its power of inspiring the human mind. As is well known to you, it is held in high esteem in Western countries, while in our country, to our greatest regret, it still remains utterly ignored. We, therefore, should strive together to elevate the quality of our painting, avoiding the evils of frivolity, and it is our responsibility as pioneers in this art to arouse the public mind through noble works in order to have it at last flourish throughout the country."[39]

During these years Takahashi undertook several ambitious projects to further the promotion of Western-style painting in Japan. These included annual participation in the National

[37] See Tsuda, pp. 584-88.

[38] Through the whole period of its existence there were more than 150 who entered the school, among them Andō Chūtarō, Harada Naojirō, Kawabata Gyokushō, and Araki Kampo (the latter two in traditional painting).

[39] Takahashi Documents. Quoted also in Kumamoto, p. 64. The exhibits continued until 1882. The main works of Takahashi painted after 1875 were first shown in this exhibit.

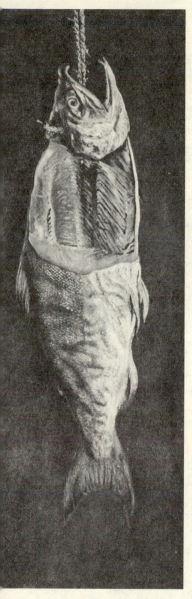

I. Takahashi Yuichi. "Sake." Oil on paper, ca. 1877.

II. Takahashi Yuichi. "Oiran-zu." Ca. 1872.

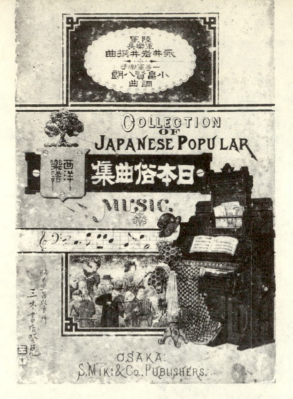

I. Cover of *Collection of Japanese Popular Music*
(1892).

II. Illustration in *Tekukin Dokukeiko* (1894).

Industrial Exposition beginning in 1877, a commission to paint the portrait of the Meiji Emperor in 1879, the expansion of his school in the same year,[40] and the publication of an art magazine (the first of its kind in Japan) in 1880.[41] As was common among early Meiji intellectuals, a strong sense of national identity inspired these activities. "Art, the criterion of the level of civilization in a country," he wrote at one point, "must be encouraged at every opportunity, especially today when Japan finds it necessary to demonstrate its inviolable national sovereignty and prestige so that she may surpass even the other advanced nations of the world." (Takahashi Documents)

Examples of Takahashi's Pictorial Realism

To illustrate more concretely the type of realism sought by Takahashi, let us look closely at two representative still lifes. The dimensions of the first, *Sake* (Plate I) are unusual—139 cm. by 46 cm.[42] A single, salted salmon is vertically suspended slightly left of center in the composition. The upper part of the body has been cut away exposing red flesh. A straw rope pass-

[40] At this time Takahashi sold about 35 canvases to the Kotohira Shrine and received 200 yen in payment.

[41] It was called *Gayū sekichin*. Its main purpose was to "develop a harmonious spirit within the country through visual arts." It introduced works from Japanese, Chinese, and European art treatises to biographies of Da Vinci and Michelangelo, but it ceased publishing after only five issues. (Meiji Shimbun Zasshi Bunko Collection of the University of Tokyo.)

[42] Otama, the Japanese wife of Vicenzo Ragusa, the Italian instructor of sculpture at the Art School of the Imperial Engineering College, explained one day why Takahashi's *Sake* had been given such an unusual shape: "If an oil painting is horizontal, it can't be hung in a *tokonoma*. So, artists at that time used to paint on a long, narrow board so that it could be hung on a pillar." Kimura Ki, *Ragusa Otama* (1931), quoted in Sasaki's article. Obviously this cannot be the only reason, but it shows how free oil-painters still were in early Meiji in their attitude toward the European norms of painting. Such an attitude must have seemed, as Takashina points out, like a sacrilege to a faithful student of Western tradition like Kuroda Seiki, who was trained in its "homeland" (*homba*).

ing through the open mouth is drawn tight by the weight of the fish and casts a shadow against the brown background.

This dark reflection together with the blurred shadow of the fish indicates the thickness of the unseen side of the fish. The viewer's eye is held by the flesh, the full, dusky red flesh. Two lines intensify this sense of richness, a black stroke, suggesting rising skin, running from the head to the shoulder, and the line of the belly, glistening with oil. The lower part of the body has not been cut away. Here the salted skin is puckered, drawn together like waves. The lower part of the body gives a sense of hardness and volume. This weight accounts for the strain on the rope. Weight, the very fullness and density of the fish, is concentrated also in the two fins which incline outwards. They act as a plummet to indicate the downward pull of gravity.

The painting of the straw rope and the gills is careful but not meticulous. An overall variation in the brushwork remains, close painting in the head, a rougher texture in the upper part of the body, and detailed execution in the lower portion. The brush line of the fins becomes rapid and sharp. This harmonious movement accentuates the weight of the body. The source of light is on the right. There is a faint crimson and blue detectable in the honey color of the gills and lower part of the body. A whole range of colors, the vermilion of the flesh, the gradations of brown in the background, imitate some mysterious melody. The color and detail is nowhere fussy. There is a final silence, a restfulness here.

The attitude of the artist is one of respectful truthfulness to the material reality of the salmon. It is a relentless pursuit of the real quality of the subject. We find it again in other canvases. *Tōfu* catches the dampness of a chopping board wet with soggy bean-curd and scratched by repeated cuttings. *Bolts of Cloth* records exactly the soft folds of fabric; *Reader and Notebook*, the creases of paper.

This realism emerges in another painting, which we will

consider at some length. *Oiran-zu* (*The Picture of a Courtesan*) (Plate II) might be classified as a "genre" work. It was executed at the request of a patron who lamented the disappearance from current fashion of a particular style of dressing a woman's hair, "Hyōgo mage." Yet Takahashi seems to have disregarded this aspect of his commission, to have set aside documentary interest in recording a disappearing fashion. The artist's eye becomes instead an instrument attuned to the material and the objective aspect of the thing before it. His approach is also designed to capture the human quality of the woman. Twenty candy-colored tortoise-shell combs are depicted with brilliant fidelity—filtering the sunlight, pressed downward, circling the head like a fan. The hair itself below the combs is not in good order. The white collar is painted in thick colors, strongly done. Hair falls around it. The eyebrows are thin. And the eyes look off into the distance. High, white cheek-bones protrude. The cheeks are fleshy, with a cherry tint. The nose is small. The somewhat pointed red lips are painted forcefully. It is not the face of a great beauty that shows its three-quarter pose against the dark green background.

A certain crudity about the brushwork is generally remarked in criticism of this work. There is an awkwardness about the nose, the base of the throat, and the shoulder of the dress. But this contributes to the portrait of a middle-aged courtesan, almost enveloped in her gorgeous dress, splendid headgear rising behind. She is dauntless, despite submission to her profession. Nakano Shigeharu points out that the artist is not interested in repeating conventional views of courtesans, sanctified by the *ukiyo-e* tradition. His interest is kindled here by the direct challenge of a single courtesan.

With good reason these paintings are called realistic. The choice of title offers the first indication of the realistic intention of Takahashi's art. He discovered in the common articles of Meiji kitchens and living rooms a beauty especially suited to expression in oil. He made simple items into "wholly valid subjects for self-contained easel pictures."[43] Until this time there had been no example of a subject like his salmon or his textiles, boldly commanding the composition, rendered solely for the sake of their own naked beauty. The popular ornamental painting of the Tokugawa, *kachō-ga* (paintings of flowers and birds), hardly qualifies as legitimate still life. Even *ukiyo-e* does not equal Takahashi in bestowing a new "prestige" upon the everyday utensils of the household. With Takahashi's revolutionary act the genre of still life made its first appearance in Japanese painting. Only haiku already had a tradition of making familiar objects poetic. Haiku was poetry not limited to the conventionally beautiful. A number of the artistic effects described above appear much earlier in haiku. The dried salmon (*karazake*), for example, was used to suggest winter.

Karazake mo	Dried salmon
Kūya no yase mo	And an emaciated saint,
kan no uchi	Deep in winter. (Bashō)

Karazake no	Ringing against
hone ni hibiku ya	Dried salmon —— hard!
goya no kane	Bells of Matins. (Buson)

When Takahashi confronted the object he was to paint, his interest was not in its superficial elegance. Nor was he interested in what might be called "spiritual significance." He sought to ascertain the surface, the volume, the density and weight of what was before his eye, carefully and exactly, making use of a new medium, oil. Once he had "located" the object in its place on a table top, for example, he set about shaping an atmosphere which could contain it. All his effort in the creative act was concentrated at this point—realizing on canvas what he had in hand. This posture vis-à-vis the object, this pursuit of it, loosed a discernible ardor in the picture. Nakano Shigeharu wrote of it in this short but penetrating passage

[43] Max J. Friedländer, *On Art and Connoisseurship* (Beacon Paperbacks, 1960), p. 131.

about Takahashi: "He was possessed, maddened even, by his passion to lay hold of the real."[44]

He confronted his subject squarely, "positively." This attitude, as mentioned above, may be perceived in the latter part of the eighteenth century. It was with Takahashi, however, that the attitude found, in his sure and certain mastery of a painting technique, competent expression. The introduction of the use of oils was the crucial factor. In the process of mastering this new medium Takahashi was actually putting away from himself the skill and subtlety which flowed so readily from traditional techniques of painting. It was the very resistance that oil as a medium gave to one unskilled in its use which stroke by stroke assured the completeness of his victory over older ways of painting and of seeing. The process restrained the subjective element, all too ready to beguile him back into conventional methods. Cut off from tradition, he was free to establish a fresh perspective. *Sake* and *Oiran* convey the feverish joy which came with this new experience.

The "realism" which Takahashi discovered severed him from two important streams in the history of Japanese art. It set him in opposition to the "subjective" view which was clearly predominant in two other contemporary factions. He could no longer share the almost religious ecstasy rising from the fusion of "subjective" and "objective" worlds inspiring Muromachi *suiboku* painters, Edo Literati painters, and traditionalist contemporary schools. At the same time the discovery cut him off from the Impressionist school, which rose to prominence about the time of his death and dominated oil painting during the following decades.

Takahashi's Realism in the Cultural History of Early Meiji

Most of Takahashi's work is undated and much even unsigned. The two pictures discussed above can be dated

[44] Nakano Shigeharu, "Saitō Mokichi ron nōto," in *Nakano Shigeharu zenshū* (Chikuma shobō, 1959), II, 464.

approximately by comparison with similar works and with the help of contemporary documents. *Courtesan* was probably done around 1872, *Sake* finished sometime between 1877 and 1879. Most of the Kotohira collection dates to the years around 1878.[45] It is remarkable that the maturity of Takahashi's art should have come so early in the Meiji period. It was a time when but few other artists, with the exception of Kawakami Tōgai and Kunisawa Shinkurō, were at work. There was no recognized artistic movement as such. Takahashi worked within a society caught in a sudden and chaotic political transition.

Perhaps Sansom had in mind *ukiyo-e* artists at the end of the tradition like Hokusai, Kuniyoshi, and Kiyochika when he commented: "The aesthetic bent of the Japanese makes them peculiarly sensitive to fleeting movements on the surface of life; and because their visual perception is acute their artists are often quicker than their writers to seize upon changes in popular taste or shifts of public interest."[46] The same thing could surely be said of Takahashi. He was sensitive to the "shifts of public interest" at a very fundamental level, his art recording as it did the very process of a change in the ways of thinking and feeling which the nation at large was experiencing. It is difficult to find an exact counterpart to Takahashi among other artists and writers of the day. His realism is closer to the positivism we find in the intellectual currents of the period, in the thought of a person like Fukuzawa for example, or Nishi Amane. The perspective of Fukuzawa's *Bummeiron no gairyaku* or Nishi's treatises in the *Meiroku-zasshi* or the *Bei-Ō kairan jikki* of Kume Kunitake is more akin to the realism of Takahashi than the work of any other artist or writer of the day. It is a practical, non-speculative, experimental, rationalistic perspective, a way of watching the world which adheres closely to the concrete and strives to be precise. It includes that type of

[45] See Kumamoto, *Kindai Nippon bitjutsu no kenkyū*, pp. 71-72, and Sasaki.

[46] George B. Sansom, *The Western World and Japan* (New York, 1962), p. 378.

political utilitarianism familiar to the period. "They had to learn how to measure a thing's length, its breadth, its depth, its surface area, its volume, its density. It was the way they had to take in learning how to see and to measure in close accord with the thing itself."[47]

Of the works mentioned above, the *Bei-Ō kairan jikki* is the least well known. Kume (1839-1931), a samurai of Saga *han*, was a noted master of Chinese classics. He accompanied the Iwakura Embassy to the United States and Europe from 1871 through 1873. The work in question is the official report of the mission. It is exceptional for the quantity, the scope and detail of its observations. It is certainly a rich example of a study of Western civilization made by a Japanese.[48] In passages about the shipbuilding yards at Liverpool or the iron factories at Newcastle, Kume comments on the shortcomings of most Japanese of his time—their addiction to superficial ingenuity, to clever improvisation or, on the other hand, to lofty but abstract speculation. He admires the industrial plans and models of Europe. His sympathy is with experiments carefully and accurately conceived, with the broad spirit of investigation.[49] The same type of reflection inspired comments written after a visit to the Conservatoire des Arts et Métiers in Paris: "Ideas don't fall down to you from heaven. You have to know the thing involved. You have to see its shape. You have to learn its technique."[50] There is a correspondence between Takahashi's

---

[47] Nakano, p. 463.

[48] See Eugene Soviak's account, pp. 7ff. Also Haga, "Meiji shoki ichi chishikijin no seiyō taiken," in *Shimada Kinji kyōju kanreki kinen rombunshū: Hikaku bungaku, hikaku bunka* (Kōbundō, 1961).

[49] Kume Kunitake, *Tokumei zenken taishi Bei-Ō kairan jikki* (Tokyo, 1878), II, 145, 277-78.

[50] Kume, III, 59. Kume's *Journal* refers several times to the problems of the fine arts. While visiting an art school, he frowned at the "scandalous scene" of students sketching nude models (III, 369). As for Western painting in general, he showed a reaction somewhat similar to that of Fenollosa's when he said: "Western painting is too heavily ornate to be tasteful. . . . Unworldly elegance is the quality for which the Japanese are the most gifted" (III, 84).

struggles as a painter and Kume's experiences as an observer of the Western scene.

Others too were caught up in the passion to discover the natural order of things (*kyūri*). Ichikawa Wataru was only a minor official during the Bakufu mission to Europe of 1862. Still, this zest for observation seized him, prompting him to measure the breadth and the length of the train rails in Suez. The opulence of the Hôtel du Louvre in Paris so fascinated him that he recorded in detail its architectural plan, the furniture and ornaments of its rooms.[51] This careful record strained to the limits the literary Chinese style in which he wrote.

An intellectual who might be called the incarnation of the positivism of the period is the Confucianist and botanist Kurimoto Joun (1822-97), a man of varied career. He acted on the medical board of the Bakufu, the body commissioned to develop Hokkaido, and the Bakufu's office of foreign affairs. A memoir from his term as Minister in Paris (1867-68) is a gem as a travel account in classical Chinese. He calls the record *Gyōsō tsuiroku* (Memoirs at the Window at Dawn).[52] It reveals the same powerful intellectual curiosity. At a later time one of Kurimoto's disciples discovered the study during his own stay in France, noting the "amazing intellectual vigor of this eminent materialist." This was Shimazaki Tōson, who read this record while laying the groundwork in Paris for his own novel, *Yoake mae*.

A similar attitude, call it "positivistic" or, as Tōson did, "materialistic," is apparent not only in the reports of Meiji technicians and in the records of representatives abroad, but eventually in literature itself, though as Sansom points out, some time after it appears in the canvases of artists. The pioneer work toward a new realistic literature was Tsubouchi Shōyō's *Essence of the Novel* (1885). The path was advanced

[51] Ichikawa Wataru, "Biyō ōkō manroku," in *Kengai shisetsu nikki sanshū* (Nippon shiseki kyōkai sōsho), II, 303-304, 326-29.

[52] Reprinted, in *Meiji bunka zenshū* (Nippon Hyōronsha, 1928), XVI (Gaikoku bunka hen), 170-88.

by Futabatei Shimei's novel *Ukigumo* (1887) with prose close
to the spoken language. But to find a counterpart to Takahashi
Yuichi's pictorial realism it is necessary to go to the prose of
Mori Ōgai and to the *waka* of Masaoka Shiki. Indeed, Ōgai
gained a respectable knowledge of the visual arts while in
Germany and counted as one of his close friends Harada Naojirō, a student of Takahashi. After his return to Japan in 1888,
Ōgai became one of the leading aestheticians and art critics of
the Meiji period.

A young French comparativist, Jean-Jacques Origas, devotes
an essay to a close analysis of the style of two of Ōgai's works,
Fumizukai and *Maihime*, in order to indicate their particular
way of looking at the outer world.[53] He concludes that Ōgai
relies less on adjectives than on the structure of his phrases,
less on suggesting the mood of a scene than on giving its exact
details. This becomes clearer by comparison with Tsubouchi's
Saikun (1889). Tsubouchi avoids a graphic style of description
which might present his characters, their acts and spatial relations, directly. He relies on a single touch, a lightly drawn line.
Ōgai, however, casts an almost defiant eye at whatever he confronts, seizing it part by part. Ōgai lays hold of the material
world, setting a siege about it (*ryōryaku*) as he describes his
character Rodin as doing: "Rodin looked at Hanako's small
compact body—all, from the hair, clumsily arranged in the
high mode, to the feet, in their white *tabi* slipped into *chiyoda
zōri*—looking as though to lay siege with his glance, and then
he grasped the small but firm hand." Ōgai's method corresponds to the realism of the artist Takahashi. Ōgai gives us
the right word for it.[54] Takahashi was *laying his own siege* as

[53] Jean-Jacques Origas, "Mono to me, wakaki Ōgai no buntai ni
tsuite," *Kokubungaku kenkyū* (Waseda University), No. 30 (1964).

[54] In another place Ōgai formulates the idea of *ryōryaku* as follows:
"In order for one to observe nature it is paramount to grasp it through
an *Anschauung* (intuitive perception of the whole). Once the siege
of nature is laid through an *Anschauung*, nature comes by itself to
live in a work of art." "Shintō-go," in *Ōgai zenshū* (Iwanami, 1937),
XVIII, 238.

he sat before the piece of bean-curd, the salted salmon, the courtesan.

Masaoka Shiki began to study Western methods of painting as he promoted a remarkably visual type of "sketch" as a literary mode. "I put a blade of grass by my pillow. I sketch it truthfully. Am I not little by little unfolding the secret of the universe? I think I am."[55] There was no place in the process for meager "subjectivism" or for worn-out idealism. His aim was to stick close to the object. "First arrange the lines. Then sketch and again sketch."[56]

Kurenai no	Crimson.
nishaku nobitaru	And already two-feet tall,
bara no me no	Rose buds and thorns,
hari yawaraka ni	With spring rain softly falling.
harusame no furu	Softly falling.
Kame ni sasu	Wisteria in a vase.
fuji no hanafusa	A tassel spills over.
mijikakereba	Too short,
tatami no ue ni	It never quite
todokazarikeri	Touches the mats.

Such poems embody his idea of the "sketch" in poetry. They use ordinary words. The visual element in them is predominant. Shiki is a poet "crazed" with objects in the real world. Together with Takahashi, Shiki was restoring the visual sense of the Japanese: "Revitalize the way a man sees and you restore mankind."[57]

Takahashi's pursuit of realism in Western-style painting was inspired by the most basic and deep-seated needs of the Japanese during the Meiji period. Fenollosa and the Japanese who listened to him misunderstood this. Even today it is misunder-

[55] Masaoka Shiki, "Byōshō rokushaku," in Gendai Nihon bungaku zenshū (Chikuma Shobō, 1955), VI, 92.

[56] A letter-poem to Katori Hotsuma (April 25, 1899), quoted in Saitō Mokichi, Masaoka Shiki (Sogensha, 1943), p. 214.

[57] Nakano, p. 459.

stood in some quarters by those who think that his work was a single, local expression, one surface phenomenon in the process of Westernization. In fact it corresponded to a change in the Japanese consciousness at the most fundamental level.

Reaction and Its Sequel

The opening of the Art School of the Imperial College of Engineering (Kōbu Bijutsu Gakkō) in the autumn of 1876 under the supervision of Itō Hirobumi, Minister of Industry, and the appointment of the Italian artist Antonio Fontanesi (1818-82) as instructor there, must have been highly encouraging developments for Takahashi. He was a personal acquaintance of the Italian Ambassador, Count Alessandro Fe, who supported the proposal for a new art school and introduced him to Fontanesi. Takahashi entered his own son, Genkichi, and several of his pupils in the school. Fontanesi discerned exactly what was needed by early Meiji painting at the time and proceeded to teach fundamentals. Stressing from the outset the indispensability of studies in geometry, perspective, and anatomy, he insisted that a scientific view of nature lay behind Western painting. Though he himself was a painter of pastoral scenes reminiscent of the Barbizon school, with strong romantic inclinations, he advocated the most orthodox training to his Japanese students, reprimanding those among them who were unable to break away from the Literati style in their freehand sketching: "If you live to be eighty years old, then you may be permitted to do this."[58] It is not difficult to imagine that Takahashi may have discovered there an affirmation of his own thought and work up to this time.

Perhaps Fontanesi's influence can be found in the landscape paintings of Takahashi's later period.[59] From about the time of *A View of Mt. Kotohira* (60 x 139 cm.), in 1880, he finally divorces himself from the formula of the *meisho-zue* and

[58] See Kumamoto, "Antonio Fontanesi ni tsuite," p. 129.
[59] There are notes from "Mr. Fontanesi's lecture" in the Takahashi Documents. They deal mainly with landscape painting.

begins to penetrate nature with his own eyes. This becomes clear in *Entrance to the Cave of Kurikoyama* (100 x 147 cm.) and *Tokiwa Bridge over the Sukawa River* (105 x 151 cm.), painted during a trip to the Tōhoku in 1881. Fontanesi's touch may be seen in the choice of angle of vision, the economy of brush stroke, and the graduation of dark tones. But more important there is here a maturity stemming from Takahashi's own experiences with the still life. As a luscious, melancholy poet of nature, the Italian painter suggests Thomas Gray's *Elegy*, which was translated by the *shintai-shi* poets precisely at this time (1882). However, in Takahashi's landscapes this literary lyricism is not to be found. It is the realist of *Sake* and *Tōfu* who pursues nature on this journey to remote Japan and constructs on his canvases a spatial reality highly charged with tension yet at the same time imperturbably cool and dry. Mountain sides covered with dark woods dominate a scene as a cave yawns before us. Elsewhere a stone bridge bestrides the canvas, solid and ponderous.

But during the second decade of the Meiji period, while Takahashi was directing his efforts to exhibits, an art magazine, and other educational activities, the turning point of the era arrived. It took the form of a nationalistic reaction to the Europeanization process. In the autumn of 1878, after two years in Tokyo, Fontanesi, then sixty, left promising students and unfinished projects to return to Turin. Not only ill, he was in addition crushed by the Government's decision to postpone construction of a new building for the Art School because of the expenses incurred by the Satsuma Rebellion.[60] That same autumn an ambitious young philosopher from Boston, twenty-five years old, arrived to assume a teaching position at the University of Tokyo. The replacement of Fontanesi by Ernest Fenollosa (1853-1908) was not, of course, enough to cause an immediate about-face in the artistic trend of Japan. Takahashi recalls in his *Rireki* that Fenollosa called on him at his school,

[60] Takahashi grieved over their parting and they exchanged paintings (*Rireki*).

Tenkai Gakusha, in 1880 and, arguing for the promotion of Western-style painting, promised to make subsequent visits and even to give lectures on Western art at the School. Deeply interested in anything concerning Western painting, Takahashi paid several visits to Fenollosa's residence on the Hongō campus. At this time he received one of Fenollosa's own paintings, most likely a dark-toned landscape of the Barbizon school.[61] But soon afterward, before the promised lectures could be delivered, Takahashi records that "Mr. Fenollosa has been converted to the traditional Japanese school of painting" and "has been freed from his former promise."

It was quite natural for Takahashi to expect a successor to Fontanesi in this American professor at the Imperial University who had studied esthetics at Harvard. Fenollosa's deep commitment to the study of the artistic tradition of Japan, on the other hand, was a sudden turn of interest, unexpected even by Fenollosa himself. Ever since his first glimpses of Japanese art in 1879, the year before his visit to Takahashi, his wonder and enthusiasm for these previously unknown treasures had been steadily growing. These two men, Takahashi and Fenollosa, were each in quest of the other's cultural past. Yet it was a far more burdensome task for an early Meiji painter to set himself free from the Tokugawa traditions of painting than for a pupil of a certain Emil Otto Grundmann[62] to denounce Western art in the most general terms.

We need not discuss in great detail the content of *Bijutsu shin setsu* (Truth of Fine Arts),[63] Fenollosa's well-known speech delivered at the Ryūchikai meeting in May of 1882, and its effect upon the rapid shift in the art policy of the Government authorities. The esthetic based on the Hegelian "idea"

[61] This landscape is presumed to be a work of Fenollosa which remains today in the collection of the Tokyo College of Fine Arts. See Odakane Tarō, "Ernest Fenollosa no bijutsu undō," *Bijutsu kenkyū*, Nos. 110-12 (Feb.-April, 1941).

[62] Lawrence W. Chisolm, *Fenollosa: The Far East and American Culture* (New Haven, 1963), p. 29.

[63] Reprinted in *Meiji bunka zenshū*, XII, 157-74.

(*myōsō*) presented by Fenollosa in this speech, stale and vulgarized as it may seem, no doubt provided useful criteria for problem-solving, given the level of art criticism of the time. The speech persuaded the Japanese to preserve the universal values of the arts of Japan's past, which had been destroyed or neglected during "the violence of foreign fever"[64] following upon the *haibutsu kishaku* (exterminate Buddhism) movement.

However, this sudden fiery burst of enthusiasm for classical Japanese art led Fenollosa to believe mistakenly that the degree of past excellence could be attained in the present. His discussion of the relative values of Japanese and Western art based on an extremely vague and one-sided generalization and the resulting wholesale rejection of Japanese oil painting involved regrettably misleading propositions for the development of Japanese painting as a whole. While Fenollosa's enthusiasm for one of the most fruitless academies in art history, the Kanō school, and his attacks on the genre of Literati painting, including geniuses such as Ike no Taiga and Yosa Buson, were alarmingly shortsighted, the judgment may remain a question of individual taste in art. It is true that oil painting in Japan at that time was by and large still at a clumsy, infantile stage. Exactly for this reason, it did not yet have enough established influence to "crush traditional Japanese painting" as Fenollosa feared. On the contrary it was encouragement, above all, which was needed. Those schools of Japanese painting which Fenollosa celebrated—Kanō, Tosa, and Shijō—were already cringing in defeat, their lifeblood and raison d'être vanished.

"Art is a sensitive barometer to measure the buoyancy of spirit," says Fenollosa in his Preface to *Epochs of Chinese and Japanese Art*. The realistic, Western-style painting of Takahashi represented "the spiritual buoyancy" of nineteenth-century Japan. Far from being merely the product of a frivolous craze for things Western, it was the zenith of a long, steadfast pursuit, spurred in the remote Bakumatsu period by an utterly

[64] Sansom, *The Western World and Japan*, p. 381.

personal experience and advanced by considerable inner drive. Invigorated by the legacy of eighteenth-century rationalism, Takahashi's art finally culminated in a unique form of realism. While it found broad confirmation and support in the contemporary "positivistic" intellectual milieu which had grown out of the "self-improvement" process of the Japanese in the Restoration period, it already foreshadowed elements of the coming trend toward realism in literature. Takahashi's artistic achievement thus had its roots deep in the changing national life of nineteenth-century Japan and endowed the whole realm of Japanese art with unique and enduring values.

This newly forged and genuine artistic style was to be cast aside by the Japanese on the initiative of a Westerner. As Lawrence W. Chisolm points out, "Ironically, it was easier for Fenollosa as a Westerner to lead the national revival. . . . Western approval was important, particularly for anti-Western opinion."[65] Adulation for a Westerner's opinion resulted in a hasty and intolerant rejection of Western culture. Following the Fenollosa speech by only a few months, the first government art exhibition, in the autumn of 1882, excluded Western-style oil painting. The second exhibit in 1884 did the same. Moreover, the Art School of the Imperial Engineering College was closed at the end of 1882. The nationalistic reaction in the area of fine arts seemed to have reached a fanatic stage when, in 1885, the traditional technique of brush and *sumi* was restored in elementary art instruction, replacing the pen and pencil drawing which had been practiced for nearly ten years. Fenollosa, his aide-de-camp Okakura Tenshin, some minor painters of the Kanō school, and a few officials of the Ministry of Education took the lead in this strange regressive movement.

Western-style painters in Japan were soon forced into pathetic immobility under the pressures of these radical revivalists allied with political authorities. They could not, of course, remain utterly hushed. They tried to raise a protest against Fenollosa and his faction. Among the Takahashi Yuichi Docu-

[65] Chisolm, p. 46.

ments are several drafts of protest memorials, repeatedly corrected and revised, which seem to have been prepared in the middle of this critical period.

> There is nothing wrong with the recent tendency to encourage the native arts of Japan. I regret only the inappropriately one-sided way in which it is being carried on. The artistic genius of one nation is a heavenly gift and can never disappear from creative work whatever new methods and means of expression may be developed in the process of creation. On the contrary, at some junctures, contradictory as it may seem, innovation itself becomes vital for a more perfect manifestation of the native genius. The present reform movement encouraging us to revive and cling to trifles of obsolete models and canons is doomed to be fruitless.

This statement by Takahashi seems more tolerant, more self-confident and in closer touch with the actual process of artistic creation than the Fenollosan provincialism. In another document he advocates:

> Art in the days of old had its own flavor. But it is a law of nature that taste and style in art evolve along with the spirit of the times. . . . What is most needed for Japanese artists today is to inquire into and so to acquire the theory and precise methods of Western painting. Frivolous and illusory is the attempt of some of them to reject Western painting as a whole before gaining any impartial and full understanding of it, by caviling at its minor defects in a few examples of no significance, while, on the other hand magnifying traditional Japanese painting, primitive and deformed as it is, as something beyond all other nations' achievements.[66]

In the face of this rising Japanism, Takahashi was unyielding in his deep distrust of the traditional schools and in his firm conviction of the necessity for Western-style realism. Takahashi's very existence was a strong refutation of Fenollosa's

---

[66] No date, no title, like many other drafts in the Documents.

posture with regard to contemporary Japanese art. Indeed, contrasting *Sake* with the renowned *Hibo Kannon* (*Kannon, the Mother of Compassion*) (1888) of Fenollosa's protégé Kanō Hōgai, the feeble mannerism and postiche idealism of the latter are inescapably evident.

It is doubtful that Takahashi's memorials were in fact presented to the authorities. What is certain, however, is that the protest movement did not produce any effect. In 1884, after having put an end to the eleven-year history of his school, Tenkai Gakusha, Takahashi took his second trip to the Northeast. It was, so to speak, a barnstorming tour in order to make sketches of a great variety of construction works, bridges, dikes, and tunnels, which were commissioned by Mishima Tsūyō, governor of Tochigi, Fukushima, and Yamagata Prefectures. Three albums of 130 hand-colored lithographs developed from these sketches, delicately and rhythmically delineated, vividly portray life in this remote Tōhoku area changing rapidly under central leadership.[67] This was the last significant work of Takahashi.[68] In 1889, after years of enforced standstill, Western-style painting in Japan took fresh inspiration from the Meiji Art Society, enrolling as its leading members Harada Naojirō, Yamamoto Hōsui and Asai Chū, all recently returned from Europe. They were encouraged by Mori Ōgai, the new star of art criticism and close friend of Harada, but Takahashi preferred to remain an outsider.[69]

[67] I have seen a copy belonging to the Local History Collection of Yamagata University. Original sketches are in the hands of the Mishima family. Takahashi's letters written during this trip are said to be in the possession of Mr. Miyao Shigeo.

[68] There are some historical paintings of later date, dealing with such themes as Kusunoki Masatsura and Oda Nobunaga (both 1892), which were condescendingly commissioned by the Imperial Household Office. Unfortunately these are pitiful works done by an old, bedridden artist, forced to compromise with fashionable subjects.

[69] Five years later the Society was already branded as "old school" or "resin school" (*yani-ha*) and was replaced in influence by a new group of more fashionable young artists (called "purple school"),

Takahashi Yuichi died on July 6, 1894, at the age of sixty-six, without having formed any meaningful affiliation with Kuroda Seiki or Yokoyama Taikan (1868-1958), the two leaders of the next generation of artists. This "eminent materialist" had engraved upon his tomb stone his Buddhist name: Jissai-in Shin-ō Yuichi-koji (Yuichi the Positivist Faithful to Truth).

---

with Kuroda Seiki and Kume Keiichirō, son of Kunitake, as its leaders. Change was swift in all fields of Meiji society.

CHAPTER VII

The Modern Music of Meiji Japan

WILLIAM P. MALM

THE history of the course of music in Japan during the Meiji period has already been discussed in various English-language publications.[1] Thus, it will be necessary here merely to outline the major historical events in Japan's musical life from the middle of the nineteenth century to approximately the period of World War I. The purpose of this study is to comment on the manner in which these events took place and to meditate on what their significance was to the course of the music that followed. Musical examples will be used from the more popular forms of Meiji music in order to show in specific terms what the confrontation of East and West really meant to the everyday musical habits of Japanese during this fascinating era.

The State of Traditional Music
in the Mid-nineteenth Century

Western music was introduced into Japan at a time when there was considerable activity in a variety of musical forms. While court music (*gagaku*) and the *nō* drama continued in a rather perfunctory way throughout the nineteenth century, various forms of shamisen music such as *nagauta* and *kiyomoto* were actually at the height of their development and creativity. It was during this time that much of the basic repertoire of these newer forms, still played today, was composed. In addition it was in this period that the practice of *ozashiki*, i.e., concert performances of shamisen music, became common. This weaning of the music from the kabuki theatre allowed

---

[1] See particularly *Japanese Music and Drama in the Meiji Era*, ed. Komiya Toyotaka, trans. E. Seidensticker and D. Keene (Tokyo: Ōbunsha, 1956).

composers to experiment with new forms and new sources of inspiration. In *nagauta* the results are seen in such pieces as "Azuma hakkei" (1818), which deals with famous scenic views, and "Tsuru kame" (1851), which is based on a *nō* play. A less pleasant but nevertheless significant proof of the viable state of traditional music in the nineteenth century was the endless school feuds, family quarrels, and creations of new guilds of musicians.[2] Thus it was that these various traditional forms were hardly affected at first by the early actions of the Meiji restoration.

The state of affairs in the worlds of koto, shakuhachi, and biwa music was more directly affected. The basic styles of koto playing and much of its standard repertoire had been established in the eighteenth century under the influence of Ikuta Kengyō (1655-1715) and Yamada Kengyō (1757-1817). Further developments were found in the fields of solo literature (*danmono*) and chamber music (*sankyoku*) in the nineteenth century. However, the connection of koto music with the special rights of the blind caused a considerable upheaval in the political structure of the koto world when these ancient rights were changed under Meiji law. A similar social change occurred in shakuhachi music when the exclusive rights of the Fuke sect of Buddhism to the playing of shakuhachi were abolished and opportunities for new kinds of students and teachers were created. Fortunately for both shakuhachi and koto music, these two traditions had developed notation systems[3] suitable to the requirements of their particular style so that new markets for their music could be reached without depending exclusively on the traditional rote learning technique. Such systems were hardly known in shamisen music before the twentieth century.[4]

[2] For such details see Machida Kashō, "Japanese Music and Dance," *ibid.*, pp. 329-441.

[3] For examples see the article "Kifuhō" in *Ongaku jiten*, III (Tokyo: Heibonsha, 1955), 93-96.

[4] Rare eighteenth- and nineteenth-century examples as well as the two standard twentieth-century forms are shown on pages 96-98,

The biwa was primarily of regional interest by the nineteenth century. The recitation to biwa accompaniment of the famous epics of the Heike (Heike-biwa) were still performed during the Edo period under the protection of the shogunate but the art nearly disappeared when this patronage was withdrawn in Meiji times. However, the southern traditions of Satsuma and Chikuzen biwa actually advanced during the late nineteenth century as the power and influence of Satsuma increased in national affairs. Thus this music moved to Tokyo as part of the general flow of men and ideas from Kyushu to the new circles of power.

The brief survey given above shows that, while the very beginnings of Meiji reform did have fundamental effect on the social structure of several Japanese music traditions, the strength (or perhaps inertia) of other traditions led them along basically unaltered paths when Western music first appeared. However, the intimate relation of Western music to the new Japanese educational system soon forced traditional music to take note of its new rival.

The Introduction of Western Music into Japan in the Meiji Era

We can divide the first forms of Western music found in Japan into three basic types: church music, military music, and music in the schools. In all three cases Western music was not acquired by the Japanese out of any special interest in its qualities per se, but rather as necessary parts of a Western-derived table of organization for the particular institution in question.

Church Music

By the middle of the nineteenth century musical remnants of the sixteenth-century Christian tradition in Japan were extremely rare. With the establishment of religious freedom

---

op. cit. The latter are based on the French Chevé number system, which was introduced into the Japanese schools by Luther W. Mason.

in 1872, the Protestant hymn became the dominant Christian musical form. The first collection of hymns published in Japan appeared in 1878 and was soon followed by many more as the number of denominations increased and the popularity of the form grew. Interdenominational collections became more common after 1890. Japan acquired a standard set of Christian musical pieces. The simple, foursquared style of these works exerted a strong influence on many of the early Western-style Japanese song writers. A perfect case is "Meiji setsu," shown in Example 1. It is interesting to note that a similar "Christian" sound can be heard in the early nationalistic songs of many twentieth-century African nations where the first musical training of the native peoples likewise occurred under church auspices.

Military Music

Admiral Perry made good use of his bands during his first visit to Japan as can be seen by both his own artist's lithographs and various Japanese woodblock prints.[5] However, the 1869 request of the Satsuma domain that William Fenton, band leader of the British Tenth Marine Battalion, train thirty men in band music was motivated primarily by a desire to complete their military table of organization rather than any great fascination with the music as such. The national military ministries followed suit in 1871 and, under the guidance of English, French, Italian, and German musicians, a tradition of military music became firmly established within the Meiji Western-style culture. The military bands provided Japan's first public concerts of Western ensemble music, beginning with a Navy band performance at the Shimbashi Railway Building on September 12, 1872, on the occasion of the opening of the first railway. The best-known location for later concerts was the famous Rokumeikan Club which, in the eighties, was the location for many foreign-style parties (see pp. 94-95).

[5] See the plates opposite pages 375 and 486 in Francis Hawks' *Narrative of the Expedition of an American Squadron . . .* (New York: Appleton, 1857).

Example 1: Meiji setsu

Text of Example 1: Meiji setsu

Ajia no higashi hi izuru tokoro,	The Eastern sun of Asia rises,
hijiri no kimi no arawaremashite	His Majesty appears.
furuki Ametsuchi tozaseru kiri o	And the Universe covered of old with mist
ōmi hikari ni kumanaku harai	He purifies through with a great light.
oshie amaneku michi akirabeku	His teachings open wide pathways,
osametamaeru miyo tōto	Graciously ruling over us, Noble Prince.

In addition to introducing Western music in general, the military bands also helped to create a body of patriotic music, the most notable example of which was the national anthem. The manner in which it developed is an excellent illustration of the relation of the early military band leaders to the growth of music in Meiji Japan. There are several different versions of the story but most agree that it was the British bandmaster Fenton who first noted the lack of a national anthem during his teaching sessions with the young men of Satsuma. According to the most recent study[6] he sent one of his students, Ekawa Yogorō, to find a proper verse which Fenton could then use to compose an anthem for Japan. Ekawa went to a Captain Oyama of the Satsuma domain who, in consultation with some gentlemen who happened to be in his Tokyo house at that moment, produced the old poem "Kimi ga yo." There is some disagreement over whether he picked the poem from the *Kokinshū*, a Shintō dance poem, or the Satsuma-biwa composition, "Hōraisan." In any event, Fenton used this text for the composition premiered on September 18th, 1870, as an unofficial national anthem. As can be seen in Example 2A, the piece is almost unsingable from either a Western or a Japanese point of view.

Fenton became director of the Navy band in 1871 and his tune for the anthem continued to be used until at least 1876 at which time its appeal began to wane. Several revisions were tried, but none seemed appropriate as a piece expressing respect for the emperor. It is interesting to note that the poem and the music were emperor-oriented rather than directly patriotic. This typical Meiji orientation created difficulties for the eventual form of the national anthem when, after World War II, the position of the emperor was de-emphasized. The difficulties in the 1870's, however, were more pragmatic. Japanese official imperial and diplomatic protocol required the performance of appropriate musical selections, while the Japanese Navy found

[6] Masuko Tokuzō, *Kimigayo no kenkyū* (Tokyo: Shinsei Shobō, 1965).

itself unable to answer in kind when it heard the national anthems of other nations performed at flag ceremonies on neighboring foreign ships.

In an attempt to find a proper anthem, the Navy invited court musicians from the palace to teach some bandmen *gagaku* in the hopes that one of them would then be able to devise an appropriate Japanese composition.[7] However, the difficulty of the court instruments as well as, perhaps, the slow traditional teaching methods, discouraged the band musicians. The Navy then sent an official request to the Imperial Music Bureau for a national anthem to be composed by a member of the court orchestra. A committee of court musicians assisted by Franz Eckert, the German replacement for the repatriated Mr. Fenton, eventually selected a composition by Hayashi Hiromori (1831-96), the second-ranking member of the orchestra. Hayashi was a traditional musician and apparently had little knowledge of or liking for Western music. He produced a piece in the Ichikotsu mode of the gagaku tone system[8] and wrote it out in traditional court vocal notation so that it could be performed by the court musicians. The melody, shown in Example 2B, was put into Western notation by Eckert and then harmonized and arranged for band. In this setting the piece was premiered on November 3, 1880. Thus, at the beginning the national anthem existed in both a traditional and a Western setting.

Another setting of the poem was found in the first public school song books (the *Shōgaku shokashi shōden* of 1881) but, as can be seen in Example 2C, it was very Western in form and, like Fenton's original setting, it lost official favor even though it was widely sung throughout Japan's first public schools.

[7] At the same time several court musicians were trained to play Western music in order that they could function in both capacities in the Court (as they continue to do today).

[8] The various modes of the *gagaku* tone system can be seen in the author's *Japanese Music and Musical Instruments* (Tokyo: Tuttle, 1959), p. 101.

Example 2A: Kimi ga yo

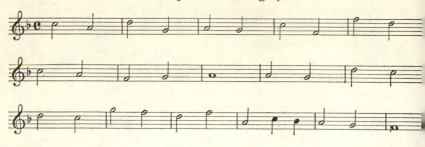

Example 2B

Example 2C

Text of Examples 2A, B, and C: Kimi ga yo

kimi ga yo wa	The reign of my Lord
chiyo ni yachiyo ni	A thousand ages, eight thousand ages;
sazare ishi no	So long that a tiny pebble
iwao to narite	Will grow into a rock
koke no musu made	All covered with moss.

We shall see later how military traditions affected other aspects of Japanese musical life. In the case of the national anthem, however, we have a unique instance of traditional elements taking precedence over the Western forms. A more typical example of the Meiji military style of music in Japan is seen in Example 3, the 1894 march "Yūkan naru suihei." Note that despite its harmonically oriented, foursquared tune and incessant dotted rhythm, it does exploit a five-toned (pentatonic) scale in the manner of some oriental and folk melodies. The same scale can be seen in the various versions of "Kimi ga yo" in Example 2; this widespread scale was considered by many Western and Japanese writers to be a bridge over which the great musical meeting of East and West could take place. Such an attitude was certainly evident in the creation of Japanese school music.

Public School Music

The story of the founding of the Japanese public school music system under the guidance of Izawa Shūji (1851-1917) and the American, Luther Whiting Mason (1828-96), has been related in English several times.[9] We need make note here only of a few special points about its founding. In the original petition sent by Izawa and Mekata Tanetarō (director of Japanese students in America) an emphasis was laid on national music. The term was explained in the following manner:

The worth-while examples of traditional Japanese songs and music should be studied afresh, and their inadequacies supplemented from the west. National songs can then be written which every Japanese, of high or low birth, of refinement or simplicity, can sing on all occasions, and a distinctive Japanese music will be promoted.[10]

[9] The most recent is Elizabeth May, *The Influence of the Meiji Period on Japanese Children's Music* (Berkeley: University of California Press, 1963), pp. 56-57.
[10] Quoted in Nomura Kōichi's "Occidental Music," in *Japanese Music and Drama in the Meiji Era*, p. 463.

Example 3: Yūkan naru suihei

Text of Example 3: Yūkan naru suihei

kemuri mo miezu kumo mo naku	There's not a sign of smoke, nor even a cloud;
kaze mo okorazu nami tatazu	Not even a breeze; the waves are still.
kagami no gotoki kōkai wa	The Yellow Sea is like a mirror
kumori sometari toki no ma ni	Just as the sky is filled with color.
sora ni shirarenu ikazuchi ka	An unknown thunder in the sky?
nami ni kirameku inazuma ka	A brilliant lightning on the waves?
kemuri wa sora o tachi komete	The smoke rises to the sky,
amatsu hi kage mo iro kurashi	And darkens even the heavenly light.
tatakai ima ya takenawa ni	The battle is now at its height!
tsutome tsuku seru masurao no	The dead bodies of the valiant heroes who gave their last
tōtoki chi mote kampan wa	full measure of devotion, cover the deck made crimson
kara kurenai ni kazararetsu	By their precious blood.

This statement points up two basic attitudes. First, it expresses a desire to blend the best of East and West and, secondly, it implies that Eastern music is artistically inferior to Western. Both these points are made again in Izawa's 1879 "Plan for the Study of Music."[11] Following the best Japanese tradition of compromise, he avoids the idea of teaching Western music exclusively or of working on the cultivation and improvement of Japanese music alone. "We should take a middle course between the two views, and by blending Eastern and Western music establish a kind of music which is suitable for the Japan of today."[12] In looking for a kind of music in which such a blend can take place he chooses first children's songs. "This is because the elements which compose Western and Japanese music do not differ in the slightest, and it is only the methods of combining the elements which are dissimilar. Therefore, in the case of simple compositions like children's songs the differences are exceedingly small . . ."[13] It should be noted that Izawa was not a musician and therefore produced rather far-reaching ground rules for the future of music without any profound knowledge of the art itself. One wonders, in fact, if there is any significance in the fact that Izawa's previous position was that of the director of a school for the deaf and dumb.

The arrival of Mason in 1880 put a fully professional musician on the staff. He immediately began to apply his Boston public school techniques to selected elementary and normal schools in Japan. A program of teacher training was also started. In October of 1880 twenty-two students were enrolled in a course of "blended" music studies in what was to be known by 1890 as the Tokyo Music School. Shamisen and court musicians were mixed with beginners and lessons were given on koto and the bowed *kokyū* as well as piano, organ, and violin. The first program given by students and teachers of this organization included both Western and Japanese music. The singing curriculum included both Western melodies and

[11] *Ibid.*, p. 464. [12] *Ibid.*, p. 466. [13] *Ibid.*, p. 467.

arranged *gagaku* and koto melodies. In keeping with the original goals of Mason and Izawa, however, a major part of the publishing efforts were directed towards children's school song books. The first of these, the *Shogaku shokashi shoden* (1881), contained thirty-three songs, half of Western origin and half composed by Mason with the aid of Japanese assistants. These first "blended" pieces were arranged in a curious if pragmatic way. In the case of the Western pieces Mason met with a group of imperial court musicians and a blind poet. He played through various Western pieces and had their texts explained. When a tune was liked by the Japanese it was played several times for the poet who then went to work on a suitable Japanese text. In this way "The Bluebells of Scotland" became "Utsukushiki" and "Auld Lang Syne" was filled with fireflies ("Hotaru no hikari"). The choice of new Japanese pieces is discussed less clearly though we do have a report of the manner in which Mason set about revising Japanese music in conjunction with Izawa, a koto player, some court musicians, and a man knowledgeable in Japanese literature.

A general council is held on a certain day to determine whether the piece is fit for revision or not. The music, as well as the words, is tried by a concert of koto, kokiu, shamisen, shakuhachi, etc. If the music is good and the words are not, the words are revised, but if both music and words are unsuitable the piece is rejected. After the words are reformed, a trial will be made again by the same concert as before. On this trial, if the words be found unfit for the music, they will be corrected or revised, again and again, until all is right . . .

When a piece is finished after passing the various steps above enumerated, it is harmonized, so far as the natural beauty of Japanese music can be retained, according to the principles of modern music, in order to make it on an equality with European music.[14]

[14] Quoted from Izawa in May, pp. 56-57.

Note in this description that the performances were given in traditional, un-harmonized versions but always with the intent of finding pieces which could eventually be harmonized. At no point in the preparation of materials for the schools do we find any indication of a desire to find pieces which could be played on traditional instruments in a traditional way in the classroom situation.

In most of the musical compilations one is struck by the extensive use of court musicians and poets as the major consultants on tunes and texts. It is small wonder that children found the melodies difficult and the words hard to understand. It would be rather like starting American children with pieces based on Gregorian chant which used Shakespeare sonnets for text. Court music had and still has about as much relation to the general Japanese public as the various collegiate medieval instrumental ensembles have to the American populace. One wonders if the steady increase in Western-style pieces vis-à-vis Japanese-inspired works in later song collections would have been so great if musicians from the more "vulgar" world of the Japanese theatre had been more active in the formation of these books.

There was a committee devoted to the study of Japanese music (the *Hōgaku chōsa gakari*) within the structure of the Tokyo Music School. However, such a committee was not really active until 1907, long after the basic public school repertory was formed. We noted earlier that the koto and *kokyū* were used from the very start in the training of Music School students but neglected to say that they were used mostly for playing Western music since there was a shortage of pianos and violins. Genuine koto music (*sōkyoku*) had been the concern of the school as well and in 1888 it published a *Collection of Japanese Koto Music* which consisted of well-known traditional pieces notated in five-line Western style. In addition, *nagauta* shamisen music was also available at the school. However, none of these activities seemed to have really affected what happened in the public school classrooms. Though Izawa recommended in 1884[15] the use of koto and *kokyū* in primary grades (since organs, pianos, and violins were expensive to provide), there seems to be little evidence to show that this procedure was used as anything more than a stopgap until "proper" instruments could be made available. As for the traditional music itself, one need only read Izawa's statement that "Such popular music as is so deeply rooted in the hearts of the people, cannot be eradicated entirely, but may be revised by degrees"[16] to realize that the reforms discussed earlier implied something more than mere harmonization. He says in addition that "Some special arrangements will be made for those who wish to learn particularly this kind of music. . . . After this is done, the old immoral music will be forbidden."[17] The special arrangements were never made and the reformed traditional music lay stillborn between the scholastic and the professional worlds.

Most of the early students at the Tokyo Music School had previous Japanese music training and in theory they could specialize on either a Western or a Japanese instrument.[18] However, these early traditional musicians were at the school primarily to learn Western music and music systems rather than to contribute their own special talents to the experiments going on around them. In addition, as the program developed the goals and backgrounds became different for students majoring in Western instruments and those majoring in traditional instruments. The Japanese piano student came out of no special social or professional background since the instrument was quite new to his culture. Such a student, at least at the early stages, knew that he was being trained primarily as a public school teacher. The koto student, by contrast, came out of

---

[15] Izawa Shuji, *Report . . . on the Result of the Investigation Concerning Music* (Tokyo: The Institute of Music, 1884), p. 48.

[16] *Ibid.*, pp. 61-63. He refers here to vulgar music (*zokkyoku*) not to popular music in the modern Western sense of the term.

[17] *Ibid.*, p. 64.

[18] This choice is still possible in the present day inheritor of the Tokyo Music School, the Geijitsu Daigaku, Ongaku-bu.

a long tradition of guilds, special teacher-student relations, and a world in which the acquisition of a professional name (*natori*)[19] and a professional performing and private teaching career were still the primary goals. With such a legacy it was unlikely that these persons would go into the public schools. The repertoire they had learned on their traditional instruments was not the same as that found in the school song books. Thus it was a combination of a legacy from an Edo-style musical life and a Western-oriented music education system with a Victorian view of what was proper music that drove a wedge between the best of the East and the West and shattered Izawa's dream of a blend.

The exclusion of musicians of the Edo world from public school music may have been a matter of social status as well as the situational connotations of the music they played. Musicians and actors, though often rich and famous, had traditionally been low on the Edo period social ladder. Since the reforms were taking place under the aegis of an imperially oriented bureaucracy, they naturally turned to the only set of musicians traditionally associated with the more refined courtly life and untainted by the popular theatre, the geisha house, or the topical subjects heard in the streets. Had the shogun been the one to undertake these reforms he would probably have been equally hard on theatre music,[20] but he might at least have included artists from the *nō* drama. Perhaps the years of patronage from the shogunate for such forms as *nō*, biwa, and shakuhachi music made them less acceptable when the new era began.

An awareness of the position of such traditional musicians outside the power structure of the Meiji musical establishment

---

[19] It was quite a shock to the Japanese music world when a group of shamisen students at the University of Fine Arts and their teachers rejected their professional Kineya and Yoshizumi names to form the Toon-kai. This happened in 1959.

[20] His actual attitude can be seen in Donald Shively's "Bakufu versus Kabuki," *Harvard Journal of Asiatic Studies*, XVIII (Dec., 1955), 326-56.

is crucial to an understanding of the direction in which musical modernization continued throughout the Meiji. Had musicians from the popular, plebian forms been consulted on the choice of school music, Japanese children might have learned to relate more quickly to the living worlds of both Western and Eastern music. As it was, they were taught the modern music of the West and an artificial version of old-fashioned music from their own country.

Since the older, stiffer style of the Japanese pieces compared poorly with the lyricism of "Annie Laurie" or "The Last Rose of Summer," the latter became more popular. This led Japanese composers to write pieces in imitation of the Western styles or in a pseudo-Japanese style based on pre-Meiji children's songs from Japan.

Three levels of school songs can be seen in Examples 4, 5, and 6. Example 4 shows the unadorned use of a foreign melody with Japanese text. It refers in its text to the rage for music boxes (*orugoru* in Meiji Japanese) which were a popular import item until local industrial acumen completely reversed the flow. Example 5 is a rather amazing illustration of a Japanese composition which combines Stephen Foster with Protestant hymn style while singing of the Japanese tradition of kite flying. Example 6 is couched in the more traditional style of Japanese children's game songs though one suspects a possible influence from the rhythm of military songs (compare with

Example 4: Amaririsu

Text of Example 4: Amaririsu

minna de kikō	Everyone, listen together
tanoshii orugoru o	To the merry music-box
ra ri ra ri ra ri ra	La li la li, la li la
shirabe wa Amaririsu	The melody is Amaryllis

Example 5

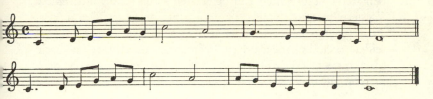

Text of Example 5

tobe tobe tonbi sora takaku
nake nake tonbi ao zora ni

pin yorō, pin yorō, pin yorō,
   pin yorō
tanoshige ni wa o kaite

Fly, kite, fly, high in the sky.
Sing, kite, sing, in the blue
   sky

Pin yorō, pin yorō, pin yorō,
   pin yorō,
Merrily flying in a circle.

Example 6: Kakurembo

Text of Example 6: Kakurembo

kakurembo surumono to
   yottoi de
jan ken pon yo aiko desho
mō ii kai, māda da yo
mō ii kai, māda da yo
mō ii yo, mō ii yo

Let's play hide and seek and

Jan ken pon
Ready? Not yet!
Ready? Not yet!
Ready! Ready!

Example 3). Note that all three examples use the standard pentatonic scale which can be related to either an incomplete Western major or natural minor scale or to *gagaku* modes. The half-step laden scale (the *in*) so popular in Edo music seldom occurs in the modern "reformed" collections. The basic gagaku scales (*ryō* and *ritsu*) and the Edo *in* scale are shown in Example 7 for the sake of comparison.[21]

Example 7

The lack of pieces in the *in* scale would, of course, be a natural result of the tonal prejudices of the *gagaku* musicians on the committee as well as the difficulty of relating it to more "modern" Western scales. This scale was very familiar to the koto and shakuhachi musicians, but perhaps using such a scale in school songs in Japan might have had a social connotation analogous with the use of a blues piece in an American kindergarten.

[21] A detailed explanation of the Japanese tone system seems inappropriate to the nature of this paper. Those wishing further information should consult the author's *Japanese Music and Musical Instruments*. The modal possibilities of the *yō-in* system are found on page 61 of the author's *Nagauta: The Heart of Kabuki Music* (Tokyo: Tuttle, 1963).

The Legacy of Meiji School Music

Since many of the edifying, Confucian-laden songs of the early Meiji children's books were somewhat less than enthusiastically received by the students, other sources of inspiration were sought. The Japanese composer took to the street to find more popular idioms, but his ears were still Western-oriented. He did not pick the continuing popular music tradition of Edo, or its Meiji offspring, about which we will speak in more detail later. Rather, the one form that most affected the content of middle Meiji song books was the *gunka*, the military song, particularly as it flourished during the time of the Russo-Japanese War. Tunes with the qualities of Example 3 have been standard in children's song books ever since as can be seen in a twentieth-century piece shown in Example 8. A similar style of song but of even less musical interest was the so-called railroad songs. These short songs were used in the early 1900's as aids in the memorization of all kinds of subject matter from geography to arithmetic.

The Japanese public school repertoire has remained basically unchanged in style since the Meiji period. Students wearing nineteenth-century-style dark uniforms continue to sing Stephen Foster long after the demise of his popularity in American schools. These songs are classical examples of marginal survival, with one important difference. A young Japanese can, perhaps, rightly claim "Jeannie with the Light Brown Hair" as a Japanese national song since both his father and his grandfather sang it before him.

Japanese school-song composers continue to produce new pieces following the general patterns of the examples given above. Such changes as have occurred result primarily from reactions to the latest fads in American music education or to the pronouncements of the German school. However, even though the public school music tradition contributed little to the creative side of the arts in the Meiji period, it exerted a powerful influence on the musical habits of young Japanese. It

Example 8: Kitaeru ashi

Text of Example 8: Kitaeru ashi

ōzora harete fuka midori	The sky is clear and deep blue.
kokoro wa hitotsu, hi wa urara	The sun is bright. All together now
ashi nami soroe, gun gun aruke	Keep in step, marching onward
minna genki de, kitaeru ashi da	Everyone with spirit— well-trained feet.

trained them to learn music by note rather than by the traditional rote system.[22] It put into their ears songs and tonalities only occasionally related to the immediate musical traditions in existence at the end of the Edo period. It also inculcated the young with the attitude that the proper rendition of a melody was in a harmonized form. This last point led to an emphasis in middle and high schools on choral singing which in turn led to a need for post-graduate organizations dedicated to the continuation of this tradition. The traditional music world had no place for such performance practices. There was really no

[22] Curiously enough, the West has recently become excited over the so-called "Suzuki Method" of violin playing in which the rote tradition of old Japan has been applied to a Western instrument.

place for their talents in the Western-art-music world either, for at that time large choral organizations hardly existed in Japan. Later, however, labor union, leftist, and other militant groups of the Taishō and Shōwa periods found that the formation of choral groups was an excellent way to recruit the young as well as a good means of maintaining solidarity among its established membership. The continuing importance of this Meiji musical change can be seen in the 1955 Stalin Peace Prize won by Seki Akiko for her work in organizing workers' and students' choruses as part of the Japanese *utagoe* movement.[23] The mass singing sessions of the militant Sōka Gakkai Buddhist sect are an even more recent example. Surely Izawa and Mason had no idea their modernization attempts within public school music systems would have such divergent extra-curricular results. Yet in the long view these may be some of the most important aspects of at least the social history of the uses of music in Japan since the Meiji. If one wishes to look for more creative elements in the study of Meiji music, as they affected the lives of the general Japanese public, the field of popular music offers a more fruitful area for discussion.

Japanese Popular Music in the Meiji Period

Every urban society has had some kind of topical, easily learned music which tended to be understood by all classes of people. The cities of the Edo period were no exception. The words *ryūkōka* or *hayariuta*[24] designated most of the topical songs of the streets, tea houses, and music halls. During the Meiji period the subject matter covered by such songs was

[23] A detailed account of the activities of this group can be found in a special August, 1956, issue of *Chisei* magazine.

[24] The distinction between these two terms is not always clear. See related articles in *Ongaku jiten*, VIII, 149 and II, 152. *Hayariuta* most often refers to older popular music while *ryūkōka* is applied to any kind of popular music including Western products. See also Tanabe Hisao, *Meiji ongaku monogatari* (Tokyo: Seiabō, 1964). There is a good record album of popular music from the period, *Meiji Taishō ryūkōka-shi*, Nippon Victor SJV-320-1.

highly varied. For example, the well-known Meiji phrase "*Yoi ja nai ka*" (Isn't it good?) can be included in this category. It was chanted or sung by great masses of people who, it is reported,[25] were used by Shintō priests in street demonstrations which, while ostensibly related to the *ofuda ori* scattering of magic charms were, in fact, part of the political pressure used in support of the Imperial Restoration. These priests connected the ideas of the Land of the Gods, the Emperor, and Divine Protection into a popular religious-political movement which is barely evident in the words of the "*Yoi ja nai ka*" chants, two verses of which translate as follows:[26]

> Isn't it fine, the Sumida River?
> For flowers, for moon,
> For snow-viewing, too
> Isn't it fine, that we do not become angry
> Talking together
> Hearts understanding each other?

A more direct form of political music is seen in the song "*Dynamite bushi*" which was popular in the period of 1886-88. Supposedly it was sung by followers of Ōi Kentarō after his arrest and imprisonment. In any event it does reflect a more activist view of political techniques as seen in its first verse, which translates as follows:[27]

> Yamato spirit is polished with rain
> From the tears of the advocates of People's Rights.
> Promote the national interest
> And the people's happiness
> Foster the National Resources
> Because if this is not done—
> Dynamite! Bang!

[25] Fujisawa Morihiko, *Hayariuta hyakunen-shi* (Tokyo: Daiichi, 1951), p. 65.
[26] Fujisawa, pp. 65-66.
[27] The original text is found in Fujisawa, p. 247.

There was a great host of similar popular, political or patriotic tunes such as the "Count Our People's Rights Song" (*Minken kazoe-bushi*) or "Keep Our Glorious Peace for A Thousand Years Song" (*Taihei medeta chiyo bokure-bushi*) but most of their jogging tunes have faded with the years and the demise of old party members. The melodies seemed to have been as dull as their poetry and are a loss more in the historical sense than in the musical one. Like the children's songs already discussed, they tended to be imitations of Western marches and late nineteenth century popular styles. The 1901 piece, "The Song of Perry's Arrival" (*Peruri torai no uta*), shown in Example 9, illustrates such a mastery of the technique of writing hack patriotic melodies in the Western diatonic scale system. The 1900 piece, "Strike Song" (*Sutoraiki-bushi*), shown in Example 10, would seem to confound our statement with its *in* scale tendency and shamisen accompaniment. However, as the text reveals, this particular strike was that of a Nagoya house of prostitution, the Aurora, and thus the music might logically be expected to reflect the more traditional training of the strikers involved. Note how much freer in phrase structure and rhythm this more indigenously Japanese popular tune is compared with the Western-style compositions we have viewed so far. We can only hope that this more imaginative, native piece was of some value in improving the working conditions for what truly might be called a group of outraged workers.

In addition to these rather specific topical tunes, there were in the late Edo period and in the Meiji era many songs that could be called novelty tunes. Many of these revolved around a nonsense syllable which was used as exclamations (*hayashi kotoba*) at the end of verses or phrases or as onomatopoetics. The Edo piece "*Kochae-bushi*"[28] is an example of an ending exclamation, while in the song "*Chonkina*" is filled with imitations of the shamisen. The latter is said to have been noted

[28] The music can be seen in *Gesammeltewerke der Welt Musik* (Nihon ongaku shū), XIX (Tokyo: Shunjū Kaisha, 1931), 15. The other pieces mentioned in this category can also be found in this work.

Example 9: Peruri torai no uta

Text of Example 9: Peruri torai no uta

Kaei mu tose no natsu no
   goro
uranari kitaru tenkan wa
nami shizuka naru sagami
   nada
miru miru chikazue uragako

In the summer of the sixth
   year of Kaei,
A line of iron clad ships
And many riders too, in the
   calm Sagami Bay.

III. Even the ships' names
      were noble and
      Commodore Perry's
      party too.

IV. If you don't sign a
      transport pact in the
      Pacific Ocean

V. The future hinges on
      us, and probably in
      fifty years

VI. The samurai path and
      commerce too will push
      forward in the East.

Example 10: Strike Song

Text of Example 10: Strike Song

nani o kuyo kuyo Kawabata
   Yanagi

kogaruru nan to shiyō

mizu no nagare o mite
   kurasu

shinonome no sutoraiki

saritowa tsurai ne 'tte na koto

osshaimashita ka ne

What are you worrying about,
   Kawabata Yanagi?

Pining, "What shall we do?"

They live watching the river
   flow.

The Aurora strike. . . .

You said something like

"That's really tough."

(Continued)

Text of Example 10: Strike Song (*continued*)

jiyū haigyō de kuruwa wa deta ga	They left the quarter by freely closing shop,
sorekara nan to shiyō	But then "What shall we do?"
yukiba ga nai no de kuzuhiroi	Having nowhere to go, they became ragpickers.
ukareme no sutoraiki	The prostitute strike,
sari to wa tsurai ne 'tte na koto	And you said something like
osshaimashita ka ne	"That's really tough."

in Pierre Loti's *Madame Chrysanthemum*[29] though it was not carried over into *Madame Butterfly* by Puccini.

Meiji extensions of this tradition are found in the 1869 piece "*Gichonchon*" and the best known variant, the 1887 piece "*Oppekepē-bushi*" which imitates the sound of a bugle. The latter piece shown in Example 11 belongs to that type of nonsense syllable song which since Edo times has been basically a patter song in which topical news, stories, and gossip are spoken against a *shamisen ostinato*. Readers familiar with the talking blues of Woody Guthrie and other American folk musicians will recognize this performance technique. In Japan it was used greatly in the music halls and by *rakugo* artists, one of the most famous practitioners being Kawakami Otojirō (1864-1911), an important pioneer in the Shimpa theatre movement.[30] "*Oppekepē-bushi*," like its American counterpart, used texts that were primarily political, topical, and of a protesting nature.

In our discussion of Meiji popular music so far we have tried to emphasize its eclectic, opportunistic qualities and show how it was able to use musical characteristics from both the Edo and the Western traditions since, unlike public school music, it was

[29] See notes, *ibid.*, p. 204.
[30] A short resume of his career may be found in *Japanese Music and Drama in the Meiji Era*, pp. 265-74.

Example 11: Oppekepē bushi

Text of Example 11: Oppekepē bushi

Beika tōki no konnichi ni	In these days when the price of rice is rising,
saimin konkyū kaerimizu	you completely ignore the plight of the poor,
mebuka ni kabutta taka bōshi	covering your eyes with tall hats,
kin no yubiwa ni kindokei	wearing gold rings and gold watches,
kemmon kiken ni hiza o mage	you bow to men of influence and position
geisha hōkan ni kane o maki	and spend your money on geisha and entertainers,
uchi niwa kome o kura ni tsumi	and piling up rice in your storehouse at home,
dōhō kyōdai migoroshi ka	will you let your fellow countrymen perish?
ikura jihi naki yokushin mo	Such selfishness without compassion
amari hidō na hakujō na	is completely heartless and inhuman.

(Continued)

283

Text of Example 11: Oppekepē bushi (*continued*)

tadashi wa meido no omiyage ka	But if you think you can get to Paradise
jigoku de Emma ni menkai shi	by the special favors of Purgatory
wairo tsukōte gokuraku e	or by using a bribe when you encounter
ikeru kae ikenai yo	the King of Hades in hell you'll never get there!
oppekepē, oppekepeppō peppoppō.	*oppekepē, oppekepeppō peppoppō.*

unencumbered by doctrinaire goals. One of the most famous Meiji examples of popular music's talent for compromise is the song, "*Norumanton-gō chimbotsu no uta,*" which concerned itself with the 1887 wreck of a British freighter off the Japanese coast. The tune is said to have been derived from the 1885 march, "*Battō-tai,*" written for the imperial army by their French bandmaster, Charles Leroux. Examples 12A and 12B give both the original piece (*Battō-tai*) and the start of the popular song. Leroux's march is a rather long-winded piece beginning in the minor mode and ending with a trio in the parallel major key. It is, perhaps, one of the last remnants of the kind of military music that was written during the Napoleonic period. The popular song version (12B) cuts the original piece down to a standard sixteen bars and places it in the Japanese *in* scale.

There is yet another piece which is said to have been derived from Leroux's march.[31] It is a 1907 music hall piece called "*Rappa-bushi.*" It is in the bugle song tradition so popular after the Russo-Japanese War. As shown in Example 12C it has become a very distant relative of "*Battō-tai*" and seems to be a half-breed in both its origin and its tonal system.

[31] Sonobe Saburō, *Nihon minshū kayōshi kō* (Tokyo: Asahi Shimbunsha, 1962), pp. 67-68.

Example 12A: Battō-tai

Text of Example 12A: Battō-tai

ware wa kangun waga teki wa	The enemy of our Imperial army.
tenchi irezaru chōteki zo	Heaven and Earth do not permit enemies of the Emperor.
teki no taishō taru mono wa	The general of the enemy

(Continued)

Text of Example 12A: Battō-tai (*continued*)

kokin musō no eiyū de	Is a peerless hero of all ages,
kore ni shitagau tsuwamono wa	and the soldiers who follow him
tomo ni hyōkan kesshi no shi	Are also fierce do-or-die men
kijin ni hajinu yū aru mo	With courage worthy of the gods.
ten no yurusanu hangyaku o	Since ancient times, men who try to stir up
okoseshi mono wa mukashi yori	Heaven-forbidden treason
sakaeshi tameshi arazaru zo	Have never been successful.
teki no horoburu sore made wa	Until the enemy is vanquished
susume ya susume ya morotomo ni	Advance, advance, all together,
tamachiru tsurugi nukitsurete	Drawing our bullet-scattering swords
shi suru kakugote susumubeshi	We must advance prepared to die.

Another source of materials for an understanding of the changes in the Japanese musical scene on the popular level is found in the many printed collections of popular music. Most of these books rely on the number system mentioned earlier though many of them use both Western five-line notation along with the number notation. This double notation tradition is still used in popular and folk song collections printed in Japan today. Such is the case in the *Collection of Japanese Popular Music* edited by Y. Nagai, bandmaster at Osaka castle, and K. Kobatake, "first class saxaphonist" (sic) of the same, and published by the Miki Company of Osaka in 1892. This little volume is informative in many ways. The cover, shown in Plate I, carries both an English and Japanese title (*Nihon zok-kyoku shū*) and is illustrated by a kimono-clad girl playing a

Example 12B: Norumanton-gō chimbotsu no uta

Text of Example 12B: Norumanton-gō chimbotsu no uta

kishi utsu nami no oto takaku	The loud noise of waves hitting the bank,
yowa no arashi ni yume samete	Dreams fade in the midnight storm.
ao unabara o nagametsutsu	As I keep watching the blue sea,
waga harakara wa izuko zo to	Where are my brothers and sisters?
yobedo sakebedo koe wa naku	Although I call, although I scream, there comes no voice.
tazune sagasedo kagemonashi	Although I seek, although I search, there comes no form.

pump organ which appropriately carries the Miki trademark. A vignette beyond her shows eight Japanese gentlemen playing respectively two bugles, a clarinet, bass viol, violin, accordion (the only man dressed in hakama), Chinese flute, and a Chinese moon guitar (*gekkin*). There is also one girl shown playing the shamisen. The Chinese instruments relate to yet another musical facet of Meiji life, the brief flurry of interest (begun in the Edo period) in forming Chinese instrumental ensembles. This so-called *minshingaku* or *seigaku* tradition

Example 12C: Rappa-bushi

Text of Example 12C: Rappa-bushi

ima naru tokei wa hachi ji han	The clock is now striking half past eight.
sore ni okurerya jūeisō	Anybody late will be thrown in the brig.
kondo no yasumi ga nai ja nashi	Even on Sundays
hanase gunto ni sabi ga tsuku	An idle sword will get rusty
toko tottotto	*Toko tottotto*

created a separate market for music books published in Chinese notation. Some of the instruments used in these ensembles, particularly the moon guitar, were put to more plebian use as shown in this illustration.

The 1892 song collection has an English and a Japanese preface, one in each "front" of the book. The English preface is printed in florid type and begins, "The work of Japanese Popular Music to a class of both foreigners and Japanese amateurs, is doubtless a new type to many into whose hands this book may fall," and moves on to ever more involved and incomprehensible verbiage, the triumph of which is the following paragraph:

As for those who desire to know what is to be played in Japanese "Egyptian hall," or, by "Menageric," this book will no doubt suit to them, to whom our desire is this that, if great economy would render and the requirement might meet, the extent of which distribution should more or less have given them the benefit.

The preface ends with thanks to a Mr. Sakai, "who has completely assisted us during the course of preparation of this work, especially for aids of English readers."

The Japanese preface in Edo script extols the beauties of the music, and continues with an author's explanation of the great flourishing of music in Japan and the ability of one to play these old and new Japanese songs on any instrument thanks to the notation system. Next there is a twelve-page explanation of the notation system using the violin fingerboard as the basic frame of reference and including certain other rudiments of music such as rhythm and Italian tempo markings. The introduction ends with one page each devoted to special instructions for the accordion, violin, and organ, plus an additional three pages of advertisements concerning each of these instruments.

A perusal of the actual musical content shows that the editors have indeed included Edo pieces and more recent favorites. The 1811 *nagauta* piece, "*Echigo jishi*," is represented by an excerpt, while two versions are given of "*Kappore*," a very popular Meiji stage dance (*buyō*) which developed out of a late Edo period folk-style shrine dance. The piece "*O Edo nihombashi*" appears. Its text is related to an old seventeenth-century song, "*Hakone-bushi*," as well as to the Meiji piece, "*Kochae-bushi*," which in turn belongs to the novelty tune category discussed earlier.[32] A famous limerick song from the Edo period, "*Dodoitsu*" is included as well as a piece, "*Ryūkyū-bushi*." The latter originated as a Ryukyuan song brought to Japan in the Edo period. During Meiji it was revived in the pleasure districts with several new verses added of a distinctly more mod-

---

[32] See Atsumi Seitarō, *Hōgaku buyō jiten* (Tokyo: Tomoyama Shobō, 1956), p. 258.

ern flavor such as the following: "Liquor, brandy, champagne, beer. I want to see a drunken brawl."[33]

From a purely musical standpoint two salient features emerge from this collection. All the twenty-six pieces are firmly rooted in the Edo-oriented *yō-in* scale system; the *ryō-ritsu* traditions of *gagaku* found in the school books have little place here. The second feature of this music collection is how very inappropriately it is arranged for Western instruments. Most of it is filled with disjunct skips and occasional double notes which are much more appropriate to the shamisen than to the organ or accordion. We find in this collection, then, the other side of the musical coin. If the school collections were ill-suited for the use of traditional instruments, many of the public popular song collections were equally unrewarding on Western instruments even though, in the latter case, flexibility was intended.

A charming illustration of the optimism of the general public and the music publishers concerning the inevitable blend of traditional and Western music in Japan is found in an illustration from an 1894 self-instruction book for the accordion shown in Plate II.[34] Two well-dressed Japanese ladies are shown sitting before a properly arranged tokonoma, warming themselves by a hibachi and playing duets on the accordion and shamisen. The notation used in this book is numerical with a special set of Japanese numbers for the buttons on the accordion (or perhaps more accurately a concertina). The repertoire begins with the national anthem, *"Chō-chō,"* and *"Haru no yayoi"* and then moves on to three *minshingaku* pieces. The remaining twenty-two pieces are popular Meiji songs including many of the same works found in the 1892 collection discussed above.

[33] This text is from *Nihon zokkyoku shū,* p. 9. Additional verses and the historical material are found in Nakauchi Chōji, *Nihon onkyoku zenshū*: Vol. VII, *Zokkyoku zenshū* (Tokyo: Nihon Onkyoku Zenshū Kankōkai, 1927), 124.

[34] *Tekukin dokukeiko,* ed. T. Miyaji (Osaka: Yushogenhan, 1894).

The continual success of pieces in the more popular idiom eventually led to the creation of works by better composers. The best known is the 1901 composition *"Kōjō no tsuki"* by Taki Rentarō (1879-1903) shown in Example 13. Note that it

Example 13: Kōjō no tsuki

Text of Example 13: Kōjō no tsuki

Haru kōrō no hana no en	At the flower-viewing party of the spring castle,
meguru sakazuki kage sashite	Circling sake cups are shaded by
chiyo no matsu ga e, wake ideshi	Ancient pine trees with branches inseparable.
mukashi no hikari, ima izuko	Where is the ancient glory?

also emphasizes the *in* scale except for a compromising E sharp in measure three which turns the opening phrase towards the standard Western minor scale. This note is found in the fully harmonized version of the piece, which, perhaps as a result of Taki's training in Germany, sounds very much like Schubert. However, it is interesting to note that many Japanese who learned the piece orally return this note to its native position on E natural. For all of the westernization of Japanese musical life, the pieces reflecting the older tonal sounds seem still to strike a responsive chord in the hearts of the Japanese man in the street.

Composition in the Meiji Period

We have spent some time discussing popular music not only because it is a useful reflection of the habits of the Japanese people but also because, during this period, there is little one can say about the composition of more serious Western-style music in Japan. We have noted earlier that the emphasis of the Tokyo Music School was on instrumental ability and teacher training. In such a situation, composition was very slow to develop except among those fortunate graduates who were able to study abroad. One of the first distinguished alumnae of this school, Kōda Nobu (1870-1946) is said to have written a sonata in 1897. The famous composer of popular and children's songs mentioned earlier, Taki Rentarō, wrote at least a minuet and another short instrumental piece.[35] In 1905 Kitamura Suehara (1872-1931) wrote a cantata-like piece, "*Roei no yume*" based on events from the Russo-Japanese War. This has been considered by some to be the first Japanese operatic work and can perhaps be compared in quality with a 1906 production of the *nō* play, "*Hagoromo*," which used Western-style singers and a piano-organ accompaniment.[36] However, by the end of the Meiji period (1912) no really significant Western-style compositions were available for the several competent Japanese performers who now began to appear. The first big name in composition, Yamada Koscak (Kōsaku) (b. 1886), was just starting his intensive musical training in Germany at this time, while most of the others who were to become important in the development of this field were still children or not yet born when the Meiji period closed. Nevertheless, the major problem

[35] Togashi Yasushi, *Nihon no Sakkyokuka* (Tokyo: Ongaku no Tomo Sha, 1956), pp. 11-14.
[36] Iwaki Heijirō, "How Japan's Musical Awakening was Brought About," *Musical America*, 31 (Jan., 1930), 29-31.

they were to inherit was already firmly established by this time, namely, what kind of compromise should the sensitive Japanese composer make between his own cultural background and that of the West? The answers of these Western-style composers to this question begin to appear in the Taishō period, but some answers from composers in the traditional genres were already available.

Since koto was one of the instruments most closely connected with the Tokyo Music School, it is not surprising to find koto musicians involved in new compositional experiments. They concentrated on two areas: new tunings, and new techniques and sonorities derived from Western ideals. We shall discuss them in that order.

The experiments with new tunings was a logical one in the case of the koto since the pitch of each of its thirteen strings is controlled by an individual movable bridge. Even before the Meiji period there were over a dozen common tunings for the instrument. In fact, the three main sources of Meiji tuning experiments—Chinese modes, *gagaku* modes, and Western scales—had already been tried before the new era began. The first known use of the Western scale in koto music is found in a piece, "*Oranda manzai*," written by Ishimura Kengyō sometime between 1804 and 1817. The "Holland" (Oranda) in the title refers to the Edo period term for the major scale, the *oranda-chōshi*, the Holland tuning. It also became known later as the *orugoru-chōshi* after the sound of the imported music boxes (*orugoru*). As shown in Example 14, the use of the new scale system in this piece was rather ambiguous. While the basic tonality of the passage transcribed is the *in* scale built on D, the shamisen seems to launch into the major mode in measures five through seven while the koto continues in the previous scale system with only one concession to the new tonality, the E natural in measure seven. Thereafter both instruments settle back into the traditional tone system. This short clash of tonalities is rather unique in koto music and by the Meiji era it was possible to compose an entire piece in major. In general,

Example 14: Oranda manzai

however, the major mode was never as popular in koto music as various harmonized compositions in a compromised *in* scale[37] or in a *gagaku* mode.

The use of *gagaku* modes was relatively simple for Meiji composers since the koto was originally a *gagaku* instrument.

[37] A technical discussion of the reasons behind the particular kind of scale mixtures that occurred between Western and Japanese systems can be read in Michio Kitahara's "Kayokyoku: An Example of Syncretism Involving Scale and Mode," *Ethnomusicology*, x (Sept., 1966), 271-84.

This gave the composers not only other tunings but also certain melodic characteristics found in the stereotyped patterns of the older koto music. This can be seen by comparing the typical *shizugaki* pattern played on the *gagaku* koto (the *gaku-so*) shown in Example 15 with Example 16, part of an

Example 15: Shizugaki Pattern

Example 16: Kōbai

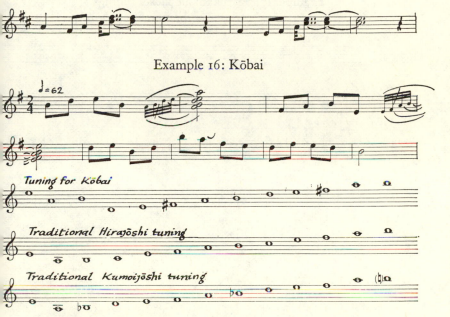

instrumental interlude from the 1904 piece "*Kōbai*" by Suzuki Teruo (1875-1931).[38] The tuning of this piece is based on the *gagaku oshiki* mode. To show how much of a change this is from traditional practice, the actual tuning of the strings for this piece have been included in Example 16 immediately above two common koto tunings of the Edo period.

[38] The composer went under several names including Suzuki Koson, Nachi Shuse, and Nachi Toshinobu. See *Ongaku jiten*, v, p. 241; and Tanabe Hisao, *Nihon ongaku-shi* (Tokyo: Tokyo Denki Daigaku, 1963), p. 254.

The Chinese-style tuning was called *kankan-chōshi* and was derived from the Chinese-inspired *minshingaku* mentioned earlier. In the 1888 composition, "*Mikuni no homare*," the Osaka musician, Kikutaka Kengyō, has tuned two koto differently as seen in Example 17. A short excerpt from the open-

Example 17: Two kankan-chōshi tunings
for "Mikuni no homare"

ing of the piece is shown. Perhaps the upward sliding note is meant to give the music a Chinese sound. The music that follows is not particularly unique though the piece is of historical interest since it was written in direct praise of the Meiji government.[39]

[39] *Ongaku jiten*, x, 136. The text and commentary on all the pieces in this section of the paper are found in the notes by Kikkawa Eiji to the Nippon Victor record album SLR-510-3, *Sōkyoku to jiuta no rekishi*. The notations of these pieces were made by the author from

The use of two different tunings in *"Mikuni no homare"* relates in part to the new technical advances in koto music during the Meiji era. It had been common practice throughout the late Edo period to add second koto parts to pieces as upper obligatos. However, in Meiji we often find that there is a greater interest in exploiting the lower range of koto sounds. This technique seems to be inspired by the bass parts so evident in the Western music heard in Japan at that time. Such an interest in creating a bass line is quite obvious in the excerpt shown in Example 18 from the 1907 piece *"Mitsu no keshiki"*

Example 18: Mitsu no keshiki

by Kikutaka Kengyō (1846-1910). We can see in this piece the beginnings of the great struggle between a music tradition which is basically melodically oriented and a world in which chords are a presumed underpinning for every tune. Pianistic effects were tried on the koto by plucking the strings with both hands while typical violin harmonies were added to the sounds available on the koto. All these attempts to produce a richer

---

this album and are not necessarily those of the original scores, which were not available at the time of writing.

sonority and a clearer bass line in koto ensembles were cli-
maxed in 1921 when Miyagi Michio (1894-1956), a young blind
koto player recently returned from Korea, used a seventeen-
stringed bass koto in the composition "*Rakuyō no odori.*" The
opening of this piece is shown in Example 19. From the opening cadenzas to the full bodied tutti section this composition
speaks of a new music for a new Japan.

By the time we reach "*Rakuyō no odori*" we have passed
beyond the formative period of Meiji and are entering into an
era of more daring innovation in both Western and traditional
music in Japan. After World War I Japanese music history is
filled with the formation of new musical societies, concert
ensembles, and composers' alliances. Thus, it would seem that
we have traced the flow of musical modernization in Japan
from its headwaters to a point at which flood gates were suddenly opened. It remains for us to assess the degree of modernization that actually did take place during the Meiji period.

How Modernized Was Meiji Music?

We have spoken about several different kinds of music in
the Meiji period but our emphasis has been primarily upon
school and popular music. The reason for this is that these two
forms seem to be the most significant in terms of lasting
changes brought about in the modernization of Japanese musical life. Church music and military music were basically stuck
onto Japanese culture and, while both popular in their own
way, did not become significant factors in Japanese music after
World War I. Traditional music did react in its own ways as
shown earlier but for the most part remained in the musical
frame of reference which was traditional in nature. By the
end of Meiji, Western-style composition had hardly begun.
School music and popular song, however, were at their height
by the end of the period.

We have shown that the tonalities and tunes of the school
tradition and the popular songs were often quite different and
that the influence of one upon the other was rather slight as

Example 19: Rakuyō no odori

compared with their separate borrowings from other styles. In the period after Meiji, popular music continued its eclectic course and thus has kept its creativity along with its heavy doses of banality sweetened by an occasional catchy or touching song. School music has barely changed in the last fifty years in Japan and thus it still is without a direct connection with the outside world.

The importance of school music is not its repertoire or style but rather its orientation. The fact that the first music appreciation records dealing with Japanese music for use in the middle schools appeared in 1960 is rather ample proof that the public schools were patently disinterested in that genre. The dreams of Izawa came to no reality. However, the training of generations of Japanese youth to a harmonically oriented music has created a series of mental blocks which shut out the special musical potentials of traditional styles. Since musicians in Japan were at one time students too, most of them suffer from the same problem. It has only been with the violent shift of social and intellectual ideas that followed World War II that some Japanese composers have been able to see greater possibilities in their native idioms than merely the harmonization of Japanese tunes. The recent experiments of such composers as Mamiya Michio, Takemitsu Tōru, and Mayazumi Toshirō may indeed have been aided by the fact that Western composers themselves have been seeking totally new orientations and structures in their music. Whatever the reason, the results are far more original and filled with potentials for creative developments than the products we have previously been discussing.

If modernization means "making to conform to present usage, style, or taste," then only parts of the Meiji musical scene can be called truly modern. However, the fascination of Meiji music lies primarily in the many old-fashioned legacies that managed to merge with the new trends and to create products which could be accepted as historically modern but which still could never be mistaken as anything but Japanese.

PART THREE

The Search for Identity in Literature

Introduction

THE development of modern literary forms was a slower and more complex process than producing the first successful oil paintings. In the creation of an artistic work, the process from observation to expression is more direct for a painter than for a writer of fiction. In addition to the different problems posed by the intellectual process of the writer, Japanese authors had the difficulty of evolving genre forms and a literary style for a society that was passing through the most awkward years of its adaptation to the modern world. It was necessary to evolve a language style appropriate to modern writing, one that was both precise and graceful, that would harmonize with the modern colloquial language and yet retain literary quality. It took time to gain a mature conception of the European novel or play. Familiarity with Western literature came through a tutorial process, first by translating Western novels into Japanese. This inspired a vogue for writing political novels in the eighties. Although these novels had little literary merit, they contributed to shaping the concept and practice of fiction writing and to its acceptance as an activity proper for men of education and social standing. The first serious attempts at writing modern fiction were made in the late eighties by Futabatei Shimei and Mori Ōgai, but it was almost two more decades before mature practice of the art in a language style suited to the genre became prevalent, and before a reading public was prepared to recognize this writing as literature.

This stage of development in the novel was reached just after the turn of the century in the realistic novels of Shimazaki Tōson, discussed here by Professor McClellan, and in the writings of Natsume Sōseki and those of their contemporaries. Although Tōson and Sōseki are very different writers, we find in both authors the close observation and careful depiction of contemporary society undergoing change, and especially the psychological strain of these changes on intellectuals and on the authors themselves. Professor Hibbett's study of Sōseki's psychological novels demonstrates how much the modern artist differs from the premodern. He must arrive at his own individual view of the world to a far greater extent than was necessary (or permitted) in the more ordered traditional society. In searching for an understanding of himself and his role in society, he undergoes an intense personal crisis. He must deal with a society that is becoming increasingly complex and impersonal.

Sōseki was a student of English literature who rediscovered Japanese literature and then found his calling in combining the two traditions. It was through his close friend Shiki that his appreciation of Japanese poetry was revived. Shiki is known best as a haiku poet, but his role in reinvigorating the classical tanka form, described in Professor Brower's paper, illustrates how in this genre too his principle of direct, realistic description drew both from the tradition of Western painting and from the directness of the Japanese poetic style of the eighth-century anthology, the *Manyōshū*.

Two other forms of literary activity are represented, in Professor Seidensticker's paper on the critic Kobayashi Hideo and Professor Ortolani's discussion of the playwright Fukuda Tsuneari. These writers began their work several decades later and have continued as leaders in their fields in the postwar period. They are not concerned merely with assessing the spirit of the contemporary Japanese intellectual; they have conducted their own individual rediscovery of Japanese culture and their own reinterpretation of the West. To evaluate the performance of contemporary writers and thinkers or to write for a present-day audience, they have felt impelled to reexamine Western culture and Japanese tradition, which together have produced the intricately blended product that is modern Japan.

CHAPTER VIII

Natsume Sōseki and the Psychological Novel

HOWARD S. HIBBETT

THE psychological novel is often regarded as one of those ingenious Western inventions, such as the camera or the phonograph, which were eagerly imported into Japan and then produced by the Japanese themselves in impressive numbers. No doubt the overwhelming influence of Russian, French, and English fiction accounts for much of the technical skill of certain Meiji novelists, beginning in the late 1880's with Futabatei Shimei, at depicting the inner lives of characters—usually frustrated intellectuals—from their own world. Both in structure and in finely grained realistic detail their novels are indebted to Western prototypes, as are many of the ideas embodied in them. But literary history seldom fosters confidence in the inevitability of progress, least of all at a time of rapid cultural change, though it amply illustrates the influence of technologies and ideologies on the arts. The novels of Natsume Sōseki (1867-1916) represent a unique achievement in modern Japanese literature, rather than a mere stage in its development; and an exploration of their special qualities leads into the labyrinth of his personality and of the socio-cultural milieu in which he lived. His mastery of the psychological novel reflects the complex experience of a man who was at once highly idiosyncratic and sensitive to the pressures of his age.

Of course the assiduous student of comparative literature need not be daunted by Sōseki's splendidly evasive answer ("There is hardly a book I have read that has not had some influence on me") to the interviewer who asked him about the influence of Meredith on his work. (34.213)[1] But even clear-

[1] Parenthetical references throughout this paper are to *Sōseki zenshū* (Iwanami Shoten, 34 vols., 1956-57). For a convenient bibliographical

cut relationships—the acknowledged influence of X on Y—
rarely afford much insight into the qualities of a master, except
for his capacity to transform techniques and materials to his
own ends. And here the problem is complicated by the fact that
Sōseki had read so widely in several languages, including the
Chinese, and in the vast range of European thought and literature to which he had access through his remarkable command
of English. If we must seek his antecedents among such dissimilar writers as Jane Austen and Dostoevsky, we can scarcely
expect to trace a clear line of descent from the Western to the
Japanese psychological novel. Nor can we overlook the fact
that Sōseki, who wrote embarrassingly bad English verse, was
an accomplished poet in Chinese forms—his *kanshi* are the
finest of the modern era—and in haiku. Even his grimmer
novels are enhanced by impressionistic touches in the long
native tradition of aesthetic sensibility.

Again, it is not irrelevant that the Japanese literary tradition
includes the first great psychological novel of the world, the
Genji monogatari, and that even its earliest literary criticism,
in the preface to the *Kokinshū*, recognizes the primary importance of the emotions in literature. Murasaki's apologia for the
art of fiction begins by asserting its claims against those of history, with a Balzacian eye for particulars rather than an Aristotelian concern for universals, but she goes on to stress the role
of the author as a witness who is emotionally involved: "The
storyteller's own experience of men and things . . . has moved
him to an emotion so passionate that he can no longer keep it
shut up in his heart."[2] Poetic truth, analogous to the expedient
teachings (*hōben*) of the Buddhist scriptures, is the novelist's
aim, and his justification for a subjective stress on feelings
instead of facts. The diary and the fragmentary but reflective

---

guide to Sōseki, see *Kindai bungaku kenkyū hikkei* (Gakutōsha, 1961),
pp. 197-206, as well as the fuller survey in Naruse Masakatsu, et al.,
Ōgai Sōseki (*Kokugo kokubungaku kenkyūshi taisei*, Vol. 14, Sansei-
dō, 1965).

[2] Arthur Waley, tr., *The Tale of Genji* (New York, 1935), p. 501.

essay (*zuihitsu*) are other subjective genres that contribute to this long literary tradition.

To be sure, Heian modes of psychological realism derive from an unselfconscious subjectivity which is in sharp contrast to the self-preoccupation of modern Japanese novelists, the "awareness of being different" common to all variations of their response to the West. In the later works of Sōseki even the traditional reliance on intuition and aesthetic sensibility seems to have been largely supplanted by analytical, intellectual tendencies, a respect in which his novels owe a particularly heavy debt to the West. Kawabata Yasunari, who calls them "the most mature psychological fiction of modern Japan,"[3] goes on to discuss a kind of "Japanese psychological analysis," more contemplative than rigorously analytical, which is characteristic of the egocentric "I-novel" (*watakushi shōsetsu*)—and, it may be added, of Kawabata's own superb blending of traditional and modern techniques. Yet these are distinctions among essentially introspective novelists, even though their pages are usually filled with conflict between the individual and his family, rather than within himself. Partly as a consequence of the search for a modern "self" (*jiga*), and of the frustrations of a slowly developing individualism, some degree of alienation and isolation has set the Japanese novelist off from his society at the same time that he has attempted to deal with these problems by the method of introspection.

An uneasy, self-critical individualism, then, has been both a crucial theme of the modern Japanese psychological novel and the basis of its chief technical innovation. For Sōseki, individualism was a subject for profound reflection, expressed both dramatically in his novels and abstractly in lectures and essays. As a novelist he found this problem central to his vocation: by a process of critical self-examination, familar enough in the development of modern Western literature but exceptionally difficult in the social and cultural circumstances of Meiji Japan, he made his own tortured experience the focus of a more pene-

[3] *Shōsetsu no kōsei* (Gan Bunko, 1946), p. 121.

trating gaze than that of any of the obviously "autobiographical" novelists. Because Sōseki permitted himself a wide range of fictional invention, unlike the writers who tended to regard naked self-revelation as the height of sincerity, he felt free to direct his keen intelligence toward his own innermost feelings—his anxiety, his guilt, his ambivalent sense of pride and humiliation. And these feelings, however exacerbated by his psychological predisposition toward them, were closely related to his role as an intellectual, a student of Western culture, and thus had an immediate appeal to the members of the self-conscious late Meiji intellectual elite—and to the wider circle of educated people whose attitudes they helped to formulate. Further, and more important, his novels were charged with wit, drama, and intense emotional force. As a novelist of alienation, Sōseki had the Chekhovian gift of depicting boredom and depression without being boring or depressing, and the memorably unhappy characters of his fictional world have always engaged the sympathies of a broad reading public.

Yet Sōseki's literary success was not easily won. His debut as a novelist was preceded by many years of study and teaching, against a background of poverty, domestic discord, and neurotic suffering. Throughout his increasingly brilliant career he struggled to portray an existential despair which only his stoic self-discipline enabled him to confront. The evidence that he eventually exorcised his private demons is scanty and unconvincing. If in late years he seemed to have only a lingering uneasiness about his vocation, unlike the radical lack of confidence of Futabatei Shimei, for example, he never ceased to emphasize the bitterness of isolation, alienation, loneliness—which his protagonist in *Kokoro* explained as "the price we have to pay for being born in this modern age, so full of freedom, independence, and our own egotistical selves." (12.33)[4] Even the lecture on "My Individualism" (*Watakushi no kojin shugi*) which he delivered at the Gakushūin in 1914, only two years before his death, had somewhat lugubrious undertones

[4] Edwin McClellan, tr. (Chicago, 1957), p. 30.

for the occasion of an inspirational talk by a famous man of letters. The deceptively mild adjective *sabishii*—"lonely"—re-echoes as a description of the "other side" of individualism. "Thus, on the other side lurks a loneliness of which people are unaware. Since I choose to seek my own way, apart from any faction, and similarly do not hinder others from seeking theirs, it is inevitable that we must sometimes go off in our separate directions. That is lonely." (21.152) To find the right "way" (*michi*) may take ten years, or twenty, or a lifetime of work, he had told his young audience, but to attain that self-realization would be worth any sacrifice. "No doubt some of you will experience the sort of anguish which I have suffered." (21.143)

Although Sōseki's sketchy account of his trials earlier in the lecture is understandably reticent, he does recall some of the vagaries of his education—being required to memorize a chronological list of the works of Sir Walter Scott, for instance—and especially his own groping attempts to understand the meaning of literature. His apprenticeship as a writer was long delayed by his misdirected but indispensable scholarly efforts, for him an extended intellectual "moratorium" which helped him to achieve a place "among the great men who came upon their most decisive contribution only after a change of direction and not without neurotic involvement at the time of the break-through to their specific creativity."[5] A member of the troubled generation that grew up with the Meiji era, Sōseki was born in the year before Kitamura Tōkoku, a few years before the literary constellation of Doppo, Katai, Shūsei, and Tōson, and shared the rebellious independence—and the uncertainties—of the many young men educated under the new Western-influenced school system yet unable either to play their anticipated role in molding the future of the nation or to overcome their nostalgia for the secure values and social harmony of the forsaken past. By the time he found his métier as a novelist, Japanese intellectuals had entered the period of disillusionment and disaffection that followed the Russo-Japanese War. Like Bashō,

[5] Erik H. Erikson, *Young Man Luther* (New York, 1962), p. 45.

Sōseki lived the traditional span of fifty years and accomplished his most important work only in his last decade.

Indeed, it was during and after his last prolonged attack of mental suffering that Sōseki produced his finest novels—the novels in which he expressed his deepest insights into his own character and created psychological fiction of unsurpassed brilliance. Biographers have drawn heavily on these works, most of all on *Michikusa*, his one transparently autobiographical novel; and critics have usually identified Sōseki with their unhappy protagonists (in spite of his insistence on the freedom to invent whatever he pleased) as well as with the successively older and more dejected protagonists of the series of novels which preceded them. Psychiatrists have also stressed the importance of these late works for the understanding of Sōseki's own mental difficulties. *Kōjin*, which he began in 1912 shortly after the onset of the attack, has been used as the major document in Chitani Shichirō's detailed pathography, *Sōseki no byōseki*,[6] the most ambitious study of its kind. Perhaps the chief point demonstrated by the extensive literature on Sōseki— more extensive than on any other modern Japanese writer—is that a wider, rather than a narrower scrutiny of the collected works and of the primary biographical sources remains the best way to minimize (though it cannot eliminate) the danger of circular argument from *vie* to *oeuvre* and back again. For-

---

[6] (Keisō Shobō, 1963). But see also Shiozaki Yoshio, *Sōseki, Ryūnosuke no seishin ijō* (Hakuyōsha, 1957), a less dogmatic analysis based on a wider range of sources. Though emphasizing Sōseki's delusional states, Dr. Shiozaki ascribes most of his mental difficulties to reactive character traits instilled by early environmental influences. A broad study of Sōseki's personality, with more attention to social and cultural factors, will be found in the forthcoming work *Alienation and the Japanese Intellectual*, by George DeVos and Hiroshi Wagatsuma. Very different in aim and method are some recent studies by Doi Takeo: a chapter on *Michikusa* in *Seishin bunseki* (Sōgensha, 1967) and a series of articles on Sōseki's novels in *Kaishaku to kanshō*, beginning with *Botchan* in Vol. 32, No. 11 (1967), pp. 179-86. Dr. Doi analyzes Sōseki's novels on their own terms, without reference to the author's life, but uses psychoanalytic concepts in interpreting them.

tunately, there is a mass of biographical material—diaries, letters, memoirs, essays—to be scrutinized. Sōseki is obviously a tempting subject for a case study of the vexed question of the relations between art and neurosis: it is no wonder that psychiatrists as well as literary scholars have interrogated the novels in trying to reveal the hidden secrets of his life, nor, in view of the complexity of the interrelationship between art and life, that they have as yet failed to discover many of what Proust called "the secret links, the necessary metamorphoses existing between the life of a writer and his work, between reality and art."[7]

Still, for a novelist of such an introspective cast of mind as Sōseki, an analysis of his achievement as a writer of psychological fiction requires some confrontation of the psychology of the author with psychology in the novels. This is not to imply that all the available evidence is sufficient to diagnose "the case of Sōseki" and then duly employ this finding as a diagnostic tool to reveal the hidden patterns within his fiction. Even Dr. Chitani, a translator of Ludwig Klages and a constitutional psychiatrist who has long specialized in endogenous depression, makes a weak argument, both from a literary-biographical point of view and from that of many of his fellow psychiatrists, for his diagnosis of Sōseki as a victim of *naiinsei utsubyō* (*endogene Depression*, in the German terminology of his school). For all his care to avoid faulty interpretations (a colleague sent him a psychoanalytic study of Sōseki,[8] he tells us,

---

[7] *Jean Santeuil* (Paris, 1952), I, 54.

[8] Kitayama Takashi, *Natsume Sōseki no seishin bunseki* (Okakura Shobō, 1938). This pioneering work, one of a series which included "psychoanalyses" of Issa and Napoleon, applied Freudian concepts with more enthusiasm than discrimination. Still, it anticipates most of the later efforts of Ara Masahito and others to analyze the "dark aspect" of Sōseki. Another early study of Sōseki's inner world is Yoshida Rokurō, *Sakka izen no Sōseki* (Shibundō, 1942). Yoshida writes in the familiar intuitive, impressionistic vein of Japanese literary criticism, but his views have influenced the work of Etō Jun, whose *Natsume Sōseki* (Tokyo Raifu-sha, 1956; rev. ed., Keisō Shobō,

but he has never glanced into it), Dr. Chitani's pathography itself suffers from an excessive narrowing of attention to the three critical periods of Sōseki's life—especially to the third of these and to its product *Kōjin*—in which his depressions appear to have been most severe.

As Dr. Chitani points out, Sōseki's condition has been variously attributed to such grave maladies as schizophrenia, paranoia, a borderline schizoid manic-depressive state, and the virulent influence of Rousseau. In his own study, which omits any account of Sōseki's life before the first clearly defined attack (in 1894 at the age of twenty-seven), a heavy stress on biologically determined periodicity has the effect of remolding life and works into the shape of a considerably simplified case history. A notably unhappy childhood is by no means the sole explanation of Sōseki's lifelong depressive tendencies, or of all his other disturbing behavior, nor is it quite the same "cold, sad shadow" darkening his childhood memories, as he recalls them in his final memoirs *Garasudo no naka*, that extends over all his mature novels. But Sōseki himself felt an increasing need to probe the old wounds of his childhood and youth; and the relationship between these motifs from his past and the themes of all his work, including his later novels, illustrates the importance which his early experiences had for him.

To be sure, it was only in *Michikusa*, written the year before his death, that Sōseki approached, though he scarcely approximated, the directness of autobiographical reference of the Naturalists and of their successors, the I-novelists. After *Botchan* he discarded the satirical, comic mask which had protected him in his self-portrait as Mr. Kushami in *Wagahai wa neko de aru*, his earliest success; and after the experiment of writing a "haiku novel" (*Kusamakura*), he abandoned, at least in his novels, even the defense of aesthetic withdrawal from the prob-

---

1965) is the most stimulating of the many postwar studies. Etō has perhaps done more than any other critic to "peel away the myth" from the image of Sōseki fashioned by his loyal pupils and enshrined in the standard biography by Komiya Toyotaka.

lems which most disturbed him. From time to time he continued to indulge a taste for fantasy first expressed in *Rondontō* and several other strange, romantic short stories, but in general his fictional method was a low-keyed dramatic shaping of materials related only obliquely to his own experience. For this he was criticized by many of his contemporaries as lacking in "sincerity"—the virtue which sanctioned the almost ritual self-exposure of members of the confessionalist school. Startling as this criticism might seem, except in the context of a moralizing insistence on the frank identification of author and protagonist, Sōseki occasionally felt it necessary to assert the value of fiction, of the "fabricated" (*koshiraemono*), and to disclaim such autobiographical elements as were thought to exist in his novels. Yet the intensity of feeling beneath their polished surface suggests a strong emotional involvement with his material, in spite of the distance which he was careful to maintain between himself and his readers. His plots are often built around oddly similar triangles (a woman loved by two men who are close friends, one of them harrowed by guilt or suspicion) which are only incidentally related to the familiar adultery theme of modern Western fiction. Sōseki's sources appear to go back far beyond his conventionally dutiful married life, and the imported conventions of the European novel, to emotions which were already stirred in him by the traumatic events of his childhood. It is hardly surprising that the massive documentation of his life yields no support to the frequent assumption that he was once in love with another woman. Again, one is reminded of Bashō, whose most lurid biographers have been able to produce nothing more Byronic than an insubstantial theory that he may, just possibly, have had a mistress.

Early in 1915, before beginning *Michikusa*, Sōseki wrote a series of desultory memoirs in the course of which he looked back on his childhood as the youngest son of a proud but, after the unsettling changes of the Restoration, somewhat impoverished family of hereditary local official status. Twice sent out to be cared for by other, socially inferior families, he was nine years old before he was reluctantly brought home to live with his actual parents, after "some strange trouble occurred in the family that had adopted me." His foster parents (as he later learned them to be) had had only a quasi-filial relationship with the older couple whom he had been told were his grand-parents, and who were in fact his parents. This formidable identity confusion, still later to be confounded by legal complications, was not readily resolved. "When I was taken from Asakusa to Ushigome, I had no idea that I had returned to my real home, and still thought of my parents only as my grandparents. Quite unsuspectingly, I went on calling them grand-father and grandmother as usual. For their part, possibly thinking it unwise to correct me abruptly, they gave no indication that I was really their son." (17.177)

One night a maidservant was kind enough to dispel his illusion, he tells us, which made him extremely happy. "I was happy not because I had learned the truth from her but simply because of her kindness to me." (17.178) His gratitude to the maid suggests that she was another of the several substitute mothers to whom he had had to turn for affection. Apparently his "real mother" (*jitsubo*) remained a more or less remote figure to him, though he was already fourteen years old when she died. Born to her at forty, the last of her three daughters and five sons, he had been a considerable embarrassment to his aging parents as well as an additional burden at a time when the family fortunes were declining. (Ironically, especially in view of his later exaggerated concern for money, he was given the name Kinnosuke, with the character for "gold," in order to avert the danger that a child born on the inauspicious day of February 9, 1867 would become a great thief.) But her aloofness seems to have strengthened his sense of mingled awe and admiration, to judge from the passage about her in his memoirs.

I should like to write something here in memory of my mother, but I am afraid I can only summon up a few reminiscences of her.

314

Mother's name was Chie, a word that is still dear to me. I feel as if it were her name alone, and could not belong to any other woman. Fortunately, I have never met another woman named Chie. . . .

Being mischievous and stubborn, I was not treated by Mother with the indulgence usually shown toward a youngest child. Yet my memories of her are always warmed by the feeling that of all my family it was she who gave me the most affection. However that may be, she was without doubt a woman of grace and refinement. And everyone could see that she was more intelligent than Father. Even my difficult elder brother held her in great respect.

"Mother doesn't say a word, but there's something awesome about her."

I can still call up this remark of his out of the dark, distant past. But it is only a fragmentary memory, as uncertain as a text restored from a watery, flowing script. And beyond these few fragments everything about my mother seems like a dream. (17.192-95)

Sōseki's (Kinnosuke's) father, though much older, outlived his wife for sixteen years. He emerges only briefly in the memoirs, and in a harsh light: "I remember in particular how cruelly my father treated me." (17.177)

In contrast, Sōseki's young foster parents Shiobara Shōnosuke and his wife Yasu were very indulgent with him, as were doubtless the shopkeeper and his wife (a sister of one of the Natsume family's maids) who had taken care of him in infancy. But the time-honored Japanese institution of the wet nurse, and the practice of putting a younger child out to adoption with a family linked by ties of obligation, turned out badly in his case when he felt himself caught in a web of deception spun by the Shiobaras' efforts to claim his filial gratitude for their own selfish purposes. Shiobara had once been a dependent of the Natsume family, and was further indebted to the elder Natsume for having been reinstated in his father's office as ward chief (*nanushi*) in Yotsuya, from which he was afterward transferred to a position in Asakusa. Later it was discovered that he had used his office to register the boy as his real son, a device which would have enabled him to make a legal claim for support in his old age. This piece of chicanery came to light as a result of the "strange trouble" when Shiobara, after taking up with a widow in the neighborhood, began to have violent quarrels with his wife, was divorced by her, and, what was worse, was deprived of his foster son by the Natsumes, who took both wife and child back to their own home. Although Sōseki's feelings of distrust were heightened by these incidents, and by the numerous attempts of Shiobara to claim money from him, his awareness of hypocrisy and deception seems to have been awakened early by the anxious solicitude of his foster parents. At the same time, their rivalry for his affections must have strengthened his narcissistic defenses, among them a thoroughly instilled sense of being a superior person, as well as created an unconscious guilt for his evident advantage over his rival in this ultimately and dramatically shattered family triangle. Indeed, the vicissitudes of his childhood appear to have influenced him decisively toward his deep-seated sense of doubt and mistrust, his endless search for autonomy, partly within and partly in defiance of the traditional value system, and his lifelong burden of anxiety. We need not hypothesize secret love affairs to account for fantasies of obscure sexual guilt which are embodied in so much of his fiction.

Thus, by the age of nine, back in his gloomy, out-of-the-way ancestral home at Ushigome, Sōseki was already well prepared for a lifetime in which events would conspire to intensify his hatred for the father, "real" or foster, and for all those other menacing figures of authority—policemen, detectives, rich men, politicians, government and university officials, even teachers, a role he himself was to play. His unconscious identification with these more or less aggressive males, sometimes revealed by flashes of envy, sometimes by literary fantasies, contributed to an ambivalent pattern of alternating rebellion and passivity as Sōseki attempted to extract from an untrustworthy world the warmth and regard which he kept telling himself he ought not to expect from it. This is by no means to imply that his future development had already been determined, or that "external" social forces—to say nothing of his wife—were not to modify the often pathological tendencies in his struggle against a universe of deception. Throughout his life Sōseki attempted with varying success to find a solution in art, in morals, in the role of the intellectual, to problems which had a special urgency for him because of the hidden personal feelings which he projected into them.

Like so many other men of his generation, Sōseki saw his own difficulties as symbolic of the historical predicament of his nation. After decades of study of Western culture he came to the conclusion that even such arduous efforts had yielded only a superficial result, and at the cost of excessive nervous strain. He remained acutely conscious of his position in society as an intellectual—a responsible artist and moralist—and of his cultural identity as a Japanese. But his powerful critical intelligence, colored by an extremely pessimistic temperament, readily discerned the inadequacies both of the alien culture as adopted in Japan since Meiji and of the pure native virtues increasingly eulogized during his adult lifetime. His own desperate search for autonomy—for "individualism"—betrayed at last its relation to the selfish egoism which he had tried to externalize in those persecuting "others" for whom he felt such contempt. Sōseki's novels are the expression of an exemplary creative vigor maintained even during barely subclinical mental illness. However, this illness was itself attuned with paranoid ingenuity to the realities of his environment. Given the pervasive strength of the sense of cultural identity in Japan, it is natural that Sōseki, both as a novelist and as a man, has been customarily seen by Japanese critics as a representative though towering figure of the Meiji intellectual.

Still, to view Sōseki as a public figure with an unhappy but irrelevant private life would be as vitiating as to try to analyze his achievements in the psychological novel without taking into account his heroic efforts to understand his own mental suffering. The fact that he customarily identified his anxieties with the problems of the age is itself at once an influence of the climate of his times, his actual role as an intellectual, and (as he came to recognize) his own inner needs. Because his novels are works of art which express his most intimate feelings and which convey the full complexity of the man, including his irrational, romantic side, they are incomparably more vital than the fairly mellow wisdom of his celebrated lectures and essays. Even his memoirs are reticent, unlike his widow's acidulous *Memories of Sōseki* (*Sōseki no omoide*) or the several books of reminiscences by their younger son Shinroku. It was through the medium of the novel, paradoxically freest to pursue psychological truth when camouflaged by the resources of the imagination, that he was able to confront some of the darker aspects of his own character—not only the notorious neurotic rages, on the whole reserved for his family, but the fastidious intolerance, the stubbornness, meanness, pride, and egotism which were indissolubly allied with his many admirable qualities.

Numerous anecdotes attest to the existence of this meaningful mélange of qualities in Sōseki since his early school years. Even the trivial errors of adults bothered him: he was once distressed to notice that his teacher had written *Kigensetsu* (Empire Day) on the blackboard with *gomben* instead of *itohen* in the first character. He could not resist surreptitiously correcting this mistake while the teacher was out of the room— and for years was haunted by guilt for his premature assumption of authority. His adolescent shyness and isolation were natural enough, after the experience of having been treated as an orphan by his own parents, but even when these difficulties had been mitigated by the friendships of his later school years Sōseki often expressed melancholy feelings in letters to his closest friend, the militant young haiku poet Masaoka Shiki. He had become acquainted with Shiki in 1889, not long before taking the comically perverse pen name of Sōseki (rinse-stone) and beginning his own distinguished career as a haiku poet. At twenty-three, in a letter dated August 9, 1889 and addressed to Shiki in his provincial home town of Matsuyama, Sōseki is characteristically depressed: "Lately, I have come to feel disgusted with life. No matter how hard I try to change my attitude, I cannot help feeling disgusted. And yet I lack the courage to commit suicide—does that mean I am still somewhat human?" (27.17-18) He goes on to diagnose his mental condition as "the disease of misanthropy" (Misanthropic*byō*, with the adjective in English). On November 11, 1891, he writes to Shiki: "Last year I was sick of life, and this year I am still sick of life." (27.39) A few months earlier, before the beginning of his second year in the English literature department of the Tokyo Imperial University, he had told Shiki he was beginning to realize that it was inconceivable for him to become a "Captain of Western literature" (27.29)—that is, as he described it in retrospect, to fulfill his ambition to "master English, write works of high literary value in the foreign tongue, and astonish the Westerners." (34.165)

By the time he was graduated from the university in July of 1893 Sōseki was on the verge of his first critical period of mental disturbance. His knowledge of Chinese literature, which he had long admired, and Japanese literature, an interest fostered especially by Shiki, only served to heighten his uneasiness about his beginning career as a scholar-teacher of English. Disabused of the notion that English literature must be fundamentally the same as Chinese, he found himself obliged to begin practicing his doubtful vocation. Even during subsequent years of teaching in the provinces and of furious study in England he never overcame the sense of having been deceived by English literature, by the dubious alien culture which was invading Japan and which he had wished to study "for the sake of his country." In 1907 when he finally published his *Bungakuron*, the massive but productive failure that was the chief result of many years of scholarship, he prefaced it by explaining that because of his high esteem for Chinese literature, he had wrongly supposed English literature to be an equally rewarding field for a lifetime of study.

Years later, in his lecture on individualism, he again attributed the "uneasiness" (*fuan*) of his early manhood primarily to frustration and disillusionment as a student of English.

My three years at the university ended in the utter failure of my attempt to understand the nature of literature. It is not too much to say that this was the basic cause of my anxiety.

With that uncertain attitude I went out into the world and became, or rather was made into, a teacher. . . . I spent my days in secret melancholy, wondering what would become of me.

Troubled by this sort of uneasiness, I graduated from the university; I took the same uneasiness along to Matsuyama and Kumamoto; even when I went abroad I had the same kind of uneasiness with me, hidden away in the bottom of my heart. (21.137-38)

Apparently Sōseki's first extended period of severe "neurasthenia" (*shinkei suijaku*, then as now the common term for any sort of nervous exhaustion, nervous breakdown, or the like) began in the summer of 1894, shortly after he had suffered from what he thought to be tuberculosis, and lasted for about a year. Toward the end of this period, in April, 1895, he suddenly resigned from his teaching post in Tokyo and went to teach at a middle school in the small town of Matsuyama in Shikoku. The reasons for this self-imposed exile have never been clear, except that Sōseki felt obliged to escape from Tokyo. His choice of Matsuyama reflects another influence of his friend Shiki, whom he had visited there in 1892; in August, 1895, Shiki came back to convalesce after an attack of tuberculosis while in China as a war correspondent, and stayed with Sōseki for more than a month before returning to Tokyo. In late December Sōseki came to Tokyo to meet Nakane Kyōko, a prospective match, and promptly became engaged. In April of 1896 he took up a new position at the Fifth Higher School in Kumamoto, where, in June, he was married. His four years there were comparatively calm, in spite of his wife's tendency to hysterical outbursts and his own *shinkei suijaku* during her uncomfortable pregnancy of late 1898, after a miscarriage the year before. Their first child, a daughter, was born in May, 1899, and the following year he was sent by his government to study in England.

Sōseki's poverty and loneliness during the two years in London, his sense of alienation, his frantic efforts to discover the nature of literature and of cultural differences, and the severe "nervous breakdown" of which he began to show symptoms in the summer of 1901 are well documented in his own writings. The "Bicycle Diary" (*Jitensha nikki*) published soon after his return to Japan describes an attempted cure by cycling, which had been suggested by a friend, as well as something of the deepening suspicions which he held against his several English landladies, so kindly on the surface but constantly spying on him and defaming him, as indeed all the English seemed to be doing, behind his back. Perhaps there was some basis in fact for these suspicions, in view of his odd behavior, if not for his similar earlier suspicions of the nuns at the Hōzōin temple where he had once lodged in Tokyo and of those whom he believed to be spying on him in Matsuyama. But the incident reported by Sōseki's wife as occurring a few days after his return from London confirms other evidence that he was subject to persistent delusions. To account for striking their eldest daughter, who had been sitting quietly on the other side of the *hibachi* from him, he said that a small copper coin that was lying on the rim of the *hibachi* must have been put there as a deliberate insult:

> While in London, he told me, he was taking a walk one day and a beggar made a pitiful appeal to him for money, so he gave the man a copper. Then when he went home to

his boarding house, he was shocked to find the same kind of coin sitting on the window sill of the bathroom. Such impudence! He had always thought his landlady followed him and spied on him like a detective, and sure enough she was watching everything he did, just as he had supposed. And now the disgusting old woman had brazenly put that coin where she knew he would see it, as if to let him know he was being watched. He said that he had been really infuriated by her insolence—and there on the rim of the *hibachi* lay the same sort of copper coin! Thinking his daughter had tried to make a fool of him, he had struck her.[9]

Meanwhile, his unpleasant relations with his wife had not been improved by their long separation, during which she seldom wrote him (twice in the first six months, while he was awaiting news of the birth of their second child); and his own letters, even after almost two years' absence, were not without nagging complaints of such faults as her late rising ("Any woman who sleeps till nine or ten must be a concubine, a prostitute, or of the lower classes"). (27.173)

Sōseki's financial difficulties after returning made it necessary for him to teach at the First Higher School as well as at the Imperial University, where he was appointed Lecturer on English Literature in succession to Lafcadio Hearn. His debut at the university was not welcomed by the students, who at first found his cool, rational style less engrossing than the highly romantic "Japanese" manner of Hearn, whose retirement they had opposed. And then there were the university authorities, toward whom Sōseki felt a strong antipathy. His refusal to take charge of an English language examination in 1906, the year before he left to join the staff of the *Asahi shimbun*, was no less symptomatic than his indignant refusal of a doctorate from the Ministry of Education in 1911. In a letter to a scandalized senior colleague explaining why he had refused to give the examination, he said that he believed it to be outside his

---

[9] Natsume Kyōko, *Sōseki no omoide* (Kaizōsha, 1928), p. 132.

duty, which was simply to lecture six hours a week, and that
he was too busy. (28.23) Two days later, in response to his
friend's reply, he added that if he had any free time he ought
to spend it reading, even a single page. The university was at
fault for its degenerate formalism—indeed the twentieth century was hopelessly degenerate. "A Dean needn't think he has
become a great man in history! He ought to realize that there
are *some* odd people in the world, and that even with a mere
lecturer he can't have everything his own way!" (28.27)

Sōseki's second protracted mental crisis continued for more
than a year after his return from London. His sudden rages,
midnight outbursts in his study, and unpredictably violent
behavior became so alarming during the early summer rainy
season of 1903 that Mrs. Natsume asked her doctor to find a
pretext for examining him. He did, and told her that it seemed
to be no ordinary *shinkei suijaku*—he thought Mr. Natsume
should see a specialist, Dr. Kure of the University Department
of Psychiatry. The marital discord of the Natsumes was aggravated at that time by her third pregnancy, and in July she left
with the children for what turned out to be a two months' stay
at her parents' home. Meanwhile, Dr. Kure reported to her that
her husband's illness was incurable, and would recur from
time to time. "After that he explained the disease to me in
detail. I thought to myself *'Naruhodo!'*" After an elder brother's intercession, she tells us, Sōseki agreed to let her come
back: "After all, we both have *shinkei suijaku.*"[10]

In October their third daughter was born, and Sōseki's condition became worse, improving slightly toward the summer
of 1904. All the while, however, he continued to lecture, to
write, and, a new avocation which helped to soothe his irri-
tability, to paint in water colors. His lectures on *Macbeth* were
so shrewd and witty that he overcame the poor reputation of
those on *Silas Marner*; and in the January, 1904 issue of *Teikoku bungaku* he published an essay on "The Ghost of Mac-

[10] *Sōseki no omoide*, pp. 141-42.

beth," followed in the February *Eibungaku sōshi* by translations from Ossian, including "The Songs of Selma" already
well known from *Werther*. These modest successes were mentioned by Sōseki in the satirical style of self-mockery which
was the dominant tone of his prose writings from the time of
the "Bicycle Diary" until he became an established writer. In
one of his "Fragments" (*Dampen*), probably written in 1904
as an early sketch in the manner of *Wagahai wa neko de aru*,
he accords himself a degree of ironic praise while supposedly
overhearing a student and a maidservant in a lodging house
across the street mimic a conversation about him:

> As a result of their various researches, these students use
> many kinds of voices each in its proper way. Sometimes they
> imitate a certain professor, or a school teacher. They are men
> of many accomplishments. It is none of my business, but if
> they learned how to imitate actors instead of teachers they
> might be able to earn some pocket money. It is too bad that
> their imitations are of no use whatever, except to startle me.
> Here is a sample.
> Man (student imitating a professor): . . . have been very
>   popular.
> Woman: Wait till his "Songs of Selma" comes out!
> Man: And that recent piece of his about Macbeth's ghost
>   in *Teikoku bungaku* has had a lot of praise. (I was
>   delighted, and privately expressed my gratitude.)
> Woman: Really? How kind of everyone to say so . . . (Some-
>   how she sounded like my mother.) He has quite a good
>   head, in spite of what you might think. (She was obvi-
>   ously partial to me, but I was a little unhappy with that
>   "in spite of what you might think.") My, how obstinate
>   he is! . . .
> Man: By the way, how old is he?
> Woman (scornfully): He's already thirty-eight! (The fact
>   is, I *am* thirty-eight. Mother's sagacity astonished me.)
>   (24.88-89)

Similar passages of humorously detached self-ridicule in *Neko* and *Botchan* reflect some awareness of what, in the unsympathetic light of Mrs. Natsume's memoirs, appear to be systematic delusions of persecution and reference. But his wife's naïve account of life at the Natsumes' has the ring of authenticity:

He behaved very peculiarly toward a student who lived in a boarding house across from us, and even his published diary has a dreamy story of that student talking about him. Natsume's own study was directly overlooked by the boy's second-floor room; every evening there would be a light in that window and you could hear him read his school books in a high-pitched voice. It seems he had the habit of reading out loud whenever he was working at his desk by the window. Sometimes his friends would come to see him, and they would talk loudly too. It always sounded like rude gossip to Natsume's abnormally sensitive ears. And he was terribly nervous about being watched, peeped down at from a high place. Besides, since most schools begin around the same time in the morning, the student would be getting ready to leave just as Natsume was leaving, and would walk along after him. So Natsume made up his mind that he was being followed by a detective, in a student's disguise. It was pretty awkward for the student.

In the morning Natsume would get up and wash his face, and then, before breakfast, go to the window of his study and deliberately shout up toward that room, "Hello, Detective! When are you leaving for school today?" or "Detective! I'll be going at such-and-such a time!" . . . He did that every morning, so the student must have thought he was some kind of lunatic. It *was* odd of him to insist on calling the boy's attention that way, so earnestly, before he would sit down to breakfast.[11]

[11] *Sōseki no omoide*, pp. 155-57.

Delusions of hearing, whether of accusations, criticisms, conspiracies, or exceedingly subtle kinds of persecution, may be deduced even from Sōseki's diary of late 1914, near the end of his third mental crisis. Not only are his wife and maids accused of conspiring against him, a longstanding suspicion, but at times there are even complaints about his young friends, whose letters and visits were such a consolation to him. For example, one entry remarks on what, to Sōseki's acutely sensitized hearing, seems altogether too malicious to be the ordinary Japanese habit (especially at moments of tension or discomposure) of drawing in a breath with a slight hiss. His maid has been doing this intentionally, he says, and if forced to stop would only find some new way of tormenting him. He has tried to hint his displeasure by hissing back at her—but now others are taking up the practice:

One day I had to go to see Mr. Sasaki Nobutsuna in Hongō. And there was someone in the streetcar who hissed through his teeth like our maid. I hissed too. Then the other man stopped. After arriving at Mr. Sasaki's house I learned that we would have to go on to Ōtsuka's, and while I was waiting for him to get ready I again heard sounds of that kind, coming from the next room. I repeated as many as I heard. Fortunately, I escaped such unpleasant sounds at Ōtsuka's house. The night before that, Matsune had come to see me, and had hissed the same way. When I asked him whether he had a toothache, he said he did but had no time to go to a dentist. He certainly didn't look as if his teeth ached. That was Saturday. It was Sunday when I went to Sasaki's. On Wednesday Naka and Abe came. . . . Suddenly Abe began to hiss through his teeth the same way. Since he did this over and over again, I asked if he had a toothache. But his answer was a little different from Matsune's. This time the reply was that he had no pain but felt something strange between his teeth—and he made the noise again. I told him if you're as old as I am your gums shrink and matter lodges there, so you can't help making whistling sounds in order to blow it out. I hissed too, apologizing for having to make such rude noises in the presence of a guest. Still Abe didn't stop, he kept on and on with those unpleasant sounds. I was compelled to advise him to stop it. He replied that he would. But he repeated it once more and said "Oh, excuse me!" before he actually *did* stop. Even now our maid goes on hissing, particularly when my wife is out of the house. Either she is doing it under my wife's orders, or, to interpret it another way, she is taking such a liberty because of her absence. If it is the former, my wife is behaving outrageously; if the latter, the maids respect only her and are making a fool of me, their master. Moreover, when they openly do other things to me they always choose a time when she is not at home. Does my wife think she can evade her responsibility that way? If she does, she is an incredibly cold, shallow woman. (26.145-47)

Sōseki's second and perhaps worst period of crisis ended at about the time he began writing fiction—gloomy, fanciful stories set in England and the first of many installments of *Wagahai wa neko de aru*, the caricatural satire of his own intellectual milieu that immediately made him famous. By April, 1907, when he resigned from his teaching positions and joined the staff of the *Asahi*, Sōseki had already finished his experimental novels in the vein of Edo wit (*Neko, Botchan*) and haiku (*Kusamakura*), and had begun, with *Nowaki*, the series of somber psychological novels in which he deals seriously with characters haunted by his own sense of isolation and suffering. That even his closest alter egos are sometimes idealized and always more or less fictionalized is not only a matter of artistic technique, a symptom of the benign "splitting of the ego" which is a common practice of modern novelists, but one of the modes of defense without which he could not have tolerated the necessary exposure of painful psychological insights. Profound self-observation is essential to the modern psychological novel; and Sōseki's morbid hypersensitivity, his often arrogant pride, and his Edo-Victorian sense of propriety and decency made this work at once excruciatingly difficult and personally as well as artistically rewarding. The burdens of the past, conscious and unconscious, must have weighed all the more heavily on him because of his high ethical standards and the outward blamelessness of his life. He was an example of Dostoevsky's extreme case of the moral man: "In every man's memory there are things which he does not reveal to everyone, but only to his friends. There are also things which he does not reveal to his friends, but at best to himself and under a pledge of secrecy. And finally there are things which man hesitates to reveal even to himself, and every decent person accumulates a considerable quantity of such things. In fact, you might say the more decent a person is, the greater the number of such things that he carries around with him."[12] In Sōseki's novels both kinds of revelation, along with evidences of the force of repressed memories, occupy an increasingly large place.

Although Sōseki's fame grew swiftly and steadily from the time when, almost forty, he at last found his true vocation, he continued to suffer from the mental difficulties of his years of uncertainty and preparation. In 1910, after a violent attack of gastric ulcers, he experienced a dramatic mental "patho-cure," widely interpreted as a kind of *satori*. Much has been written about his efforts to "escape the self" and to achieve a philosophical if not religious calm in the face of death. However, such efforts had long been anticipated by various modes of withdrawal (especially painting and Chinese poetry, which helped to sustain him until the end); and he continued to strive for freedom from anxiety without conspicuous success during all his later years. These years were filled with personal tragedy: relapses of physical illness, the sudden death of a two-year-old daughter in 1911, and from 1913 through much of 1914 his third period of sustained mental crisis. Yet they also saw his greatest achievements as a novelist: *Kōjin, Kokoro,*

[12] *Notes From Underground,* xi.

Michikusa, and *Meian*, the novels which are stored with his richest psychological insights and which are the culmination of his art.

Sōseki began writing *Kōjin* at the end of November in 1912, and its first installment appeared in the *Asahi shimbun* on December 6. That year had seen the end of an era: the death of the Emperor Meiji on July 30, followed by the powerful emotional drama of the suicide of General and Countess Nogi on September 13, the day of the Emperor's funeral. Sōseki's mood had darkened greatly since midsummer, and he complained that the writing did not go well. During the first half of 1913 his mental condition was particularly bad, although it was relieved, as usual, by one of his recurrent ulcer attacks. This time he was confined to bed for about two months, beginning in late March, and was obliged to discontinue his novel until the fall. Its fourth and final section was published between September 16 and November 15. Before his illness Sōseki had planned to wind up his already lengthy work as quickly as possible, but in its last section, almost a third of the novel, he abandons the subordinate characters and the plot to end with a brooding, analytical, deeply introspective study of his protagonist. It is in this moving coda that Sōseki's self-analysis achieves its most penetrating insights.

Kōjin begins with a rather tedious account by the narrator, a young man named Jirō, of such conventional marital and romantic problems as matchmaking, a childless marriage, and frustrated love, a subplot enlivened by the newspaper-novel technique of contrived suspense and neatly turned installments. But there is a pathological element foreshadowing later troubles: Misawa, the "Friend" (*Tomodachi*) of the title of this section, is discovered in a hospital with what seems to be a case of ulcers, which also happens to be the illness of a young woman to whom they are both attracted; later he confesses to Jirō about another pathetic young woman, touched by madness, who had been in love with him but had died. And there is the familiar guilty triangle of Sōseki's novels, with its disturbing tensions between friends. Jirō, though a sensible, well-balanced type of the younger son, is acutely sensitive to his friend's feelings and his own. He notes Misawa's obstinacy and selfishness in trying to keep him from leaving the city, but not without reflecting on his own attitude: "I was well aware of my own selfishness in trying to abandon the patient as soon as possible." (11.32) After their friendship has been strained by his attraction toward the sick girl, Jirō analyzes their feelings subtly, and despairingly.

"My interest in her had languished, but I didn't care to see Misawa so intimate with her. . . . In that way a veiled, unconscious enmity existed between us. The innate human qualities of selfishness and jealousy were aroused. . . . I felt ashamed of myself for being so furtive about it. At the same time, I resented Misawa's furtiveness. Yet I realized that, such is the base nature of man, as long as we lived we could never eradicate this furtiveness. I became very depressed. And beyond that, sad." (11.54)

Misawa leaves, and the next day Jirō's elder brother Ichirō arrives with his wife Nao and their mother. Thereafter Jirō is preoccupied with family matters, especially those centering on Ichirō, though later in the novel Misawa reappears, to suggest a possible bride for him. (By then, marriage seems a dismal prospect, in view of the hostility between Ichirō and Nao.) We learn little by little of Ichirō's difficult character, his "bad moods" which so often plunge the household in gloom, as well as the few pleasanter qualities of his complex personality. Both Ichirō and Nao are seen from outside, chiefly through the comments of Jirō and his mother, but Nao remains somewhat enigmatic while Ichirō is depicted more and more vividly, if unflatteringly. From the first Jirō's admiration for his brother has been tempered by his awareness of qualities similar to those discerned in Sōseki by his wife, among others:

My brother was a scholar and a thinker. He was also a good man, with the pure nature of a poet. Only, as the eldest son, he had a certain willfulness. If you ask me, he had been much more spoiled than the usual eldest son. . . . Once he became irritable he would wear a sour expression for days on end, and never utter a word. Still, when he was with others, he was a changed man—an excellent companion, amiable, tolerant, and gentlemanly. That is why all his friends believed him to be a fine man with a calm disposition. (11.77-78)

Soon it appears that Ichirō's behavior is not merely willful: "He would get in a bad mood from little, trifling things, and our cheerful house would fill with a gloomy air. My mother would frown and say under her breath to me, 'Ichirō's illness has flared up again.' In my happiness at being treated as Mother's confidant, I would say, 'It's just a habit, leave him alone.' Not only did my brother have a difficult temperament, he also, out of a sense of justice, abhorred the thought of anything, however trivial, going on behind his back." (11.79)

Nao shares Ichirō's surface coldness and pride and, like him, denies the love that both of them need. But he is haunted by fear of deception, and asks Jirō, with whom he suspects her to be in love, to try to discover her feelings—even to be an agent provocateur by arranging to go on an overnight trip with her. Jirō is properly horrified by this request; yet when a sudden storm forces him to spend a night alone with his brother's wife he finds that she is by no means so cold toward him as she is toward her husband. After the suppressed erotic excitement of this encounter, a significantly passive variant on the blatant use of coincidence in Japanese drama and fiction, Jirō not only feels guilty toward Ichirō but has a trace of Nao's coolly rebellious attitude toward his superior authority. Ichirō's suspicions had brought him to the point of seeming "hysterical" (*hisuteriteki*) to his brother, as close to delusion as anything in Sōseki's novels; and Jirō, who has been told by Ichirō that he will suspect him for the rest of his life, finds himself both the obscurely guilty accomplice of Nao and, like his brother, indeed all men, the object of her contempt. It is almost as bad as being married.

At home again in Tokyo, the family settles down to its usual routine: Ichirō, when he is not at the unnamed university where he teaches, spends most of his time secluded in his study, withdrawn from his cold wife and fearful daughter. Jirō is distressed by his brother's growing estrangement from the rest of the family, and decides to find lodgings elsewhere. Ichirō asks if he will be leaving home alone, and laughs, again with a note of hysteria in his voice. There are other reasons to fear for Ichirō's sanity: his colleague and closest friend, Mr. H, has reported his strange silences in the lecture room, and suggested that it might indicate a nervous breakdown. But the long winter passes uneventfully, no more drearily than usual, and the final section begins with Jirō, like the young narrator of *Kokoro*, enjoying a momentary, illusory feeling of hope as he "breathes in the scent of spring."

The title of the last section is *Jinrō* ("Anguish," a Buddhist term for the passions, desires, and troubles of this world), and its ominous shadow deepens as the novel slowly draws to its close. Sōseki felt obliged to complete it, he told a friend, because that was a vital necessity to his own life—"even though it may look stupid or insane to others, and have no benefit to society or family or anyone else," . . . "I am not by nature an unkind person, but at present I am so concerned with myself that I cannot be kind to others." (30.194-95) There is no doubt of his sense of obligation toward his *Asahi* patrons, and toward the readers who were awaiting the resumption of their daily serial, but he seems to have had an inner need as compelling as that of the Sensei in *Kokoro*, whose decision to commit suicide followed swiftly on the suicide of General Nogi but who felt obliged to record his experience before yielding to death: "Please understand, I did not write this merely to pass the time away. My own past, which made me what I am, is a part of human experience. Only I can tell it. I do not think that my effort to do so honestly has been entirely purposeless. If my story helps you and others to understand even a part of what we are, I shall be satisfied. . . . I did not write simply to keep my promise to you. More compelling than the promise was the necessity which I felt within me to write this story." (12.233-34)[13]

Both *Kōjin* and *Kokoro* end with long, revealing letters, after the subject, Ichirō or the older Sensei, has been offstage for some time; ànd the revelation of Ichirō's keen but more vaguely motivated anxieties is similarly dependent on the role of the friend, the one link—however weak—to the possibilities of trust which were blighted long ago and which are so conspicuously absent in marriage. "What brings your heart and my heart together? And what is it that separates them?" Ichirō asks his friend Mr. H, who replies with the German proverb "Keine Brücke führt von Mensch zu Mensch." (11.302-03) But there is no such meeting of minds, if not hearts, when the Sensei's wife asks wistfully, "Can't a man's heart and a woman's heart ever become a part of each other, so that they are one?" (12.229) The Sensei's noncommittal answer ("Perhaps, when the man and the woman are young") only emphasizes the gulf between them.[14] We last see Ichirō and his friend alone together, his wife and family barely visible in the background, and it is thanks to the friend that we—and Ichirō—are able to understand more of the nature of his suffering. There is evidently a strong transference element in his friendship, its emotional tension heightened by reaction to the friend as if he were someone from the past, an intensified tie which is in part a compensation for distorted and unsatisfactory relationships to others in the present.

Mr. H, having observed Ichirō's worsening behavior, agrees to take him off on a holiday trip, and to report by letter to Jirō if there is anything worth reporting. His letter, which arrives ten days after their departure, turns out to be long enough to occupy twenty-five installments in the *Asahi*. Not only the earlier subplots but the superficially dramatic problems raised by

---

[13] McClellan, p. 247.   [14] McClellan, p. 242.

the Nao-Jirō-Ichirō triangle have been discarded, as Sōseki completes his novel. Mr. H is fully conscious of his role as a concerned observer, a more effective agent than Nao, Jirō, or their parents in the therapy of this desperately ill patient; he almost seems aware of the *counter*-transference (the narcissistic hazard of self-analysis) which can blur his own vision. As with even the closest of Sōseki's alter egos, always satirized, idealized, or transformed to meet the requirements of a fictional role, the faithful and responsible Mr. H (an able, dedicated writer, for all his modesty) provides in himself as well as through his vision only a partial portrait of the artist: "Probably the Ichirō I have seen is not the Ichirō that the rest of you know. Doubtless I understand him in a different way too. If this letter has been worth the effort of writing, that is where its value lies. Please accept it as another image of the same person, seen from a different point of view." (11.334)

In the conclusion of the letter—the novel—Mr. H returns to the theme of death, which, with madness and religion, has been one of the avenues of escape from anguish which Ichirō was already discussing earnestly with him before they left on their trip. At Numazu, on their first night away from Tokyo, Ichirō had given up their game of *go* (the black and white stones seemed to be fusing into menacing patterns before his eyes) and confessed his mental state of unrelenting anxiety, behind his appearance of calm. "Ichirō suffers because nothing he does seems to him either an end or a means. He is constantly uneasy. . . . He says that when he imagines what all this is coming to, it frightens him so much that he breaks out in a cold sweat. He says he is overwhelmed with fear." When Mr. H attempts to console him by suggesting that this is the general uneasiness of the human condition, Ichirō agrees, to the extent of attributing its origin to the unsettled age they live in: "Our uneasiness comes from scientific progress. Science does not know where to stop and has never let us stop either. . . . No one knows where it will take us. It is really terrifying." But then he goes on to claim that his own fear is unique: "That is because I alone in my own lifetime must experience a fate to be arrived at by all mankind, after many centuries. . . . In short, I combine within myself the anxieties of all mankind, and I experience a fear which concentrates that anxiety into every moment of the day." (11.293-95)

They arrive at last at Shūzenji (the scene of Sōseki's fateful illness), where Ichirō confides further in Mr. H:

For the first time I heard the touching confession that your brother is as lonely at home as he is in society. Besides harboring doubts about me, his good friend, he always suspects somebody or other in his family. To him, even his father and mother are vessels of falsehood. His wife seems worst of all. He told me he had struck her recently. . . . Strangely enough, your brother vividly described his unpleasant behavior toward his wife and yet said nothing definite about the cause for such extreme behavior. All he said was that his whole environment was composed of falsehoods. But he made no attempt to reconstruct any of them for me. I could not understand why your brother became so excited over that vague-sounding term "falsehood." (11.304-05)

Mr. H's analysis of Ichirō is, however, at once sympathetic, even adulatory, and acute:

Ichirō is a sensitive person. He is aesthetically, morally, and intellectually hypersensitive, with the result that he seems to have been born to torment himself. For him there can be no thick-skinned indifference as to whether he chooses one thing or the other. It absolutely must be a particular one. Moreover, if it is that one, and the shape or the degree or the shade of color is not just as he wishes, he will not accept it. His life proceeds step by step as if crossing the perilous tightwire of his own choices. . . . Ichirō has always had superior introspective powers, and now, as a result of too much reflection, is suffering under their pressure. Whatever his state of mind, he can never go ahead until he has stopped

335

to scrutinize it. The course of your brother's life is momentarily interrupted time after time—it must be as harassing as being called from dinner to the telephone every other minute. . . . He wants to be happy, but he only studies happiness. No matter how far his study advances, happiness remains on the other side. (11.306-08)

By the end of the letter Mr. H has discerned further contradictions in his friend's character: Ichirō's need for personal autonomy conflicts with his need for love, his highest values block him in his search for happiness, his overvalued intellect is itself a source of pain. "Even now, I have not the slightest doubt that your brother's mind is far more exact and well-ordered than mine. But as a human being, when you compare him with his former self, he appears to be in some disorder. The cause of that disorder, if you come to think of it, is nothing less than the functioning of his well-ordered mind." (11.314) Ichirō's own insights are remarkable, as perhaps might be expected in view of his compulsive introspection and rather tiresomely reiterated intellectual superiority. His last quoted statement reveals a clear recognition of his guilt toward his wife—to become one of the themes of *Michikusa*. "I have no idea how much harm I have already done to her. It takes a lot of nerve to seek happiness from a woman you have ruined, don't you think?" (11.332) By this time his suspicions of Nao have been forgotten in his self-preoccupation, left far behind along with the other dramatic elements that dominated the earlier parts of the novel. In spite of his friend's flicker of hope, Ichirō is alone in hopeless isolation.

Thus Sōseki ends his long novel with an unresolved situation closely identified with his own dilemma, at an aesthetic distance which has been steadily diminished from the late and leisurely introduction of his protagonist as a cold, withdrawn, difficult personality. If the unfinished portrait of Ichirō suggests the limitations as well as the achievements of Sōseki's self-analysis, the structural weaknesses of the novel—its lack of unity, in particular—are not irrelevant to the fact that "it contains the most fully articulated statement of Sōseki's main theme, man's isolation."[15] The wealth of psychological insight beyond that of the earlier novels is not matched by a corresponding ability to use it effectively for the purposes of the novel. But without the exploratory technique of *Kōjin* Sōseki might never have arrived at the mastery of the psychological novel attained in *Kokoro, Michikusa,* and *Meian.*

In *Kokoro* Sōseki achieves his greatest dramatic intensity—and an extremity of despair—in the statement of the theme of isolation. Loneliness in marriage again casts the sort of dark shadow (a frequent image) which overhangs even friendship, the last hope in life. Paradoxically, too, Sōseki's voluminous correspondence with his friends is also often concerned with the theme of loneliness, seen as the necessary but almost intolerable condition of the artist. His gratitude for Abe Jirō's praise of *Mon* sounds as if he were a struggling, unknown writer, rather than the famous Sensei with his circle of devoted pupils. (30.136-37) On December 4, 1912, shortly after beginning *Kōjin,* he writes to Tsuda Seifū: "Much as I wish to be content with loneliness, I am naturally happier if I can win even one friend to my side. That is probably because I lack a purely artistic temperament." (30.152) Again, the following March, he thanks another friend for his admiration, because lately he had felt there was no one in the world who would stand by him. (30.178)

In his essays and lectures of these years Sōseki often takes up the theme of the artist's isolation at his lonely task—a deeper loneliness than that of his contemporaries, each more or less afflicted with it in an age of self-centered individualism—and of the value to himself, as well as to others, of heroic devotion to the duty of introspection and self-revelation. In a letter of January 7, 1914, a few months before beginning to write *Kokoro,* he defines a novel as "a faithful account of the author's

[15] McClellan, "An Introduction to Sōseki," *Harvard Journal of Asiatic Studies,* XXII (1959), 208.

own life or fate" (31.5); and a week later, replying to a friend who had suggested Mendelism as a useful addition to the scientific resources of the writer, he asserts that Mendelism is "too simple" for application to the human psyche, that, similarly, "the discoveries of experimental psychology represent only a very small fragment" of the world of mental phenomena with which he must deal, and that he can only rely on his powers of self-analysis:

> Since I am myself concerned with literature, I cannot view literary psychology purely scientifically. Even if I tried, it would remain something quite remote, I am not in the least inclined to investigate it. My method is always to analyze my own psychological phenomena. For me, that explains things most satisfactorily. If it is at times inadequate, I can only believe that that is because of the complexity of the phenomena themselves, not because it is a bad method. (31.7-8)

The portrait of the lonely, melancholy Sensei in *Kokoro* is sketched much more economically than that of Ichirō in *Kōjin*, but becomes at last a self-portrait rather than a single arresting figure dominating a gallery of other characters: the even longer letter which concludes this novel is Sensei's own confession, the fulfillment of his promise to a young student who is his only friend but also of his duty to record his past—his share of human experience—and of his own inner need. He confesses to having betrayed a friend, a betrayal that led to suicide and to the guilt and isolation that have driven him toward the same fate; and the first half of the novel, narrated by the student-friend to whom he wrote the letter, records another, more subtle betrayal—a failure to respond to a cry for help—and thus mirrors both Sensei's tragic error and his expiatory act of self-revelation. Since this primary narrator is looking back from a sadder and wiser maturity at his own youth as well as at Sensei, he has from the first a level of understanding which reveals the development of his introspective character at the same time that it enhances the suspense and the significance of his story: "A man capable of love, or I should say rather a man who was by nature incapable of not loving; but a man who could not whole-heartedly accept the love of another—such a one was Sensei." (12.15)[16] Such a one, we are tempted to add, was Sōseki, another "Sensei" who was unable to satisfy his urgent emotional needs.

Many other details from *Kokoro* could be gathered to illustrate what we know of Sōseki's character, and of the meaningful interrelationship of traits attested by such sources as the photographs of his neatly ordered study, say, or the volumes of testimony to the sense of injustice which was sharpened by his pride, his obstinacy, and his anxiety:

> Indeed, Sensei was a very tidy person. His study, for instance, was always in perfect order. . . .
>
> "Sensei is rather fastidious, isn't he?" I once said to his wife . . . Sensei, who was listening to us, said with a laugh, "To tell the truth, I have a fastidious mind. That is why I am always worrying. When you think about it, it's a terrible nuisance to have a nature like mine."
>
> What he meant by "a fastidious mind," I did not know. Neither, it seemed, did his wife. Perhaps he meant to say that he was too intensely conscious of right or wrong, or perhaps he meant that his fastidiousness amounted to something like a morbid love of cleanliness. (12.69)[17]

But the deepest stratum in Sensei's character is his distrust— of all humanity, he insists, with the same magnifying tendency that leads him to interpret his loneliness as the price for being born in an age of individualism. It is because of this pervasive distrust, ranging from self-distrust to distrust projected into society at large, that Sensei warns his young friend against future disillusionment. He is aware of the student's over-estimation of him, of the youthful inclination to become blindly

[16] McClellan, *Kokoro*, p. 12.   [17] McClellan, pp. 69-70.

devoted to a single cause, and warns against the danger of hostility that underlies their friendship.

> "At any rate," he continued, "don't put too much trust in me. You will learn to regret it if you do. And if you ever allow yourself to feel betrayed, you will then find yourself being cruelly vindictive."
>
> "What do you mean?"
>
> "The memory that you once sat at my feet will begin to haunt you, and in bitterness and shame, you will want to degrade me. I do not want your admiration now, because I do not want your insults in the future." (12.32-33)[18]

The identification between Sensei and the student's father is clearly indicated, as is the futility of a substitution which will only lead to another estrangement and loss: the student's development as an individual—scarcely assured by his graduation from the university—can only come with freedom from this seemingly beneficial dependency. And Sensei's caution reflects fear of what he himself will lose.

The solution of this dilemma is heroic, in its way, like the death of General Nogi which is its immediate occasion. Of course suicide alone does not suffice: both the General and Sensei feel obliged to leave a testament. Sensei's confession of the betrayal of a friend, the result of a guilty triangle such as is so often described by Sōseki, is a brilliant novel within the novel, like Mr. H's letter in *Kōjin*. But since the confession itself fulfills a promise, one given most reluctantly in a desperate effort to establish a link of trust, it illuminates a transference relationship even more critical than that of Ichirō and Mr. H. By the time he writes his own memoir of their friendship the narrator has realized that Sensei would not have welcomed an attempt to study him: "Had I been curious in an impersonal and analytical way, the bond between us would surely not have lasted. I was, of course, not aware of all this at the time. I hate to think what might have happened had I acted differently.

---

[18] McClellan, p. 30.

Even in his relationship with me, he was in constant dread of being coldly analyzed." (12.17)[19] Yet he speculates, correctly, that Sensei is given to self-scrutiny. It is perhaps for this reason that Sensei's evasions become intolerable, and that he is at last driven to accuse the older man of hiding something from him. Characteristically, Sensei would prefer to interpret the "something" as purely intellectual, on the safe, impersonal plane of ideas, and thus to feel justified in denying that deception.

"It would appear that you are unable to distinguish between my ideas at present and the events of my past. I am not much of a thinker, but the few ideas that I do have, I have no wish to hide from others. I have no reason to. But if you are suggesting that I should tell you all about my past—well, that's another matter entirely."

"I do not agree with you. I value your opinions because they are the results of your experience. Your opinions would be worthless otherwise." . . .

Sensei is shaken by this disarmingly direct attempt to penetrate the human reality behind his elaborate intellectual defenses, and can only appeal to the proprieties of their unequal status by calling him "an audacious young man." But the student persists:

"No sir, I am simply being sincere. And in all sincerity, I wish to learn about life."

"Even to the extent of digging up my past?"

Suddenly, I was afraid. I felt as though the man sitting opposite me were some kind of criminal, instead of the Sensei that I had come to respect. Sensei's face was pale.

"I wonder if you are being really sincere," he said. "Because of what happened to me, I have come to doubt everybody. In truth, I doubt you, too. But for some reason, I do not want to doubt you. It may be because you seem so simple. Before I die, I should like to have one friend that I can truly

19 McClellan, pp. 13-14.

trust. I wonder if you can be that friend. Are you really sincere?" (12.67-68)[20]

The friend on whom this character was modeled, according to the handy little desk-side *Dictionary of Models of Modern Masterpieces* (*Kindai meisaku moderu jiten*), was Komiya Toyotaka, Sōseki's favorite protégé and conscientious biographer.[21] But there is no evidence to justify selecting only a single key from among Sōseki's many younger friends, nor should it be overlooked that the character is an image vitalized by memories of his own youth. Inevitably, observation is complemented by self-observation, by exploring deeper layers of memory, as Chateaubriand implied in an aphorism which anticipates the necessary discipline of the psychological novelist: "The only heart one paints well is one's own, while attaching it to someone else, and indeed the greater part of genius is composed of memories."[22]

Sōseki's next work, after completing *Kokoro* by August of 1914 and delivering his lecture on individualism in November, was *Garasudo no naka*, which he began around the end of the year during a period of relative calm that was to continue until his last illness. These memoirs are his most personal, and precede his one autobiographical novel, *Michikusa*, written later in 1915. Yet *Garasudo no naka* is still a tantalizingly reticent work, contrasting in its bland reflective tone with the tension, sometimes heightening to anguish, of the novels. As Sōseki points out near the end, he has had no intention of being indiscreet:

Although I am not so vain as to wish to deceive others by telling lies, neither have I seen fit to expose the worst, the basest things about me, or my most shameful faults. Someone has said that however far one may seek the truth—in the *Confessions* of St. Augustine, of Rousseau, the *Confessions of an English Opium Eater*—it lies beyond the powers

[20] McClellan, pp. 67-68.   [21] (Shibundō, 1960), pp. 129-31.
[22] *Le Génie du christianisme*, II.

of human description. And what I have written is not even a confession. My sins (if they can be called sins) have perhaps been depicted only in their brightest aspect. (17.197-98)

In *Michikusa*, on the other hand, the darker aspects of Kenzō, its protagonist, are depicted a good deal more thoroughly than the bright. The same is true of the portraits of Kenzō's sullen hysterical wife Osumi (a not unsympathetic but fitting companion-piece to Mrs. Natsume's portrait of her late husband in *Sōseki no omoide*) and of most of the half-dozen other relatives who may be identified from the *Moderu jiten*. But even here Sōseki's critical and self-analytic tendencies distinguish him from the author-protagonists of the usual I-novel, as it had begun to flourish by this time. It is not so much because of his fictional techniques—compressing the events of 1903 to 1905 into the single year of his return from London, turning the whole plot on an episode involving his foster father in 1909, and so on—as because of his warily introspective attitude. Even when closely following the external events of his own life Sōseki's chief interest remains the analytical one of observing his reactions to them, and from a certain distance. The time-setting of *Michikusa* enables him to view himself at the comparatively safe remove of a decade, even though some of the elements—in particular the scarifying marital conflict—must also reflect recent experience, while others draw on childhood memories more painful than those which occupy such a prominent place in *Garasudo no naka*. Still, the year after his return from London was one of severe mental suffering for Sōseki, part of his second crisis; and because he wrote *Michikusa* soon after recovering from a third crisis which had set in despite his success in his vocation and his new perspective on life after grave physical illness, he must have felt a need like that of Sensei in *Kokoro*—to understand and communicate the significance of his own long-past experiences.

From the vantage point of the mature psychological novelist there is striking insight into the neurotic difficulties of the hard-pressed Kenzō. Apart from the actual external pressures of his distasteful work as a university teacher and of the financial burdens imposed by various relatives, Kenzō suffers from inner tyrannies such as his obsessive hoarding of time ("he was unaware that his attitude toward time was nothing short of miserly") and his compulsive work habits. (13.9) Nor does he realize that all his learning, his logic, his strong sense of intellectual superiority are not enough to solve his domestic problems. His wife is even so unfair as to tax him with unkind remarks he is supposed to have made while delirious from a high fever:

> "If you didn't think such thoughts you'd never say them, no matter how sick you were!"
> Kenzō was the sort of man who would immediately try to argue his wife down, rather than ask himself how much truth there might be in her words. . . . He was unaware that he was using the authority of logic to deceive himself. (13.25)

But Kenzō *is* aware that his troubles stem at least in part from his nervous temperament, which, however, under the pressures of work, helps to distract him from memories of his foster parents and of his "unhappy past":

> Fortunately, under his present circumstances he had no time to worry about such things. As soon as he came home and changed his clothes he went into his study. He always felt that his narrow six-mat room was heaped high with work to do. But in fact his nerves were far less taxed by the work itself than by the thought that he *had* to do it. Naturally he became irritable. . . .
> Many who knew him said that he was getting neurotic. Kenzō himself believed that it was just his temperament. (13.8-9)

Although Kenzō assures himself that he is too busy to worry about the past, remembered scenes from his childhood occupy a large place in *Michikusa*. He has especially bitter memories of his two "fathers," adoptive and "real," each selfish, hypocritical, and deceptive in his own way. "From the viewpoint of both his fathers, Kenzō was not a human being but a kind of property. The only difference was that his real father treated him as rubbish, while his foster father thought he might eventually be of some use." (13.203-04) The doubling of this hostile image helps to explain the peculiarly sinister force of Shimada—the foster father—in the suspenseful, detective-story-like development of the plot. There are mysteries in the past which Kenzō believes himself to have penetrated, but they continue to disturb the present. In the midst of this struggle to establish his identity as a free individual, he cannot avoid diverting much of his energy to coping with the obsessive problems of the past—problems personified by Shimada's attempt to enforce its claim on him. In spite of his considerable success in this struggle, Kenzō lacks the essential self-knowledge to find a secure place for himself in the world; indeed, the very degree of his success, present and anticipated, is the measure of his growing isolation.

"But how did I become the man I am now?" The question always seemed disturbingly strange to him. Along with the strangeness there was a good deal of mingled pride that he had been able to fight his way through successfully against his environment. And of course he also took some pride in accomplishments which had not yet been realized.

He looked at the contrast between the past and the present, wondering how the present could have developed out of the past. Yet he was unaware of how much he was suffering because of the present.

Thanks to the present, his relations with Shimada were broken off. For the same reason, he disliked Otsune and was unable to feel at ease with his brother and sister; no doubt that was also why he was gradually becoming more distant from his wife's father. Viewed from a different angle, Kenzō had made himself into a pitiful man who could not get along with others. (13.204)

Kenzō, after all, is not so different from the eminent author who lectured in 1914 to the students of the Gakushūin about the value of individualism and the loneliness that was its price.

For Sōseki, born in the Tokugawa period but whose age—calculated in Western fashion—was that of the Meiji era itself, individualism and alienation were the inescapable conditions of a modern consciousness. Individualism could be viewed as a virtue, all the more admirable because of the difficulty of achieving it, but the loneliness which was its shadow had an especially poignant reality for him. Egoism, "modern man's vain sense of a self-made self,"[23] had always been associated with uneasiness for Sōseki, and as his courageous efforts toward self-discovery continued, he found in himself an aggressive element which he shared with those "others" whom he had feared and despised. He died before completing *Meian*, in which this problem is treated on an almost symphonic scale, after the doleful chamber music of *Kokoro* and *Michikusa*; and this last and, even unfinished, perhaps finest of his works demonstrates the artistic powers which he developed in the course of a career of expressing his own deepest feelings and, inevitably, those of his time. If his early novels reflect more clearly the surface changes of his society, it is in the later novels, in which he probes his own darkest psychological problems, that he symbolizes the widespread anxiety beneath those exciting changes. And his efforts helped to create an instrument—the modern Japanese psychological novel—of unequaled sensitivity for the recording of the forms of consciousness which emerged so dramatically in his era.

[23] Erikson, *Insight and Responsibility* (New York, 1964), p. 146.

CHAPTER IX

Tōson and the Autobiographical Novel

EDWIN McCLELLAN

THE writers of the *shizen shugi*, or naturalistic, school—Shimazaki Tōson (1872-1943), Tayama Katai (1871-1930), Tokuda Shūsei (1871-1943), Masamune Hakuchō (1879-1962)—who formed a powerful literary clique for about a decade after the publication of Katai's *Futon* ("bed quilt," 1907) and Tōson's *Hakai* ("broken commandment," 1906), have since lost much of their popularity; and it is possible that soon, their numerous detractors will have successfully obliterated whatever real claim to distinction they may have had. Certainly Tōson, the most famous of the naturalists, is already the least respected of the late Meiji "giants," his critical reputation having suffered far more in recent years than either Natsume Sōseki's (1867-1916) or Mori Ōgai's (1862-1922).

Much of the unfriendly criticism of the naturalists is surely justified. They were doctrinaire, and no doubt discouraged, intentionally or not, the writing of fiction more imaginative, less concerned with the mundane, than their own. It is probable too that they played a large part in fostering the prejudice which even now exists in Japan against fiction that stimulates and entertains, against the adventurousness of such writers as Tanizaki Jun'ichirō and Mishima Yukio; and that by helping to establish that peculiarly Japanese phenomenon, the *shishōsetsu*, or the autobiographical novel, with its emphasis on impressionistic description, lyricism, and "truthfulness," they encouraged the notion that the more creative kind of fiction was "popular," that the "pure" novelist was one who controlled his imagination to the point where it was hardly detectable in his writings.

Much of what is said about the naturalists can be, and almost

347

always is, applied to Tōson; for he was not only the most successful of his school, but the most representative. He wrote six full-length novels in his long career—*Hakai, Haru* ("spring," 1908), *Ie* ("the house," 1911), *Sakura no mi no juku suru toki* ("when the cherries ripen," 1917), *Shinsei* ("new life," 1919), and *Yoakemae* ("before the dawn," 1935). Of these, only the first is fiction in the full sense. The last, *Yoakemae*, is based on the life of his father; and the rest are all more or less autobiographical. They are on the whole heavily written, loosely constructed, and conspicuously lacking in drama. The characterizations are thin, and intelligent examination of motive is usually sacrificed for description of the surface scene, so that one does not understand Tōson's people as one does, say, Sōseki's. In other words, Tōson's novels for the most part make very dull reading; and even the frequently beautiful lyrical passages begin to seem not sufficient compensation for the absence of plot and drama. At any rate, because despite his weaknesses as a novelist he enjoyed for many years a position of eminence, it is likely that he was as responsible as any single writer could be for the prevalence of the idea in Japan that the novel need not or should not be a creation of the dramatic imagination.

Even if one does not go so far as to insist on the generally negative influence of Tōson, one will have to admit that his contribution to the modern Japanese novel was nowhere near as significant as Sōseki's. The impressionistic autobiographical novel of Tōson was an arid form, capable of little development. After *Ie*, his third novel, Tōson essentially stopped growing. And it is significant that *Ie* still remains the best example of the genre, and that he has had no noteworthy descendants; whereas it can be said of Sōseki, the freewheeling intellectual story-teller, that he paved the way for such men as Tanizaki and Mishima.

It so happens that Sōseki's last completed novel, *Michikusa* ("grass on the wayside," 1915), is autobiographical. And it is interesting to see how different is his approach from Tōson's.

Sōseki, even when writing in a form which had by 1915 come to be largely identified with the impressionistic naturalism of Tōson, remains a story-teller whose main concern is to draw people as vividly as possible. The following is a passage from that novel. (Kenzō, the main character—i.e., Sōseki—was as a child adopted by Shimada. He was then taken back by his real parents when it became clear that Shimada was not an ideal foster father. Years later, when the novel begins, Shimada appears again and forces his way into Kenzō's life, with the intention of getting money out of him. The meeting described here is one of several that take place in Kenzō's house.)

Not every house in those days had electricity, and the living room now was as usual illuminated by the weak glow of an oil lamp.

The oil cup fitted into a flat, round saucer which rested on a thin bamboo stem. The stem had a round base, about the size of the saucer, so that the entire pedestal looked like a small hand drum.

Shimada had the lamp by him, and was fussing with the wick. Not bothering to look up as Kenzō entered, he said: "The flame needs adjusting. It's smoking too much."

The lamp had always been a temperamental one, and if the wick was not trimmed with particular care, it would smoke profusely. Noting that its chimney was indeed getting quite black, Kenzō said, "Let's have the maid bring us another one." But the suggestion was received with a marked lack of enthusiasm by Shimada, who now brought his face close to the glass shade with its busy floral design and peered through the transparent patches. "What can be the matter with it," he mumbled anxiously.

How like him, Kenzō thought, to be so offended by an inefficient lamp.

Shimada had always wanted everything to be neat and orderly. It was as though he was trying to make up for his own lack of morals by worrying unduly about dust in the corridors and rubbish in the garden. He was in the habit of rushing about with broom in hand, Kenzō remembered, searching for dirt in the remotest corners. And when anything got broken, he would try to mend it himself, no matter how difficult the job or how time-consuming. Of course, meanness played a large role here. A copper coin in the hand seemed to Shimada worth much more than time or labor. "We can mend it ourselves," he would say. "To get someone else to do an easy job like that would be sheer waste of money."

He lived in constant dread of wasting money. That there were other things that could be wasted, he seemed never to learn.

"The trouble with him," Ofuji once said to Kenzō, "is that he is too conscientious." This was soon after she and Shimada were married. Naive as he was then, Kenzō knew that "conscientious" was not the word for Shimada's trouble; and guessing that Ofuji knew it too and was merely trying to defend her husband's reputation, he was decent enough to say nothing at the time.

But now he wondered whether Ofuji was not right in a sense after all. Perhaps the wastefulness of this man's life had indeed been due to a kind of conscientiousness; with capacities far outmatched by his greed, he had spent all these years desperately trying to satisfy it.

With growing pity Kenzō watched Shimada who was still staring intently at the flame, his sunken eyes almost touching the glass shade. He said to himself, that is what is left of a lifetime. And as he thought of the meaninglessness of this old man's life, he could not help wondering how he himself would grow old.

He had always disliked the word "god." But at this moment he asked himself the question: if god were to look at my own life, would he think it was much different from this greedy old man's?

Shimada had accidentally turned the wick up too high,

and the room suddenly became very bright. In a dither he quickly turned it down; now the flame was feebler than ever. "It certainly needs fixing," he said.

Kenzō summoned the maid and asked her to bring another lamp.[1]

Very different from the above is the following passage from *Shinsei*, where Tōson describes the loneliness of Kishimoto— i.e., himself—in exile in Paris. It is as typical of Tōson as the other passage is of Sōseki. There is lyricism here, but no drama. Sōseki's characters are life-size; but Tōson's character is hardly more than part of the surrounding scene, and we see him from a distance. Even when Tōson's intention is to depict a character's state of mind, he tends only to convey the general mood. His portrayal of Kishimoto has none of the precision, the boldness, of Sōseki's portrayal of Shimada.

The most pleasant season in Paris arrived. Of those trees on the old dignified boulevards, the first to herald the coming of spring were the chestnut trees. Then the buds on the plane trees burst into leaf, and as the leaves grew larger and darker, the whole city, it seemed, became a world of green. One could see, over the stone fences, the hollies in the private gardens beginning to bloom; soon, their white and purple blossoms would be in full flower. It was a lovely time of the year, and Kishimoto felt his spirits reviving.

Yet, though he felt refreshed, he felt that he could not relax. It was not that he had come to France with any thought of seeking a life of comfort. All he asked was that he be allowed to find peace of mind, which he needed so much. But so far he had not found it. Why could he not feel, he asked himself, that all he had done was to move his study temporarily from Tokyo to the boarding house in Paris? Slightly irritated at himself, he left his room and went outside. The plane trees by the maternity hospital cast their

---

[1] *Sōseki zenshū* (20 vols., Sōseki zenshū kankōkai, Tokyo, 1928), IX, 371-73.

shadows on the sidewalk. A group of schoolboys with their teacher walked past, bathed in the warm sunshine. They were probably on their way to a picnic. Their French eyes were full of curiosity as they looked at Kishimoto. He stood and watched these innocent boys and thought of his own sons far away. Shigeru, the younger one, was now in his first year at school. Kishimoto imagined him walking to school with his brother Senta.

He walked on towards the observatory. There too he found little children. They were playing in the shade of the tall, calm chestnut trees. High above were the flowers, full blown; and it seemed to Kishimoto that these were stage lights, casting their gentle glow on the spring scene below.

Fresh memories came back to him of the time he arrived in Marseilles and stepped onto European soil for the first time in his life. He felt as though he had never stopped walking since. Remaining indoors under the roof of a French tenement was to him little different from walking in his leather shoes on the cold stone pavements of Paris. He could not find true rest anywhere. He had gone to parks, stood in front of shop windows, sat down in strange coffee shops, not because he wanted to but simply because there had been nothing else for him to do. There had been periods when he would wander in this aimless fashion for days on end. Indeed, one could say he had spent the entire year in this alien land like a lost child. What a way to live, he thought, with a touch of incredulity.

When he got back to his room he was quite exhausted by the long walk under the fresh young leaves. He had seen so many streets that day. He went to the window and stood there, utterly forlorn. Far away in the sky were fluffy white clouds like those he remembered seeing from the mountains of Shinano. Blown about by the early spring breeze, they changed their shape endlessly. He watched them alone, with no one beside him to share his thoughts. The work he had brought with him from Japan lay on his desk untouched.

But there were his children in Tokyo that he had to support; he must somehow get down to work. I have become home-sick, he thought disgustedly. He felt the strain of exile so acutely then that he could have thrown himself onto the bare wooden floor and wept.[2]

Descriptive passages of this kind, at least as effective, can be found in Sōseki's novels too. But there, they provide relief from those more dramatic moments when the author gets closer to the characters; while in Tōson's novels, they seem to form the core.

One is tempted to characterize this difference by thinking of Sōseki as an essentially "Western" novelist and of Tōson as a "traditional" one. Sōseki himself was not over-admiring of tra-ditional Japanese literature,[3] and despite much that is Japanese in them, such novels of his mature period as *Kōjin* ("passer-by," 1913), *Kokoro* ("the heart," 1914) and *Michikusa* do owe their inspiration, it seems, to the Western psychological novel. There is in them a combining of drama and intellectuality such as cannot be found in Tōson's most representative novels. Unlike Sōseki, Tōson constantly talked of Japanese writers of the past. And his own technique, which he chose to call "impressionistic," he thought he could find in Sei Shōnagon and Saikaku.[4] Moreover, he sometimes would refer to himself as a poet turned novelist; and in so doing, he was seeing him-self as a part of the tradition that produced Bashō and Issa.[5]

There is then the fact of his having favored the *shishōsetsu* form. As Howard Hibbett has pointed out, this modern Japa-

[2] *Shimazaki Tōson zenshū* (19 vols., Shinchōsha, Tokyo, 1948-52), VI, 142-44.

[3] See, for example, *Sōseki zenshū*, XX, 425-26.

[4] *Tōson zenshū*, XIV, 35.

[5] "My good masters have been those poets of the *Manyōshū* . . . and such men as Bashō and Issa who showed me how much there was to be found anew in our ordinary, common language." (*Tōson zenshū*, XVIII, 125.) "Even when reading Issa's diary, one can see how deep-rooted our long tradition of detailed realism is." (XV, 16.) See also XVII, 304.

nese genre has characteristics reminiscent of the traditional essay, the *zuihitsu*.[6] It is not strictly a confessional form, for in the place of rigorous self-examination, there is description of the surface scene—instead of psychological insight, melancholy lyricism. Also, in writing *shishōsetsu*, Tōson might very well have been giving expression to the traditional Japanese conviction that poetry and the essay are the respectable literary forms, while fiction is for the vulgar. Poetry and the essay are "true"; fiction, on the other hand, is made up, and therefore by definition lacks seriousness.

However, for all the seemingly traditional traits in Tōson, he was in his own way as modern a writer as Sōseki was. And though his conception of the novel was inherently limited and as a result his long-term contribution was not as positive as Sōseki's, he still remains one of the key figures of Meiji literature, if only because his career mirrors so clearly certain crucial aspects of Meiji literary history in a way that the career of the more original, more creative Sōseki does not.

With one or two exceptions, those writers who were active before the emergence in the first decade of this century of such men as Sōseki, Tōson and Nagai Kafū (1876-1959) tended to be either uninformed or at best undiscriminating about Western literature;[7] so that Bulwer-Lytton, say, would seem to them as impressive as Disraeli and Disraeli as impressive as any of the other European novelists. For example, political novels—a post-Restoration phenomenon in Japan—were written by politically minded men who thought Disraeli was a serious novelist simply because the things he wrote about were respectable. The subtlety of his language and the sophistication of his understanding of people were lost to the authors of *Kajin no kigū*

[6] Howard S. Hibbett, "The Portrait of the Artist in Japanese Fiction," *Far Eastern Quarterly*, XIV (1955), 347-54.

[7] The one outstanding exception is Futabatei Shimei (1864-1909), whose *Ukigumo* ("the fleeting cloud") appeared as early as 1887, and who seems to have had an unusually sophisticated understanding of Russian novelists. See Marleigh Grayer Ryan, *Japan's First Modern Novel*: Ukigumo *of Futabatei Shimei* (New York, 1967).

("a chance meeting with two fair ladies," 1885) and *Setchūbai* ("plum blossoms in the snow," 1886).[8]

Tōson, on the other hand, read Western novelists with cultivated intelligence and prejudice, so that Zola seemed at times funny and Flaubert frightening.[9] Dostoevski's large themes bored him; but those incidental passages, where shadowy, unknown figures would appear before one's eyes and in a moment disappear, perhaps into some doorway, haunted him.[10] He read these novelists not as a would-be imitator with limited comprehension of the original, but critically as a fellow novelist.

What seems to be important is not that he understood Western literature better than his predecessors, but rather that he understood better than they the best examples—whether Western or not—of a particular literary form, and read them with an attitude that was all his own. And it can be argued that his awareness of what he could and could not do in his own context was conditioned by his intelligent understanding of what the Western novelists had succeeded in doing in theirs. The peculiar limitations of the kind of novel he came to write, the seemingly traditional qualities he brought to it, are, paradoxical

[8] The content of *Kajin no kigū* by Tōkai Sanshi (1852-1922) is summarized in *Introduction to Classic Japanese Literature* (Kokusai bunka shinkokai, Tokyo, 1948), 365-71. *Setchūbai* by Suehiro Tetchō (1849-96) is perhaps not as incredible, in that the cast is all Japanese, and lacks such exotic figures as Louis Kossuth, Fannie Parnell, Arabi Pasha, a Chinese cook who is "the impoverished scion of a once distinguished family," a Spanish general, etc. However, it is no better as a novel. The hero is an idealistic young politician, and the heroine is a progressive and beautiful girl who admires him for his idealism. Little does she know that he is actually the young man whom her father had once taken care of, and whom the latter had designated her fiancé. Towards the end, however, after he has survived all the villainous attempts by his rivals and her very wicked uncle to ruin his career, his real identity becomes known to the girl when she seees his own photograph in one of her albums and he exclaims, "But that's me!" And she exclaims, "Then you must be . . ." As for the reasons why they had not recognized each other before, they are far too complicated to be explained here.

[9] *Tōson zenshū*, XIV, 126.　　　[10] *Tōson zenshū*, XV, 30.

though this may seem, a sign of his modernity. His lack of sympathy for Dostoevski's intellectuality and his admiration for his impressionistic passages reflect a consciousness not so much of Dostoevski's limitations as of his own, a consciousness of distinctions that was beyond the capacity of his predecessors. And when he implied the similarity of his approach to that of the "impressionistic" Japanese writers of the past, he was not being a traditionalist so much as a twentieth-century writer who, having understood the richness of the Western novel, was rationalizing his weaknesses by reference to tradition.

Tōson, then, was as different as any of his contemporaries was from those writers that had come before. Despite their narrowness, his novels constituted as great a departure as any from what had previously been written. And it is perhaps by seeing even his failure, specifically the weaknesses inherent in a *shishōsetsu* writer, as a part of his modernity that we can understand not only the nature of his contribution but the kind of obstacles encountered by a Japanese writer attempting to write a modern novel in the early twentieth century.

Tōson's first novel and only long work of genuine fiction, *Hakai*, is still one of the most famous novels of the Meiji period. It is regarded, quite justly, as a pioneer work of modern realism.[11] It is, as are Kafū's *Yume no onna* ("the woman of the dream," 1903)[12] and Sōseki's *Nowaki* ("autumn wind," 1907),[13] one of the very first works of this period which are separated, by the relatively complex way in which the charac-

---

[11] "*Hakai* was *Ukigumo*'s spiritual heir and established the modern novel in Japan." (Kawazoe Kunimoto, *Nihon shizen shugi no bungaku oyobi sono shūhen*, Tokyo, 1957, p. 64.) "*Hakai* was the first great triumph of Japanese realism." (Sugiura Mimpei, "Shimazaki Tōson," *Nihon bungaku kōza*, Kawade Shobō, Tokyo, 1952, VI, 153.)

[12] This remarkable novel is discussed by Edward Seidensticker in his excellent study, *Kafū the Scribbler* (Stanford University Press, 1965), pp. 14-17.

[13] This novel is discussed, as are some other novels by Sōseki, in Edwin McClellan, *Two Japanese Novelists: Sōseki and Tōson* (University of Chicago Press, 1969).

ters are handled, by the modernness of the language used, and by the content, from what preceded them. One scholar has commented that before the appearance of such "novels in the European sense," only *monogatari*, or romances, were being written.[14] Whether we accept this manner of distinguishing or not, the fact is that when we look at some of the more representative works which appeared before *Hakai*, we see what a considerable achievement it was.

Tsubouchi Shōyō's (1859-1935) *Tōsei shosei katagi* ("the character of the modern student," 1885) may serve as an example. His *Shōsetsu shinzui* ("the essence of the novel," 1885)[15] is probably the most famous work of literary criticism of the Meiji period. In it he attacked the vulgarity and childishness of Japanese writers, and demanded that they emulate the seriousness of their Western colleagues. More dignity, more realism, more intelligence was what he wanted to see. It is not a distinguished piece of literary criticism, but presumably it was for Shōyō's contemporaries a startling document. At any rate, what is interesting is that the same man should have written a novel quite so appallingly bad as *Tōsei shosei katagi*.

The novel has an enormous cast of characters—surely larger than that of any other supposedly respectable Meiji novel— most of whom are given roughly equal attention by the author, and all of whom are cardboard; the result being that the reader must have an unusually good memory for names if he is to follow the plot, or plots, at all. Perhaps it was meant to be a work of social criticism; for the title suggests that it is concerned with the manners of contemporary university students. However, it is mostly a collection of pointless anecdotes about students' escapades, arbitrarily tied together by a kind of main plot which is occasionally allowed to emerge from the veritable jungle of subplots and sub-subplots.

[14] Yoshida Seiichi, *Meiji Taishō bungakushi* (Tokyo, 1956), pp. 161-62.

[15] See Donald Keene, *Modern Japanese Literature* (New York, 1956), pp. 55-58.

The reader, if he is sufficiently hardy, will in time gather that two students, Komachida and Moriyama, who are good friends, are perhaps meant to be slightly more important than their numerous colleagues. Komachida is interested in a young geisha, Tanoji. When he was a boy, his father had taken into their house a little girl whom his mistress had found wandering in the streets. But when the father went bankrupt, the mistress and the girl had had to go. Moriyama similarly had once had a younger sister. But years before, during the civil disturbances, the girl had disappeared. Then there is the villainess, Ohide. She has a geisha daughter, an associate of Tanoji, by the name of Kaodori. In the very same battle in which the Moriyama girl had been lost, Ohide had momentarily mislaid her child, and picked up by mistake another baby girl. On realizing her error she had immediately thrown her away, but had kept the purse she had found on her. On it is embroidered a family crest—the Moriyama crest, of course. Now hearing that Moriyama's father is still looking for his daughter, she and Kaodori go to him and show him the purse as proof of Kaodori's identity. Mr. Moriyama is about to be fooled when a strange old man bursts in and tells him that Kaodori is an imposter. He knows all about Ohide's evil plot, the old man says, because he has overheard her conspiring with her daughter; he was not going to do anything about it, but he has just discovered that the little girl his sister—now long dead—once looked after was none other than Tanoji, and he has good reason to believe that she, not Kaodori, is Mr. Moriyama's daughter. It turns out besides that Tanoji is the girl Komachida's father's mistress had picked up. Tanoji, then, is a lady, worthy after all of Komachida's attentions. She had once been a kind of stepsister to him too. And most exciting of all, she is his best friend's sister. On this happily incestuous note, the novel comes to an end.

Perhaps more sophisticated is Yamada Bimyō's (1868-1910) *Musashino* ("Musashi Plain," 1887), much admired in its day for its modern style and "realistic" content. The time of the story is about five hundred years ago. Two warriors—a young man and his father-in-law—are making their way across the plain. They are obviously model types—restrained and gentle, loyal and brave. But unfortunately they are waylaid by a band of enemy warriors and killed. The scene shifts to a lonely cottage, far away from the plain. There we find the two men's wives—mother and daughter—wondering what has become of them. The next morning the mother wakes up to find that her daughter, armed with a halberd, has gone to look for the two men. In the next scene, a fugitive warrior comes to the cottage. The mother finds out from him that both her husband and her son-in-law have been killed. And when she mentions her daughter, the warrior tells her that on his way he saw the body of a young woman in armor, with a halberd beside her, lying by the mountain road. She had obviously been killed by bears, he says. And that is the end of the story.

The comment that Bimyō throws in at the end is significant, in that it gives us an idea of what he, and his contemporaries presumably, thought was so novel about the content of *Musashino*: "If this had been a superficial work, the two warriors would have escaped from the enemy."[16] The same of course could be said of the heroic young lady. In other words, *Musashino* is "realistic" because "good" people are killed in it—rather senselessly, one might add; it is "modern" because it is free of didacticism, and Bimyō, unlike Shōyō, does not allow virtue to be rewarded.

Konjiki yasha ("gold demon," 1897-1903) by Ozaki Kōyō (1867-1903) is perhaps the most famous of all Meiji novels. Several movies have been made of it; and surely no lovers in modern Japanese fiction are more familiar to the public than Miya and Kan'ichi. Kan'ichi is an orphan, and has been brought up by Miya's father. He is a college student. It is understood by all that he and Miya will marry. However, when a very rich young banker, Tomiyama, proposes to Miya, she

[16] *Bimyō senshū* (2 Vols., Ritsumeikan shuppanbu, Kyoto, 1935), I, 17.

and her parents succumb to the lure of money and decide to break her engagement to Kan'ichi. Kan'ichi, when informed of the decision, is incredulous, and immediately goes to Atami where Miya is holidaying with her mother. He must hear what the girl herself has to say. The two meet in a lonely spot. It is evening, and a full moon shines brightly on the sea below and the pines nearby. When Miya tearfully admits that what he has heard is true, Kan'ichi cries out:

"Ah Mii-san! This is the last night we shall be together like this. After this night, you will never console me again, I shall never speak to you again. The seventeenth of January, Mii-san, remember it well. Oh where shall I be gazing at the moon on this same night next year! The year after that, ten years from now, for the rest of my life, I shall remember this night. How can I forget it, even if I die? Remember, Mii-san, the seventeenth of January. On this night next year my tears will veil the moon. And then, Mii-san, and then you will know that I am somewhere haunted by the memory of this night, and crying as I am now."[17]

Miya marries Tomiyama in due course. She has everything, except love. Very soon she realizes what a terrible mistake she has made, and begins to pine for Kan'ichi. He, in the meantime, has become a notoriously mean usurer. He is going to become rich, and will have his revenge not only on Miya but on mankind. Before he could finish the novel Kōyō died, so that we do not know what finally happens to the ill-starred lovers.

Konjiki yasha is a work of some distinction. It is elegantly written (Kōyō had a great command of the language), and is more dignified than most works of fiction by Sōseki's and Tōson's predecessors. But when all is said and done it is rather

---

[17] *Ozaki Kōyō zenshū* (Chūō Kōronsha, Tokyo, 1941), vi, 72. Only Vols. v, vi, and ix of this edition have appeared.

low-brow, with the usual cast of cardboard characters. Kan'ichi, for example, who changes from clean-cut college student to mean usurer, may be an improvement on the hero who never ceases to be virtuous, but the change is after all mechanical. And the usurer that Kan'ichi goes to work for is named Wani-buchi, or "crocodile pool."

According to one commentary, Ozaki Kōyō "... in this novel attempts to show that no matter how potent money appears to be, its power over human life is after all evanescent; while love, although apparently weak in comparison, possesses in actual fact the quality of permanence."[18] One suspects that this is not an entirely inaccurate interpretation of Kōyō's intentions.

Tōson, then, seems to have understood much more clearly than such writers as these what were the qualities necessary to the modern realistic novel. *Hakai* is a surprisingly intelligent novel for its time; its characters, for all their theatricality, are incomparably more complicated psychologically than those we are accustomed to seeing in earlier Meiji fiction. Its protagonist, Ushimatsu, is not only a complex personality but often believably so; moreover, he is a strikingly modern hero, in that he is conceived as an intellectual alone in an alien world.[19]

Ushimatsu is an *eta*. However, by hiding this fact, he has managed to go through the prefectural normal college and get a post as school teacher. The novel concerns the strain this deception places on him, his persecution by those of his col-

---

[18] *Introduction to Classic Japanese Literature*, 377.

[19] Any hero of course is alone in that he stands out above the rest and receives more attention. But isolation is a necessary condition of Tōson's and Sōseki's protagonists. The protagonists may not revel in it, but it gives them their raison d'être as characters. They are fairly ordinary people, but they demand attention because they are alone and are conscious of it. Isolation gives them the distinction they need as heroes. They do not have to be intellectuals, but they tend to be, for they are introspective. Sōseki's or Tōson's hero may die mad, as in Tōson's *Yoakemae*, or commit suicide, as in Sōseki's *Kokoro*, or continue to lead a life of quiet desperation, as in Sōseki's *Michikusa* or Tōson's *Ie*.

leagues who suspect his origin, and his final decision to confess publicly his secret.[20]

It is this decision that the title ("broken commandment") refers to, for his father had once admonished him never to tell anyone of his *eta* birth. But one of the features of *Hakai* that makes it a pioneer work is that filial obedience becomes for Ushimatsu a means of rationalizing his fear of being found out.

There is a character in the novel by the name of Inoko who is also an *eta*. Inoko, however, does not lie about his birth, and has dedicated his life to fighting the unjust persecution of his kind. Ushimatsu admires him, and one day goes to see him intending to tell him that he too is an *eta*. But in the end he fails to do so. This is how Tōson describes Ushimatsu's state of mind as he leaves Inoko:

> . . . he thought of his own conduct and he wanted to cry. To comfort himself, he tried to think of all the reasons why he shouldn't have told him: there was the promise he had made to his father; there was his uncle to consider too; and once he divulged his secret, what was to prevent Inoko from telling his wife, who, being a woman, would then in all likelihood talk about it to someone else? No, once it got started, there would be no end to it. Why should he, he asked himself, force on himself an *eta*'s identity at this point? Hadn't he passed as an ordinary person so far? And wasn't it perfectly reasonable that he should want to go on doing so?
>
> But he knew that these were rationalizations; he was merely trying to cheat himself. He could not, after all, forgive himself for not having told Inoko.[21]

The villains too are conceived with some subtlety. There is a politician, Takayanagi. He has just married an *eta* girl for money, and if her origin were to be discovered, he would be

---

[20] *Hakai* is described more fully, as are the other novels by Tōson, in Edwin McClellan, *Two Japanese Novelists: Sōseki and Tōson*.

[21] *Tōson zenshū*, III, 118-19.

ruined. He has learned through her that Ushimatsu is an *eta*.
Ushimatsu, then, must know about her. He tries at first to
befriend Ushimatsu, but the latter rejects his overtures, mainly
through fear. His next recourse is to ruin Ushimatsu's reputation. He tells a junior colleague of Ushimatsu's, Bumpei, who
covets Ushimatsu's post. Bumpei in turn tells the principal, a
wily academic bureaucrat.

At the end of one of the corridors, where there was a
flight of stairs leading to the second floor, the two met to
have their talk. Few students came that way, and it was a
comparatively quiet spot. Ushimatsu, the two knew, was
busy elsewhere with his students. They stood side by side,
leaning against the grey wall.

"And who told you about Ushimatsu?" asked the principal.

Bumpei smiled and said: "You'd be surprised, sir—very
surprised."

"I couldn't even begin to guess."

"Well, as a matter of fact, this man asked me not to mention his name. He felt that he shouldn't get involved in a
matter that would affect so seriously the reputation of
another. But I assure you, he is a thoroughly reliable source
of information. Wouldn't you say, sir, that a candidate for
the Diet was reliable?"

"A candidate for the Diet?"

"You know who I mean."

"You don't mean the man who recently came back with
a bride?"

"Getting warm, sir, getting warm."

"I see. In which case, he probably heard about it while he
was travelling around the country. Well, things like that
always come out in the end. Let it be a lesson to all of us."
The principal gave a sigh. He continued: "It's a bit of a
shock, I must say. Ushimatsu an *eta*! I'd never have believed
it."

"To be honest, I was a bit taken aback too, sir."

"But look at his face—there isn't a thing there that would indicate his lowly origin."

"That's why, I suppose, he managed to fool everybody."

"Maybe so, maybe so. At a glance, no one could tell, wouldn't you say?"

"Appearances are misleading at the best of times, sir. But what about his character?"

"I shouldn't have thought you could conclude much from that."

"But Principal, hasn't his behavior in general struck you as a little odd? Observe him carefully next time. You'll notice, for example, that there's a very furtive look in his eyes."

The principal laughed. He said: "You could hardly take that to be proof of his *eta* birth."[22]

But the principal is willing enough to be convinced. Ushimatsu has never seemed to him an all-Japanese sport. And so in the end we find him saying: "I always thought there was something strange about him. Why should he behave in that gloomy way of his, if he had nothing to hide?"

Wily or hypocritical bureaucratic types are commonly encountered villains in Japanese literature of the period, and Tōson's principal is in a sense a fairly stock figure.[23] He is nevertheless an original enough creation, a far more interesting and believable character than Shōyō's or Kōyō's villains. And because of the very moderation with which Tōson presents him, the above is as sinister a piece of dialogue as one is likely to find in Meiji fiction.

The seemingly strange thing, then, is that after writing this deservedly successful novel, in which he showed imagination

[22] *Ibid.*, 170-71.

[23] There is the protagonist's bureau chief in Futabatei's *Ukigumo*, for example, or the school principal in Nagai Kafū's *Jigoku no hana* ("hell flowers," 1902) who rapes the heroine.

and insight in his handling of character, and in which is evident the remarkably advanced notion that modern realism must to a great extent depend for its drama on subtle characterization, Tōson should have proceeded to write the autobiographical *Haru*, and continued throughout the rest of his career to write novels based on his own experiences; that after having shown that he could write realistic, "made-up" fiction in the Western manner, he should have moved to a form where drama, tight plotting, and close examination of character and motive were replaced by descriptive lyricism, where those qualities we deem most necessary in fiction came to be for the most part ignored. But perhaps this move from *Hakai* to *Haru* was a natural outcome of his modernity, and the very qualities which made it possible for him to write the kind of modern psychological novel that his predecessors could not were partly responsible also for his retreat to the peculiarly limited *shishōsetsu*.

Viewed purely critically, without reference to the historical context, *Hakai* is not a distinguished novel. It has a very bad ending, for instance. Ushimatsu tearfully announces to his class that he is an *eta*, and asks the boys to forgive him for having lied to them. The boys are very touched; they immediately go to the principal and plead with him to keep Ushimatsu on the staff. However, fortunately for the principal and presumably for Ushimatsu also, a rich *eta* steps in and offers him a job on a ranch in Texas. Ushimatsu will sail happily for his new job and home with his sweetheart, who has remained staunchly loyal throughout. But aside from this, a glaring fault of the novel is that the author constantly fails to maintain his detachment and becomes much too emotionally involved with his hero. It is, in other words, frequently sentimental, despite the fact that Tōson's initial conception of Ushimatsu is on the whole free of sentimentality. For example, as Inoko is attacked and mortally hurt by the politician's hired toughs and Ushimatsu too late rushes to his side, Tōson writes, allowing his own language to be colored by the emotion of his protagonist:

"Alas, Inoko's body was already cold. How hard it was for Ushimatsu to take final leave of his mentor! He laid his face against the blood-drained face of the dead man and exclaimed, 'Maître, maître!' "[24]

The sentimentality, or emotionalism, of Tōson, however, is rather different from that of, say, Kōyō. That is, the objects of their respective sentimental attitudes are different. Ushimatsu is an isolated intellectual, persecuted by the likes of the principal and Bumpei not only because they suspect he is an *eta* but because he is different (or "gloomy," as the principal calls him). Kan'ichi, on the other hand, is a shallowly conceived figure of melodrama, whose plight is not necessitated by qualities peculiar to himself. So that whereas the emotionalism of Tōson comes from some sort of personal emotional investment in his protagonist, that of Kōyō is little more than a professional requirement.

And so though emotionalism is indeed a major weakness in *Hakai*, it does also reflect a rather significant new quality which Tōson brought to the Meiji novel—an emotional commitment to what one is saying, a seriousness of intention—and which the writers before him seemed to lack. Of course the absence of emotionalism in a novelist may be a virtue; but it is a virtue when we mean by it detached understanding which represents a step forward, say, from direct identification of the novelist with his characters. In Tōson's predecessors it showed rather a lack of concern, an inability to become involved in what they were writing about. They had not yet reached the stage, as it were, of over-identifying, let alone that of clinical detachment.

Tōson was apt to talk about "the sense of discovery," "insight into reality" and the like that he thought he found in the best writers of the past, both Japanese and Western.[25] Solemn statements of this sort can make us shy, but the fact is that he was

---

[24] *Tōson zenshū*, III, 253.

[25] For example: "One must realize that literature that excels is born when the writer sees life exactly as it is." (*Tōson zenshū*, XIV, 7.)

referring to a very important aspect of the development of the modern Japanese novel. The lack of involvement on the part of writers like Shōyō, Bimyō and Kōyō was indeed a reflection of their inability to understand that realism in fiction must at least in part grow out of the desire to communicate such "insight."

The relatively mature realism of *Hakai*, then, is due more to the presence of such a desire in Tōson than to some readily identifiable influence of the Western novel. And it is not at all paradoxical that the realism of his novels should be ultimately traceable to the romantic poetry of his early period when he was one of that group of passionate young writers who ran the literary journal, *Bungakkai* ("the world of literature," 1893-98). For it was through his association with the *Bungakkai* group and its leader, Kitamura Tōkoku (1868-94)[26] that he first learned to express his consciousness of his own identity, of the loneliness of modern youth; and it was this consciousness which led him eventually to write his so-called naturalistic novels, and which was mostly responsible for their modernity.

The romanticism of the young Tōson, and perhaps of the *Bungakkai* group as a whole, was characterized by self-centeredness, an adolescent yearning for things unattainable and things remembered (and perhaps for adolescence itself),[27] a deep regard for one's own feelings and a tendency to see literature as a means of exhibiting these, a sense of separation from the rest of society, and an inability, or unwillingness, to

[26] See Francis Mathy, "Kitamura Tōkoku: The Early Years," *Monumenta Nipponica*, xviii (1963), 1-44; "Kitamura Tōkoku: Essays on the Inner Life," *Monumenta Nipponica*, xix (1964), 66-110; and "Kitamura Tōkoku: Final Essays," *Monumenta Nipponica*, xx (1965), 41-63.

[27] One remembers that Higuchi Ichiyō's (1872-96) beautiful *Takekurabe* ("growing up") appeared in *Bungakkai* in 1895. The children in it live apart from their elders, none of whom understand the pain of growing up. It is a modern work, partly because it is concerned with the loneliness of adolescence. See Edward Seidensticker's translation of it in Donald Keene, *Modern Japanese Literature*, pp. 70-110.

express oneself in a context other than that of one's own emotional world.

What is modern about them is that though they spoke frequently of the English romantic poets, for example, they turned to these more to find expression of what they felt than to seek inspiration; and their sense of separation, it would seem, grew out of the native context. In one scene in *Haru*, Kitamura Tōkoku (called Aoki in the novel) is described as follows:

> After the drinking had begun, Aoki became deadly serious and in a tone of deep indignation began to attack those who in their thinking were still slaves to convention. He cited examples of false patriots, ignorant optimists, worldly clerics, and worthless idols of the public. Even among men who behaved with greater dignity than these, he said bitterly, there were many who were in fact contemptible hypocrites. Japan had become a graveyard of the young. There was no freshness of spirit, no originality. What did one see but a docile, mindless acceptance of everything?
>
> Destroy! Yes, destroy! Then perhaps we can begin anew.[28]

It is easy to criticize *Bungakkai* romanticism for its intellectual naïveté and formlessness. But it did represent a truly new awakening of the heart, and helped to introduce qualities peculiar to late Meiji literature, romantic yearning and the dignifying of loneliness. In a collection of verse that Tōson brought out in 1897, called *Wakanashū* ("a collection of young leaves"), we find this:

> I am like the morning cloud
> That brought rain the night before;
> Or I am like the evening rain
> That tomorrow will be a floating cloud.

> Like leaves that have fallen
> I was carried by the wind;
> And with the clouds of the morning
> Came over the river at night.

[28] *Tōson zenshū*, IV, 90.

Perhaps here, in Miyagi Plain,
In this ancient wilderness without a path
I shall cease to wander,
And find some rest.

The grass has withered under the northern sun;
And in this barrenness of Miyagi Plain
My troubled heart
Shall find a home.

In loneliness I listen to the northern wind;
To my ears it is like the sound of the harp;
And to my eyes the stones
Are like flowers in bloom.[29]

Because his novels are often so heavily written, and perhaps because of our preconceptions about naturalism, we can miss this romantic spirit which underlies all of Tōson's novels. The close attention to detail is not there for its own sake. It is there because the surroundings echo the emotions of the lonely observer; they are an extension, so to speak, of Miyagi Plain. And it is by reference to this romantic spirit that we can begin to see the implications of his move from *Hakai* to *Haru*, and the nature of one major course of development towards realism in Japan.

Haru is not easy to describe, for the simple reason that it has no tangible story to get hold of. It seems to have almost no plot. The main character is a young writer and poet, Kishimoto (Tōson), and surrounding him are the *Bungakkai* group, led by Aoki (Kitamura Tōkoku), and their various relatives and acquaintances. Kishimoto is in love with a girl whom he had come to know while teaching in a women's college. However she hardly ever appears in the book. She marries someone else, and dies soon thereafter. Kishimoto is a lost soul, not only because of his doomed love affair but because of a general sense of aimlessness. Aoki is embittered by poverty and, the reader

---

[29] *Tōson zenshū*, II, 24-25.

supposes, by what he considers his own failure. He kills himself; and Kishimoto now feels even less prepared than before to cope with life. But he must survive somehow, and when he is given an opportunity to go to Sendai in the northeast to teach, he decides to leave Tokyo and his friends and start afresh. The novel comes to an end as the train leaves for Sendai:

> He could hear the melancholy sound of the rain outside. He leaned his head against the window and dreamed hopefully of all that the future might hold for him. He was utterly exhausted. He thought: "I do want to live—even I." The scene outside flashed past his eyes—the grey sky, the trees and grass shining wet, thin mist rising from the rain-soaked ground, hens huddled forlornly under the eaves. Weary of the journey through the rain, most of the other travellers had gone to sleep. The rain, which had been falling steadily, suddenly began to pour down.[30]

Haru is not as carefully plotted as *Hakai*, and it meanders in a way that the other does not; its characters are not half so vividly drawn, nor are they shown in as dramatic situations. It is in some important respects, then, less of a novel than *Hakai*. Nevertheless, it is a work of greater seriousness. It is less contrived, less melodramatic, and finally more intelligent. Because Tōson was writing about his own youth and about people he had once known, he could be more himself, and more serious, than when writing about imaginary people and situations; he could concentrate more on expressing himself than on entertaining the reader, and wander freely as a prose lyricist in a world where there were no handsome *eta* school teachers and unpleasant school principals. In his handling of Ushimatsu he had not shown sufficient detachment; the subjectivity, the need to identify, had been too strong. The romantic poet turned novelist had to speak in his own voice, and to

[30] *Tōson zenshū*, IV, 248.

do so in *Haru* was more appropriate than to do so in a novel like *Hakai*.

Perhaps in going to his own past for his material Tōson was admitting his lack of fictional imagination. Certainly one of the great failings of *Haru*—and of his other autobiographical novels that followed—is the absence of this important quality. But however unsatisfactory *Haru* may be as a novel, Tōson did in writing it introduce to his medium the concern of the lyric poet for truthful depiction of what he sees and feels. And with the concern came the kind of artistry that we do not find in novels that appeared before it. Even the most successful scenes in *Hakai* do not have quite the subtle emotional coloring, the restraint, the dependence on things unsaid, the suggestion of significance through sheer objective description of the scene, that we find in the best passages in *Haru*. And the effectiveness of these passages does not depend upon rich and complicated imagery, or the elegance of individual sentences, but upon the starkness and economy of the language which is purposely prosaic because the writer's intention is to convey the total quality of a scene, as he sees it, as faithfully as possible.

Here is a typical passage. Kishimoto is staying with Aoki and his wife, Misao, who live in a rented room in a temple. The Aokis have a child, Tsuruko. It is early morning, and Kishimoto and Aoki are about to go to the nearby sea to wash their faces.

Aoki seemed somewhat revived by the fresh air outside. The railway, like a rough intruder, cut through the temple grounds, and the two had to go across it to get to the village. They went down and then up some stone steps, and reached the old entrance gate at the top of the hill. Misao, carrying the child on her back, accompanied them thus far.

"Tsū-chan wants to go with daddy," she said. "Do take her with you."

Aoki stopped and said, "I can hardly do that. You know she'll be in the way."

"But she wants to go badly. Look at her." She then turned to the child and said, "Go along, then, go along with daddy."

Tsuruko reached out for her father.

"She'll be in the way, I tell you," Aoki said, then added feebly, "can't you see, I've got company." He almost pushed away the clinging child. "You take care of her."

"Please," said Misao.

Pursued by the child's pleading cries Aoki fled from the scene, and disappeared around the corner of a fisherman's hut. Kishimoto watched helplessly, not knowing whose side he should be on.

They walked on sand until they came to a pine grove. The morning sun was already very strong, and it hurt to look at the glittering water. They were young, and were not content merely to wash their faces. Throwing off their clothes they jumped in and raced each other towards the oncoming waves.

The sea was rough, and Kishimoto was often close to being washed under. Aoki had been brought up in these parts, and was the better swimmer. Cheered by the thought that he was not so feeble after all, he imitated Kishimoto who was splashing about playfully. Then they heard the ominous sound of weighted fish-hooks flying through the air towards them. The whole beach now seemed to be covered with fishermen. The two began desperately to swim towards shore, away from the hooks that were falling all around them. They were forced back at first by high receding waves, but the next moment they felt themselves being carried in. There was a deafening roar, and at last they stood up in the midst of foaming water.

It was a good day for the fisherfolk. The two sat down and watched the women and children pull in the bonito. The sand felt warm and inviting, and Kishimoto thought he would just lie for a while and bask in the sun, forgetful of everything. But his memories would not leave him alone. Water trickled out of his ears; this reminded him of the days when he used to swim in the river by Ryōgoku. And he remembered that nine months had gone by since he left home. He had gone to many strange places in that time, he thought, even as far as the distant northeast. Aoki sat still, hugging his knees. There was disillusionment, and exhaustion, in his eyes. Kishimoto saw him hang down his head wearily until it almost touched his knees, then close his eyes. He seemed to be listening to the waves beating against the shore.

Soon they were ready to go. They cut across the village and followed the sandy path to the temple gate. There they found Misao with the child on her back.

"Tsū-chan," Aoki said. He hardly ever called her that. In spite of her sex he usually called her *"bōzu."*

Misao said nothing, and started to walk away. Aoki quickly caught up with her. "Tsū-chan," he said again fondly. He smiled at her, then put out his hand; he seemed to be asking for forgiveness. Misao stood there, gazing at her husband. She gave a sigh, then continued on her way. Aoki was taken aback. Guiltily he watched his wife go down the steps and cross the railway. "Misao! Misao!" he called pleadingly.[31]

This is one of the most haunting scenes to be found in any Japanese novel of the period. It is beautifully executed. It has balance, in that it has just the right degree of focus, just the right touch of suppression of emotion, of muting of voices. But it is not the technique surely that is finally responsible for whatever beauty there is here. Rather, it is the emotion contained in Tōson's memory of the scene and his desire to express it that has made the artistry possible. What touches us is the credibility of the emotion Tōson wishes to convey; and this credibility, so new to the Japanese novel then, stems from his conception of the form as a proper means of saying something that is very close to him.

[31] *Ibid.*, 61-64.

A collection of such scenes, no matter how well done they may be individually, does not necessarily make a good novel. *Haru*, then, fails because it does not tell enough of a story. But the very fact that it lacks *Hakai*'s clarity of design is in itself an indication of its greater sophistication. It is not strictly about *Bungakkai* or Kitamura Tōkoku, or about himself; rather, it is an expression of his nostalgia for the days of his youth and for friends long lost, of the pain still remembered of loneliness and unrequited love. It is a novel written in homage to the romantic spirit of the 1890's, that spirit which remained to his last years Tōson's major trait, and which was the basis for his realism, or naturalism. At any rate, in the abstractness of *Haru*'s theme, in the mostly lyrical nature of Tōson's purpose, and in the meaningfulness to himself of what he wants to say, we find a new dimension being added to the Meiji novel.

That Tōson's contribution should have been at the cost of the more imaginative aspects of fiction is perhaps unfortunate. But what we have to take into account is that it must have been very hard for Tōson and the other writers of his time to make up a story that seemed real to the reader and to themselves. The writing of realistic fiction which imitates life convincingly and which stimulates the reader emotionally or intellectually is after all a habit acquired after generations of practice. It is a convention with its inherited language that provides ready-made means of depicting the complexities of human life. With such means at his disposal, the novelist then can concentrate on the imaginative aspects of his craft. Realistic fiction, as we understand it, presupposes the existence of several factors: the right audience—i.e., readers who will go to fiction with certain expectations—and the author's confidence in the existence of such an audience; the right kind of language—i.e., a language which can combine elegance with precision, indeed a language whose elegance largely depends upon precision, and which resembles the language used in everyday life; a tradition which helps to attract to the art men with certain abilities, men who assume that it offers a certain range of expression; the ability to articulate, not only on the writer's part but on the part of a sizeable segment of the reading public, problems of individual psychology, for instance, which cannot be neatly categorized by reference to publicly acknowledged moral certainties; an interest in what the romancers would consider prosaic and mundane; and an inclination to eschew the fantastic.

In the first half of the Meiji period these factors were for the most part non-existent. For example, fiction was held in such low esteem that it attracted to it more or less vulgar entertainers such as Kanagaki Robun (1829-94)[32] or amateurs with axes to grind such as Tōkai Sanshi (1852-1922), the author of *Kajin no kigū*; and it was only in the late 1880's, when the likes of Futabatei Shimei (1864-1909)[33] and Yamada Bimyō

[32] His best known work is perhaps *Seiyō dōchū hizakurige* ("a walking tour of the West," 1870). A brief description of one typical scene may give the reader an adequate idea of the sort of work it is. Kitahachi and Yajirobē, the two main characters, are low-class citizens of Tokyo. Their boss is going to England on a tour of observation, and he takes them with him. Accompanying them is Tsūjirō, the interpreter. They reach Aden. While sightseeing in that city Tsūjirō and Kitahachi get lost, and wander into the nearby hills. There they encounter a huge hairy beast eating fruit. (The author explains that the beast is a kind of orangutan.) They are frightened, and run away. They come upon a tent. (All "Indians" in the mountains live this way, we are told.) They go in and find five or six natives, all very surprised to see the two strangers. Tsūjirō says in English: "Ai Jappan, kiruiru oppu ze dōto." ("I Japan, clear up the doubt.") He then bows, and flaps his arms up and down: "Purē dō notto bi engurī." ("Pray do not be angry.") The natives understand perfectly, and give them a meal. The two go to sleep, and wake up some time later to find themselves stark naked. The natives have run off with their clothes.

[33] It is a wonder that Futabatei's *Ukigumo* should have appeared so early (1887). Yet it is understandable too that it should have been left unfinished (if it is complete, then the ending is very peculiar), that he never wrote anything half so good again, that it should contain such incongruous, half-hearted comic insertions and bizarre asides, and that it should have had so little immediate influence. See Donald Keene, *Modern Japanese Literature*, pp. 59-69.

appeared, that men with serious literary ambitions began to write fiction.[34] Again, it was only with the emergence of Sōseki and Tōson that the great problem of *gembun itchi,* or the fusion of the written language with the spoken, seemed finally solved, and the novelist at last began to write easily and confidently in a language suited to the modern realistic novel.

It is not particularly surprising, then, that in the first mature phase of the development of realism in modern Japan it should have appeared most conspicuously in the autobiographical novel. To create a language suitable for the realistic novel, to avoid such technical crudities as ponderous asides (to bring oneself to assume that an audience exists which recognizes the implicit language of the novelist), to avoid melodrama—all this surely was an enormous task for the Meiji writer. To ask that Tōson should also have mastered structure, dramatic development, the art of telling an interesting story, and gone outside of the realm of personal experience is to overlook the limitations of his own time.

Even Sōseki, who had a richer imagination than the other distinguished writers of his time, was apt to exaggerate, to be a little "popular." And it does seem that his autobiographical *Michikusa* is more subtle, more real than *Kokoro.* As for Mori Ōgai, who is most admired for his historical novellas, it can hardly be claimed that he had much imagination as a novelist.[35] Tōson's going to his own life for his material was no less imaginative than Ōgai's going to history for his.

One reason for Tōson's success in spite of his weaknesses

[34] Tōson suggests that even at the time of the publication of his *Hakai* (1905) writers were regarded as tradesmen. (*Tōson zenshū,* xv, 203.)

[35] Of his longer works of fiction that are not historical, *Gan* ("wild geese," 1911-15) is perhaps the most successful. Yet it is on the whole a rather pointless story, with an extraordinarily limp ending. And one cannot but feel that the late Meiji wistfulness we find in it had already been better handled by Sōseki in *Sanshirō* (1908), or by Ichiyō in *Takekurabe.*

must have been that he reflected closely the particular stage of development the Japanese novel had reached; and he was able to communicate better than most writers of the late 1890's and early 1900's the new awareness of self and the accompanying sense of loneliness that he shared with the young men of the time. With this awareness too came something inherent in his romanticism, the relating of the lonely self to sympathetic nature surrounding 'oneself.

Tōson has been taken to task for not putting himself and his experiences in a larger context, for not relating these to a world larger than his own immediate environment.[36] It is true that his realism is descriptive rather than critical, and he seems mostly unaware of what one might call the social context.[37] (One wonders whether such unawareness is not a part of his inability to create, to write imaginative fiction. Even Jane Austen's tiny world provides a context for her characters, so that their pettiest actions begin to have some significance. And if a writer has no basis for giving significance in this sense to what his characters do, then perhaps he has no incentive to tell a story.) But there is the context of nature in his novels; and it does seem that the introduction of this context to the novel was in itself an innovation. And in placing the "I" in it, he was at least able to describe some aspects of human experience with conviction.

In the novel at least, realism seems to depend to a large extent on the conviction that the private world is interesting in its own right, that no embellishment is needed in the detailed

---

[36] For an example of such criticism, see Satō Haruo and Uno Kōji, *Meiji bungaku sakka ron* (2 vols., Tokyo, 1943), II, 274-75.

[37] This can be said of so many Japanese writers. When "nature" takes the place of "society," the novel tends to be introspective, uneventful, with the novelist retreating into the self. But the "I" novel is not the only form of retreat for the novelist: he may dress up his characters in fancy costume, as Akutagawa Ryūnosuke (1892-1927) does; or like Kafū, turn to the world of prostitutes and bars.

depiction of it. Such conviction comes at first perhaps as a discovery. In any event, it seems to have been present in the Heian period, and again in the Genroku; and it had to emerge anew in Meiji. A conspicuous instance of the emergence of this conviction, or self-awareness, was Tōson's romanticism, which led to the writing of *Haru*.

CHAPTER X

Masaoka Shiki and Tanka Reform

ROBERT H. BROWER

THE literary experience of the last eighty years has settled the fate of the thirty-one syllable tanka, or waka as it is also called, to the satisfaction of most Japanese literary men and intellectuals. For as in the West, the history of modern literature in Japan is pre-eminently the history of the novel and to a lesser extent of other literary forms, including the new-style poetry, borrowed from Western literature. The tanka, traditionally the most aristocratic form of Japanese literature— the form par excellence for the expression of the characteristically Japanese lyrical response to the beauty and sadness of the world—has been shouldered into an increasingly lonely corner of serious Japanese literary activity. The great heritage of the past remains, but few important Japanese poets any longer devote themselves wholeheartedly to the tanka, as the poets of the past once did. Nevertheless, the tanka was held in as much veneration in the mid-nineteenth century as it had ever been in the classical past, and it survives stubbornly today. Whether it can only survive as what Professor Kuwabara Takeo has termed *daini geijutsu*, or "second-class art," is a question that the Japanese must decide for themselves.[1]

[1] Kuwabara Takeo, Professor of French Literature at Kyoto University, published his controversial article, "Daini Geijutsu," in the November, 1946 issue of *Sekai*. The article was specifically an attack upon the "feudalistic" schools of contemporary haiku, but it was taken as applying to the tanka as well, and the term "second-class art" has been widely applied since to both of the brief forms of traditional Japanese poetry. Kuwabara's criticisms of the haiku and its practitioners in post-World War II Japan are in many respects similar to the criticisms of the traditional poetic forms by the editors of the *Shintaishishō* and others in the 1880's (see below).

In this paper I shall discuss the life and work of Masaoka Shiki (1867-1902) in the context of tanka reform and the re-evaluation of the Japanese poetic heritage in the Meiji period. For although Shiki's ideas for tanka reform were simple and limited, to an appreciable extent today common Japanese attitudes toward poetry and the Japanese poetic heritage are affected by his prescriptive ideal of "realistic description" or "copying from life" (*shasei*), his glorification of the *Manyōshū* and of certain pre-modern poets who composed in the "*Manyō* style," and his total rejection of the main classical tradition of Japanese poetry. Although Shiki did not himself intend the emphases that have since been given to some of his ideas, his principles have been largely re-interpreted and re-shaped by his followers into a view of poetry that places the highest value on that peculiarly Japanese ideal of "sincerity"—on expressing the real "just as it is"—with an accompanying suspicion of imagination, convention, and tradition. In the resulting confusion between biography and art, the tragic figure of Shiki himself as a gifted young poet who died at the age of thirty-five has played a substantial role. In order to understand Shiki's significance as a tanka reformer, however, it is first necessary to say a few words about his predecessors.

By the early Meiji period, the art of the waka had long since become a traditional art, with a diction that was rigidly fixed and a conventionally limited range of acceptable poetic treatment and expression. It was studied, mastered, and passed on from teacher to pupil with increasingly less emphasis upon earlier classical ideals of originality of treatment within its deliberately restricted range. To some of the Western-oriented young literati of Meiji, it seemed that the tanka must be abandoned entirely for new, freer forms adapted from Western poetry. This was the view of the three young professors of Tokyo University who together published the epoch-making "Selections from Poetry in the New Style" (*Shintaishishō*) in 1882.[2] At the same time, the traditional schools of tanka

[2] The *Shintaishishō* was a collection of nineteen translations from

poetry—the Palace School, comprising principally the latter-day descendants of the once vigorous Nijō, Reizei, and Asukai families of Court poets; and the Keien School, descended from the famous Tokugawa poet-scholar Kagawa Kageki (1768-1843)—continued to rehearse with unwearying monotony the threadbare clichés of a long-since attenuated tradition. Many of the conservative poets taught poetry for their livelihood, and had an economic stake in the perpetuation of their traditions among the younger generation. It was from their ranks that were chosen the men to perform various ceremonial functions involving poetry for the Imperial Household. They officiated over the annual New Year's poetry ceremony (*Uta Gokai Hajime*), and one of their number was appointed first head of the Imperial Bureau of Poetry in 1888.[3] The inertia of these conservative poetic schools was awesome, and their influence among the traditional establishment pervasive.

During the 1880's the debate over the fate of the tanka was carried on for the most part by men who did not think of themselves primarily as poets; the fact helps explain why some of them were so ready to cast the tanka into eternal oblivion. With the rising tide of cultural conservatism towards the end of the decade, however, it came to be felt that the adoption of new forms from Western literature need not involve the total rejection of the traditional forms. The tanka was to be allowed to survive, and was even to be encouraged as a form particularly suited to the Japanese lyrical genius, but it was to be

---

English poetry (including one French poem translated from an English version) and five original compositions by the compilers, each of whom contributed a preface. In his preface, Toyama Masakazu (1848-1900) expressed the general contempt for the brief forms of traditional poetry: "The kind of ideas that can be expressed in thirty-one syllables or in the *senryū* [haiku] form are no more substantial than a bit of fireworks or a shooting star." (Quoted in Koizumi Tōzō, *Kindai Tankashi, Meijihen* [Hakuyōsha, 1955], p. 126).

[3] Takasaki Masakaze (1836-1912), a poet of the Keien School and teacher of poetry to the Meiji Emperor and Empress.

rejuvenated with freedom of diction, use of the common language, and a spirit of masculine vigor.[4]

Considerably after such major landmarks in the modernization of Japanese literature as Tsubouchi Shōyō's *Essence of the Novel* (1885) and Futabatei Shimei's pioneering novel *Ukigumo* (1887) had appeared, groups of poets began to form for the purpose of bringing a new personalism and freedom of expression to the tanka. The first such group was the Asaka Society, founded in 1893 by the literary scholar Ochiai Naobumi (1861-1903). Naobumi's unwillingness to make sharp or sudden breaks with tradition gave the society a considerably less than revolutionary character, but the group came to include such important young poets as Yosano Tekkan (or Hiroshi; 1873-1933), himself the son of one of the more independent poets of the late Tokugawa period. Tekkan became literary editor for the newspaper *Niroku Shimpō* through the influence of Naobumi, and in May, 1894, two months before the outbreak of the Sino-Japanese War, he launched an attack upon the traditional schools of tanka poetry in a series of articles entitled *Bōkoku no On*, or "Tones Ruinous to the Nation."

On the eve of Meiji Japan's first momentous adventure in military conquest, Tekkan was fired with patriotic zeal. Like earlier advocates of tanka reform, he deplored the lack of robust, virile qualities—what the Tokugawa National Scholar (*kokugakusha*) Kamo no Mabuchi (1697-1769) had called *masuraoburi*—in the modern tanka. Using an odd dialectic that confounded Confucian and utilitarian elements with Buddhist doctrines of secular change and decline, Tekkan argued that literature was symptomatic of the state of moral health of the society which produced it. The modern tanka, he declared, was unvirile and effete; it sounded the "tones ruinous to the nation."

---

[4] This was the view expounded by the literary scholars Hagino Yoshiyuki (1860-1924) and Konakamura (Ikebe) Yoshikata (1861-1923) in their influential collection of essays, *Kokugaku Waka Kairyōron* (1887).

The true man, said Tekkan, encompassed the whole world in a single utterance and celebrated the universe in his poetry.[5]

Coming at a time of national crisis and patriotic exhilaration, the curious moral mélange of "Tones Ruinous to the Nation" is said to have brought Tekkan a large and enthusiastic following among the youth of the day. He provided no specific examples of what he meant by a new, robust, poetic style, however, until the publication of his first collection of poems, *Tōzai Namboku*, in 1896, after his return from a brief period in Korea as a Japanese language teacher. The collection included a number of such poems as the following, composed while he was in Korea.

Onoe ni wa	On the mountain ridge, how
Itaku mo tora no	loudly the tiger roars! The
Hoyuru kana	sound foretells the rising wind
Yūbe wa kaze ni	that will come with evening.
Naran to suran.[6]	

The poem is based on the popular saying that a tiger calls up the wind by its roaring. But the image of the tiger is really the only unconventional element in the poem. Tekkan demonstrated his masculine vigor—and earned the nickname "Tiger Tekkan"—by the frequent use of such images as tigers and swords in his first collection. Nevertheless, in the melodramatic atmosphere of these early poems were the seeds of the so-called Romantic movement in the modern tanka.

Ultimately, Tekkan founded the New Poetry Society (Shinshisha) in 1899, and in April of 1900 appeared the first issue of the Society's famous journal *Myōjō*. Both society and journal

---

[5] Koizumi, *Kindai Tankashi*, pp. 257-58.

[6] Kimata Osamu, *Kindai Tanka no Kanshō to Hihyō* (Meiji Shoin, 1964), pp. 54-55. In the present essay, I have provided only a prose paraphrase for each poem quoted, expecting that most readers will be able to approach the originals directly, and lest any more elaborate translations seem to obscure the critical issues involved.

were devoted to poetry in the new style as well as to the tanka, and extended a particular welcome to aspiring young poets who were not associated with the traditional schools. The poets of the *Myōjō* School tried to express in their poetry a sense of individualism and freedom from traditional social restraints that often bordered on the comic and at times became sensationally autobiographical. However, in their emphasis upon the tanka as a vehicle for the expression of personal lyricism, they could feel that they were restoring to the form a vital personalism that it had lost. For the eight years of its publication until its last issue in 1909, *Myōjō* was the major journal of the modern tanka, and the passionate romanticism of such gifted poets as Tekkan's wife Akiko (1878-1942) brought a new intensity of personal conviction to the form.

During the early 1890's, while Tekkan and his friends were preparing the way for the burgeoning romanticism of the *Myōjō* poets, Masaoka Shiki was immersed in his own vigorous movement to reform the traditional haiku. The son of a minor official of the Matsuyama fief in Shikoku, Shiki had been given an excellent old-fashioned education, including a thorough grounding in the Chinese classics and Chinese poetry. In 1883, however, he had come up to Tokyo to continue his education in the city where everything interesting and worthwhile in life seemed to be concentrated. Full of enthusiasm for liberal ideas and popular rights, Shiki had expected to study philosophy at the university and mark out a brilliant career in politics.

In 1885, Shiki entered the First Higher Middle School, preparatory for seeking entrance to Tokyo University. A mutual fondness for the comic monologues (*rakugo*) of the variety halls appears to have first drawn him to his fellow-student and lifelong friend, Natsume Sōseki. At a time when Sōseki still thought of himself as a prospective architect, Shiki half-seriously foretold, with divining sticks and diagrams, that he would become a celebrated man of letters, amazing even the foreigners. In turn, Sōseki was overcome with admiration for Shiki's literary accomplishments on reading his friend's *Shi-*

chisōshū, a book of original haiku, prose sketches, and poems in Chinese hastily put together over the summer holidays of 1888.[7]

During that same summer of 1888, Shiki had already begun to cough blood, and in May of the following year came the first bad tubercular hemorrhage and the unhappy realization that a political career was not for him. Although he went on to the university in 1890, Shiki had already begun to channel his energy and reforming zeal into the haiku. He withdrew from the university after failing the second-year qualifying examinations in 1892, and in the autumn he obtained a post on the nationalistic newspaper *Nihon.* The position brought the opportunity to publish a series of "talks on haiku," travel sketches, and the like, as well as haiku by himself and the enthusiastic group of friends and disciples who had gathered about him. In 1893 he published in *Nihon* his series of attacks on the conventional haiku, *Bunkai Yattsuatari,* and began his series of essays on Bashō, *Bashō Zatsudan.* It was at this point that he discovered the descriptive poetry of the great eighteenth-century haiku master Buson (1716-83), and he was eager to share the experience. Haiku parties, discussion groups, and planning sessions were of almost daily occurrence at his house in Negishi, where his illness often kept him confined.

It was probably in 1894 that Shiki first met the Western-style painter Nakamura Fusetsu (1866-1943) (later the illustrator for the first edition of Shimazaki Tōson's collection of new-style poetry, *Wakanashū*). Like many other Japanese painters of the day, Nakamura was fascinated with Western materials and with the principles and techniques of illusionist realism. Shiki was intrigued with his ideas, and borrowed from him a useful term—*shasei,* or "copying from life." He quickly gave the name *shasei* to his literary ideal of "realistic description" in the haiku, using it in his later writings interchangeably with *shajitsu.*

In May of 1894, Tekkan published his *Bōkoku no On* and emerged as the new champion of tanka reform. Shiki also was

[7] Kusumoto Kenkichi, *Masaoka Shiki* (Meiji Shoin, 1966), pp. 65-69.

caught up in the nationalistic spirit of the day. When the Sino-Japanese War broke out in July, he wanted to play a part in the glorious effort. Clearly, his health would not permit him to become a hero in the front lines, but at length, against the advice and pleading of all his friends, he set out for Manchuria as a war correspondent. Events moved quickly, however, while the government kept him waiting for his papers. Truce had already been declared before his ship finally left Japan in early April, and little more than a month later the war was over and he was on the way home. He had spent the unromantic interval in Manchuria, experiencing there and on the trip home the discomforts attendant upon the low status of war correspondents with the Japanese military establishment.

As his friends had predicted, this ill-advised expedition had been too much for Shiki's strength. On the return trip he suffered a severe lung hemorrhage; by the time the ship docked in Kobe, he was coughing blood every time he tried to walk. He was carried to the hospital, and there told that he must have complete rest or die. Several weeks of slow recuperation followed, while his mother and favorite haiku disciple Hekigotō (1873-1937) attended him. At the end of July he was transferred to the convalescent hospital at Suma, and in mid-August had recovered sufficiently to make the trip home to Matsuyama. There he moved in with Sōseki, who at this period was teaching in the Matsuyama Middle School. With returning strength came returning enthusiasm, and Shiki was soon busily directing the local haiku society, the Shōfūkai, and converting its members to the principles of *shasei*.

Shiki returned to Tokyo in October, 1895. His mind was as vigorous as ever, and his enthusiastic temperament only the keener for illness, but the disease had now begun to attack the spine. He was soon almost permanently bedridden. For his last six years until his death in December, 1902, his house at Negishi was headquarters for his devoted group of haiku disciples, and also from March, 1899, for the newly-formed Negishi Tanka Society. Throughout these last years Shiki carried on with almost unbelievable energy—writing, dictating, editing, publishing. It is not difficult to understand why his premature death at the age of thirty-five should have been so deeply felt, or why his memory soon became a cult with his most loyal followers.

Shiki had received a bit of formal instruction in the tanka from an old-fashioned teacher in Matsuyama as early as the summer of 1883, even before he became seriously interested in the haiku. But his understanding of the literature of the thirty-one syllable form was still what any trained tanka poet would have called rudimentary when in 1893 he began to fire his first occasional shots at the conventional waka poets in the pages of *Nihon*.[8] In the summer of 1893 he had chanced to meet Tekkan's friend and fellow poet Ayukai Kaien (1864-1946) at Sendai, and Kaien had talked enthusiastically about the need for reform in the tanka. But as Tekkan was at pains to point out some years later:

> Shiki was at that time absorbed in reforming the haiku; his proficiency in waka was still at an extremely elementary stage. In the summer of 1893 when Kaien and I went to Matsushima, Shiki was also vacationing in the area, and he and Kaien happened to run into each other. Kaien pointed out to Shiki in great detail why the waka should be reformed, but Shiki replied that although he shared Kaien's feelings, he himself had not yet studied the waka, so that he had not the slightest idea of what the standards for judging it might be. However, lately he had been finding the *Kokinshū* very interesting. That he was at the stage of "finding the *Kokinshū* very interesting" convinced us that although he may have been very well informed about haiku, his study of waka was still at the most elementary level.[9]

[8] E.g., in his *Bunkai Yattsuatari*, published from March to May, 1893. Cf. *Shiki Zenshū* (Kaizōsha, 1929-31), XVII, 19-20. All references to Shiki's collected works in this paper are to the twenty-two volume Kaizōsha edition, cited hereafter as *Zenshū*.

[9] *Shimpa Waka Taiyō* (1902), quoted in Usui Yoshimi, "Kaisetsu,"

Shiki's notions of what was good and bad in the waka remained fairly conventional until 1894. At this point he experienced a rather sudden change of heart—an emotional revulsion against the classical *Kokinshū* and a correspondingly fervent conversion to the *Manyōshū*, the first great anthology of Japanese poetry, compiled in the eighth century, and revered by the National Scholars of the Tokugawa period as the supreme expression of the pure Japanese spirit. The suddenness of the conversion suggests that it was prompted more by men and events than by any deep study of the tanka tradition. The patriotic praise of the *Manyōshū* in the writings of others may have had something to do with it: Tekkan, for example, declared in his *Bōkoku no On* that there had been no great poets in Japan since the *Manyōshū*. More important, through his association with Kuga Katsunan (1857-1907), the nationalistic editor of *Nihon*, Shiki had been lately introduced to such minor but independent poets as Amada Guan (1854-1904), Maruyama Sakura (1840-99), and Fukumoto Nichinan (1857-1921). Unlike the poets of the major conservative schools, these men looked back to Kamo no Mabuchi as their authority, sharing his admiration for the *Manyōshū* and for the *Manyō*-style poetry of the young Kamakura shogun, Minamoto Sanetomo (1192-1219). They also composed poems of their own with the archaic grammar and diction of the "*Manyō* style." Shiki probably derived from them his enthusiasm for Sanetomo as well as the highly romantic, primitivistic view of the *Manyōshū* that he first set forth in his *Bungaku Mangen* in 1894: "The men of that age were unsophisticated and did not make any effort to compose poems that were particularly beautiful or

---

Masaoka Shiki, Itō Sachio, Nagatsuka Takashi Shū in *Gendai Nihon Bungaku Zenshū*, VI (Chikuma Shobō, 1956), 419. The *Kokinshū* was the first imperial anthology of Japanese court poetry, compiled in 905. It was traditionally regarded as the canonical authority for all acceptable poetic styles and decorum, and in the late Tokugawa and early Meiji period was especially revered by Kagawa Kageki and the poets of his Keien School.

elegant. Rather, I feel that they put into poetry directly whatever they thought or felt, so that whatever the poem, it was straightforward and direct in its appeal, simple and without a particle of vulgarity."[10]

For three years after his return from Manchuria, Shiki continued to devote most of his energies to the haiku. Increasingly, however, he turned to the tanka, composing many poems as well as publishing occasional comments on the waka in *Nihon*. Tekkan had asked him along with a number of others to contribute a prefatory paragraph to his first collection of poems in 1896, and in what he wrote, Shiki hinted that he envied Tekkan for being first in the field of tanka reform: "I too wished to join the dance, beating my broken bell and flourishing my rusty halberd, but I was unprepared for the task. Now I am filled with chagrin that Tekkan has taken the initiative from me."[11]

By 1898, however, Shiki's haiku school was established as dominant, and he could thenceforth devote some of his reforming zeal to the waka. The first and most extended major statement of his views was the ten installments of his "Open Letter to the Waka Poets" (*Utayomi ni Atauru Sho*), published in *Nihon* in February and March, 1898. Coming in the midst of Tekkan's already well-advanced campaign of reform, Shiki's manifesto was something of an anticlimax. Nevertheless, its forceful language impressed Shiki's following and the readers of *Nihon*, and the "Open Letter" has since become a kind of classic of modern Japanese literary polemics. The opening section will serve to illustrate Shiki's style, as well as his admiration for the *Manyōshū* and Sanetomo.

In recent years . . . the art of Japanese poetry has not shown any signs of development. In fact, to speak forthrightly, it has shown no signs of development since the *Manyōshū* and Sanetomo. How lamentable that Sanetomo should have met his tragic death before he attained even the age of thirty,

[10] *Zenshū*, XVII, 87.   [11] *Zenshū*, IX, 170.

when his whole life still lay before him! Had he been allowed to live another ten years, who can tell what numbers of great poems he might have left behind? As it is, I regard him as a poet of the first rank. He neither slavishly copies Hitomaro and Akahito, nor, it need scarcely be said, does he blindly follow Tsurayuki and Teika.[12] Possessing his own special character, he towers up, competing in loftiness with the mountain peaks and with the sun and moon in his splendor. Truly he inspires awe and respect, making us instinctively fall to our knees before him. He has been regarded over the centuries as of mediocre talent, but this is certainly a mistaken view. . . . For the poetry of Sanetomo is not merely adequate—it has skill, insight, force. It is untainted by the fads of the day, disdaining to cater to the popular tastes of his time; it should not even be mentioned on the same day as the products of the mass of dilettantes and moribund courtier-poets. Surely it would be impossible without superior discernment and intelligence to compose poetry with the strength of Sanetomo's verse. It was Mabuchi who first gave Sanetomo high praise, but still I feel that Mabuchi's praise falls short. . . .

Mabuchi was one of the most astute critics of poetry in early modern times, and his devotion to the *Manyōshū* is truly remarkable in view of the time in which he lived. But I still feel that his praise . . . was inadequate. Mabuchi's repeated insistence that even in the *Manyōshū* there are good styles and bad gives the impression that he feared people would attack him, singling out some of the more crabbed poems in the *Manyōshū* to prove that the collection as a whole is worthless. . . . On reading through Mabuchi's col-

[12] Kakinomoto Hitomaro (fl. ca. 680-710) and Yamabe Akahito (d. ?736) were two of the greatest poets of the *Manyōshū*; and Ki no Tsurayuki (868-?945) was a major poet of the early Heian period and chief compiler of the *Kokinshū*; Fujiwara Teika (1162-1241) was a leading poet of the late Heian, a compiler of the eighth imperial anthology, the *Shinkokinshū* (ca. 1206), and the most influential critic of court poetry.

lected poems, I was shocked to find that his understanding of the *Manyōshū* was far less perfect than I had expected.[13]

To Shiki, the fault of the *Kokinshū* lay in the vulgar "wit" (*rikutsu*) that seemed to him the basis for most of its poems—the equivalent in the waka of the frivolous "*tsukinami* style" that he had attacked in the haiku. And the great mistake of the poets since the time of the *Kokinshū* had been to perpetuate this vulgar standard:

Tsurayuki is a bad poet, and the *Kokinshū* a worthless collection. Yet although the cult of Tsurayuki and the *Kokinshū* is patently ridiculous, I must confess that until a few years ago I was one of the devotees of the collection, so that I can well understand why most people today venerate it. While under its spell I was convinced that poetry was synonymous with elegant beauty and that the *Kokinshū* was the refined essence of this quality. Now I feel the disenchantment of a lover whose eyes are opened one morning after three years of blind infatuation, and who is chagrined and angry that he could have been so long deceived by such a weak-spirited woman. Take down the *Kokinshū* and open it to the first page. The first thing you will come upon is this really disgustingly insipid poem:

Toshi no uchi ni	Spring has come within the
Haru wa kinikeri	old year: shall we call the year
Hitotose o	"this year," or shall we call it
Kozo to ya iwan	"last year?"
Kotoshi to ya iwan.	

The poem is so silly that it fails to rise even to the level of vulgar wit, as if one were to say, "This child of mixed blood, born between a Japanese and a foreigner—are we to call it 'Japanese,' or should we call it 'foreigner'?" And the rest of the poems in the anthology are much the same: all of them are concerned with some trivial play on words or shallow wit

---

[13] *Zenshū*, VI, 10-11.

and reasoning. . . . If I must bestow some praise on the *Kokinshū*, I should say that its single merit is that although the poems are bad, it at least established a certain individual style that differentiates it from the *Manyōshū*, so that anyone might find a certain novelty in it on first reading. But I cannot understand what possessed those fools in later generations who believed that true art could only be achieved by imitating the *Kokinshū*. Even this might be allowable for ten years or even twenty, but that they should be still slavishly imitating it after two hundred, nay, three hundred years, shows a lack of discernment that is truly astonishing. Whether this imperial anthology or that imperial anthology, every last one of them is merely the dregs of the dregs of the *Kokinshū*.[14]

Shiki goes on in much the same tone to excoriate the contemporary waka poets for knowing nothing about haiku or Chinese poetry; for being smugly convinced that no form of literature can be as fine as their tanka; for refusing to recognize the beauty of any but a smoothly mellifluous poetic cadence, and the like. Despite the obvious unfairness of his sweeping charges, however, his specific criticisms of poets and poems are often lively and pointed, and his arguments also have the considerable merit of treating poetry for the most part in the proper literary terms. At the same time, notwithstanding the expansiveness of his avowed principles—his call for complete freedom of diction, or to "study and learn from all literature, old and new, high and low, East and West"—the conclusion of the "Open Letter" shows that Shiki's basic esthetic ideal was actually rather more conservative than revolutionary. Fundamentally, it was the haiku standard of *fūryū*, or "poetic elegance"—an ideal significantly different from the waka concept of elegant beauty, but in its way just as traditional. The ultimate test of what should and should not be treated in poetry therefore came down to the question of

[14] *Zenshū*, VI, 13.

whether the material was "beautiful," or could be rendered beautiful by the basic techniques of composition, contrast, and arrangement (*haigō*) of the haiku:

When I say to treat new and unusual materials in your poems, some people will bring forth such "machinery of civilization" as trains and railroads, but such notions are very mistaken. The machinery of civilization consists for the most part of inelegant, unpoetic things, which are difficult to put into poems. However, if one wishes to make the attempt, there is nothing for it but to arrange and harmonize these things with other materials that are tasteful. To treat them without such harmonizing material—to say, for example, "The wind blows along the railroad tracks"—this is utterly flat and tasteless. It will give at least a somewhat better appearance if one combines these things with other materials, saying, for example, that violets are blooming beside the railroad tracks, or that the poppies scatter or the pampas grass waves in the wake of the passing train, and the like. Another good way of treating such unpoetic materials is from a distant point of view. One means of effacing their prosaic, tasteless qualities is to say, for example, that the train can be seen across the field of rape flowers, or that the train is passing in the distance beyond the broad fields of summer grass.[15]

The basic conservatism of Shiki's view of the poetic suggests that by "realistic description" he really meant something rather different from describing whatever happens to be at hand "just as it is." The concept is simple and limited (though no less artistically valid), notwithstanding Saitō Mokichi's later elaboration of it into a philosophical concept. Shiki's realistic description in the tanka is basically a poetic mode, a way of treating certain poetic materials. The effect of the treatment when it is successful is to give the illusion of reality—to present a scene or a situation that seems somehow "objective" and "true"—but the techniques may be as conventional and "artificial" as the

---

[15] *Zenshū*, VI, 42.

careful arranging of the haiku masters, or the conceits of Tsurayuki.

For the first public demonstration of his principles, Shiki asked eleven friends, mostly haiku disciples and newspaper people connected with *Nihon*, to select ten poems each from among his tanka. The results were published on successive days in *Nihon* in February, 1898, under the title "Ten Poems from a Hundred" (*Hyakuchū Jisshu*). Many of the poems are surprisingly conventional in view of Shiki's announced program of reform; some have no more strikingly novel effect than is conveyed by an unusual word or image. Such touches, however, seemed considerably more bold and daring to Shiki's Japanese readers in 1898 than they do to a Japanese or a Westerner today. The traditional aspect of Shiki's approach to tanka composition is perhaps best shown by the simple fact that nearly all of the poems in the series are "compositions on topics" (*daiei*). In both the conventional waka and haiku the great majority of poems were *daiei*, and the imagery, tone, and even details of treatment of such poems were determined in greater or less degree by their imagistic or situational topics, which were conventional and often fictional. The poet's task was to compose a poem on the topic that expressed its "essential nature" (*hon'i*) in terms of his own imaginative experience. Shiki clearly felt no conflict between his mode of descriptive realism and the imaginative treatment of fictional situations, as the following poem with its two imaginary lovers suggests:

> *Tobari tarete*　　The shades hang down about
> *Kimi imada samezu*　the bed where my love lies, not
> *Kurenai no*　　yet awake, while the morning
> *Botan no hana ni*　sun touches the peonies.
> *Asahi sasu nari.*[16]

At the same time, it is impossible to make clear in translation the significance of Shiki's deliberate use in this poem of the more modern, haiku-derived Chinese loan word *botan* for

[16] *Zenshū*, VII, 47.

"peony" instead of the traditional Japanese *fukamigusa*. But that the choice was deliberate, and was intended to convey Shiki's vivid sense of the bold beauty of the flower, is shown in this passage from his "Open Letter":

> It is distressing that whenever the waka is mentioned it leads to an argument about diction. There are people who insist that in waka the right word for "peony" is not *botan* but *fukamigusa*, or that such-and-such a word is not used this way but has to be used in such-and-such a way according to rule. Such ideas are fundamentally different from mine. My own idea is not to say it in exactly the same way as the ancients did, nor to attempt to follow the established practice. *My fundamental principle is to express as clearly as I can the poetic quality that I myself feel to be beautiful* [italics Shiki's]. Consequently, if I feel that common language would most appropriately express my esthetic feeling, I should discard elegant diction and use common language. Although I may sometimes treat a subject in accordance with the traditional, established practice, when I do so it is not that I have followed the established practice simply because it is there. I have employed it because such treatment is most appropriate to the expression of beauty. And although people speak of the established practices of the ancients, the ancients themselves usually employed the expressions they did because for them they were new. With respect to the difference between *botan* and *fukamigusa*, to us the word *botan* conveys more quickly and vividly the image of a peony. Also, the sound of the word *botan* has more strength and is better suited to the bigness and coolness that are the qualities of a real peony blossom. Consequently, if one is trying to express objectively the beauty of a peony, the word *botan* should usually be the better one to use.[17]

Because of Shiki's background and objectives, the structural difference between the seventeen-syllable haiku and the thirty-

[17] *Zenshū*, VI, 41-42.

one syllable tanka, and the difference between their traditional worlds, at first seemed of little consequence. It is not surprising that he drew heavily on his experience with haiku for his first attempts at tanka in the style of "descriptive realism"—or that the results should often seem more remarkable for their novelty of technique than for a conviction of vital experience. Sometimes the carefully arranged pattern seems the whole raison d'etre of the poem:

Ensaki ni
Tamamaku bashō
Tama tokete
Goshaku no midori
Chōzubachi o ōu.[18]

At the veranda's edge, the tightly-curled young plantain unfolds its leaves, and five feet of green cover the wash basin.

The diction is unconventional in this poem, for the haiku summer image of the plantain and the plebeian veranda and wash basin are not found in the classical tanka. The repetition of *tama* in the third line and the extra syllable in the last are also somewhat unusual. But the haiku-like pattern is the most striking characteristic of the poem.

The following poem treats a larger scene with much the same technique.

Neshizumaru
Sato no tomoshibi
Mina kiete
Amanogawa shiroshi
Takeyabu no ue ni.[19]

All the lamps go out as the country village hushes into sleep; the Milky Way is white above the bamboo grove.

Again, the carefully arranged pattern of change, leading from the lights of the village to the stars of the Milky Way and from the village with its sleeping inhabitants to the lonely bamboo grove, gives the poem the effect of deliberate arrangement that seemed to Shiki's readers so obviously derived from his haiku practice.

[18] *Zenshū*, VII, 47.   [19] *Zenshū*, VII, 58.

Shiki's "Open Letter" and "Ten Poems from a Hundred" predictably aroused a good deal of protest. Shiki had acted in haste, and before he really knew a great deal of what he was talking about. One important reason for his decision to launch his campaign when he did was that his conservative employer, Kuga Katsunan, had been recently publishing in *Nihon* poems by poets of the "Imperial Poetry Bureau School." This annoyed Shiki and determined him to act. Once begun, he was determined to keep on. In a letter to Sōseki dated March 28, 1898, he wrote, "I have my tanka enemies both within and without. It is entertaining to deal with the outsiders, but I am at a loss to cope with the enemies on the inside. I mean my seniors on the newspaper and the complaints of other people senior to me with whom I have social contacts. . . : Having frequently gotten into trouble before with my comments about poetry, this time I was careful to request permission in advance before I started publishing. Now that I have begun, I will never turn back until I die."[20]

In spite of his failing health, Shiki threw himself into his work on the tanka with all his native enthusiasm. On March 18 he wrote to Guan: "Since the end of last month I have stayed up until two or three o'clock every morning, working on tanka poetry. I suppose that is largely why I have been feeling rather weak recently."[21]

The Negishi Poetry Society met for the first time at Shiki's house on March 25, 1898. Those present were all members of Shiki's haiku circle, and the society did not meet again until nearly a year later. It can hardly be said that the "Open Letter" and the "Ten Poems from a Hundred" had brought the world of the tanka flocking to Shiki's door. Nevertheless, a good deal of curiosity had been aroused among other poetry groups, partly because Shiki had signed his work with the pen name Takenosatobito (The Man of the Bamboo Village), and few people outside his own circle knew who he was. Among the

[20] Quoted in Koizumi, *Kindai Tankashi*, p. 513.
[21] *Ibid.*

curious were the young poets who had recently formed about
Sasaki Nobutsuna and begun to publish the poetry magazine
Kokoro no Hana. At length two of them, Katori Hozuma
(1874-1954) and Oka Fumoto (1877-1951) paid a call on Shiki
and were received with great cordiality. By the end of the visit
they had determined to become Shiki's disciples. They attended
the second meeting of the society in March, 1899, and thereafter, although the meetings almost always included haiku
poets, new men whose primary interest was in the tanka steadily appeared. One or more topics—"Travel," "The Yellow
Rose," "The Summer Moon," and the like—were assigned
before each meeting, and the participants brought with them
for discussion the ten poems or so they had composed. Beginning in July, 1899, the proceedings of the society began to be
published in *Nihon*; by the end of the year Shiki was soliciting
poems from readers for what had become a regular poetry column. Among these readers were Itō Sachio (1864-1913) and
Nagatsuka Takashi (1879-1915), who soon became Shiki's most
ardent disciples.

Shiki composed tanka almost constantly from 1898 on. His
poems are often in groups of eight or ten, treating the same
topic, or all ending with the same word. The following poem
is from a sequence of eight, all ending in *ware wa* (I . . .), published in *Nihon* in 1898.

> *Yoshiwara no*   From the Yoshiwara, the sound
> *Taiko kikoete*   of a drum is heard, while all
>   *Fukuru yo ni*   alone in the deepening night I
> *Hitori haiku no*   sort haiku.
> *Bunrui su ware wa.*[22]

The contrast between the gay world of the pleasure quarters
implied by the sound of the drum and the solitary Shiki
absorbed in his work suggests a tone of loneliness—a lyrical
element that is lacking in so much of Shiki's poetry. Indeed,

[22] *Zenshū*, VII, 109.

the biographical reference—it is said that it refers to a time two years before, when Shiki was working intensively on haiku—makes the poem one of Shiki's most admired today.[23] It is also valued for its "pictorial quality." The order of the Japanese syntax cannot be reproduced in English, but the effect of the final *ware wa* is as if Shiki were explaining a photograph—saying, "Here I am, sorting haiku late at night. . . ."

Another poem is from a set actually composed on a series of pictures, and all ending with the substantive *tokoro* (place, time).

Ko no moto ni	The elephants and serpents
Fuseru Hotoke o	weeping and worshipping the
Uchiogami	reclining Buddha under the
Zō hebidomo no	tree.
Nakiiru tokoro.[24]	

The picture on which the poem was based depicted the death of the Buddha. Shiki was trying, of course, to capture the essential details of the picture, and to render them "realistically." The effort to achieve this realistic description absorbed and excited him and the followers who gathered about him, but the poetic result in this instance is flat and prosaic, like a caption.

The "realistic" technique of such poems is based on the premise that what is objectively true can be discovered and expressed "objectively." It also implies the assumption that the truth so expressed has an importance both to the poet (or the speaker of his poem) and the audience. It is perhaps not surprising that the quasi-scientific ideal should impel Shiki characteristically to eschew some of the basic subjective means—metaphor, symbol, and other techniques—by which poets commonly convey their imaginative apprehension of what is true and significant and their feelings and attitudes towards experience. But Shiki's obsession with Realism also often led him to neglect the expression of feeling which is the life blood of such a brief

[23] Kimata, *Kindai Tanka no Kanshō to Hihyō*, p. 73.
[24] *Zenshū*, VII, 130.

poetic form as the tanka, and in turn has led some later critics to characterize him as "anti-lyrical."[25]

The effort to express the real in as exact terms as possible sometimes leads in Shiki's poetry to the treatment of greatly reduced materials almost microscopically observed—to "painting the stripes on the tulip," as in this poem from a set of ten composed in April, 1900.

Kurenai no	The spring rain falls softening
Nishaku nobitaru	the thorns of the rosebush,
Bara no me no	whose canes have grown to two
Hari yawaraka ni	feet of crimson.
Harusame no furu.[26]	

Shiki's esthetic ideal of beauty in nature—the *furyu* of haiku—is conveyed by the traditional tonal associations of the spring rain and the lovely contrast it makes with the crimson canes of the rose bush. But the significance of the realistic technique lies rather in the minute detail of the thorns and the exact qualification in the second line: the rose canes have grown not "quickly" or "suddenly," but to "two feet." Our response must depend on the extent to which we can appreciate the importance of Shiki's choice.

The "accuracy" of "two feet of crimson" is basically more subjective and impressionistic than scientific, and in poetry such details inevitably involve the feelings as well as the intellect. While denying himself so many of the traditional resources of Japanese poetry, Shiki argued that his kind of "objectivity" (i.e., description) should evoke an emotional response just as surely as more avowedly subjective kinds of poetic treatment. "Even though a poem may be composed in a completely objective fashion," he wrote in his "Open Letter," "it goes without saying that it is based on feeling. Thus, if one puts into a poem just as it is the description of a willow tree swaying in the

[25] See, for example, Chapter 7, "Shiki no Han-Jōjō Seishin," in Kusumoto, *Masaoka Shiki*, pp. 77-93.
[26] *Zenshū*, VII, 218.

breeze at the foot of a bridge, even though the poem is objective, the reason for composing the poem is that the poet felt this objective scene to be beautiful. Therefore it is of course based on emotion, and it is only a question of adding or not adding the statement that it is beautiful or pretty or happy or pleasurable."[27]

Another feature of Shiki's poem should be pointed out. This is the function of the adverbial phrase *yawaraka ni* (softly) in the fourth line. In the Japanese syntax, the phrase is a kind of pivot word, serving not only as an adverbial phrase to qualify the falling spring rain in the last line, but also as a predicate for the noun *hari* (thorns). The effect is not the conventional word play of the *kakekotoba* or pivot word, but a kind of "yoking," or zeugma, it may be called. The quality of softness is attributed to the thorns, and a relationship established between the thorns and the rain that touches them. The softness of rose thorns is a subjective impression of the speaker of the poem; it is not describing things objectively, "just as they are."

Shiki's critics have not failed to notice his use of the technique in this poem, but the discovery of such rhetorical "tricks" has made them uneasy, and many have either denied the technique or, failing that, denied that Shiki was conscious of what he was doing.[28] Conscious or not, the technique, as well as many other elements of Shiki's ideal and practice of *shasei*, may be found in the poetry and ideals of a period and group of the very Court poets whose tradition Shiki so flatly rejected. In the late thirteenth century and early fourteenth, the innovating Kyōgoku-Reizei Court poets attempted to bring a new freshness and intensity to their tradition and to express their poetic impressions of the natural world through a descriptive poetry in many ways strikingly similar to Shiki's.[29] The

[27] *Zenshū*, VI, 25-26.

[28] Cf. Kimata, *Kindai Tanka* . . . , p. 80.

[29] For a discussion of the Kyōgoku-Reizei poets, see Robert H. Brower and Earl Miner, *Japanese Court Poetry* (Stanford University Press, 1961), Chapter 7, *passim*.

motives behind the poetic results were also similar in some respects. The realism of the Kyōgoku-Reizei poets was intellectually motivated by their interest in such things as Zen Buddhism and Chinese poetry and painting of the Sung period— not by the techniques of illusionist realism in Western painting or the desire to return to the "artless realism" of the *Manyōshū*. But in their effort to express as "realistically" as possible the quasi-Platonic essences of their conventional topics, they explored as completely as they could the possibilities of the descriptive mode in their nature poetry. In their new styles they avoided the more obvious kinds of subjective wit of the traditional "*Kokinshū* style," using colloquial diction and images and such techniques as repetition to convey the exact nature of a moment of experience. And in place of the traditional pivot word (*kakekotoba*), they developed the analogous technique of "yoking" two syntactic units by a single word, usually an adjective, that relates to both, as in the following poem by Kyōgoku Tamekane (1254-1332).

> *Eda ni moru*　　　　In the rareness of the rays of
> *Asahi no kage no*　　the morning sun, the coolness
> *Sukunasa ni*　　　　 is *deep* within the bamboo
> *Suzushisa fukaki*　　 grove.
> *Take no oku kana.*[30]

Here the adjective *fukaki* both serves as a predicate for the substantive *suzushisa* (the coolness is deep) and modifies the phrase *take no oku* (deep within the bamboo grove).

It is doubtful that Shiki more than glanced at the poetry of the Kyōgoku-Reizei poets, and his use of a similar technique is probably not due to conscious borrowing. Nevertheless, the coincidence is but one similarity between Shiki's descriptive techniques and those of the Kyōgoku-Reizei poets, as more extensive comparison would show. It also helps to clarify the underlying subjectivity of Shiki's poetry of "realistic description."

[30] *Ibid.*, p. 366.

The treatment of greatly reduced materials "exactly as they are" often results in a greatly decreased esthetic distance between the poet and his materials and an increased distance between the poet and us, his audience. We may concede that the thing itself and the experience of perceiving it are of over-riding significance to the poet, but it often becomes extraordinarily difficult to follow him into the experience. The difficulty is particularly great with such a brief form as the tanka if the experience is not presented in terms of conventional tonal symbols or even of normal values and experience that we can understand. The problem is crucial to Shiki's poetry, and deserves to be examined in some detail.

The following poem has been extravagantly admired by the poets and critics of the *Araragi* School, the heirs of Shiki's reforms.

Kame ni sasu	The spray of wisteria put in
Fuji no hanabusa	the vase is so short that it does
Mijikakereba	not reach the floor.
Tatami no ue ni	
Todokazarikeri.[31]	

Taken by itself, the poem seems very flat and prosaic. The subjectivity of the conception is of course implicit in the selection of imagistic detail, and explicit in the statement that because one thing is so, another is not—a rhetorical element that again reminds us of the practice of the late classical poets. But what does the poem mean? we ask. What is the tone of the poem?

Within the tanka tradition in which Shiki was perforce working, the obvious thing is to look first to the natural images of the poem for clues to meaning, for centuries of poetic development had endowed such images with complex tonal associations of beauty or transcience or sadness. The single natural image in this poem is the wisteria, a spring image traditionally treated in terms of appreciation for the graceful shape and color

[31] *Zenshū*, VIII, 187-88.

of the flowers, whether purple or white, often compared by the Court poets to the waves of the sea (*fujinami*) and the like. Unlike cherry blossoms or autumn leaves, which suggest evanescence as well as beauty, the wisteria is more neutral; it is simply beautiful. Is the poet, then, complaining that the wisteria in this instance is not graceful because it fails to sweep to the floor like the conventional wisteria of older poetry? Probably not, for such treatment would violate the convention that the wisteria must be presented as beautiful—the convention that governs this similar poem by Shiki's older contemporary, Ochiai Naobumi.

Kogame o ba	Though I have placed the vase
Tsukue no ue ni	upon the table, the spray of
Nosetaredo	white wisteria is still too long,
Mada mada nagashi	yes, too long.
Shirafuji no hana.[32]	

The images of the wisteria and the vase are very similar in the two poems, and like Shiki's (which might almost be taken as an allusive variation on it) this poem treats the length of the wisteria spray. The conventional beauty of the flower is conveyed by the image and the speaker's appreciation of it by exclaiming over its length. We may not respond to Naobumi's poem with appreciation, but at least we feel we can understand it.

It might be concluded that Shiki's poem plays itself off, as it were, against convention; that is, that it might have such an implication as, "The wisteria of tradition is beautiful because of its graceful length, but this real spray before me is so short that it does not reach the floor. This is the beauty of truth as opposed to the elegant fictions of literary convention." Such an interpretation of the "meaning" of Shiki's poem may be far-fetched, but it is not entirely unjustified unless one is to disregard the tanka tradition completely.

[32] Quoted in Kusumoto, *Masaoka Shiki*, p. 159.

Historically, of course, Shiki's poem has been esteemed for quite other reasons. To understand these reasons, and to try to appreciate the poem in something of the same way that Shiki's admirers have done, one must look for more specific help than the experience of reading many older poems on wisteria or the tradition as a whole can provide. One turns next to the circumstances of composition. Again, this is to approach the poem in a traditional way. Innumerable older poems from the *Manyōshū* on were provided with accompanying prose explanations or were later glossed by tradition with accounts of when, where, and why they were composed; many can scarcely be understood otherwise. The close connection between poetry and its occasional contexts is shown by the innumerable classical diaries, collections of "tales of poems," and novels that are studded with poems. However, the standard for judging such contextual poems, as they may be called, and the poems treating a conventional topic were not the same. The poem on the topic must be "complete," whereas the contextual poem need not stand alone as single expression.

The place to go with Shiki's poem, then, is to the surrounding context which Shiki himself provided. This is to be found in his journal *Bokujū Itteki* under the date, April 28, 1901. Here we find the poem as the first in a set of ten with the following headnote: "I was lying on my back after the evening meal had been cleared away, and happened to glance to the left. On the table was an arrangement of wisteria. It had been carefully watered, and the blossoms were just at their peak. Murmuring to myself how elegant and lovely they looked, I was reminded somehow of the days of the old romances, and as I mused on all this, to my surprise I felt moved to compose some poems. Since I had been growing more and more out of the habit of composition for many days now, it was with some uncertainty that I took up my brush."[33] The ten poems, beginning with the one under discussion, follow, and are in turn followed by a postscript: "Although there are many points in

[33] *Zenshū*, VIII, 187.

these poems that make me uneasy, this brief literary interlude
brought me the first such solace I had felt in many days. What
a strange spring night it was."[34]

Without presenting the whole set of ten poems here, some
sense of the immediate context of the first poem may be gained
from the four that follow it.

Kame ni sasu
Fuji no hanabusa
Hitofusa wa
Kasaneshi fumi no
Ue ni taretari.

A single strand of the spray
of wisteria put in the vase
hangs down over the pile of
books.

Fujinami no
Hana o shi mireba
Nara no mikado
Kyō no mikado no
Mukashi koishi mo.

When I gaze upon the blossoms of rippling wisteria, I
long for the past of the emperors of Nara, of the emperors of Kyoto.

Fujinami no
Hana no murasaki
E ni kakaba
Koki murasaki ni
Kakubekarikeri.

If I were to paint the purple
of the rippling wisteria blossoms in a picture, I would
paint it deep purple.

Kame ni sasu
Fuji no hanabusa
Hana tarete
Yamai no toko ni
Haru kuren to su.

The spray of wisteria put in
the vase; the blossoms hang
down, and as I lie ill, spring is
about to end.

Shiki implies that the poems were rather negligently dashed
off in a mood of romantic nostalgia—a mood that pervades the
third poem and is colored in the fifth with a consciousness of
the passage of time and beauty and a sense of his own
approaching end. The third poem, especially, uses *Manyō* diction to help convey a romantic longing for the bygone glories

[34] *Zenshū*, VIII, 189.

of old Japan very like the mood of reflective melancholy expressed in many old poems. The prevailing mood thus seems more calm and reflective than exalted or intense.

To return to the first poem, the surrounding context helps to explain the rather cryptic statement. We gather from the context that the poem treats a real spray of wisteria in a real vase beside Shiki's bed, but in a curiously matter-of-fact way. What, it may be asked, makes it a good poem? Or, to put it in other terms, what makes it the epitome of "realistic description?" Saitō Mokichi, for many years editor of the poetry magazine *Araragi* and the most important exponent of Shiki's ideas, wrote of the poem in the July, 1912 issue of *Araragi*:

It is a plain composition, but it is a rare poem that has the deep savor of this one. People may laugh at me for such a statement and say it is just my own arbitrary opinion; others may indignantly ask what I mean by speaking this way about such an insignificant poem, as if I were Columbus with the egg. I cannot help that, but just the same, I wonder if I am being too hasty in concluding that the poets of "technique" and "imagination" would not be able to compose a poem like this to begin with. I should also like to propose this poem as the handiest example of what a poem is like that expresses the "fresh, sharp perception" that is so much talked of these days. . . . No doubt the general run of poets would even be unanimous in feeling that something is lacking in this kind of expression, founded as it is on a childlike first impression. No doubt they would even think it worthless. And so when they come to the point of composing poems themselves, they hurriedly invent all kinds of feelings. Then they express them so as to give the impression that they are richly gifted poets, as if they had a profound sense of what they were saying. Even such people may yet be considered acceptable. But when it comes to those of lesser talent, their sensitivities are so dull that they would not even be capable to begin with of such a first impression as this poem expresses.

That being the case, they go on composing poems that give the impression that they are the most profound of poets. Instead of proceeding from their own real impressions, they make poems up out of thin air.[35]

Some years later, in 1929, Mokichi wrote of the same poem,

People do not realize that the poem . . . is the voice of the poet's own irrepressible subjective being. The reason that he exclaims, "It does not reach the floor," as if it were a matter of such great import, is that to the poet this is the voice of truth. This poet, for whom it had become completely impossible to come into direct contact with the majesty of the mountain peaks or the surging motion of the sea, turned to the spray of flowers in a vase at his bedside and expressed his solitary thought in this poem. For this reason, the subjectivity of the poet gives a kind of profound tone and cadence to the poem that echoes in the reader's heart.[36]

What makes such criticism as Mokichi's possible is the context of the poem in Shiki's journal, and ultimately the total context of Shiki's tragically short life. The poem is good, not because of a complex or artful simplicity, but because it is a true impression of a particular poet. Behind this true impression stands that romanticized but nonetheless moving image of the dying Shiki who pours into this artless creation a profound conviction of his own subjective perception of truth.

Much of the discussion that has centered about the poem has been concerned with the significance that should be attached to the crucial adjective form *mijikakereba* ("because it is short," "is so short that . . .") in the third line. The expression gives the poem the cause-and-effect construction that in many forms and guises typifies the "wit" or "reasoning" (*rikutsu*) of the "*Kokinshū* style," and is often found in such a milder, less witty form as this in the poetry of the Kyōgoku-Reizei poets. The consensus seems to be that Shiki did not really mean

---

[35] Quoted in Kimata, *Kindai Tanka* . . . , p. 84.
[36] *Ibid.*

"because"—that he intended instead a simple statement of fact: "The spray of wisteria is short *and* does not reach the floor." As one commentator has put it,

> The gist of the arguments is that *mijikakereba* does not express a reason (*rikutsu*). Rather, the poem expresses straightforwardly the appearance of the spray of wisteria just as the poet saw it just as he lay there on his back. In other words, this is a work in which the poet directly demonstrates the method of realistic description that he has advocated. If we repeat the poem over a number of times to ourselves, bearing in mind the feelings expressed in the headnote, we will soon cease to feel that there is any reasoning involved, and will be able to sense the breathing of the invalid poet Shiki. By *mijikakereba*, he has expressed pretty much the meaning of *mijikakute* ("is short, and . . ."), and in the deliberate choice of *mijikakereba* with its extra syllable, we must also consider that Shiki was giving attention to the poetic cadence.[37]

It is so easy to read things into a tanka, and so easy to scoff at those who do. If biography seems to play an unwontedly large role in creating the reputation of some of Shiki's more prosaic compositions, it is still possible to appreciate such a poem as this within the context of the mixed prose and poetry of Shiki's journal and the tone of sad melancholy that pervades the whole.

Shiki's poetry necessarily became more circumscribed as he turned increasingly to his immediate surroundings for subjects and materials. He had earlier tried his hand at the new-style poetry, particularly in the years before embarking on his tanka reform in 1898. He also wrote patriotic chōka on the Emperor's Birthday or "Celebrating the Marriage of the Crown Prince" in 1900, and called upon the readers of his column in *Nihon* to send in poems on such topics as "On Reading the *Heike Monogatari*." But when one considers the wide range of sub-

---

[37] *Ibid.*, pp. 84-85.

jects and themes treated in older poetry or the almost graphic references to love making in the sensationally autobiographical poems of Yosano Akiko, Shiki's poetry seems almost unduly restricted. He wrote no love poetry, for example, apart from a few early treatments of fictional topics. Within the framework of the total cumulative development of the tanka tradition, even some of his best nature poetry seems pale and bloodless by comparison with the more exciting poems of the Kyōgoku-Reizei poets, who made a comparable attempt to present the real.

In avoiding the higher flights and even the fictional treatment of such subjects as love, Shiki was no doubt following the natural inclinations of his "anti-lyrical" temperament as well as directing his intense energy into the effort to present the real. If he was often prosaic, he seems to have felt in the poetry of the "idealists"—that is, such exponents of the more strongly lyrical as the poets of the *Myōjō* school—something of the uncomfortable self-dramatization that often mars their work. Like his friend Sōseki, Shiki seems to have had a kind of exaggerated dread of appearing ridiculous. Such concerns led him away from certain poetic subjects and treatments, and to the end of his life underlay his preoccupation with *shasei*. In June, 1902, only a few months before his death, he wrote in his journal *Byōshō Rokushaku*:

In both painting and poetry there are many who advocate what is called idealism, but such people do not even understand the flavor of realistic description. . . . I do not mean to say that idealism is necessarily bad, but it is a fact that the majority of works in which the conception is expressed as idealism are bad. . . . A work of realistic description may appear at first sight to be shallow, but the more deeply it is savored, the greater its variety and the deeper its poetic taste. . . . It often happens that that fellow idealism tries to reach the top of the roof in one jump but only succeeds instead in falling into the pond. Although realistic description may be plain and flat, it does not fail in this way. And when one has succeeded in embodying the height of poetic taste within the plain and simple, its marvelous effect is indescribable.[38]

Despite Shiki's "anti-lyricism," his poetry became increasingly autobiographical as he turned more to his immediate surroundings for poetic inspiration. That is, the speaker of his later poems is almost always avowedly himself, so that we are increasingly aware of the particular circumstances of Shiki the poet and the man in the background or context of the poem. This confusion or blurring of the distinction between the poetic speaker and the poet can be found in poetry throughout the tanka tradition. Even in periods most given to "compositions on topics," there was a strong undercurrent of autobiographical poetry as well as a latent feeling that somehow such poetry was more "sincere." As the autobiographical strain becomes more pronounced in Shiki's poetry, the poetry becomes more traditional in this sense, and perhaps feeling himself more in the mainstream of Japanese poetry, Shiki began to turn more to tradition—specifically, the *Manyōshū*—and to incorporate recognizable elements of traditional rhetoric and diction into his poems. The tendency can be seen in the third poem in the series on the wisteria discussed above, and also in such examples as this first poem from the famous set of ten in his journal *Bokujū Itteki* under the date May 4, 1902. The head-note says simply, "On forcing myself to pick up my brush."

Saogami no	How sad the parting with the
Wakare kanashi mo	Spring Goddess of Sao when I
Kon haru ni	shall not again meet the return-
Futatabi awan to	ing spring.
Ware naranaku ni.[39]	

The "I" of the poem is of course Shiki himself, but the archaic diction and cadence conjures up a romantic picture of the *Manyōshū* within which Shiki's personal lament is, as it

---

[38] *Zenshū*, VIII, 309. [39] *Zenshū*, VIII, 194.

were, costumed. The most striking characteristics of the "*Manyō* style" here are the full stop at the end of the second line, which gives the poem as a whole the so-called "five-seven cadence" of much *Manyō* poetry; the relative heaviness of the fourth line with its extra syllable; the archaic combination of the adjective indicative with the exclamatory particle *mo* in the *kanashi mo* of line two; and the adjective-substantive form *naranaku* followed by the copula infinitive *ni* in the last line. The details of archaic grammar contrast strikingly with the neutral poetic grammar of Shiki's day, old though that too was; the grammatical elements are arranged in a composition that is palpably in the *Manyō* manner. The effect is a combination of direct imitation and general allusion that is difficult to evaluate. It may be illuminated by comparison with the allusive variations upon *Manyō* and later poetry of the medieval poets, but it must also be considered in the light of Shiki's attitude toward the *Manyōshū* and its imitators. The cult of the *Manyōshū* represents the romantic side of Shiki's program for tanka reform, and must be examined in some detail.

To begin, something should be said about the role of the *Manyōshū* in Japanese literary history before the Meiji period. It is perhaps needless to emphasize that the best poetry of the *Manyōshū* conveys a vivid sense of immediacy and direct involvement of man in his world that is most often the product of a highly sophisticated art. Nevertheless, the poetic effect could easily be taken for artless simplicity, and in the classical periods, when Japanese poetry came to emphasize increasing complexity within a more restricted range, poets began to look back on the *Manyōshū* with a certain nostalgia. The world that its poetry seemed to represent took on the romantic aura of a simpler, better age; its poetry seemed free, unsophisticated, and spontaneous, albeit archaic and somewhat crude. The *Kokinshū*, with its more mannered subjectivity and limited range of poetic expression, became the standard for poetic decorum in the classical periods, but in age after age, poets turned to the *Manyōshū* for simpler modes or invoked its "freedom" to justify innovations of their own. In the twelfth and thirteenth centuries, poets and scholars began to study the *Manyōshū* with increasing seriousness, emulating its descriptive poetry, and to some extent using it as a source for poetic allusion. Few poets, however, saw anything to be gained by reviving the archaic language or directly imitating the more robust rhythms of *Manyō* poetry with the apparent exception of the talented but eccentric young Minamoto Sanetomo. Sanetomo was the son of the famous Yoritomo, and succeeded his brother Yoriie as the third Kamakura shogun, but was assassinated at the age of twenty-seven. His *Manyō*-inspired poetry, little regarded during his lifetime, was more or less forgotten after his death.[40] In the Tokugawa period, the *Manyōshū* was intensively studied and the *Manyō* spirit of "sincerity" (*makoto*) was extolled by the National Scholars. Nevertheless, Kamo no Mabuchi and his exalted pupil and patron Tayasu Munetake (1715-71) evoked widespread opposition by advocating direct imitation of *Manyō* diction and styles. Mabuchi also "discovered" the *Manyō*-style poetry of Sanetomo and was largely responsible for creating an image of him as a tragic young poet of genius.

The admiration of Mabuchi and other scholars of National Learning for the *Manyōshū* was mixed with notions of Japanese cultural superiority, the divine origins of the land and people, and the "purity" of ancient Japanese culture before it became "tainted" by the Chinese. Mabuchi's disciples and their pupils inherited his special interests in the *Manyōshū* and Sanetomo, forming a group of scholars and poets, the "Edo School," that continued into the Meiji period and provided some opposition to the dominant traditional schools of poetry.

It has been seen that Shiki embraced the *Manyōshū* rather suddenly just before the Sino-Japanese War, and that this change in his literary preferences was probably due in large part to his association with such Edo School poets as Guan and Nichinan. Shiki seems never to have modified his romantic

---

[40] For a discussion of Sanetomo and his poetry, see Brower and Miner, *Japanese Court Poetry*, pp. 329-37.

413

conception of the artless realism and robust vigor of *Manyō* poetry. Until perhaps as late as 1900, when the Negishi Tanka Society met for several sessions to read and study the *Manyō-shū*, Shiki saw the anthology through the writings of Mabuchi and under the guidance of Guan and others rather than by approaching it directly.[41] At any rate, in the years following the "Open Letter," he published numerous articles on, or touching on, the *Manyōshū*, discussing its eccentric poems, its characteristic rhythms and patterns of extra syllables, the interpretation of specific poems, and the like. During these last four years, he moved from expressed admiration to imitation of the *Manyōshū* in his poetry, and to ever more enthusiastic praise for those poets of the past who had imitated it in theirs.

To judge from his own account, it was a momentous event in Shiki's life when his friend and disciple Akaki Kakudō (1879-1948) sent him from Okayama an article from a local newspaper on an obscure samurai poet-scholar of the last century named Hiraga Motoyoshi (1800-68), enclosing a copy of as many of Motoyoshi's poems as he could find. Shiki wrote of his consequent discovery of Motoyoshi and his *Manyō*-style poetry in several successive daily entries in his journal *Bokujū Itteki*, beginning on February 14, 1901. A few passages will indicate the intensity of his enthusiasm.

If one could gather every last poet of the Tokugawa period together in one room and test them with the question, "In which of the several hundred collections of poetry that have come down from antiquity are the most good poems?" those who would answer "The *Manyōshū*" would be only Kamo no Mabuchi and perhaps three or four others. If one then asked, "Well then, which anthology should we study as a model for composing our own poems?" the only one who would answer unhesitatingly, "The *Manyōshū*" would be Hiraga Motoyoshi. Truly, Hiraga Motoyoshi, the poet of Bizen, is the only person who, through the long millennium

[41] Cf. Koizumi, *Kindai Tankashi*, pp. 570-71.

414

since the *Manyōshū*, has recognized the true value of the *Manyōshū* and has imitated it, leaving to the world poems in the *Manyō* style. Such a man as Mabuchi went no further than to see the outer shell of the *Manyōshū*. . . . Although the waka poets are in complete agreement in honoring the *Manyōshū* and in regarding Hitomaro as a Saint of Poetry, they have never even tried to compose a poem in the *Manyō* style. That during this period only one man, Hiraga Moto-yoshi, should appear and compose poetry in the *Manyō* style is something of a miracle, is it not? There were no older poets to instruct him . . . and no younger poets to welcome his poems. . . . Yet there he stood, grandly apart from the vulgar crowd, composing poems . . . for his own pleasure and paying no attention whatever to what others thought. Surely this could never have been unless he had had great confidence in his heart.[42]

Motoyoshi's poems are in pure *Manyō* style. Consequently, we find in them none of the detestable wit and empty rhetoric of the poetry from the *Kokinshū* on. Furthermore, he never composed a poem except on a real event or a real scene. Consequently, his poetry is sincere and compelling, and its archaic beauty is completely untainted by the artificial technique and effeminate delicacy of the ages following the *Manyōshū*.[43]

Among Motoyoshi's poems there are a very great many in which he uses the words "beloved" (*imo*) or "my beloved" (*wagimoko*). For this reason he is said to have been nick-named "Wagimoko Sensei." But actually, Motoyoshi probably used this word so much because, owing to his passionate nature, his love for his mistress naturally appeared in a great many of his poems. When one considers how he never composed a poem except upon something that actually happened in real life, his "beloved" poems, too, should not be regarded as mere idle fancy. The poetry of love, which had been no

[42] *Zenshū*, VIII, 112-13.　　[43] *Zenshū*, VIII, 114.

more than empty words since the *Koķinshū*, returned to the ancient age of the *Manyōshū* with Motoyoshi and succeeded in re-establishing its source of inspiration in human feeling.[44]

Motoyoshi pours out his passion along with his dissatisfactions with life and occasionally strikes an eccentric note, but he is a man who by nature based himself upon a stubborn faith and a transcendent vision and who made it his duty to preserve his own individuality of outlook. He was by no means the type of man who would end as a captive of love. Thus, just as the word "my beloved" appears in his poems, so his frequent use of the word "brave warrior" gives evidence enough that he aimed to be a man of splendid, heroic character.[45]

Shiki's praise of Motoyoshi shows more than enthusiasm for an imitator of the *Manyōshū*. It shows how during these last years Shiki had come to esteem poetry for its supposed biographical integrity—for its biographical "truth" as much as for its "realistic description." His praise of Motoyoshi, like his admiration for the artless realism of the *Manyōshū*, is positively naïve in its assumption that because the poet says a thing it must necessarily be biographically true and "sincere." The enthusiasm for Motoyoshi as a poet of the *Manyō* style is also strongly colored by sympathy for the particular circumstances of his eccentric life. It is perhaps not entirely wrong to suggest that Shiki's romantic praise of Motoyoshi—and even more his earlier praise of Sanetomo—was influenced by the fact that he saw in them a reflection of himself. The militant Shiki, too, was a man of "stubborn faith and transcendent vision" who "disdained to cater to the popular tastes of his time."

Shiki had too much good taste to be entirely taken in by the sound of his own words. Although he was nearly blinded by the glorious fact of Motoyoshi's imitation of the *Manyōshū*, he could still see, as most readers of Motoyoshi today could hardly

[44] *Zenshū*, VIII, 118.   [45] *Zenshū*, VIII, 121-22.

fail to do, that "his poetic conceptions are rather ordinary and unvaried."[46] Nevertheless, the praise is extreme enough, and it suggests that in his zeal for the *Manyōshū* Shiki did not think very far beyond his first premise—that it was a good thing to imitate it.

If Shiki's own poetry in the *Manyō* style may be examined in the light of this simple enthusiasm, it cannot be regarded as an attempt to achieve a rich or complex artistic effect. It is not the sophisticated quasi-pastoralism of the classical poets, who as far back as Tsurayuki used old techniques and diction associated with the *Manyōshū* to re-create an image in the present of a simpler past. Shiki's use of the *Manyōshū* is not for metaphor as the evocation of the ancient anthology in the allusive variations of the classical poets contrasts the past with the present to convey the sense of the sad passage of time. Shiki's *Manyō* poetry is, in short, imitation—more skillful, perhaps, but basically no different from Sanetomo's or Mabuchi's or Motoyoshi's. The argument for it seems to be very like the usual arguments for imitation. The *Manyōshū* is simple, forthright, direct, and full of realism and vigor. These are all qualities of good poetry. Consequently, if we imitate the *Manyōshū*, our own poetry will have these qualities; it, too, will be simple, forthright, direct, and full of realism and vigor.

Although it is difficult to see any greater complexity of motive behind Shiki's imitation of the *Manyōshū*, it must be remembered that his reforms were put forward at a time when the traditional schools of waka poets were very much of a physical and literary reality. Judging only from the contemporary state of the poetry of these schools, it could easily seem to Shiki that if imitation were called for, the *Manyōshū* was far preferable to the *Kokinshū*. And we can respond with sympathy to Shiki's *Manyō* poetry, if, like most Japanese readers of it today, we react to such poems as those on the end of spring and his own approaching death within the larger context of his *Bokujū Itteki* and our general knowledge of the

46 *Zenshū*, VIII, 125.

circumstances of his life. To read the poems in this fashion is to forego strict literary judgment, but it is also to take the later poetry of Shiki on what seem to be to a large extent his own implicit terms. Such of his followers as Itō Sachio and later Saitō Mokichi espoused his *Manyō* style because they too saw in the *Manyōshū* values with which they hoped imitation might endow their poetry. If we respond with sympathy to this poetry, however, most of us probably do so in spite of the *ka mo*'s and *naku ni*'s.

Shiki's poetic reputation today rests primarily on his haiku and on a body of plain descriptive poetry that has the haiku-like vividness of precise detail. His principle of "realistic description" was a quasi-scientific principle directly influenced by conceptions of illusionist realism in Western-style painting. His advocacy of the *Manyōshū* was an echo of the antiquarianism of Kamo no Mabuchi and the scholars of National Learning. Underlying these two very differently inspired aspects of Shiki's reform movement, however, can be seen the ideal of "sincerity"—that peculiarly Japanese virtue so often brought forward to justify the products of the struggle to create a modern literature in the Meiji period. The basic "sincerity" combined with the very simplicity of Shiki's two main enthusiasms made it possible for his followers to elaborate upon them. Thus, while Nagatsuka Takashi strove to carry on Shiki's *shasei* as a simple poetic technique, Itō Sachio could develop it into a justification for the tanka as an outpouring of the heart—a *sakebi* or lyric cry. And Saitō Mokichi, by the age-old method of pseudo-etymology, could find justification for investing the Chinese characters of Shiki's *shasei* with the all-embracing significance of "describing human life." Accidents of Japanese literary history in the early twentieth century—the end of the *Myōjō* movement and the failure of important younger poets to emerge from it—enabled these poets to attain an influence that they would not perhaps otherwise have had. Through their poetry and their critical writings, Shiki still affects common attitudes towards Japanese poetry today.

CHAPTER XI

Kobayashi Hideo

EDWARD SEIDENSTICKER

· I ·

WE HEAR the cry: "Japanese intelligentsia, return to Japan." I can see some reason in it, and at the same time I sense fear. I seem to hear it saying how strong an element of fear of the West there was in our erstwhile adulation of the West. The intelligentsia, and other people as well, ordered to return to something, have nowhere to return to but themselves, the selves of the present moment. And how tongue-tied we Japanese are when we try to talk of what we are at the present moment!

We have never ceased being Japanese. We have but thought from time to time we have done so. To be sure, such ideologies as liberalism and Marxism are Occidental, but when we look back upon ideologies and isms and the like we must be struck with the very Japanese manner in which we have adopted them. It is easy enough to understand an ism, but it takes a great deal of time to see how very much one's way of comprehending is like oneself, how Japanese it is. None of the many ideologies we have learned has the power to change a human being radically; and we have failed to capture the unchanging image of the Japanese that is there.

It can never be said that the ideology of the West has poisoned us. To treat so simply of the past through which one has come is to insult the life one lives now, both in the case of the individual and in matters of broader cultural history. Various forms and organizations in modern Japanese society are very clearly Westernized, but there is nothing clear about the Westernization of spiritual life that lies beyond the reach of the eye. . . .

419

The illusion that Western ideology has quite painted our spirits over comes from seeing only the intellectual forms themselves, and overlooking the subtle ways in which ideology lives within the human being. In the subtlety is the contemporary Japanese. (IV, 187)[1]

It is a remarkable statement, calm and reasonable at a time when men of reason, believers in the omnipotence of science, were being hysterical, and yet coming from a man who did not then believe and never has much believed in reason and science. Back from a trip to the continent, where The Incident was then going into its second year, Kobayashi Hideo chose not to avail himself of an opportunity to join "national spiritual mobilization," in which movement some of his best friends were very active. Instead, in these "Impressions of Manchuria" (*Manshū no inshō*), he reminded his readers of the old paradox: the "Japanese spirit" is never less in danger of faltering and failing than when it is partaking most generously of foreign nutriments.

He might have made himself a case in point. Student of French symbolism, adviser to very up-to-date Japanese symbolist poets, he somehow does not look at home among French critics. Such Frenchmen as Sainte-Beuve may have shared his suspicion of neatly sealed systems, but the Japanese are not wrong when they think themselves different from the intellectualizing West—and of course the French have been among the chief intellectualizers. Brief insight figures much more prominently than sustained building in the Japanese artistic and critical traditon. The Japanese are not their most loveable, perhaps, when they burst into lyrics of self-congratulation on the superiority of intuition to reason. Badly done, the strain is as tiresome as a strain can be. Eloquently and imaginatively done, however, it can be the very music of the race.

Kobayashi is one of the satraps of modern Japanese literary

[1] All references in this paper are to the eight-volume *Kobayashi Hideo zenshū* published by Shinchōsha between 1955 and 1957.

criticism. Among his predecessors probably only Masamune Hakuchō approached him in influence, and only Kitamura Tōkoku in eloquence. Yet his suspicion of closed systems sometimes becomes almost a suspicion of contrivance in general, and so a suspicion of art itself; and its obverse, a steadfast belief in the uncomplicated act and the unclouded heart, leads perilously close to a breaking down of the distinction between life and art, and so to a denial of the critic's own reason for being. Much of Kobayashi's best writing is in fact scarcely literary criticism at all. Its concern is more moral than literary.

The blurring has its origins in fundamentals. What should a critic be, and what should he look for in a writer? Kobayashi's point of departure as a critic is a highly subjective one, sometimes almost solipsist. Criticism is self-awareness. As is the case with Emerson, the act of creating comes to seem as important as the object created, the act of criticizing as important as what is said of the object criticized. The critic seems to be saying: "The fact that I am here writing this essay and thereby improving my awareness of myself is as important as anything I am writing."

Again, the basis of criticism is sympathy. Over desert expanses of time, the lonely critic reaches out for fellow life. The writer does the same thing, and the openness of heart with which he apprehends his subject becomes a major test, perhaps *the* major test, in judging what he has done; and so the temptation becomes strong to judge the writer rather than the writing. Artist and critic alike are by way of becoming no more than men of sympathy and sincerity. If they are that all is well. A void seems to open up for art and criticism to go tumbling into.

It need not surprise us that as a practicing critic Kobayashi has been erratic, and has sometimes seemed even a touch malign. Critics who venture judgments on their contemporaries tend to be wrong from time to time, and yet are not held to fail as critics by virtue of that fact. Were they always right, there would be no unrecognized geniuses, no Hölderlins for us of later generations to congratulate ourselves for having at length recognized. With a critic like Kobayashi the problem is more complicated. If, at least by implication, he constantly betrays doubts about the importance of literature, and yet has been a man of very great influence upon the intellectual moods of his day, then much of his own importance must lie in a realm other than practical literary criticism. He may be wrong in everything he has to say about his friends and enemies, and still not be a lightweight, so to speak. We all know that Kiku-chi Kan (Hiroshi) was a bad novelist, and Kobayashi Hideo has praised him to the skies. We all know that Kawabata Yasu-nari is a good novelist, and Kobayashi has had some rather slighting things to say about him. Of that wonderfully skillful storyteller Akutagawa he has had extremely biting things to say, and with tiring repetitiousness. The fact that Kobayashi should have drawn from deep native wells of anti-reason and anti-artifice when he made them, and that so many people should have listened so attentively, and nodded so approvingly, is important all the same.

His admirers may also be confusing life and art, and thereby saying something about themselves and about him. As he has done by the objects of his criticism, so may his critics, including myself, sometimes do by him. The man is as interesting as his work. Quite aside from the validity of his ideas, the steadiness with which he has held to them, in the most difficult circumstances, is remarkable. His belief in straightforwardness and action led him to support the war, at a time when to oppose it would have been more courageous. He cannot be accused of cowardice, however, for the principles that brought out his patriotism had in his youth made him the enemy of those advocates of "scientific" criticism, the Marxists, who were more powerful by far than he, and since the war the same principles have earned him the designation "feudal." He was not among the shrill patriots during the war, and he has not been among the shrill peace-mongers since. Given the number of

Japanese intellectuals who, now bellicose and now peaceful, have followed each fad in turn, such firmness is admirable.

· II ·

Kobayashi Hideo was in his late twenties and recently graduated from the French department of Tokyo Imperial University when he first attracted attention as a critic. In 1929 he won second prize in a contest sponsored by the magazine *Kaizō*. First prize was won by the Communist Miyamoto Kenji. The contest was a frontal clash, for Kobayashi's entry, called "All Sorts of Designs" (*Samazama naru ishō*), was a denial of ideology and dogma in general, and most particularly of Marxism. Kobayashi is said to have been bitterly disappointed that he did not win first prize. He had made a very careful appraisal of the judges, and thought he knew exactly what they would take.

He may have thought that they would take obfuscation. Kobayashi's later style is sometimes hard to penetrate, full of paradox and aphorism; but few of his essays are as maddening as this one. Some understanding of his later work seems almost imperative if one is to guess at the meaning. Can it be, one wonders, that the judges awarded him second prize rather than admit that they had no notion what he was talking about?

Still, ideas are there, and some of them are basic to the whole of Kobayashi's thought, or rejection of thought. There may have been a certain amount of youthful sporting with judges along the way, but there can be little doubt that the heart of the essay is sincerity itself. He is behaving as he would have serious authors behave, and implicit in the essay is the assertion that the critic himself can be as serious a writer as the best of them.

The basis of criticism, we learn, is self-cultivation. "How is a person to distinguish criticism from self-awareness [*jiishiki*]? . . . Criticism aimed at oneself, criticism aimed at others—it is one thing, not two." (1, 104)

423

And so it is with literature in general. "I do not like the expression art for the sake of the proletariat, and I do not like the expression art for art's sake. . . . In the final analysis they say nothing. Which is the more difficult, to fight for the sake of the country or to fight for the sake of oneself? It is easy to order a person to produce art for the sake of the proletariat or for the sake of himself alone; but for the artist so instructed the two are equally difficult." (1, 106)

Creators of systems are no different from creators of specifics. Marx is no different from Balzac. Each had his "destiny" (*shukumei*), a word that seems to have close affinities with the existentialist "contingency." "The logical relationship between theory and action in the individual case of Balzac had to be the same in the individual case of Marx. . . . When the two sought to set down the basic character of the day in which they lived, they wished for nothing, as the condition for their work, other than the living reality before their eyes. Each of the two had his different destiny, that is all." (1, 114-15)

Each, having grasped his destiny, produces his "design," grows it as his skin. It is what keeps him from dissolution. "Designs" are possible, but not significant, without the necessary awareness of destiny. "Art for art's sake" is a feigning. Materialist theories of "art for the proletariat" tend, in these later days, to be easy solutions for those who have not been through the necessary crisis. And so, in conclusion:

"I believe that I have made my way among at least the more important of the various designs we see in the Japanese literary world today. I have not, in a search for something better, wished to ridicule them. I have but sought to believe in all designs, so as not to believe too much in any one of them." (1, 116)

After puzzling over this first important essay, and leaving it and returning to puzzle over it again, the reader may conclude that it need not have been as difficult as it is (though if it had come right out and said what it was up to it might not have won a prize). Yet much of what Kobayashi was to argue through the Decade of the Assassinations and the Decade of the Disaster and after is already there: the suspicion of systems and concepts, and especially of Japanese conceptualizers and systematizers; the belief in the intensely subjective nature of literary creation, and its association with personal crisis; the confidence that the critical act is itself an act of literary creation. It will also be apparent that literature shows a distressing tendency to get mixed up with all sorts of other things. Marx and Balzac faced their destinies and formed their designs against it, and the designs are of the same order. There is a suspicion of the claims of literature to uniqueness.

On one problem Kobayashi was to waver somewhat: the relation of the author to society. The rejection of concept seems very much like a rejection of the social applicability of literature, and the truest reality that of the "I-novelist," alone with his self-awareness. Indeed the critic himself becomes a sort of I-novelist.

In most other matters he remained remarkably steadfast. The self-consciously and too confidently intellectual in its various guises—science, concept, analysis, "psychologism"—remained the enemy. The best writer was he in whose case the confrontation and the work of art, the act and its expression, were one. For the young Kobayashi, the writer who came nearest to the ideal was Shiga Naoya.

If his graduation essay on Rimbaud be excepted, Kobayashi's first monograph, which appeared in 1929, the year of the "designs," was on Shiga. Excerpts follow.

> The problem of Shiga Naoya is the problem of the ultra-egoist [the English word is used]. His fascination lies in the most individual acts of the most individual self-awareness (*jiishiki*). He is not important for having harvested a world view. His importance lies rather in a harvest of acts. What he sings of is always the present and portents of the future (*yochō*). Reminiscence in the true sense of the word is not to be found in his works. (1, 119)

There can be few among modern writers who are as far from such sorts [examples have been given of doubting French writers] as Shiga Naoya. The word "classical" is a vague, misty one, but if it means an intimate harmony between reason (*richi*) and desire (*yokujō*), then Shiga Naoya is a truly classical person. (I, 120)

"The consequences of murder were no concern now. Perhaps I would be put in prison. But I could not measure how much better life in prison would be than my life now. I would take care of that time when it came. It would be enough if I somehow disposed of matters as they arose. Perhaps I would dispose and dispose and never have done with disposing. But if I had to work at it to the very end then that would become my real life." ("Han's Crime": *Han no hanzai*.)

Such is the fundamental form that Shiga's thought (*shisaku*) takes. It is really less a form of thought than a mode (*kitei*) of action. He admits of no gap between thought and action. (I, 120)

I do not know whether or not I am correct in describing his nerves as classical; but it is clear that the word "nervous" has for him a far more significant meaning than for most modern men. What appears to be the most distal of nerves always clings with a persistence like the tiniest little decorative flourish in Chopin, a toothache echoing to the pit of the stomach. (I, 122)

Shiga is not a person of thought or of passive sensation (*kankaku*). Above all he is a man of action. (I, 123)

Impressions (*inshō*) for him are truly direct, like the snake raising its head to the sound of the flute, the wings of the ptarmigan turning white with the onset of winter. The directness of the impressions allows no hesitation in the choice of words. The wave pattern upon the water is caught while it is still spreading. (I, 123)

His spirit does not know drama. His trials are those of a growing tree. (I, 127)

If there are among you those who do not weep, that is not because your hearts have dried up, it is because your brains, not all that clever in the first place, have been pushed beyond their pace. It is not hard to make conceptual persons (*kannenteki na ningen*) weep sentimental or nervous tears. (I, 127)

The last quotation has reference to "Reconciliation" (*Wakai*), a thin story about a boy who at first thinks his father beastly and then later does not. It has been preceded by a flat declaration that everyone weeps upon reading "Reconciliation," for "the author's powerful naturalness hits directly at the tear glands." The critic at such times seems near abandoning literary standards, and an awareness of the danger may be responsible for that bit of name-calling at us who do not weep.

Almost a decade later, in 1938, Kobayashi wrote a second important essay on Shiga. His admiration for "Reconciliation" and Shiga had not diminished, but the heart of the novel shifts somewhat in the second essay. It becomes the believability of the characters. Shiga, we learn, has created a single character, active in more than one work: Ōtsu Junkichi in "Reconciliation" and Tokitō Kensaku in the more ambitious *Journey through Darkness* (*Anya kōro*). A single character—but what a character he is! Not just any ordinary, believable inhabitant of a novel, but rather a subject and object of love, *Journey through Darkness* being a love story, Tokitō Kensaku emerging as a character in the round because the object not merely of observation but of affection.

Do we not have here an example of an author's love apprehending a character in a remarkably objective fashion? . . . Love is, more than anything, action, will. It is not something that merely is, it is something that men find, invent, protect. . . .
Kensaku has no liking for the sport so beloved of the modern writer, translating spiritual anguish into words and then stumbling over the words. His pain comes directly from

427

life, and does not seek the good offices of words. (IV, 141, 143-44)

Kobayashi does not push the problem of characterization very far, however, and the evidence in the second Shiga essay as in the first is that he is not all that much interested in what it is that makes a novel a novel. We learn that Shiga is a realistic poet in the *Manyōshū* tradition ("What are observations without individual style?" IV, 137), and that he is a moralist the efficacy of whose moralizing comes from its being in the act and not in the abstraction: "The fact that Shiga's character as a moralist has not shown itself openly, the reader will agree upon looking at this work [*Journey through Darkness*], is due to the purity of the moral. It is, in a word, the pursuit of happiness in a very profound sense." (IV, 143)

Sympathy, immediacy, commitment to art-as-act: these are Shiga Naoya. His opposite is Akutagawa, cold, withdrawn, analytical, morbidly given to "psychologism." Attacks on Akutagawa dot Kobayashi's writings about modern Japanese fiction.

Here is a stricture from a 1932 essay called "Anxiety in Modern Literature" (*Gendai bungaku no fuan*):

We writers used to speak of people whose characters were bankrupt (*seikaku hasansha*). . . . What were they driven by? By what they called the vulgar, irritating to their delicate sensibilities, by the vulgar utilitarianism they so disliked. This dislike, turned inward and joined to the traditonal naturalist fondness for self-culivation, was the song of character bankruptcy. . . . The most classical and pitiable singer of this classical song was Akutagawa Ryūnosuke. Critics frequently describe Akutagawa as the embodiment of the modern intellectual and his fate. I think the view a mistake. This singularly talented man left behind only delicate meditations. This essayist who failed to portray a single human being—it is extremely doubtful whether he had keener human perceptions than all those naturalists whose reputations fail to approach his. (II, 59)

Here is another, a slightly later one, from an essay "On Paradox" (*Gyakusetsu ni tsuite*):

One witnessed a curious phenomenon: a semi-intellectual writer like Akutagawa, who sought to pin man down with sharp and clever words, seemed more of a realist than those belittlers of the intellect who, albeit on a small scale, wrote of man as he was. The intellectual writer of a few years ago was no more of a realist than the naturalist writer who preceded him. Both were sentimental poets. All that made the former seem more realistic was the cloak of paradox he wore. (II, 171-72)

And another, from a 1941 essay in the course of which Akutagawa's treatment of General Nogi is contrasted with that of the American journalist Stanley Washburn:

Because Akutagawa's sort of analysis differs little from inquiry into how much General Nogi weighed, the more he concentrates his technique upon it, the more the result, quite against his wishes, becomes caricature. . . . Washburn, by contrast, perceives the extraordinary tragedy enacted inevitably by a man of Nogi's extraordinary spiritual strength. . . . He does not make sport of the general's humanity. (VI, 87)

Akutagawa, although the favorite target, is not the only one. Here, written in 1941, is an appraisal of Kawabata Yasunari as a novelist:

People are fond of describing the cold reason (*richi*) and the beautiful lyricism in the novels of Kawabata Yasunari. This is benighted nonsense. Kawabata Yasunari has not written a single novel. One has but to read his works with a modicum of care to see how indifferent he is to the matters that ought to be the objects of the novelist's interest: what

our everyday life is like, how we collide with and how we
give in to social forms and customs, what sort of complications arise between persons of different views and different
characters. Note how lacking he is in the talent even to distinguish two men, two women from each other. (VI, 108-109)

Elsewhere (IV, 23) the literary movement to which Kawabata
belonged is called "less literary than stylistic."

And here, in the late 1930s, the Proletarian writers are
charged with bleeding mankind in another fashion: "Because
they believed in a social base into which thought had sunk its
roots, they naturally tended to believe that giving individual
and human form to thought was no problem. The scientific
and universal nature of their beliefs but complicated the fundamental technical problem of the writer [novelist?], the indi-
vidualization and humanization of thought." (IV, 117)

Here, from a 1931 review of a novel called *The Anjō Brothers* (*Anjōke no kyōdai*), are some remarks on the inferiority
of Satomi Ton, a friend and colleague of Shiga Naoya's, as a
novelist:

> For Shiga the flow of life-feeling (*seikatsu kanjō*) is
> entirely unconscious. It is, in other words, absolute, self-evi-
> dent, something that it would be foolish to discuss, to com-
> ment upon. However much his own mind (*shinri*) may be
> disturbed within the flow, the style is of an unchanging den-
> sity. Whatever characters may come into his ken, they
> are always viewed with the same exactness. More precisely,
> each is viewed in the light of his own special psychological
> interest, but they are all treated with the same correctness in
> terms of writer's theory (*sakka riron*). Although each of
> them is observed only in fragments, each comes to us whole
> and independent.
>
> For Satomi, life-feeling is an object that must be discussed
> and interpreted for purposes of self-cultivation, an adversary
> one must not for an instant lose hold of. And what, in sum,
> does this mean?

In this novel the observing eye of the hero, Shōzō, moves here and there in varied fashion. It is warm, cold, amiable, perverse, and as it changes the various characters and their backgrounds develop. To take an example: when the older brother, Bunkichi, commits suicide, the observing eye is filled with hatred and malice. No other character is allowed to act except through the malice. It is no exaggeration to say that in this passage there is not a single living individual. All must cater to Shōzō. . . . Why, but fragmentarily if need be, does the author not *show* the reader the spoiled adult Bunkichi is? He but tells us over and over again that Bunkichi is spoiled, a thoroughly impossible person. (II, 13-14)

One need not be in sympathy with the specific judgments to see that the argument—a sort of argument against arguments—is clear and forceful. Kobayashi's attack is concentrated upon the various forms of "realism" in which analysis and withdrawal preclude the essential crisis, that coming to grips with "destiny" and imposing designs upon it. Notions of what is important to any particular genre seem to disappear.

Over and over again Kobayashi says that concepts and techniques are easy to swallow, but very difficult indeed to live in the flesh. "The intellectual of today stops at confession and excludes the flesh and blood that is the writer, and makes himself but a puppet of technical theories." This (II, 59) is from the 1932 essay already quoted, in which Akutagawa comes off so badly. Among techniques the worst is introspective self-analysis, and because of it Akutagawa and his sort, in the same essay, are found to compare badly with Dostoyevsky. "They had the notion of bankruptcy of character, but they had not yet even once beheld a scene in which it became a human actor. Beholding such a scene, they fell back bemused. For want of a better solution, they called it unnatural, eccentric, and they did not again undertake to read the great man's novels." (II, 60) Beyond Dostoyevsky's great powers of analysis, we learn in a slightly later essay, lay nature, unshakable, and because of it "what he [Dostoyevsky] sought was not analysis but synthesis." (II, 69)

Almost a decade later, on the eve of Pearl Harbor, "psychologism," another term for obsessive character analysis, continued to be the enemy. The following is from a 1941 essay on the critic and novelist Hayashi Fusao, who would have no truck with that enemy:

> A feeble uneasiness is taken for a strong spirit of doubt, mechanical distinctions are taken for clear, sharp judgment, boredom from a loss of things to think about is thought to be deep contemplation, the reader thus thinks himself a man of thought, and a person who has merely lost all capacity for decision is thought to be the possessor of an interesting and complex character. . . . Such is the true aspect of the psychologism (*shinri shugi*) running rampant over our modern literature.
>
> I seek the criterion for separating the true from the false in whether or not a piece of modern writing has fallen into the trap laid by this psychologism. (VI, 72)

The point could not be made too often. It was made again the same year, in the essay in which Akutagawa (what varied adversaries he was forced to take on!) was bettered in his contest with Stanley Washburn:

"Is it not stupid arrogance to think that a human being is to be captured better by observation (*kansatsu*) than by respect and sympathy and fellow-feeling and affection?" (VI, 92)

Analyzing and conceptualizing may seem a world or so apart, the one a result of a nagging suspicion that there may be no truth and no reality, the other the result of a belief in truths into which apparently observable facts must be fitted; but their result for literature, thought Kobayashi, is the same, the wringing dry of blood. As for conceptualizing, the Marxists continued, on the eve of the war, though most of them had become noisy patriots, to be leading offenders:

Empty thought can go anywhere, my own feet can tread only a small bit of ground. We think of eternal life, I must shortly die. I cannot have many friends, I cannot have many lovers. The things to which I can give assent from my very entrails add up to but a tiny sum, the people I can love and hate can number no more than the few immediately beside me. This is the state of life for me, and it is for everyone. So it has been since society began, so it will always be. The fact that the writer does not depart from his own life means that he gives it his assent, and it alone. To give his assent is to know the true meaning of expressions like the objective world, the concrete world, real history. The ice and icicles of, let us say, the materialist view of history will teach him nothing of it. . . . There is no first and no second in the quality of ice. Nature envelops me, and the nature known as my own flesh envelops me, waterproof. (VI, 34-35)

· III ·

Kobayashi thought that the germs of these various allied ailments, scientism and psychologism and analysis and conceptualizing, came from the West. The quotation with which this paper began should be evidence enough that he did not by that fact become anti-Western. He has been no Mushakōji, drinking too deeply of the syrup of Western meliorism and then vomiting it all up. He has been rather more like Nagai Kafū, rejecting not the foreign stimuli but rather the spasms to which they seem to give rise in the native body. The trouble has been with the Japanese understanding of the West, and the danger of taking over a concept or a system without having had a part in its formation. Japanese intellectuals, although the simile is not his, have a way of joining the cheers without quite knowing what they are about.

Kobayashi's most famous exposition of the thesis that modern Japanese literature went wrong because of the importation from the West of techniques ungrounded in Japan came in 1935, in one of the most famous of all his essays, "On the 'I-novel'" (*Shishōsetsu ron*). The thesis can be traced back to his very earliest writing. The germ of it is to be detected in "All Sorts of Designs." Here is a passage from a 1931 monograph on Tanizaki Junichirō:

> It is no exaggeration to say that naturalism as it was imported into Japan was a matter of technique and nothing else. There was no positivist thought to control the writer from without, writers had no ambitious social theories about their work. . . . Most writers therefore had only themselves to turn to. They turned to polishing a "techniqueless technique" most appropriate to the nature of the Japanese writer; and the spirit of positivism was aimed not at society but at the subjective consciousness. More properly that spirit was put to the ends of self-cultivation. (1, 251)

The same influences were operating on poetry, with less baneful effects, for they fitted in rather more smoothly with domestic inclinations. Again, however, techniques were uprooted from foreign soils and brought to a field unprepared for them; and if happy flowers did from time to time appear in the field their resemblance to the foreign importation was but coincidental. They sprang from different seeds, and the gardener was under the illusion of having done more than in fact he had. The following passage was written slightly later than the celebrated essay on the I-novel:

> Our poetic tradition has been purely lyrical since the time of the *Manyōshū*. . . . Naturally, then, our poets have had nothing whatsoever in common with the movement of violent self-awareness in modern European poetry which has sought to cut away every element of prose and to create the lyric at its purest. Our poets have found only symbolist technique, and none of the intellectual spirit that produced it. They have enmeshed the symbolic in all sorts of adjectives,

"sensual," "mystical," "decadent," "sceptical" and the like, but they cannot be credited with having brought a revolution to our poetry. It had its own fully developed technique of symbolism from the outset. (IV, 36)

The 1935 essay on the I-novel has been the object of fervid debate among Japanese literary critics because in it Kobayashi seems to have some kind things to say about those old adversaries, the Proletarian writers. The essay in question is a difficult and slippery one, and Kobayashi seems to take on a deliberately enigmatic tone, at its worst a little like the evidence at the trial of the Knave of Hearts.

At the outset he quotes the novelist Kume Masao to the effect that *War and Peace, Crime and Punishment,* and *Madame Bovary* would all be considered "popular" (and therefore "impure") novels in Japan. Consciously or subconsciously, says Kobayashi, most *bunjin,* denizens of the *bundan,* the literary world, would have agreed with Kume at the time he wrote. The time was 1925, when Akutagawa was coming to the end of his career, and the Proletarian novelists were coming to the fore. In context, then, all Kobayashi really has to say of the Proletarians is that they managed to break away from the *bunjin katagi,* the prejudices and idiosyncrasies of the *bunjin.* Ideology was strong enough with some of them to force a departure from the attenuated virtuosity of Akutagawa and his predecessors.

For the sources of the *bunjin katagi* one should not be surprised, having read the Tanizaki essay, to be told to go West. After a long and involved discussion of what a time French naturalism had getting itself born, Kobayashi has this to say of Japanese naturalism, especially the father it named for itself, Tayama Katai, and its successors unto Akutagawa:

The ideological struggles of such authors were precisely what our own writers, importers of naturalist literature, found hardest to understand. "I began writing with thought, treatment, style that were under no influence from Tokugawa literature or from Ozaki Kōyō or Kōda Rohan, that were virtually unrelated to what our literary world had been. I had to have my sources. I asked what they were, and I came upon Wordsworth." So said Kunikida Doppo. At least since the latter half of the Meiji Period, all of our writers have had their Wordsworths to depend upon. Each has had his different Wordsworth: Zola, Maupassant, Flaubert. At a risk of seeming wordy, I would explain the significance of the fact thus: our writers have without question imported the individualized philosophies of Western writers insofar as they have been manifest as technique; but each philosophy has done no more than nurture the dreams of each Japanese writer. Foreign thought has been imported only as technique, and as technique alone it must live. What was imported was less thought than random thoughts (*kansō*). This has been most convenient.

The works of Maupassant, which had taken their farewell of the private life (*jisseikatsu*) of the writer, gave Katai pleasure as they gave him direction in his own private life. In these circumstances, the odd circumstances producing *The Quilt* (*Futon*), earliest of our modern I-novels, is to be found the secret of later theories of the I-novel; but at least in principle the secret is extremely simple and clear. No writer, however much of a genius he may be, can build with his own hands alone a spirit for an age, a philosophy for a society. . . . He but makes concrete in his works a philosophy that already lives among the people. . . . When Katai found Maupassant, it was not possible to contemplate a philosophy of the age that worked powerfully upon him from entirely outside his writing, either to deny that writing or to encourage and stimulate it. . . . Since then the novel, clinging tenaciously to the private life of the author, has shown astonishing technical advances in disposition of cast, nuance of character. . . .

So it is that the I-novel became the so-called "novel of mental states" (*shinkyō shōsetsu*). Confession and experience having to do with the writer's private life were polished and refined, and the "I" became progressively purer. It is for this reason, too, that the theory of the I-novel became for the *bunjin* of the day a theory of the pure novel.

Ōgai and Sōseki did not cast their lots with the I-novel movement. Men of unusual culture and education, they were probably able to see the infirmity of our naturalist novel. This discernment on their part was passed in its most correct form to Akutagawa Ryūnosuke, but the sad fact is that his constitution was not up to supporting it. Did the tragedy of Akutagawa end with his death? In what form does the I-novel appear before us now? (III, 94-96)

There is more in the I-novel essay than literature, however. Very often, with Kobayashi, what is ostensibly an exposition of a literary problem seems to have behind it, slippery and elusive, a moral discourse. Running through the essay is something known as "the socialized I" (*shakaika shita watakushi*).

In France too an I-novel movement appeared as the naturalist novel ripened. Barrès is an example, and after him Gide and Proust. Regardless of what heights they variously ascended to, the stimulus to creation was in each case the same: a yearning to revive the humanity that had become formalized under the pressures of nineteenth-century naturalist thought. Toward this end, they pursued the "I" and did not fall into error, and that was because their "I" was already fully socialized. (III, 92-93)

It continues to be debated whether Kobayashi is here departing from his early subjective notions of literature, and extending a hand to the now-reformed proletarian writers, who had at least *tried* to get out of themselves; or whether, still controlled by his earlier aversion to systems and forms as very inadequate substitutes for crises, he is urging the Japanese epigones by whom he is surrounded to give up the fight and go back to the past.

A belief in personal crisis as the source of creation does not in any case preclude feelings of loneliness, and a theory of imagination and creation based upon honesty and sympathy as the highest virtues demands a constant searching out for fellowship. Perhaps the fact that no one quite seems to know what the I-novel essay means may come from its pulling in two directions at the same time. And there is that other factor: the suspicion of fiction, and the awareness of the limits of literature in general. The problem of the "socialized I" in literature may not be as important as that of striving to be such a person in real life. Running through Kobayashi's writing in the thirties is an unshakable feeling of loneliness, of homelessness, as of being adrift in a very small boat; and with it, of course, a watch for fellow drifters.

In a 1933 essay called "Literature that has Lost its Home" (*Kokyō wo ushinatta bungaku*), Kobayashi describes how it feels to be a Tokyo man and a part of the Tokyo literary world:

> Looking back over my past, I see there not so much a Tokyo man born in a city called Tokyo, as an abstraction of a city man, born in no particular place. Writing which considers this and that about the abstraction can without doubt be literature of a sort, but it has no substantial backing. The tired heart flees society and has a strangely abstract wish to commune with nature. (II, 214-15)
>
> I suspect that our new literature, although it is a literature of the young, might be called a literature of the young who have lost their youth. Whatever the plans and intentions of the writer, the performance is uniformly abstract (*kannen-teki*). The flavor of the immediately present (*sokubutsuteki*) has been ever more wanting since the appearance of the naturalists. (II, 216)

Among the more puzzling of Kobayashi's literary verdicts is that handed down in the case of Kikuchi Kan (Hiroshi), the only man besides Shiga to whom he granted the designation genius. Kikuchi's stock is not high these days, and one may be tempted to suspect that Kobayashi let personal feelings, or just possibly political and commercial considerations, get in the way of his appraisal. The two were very close associates in the literary market place, and it does sometimes seem to be a fact in Japanese literary life that a critic's geniuses come from among his closest associates.

But Kobayashi's writings have a way of being right on one level even when they seem wrong on another. It was not so much the personal bond with Kikuchi that moved him as the access Kikuchi seemed to provide to wider fellowship, plus, of course, Kikuchi's qualifications as a man of action. The Kikuchi essay was written in 1937, when the problem of what it was that caught and held the imagination of the race, and how one went about entering that imagination, was of much concern to Kobayashi. The preoccupation with the people (*minshū*) and the popular may seem out of place in an acidulous critic of the Proletarian writers; but it is not at all out of place in the man who thought Shiga Naoya's great achievement the union of word and act, and the man who deplored the stylish withdrawal of the *bundan* from the larger world.

Kobayashi dismisses the notion that a growing tendency toward the popular (*tsūzoku*) was responsible for Kikuchi's loss of prestige with the critics. He finds, on the contrary, that there has been something *tsūzoku* about Kikuchi from the start, and, further, he finds it good. "Because his writings invite the reader into the very midst of human interest, he has disdained troublesome techniques." (IV, 40) His early, autobiographical works tend to be praised by critics, continues Kobayashi, because rarefied autobiographical writing is the opposite of the popular, and therefore good and pure. Kobayashi makes two objections. In the first place, even the early autobiographical writings are not "I-novels" of the sort beloved of the critics. We have here no tormented "I," "analyzing his heart to pieces." (IV, 42) We have rather a "complete absence of reflection-for-the-sake-of-reflection." (IV, 42)

That matter aside, the longer, more "popular" works are superior to the early, "pure" works, for they show human beings in action.

He found drama throughout human affairs (his long and short stories alike make a sort of psychological drama), but he saw no sorrow in his own position as a pioneer. The road he travelled was that of the pioneer all the same. It was not, however, the path of the conceptual (*kannenteki*) pioneer, cutting perpendicularly across that of society. The truth about his work becomes clear, I think, when one sees the pioneer walking his path and not displaying a pioneer's face. He was the first writer to feel the social quality of literature not with his head but with his body, with the very center of his individual being. . . . The Proletarian movement flooded the literary world with a debate over the social quality of literature, but it went no farther than debate. The task of actually bringing the people into literature was left to others. (IV, 46-48)

Kobayashi was not unaware of surface contradictions between the existential self and the "socialized I," and more than once explicitly blamed the split between the two upon modern Japanese culture. The wound dealt the writing and the wound dealt the writer came from the same shaft, and recognition of the fact brought of its own accord a certain discovery of brotherhood. The point was made explicitly in 1936, in an open letter to an old adversary, the Leftist critic Nakano Shigeharu:

I have always thought criticism to mean attesting to the self (*jiko shōmei*). From this principle it follows that in order to write powerful social criticism one must be in possession of a fully socialized self. Cultural conditions must be such as to permit a harmony, a balance, between the social and the individual. And how were things when I made my critical debut, believing no more than this simple principle?

You know, sir, without my telling you. One had to attempt bearing witness to one's self in a situation in which a definite self had disappeared. The paradoxical quality of my writing bespeaks a paradox forced upon it by the principle from which it began. That I have been able to say anything at all is only because I have had no dearth of opportunities to behold the comedy of critics who, wanting no part in this self-attestation, have thought they could make do with social criticism, scientific criticism. . . .

It is a time for us to meditate upon the wounds modern Japanese culture has inflicted upon us. It is not a time, I think, for the wounded to be fighting one another. (III, 162)

The transition is easy from such views about criticism to Kobayashi's views of history and war. In neither case can his ideas pass the test of literal consistency, but in both he maintains a fundamentally steady attitude toward his angels and his devil, action and imaginative sympathy on the one hand, conceptualizing on the other.

Most people's view of history is highly personal and subjective. There are those who recognize it to be so, however, and those who do not. Kobayashi has from the outset been of the former persuasion. He has long been a foe of those who argue for discernible laws of history and who think that study of the past permits prediction of the future. His belief in the uniqueness of the historical event and in the limits of historical objectivity and theory has brought accusations of soft-headedness and even sentimentality. Some of his individual judgments, to be sure, do not seem all that well judged, as when he praises Ōkawa Shūmei's "common sense and unwavering eye for history" (IV, 80); and some readers may think it unfortunate that such tear-sodden imagery is allowed to run through his historical meditations.

Yet they are on the whole consistent with his early admiration for Shiga-as-actor, and a strong preference, as the war approached and presently came, for makers of history, whether men of power or not, over searchers for patterns and scanners of *shiryō*, historical materials. In the 1937 essay that contained those warm words for Dr. Ōkawa (it is called "The Living Eye for History," *Rekishi no katsugan*) is also this passage: "The living eye for history was most apparent among historians who sought, in a day when the new positivism of the West was being voraciously devoured, to beat the discipline of history into a new shape. That eye would seem to have clouded over. It has been lost on a road that leads into the morass of historical materials. And there has been another road: the materialist view of history has sadly plundered our spirits. The path to ruin lies along the two roads." (IV, 81)

· IV ·

The case against historical repetition and in favor of the uniqueness of the individual historical happening is argued repeatedly through the thirties, and perhaps most ingeniously at the beginning of the next decade, in an essay called "The Newness of the Incident" (*Jihen no atarashisa*). The Incident in question is of course the involvement in China. Kobayashi's immediate argument is against too-easy acceptance of too-easy arguments for a "theory of leadership" (*shidō riron*) in the crisis. Oda Nobunaga had none, says Kobayashi—he but acted. Hideyoshi's great failure in Korea, on the other hand, was due to too much planning. Confidence that planning, based on the past, was the key to the future was a positive obstacle when crisis came, because it obscured recognition that the situation was new and to be dealt with in its own unique terms.

The point was more explicit in the 1937 "On War" (*Sensō ni tsuite*): "History may show ways to make general predictions, but it also teaches how dangerous are clear views of the future. He who thinks he has learned to take his seat in the future and look back down upon the present is he who has not learned the greatest lesson of history. It is this: that the real makers of history have not believed too firmly in pictures of

442

the future. They have attached themselves rather to the present, with all the vigor they possess." (IV, 87)

The most famous exposition of the thesis is the one that has come most under attack. The charge has been sentimentality. The central image is a highly wrought one, to be sure, but there is nothing inherently sentimental about a weeping mother. The only question is whether she functions appropriately. The essay, written in 1941, is that in which, among other things, Akutagawa and Stanley Washburn are seen locked in battle.

> History never repeats itself. Precisely for this reason we regret the past. History is like a gigantic accumulation of the regrets of the human race. The chain that runs through it is a feeling of reluctance to part with something, and not, I believe, a chain of cause and effect. One needs only think of a mother's feelings toward a historical fact, the death of her child. For the mother the historical fact is not just where and when and for what reason and under what conditions this happening, the child's death, took place. Its significance fails to come to life unless it is accompanied by a sense of an irreplaceable life lost irrevocably. . . . To make a historical fact, it does not suffice that there once was such an incident. There must be a sense of it as still present. The mother knows this. It may be said that for her the fact in history is not the death of the child, but rather the dead child. (VI, 81)

And slightly later in the same essay:

> Is it not because the mother, against her will, has lost a child that the inevitability of it strikes her heart? . . . Because we resist, the inevitable makes its appearance. We will not stop resisting, and so history will not stop being inevitable. This fact has no relation at all to theories of cause and effect put together in the human mind. It is an experience familiar to everyone from his everyday life, and it builds in everyone's breast an uncomplicated feeling for history. Otherwise we

would not have thought of that profound word, "fate" (*ummei*). (VI, 85)

Ummei, we learn a moment later, has been lost under such modern concepts as "psychology" and "character," and so the attack moves on by turns to Akutagawa, modern analysis in the novel, and modern "objective" historiography, deprived of ethical elements, saddled, like much of the novel, with surface techniques and a materialist view of the world, offering limitless analysis and limitless confusion. Akutagawa, bad writer of fiction, is also bad historian, losing a sense of the integrity of his subject.

Some paragraphs later, two examples of good Japanese historiography are commended to the attention of the reader. The first may not strike one as exactly the most fascinating piece of historical writing ever composed, and one may suspect that Kobayashi actually had a Chinese model, the *Shih chi*, in mind, and that ascendant nationalism set him to casting about for a Japanese alternative. It is the *Dai Nihon shi*. Certainly, from his point of view, it *would* be good history if it were as he describes it. Act is central, and appropriate to character. "Why do I so readily nod assent to the things they said and did so long ago? Their behavior is clear and entirely right for them, they say clearly what is necessary and proper. And when they die, how appropriately they do that too! Where, by comparison, have the tens and hundreds of persons in our new fiction gone every month?" (VI, 90-91)

The other example is puzzling, the more so because it is offered as the finest of histories written by Japanese. It is the *Jinnō shōtōki*, which is an attempt, if ever there was one, to force history into an ineluctable pattern, and to demand of it that it proceed into the future on a chartable line from the past. Yet the contradiction is far from complete when one remembers the praise offered in 1937 to Meiji historiography and the basic doctrine of sympathetic imagination. It was Chikafusa's humanity and his ethical inclinations that drew Kobayashi, and he would appear to have been drawn as much to the man as to the work.

One can see from his letter to Yūki Chikatomo how violently passionate he was. The sentences of the *Jinnō shōtōki* were written at the same time, in the same Oda and Seki encampments—and they are unparalleled in their calm. Only when one is in possession of this fact is one aware of the splendor with which he undertakes to describe, "not one thing disturbing his heart," the death of the Emperor Godaigo, and, still more remarkably, the death in battle of his own son Akiie. He argues over and over again in the book the need to polish the spirit—not the intellect (*gosei*) but the spirit. "Brighten and cleanse the spirit," he says, "and it will contain charity and resolve." How true the statement is—and the fundamental view of history in which he believed has not changed today and must not change in the future, whatever changeable views of history may pass over it. (vi, 95-96)

Good history comes to have affinities with good criticism, revelation of the self, attestation to the self—*jiko shōmei*. Its enemies are analysis, materialism, illusions about objectivity, a failure to acknowledge the limits of history—all vices of Taishō and post-Taishō historiography.

Kobayashi's most subtle statement of the limits and possibilities of history comes in the introduction to his longest venture in literary biography, *The Life of Dostoyevsky* (*Dostoyevsky no seikatsu*), published between 1935 and 1939. The relationship between the introduction and the biography itself will be entirely clear only to the student who has gone through the biography more carefully than I. A person may wish that he had more time for reading Japanese commentaries upon Western literature and its makers, but, alas, time is limited.[2]

___

[2] "I am not ashamed to confess that I have never read a line of the elder Crébillon's works. Life is not so long that one can afford to spend even the briefest time in the perusal of 18th-century French

The main points would seem to be, however, that specific incident and act and not abstraction is the matter of history, common sense and sympathy the qualities without which the historian fails.

Kobayashi touched upon similar matters in a famous debate with the novelist and critic Masamune Hakuchō, which took place while the life of Dostoyevsky was being serialized. Hakuchō appeared to believe that the facts of Tolstoy's death, the result, it had been revealed by literary detectives, of a quarrel with his wife, diminished Tolstoy's stature. Evidence, replied Kobayashi, of how inadequate was the Japanese naturalist grasp of human reality. In his preoccupation with biographical trivialities, Hakuchō had failed to catch the larger reality, the fact of a human being destroyed by ideas. Hakuchō, the believer in facts, failed to synthesize them into the whole fact. Paradoxical as always, Kobayashi gave some evidence in his argument of a belief in abstractions that lie outside of and shape facts, and so of making common cause, albeit obscurely, with Marxist dialecticians; but his true intent would seem to have been very different indeed.

We cannot see history, says the argument central to the Dostoyevsky introduction, apart from historical materials (*shiryō*); and historical materials are but marks inflicted upon the face of nature, marks which nature itself is in constant process of effacing.

History is myth (*shinwa*). It is myth which must, to some extent, accept the limitations imposed by the matter (*busshitsusei*) of its materials. History is a world supported by the word "history," and not by an existence which is history. What exists, including man himself, is what we can only

---

tragedians." (Aldous Huxley.) I would certainly not wish to imply that there are no riches awaiting him who *does* find time for what the Japanese have had to say about our literature; but I am grateful to Professor Nathan Glazer for calling my attention to this piece of evidence that even the most voracious of readers cannot get in everything.

think of as nature, and our powers of humanizing it are powers having to do with what does not exist. Historical materials are the resistance of nature felt by those powers. Unless they feel the resistance, anything is possible to them. . . . They can, if they wish, be present at the work of founding the universe. Where such powers of imagination are not at work, history but reveals its skeleton. . . .

The conditions for observing history are the conditions for creating history, and it is on this unstable ground that we invent the word "history." As the figure of nature becomes clearer, the desire of living being for living being encounters everywhere the resisting objects known as historical materials. The desire does not submit abjectly. In the creation of the world of history, the appraisal of external objects sets no more than passive conditions, and, however rich may be the store of historical materials, our powers of imagination are forever seeking freedom through the gaps in the mesh woven by them. . . .

A delicate balance is set up between, on the one hand, our wish to restore life to men who have returned to the earth, and, on the other, the tracks they have left upon nature. In work accomplished in such a precarious balance, one is not likely to come upon historical invariables (if the expression may be used). So it is that men have had to arm themselves with such a wide variety of theories of history (*shikan*) in answer to a simple question: what is it? (v, 9-10)

It will be observed, perhaps with discomfort, that the organization of the above discussion has had the effect of introducing Kobayashi's two most subtle and eloquent statements about history in reverse chronological order. The weeping mother was not made a symbol of history until 1941, three years after the introduction to the life of Dostoyevsky was written. They are not entirely consistent. In the earlier work two forces are seen in opposition, nature trying to obliterate man and all traces of him, man trying to humanize nature. In the later work the dehumanizing force seems to have disappeared, and history becomes the weeping mother and her awareness of the unique event. The apparent dualism, it must be admitted, does not seem ideally suited to Kobayashi and his belief in the ultimate importance of action and sympathetic awareness of action. Perhaps it is evidence of too overt and obtrusive a foreign influence, that of Bergson. What the two essays have in common is in any case more compelling than the limited range of apparent disagreement. It shows the philosopher of history and the admirer of Shiga Naoya being, on the whole, true to each other; and it helps explain his paradoxical reaction to the war, warm and cold at the same time. The superiority of act to theory argued for participation, and an awareness of the terrible loneliness of the act called for withdrawal into contemplation of the ephemeral, the *mujō*. Kobayashi's meditations upon history come nearer the heart of his thought, or determined thoughtlessness, than does his specifically literary criticism. History is action on the brink of the void.

· V ·

Dislike of feeble, uncertain Westernized intellectuals, belief in the superiority of the act to the thought, a poetic feeling for the lonely community of history, with its rich implications about the uniqueness of the community to which one happens to belong—all of these things could have made Kobayashi into a first-rate Fascist. The surprising fact is the reasonableness of his wartime behavior.

He did, it is true, surrender to the urgings of his friend Kikuchi Kan, a literary entrepreneur in war as he had been in peace, and go off to the continent to be one of the pens behind the guns. The war was also responsible for lapses in literary judgment. Kobayashi made too much of Hino Ashihei, a sort of Japanese Ernie Pyle masked as novelist. The reasons may be similar to those for his exaggerated praise of Kikuchi Kan. They are in many ways good reasons, whether the judgments themselves are or not. Like Kikuchi and unlike the *bundan*, Hino was not given to bloodless analysis and formulation; and the war seemed to offer hope of bringing a little life into a literature grown excessively "pure" and conceptual.

Perhaps, although the question is a delicate one, there were lapses in taste of a less civilized nature. "I cannot believe that it did not seem beautiful also to the gallants in the bombers. . . . I thought that they would not forget it to the end of their lives; and somehow the thought made me happy." (VI, 115) An American does not really like to hear the attack on Pearl Harbor described in such lyrical terms, and wonders how a similar passage about Hiroshima would strike a Japanese. Yet the question *is* a delicate one. Kobayashi has nothing to say, as so many of his fellow pens-behind-guns would have had, about Americans who deserve to be killed. His emphasis is rather upon Japanese who are willing to die.

The interesting fact is not that Kobayashi should have gone so far but that he should have gone no farther. In the essay with this little lyric about the view from the bombers he attributes the origins of war not to warmongers but to the human condition. Elsewhere in his writings are sharp remarks about those allies the Nazis. In a 1940 essay he describes Naziism as "not a system of organization but the incarnation of burning greed," its heart "the venom in the man Hitler." (VI, 22)

Nor, despite his trips to the continent, did he share the official, and Kikuchi's, idea that a special role or "awareness" (*kakugo*) was to be expected of writers in the crisis. He was no believer in spiritual mobilization. As early as 1937, in the essay "On War" already quoted, he had had this to say:

I can think of no "awareness" of war peculiar to the man of letters. If the time comes when I must take up arms, no doubt I shall do so happily, and even die happily. I can think of no other awareness, and I see a need for no other. . . .

Literature is a matter of peace, not of war. A writer may take any number of complicated attitudes toward peace, he

449

can take only one toward war. In a fight he must win. If he
cannot find this proposition among theories of literature,
then he would do well to give up literature. . . .

I am no blind believer in nation and race, but in no circumstances would I wish to fall victim to the malaise of historical
inevitability. . . . I can expect nothing from the intellectuals
who, having ruined their digestion and had their vitality
sapped from an overeating of ideology, are still not satisfied
and are unable to forego the pleasure of fault-finding based
on their reasoned views of history. (IV, 84-86)

Slightly later in the same essay he argues that war and politics make no choice of the means toward their ends, whereas
literature and scholarship are not allowed that luxury. The
scholar and the man of letters, while they are about their own
work, must therefore be pacifists. "I do not seek to clear away
the contradiction in my own mind. Who would be foolish
enough to think of going through life without contradictions?
When the time comes to die I think that I shall be able to die
with good grace. I am but a man. I am neither saint nor
prophet." (IV, 88)

In his "Impressions of Manchuria" the following year, he
made many of the same points again. He was not actively
opposed to spiritual mobilization, he said, but it had far too
much to say of the obvious. More important things lay behind
the slogans.

Everyone is aware of the unprecedented complexity of the
incident and the strange manner in which it has progressed.
Most people who call themselves intellectuals have been critical of the government's policies and statements. It is not of
course that they have had any particular insights and under-
standings themselves for dealing with the incident. It is only
that they have wished to produce something like criticism.
The incident has nonetheless broadened, and the solidarity of
the people has been shaken not in the slightest. And what
sort of wisdom (*chie*) is it that supports the unity? It is no

such easy matter as an unconscious unity in the blood of the Japanese race. It is a strange sort of sagacity (*sōmei*), a wisdom born of a long and truly complex and simple tradition ripened over the ages, and disciplined under the influence of the Western culture that has flooded in since Meiji. . . .

I cannot help thinking that not a single intellectual has yet spoken properly of this wisdom. The Japanese people have dealt with the incident in silence. Such, I think, is its principal characteristic. The demagogues whom it has brought forth are under the illusion that their principles of leadership have succeeded. This is an illusion which demagogues must inevitably have. . . .

Politicians and military men and scholars talk with all their might of the virtues of the Japanese people. Alas, the virtues of the Japanese people are subtle affairs that refuse to submit to their pat formulations. . . . The mutual understanding that lies behind the silence of "the other Japanese" supports but slightly the confusion of words on the surface. (IV, 188-89)

The same year, in an essay called "Powers of Expression in Contemporary Japan" (*Gendai Nihon no hyōgenryoku*), Kobayashi describes what he finds so attractive in Hino Ashihei. He has humanity and that elusive element *ninjō*. Humanity is precisely what has been lacking in both modern fiction and modern criticism—and precisely what is wanted by the ordinary reader.

The following year, in an essay called "The Incident and Literature" (*Jihen to bungaku*), the matter is spelled out further. The appeal of Hino's *Barley and Soldiers* (*Mugi to heitai*) has nothing to do with ideology, and it has a great deal to do with something very deep in the Japanese spirit from very ancient times. "In this work is brought to life a traditional spirit which we Japanese recognize with our very flesh." (V, 207) It is difficult to characterize all the modern ladies and gentlemen who, in an excess of psychological complexity, have lost track

451

of their hearts and are unable to have perfectly ordinary love
affairs; but "if in a broad sense one can call a character wanting in immediacy comical, then I think that no fiction has been
so replete with comical figures as ours of recent years." (v, 208)
The people, so sufficient unto themselves in the crisis, have had
enough of it all; hence the appeal of Hino's soldiers.

Extraordinary times, we learn some paragraphs later, do not
require an extraordinary ideology; the most ordinary and
ancient of ideologies is the only appropriate one. Literature
has no need for emergency measures, but it does have an
opportunity.

> The self-righteous solitude of pure literature is attacked in
> an atmosphere of national unanimity. The incident has but
> made the fact more conspicuous. The tendency has long been
> toward the socialization (*shakaika*) and, in a good sense, the
> popularization of literature. . . .
>
> The important thing is that the crisis brought nothing new
> from without. It but shone a strong light upon Japanese
> virtues and defects already present. The impotence of the
> bureaucrat and the ineptness of cultural policies did not begin
> only yesterday. A different situation has come upon us, to
> bring them out in the open. So it is too with the ignorance,
> political and economical, of the writer. And the courage and
> endurance of the Japanese people and the real strength of
> the Japanese economy have come to light with them.
>
> The incident is not a dangerous crisis for Japan. It is rather
> a test to be welcomed. I do not like the overuse of the expres-
> sion "extraordinary times" (*hijōji*). The choice between tak-
> ing a difficult situation as a test and taking it as a disaster
> brings individual lives to a parting of the ways. (v, 209-210)

And so the mood of the China Incident seemed to endorse
his prolonged war on the *bundan* and his espousal of Shiga
Naoya and Kikuchi Kan. That sense of a silent, communal
voice ignored in the subjectivism and niggling self-analysis of

"pure literature" also brought feelings of companionship, perhaps of having found a home at long last.

Kobayashi was of course a bad prophet. Those who, like Nagai Kafū, thought the "difficult situation" not a test but a disaster were blessed with keener foresight. It may also be charged against Kobayashi that when he wrote the remarks quoted above he had already been to China and seen with his own eyes that the Incident, whatever may have been its effect in shoring up the primitive Japanese spirit, was not at all pleasant for the Chinese. A comparison of his lyrical remarks about Hangchow with his realistic description of shattered Nanking shows that he was perfectly aware of what was going on. But after all it was possible for an American to disapprove violently of, let us say, the brutal treatment accorded the Japanese and their descendants on the American Pacific coast and to approve just as violently of what the Japanese call "the Pacific War."

The opening of the Pacific War brought a change in Kobayashi's manner. The essay containing those ecstatic remarks about Pearl Harbor was but a brief aberration, if it was that. It was written in February, 1942. Two months later he published a short essay on the Nō play "Taima." Thereafter his wartime writings had little to say of the war. He made two more trips to China, but wrote nothing about them. On the second he commenced work on a long study, or rather an impressionistic evocation, of Mozart's music. Published after the war, it is considered among his masterpieces. The emphasis is not on Mozart's sprightliness but on his sadness. The work may be considered an application on Kobayashi's theories of criticism as witness to the self. It is as much about Kobayashi Hideo as it is about Mozart, and it has been described as a sort of oblique I-novel. It is also an attempt, and a successful one, the more remarkable for its exotic subject, to do by a fellow man as Washburn did and Akutagawa did not do by General Nogi.

Other essays on Western culture appeared during the war,

but Kobayashi's major wartime pieces were on a subject that had not much concerned him before, classical Japanese literature. Six of them were collected in 1946 under the title *The Sense of Evanescence* (*Mujō to iū koto*): the title essay, "Taima," "*Tsurezuregusa*," "*Heike monogatari*," "Saigyō," and "Sanetomo." If Kobayashi thought the chief beauty of Mozart's music to be in sad, minor strains, the same can be said of his own "evanescence" collection. With the completion of the last strain, "Sanetomo," in the middle of 1943, he fell into a silence not really broken until he began serial publication of his Mozart essay in December, 1946.

The Sense of Evanescence has all the loneliness of the earlier years, but rancor at the *bundan* and at analysts and philosophers of history has been muted somewhat, and a sense of communal spirit, a sort of communion with ancient loneliness, has helped to replace it. The old loneliness has been changed by an interval of companionship. The results are less critical and expository than evocative, and have more than once been called prose poems. They do not submit to summary and are only slightly less stubborn when subjected to partial translation. Yet the latter device is the only one open to a paper of this sort. It may produce enough uneasiness to send the reader to the originals.

Here are the concluding paragraphs of "Taima":

The fair form of Chūjōhime moved diagonally across the stage. It was like a flower sprung from the mire of history. That meditations on the life and death of man could take such a simple and pure form—I suddenly thought I knew why it was able to ignore social advances. They could do no more than hover about, they could not penetrate the mask so carefully constructed. The "flower" of Zeami was hidden there, without question.

It seemed to me that there could be only pain and no profit in trying to solve a difficult riddle, why appreciation of the Nō should recently have come so in vogue. One thing seemed certain, that punishment had been meted out, punishment for having observed one another so fixedly. We had not wished to notice it, that was all. Historians rest content having called it an age of upheaval, the healthy Muromachi Period that had not a moment's doubt about the evanescence of this world and the eternity of faith.

The Muromachi Period is not far away, for I can almost believe it myself. I asked what Zeami had thought about beauty, in that day not under the tyranny of useless concepts, and I saw there not a touch of the dubious. "Exhausting the skills, the contrivances, one must know that the flower is not lost." There is a beautiful flower, and not the beauty of the flower. Our aestheticians who tax their brains over the vagueness of his "flower" are bemused. It is enough to modify the movements of the concept with the movements of the flesh, he said, for the latter are far more subtle than the former. Were he living today, he would perhaps wish to add: you would do well to mask that coarse expression, constantly imitating the movements of an unstable concept.

"I walked the night road, looking at the stars and looking at the snow. Where are the snows of yesteryear—no, it would not do to fall into *that*. I looked again at the stars and at the snow. (VI, 118-19)

Here are a pair of fragments from "Saigyō":

Saigyō was in no sense a simple poet. But there are among his poems many to make one wonder how a person as thoroughly familiar as he with the pain of "communicating the thing from heart to heart" could have been capable of such easy, effortless, soft expression. He was innately a poet, nothing more can be said; and yet each time I feel the matchless music of such poems I am astonished, and I know that hidden there is Saigyō, weary of thought. He did not know Shunzei's anguished voice in composition, but what might be called a voice of silent anguish over a mysterious something called solitude never left him. In this, one may think, lies the fact that a poem appearing to come forth with the greatest ease is cloaked in the deepest shadows. (VI, 172)

"Wavering in the wind, the smoke of Fuji disappears in the sky: my thoughts, destinations unknown."

This poem was composed on the journey of the same year, and I believe that tradition calls it his favorite among his own poems. I think tradition to be correct. He must have seen how far he had come. He must have seen how his unmanageable heart—"What is to be done with it?" was the curse cast upon him—had finally come to verse so pure, easy, bland. The spirit of any poet who thinks it vulgar has been sullied. Pain has been cleansed, Saigyō plays the strain of the anonymous poet. Through the ages men have thought of that figure, Saigyō gazing at Fuji, and, scarcely knowing it, have sent out their own laments to it. Saigyō was in the end unable to determine the destination of his own thoughts; but that very fact meant that he had determined the destination of his flesh.

"May I die under the blossoms of spring, under the Blessed Full Moon."

Presently, peacefully, the wish was granted. (VI, 174-75)

And here a fragment from "Sanetomo":

Mabuchi said that Sanetomo, studying the *Manyōshū*, became a poet who had "cast away all impure things, and bathed in the clean waters." This celebrated appraisal is quite beside the mark. I think it likely that the day never came for a dispelling of Sanetomo's anguish, and that the anguish made the sad notes, peculiarly their own, of his forthright and poignant masterpieces.

"Coming out of the Hakone Mountains they saw below them a small island upon which waves were breaking. He asked one of his attendants what this shore might be, and, told that it was the Sea of Izu, he composed a verse:

"We have come the Hakone road. Below us the Sea of Izu: waves against a small island."

456

This famous poem, said to be in the *Manyōshū* style, seems to me an intensely sad poem. Scholars of Sanetomo tell us that it was probably composed in the course of the Double Pilgrimage. No doubt they are right. He had been to the Hakone Shrine, and what had he prayed for there? Even in the introduction I can feel his loneliness. Is it that the poem transmits a sad melody to a sad heart? But a poem has its own independent form. Here it is neither bright nor large nor strong. One often hears that this poem is based on one from Book XIII of the *Manyōshū*: "We leave the Pass of Ōsaka, and all across the Sea of Ōmi the waves are like white flowers." The comparison seems to me but a sport of poetry fanciers. However I try to suppress my own feelings, the minor key of the one poem and the major key of the other sing utterly different melodies. In the *Manyōshū* the light-hearted ancient is off, white flowers in hand, to visit his love beyond Ōsaka Pass. But the other, the waves on the small island—the movement of these delicate words has in it something not of the depth of Bashō's *hosomi*, perhaps, but still akin to it. One feels that the sound of those white waves breaking, unheard by the ear, is followed by the eye, far away, and heard in the heart; and in the clear, sharp lines there is a nameless sadness. It may be thus that a musician who has lost his hearing hears music.

The Sea of Izu opens wide, and in it, far away, is a little island, and, yet smaller, the white waves move in upon it; and on beyond is the form of the poet's own heart. Such is the movement of the poem. (vi, 184-85)

· VI ·

Since the war Kobayashi has become a sort of critic-laureate. His refusal to make public confession of his war crimes and his stubborn insistence upon the virtues of such makers of the Japanese spirit as Motoori Norinaga and Miyamoto Musashi have cost him friends among the young and the Left. They did,

457

in any case, in the years just after the war. He has of recent years attracted a wide public following for the first time in his life, a possible sign that the *sengo*, the post-war period, is over. His *Hints on Thinking* (*Kangaeru hinto*), brought out by Kikuchi Kan's magazine, was one of the best sellers of 1964 and 1965.

He has not finished the study of Dostoyevsky's works that was supposed to be the companion to the life. Writers close to him have suggested that an inability to cope with Dostoyevsky's Christianity may be the root of the difficulty. Perhaps it is so. Given his views on history and criticism, it would only be proper for him to stop writing when an alien creed began putting up a wall between him and his object.

Kobayashi's early training was in French, and he thought to draw inspiration from French critics and poets, and other aliens too, Poe and certain Russians among them. How Westernized in fact has he been?

All modern Japanese have something of Europe in them, and Kobayashi's reading of European literature has been unusually wide and thoughtful. It is easy to see an affinity with Frenchmen whom he numbered among his teachers, such persons as Sainte-Beuve and Bergson. With Sainte-Beuve Kobayashi has had in common a dedication to seeking out the unifying essence in a historical or literary figure. Sainte-Beuve too was given to applying tests of sincerity, having as much to do with the personality of the writer as with the quality of the writing. Sainte-Beuve too distrusted philosophers of history, and thought that good criticism could itself be good literature. It is easy to aver that Kobayashi borrowed all these ideas.

Other ideas floated about in Europe and America and turned up in Kobayashi. Kobayashi talking about Akutagawa sounds very much like Oscar Wilde talking about Henry James. In both cases the complaint is of analysis without action, vivisection without imagination. When Kobayashi seems very near confusing art and life he also seems very near Zola, and when the act of writing, as self-awareness and self-expression, is raised to the pedestal of the writing itself, he seems as willing as Emerson to dispense with distinctions between action and art. ("Shakespeare made his Hamlet as a bird weaves its nest.") If Kobayashi often seems to have a suspicion of fiction, so did Carlyle. Kobayashi taking Masamune Hakuchō to task for failing to see the deeper truth about Tolstoy sounds like Baudelaire deploring the minute essentials in French realism.

The worship of action, the dualism between intellect and intuition and the elevating of the latter to the higher position, and a similar dualism between a synthesizing vision and an analyzing eye, the former of course being the superior—all of these are Bergsonian, and all of them lie very near the heart of the Kobayashi theory of criticism and history.

The last might be called an instance that goes beyond influence and becomes imitation, unashamed borrowing. Yet even in this most extreme case one wonders: might not the French have provided but a handy container for a stew of native concocting, a convenient frame for a native landscape? No one would accuse Bergson of having borrowed from the mystique of Tokugawa *bushidō*; but note the following distinction between the analyzing eye and the synthesizing vision, made by a Japanese long before Bergson thought of it:

Musashi is telling us that there are two ways of seeing, designated by the characters *kan* and *ken*. In his memorandum for Hosokawa Tadatoshi, he says that when, at swords' points, one faces an enemy, the eye of *kan* should be strong, that of *ken* weak. The former, he is saying, has to do with the ordinary workings of the eye. It reports that the enemy is now doing this, now doing that, it makes analytical and rational sense. The other eye brings an intuitive awareness (*chokkaku*) of the enemy's whole being. There is an eye "which sees clearly and unflinchingly." "However near the enemy comes, it keeps him as far as it wishes." "Thought (*i*) strikes the eye, heart (*kokoro*) does not." The ordinary eye strives to see, but in the heart, which does not so strive, is also an eye, the heart's own eye. Thought, striving to see, clouds that eye. And so we are told to weaken the eye of *ken*, strengthen the eye of *kan*. (VII, 163)

This is from a much-admired Kobayashi lecture called "My View of Life" (*Watakushi no jinseikan*), delivered in 1948 and revised for publication. The *kan* of *jinseikan* is the more penetrating of the two visions ascribed to Miyamoto Musashi.

So it is with most of his favorite tenets. They may look vaguely Occidental, but beneath the cosmetics their true ancestry shows. And there is the question of style. Kobayashi could and did write lucidly on some subjects. The wartime strictures against the "awareness" of the writer, for instance, are lucidity itself. His more characteristic style is cryptic, paradoxical, highly fragmented. In his very early writings he may be accused of affectation and ostentation. Once he is established as one of Kikuchi Kan's stalwarts and no longer needs to attract attention, the matter is less simple. The sphinx-like style is there for transmitting something to those who are prepared to receive it. "A good novel progresses as the reader progresses." (II, 75) So, presumably, does a good piece of criticism.

The tenets and the manner are in the old tradition. There is in that tradition little of Aristotelian analysis. It moves by example, by riddle, by mystic sign. It is lyrical rather than expository, and it is more concerned with the heart than with the mind. One thinks of exceptions. Buddhist and Confucian critics of the *Genji* were so intellectual that they never quite got around to looking at the *Genji*. Motoori Norinaga, who saw the *Genji* with clearest eye, rejected Chinese intellectuality, and, a fact that puts him in the "main stream" of Japanese criticism, never quite got around to a coherent description of his touchstone, *mono no aware*. Fujiwara Shunzei, near the sources of that stream, never even tried to tell us what he meant by *his* mystic sign, *yūgen*. One does not wish to be understood as saying that the principal strain in Japanese literary criticism is thereby inadequate. The point is that it is not Aristotelian.

So successful at synthesizing are its controlling symbols that boundaries between art and action seem to dissolve. The way of life and the way of the poet become one, art and self-discipline merge. If Kobayashi sometimes seems like Emerson, he seems even more like Shunzei and Teika. If a Bergsonian dualism can make him look a little uncomfortable on occasion, the dualism presently disappears and a primitive Japanese reluctance—the *Manyōshū* instinct, one might say—to set man and nature in opposition takes over.

Kobayashi does not like the Japanese naturalist novel. He is less hostile toward modern symbolist poetry, but he has accused it of making grander and more revolutionary claims for itself than it deserves. The irony is that he has a great deal in common with both. The symbolists thought they were doing something they had learned from the French, when they were doing something rather like what their ancestors had been doing at least since the days of Yakamochi. The naturalists too thought that they had learned from the French, and that the chasm opened up two decades before between them and the past was unbridgeable. One best understands them, even if one cannot bring oneself to admire them, by forgetting the gap.

CHAPTER XII

Fukuda Tsuneari: Modernization and Shingeki

BENITO ORTOLANI

Fukuda's Life and Work

FUKUDA TSUNEARI, critic, playwright, translator, and leader in contemporary thought and theatrical development, was born and educated in Tokyo. His entire professional career has also been spent at this center of most of Japan's modern evolution, including the *shingeki*, the "new drama" movement of the twentieth century.[1] For him *shingeki* is the symbol of Japan's modernization as it brings into one arena the artistic and intellectual problems with which Japan has struggled for the past fifty years or more.

Fukuda was born on August 25, 1912. His father, Koshirō, worked as an employee of an electric company, the Tokyo Dentō Kabushiki Kaisha, then a new symbol for modernity and progress. His father's and his mother's brothers, however, were all in traditional, centuries-old family trades—the latter as stone-masons specializing in tombstones, the former as cabinet-makers. Fukuda's father, an open-minded, self-made man, did not spare any efforts to improve his own and his children's education, and provided his first-born with the best schooling available in Japan. The young student was not able to talk at home about the world he was discovering in the classroom. Among his classmates, who belonged to privileged social groups, he felt like a stranger. Alone at school and alone at home, he developed early his characteristic of intellectual isola-

---

[1] *Shingeki* means literally "new drama" as opposed to the traditional forms including *nō*, *kabuki*, *bunraku*, etc., called *kyūgeki*, "old drama." For a general survey of *shingeki* see my article, "Shingeki: the Maturing New Drama of Japan," *Studies in Japanese Culture*, ed. Joseph Roggendorf (Tokyo: Sophia University Press, 1963), pp. 163-85.

tion—his rebellious, critical attitude, aloof from the stream. Fukuda speaks of the deep difference between his background and the artificial group-isolation of most novelists belonging to Japanese naturalism, the well-known authors of *watakushi shōsetsu* ("I-novels"), which he labels *geshuku bungaku* ("boarding-house literature"). They came from the country after their first years of schooling. In Tokyo as students they lived in boarding-houses, far from their families, cut off from their usual life and surroundings, isolated—but in an ivory tower, steeped in the artificial atmosphere of a homogeneous group, aloof from the real life of most Japanese. Fukuda, on the contrary, constantly saw his dream world of a socially privileged, intellectually progressive society, which he enjoyed at school, jarred by the reality of a non-intellectual, conservative, modest family life.

Significant in Fukuda's background also is the section of Tokyo where he lived his youth. From 1916, when he was four, until 1944, he lived in Kanda, and absorbed the unique atmosphere of that central part of Tokyo, rich in a long history, with a colorful, but strongly conservative, culture typical of the merchant world (*shitamachi*) since the Edo period. The disappearance of that familiar sight because of the destruction (both material and spiritual) of the war, is one of the "losses," the price Japan paid, in Fukuda's opinion, for a visionless modernization.

In 1925 Fukuda entered junior high school[2] where among his classmates was Takahashi Yoshitaka, who became a prominent literary essayist, and Yamazaki Shoichi, who became a scholar of Kant and of English empiricism. At this time Fukuda resented his father's strong sense of cleanliness (*keppeki-kan*), both in the material and, especially, in the puritanical, ethical meaning of the word. Eventually, this element of his father's upbringing exerted a clear influence on Fukuda's psychology. From his mother, Masa, he absorbed, on the other

[2] The present Ueno Kōtōgakkō, then called Dai-ni Tokyo Shiritsu Chūgakkō.

hand, a deep sensitiveness and the sharpness of an always suspicious, alert judgment.

In 1930 Fukuda entered senior high school[3] and in 1933 he was admitted to the English Literature Department of Tokyo Imperial University. At about this time his father retired from his job and, due to unfortunate circumstances, soon became penniless. In order to maintain his wife and five children, Tsuneari's father had to rely on his ability as a brush-writing teacher. Tsuneari himself worked as a private teacher from his first years at the university. As the first-born and only male child, he felt the responsibility of supporting himself and his parents in their old age and later of helping his sisters to get married. "I do not understand the writers who neglect their family responsibilities for literature," says Fukuda.

His early, intense interest in drama developed at this time, and he wrote his first play for the Tsukijiza,[4] the first important theatre group which dared to assert the "theatre for the theatre's sake" ideal against the dominating "proletarian" *shingeki* world of the early thirties. The play, although accepted, was never performed and was subsequently lost—for which Fukuda is now grateful.

During his university years his interest changed from drama to literary criticism. Nevertheless, he was invited to be a member of the *Engeki hyōron*, a small drama magazine produced by the group gathered around Nishizawa Yōtarō, who later became the editor of the well-known drama journal, *Higeki kigeki*. For *Engeki hyōron* Fukuda wrote his second play, *Bessō chitai*, inspired by Dostoevsky's *The Demons*, from which Fukuda took the main character, Stavrogin, and exaggerated his characteristics. No copy of the magazine containing the play seems to be preserved. He now judges this second play to be "very sentimental," an immature expression of loneliness.

[3] Urawa Kōtōgakkō, now Saitama Daigaku.

[4] Not to be mistaken for the more famous Tsukiji Shōgekijō, the Little Theatre at Tsukiji, then the main center of Marxist *shingeki* activity. The Tsukijiza did not perform at the Tsukiji theatre, but at the Hikōkan Hall.

In 1936 Fukuda graduated from Tokyo Imperial University with a thesis on D. H. Lawrence's ethics (*D. H. Lawrence no rinrikan*). After feeling attracted by William Blake, the young Fukuda found his hero in Lawrence. The reasons for his devotion to the rebellious English novelist were a subconscious resentment against his father's exaggerated puritanism and a conscious sense of antipathy, of repulsion, against the Japanese intellectualism of Protestant origin, typical of that time. Fukuda's first meeting with Christianity was a hostile approach to Protestantism. He never showed any serious interest in Marxism, simply because he has never believed in materialism. Fukuda confesses that at this period he already felt a deep longing for a superior harmony of thought (he found it concretely in Shakespeare and, later, in Catholicism),[5] but he had not yet the maturity to express these concerns. It was easier for him to indulge in sensational anti-conformity, as represented by his study of D. H. Lawrence's ethics.

After graduation Fukuda was invited by his former schoolmate, Takahashi Yoshitaka, to join the group which published the literary journal *Sakka seishin*. There he made the acquaintance of the novelists, Toyota Saburō, Takagi Taku, and Kantō Takanori, and he had his first literary essay published, *Yokomitsu Riichi*. At that time Yokomitsu was even more appreciated than Kawabata Yasunari as the representative of the Shinkankaku-ha (New Sensualists) in controversy with the ideology of the leftists. Fukuda shared D. H. Lawrence's hatred of self-justification in his fight against Yokomitsu's psychologizing. He was severely critical of Yokomitsu's excessive description of the (often questionable) motivation for each action, and this, eventually, was a factor in Fukuda's disgust with the novel and for his return to drama.

[5] Fukuda's discussion with Takeuchi Yoshimi ("Gendaiteki jōkyō to chishikijin no sekinin," *Tembō*, Sept., 1965, pp. 24-40) is a clear, published statement of his consideration of Catholicism as the key to his present *Weltanschauung*. He says of himself that he is a "Catholic driver without a license . . . ," hinting at the fact that he is not baptized.

During his postgraduate study Fukuda wrote his first essay on Shakespeare, a study of *Macbeth* (*Macbeth ron*). He accused even Shakespeare of psychologizing—an immature judgment which he now regrets. In May of the same year (1938) he accepted a post as a teacher at a junior high school in Kakegawa in Shizuoka Prefecture. In July of the following year he resigned from the position after a quarrel with the head of the school on the issue of the baseball players being admitted to the school only because of their athletic abilities.

In the meantime, because of his father's declining health, Fukuda had to support his parents and four sisters. In May, 1939, he had his second literary essay published, this one on Kamura Isota (1897-1933). Fukuda affirms that Kamura is very important because he reveals the snobbery common to all previous authors of "I-novels." Through his own *watakushi shōsetsu* Kamura brings this genre to a logical end. The preceding authors admitted their lack of success in the eyes of society— they were however inwardly convinced of being an elite, morally far superior to the very society which denied them understanding and recognition. Kamura, on the other hand, has the courage to condemn himself and his own writing on a moral level. Therefore, concludes Fukuda, Kamura openly reveals in his work the complete failure of the *watakushi shōsetsu*.

Through the recommendation of his professor, the scholar of Japanese classical literature, Nishio Minoru, Fukuda was called to be a member of the editorial staff of the magazine *Keisei*, which survived for only eight issues. In the following years he was often a part-time lecturer at Nippon University, where he taught English in the medical school, and at different high schools. He prepared his essay on Akutagawa Ryūnosuke—still his favorite author to the present time—which was first published in *Sakka seishin* (1941) and then partially in the widely read literary journals, *Bungaku* and *Shinchō*. "It was the first time," Fukuda says, "I received money for anything I wrote." During the war he had a few articles published in *Shinchō*. He deliberately used very difficult, obscure wording to avoid political censure and in order not to take the servile attitude of many literary men during that difficult period.

In 1941 Fukuda translated D. H. Lawrence's *Apocalypse*, a book which had a lasting influence on him.[6] He was convinced that it was the most important of Lawrence's works for understanding his inner world. Fukuda was unreserved in this admiration of Lawrence. He interpreted Lawrence's violent rebellion as being that of an idealist who has the courage to fight against the conformity of an insincere puritanism, without caring much about the limited objective of his idealism, that is, the exaltation of sex and instincts. In the preface to the translation of the *Apocalypse*, Fukuda wrote that this book is one of the very few which have power to change a man's life, and admits that it had actually changed his way of looking at the world, at history, and at man. Lawrence's original way of developing extreme, paradoxical judgments in his rebellious crusade against puritanism left its mark in Fukuda's way of sharply criticizing the conformist mind of many modern Japanese intellectuals. Moreover, Lawrence's influence is recognized by some Japanese critics of Fukuda's work in his "suspicious eye" in assessing the value of many modern Western writers. While prominent literary critics like Nakamura Mitsuo are often willing to point out the negative aspects of the contemporary Japanese intellectual—criticizing, for instance, the *watakushi shōsetsu*—they stand for the most part in awe before all that is foreign. Nakamura, who started from Flaubert's realism, seems to recommend assimilation of nineteenth-century European literature as a whole. Fukuda, on the contrary, looks also at European writing with a "suspicious eye."

Fukuda recently corrected his juvenile enthusiasm for Lawrence in the latest edition of his *Apocalypse* translation (1966). In his youth he walked from the front door of Lawrence's fortress out to battle, he says, without looking back to the whole of that fortress. Now he walks in again from the back

---

[6] The publication of the translation was postponed because of the war.

door, after considering all sides, and with strong reservations regarding its limitations, especially regarding the content of his idealism. A similar consideration is valid also for the two heroes of his university days, Nietzsche and Dostoevsky.

From September to December, 1942, Fukuda left Japan for the first time. He was sent to Manchuria, Mongolia, North and Central China by the Society for Promotion of Education in the Japanese Language (Nihongo Kyōiku Shinkōkai), a branch of the Ministry of Education concerned with the propagation of the Japanese language in occupied territories. Fukuda was the editor of its bulletin, *Nihongo*, conceived as a help to the teachers of Japanese in those areas. In 1944 he left the organization to become a member of the Taiheiyō Kyōkai Amerika Kenkyūshitsu, a research institute with the aim of studying America and directed by Sakanishi Shio.

In January, 1945, at the age of 33, Fukuda married Nishimoto Atsue, the daughter of an engineer in the spinning industry. Nine years younger than himself, Atsue graduated from Tokyo Women's University (Tokyo Joshi Daigaku) and then worked for the Ministry of Education in the Department of Japanese Language, where Fukuda met her when he was connected with the Ministry.[7] In 1946 they moved to Oiso and Fukuda made writing his main profession.

Fukuda is called one of the *sengo hihyōka* (postwar critics), but without the usual political (i.e., Marxist) meaning. His unique position comes from the fact that he was never involved in Marxism or militarism. This enables him to maintain his consistency as an independent thinker on problems like responsibility for, and the consequences of, the disastrous war—the object of endless discussions in the postwar years. He is excep-

[7] In the same year, 1945, Fukuda wrote a lengthy article: "Minshū no kokoro," for the journal *Tembō*. At the end of 1946 he wrote a supplement to his essay on Akutagawa (published as a serial in *Kindai bungaku*) and published his translation of Eve Curie's *Among the Warriors* (a task given to him by the Taiheiyō Kyōkai Amerika Kenkyūshitsu) with the title, *Senjin no tabi*.

tionally free from any obligation to a group or to a party line. Being in the center, he has taken a clear and objective view of both extremes from the beginning. In turn, he is constantly attacked from both sides. Of course, like all critics of his age, he started from the experiences of the war. In his controversial essays of the immediate postwar period,[8] Fukuda pointed out how unrealistic it was to reduce the experiences of the war only to the damage inflicted by physical violence. The actual moral consequences to the individual cannot be healed through a political ideology as a kind of secret substitute, or an appeasing self-justification, in the style of a Marxist messiahship.

An important part of the human spirit cannot be reduced to, or commanded by, a political ideology. Literature, for Fukuda, belongs to this most intimate part of a human being. Contrary to Marxist opinion, Fukuda considers politics and literature as two spheres to be kept most carefully separated. He thinks of politics as something which intends to set free the egoism of the masses (and of individuals in relation to others), while literature is for him something which belongs essentially to the inner "secret room" of the individual and cannot be reduced to social relations. Therefore he considers the so-called "humanism" of the Marxists to be a single-dimensional, incomplete vision of human reality. Fukuda has, however, a very sensitive feeling for politics as well. The Marxists appeal to pathos for the realization of their ideal, he says, while the dominating conservative party, Jimintō, has no part in this pathetic appeal. Fukuda feels that politics belongs to the dimension of technical competence, which excludes pathos but tries to reach an acceptable compromise, a balance for the interests (he calls it "egoism") of the masses. Literature, like art in general, transcends the sphere of technical competence, and is therefore separated from, and superior to, politics. These considerations must be interpreted in the frame of a postwar controversy mainly against the Marxists' confusion of politics and any form of art. Though they remain substantially true for Fukuda today, it is

[8] For example, "Seiji to bungaku" and "Seikatsu to geijutsu."

important to rectify a possible misunderstanding. Fukuda does recognize the need for a spiritual ideal, a *Weltanschauung*, a nucleus of thought, as a substantial foundation for any kind of really great, universal art.

Fukuda is considered to have a very personal, radical, destructive idea of the value of modern Japanese literature. He is often accused of dogmatically overthrowing its worth. Certainly he cannot be considered an optimist, or a lenient critic. For instance, in his essay "Bungei hihyōka no taido," written in the immediate postwar period, he states that the first condition for qualifying as a critic is doubt and mistrust regarding novels of the Meiji period and thereafter. In his "Kindai Nihon bungaku no keifu" (*Bungaku*, 1945-46), Fukuda passes severe judgment on the whole of modern Japanese literature. He confronts it with what his adversaries have accepted as a criterion, i.e., modern Western literature, and points out how wide the difference is. But he himself does not express his approval or disapproval of that criterion. He considers to be valid very little of the whole Japanese production—Mori Ōgai, Natsume Sōseki, and very few others—and he labels the last twenty years as a loss, a period in which art was sacrificed to a false idea of the artist. True, valid literature, independent of politics, is the lost sheep to which he refers in his famous essay "Ippiki to kyū-jūkyūhiki to." He invokes a simple, honest, and sincere fidelity to inner inspiration. More recently Fukuda has expressed some favorable judgment, in particular about parts of the work of Mishima Yukio and Ōoka Shōhei, but his concern is at present more with general trends than with single authors.

A subtle criticism of the hypocritical attitude of the so-called avant-garde intellectuals is the *leitmotiv* of his collected essays *White-painted Graves* (*Shiroku nuritaru haka*, 1948). His novel, *Horesho nikki* (1949), on the other hand, treats one of D. H. Lawrence's central themes (Ivan Morris finds in it echoes of Henry James, to Fukuda's astonishment), that is, the mere possibility of true love among humans, and it ends with a sad, pessimistic view of it.

In 1949 Fukuda completed an important book on European writers (*Seiō sakkaron*), in which he flatly condemns Japanese modernization. The mistakes of the West are, according to him, only accentuated by Japan, which is engaged in a false westernization. Fukuda writes about Shakespeare, Chekhov, T. S. Eliot, and extols David Garnett as not being polluted by today's excessive individualism. Sartre's *La Nausée* is interpreted as a catastrophe, the destruction of the modern spirit.

Kitty taifū, a play written in 1950, is one of Fukuda's finest satires.[9] It begins as a quasi-parody of Chekhov's *The Cherry Orchard*, with a salon far away from everyday reality. People who had been friends before the war meet again. By chance they come together, by chance they part, after many, hardly explicable complications. Considered mainly as a satire of contemporary Japanese intellectuals caught between blatant westernization and old, almost tribal, family ties, *Kitty taifū* is one more bitter, pessimistic description of the tragic lack of communication among human beings.

What is Art? (*Geijutsu to wa nani ka*), a book on the theory of drama and acting, was published the same year. Fukuda recognizes that he received inspiration mainly from Huizinga's *Homo Ludens* and Frazer's ethnological considerations in *The Golden Bough*. He discusses problems concerned with the origin of drama, the concept of *persona* and Aristotle's *katharsis*. In open controversy with most contemporary novelists (all accepting as absolute the doctrine: "Be yourself"), Fukuda makes the paradoxical affirmation that in the theatre the contrary is true, that is, only when you fully become somebody else do you reach your own fulfillment. *Ren'ai gassen*, a comedy in four acts completed in October of the same year, is judged by Fukuda himself as a failure. In the meantime the publisher, Koyama Shoten, chose Fukuda as one of the team for the translation of Lawrence's complete works and assigned to him the novel, *Women in Love.*

[9] It was first performed by the Bungakuza troupe in the same year.

In May 1951 Fukuda was invited to testify, as a specialist in D. H. Lawrence's work, in the trial about the obscenity of *Lady Chatterley's Lover*, just translated by Itō Sei for the same edition of Lawrence's complete works. He hesitated a long time before accepting. His testimony was an intelligent defence of Lawrence's work and ethics. Fukuda flatly denied that the novel is obscene; he considered Lawrence a puritan in his ideals of the oneness and eternity of a real marriage. Moreover, he affirmed that the novel in question is much healthier than most Japanese novels based on the usual triangle—naked love being more moral than "bikini love."

Fukuda's admiration, however, has switched now from D. H. Lawrence to T. S. Eliot, and he published a translation of *The Cocktail Party*. This play seems to Fukuda to describe perfectly what he himself would have liked to express about the possibility of love and communication among humans.

Fukuda made a very free adaptation of *Macbeth* to modern Japan with the title, *Gendai no eiyū*.[10] The theme of the play is that nowadays impostors becomes heroes, like Macbeth who, with no real qualification to be king, nevertheless became a king—the tragedy following as a consequence of this. Likewise, the groups that seized power in Japan were not qualified to lead the country and as a consequence they caused Japan's tragic defeat. The play ends as a satirical comedy. Fukuda, with reason, prefers to this long, complicated play his earlier *Yūrei yashiki*,[11] a free adaptation for an audience of children and their parents of Oscar Wilde's *The Canterville Ghost* transferred to postwar Japan; and even more his masterpiece *Ryū o nadeta otoko*,[12] which received the Fourth Yomiuri Literary Award in January 1953. The play starts from the situation at the end of Eliot's *The Cocktail Party*, transferred of

[10] Published in *Gunzō*, July 1952, and performed by the Haiyūza troupe.

[11] Published in *Shōnen shojo*, Nov., 1951, and performed by the Mingei troupe.

[12] Published by Ikeda shoten, 1952, and performed by the Bungakuza troupe.

course to Japan. Its central theme is again the possibility of true love in a country without God. This tragi-comedy of inadequateness ends with the worsening of the fundamental situation which presents no way out: the main character becomes insane. It is important to notice Fukuda's constant effort towards a superior harmony, expressed through the failure of a purely human solution of the deepest human problems. It is a key to the understanding of his criticism of the Japanese process of modernization as a blind acceptance of the explosive material progress of the West without the spiritual source of its control, recognized recently by Fukuda in Catholicism.

Minor writings of this period immediately preceding his trip to America and Europe are his serial, *Ren'ai to jinsei* for women readers, which states the fact that real love is hardly to be found in the so-called love-relation among Japanese; his translation of Hemingway's *The Old Man and the Sea*; and the novel, *Nazo no onna*, written as a serial to make money for his journey.

From September 1953 to September 1954 Fukuda traveled in the United States and Europe on an invitation from the Rockefeller Foundation. It was an extremely important year in his life. His recent experience in Japan during the trial of Lawrence's *Lady Chatterley's Lover* of a world so far unknown to him—the concrete reality of impersonal, dull bureaucracy and of unpredictable public opinion—had been for him a sad revelation of the difficulty of true human communication. His experience outside Japan deepened this feeling, since now even simple things (which could be easily and properly understood at home) became almost incommunicable abroad; and things which had become simple for the Japanese traveler became difficult to communicate at home. The problem of a genuine, undistorted interpretation for his fellow Japanese of Western culture as it really is, and the criticism of the form modernization had taken in Japan as a result of blind westernization without its spiritual *Kern*,[13] became central for him. His direct contact with Europe was a series of unforgettable revelations to him. His experience of seeing the masterpieces of the Italian Renaissance was proof of what he had previously accepted only in theory, the continuity of a vital, creative Christian Middle Age, and not the old story, still current in Japan, of a revolution against a supposed Christian dark age. The performances of Shakespeare at the Old Vic impressed him extraordinarily. Everything revealed to him the immense importance to the present time of a deep, lasting tradition and religion in the very heart of European modernization, notwithstanding its advanced process of secularization. Even America, he thought, has more tradition than Japan in its modernization process. He realized also how deeply he had been taken into the devouring maws of Japanese journalism, after being free from it a whole year. Consequently, he decided to adhere in future to a very precise program of his own work.

On his way back to Japan Fukuda decided on four fields of activity during the coming years. First, because of the impossibility of bringing to a wide Japanese public the true Shakespeare (a symbol for him of genuine Western tradition) without a new translation, he decided to translate and direct, in the Old Vic style, the main Shakespearean masterpieces. Second, he regretted the revised rules of *kana* spelling and the arbitrary limitation of Chinese characters which tended to destroy bridges to the literary past. He decided therefore on a campaign for a better standard of Japanese. Third, he would aim at the reform of the school system according to a higher spiritual ideal of education and social adjustment to present conditions. Fourth, he planned a campaign to improve the knowledge of Japanese intellectuals of the real international political situation, as he disagreed strongly with the blind acceptance of Marxist propaganda.

[13] Fukuda often uses this German word with the meaning of "central nucleus, essence, quintessence."

His publishing activity during his stay in New York was limited to a few translations.[14] Upon his return to Tokyo he wrote a radio drama, *Gake no ue*[15] which is a skillful stylistic attempt to create a type of verse, easy to declaim, based on accent and not on the traditional seven-five syllable meter of most Japanese poetry.

By May 1955, Fukuda had his first translation of Shakespeare ready. He directed his version of *Hamlet*[16] for the Bungakuza troupe, starring Akutagawa Ryūnosuke's son, Hiroshi, in the main role. This performance has an extraordinary importance in the history of *shingeki*, because for the first time the Japanese realized that Shakespeare can be vitally interesting on the stage. Until then, Shakespeare had been declaimed slowly in Tsubouchi Shōyō's solemn, classical translation, and religiously attended as a sacred duty for a "man of culture." Now the public could see, on a curtainless stage without change of decor, a fascinating human tragedy, with an imperishable life of its own, performed in understandable modern language with the speedy technique of realistic acting.

He pressed on with his translations of Shakespeare, and by 1966 had published all of the major plays in fifteen volumes.

Among Fukuda's major tragedies is *Akechi Mitsuhide* (1957), more important for its intention of providing a common platform for the *kabuki* actor, Matsumoto Kōshirō, and the *shingeki* actors of the Bungakuza troupe than for its lengthy story with overtones of Macbeth about the sixteenth-century general. Another is *Arima no miko* (1961), with its interaction of character and destiny, and based on events in the early Nara period when a central state began to be established.

[14] Translations of T. S. Eliot's *The Family Reunion, Murder in the Cathedral,* and Oscar Wilde's *De Profundis.*

[15] Broadcast in November 1954 by Chūbu Nippon Hōsō and published with the new title of *Meian* for its adaptation to the stage in *Bungakukai,* January 1955. It was performed by the Bungakuza troupe in April 1956. Published as a book by Shinchōsha, 1956.

[16] In January 1956 Fukuda received the Award of the Ministry of Education for the translation and production of *Hamlet.*

Prince Arima's pretended madness reminds one of Hamlet, and even more of Pirandello's *Henry IV*. The play is written to sound like the mixed Sino-Japanese language (*wakan-konkō-bun*) of the time, but is admirably adapted to the modern ear.

An important theatrical event in Fukuda's life was the foundation in 1963 of the new group of *shingeki* actors, Kumo (The Clouds), who rallied around him after their dramatic separation from the Bungakuza. Fukuda became the Chairman of the Board of Directors of the Institute of Dramatic Arts, the cultural foundation to which the newly established Kumo troupe was annexed, and since then has assumed one of the leading positions in the *shingeki* world. Experiments with *kabuki* actors (in 1964 Kanzaburō played the main role in *Richard III*); the invitation of leading foreign directors (for the first time in the history of *shingeki*) from England, the United States, and France to present important productions, such as *Romeo and Juliet* (1965) and O'Neill's *The Iceman Cometh* (1968); the direction of *The Taming of the Shrew* (1966) in his own translation, and of Chekhov's *The Cherry Orchard* (1968); the most successful dramatization of a recent, widely publicized event of the Japanese underworld, *Wakatte tamaru ka* (1968): these are some of the latest events in his astonishing activity as a cultural bridge between genuine Western tradition and no less genuine traditional Japanese values in a continuously changing and rapidly modernizing Japan.[17]

In the serial, *Nihon oyobi Nihonjin* (1955), Fukuda discussed the defects and virtues of the Japanese in the context of his experiences with people abroad. He criticized especially the morality of his country, stating that the Japanese moral standard of behavior is mostly an esthetic feeling, that is, an awareness of beauty or ugliness in human behavior, instead of moral

[17] Fukuda received the Yomiuri Literary Award in 1962 for *Watakushi no kokugo kyōiku*. He was in the United States for the 400th Shakespearean Anniversary in 1964. His main writings were collected in *Fukuda Tsuneari chosakushū*, 8 vols. (Shinchōsha, 1964-65) and *Fukuda Tsuneari hyōronshū*, 7 vols. (Shinchōsha, 1966).

virtue. He pointed out with serious concern the dangerous lack of a strict sense of genuine morality and inner discipline in contemporary Japan. In a series of talks for the NHK, Fukuda made some statements which were widely echoed by many intellectuals. Fukuda remarked that Japan, since the Meiji Restoration, has been losing her own culture little by little. In Western countries tradition is not sacrificed for modernization. Japan is, continues Fukuda, the most developed among the underdeveloped countries, but at what price? It is time to think seriously how much the loss of genuine Japanese culture costs Japan. Then Fukuda considers the word, "culture," and the corresponding Japanese *bunka*, to point out how different the meaning of "a man of culture" in Europe is from a *bunkajin* in Japan, where everything is *bunka*, which means merely "modern" or "up-to-date" in such phrases as *bunka jutaku* (home) and *bunka mura* (village).

The considerations in *Nihon oyobi Nihonjin* were continued the next year in his *Ichido wa kangaete okubeki koto*. Here he criticizes the lack of constitutional seriousness among most Japanese intellectuals (who have no definite idea of absolute values) in the very conception of freedom, progress, nationalism, individualism. On the other hand, in his final statement he stresses the fact that in Europe the idea of an absolute God still constitutes *the* fundamental value, the metaphysical structure which is tacitly accepted before every other value judgment, though many Europeans no longer realize it. Particularly controversial was his *Jōshiki ni kaere*, a continuation of his political considerations for world peace at the time of the riots on the occasion of the ratification of the Security Treaty in 1960. Fukuda is actually better known by the Japanese public for his anti-leftist, pro-Western political attitude than for his great merits in the literary, theatrical, and educational fields.

Fukuda's Idea of Modernization

Fukuda's writings contain numerous direct and indirect statements on modernization in general, and on its special features in Japan, which help towards a better understanding of his views on *shingeki* history.

Fukuda points out how facts, like industrialization, democracy, and technical progress, become values and objects of blind faith and worship in underdeveloped countries. In Europe the difference between such historical facts and their moral value has been kept clear. In America it has been less, yet sufficiently, acknowledged. In Japan the difference between facts and values is not yet clear, and the confusion is proportionately worse in less developed countries.

An example is the myth of progress. Fukuda is no friend of the Marxist or Marxist-inclined "progressives." He is sharp in his criticism of their transformation of progressivism into a kind of absolute: you are supposedly free to think anything you want, however you cannot be anything but progressive.[18] He distinguishes clearly between progress and progressivism. The former is a fact which has existed since the beginning of history and does not need progressivism to develop. The latter is an attitude of the spirit which transforms a fact into a supreme value, a symbol, the aim of everything, a taboo, the only emotional taboo which still exists in a modernized country which otherwise would proclaim freedom in every respect. The progressives, says Fukuda, are more concerned with what might disturb their feelings (or what can do so in the future, or might prevent them from their emotional messiahship), than with what actually stops real, objective progress. Fukuda points out how progress has never been considered as the supreme value in the Western countries. Often it was actually frowned upon as a dangerous bet, as the first step into a new world which could end in failure. In Japan progress never meant something to be regarded with suspicion, because it had already the guarantee of success in other countries.

Progress in itself, being simply a fact, is for Fukuda beyond

[18] *Jōshiki ni kaere* (Shinchōsha, 1960), pp. 67 ff. The account of Fukuda's views expressed in this section is based largely on the author's personal discussions with him, mainly in 1965.

good or evil, on a different level from moral values. It does bring necessary evils in its best conditions and at the same time advantages in its worst conditions. It is a part of the antinomic structure of reality—justice and crime, construction and destruction, altruism and egoism.

Fukuda follows the same pattern of thought when he considers the controversial subject of modernization. Since early Meiji it has been looked upon by too many Japanese not as a fact, but as a value, a matter for blind faith. The content of this new faith, as distinguished from the fact of modernization, is explained by Fukuda as follows. During innumerable centuries people believed that many phenomena in nature and in the very structure of social and political organizations were inevitable, beyond human control: for instance floods, sicknesses, social evils like misery and slavery, political troubles like wars. Extra-human powers (God, devils, original sin or the like) were invoked to explain or to change this reality. Modernization as a faith is the new belief that those phenomena can be explained, those problems can be solved by modern science, by the organized effort of men, by social reform and international institutions, etc., without any extra-human intervention.

Modernization has brought with it decentralization—the weakening or disappearance of strong religious beliefs and traditional institutions which had acted until then as active centers of spiritual unity. It has also brought secularization, the loosening of the relation between man and supernatural powers. Fukuda considers faith in modernization as a typical blunder of underdeveloped people, for he believes that we have more problems today which cannot be solved without the help of God than in the Middle Ages. Decentralization and secularization present serious dangers for the future of developing countries, deprived of spiritual unity. Fukuda considers modernization a necessary, unavoidable evil, both for the East and the West; evil, because of the actual loss of important values of the past. But since it is a necessary process it cannot be a moral evil (which presupposes a free choice). It is simply a given, concrete reality we all have to cope with—though often not at all an ideal reality, especially as far as Japan is concerned. While in the Western world modernization has negative, as well as very positive aspects, in Japan, says Fukuda, it is difficcult to find the positive ones, while all the negative are quite apparent. He affirms that in the West the disintegrating process was controlled, to a deeper extent than usually recognized, by the unifying spiritual center of the Western world. (Here Fukuda speaks of centralization, and identifies it with Christianity.) In Japan, on the contrary, the forces of centralization which were supposed to control that process did not have the same efficiency—forces such as Buddhism, Confucianism, and *bushidō*.

Modernization in Japan, therefore, is like a horse without reins. It is much more dangerous than in any Western country where, to a certain extent, Christianity still has a real impact, at least as far as the fundamental absolute values are concerned. In Japan most intellectuals make modernization itself the focus of all their efforts, in politics, finance, business, science, and culture in general. They are eager to promote modernization as the solution to every single problem, exchanging the mere fact for an absolute value.

When Fukuda states that a means to control modernization, secularization, decentralization, is necessary, most Japanese intellectuals call him a conservative and a reactionary. He counters by saying that he accepts the fact of progress, but objects to the myth, i.e., progressivism. Many Marxist or Marxist-inclined Japanese intellectuals think, when Fukuda condemns progressivism, that he considers the Emperor system or Confucianism or Buddhism as the only forces of centralization available in Japan. This he denies, for he considers that these traditional forces would only deny modernization, not control it. The conservatives and reactionaries want to kill modernization. Fukuda's solution is based on his view that modernization, although a universal phenomenon nowadays, is de facto a product of the West, imported to Japan from Europe and America. For Oriental people modernization means in reality a deep process of westernization. Therefore the only force which can control modernization in a westernized Orient is the same element which proved effective in the West. In Christianity, concretely in Catholicism, Fukuda recognizes the only spiritual, unifying force which can control modernization without denying it.

Modernization came to Japan as something planned from the top and not as a need promoted by large segments of the population. What was regarded from the governmental view as most necessary and useful for the nation was given highest priority, beginning with the Army and Navy. The power next in rank was the bureaucracy. Other important elements of modernization were the groups of intellectuals in the fields of science and education. However, independent groups are weaker, in Japan, than bureaucracy or any institution developed by the state. This appears clearly in the structure of universities and other educational or research institutions, where the public sector is stronger and more prestigious than the private. The field of the arts, which was less favored by the State, was left behind.

Another failure in Japan's modernization was the lack of unity among different fields. In each field the Japanese tried to study and import the best in Europe and America, without taking into account that all these "bests" were, in each country, often the result of the concentration of a whole country's effort in that field. Japan borrowed the model of the navy and financial world from Britain, army and fine arts (impressionism) from France, law, philosophy, medicine and music from Germany, literature (naturalism) both from France and Russia, and drama (naturalism and later expressionism) from Germany and northern Europe. The strain imposed upon the Japanese was often inhuman—they had an extremely high model to imitate in each field and tried hard to accomplish the difficult task, but without reference and coordination to the rest of the overall picture. Fukuda thinks that this lack of structural unity and of deep, indigenous background was one of the main causes for the disastrous war. Achievements in different fields had not reached the unity which could have ensured solidity in a nation's common effort.

This lack of spiritual unity is for Fukuda even more apparent in the field of literature and in the theatre, and the results even more disastrous. The considerations about *shingeki*'s history draw a sad picture of that movement; nor is Fukuda sparing in his criticism of most modern Japanese literature. The most important task of the Japanese intellectual is to regain the lost unity in order to control the "horse without reins." To control modernization there must be a central idea, a unifying faith capable of allowing progress without making a myth of it, and use it for man without using man for progress. Fukuda affirms that though the age of individualism is finished, the individual never finishes.[19]

Fukuda's Interpretation of Shingeki History

In the past most Japanese intellectuals have considered *shingeki* to be a side-phenomenon of little interest, unworthy of special study. In order to attract their attention to the history of modern drama in Japan, Fukuda has asserted that *shingeki* is the symbol of Japanese modernization[20] The reason is that in *shingeki* are brought together the problems and the shortcomings which are to be found scattered in the literature, the arts, and culture of Japan in the last fifty years. Fukuda writes, "without a reformation of *shingeki* the problem of Japan's modernization cannot be solved. . . . I long for order, for something healthy, organic, unified—and I cannot find satisfaction

---

[19] "Futatabi heiwa ronsha ni okuru," *Heiwa no rinen* (Shinchōsha, 1965), p. 71.

[20] Fukuda's most important essay concerning *shingeki* and modernization is "Engekiteki bunkaron," *Tembō*, March 1965, pp. 98-112. The history of *shingeki* and its interpretation are treated at greater length in Fukuda's "Nihon shingeki-shi gaikan," *Watakushi no engeki hakusho* (Shinchōsha, 1958), pp. 215-44.

of this desire of mine in the present Japanese literature, art, and culture."[21]

In contemporary *shingeki*, Fukuda adds, the situation is even more disastrous and distorted than in any other field. Therefore, paradoxically, Fukuda feels particularly attracted to it because he is convinced that in the very nature of theatre lies the best possibility of reconquering health, order, organic structure, and spiritual unity—the values he seeks.

In his manifesto for the foundation of the Institute of Dramatic Arts (1963) he states that in the last thirty years "the movement has gradually lost all of its original ideals, spirit, and enthusiasm. In the midst of confusion and stagnation, it does not even seem to be aware of its shortcomings; it wears a cloak of self-satisfaction."[22] In a previous work Fukuda was scathing in his criticism of *shingeki* as something without any positive knowledge—or even the desire for knowledge—of its origins, its qualities, its essence, its aims. Every contact with great achievements of Eastern or Western theatre (like the Peking Opera, the Comédie Française, the Moscow Art Theatre) would only result for most *shingeki* people in a realization of what *shingeki* does not possess: the lack, for example, of musical and ballet training, tradition, style, spirit of avant-garde and enterprise, a wide public, rhythm, first-class actors, etc.[23]

Fukuda accepts the division of *shingeki* history into seven periods as proposed by Toita Yasuji.[24] However, only the five periods before 1940 are discussed at some length in this chapter.

I. THE PERIOD OF TRIAL PLAYS (1906-13)

Like every *shingeki* historian Fukuda recognizes in the establishment of the Bungei Kyōkai (Literary Association,

---

[21] "Engekiteki bunkaron," p. 99.

[22] The English translation of the original Japanese (published at the beginning of the first issue of *Kumo* in 1963) was distributed in a leaflet on the occasion of the first performance by the Kumo Troupe of Shakespeare's *A Midsummer Night's Dream* (1963).

[23] "Nihon shingeki-shi gaikan," pp. 215-16.

[24] *Shingeki gojūnen* (Jijitsūshinsha, 1956).

1906) and of the Jiyū Gekijō (Liberal Theatre, 1909) the start-ing point of *shingeki*. These represent two separate move-ments, both of which had as their aim the modernization of the Japanese theatre. The ideals and methods of the two lead-ers, Tsubouchi Shōyō (1859-1935) and Osanai Kaoru (1881-1928), were completely different. Tsubouchi can be considered as the champion of continuity, his ideal being neither destruc-tion nor substitution, but reform—an adaptation of the tradi-tional theatre to the new times. Osanai, on the contrary, was the champion of a new beginning—a clear break with the past and the creation of a modern Japanese theatre according to contemporary Western models. One of the main differences was shown in their respective methods of actor training. Whereas Tsubouchi tried to transform students or other ama-teurs into professionals, Osanai with his friend, the *kabuki* actor Ichikawa Sadanji (1880-1940), aimed at reeducating pro-fessional *kabuki* actors to be deliberately non-professional per-formers of *shingeki*.

Tsubouchi thought of his Literary Association as something not confined to the literature of the theatre, but concerned with literature in general. Its literary journal, *Waseda bungaku*, testifies to this. Tsubouchi's interest was the reformation and modernization of Japanese literature, with particular stress on the theatre, through Shakespeare or any of the classical West-ern authors, who were considered by him as a means to this end—material for training purposes. He was not so much inter-ested in Shakespeare's message, as in the reformation of drama in Japan through Shakespeare's technique of playwriting. He had single acts or scenes from Shakespearean plays performed between *kabuki* plays, or rather scenes, as was customary in *kabuki* programs. He always thought of drama in terms of music, dance, historical subjects, and a sense of a romantic link with the past. In a word, *kabuki* for Tsubouchi was the subject to be reformed, all the rest being a means to that end. The list of the first performances of the Literary Association confirms this assertion: it shows, together with the trial scene from *The*

Merchant of Venice and a part of *Hamlet,* mainly Japanese plays with classical subjects, such as Tsubouchi's *Kaguyahime* or *Shinkyoku Urashima,* and adaptations from *kabuki* plays such as *Imoseyama onna teikin.*

Osanai and Sadanji, on the contrary, concentrated on the theatre alone. They wanted—Fukuda says, pretended—to perceive the message coming from the Western playwrights of the time, such as Ibsen, Gorki, Wedekind, and Hauptmann. They showed no interest in music, singing, and dance, which they considered to be entertainment for the masses. They wanted a realistic, psychological, spoken drama. Their first production was a complete translation of Ibsen's *John Gabriel Borkman,* that prototype of the introverted Nordic man.

As Fukuda points out, the difference between these two movements has brought about one of the main defects of today's *shingeki*: an artificial division in the evaluation of Western drama—into two unrelated fields, before and after Ibsen—and has produced endless, sterile discussions about stylization, professionalism, commercialism, and so forth. The enthusiastic followers of Osanai, who eventually assumed almost exclusive leadership in the *shingeki* world of the following decades, considered Shakespeare and the Western classics before Ibsen at the same level as *nō* and *kabuki.* They considered these to belong to a world without any connection with the vital problems of modern man—a world where dance, music, the stylization and professionalism of the actors could provide entertainment on a commercial basis for non-intellectuals, but not the discussion and the message of a new world to come needed by intellectuals for a rapid modernization of the country.

Of course, Fukuda, the great translator of the main Shakespearean plays and admirer of their universal value as realistic, spoken drama, condemns this artificial dichotomy. Fukuda confesses that, when he was young, he despised Tsubouchi and the movement centered around Waseda University, while all his enthusiasm was for Osanai and the movement centered around

Keiō University. He thought that Tsubouchi was an educationist without understanding either of the West or of its modern literature, and without natural talent for art.[25] Fukuda now regrets this juvenile judgment, and sees Tsubouchi as an honest man, who at least did not pretend to understand what he actually did not, whereas most of the people in the Osanai group made themselves ridiculous pretending a full comprehension of the West. Fukuda recognizes the great merit of men like Tsubouchi (and he includes in the list Mori Ōgai, Okakura Tenshin) in saving *kabuki* from the serious danger of suppression, after the first decade of Meiji, by a modernizing government. At this time there was harsh criticism of *kabuki* because of its feudal setting and the immoral content, "a national shame," with its too "realistic" scenes in the gay quarters. Fukuda recalls the kinship of Tsubouchi's Bungei Kyōkai to earlier societies for the reformation of the theatre, such as the Engeki Kairyō Kai (Society for the Reform of the Theatre, 1886), which became in 1888 the Nihon Engei Kyōfū Kai (Society for the Reformation of Japanese Entertainment), and in 1889 the Nihon Engei Kyōkai (Association for the Japanese Entertainments). As a member of this last society, Tsubouchi had been asked to write a play for *kabuki* actors about Fujiwara Kamatari. This was the beginning of his interest in historical plays and in his attempt to reform the theatre. Tsubouchi was not an artist, nor was he concerned with the introduction of Western artistic concepts and ideals into the Japanese theatrical world.[26] He was not even aware that there was a modern theatre movement in the West. His idea of modernizing the Japanese stage can be considered as an extension of previous efforts to defend and reform *kabuki*. A play like Ibsen's *A Doll's House* did not awaken his interest because of its new, modern problems; and, further, it offended his traditional sense of morality. Contemporary controversial plays did not appear in the program of his Bungei Kyōkai.

[25] "Engekiteki bunkaron," p. 100. [26] "Engekiteki bunkaron," p. 101.

On the other hand, Osanai was a campaigner for a new theatre after the model of the Stage Society of London, with which his friend, Sadanji, had had personal experience. His ideals were strongly influenced by the contemporary Scandinavian authors who were dominant at that time. Osanai's program was to fight against every form of commercialism and to make a new start with non-commercial, non-professional theatre. His repertoire was mainly taken from contemporary Western authors: Ibsen, Hauptmann, Gorki, Gogol, Wedekind, Pirandello, and others. Personally, Osanai was closely connected with the leading novelists of Japanese Naturalism and the New Romanticism, who were convinced that they had already written the first pages of the literature of modern Japan. Osanai was convinced, Fukuda says ironically, that he had really assimilated Western thought, that he belonged fully to the West, and that he had written the first pages of the history of the modern Japanese theatre.

Tsubouchi's Bungei Kyōkai did not last long. The last of its few performances was *Julius Caesar* in 1913. Osanai's Jiyū Gekijō had a longer life, its final performance being in 1919. But the dawn of a new era for this more vital group began with Osanai's journey abroad in 1912-13.

2. THE PERIOD OF COMMERCIALIZATION (1914-23)

By calling this period, in which many companies easily came together and as easily fell apart, the period of commercialization, Fukuda means a lowering of standards due to the prevalence of superficial imitators who seemed to inherit only the weak points of the first period.[27] Fukuda points out the fact that Osanai himself, coming back from Europe, was severely critical even of the two best groups of that time, the Kindaigeki Kyōkai (centered around Kamiyama Sōjin and Iba Takashi) and the Geijutsuza (centered around Shimamura Hōgetsu and Matsui Sumako, who had broken away from Tsubouchi's

[27] "Nihon shingeki-shi gaikan," p. 220.

Bungei Kyōkai). Tsubouchi was silent; he had abandoned the field, deeply disappointed because of criticism which was often unfair, and because his attempts at reform had not progressed well. Moreover, he was hurt personally when his two best actors had left him because he disapproved of their love affair.

Fukuda writes that the *shingeki* of these years is not worthy of being called a "movement," as some writers do, for it was no more than a typical expression of the westernized taste and sentimental mood of the Taishō period. The list of plays performed shows a clear predominance of translations of modern Western works.[28] Fukuda maintains that the *shingeki* performances had no artistic consistency, nor were the *shingeki* people conscious of being the representatives of an artistic movement, the exponents of modern drama in Japan. As playwright Takada Tamotsu once told him: "The intellectuals of that time found pleasure in the mere sight of red-haired people with pipes in their mouths and their shoulders against the mantelpiece, engaged in philosophical discussion, or just cutting meat with their knives and forks."[29] Of course, it was not only the exotic flavor of a different way of eating and dressing, of the fair color of the hair, which attracted the curiosity of the audience. The Western way of life and Western thought attracted the intellectuals of that time as symbols of freedom. However, Fukuda writes, freedom was received "from the cuticle of Western manners," very superficially, only in a sentimental way, without its deep spiritual implications.

The real problem for these men was not theatre, but art. And the word "art" (*geijutsu*) at that time was synonymous with all the new imported values, such as West, culture, civili-

[28] The list includes Ibsen's *Hedda Gabler*, *Ghosts*, *The Lady from the Sea*; Shakespeare's *Macbeth*, *The Merchant of Venice*, *King Lear*, *Othello*; Strindberg's *Miss Julia*, *The Father*; Oscar Wilde's *Salomé*, *Lady Windermere's Fan*; Shaw's *Arms and the Man*; Hauptmann's *Hanneles Himmelfahrt*, *Die versunkene Glocke*; Chekhov's *The Cherry Orchard*; Goethe's *Faust*; Maeterlinck's *Intérieur*; and Mérimée's *Carmen*.

[29] "Nihon shingeki-shi gaikan," p. 221.

zation, freedom, liberation, love, ideology, philosophy, science, and so forth. "In a word, the things that were to save us from the reality of a gray life, that is, the rosy paradise which was to save and welcome us."[30] Without this background it is impossible to understand the *shingeki* of this time, or the choice of repertoire, or even the novels. Fukuda makes the acute observation that the most successful Western plays were those which represent the reaction of playwrights from the relatively underdeveloped European countries, and their bitter criticism of their own country as compared with Paris, the Mecca. Whereas the Japanese novel succeeded later in freeing itself from this limitation, *shingeki* to a large extent still remains entangled in it. Fukuda finds that *shingeki* at this time begins to give the impression of self-satisfaction and to get away from its initial, intimate relationship with the world of the intellectuals—"the beginning of the end of their honeymoon."[31] Literature was as self-satisfied as *shingeki*, he says, and still is, although it is in the very same disastrous situation. Official criticism seems to approve of literature and to further its superiority complex, while it condemns *shingeki*'s self-satisfaction. The pretense of modernization is more easily unmasked by the theatre, which, because it must use the live voice and interpretation of Japanese actors, cannot deceive.

3. THE TSUKIJI LITTLE THEATRE MOVEMENT AND OSANAI KAORU (1924-27)

The wide destruction caused by the terrible earthquake of 1923 in the Tokyo area was an unwanted opportunity for a new start, and a unique occasion for the modernization of buildings, streets, and the mentality of many people.

The Little Theatre at Tsukiji opened on June 13, 1924. The main center of *shingeki* performances was transferred from the entertainment quarter of Asakusa to the more sophisticated area of Tsukiji, a few blocks from the Ginza. The audience

[30] "Nihon shingeki-shi gaikan," p. 222.
[31] "Engekiteki bunkaron," pp. 102-03.

was more exclusive, limited in number, and was conscious of being an elite of intellectuals, keen to study the message coming from contemporary Western playwrights. Osanai, the unequivocal leader at this period and the spirit of the new Little Theatre (the only building for decades used exclusively for *shingeki*), chose Western plays almost entirely, showing how little interest he had in Japanese playwrights of this time. The repertoire of these years was mostly translations from the German, Scandinavian, and Russian playwrights we have already mentioned, with a few representatives of Southern European countries (Pirandello, Romain Rolland and Vildrac), and Middle European countries (Molnár, Schnitzler, Čapek). The exceptions were Shakespeare, O'Neill, and Yeats.

Osanai, during his travels in Europe, had spent most of his time studying in Moscow and Berlin. The two main personalities he had met in the two capitals, Stanislavsky and Reinhardt, became the models of his future activity. Though Osanai remained the leader of the movement during this period, he met strong opposition from the new generation in his last years. The magic word, *geijutsu* (art), which in the previous period had been used to embrace so many values imported from the West, was replaced little by little by the new magic word, *seiji* (politics). More precisely, the vague humanism of the Taishō period became, at the beginning of Shōwa (the late 1920's) an openly socialistic ideology. Osanai, who, like Tsubouchi, never showed an understanding of socialism, fought against this trend, which, in the years after his death was to take over and dominate the *shingeki* world almost completely.

The words *bungakusei, engekisei,* and *kannensei* are often used by Fukuda and by many Japanese writers in critical discussion of *shingeki*. *Bungakusei* means the literary value of a play independent of its theatrical elements or its ideology. *Engekisei* is used for the theatrical elements as independent (more or less artificially and abstractly) of ideology and literature. *Kannensei* stands for the ideological, philosophical ele-

ments of the content as independent (again more or less artificially) of its theatrical or literary values.

Fukuda's ideal of good theatre is a harmonic synthesis of
literary and theatrical elements, and Shakespeare is his favorite
example of the possibility of a perfect fusion of these values.[32]
Many *shingeki* people, Fukuda writes, try to excuse their
evident lack of *engekisei*, their poor acting and directing, by
saying that most modern Western plays stress *bungakusei* in
such a way that the theatrical values become victims of the
literary elements. Fukuda protests against any artificial separation of *engekisei* and *bungakusei*: "If the former becomes
weak, the latter becomes weak too."[33] The main responsibility
for the harm inflicted both on the literature and theatre of this
time, Fukuda maintains, is *kannensei*—the use of the novel and
drama as a means of propagating a subjective ideology. The
playwright and his message became the main reason for success; the actor was reduced to a puppet maneuvered by the
threads of the text, and the play itself lost both literary and
theatrical beauty. As the expression of an ideology, the words
became aloof from a genuine theatrical text and more like a
sermon or philosophical dialogue. The result was a realistic
way of acting, weak in imagination, as contrasted to the colorful stylization of the classical theatre.

German Expressionist drama, rich in symbols and abstract
stylization, appeared at this time to offer an alternative to the
realism imposed by *kannensei*. However, for Fukuda, Expressionist drama never attained a unity between *engekisei* and
kannensei: both remained to the very end, existing separately
and pursuing different ideals. Osanai was constantly forced
by comparison with the rich theatrical elements of *kabuki* into
feeling inferior about the serious lack of *engekisei* in the young,
traditionless *shingeki* (which, moreover, had just come out of
a very weak period of commercialization), and believed he had
found in the *engekisei* of Expressionism, an answer to his

[32] "Nihon shingeki-shi gaikan," p. 227.
[33] "Nihon shingeki-shi gaikan," p. 228.

problem. No wonder, therefore, that he chose so many Expressionistic plays for the Little Theatre at Tsukiji. However, in his enthusiastic introduction of Expressionism, Osanai failed to recognize that in such a type of drama *kannensei* is more important than, and not happily synthesized with, *engekisei*.

4. THE TSUKIJI LITTLE THEATRE AND THE LEFTIST PROPAGANDA PLAYS (1928-32)

Osanai's disciples, although in open ideological disagreement with their leader, felt the responsibility of continuing his work after his death. They substituted socialism for Expressionistic ideology and were satisfied that they were carrying on, if not Osanai's *kannensei*, at least his *engekisei*. Fukuda points out how "abstract" Osanai's *engekisei* was, and how badly the new *kannensei* of socialism needed all possible help of theatrical elements. The actors were consoled only by being members of the party and serving the ideology; they could hardly be satisfied, as actors, by plays utterly lacking in theatrical elements and repeating as a constant *leitmotiv* the usual proletarian slogans, such as "Proletarians, unite!" or "Bury the lost leader!" No wonder, he continues, that *shingeki* people began, as a reaction, to idolize the concept of *engekisei* and the esthetic theories extolling the value of art since they were deprived of the corresponding reality.[34] The same thing held true for the proletarian novel and its authors also.

This is the time when *shingeki* showed increasing signs of self-sufficiency and parochialism. The actors found in their theoretical idolization of *engekisei* a satisfaction for their professionalism, and the Marxist *kannensei* provided a kind of "humanistic" messiahship which appeased their spiritual needs as intellectuals. "But the more *shingeki* tried to be independent and self-reliant, the more it cut itself off from the other arts and society; the leaders of the movement formed an exclusive society and enclosed themselves within the shell of their narrow profession." Fukuda maintains that this narrowness is one

[34] "Nihon shingeki-shi gaikan," p. 232.

of the main causes of the present state of *shingeki*: ". . . the fact is that the modern drama movement in Japan today is ridiculed constantly because of its immaturity and backwardness. It has even cut itself off from literary circles which should be its closest allies; it stubbornly refuses to open its eyes to the accomplishments of other groups."[35]

Fukuda introduces a further element for the understanding of *shingeki*'s backwardness. Osanai and his followers, such as Senda Koreya, introduced modern Western drama almost exclusively from, or through, Germany. Fukuda considers Germany an underdeveloped country, although it is close to, and is competitive with, France and England. Germany created neither Naturalism (from Ibsen of Norway and from France), nor Expressionism (from Strindberg of Sweden and Maeterlinck of Belgium), nor Socialist Realism (from Russia). The beginnings of these "isms" were developed into conscious movements only in Germany, and were used as a weapon of cultural competition with France and England. Japan followed the German pattern of introducing, first Naturalism, followed by Expressionism, and finally by Socialist Realism. However, while in the German process of evolution, transcendentalism and absolutism, that is, a strongly vital philosophical influence, actually provoked a temporary split between *engekisei* and *kannensei*, there was no reason for such a split in Japan. It happened, nevertheless, according to the German model, but very superficially. Osanai himself at the end of his life was led by his "homing instinct" to search for *engekisei* in *kabuki*—his last production was an adaptation of *Kokusen'ya kassen*, the most fantastic of Chikamatsu's plays. His followers of the leftist *shingeki*, on the other hand, grew impatient with the separation of their ideology from *shingeki*'s reality, and insisted on giving an active, but narrow-minded, political tone to their theatrical activity.

[35] From the manifesto for the foundation of the Institute of Dramatic Arts (1963).

5. THE ARTISTIC PERIOD (1933-40) TO THE PRESENT

Leftist drama, after its few years of almost complete dominance in the *shingeki* world, was suppressed by the military authorities, but, according to Fukuda, it would not have accomplished much in any case. As proof of his assertion, he points to the development after the war: the very same persons, at last completely free, soon abandoned the ideology of militant Communism and, deprived of any clear *kannensei*, ended up by stressing only theatrical values (*engekisei*). He means the two main *shingeki* groups of leftist origin, Senda's Haiyūza and Uno's Mingei. The result is today's clumsy formalism and attempts at stylization in the Haiyūza performances, and a more popular, realistic way of acting, deficient in fantasy, in the Mingei Company, which is still much closer to the proletarian spirit. Both burnt their fingers with *kannensei*, he writes, and now are vainly blowing the horn of a doubtful *bungakusei*.[36] This is the really great danger of today's *shingeki*, because Mingei and, even more, Haiyūza, with its influential school of acting, are the heirs to the Tsukiji Little Theatre.[37]

The only group which denied the hegemony of German-inspired *shingeki* was the Tsukijiza, which started in 1932 and was dissolved in 1936. The first characteristic of this group was the fact that its leading spirit was not a *sensei*,[38] but two actors, Tomoda Kyōsuke and his wife Tamura Akiko. The reason for the dissolution of the Tsukijiza was that Tomoda grew tired of the administrative work which prevented him from concentrating on acting. In the following year Kubota Mantarō, Kishida Kunio, and Iwata Toyō planned a company in which Tomoda could devote himself to acting. The tragic

[36] "Nihon shingeki-shi gaikan," p. 240.
[37] Fukuda wrote this drastic criticism in 1958, five years before the beginning of his Kumo Company.
[38] Literally "teacher," here it designates the leader of the group, a kind of autocratic *oyabun*.

death of Tomoda in the war ended this plan. The second important characteristic of the Tsukijiza was the selection of original Japanese plays as the backbone of the repertoire. Included were works by Kishida Kunio (*Mama sensei to sono otto*, *Ushiyama hoteru*), Kubota Mantarō (*Fuyu*, *Kadode*, *Odera gakkō*), Satomi Ton (*Ikiru*), Tanaka Chikao (*Ofukuro*), Koyama Yūshi (*Seto Naikai no kodomora*), Uchimura Naoya, Kawaguchi Ichirō, Morimoto Kaoru. Of the Western plays which were translated and performed, English and French were preferred to German.[39]

Fukuda considers that another factor in the artistic failure of *shingeki* during the period of the Little Theatre at Tsukiji and the heirs to Osanai's movement was the problem of translation. The lack of sensitivity to the vital importance of poetical and literary value in drama, and the misunderstanding that *bungakusei* is equal to *kannensei*, is attributed to the fact that Western plays were performed in utterly inadequate translations. The actual impression given by such translations was completely different from the beauty of the original. The Japanese words spoken on the stage did not carry the poetical and literary message of the original, with the result that *shingeki* people sought *engekisei* outside the words. "What did the audience of the Tsukiji Little Theatre actually see?" asks Fukuda caustically thinking of their claim to be seeing the real message of the Western world.[40]

On the other hand, the Tsukijiza and, later, the Bungakuza (established in 1938, followed by the Kumo Company in 1963), were on the right track in giving the greatest importance to a thorough interpretation of the foreign originals.

Fukuda concludes his interpretation of *shingeki* history with a statement in favor of *bungakusei*, for the establishment of a basic literary standard for the legitimate spoken drama.

[39] Elmer Rice's *Street Scene*; Maxwell Anderson's *Saturday's Children*; Martin Du Gard's *Le Testament du père Leleu*; and others.
[40] "Nihon engeki-shi gaikan," p. 242.

The process of modernization is particularly difficult for *shingeki* because the theatre is a group art. In an art such as painting or sculpture or the like, when an artist is able to study at the sources of modernization in a leading European country, he can attain individually a high degree of artistic achievement. It is much more difficult to westernize a whole group of artists, as in the case of *shingeki*, where director, playwrights, and actors should all be more or less on the same level and form a unit. It is true that in the case of groups such as the Army and the Navy, excellent results were reached in a very short time, but the methods of discipline and violence to the individual as used in the Army cannot be applied to the creative process of art.

Another handicap which *shingeki* had to contend with was the attitude of the intellectuals towards entertainment after the Meiji Restoration. The theatre of the Edo period was associated with the commoners of the city who had no scruples about enjoying entertainment in a very broad sense of the word. The samurai and their descendants of the Meiji period had a sense of austerity, and therefore a prejudice against any vulgar entertainment. An external sign of this change of attitude is to be seen in their attire. In the Edo period men used to wear colorful clothing. The costumes of the samurai were more colorful than the *kimono* of women today. With the Meiji Restoration such gaiety of dress was considered a kind of corruption, and a much more modest style came into use. This attitude of austerity, typical of developing countries in the process of modernization, had its influence on *shingeki*, in its lack of color and fantasy.

Another example of the change is the attitude of people toward *kabuki* actors. During the Edo period actors were officially considered on the level of outcastes, but in actuality the better actors were idolized. They had long been called *kawara kojiki* (dry-river-bed beggars), but with a nuance of affection. However, the Meiji man assumed a very serious, puritanical attitude toward them. The actors became, de facto, more truly outcastes than before, notwithstanding the formal abolition of social classes, since they were considered a distraction from the work that the nation should do. Entertainment for its own sake was frowned upon. The new intellectuals wanted a theatre which would be something of a classroom. Anything educational, intended for the transformation and Westernization of Japan, was welcome, and therefore the stage of *shingeki* became a respected means for education in the Western way of life.

Fukuda is concerned about the present situation of *shingeki*. He feels that the "art for art's sake" formula, adopted for a time by the Bungakuza under French influence, does not solve the whole problem; he finds this formula often inapplicable to the present day. The Leftists find themselves in trouble too, because their heroic stance as victims of an imperialistic system is no longer tenable in the age of freedom that has followed. Nor can they find an adequate substitute in the struggle against "American imperialism." The leftist theatre finds itself, therefore, without a clear aim. The theatre inspired by the theory of "art for art's sake" has some meaning for Fukuda as the antithesis to the theatre of the Left, but this is not sufficient in itself. Fukuda does not consider it viable for art to go alone, for art to be a supreme value without a background of supreme religious or cultural values, is a paradox. The paradox is more evident in Japan than elsewhere. In the West, the theatre had its own *Kern* for centuries before the appearance of radio, movies, and television. Western theatre reached a high degree of development and artistic perfection long before the appearance of these disintegrating mass media which, according to Fukuda, are decentralizing forces, elements of secularization. On the other hand, in Japan the movie started its extraordinary development before *shingeki* (if we exclude a few attempts of *shingeki* pioneers before the foundation of the Tsukiji Little Theatre). Fukuda, therefore, considers *shingeki*, which is the theatre's participation in the process of modernization, to be very young, at a very early stage of development. Fukuda's view that *shingeki* is symbolic of the weak points of Japan's modernization serves to explain his serious efforts both in theoretical controversies and in the practical theatre. His Institute of Dramatic Arts (Gendai Engeki Kyōkai) and the theatre group Kumo, both established in 1963, are his weapons to fight the loss of ideals in today's *shingeki* as shown in its growing commercialism and by the numerous, boring propaganda plays of the leftist groups. "We are determined to break out of the shell which hinders the modern theatre today and to start completely afresh . . . we aim at returning to the original objectives of the Literary Association and the Liberal Theatre when they were formed. We want to open the way for the development of new traditions in the Japanese theatre . . ."[41]

[41] From the manifesto for the foundation of the Institute of Dramatic Arts (1963).

PART FOUR

Philosophy, Religion, and Language

Introduction

WHEN a society is undergoing profound changes as a result of the modernization of government and industry, what effects will be felt in the cultural sphere? The third and fourth parts of this volume provide a number of examples. Japanese literature was transformed, in large measure under the influence of Western models; we find, however, that the products are more Japanese than they seemed at first glance. There is a unique blend, in which it is often difficult to determine, below the surface, just how much is Western and how much Japanese. The authors and their subjects grapple with modern problems in contemporary Japan with results that are very different both from Western literature and from earlier Japanese literature.

Part Four of this volume introduces topics that are even more complicated to discuss than literature, in that we are even less confident about the modernness of the developments.

Philosophy is represented by Professor Viglielmo's paper on Nishida Kitarō, Japan's best-known philosopher. Dealing with the first half of his life, the study gives particular attention to the stages by which Nishida worked out his philosophy. To the structure derived from his training in Western philosophy Nishida links Japanese elements, and he formulates in this way the first "modern" Japanese philosophy. This was by no means a smooth or simple process. At the same time that he was introducing some aspects of Western thought into Japan, he resisted others, and he also became interested in reinvestigating Japanese thought.

Of course his was not a fusion of all of Western philosophy with all of Japanese traditional thought. The Western thought that particularly interested Nishida was the German idealist philosophy that began its domination of the academic study of philosophy in Japan from the nineties. The Japanese intellectual tradition that Nishida rediscovered was Zen, not the Neo-

Confucianism admired by his contemporary, Inoue Tetsujirō, the person most responsible for the reorientation of philosophy at the University from English and French positivism to German idealism. Nishida's attraction to Zen recalls the experience of his close contemporary Natsume Sōseki; both these men developed Western scholarly techniques, but their latter rediscovery of Zen profoundly affected their work, adding a uniquely Japanese quality which contributed, quite likely, to their enormous following.

The final two papers concern some of the changes that have been taking place in religion and language during the last century or more. From the many major developments which have occurred in these two areas, the authors have selected for analysis specific phenomena which are especially interesting because they are not changes of the kind that make religion or language seem more "modern," at least according to our usual preconceptions that what is modern is more rational and efficient.

Dr. Carmen Blacker deals with messianic and millenarian elements in the new religions which have sprung up in modern times, especially during three periods: the middle decades of the nineteenth century, the 1920's, and the years since the Second World War. These religions appear to be means for the common, simple people of the countryside and the cities to cope with the trauma of dislocation or other disruptive changes, through a retreat to teachings that promise immediate access to a new and perfect world. The emotional faith of these movements stands at the other end of the spectrum from Nishida's eclecticism and higher mysticism, which serves to answer some questions about society for the most educated groups.

The particular feature of language analyzed by Professor Roy Miller is *keigo*, "levels of speech," the use of words and grammatical forms to express respect or politeness. Proper use of intricate nuances in levels of speech was a matter of great concern in the literature of the Heian Court a thousand years ago, and it has continued during the centuries since that time to be one of the most distinctive features of the Japanese language. Its pervasiveness and persistence are evidence of its role in the culture as an indicator defining relationships between persons and reinforcing conventions of behavior in the social system. *Keigo*, in short, is one of the features of language most deeply rooted in traditional society. But since society has changed greatly through a century of intensive modernization, what effect has there been on the use of levels of speech? While we might expect, or at least hope for, indications that usage has become simpler, more streamlined, Professor Miller demonstrates that in many respects the system has become more intricate.

The papers in this final section of the volume illustrate in another way what was already apparent in the papers on literature in the preceding part: as the society becomes more modern, there is a widening and less predictable diversity of responses, especially in cultural areas such as the arts, religion, language, to the increasing complexity of society.

CHAPTER XIII

Nishida Kitarō: The Early Years

VALDO HUMBERT VIGLIELMO

Waga kokoro	My soul
Fukaki soko ari	Has such depth
Yorokobi mo	Neither joy
Uree no nami mo	Nor the waves of sorrow
Todokaji to omou	Can reach it.[1]

NISHIDA KITARŌ's position as the foremost philosopher of modern Japan is unchallenged. Even his detractors, of whom there are many, particularly among the Marxists and quasi-Marxists, recognize his eminence and do not appear to begrudge him the title of "founder of modern Japanese philosophy." Indeed the very vehemence and frequency of their attacks on him serve only to attest to his significance. It is generally admitted that Nishida departed from the rather crude eclecticism of his predecessors and almost singlehandedly erected an indigenous Japanese philosophy. His first major work, *Zen no kenkyū* (*A Study of Good*),[2] first published in

[1] The *tanka* was written by Nishida in 1923, *Zenshū*, XII, 188. The major primary source for this paper is the *Nishida Kitarō zenshū* (*The Complete Works of Nishida Kitarō*), published by Iwanami Shoten (Tokyo, 1947-53). It contains 18 volumes, 12 in the *Zenshū* proper and 6 in the *bekkan* which includes unpublished material, letters, and the diary. A full index is to be found in XVIII, 501-14. References to the *Zenshū* will be made hereafter by the volume and page number in the text.

[2] I, 1-200. My complete English translation of this work, *A Study of Good*, was published by the Japanese National Commission for Unesco (Tokyo, 1960). The volume also contains (pp. 191-217) my translation of Shimomura Toratarō's essay, "Nishida Kitarō and Some Aspects of His Philosophical Thought," which has provided some of the basic biographical information for this paper not obtainable from primary sources.

complete form in 1911, was truly epoch-making, its impact extending to the present day. From about 1960 there has been a new upsurge of interest in Nishida, with particular reference to *Zen no kenkyū,* after more than a decade of relative inattention, and several full-length books plus numerous articles have been added to the already considerable bibliography. Perhaps the most impressive of these studies is Miyajima Hajime's *Meijiteki shisōka-zō no keisei* (*The Development of Meiji-type Thinkers*).[3] Another unmistakable sign of the new Nishida "boom" is the current publication by the venerable Iwanami Shoten of a new edition of Nishida's complete works.[4]

It is not surprising that many scholars should focus on Nishida's first work and the development of his thought prior to its publication, for, as almost all realize, Nishida's works after *Zen no kenkyū* represent only a broadening and deepening of his basic ideas as expressed in that first work. At no point in the thirty-four years of intense activity which inter-

[3] Tokyo, 1960. I am indebted to Miyajima for numerous insights into Nishida's thought, although I frequently differ from him in my interpretation. Perhaps my basic disagreement with him is that his is so often an explanation "by reduction," for he not only explains but is confident that he "explains away." He avoids the bias and invective of the Marxists and the excessive admiration, amounting almost to adulation, of Nishida's *deshi* yet falls into another trap, that of an uncritical faith in the social sciences, particularly social psychology, as capable of providing a complete explanation of any social reality. He rather blithely assumes that once he has given the social and psychological background (with an admirable wealth of detail, to be sure) to the development of Nishida's thought he has fully disposed of it. He rarely comes to grips with the true thrust of Nishida's thought, *qua* thought, and usually looks upon it as merely a kind of emanation from quantifiable, reducible, thoroughly manageable social phenomena. Nevertheless, after saying this, I must admit how useful his work has been to me, especially in enabling me to formulate my own views of Nishida vis-à-vis his.

[4] From the prospectus we learn that it will contain nineteen volumes, in contrast to the previous eighteen. I have been informed, however, that it will contain very little new material relating to Nishida's early years.

vened between the publication of *Zen no kenkyū* and his death
in 1945 did he make a radical turn in his thought or did he
reject any of the fundamental premises of his earlier work.
There is only the ever more luxuriant flowering of the buds
that emerged in *Zen no kenkyū*. Quite often the terms change,
but the substance does not. The seeds of Nishida's thought are
to be found in the years before 1911, or, more precisely, before
1906-9, since almost all of *Zen no kenkyū* had already appeared
in piecemeal fashion during those years.

What was the process whereby Nishida arrived at the philosophical position he expressed in *Zen no kenkyū*? What were
the formative influences upon him during his youth and early
adulthood that molded him into the type of thinker he subsequently became? It is these questions which have engaged the
attention of a growing number of Japanese philosophers and
scholars of Japanese intellectual history, and it is to these same
questions that I address myself in this paper.

Nishida Kitarō was born on May 19, 1870 (lunar 4th month,
19th day) in the hamlet of Mori in the village of Unoke on the
Japan Sea, in Ishikawa Prefecture not far from the city of
Kanazawa. (Today a wooden marker indicates his precise
birthplace.) When Nishida was three his family moved to
another house in the same village even closer to the sea, and
it was here, among the pine trees and sand dunes, that he
spent his childhood. In his essay of reminiscences "Aru kyōju
no taishoku no ji" (A Certain Professor's Statement Upon
Retirement) (December 1928) he himself states, rather nostal-
gically (XII, 168-71): "I was born in a poor village in the North
country. In my childhood I attended the village elementary
school, and I would play, at my parents' knees, in the pine
grove along the sandy shore."

He was the eldest son among five children; he had two older
sisters, Masa and Nao, one younger one, Sumi, and one
younger brother, Hyōjirō. His father, Yasunori,[5] was of an

---

[5] Kōsaka Masaaki gives the reading "Tokudo" in his *Nishida Kitarō
Sensei no shōgai no shisō* (*The Life and Thought of Professor Nishida*

old landholding family, from which, for generations, the village headman had been selected. His mother, Tosa, a devout Buddhist, had a deep attachment to learning, which she inculcated in her eldest son. During Nishida's childhood the family's fortunes declined, ultimately necessitating the family's moving in 1883 to the city of Kanazawa. By then, however, Nishida had already begun the first half of his life, which he rather wryly refers to as "that period when he faced a blackboard" (XII, 169), for he had already completed elementary school with considerable academic distinction, and, encouraged by his second older sister, Nao, in July 1883 he entered the Ishikawa Prefectural Normal School with the intention of becoming an elementary school teacher. He withdrew after a year, in October 1884, having contracted typhoid fever. While out of school, however, he reconsidered his career goals and decided to leave the normal school permanently. Thereafter, for two years, he studied privately under several teachers: literature under Honda Isei, mathematics under Ueyama Shōsaburō, Chinese classics under Inokuchi Mōtoku, and English under Sakuma Yoshisaburō. Ueyama is particularly noteworthy for having been a disciple of Sekiguchi Kai, a pioneer in introducing Western mathematics into Japan. In February 1886 Nishida began the study of mathematics under Hōjō Tokiyoshi, the man who undoubtedly exerted the greatest influence upon him in his entire life. In September of the same year he was allowed to enter the Ishikawa Semmongakkō, a vacancy having arisen. He studied there until 1890, when he left abruptly shortly before graduation.

His first years at Shikō, or the Fourth Higher School (officially it was the Dai-shi Kōtō Chūgakkō, or Fourth Higher

---

Kitarō) (Tokyo, 1947), p. 14. I here follow the more common reading. It is of course not impossible that both are correct. I should mention here that this work by Kōsaka also provided me with some further basic biographical information. Indeed, for want of any truly complete Nishida biography, Kōsaka's must serve as the best of the secondary sources.

Middle School), which the Ishikawa Semmongakkō became in September 1887, were full and happy ones. He himself said, in the previously-quoted essay: "My student days at Shikō were the happiest of my life. I was filled with youthful zest and I did everything I wished, heedless of the consequences" (XII, 170).

Hōjō, who continued as his mathematics teacher—and as his English teacher also—showed him special kindness. For a time Nishida even lodged at Hōjō's home. Indeed Hōjō's influence on him was so great that he seriously debated whether to make mathematics or philosophy his career. In the same essay he stated:

> At Shikō the time came for me to decide on my specialization. And I was perplexed about this problem just as many boys are. It was especially difficult for me to decide between mathematics and philosophy. I was advised by a certain teacher whom I respected to take up mathematics. In philosophy not only is skill in logic necessary but also poetic imagination. He told me that he did not know whether I had such ability. This was a thoroughly justifiable comment. I did not have enough self-confidence to deny it. Nevertheless, somehow or other, I could not bring myself to devote my entire life to dry and lifeless mathematics. While still doubting my own abilities, I finally decided upon philosophy (XII, 169-70).

Even though Nishida did not follow Hōjō's advice, he continued to have deep respect and affection for him; and despite his preference for philosophy, Nishida's continued interest in mathematics is manifest in the many references to mathematical problems and in his use of mathematical analogies throughout his work. One of his last works, completed in late January 1945, a few months before his death, is actually entitled "Sūgaku no tetsugakuteki kisozuke" (The Philosophical Foundation of Mathematics) (XI, 237-84).

Apart from Hōjō, however, there were few teachers at Shikō

who exerted a great influence upon him in the selection of his field of specialization. Kōsaka states that he does not remember Nishida's ever having spoken of any teacher at Shikō who was especially endowed with philosophical ability.[6] We must then look elsewhere for the major stimuli to Nishida's thought development at that time. We need not look far, however, for among Nishida's schoolmates there was a truly remarkable cluster of keen minds, with a broad range of interests. Nishida quickly attached himself to them, and they became a very close-knit group. Indeed many friendships were formed which were maintained throughout their lives. Even before attending Shikō Nishida had made the acquaintance of Kimura Sakae, later to become world-famous as a seismologist. They had both been students of the aforementioned Ueyama Shōsaburō. In a brief essay, "Kimura Sakae-kun no omoide" (Memories of Kimura Sakae) (November 1943) (XII, 252-56), written shortly after Kimura's death, Nishida relates how he and Kimura would study together before going to Ueyama's home for their lessons. Even though their paths separated after they left Shikō they kept up contact and saw each other from time to time. In the essay Nishida expresses admiration for Kimura's work and his pride at having had so many schoolmates like Kimura who became eminent in later life. He also cannot help but voice his sorrow that most of them have already died, and quotes from the English poem: "All, all are gone, the old familiar faces" (XII, 255).

Although Kimura was his first real friend, the boys he first met after transferring to Shikō became his closest ones. Their names read like a partial roster of "Distinguished Men of Modern Japan." We cannot but be amazed at the veritable constellation of luminaries that appeared at this school in a rather remote country town. Yet we must recognize, with Kōsaka,[7] that this was merely part of the cultural ferment of early Meiji Japan. However we explain it, it is a fact that the aforementioned Kimura and Matsumoto Bunzaburō, the scholar of

[6] Kōsaka, pp. 17-18.   [7] Kōsaka, p. 18.

Indian philosophy, were one class ahead of him, and, most amazing of all, that Fujioka Sakutarō (Tōho was his *gō*), Yamamoto Ryōkichi (his surname at birth was Kaneda; his *gō* was Chōsui) and Suzuki Daisetsu (he is better known by his *gō*; his given name was Teitarō) were *all* in his class.

Nishida gives a colorful account of the youthful Fujioka in his essay "Wakakarishi hi no Tōho" (Tōho in the Days of His Youth) (XII, 221-27). He mentions his brilliant record at school (Yamamoto Ryōkichi in another article confirms the fact that Fujioka was at the head of the class), his early and deep attachment to literature, especially Japanese literature, and his particular talent in drawing. He comments that, since his desk and Fujioka's adjoined each other, occasionally Fujioka would lean over and even sketch on Nishida's notes. Their friendship was maintained until Fujioka's early death in 1910. In his preface to Fujioka's brilliant pioneer work *Kokubungakushi kōwa* (*Discourses on the History of Japanese Literature*) (1907) (I, 414-20), Nishida gives a moving account of the suffering they both endured at the untimely deaths of their young daughters and how they attempted to console each other. This preface, an eloquent document of the bond that linked the two men, eminent in their respective fields of literary history and philosophy, also tells us a great deal about Nishida the man in contrast to Nishida the philosopher, or perhaps, more accurately, it tells us of Nishida the man as the basis for Nishida the philosopher. From these articles and from other references to Fujioka in Nishida's journal and letters, we can, therefore, learn of the impact Fujioka made on him as a young man, and we are justified in inferring that some measure of Nishida's interest in aesthetics and literature is traceable to this long and close relationship. Fujioka may even be partially responsible for the development of that poetic imagination which Nishida at first doubted he possessed but which, in *Zen no kenkyū* and his later works, he displayed at every turn, despite stylistic shortcomings and the obvious limitations of a technical philosophical vocabulary.

We turn now to Nishida's relations with his two closest friends, Yamamoto and Suzuki. Here we are no longer in doubt about the extent of the influence exerted upon him. Their extensive correspondence and the copious references to them in Nishida's journal show us how deeply they shared their experiences and how unflaggingly they encouraged and helped each other. Of course Suzuki was absent from Japan for long periods during Nishida's life but they nevertheless maintained contact. In fact it should be noted that Nishida's close relationship with Suzuki really began only after they had both completed their education and at the time when Nishida's deepening interest in Zen naturally drew him to Suzuki,[8] whose name both in Japan and in the West is now almost synonymous with Zen. Yet even in his youth Suzuki had already distinguished himself as a student and practitioner of Zen so that Nishida always looked up to him as his mentor in this area.

In another of his essays of reminiscences, "Yamamoto Chōsui-kun no omoide" (Memories of Yamamoto Chōsui) (December 1942) (XII, 245-51), written shortly after Yamamoto's death, Nishida reviews briefly the more than half century of friendship with him. His sketch of Yamamoto during his Shikō schooldays depicts an intelligent, independent-minded youth, skilled at argument either verbal or written. Nishida recalls that Yamamoto was even asked to write leading articles for the local newspaper and would dash off lengthy ones in a matter of minutes while the messenger boy waited to deliver them to the newspaper office. It is clear that Nishida's mental faculties were sharpened considerably by his close association with Yamamoto, whom he termed in English his "one and only true friend." Nishida, Yamamoto, Matsumoto, Fujioka, and others formed a literary society and brought out a privately circulated magazine (Nishida even employed a *gō*,

---

[8] See Mutai Risaku's Introduction to *Nishida Kitarō no tegami—Suzuki Daisetsu e* (*The Letters of Nishida Kitarō to Suzuki Daisetsu*) (Tokyo, 1950), p. 2.

Yūyoku, at this time), criticizing each other's writings. From Nishida's account of the young Yamamoto it would seem that the latter was not at all hesitant in expressing his views. While unfortunately copies of this magazine have not yet—and may never—come to light (Kōsaka states that Nishida once told him that Yamamoto had discovered an old copy and had sent it to him but Nishida could not find it),[9] we do have three letters of Nishida written to Yamamoto during their Shikō days. The first two have no date but are thought to have been written in 1888 or 1889 while the third is clearly dated March 13, 1889 (XVII, 3-9). These three letters are the earliest that have been preserved.

Together they present a vivid picture of the stimulating intellectual relationship between the two teen-age boys. As one might expect, the letters are filled with a youthful ardor and confidence in their mental abilities. And yet their actual content is quite surprising to those who are familiar only with the Nishida of *Zen no kenkyū* and later works. For in the first one Nishida makes a spirited attack, by following strict materialist principles, against Yamamoto's position of the immortality of the spirit. He states bluntly that everything in the universe, including man's heart and mind, is composed of the same elements and that basically there is therefore no difference between animals and plants or even between human beings and minerals. Furthermore, he contends that upon death the most complex mental powers of man dissolve into a simple, elemental energy whereby man's joys and sorrows are broken down and vanish. Towards the end of the letter he relents a bit, however, confessing that he is somehow not entirely satisfied with his theory. He admits moreover that the universe is an overwhelming mystery and that man's powers are too small to comprehend it. Thus, while the whole tone of the letter is immature in the extreme, it nevertheless serves to demonstrate that Nishida was already keenly interested in basic philosophi-

[9] Kōsaka, pp. 18-19.

cal and religious problems, although his attitude toward them is largely a negative one.

The second letter continues in much the same vein, consisting as it does of an attack upon religion, which Nishida considers as superstition created by man's fear of death and the inadequacy of his intelligence to cope with life's mysteries. He presents the familiar argument that religion begins with man's worshipping awesome forces of nature which he cannot understand. He asserts that if primitive man were to see present-day steam power and electricity, he would probably worship them as gods and that the things we worship as God today will probably be considered by future generations as similar to the totems which African natives now revere. Here again it is fascinating, and even somewhat amusing, to see that Nishida uses precisely the same arguments in this early letter which he refutes so brilliantly twenty-odd years later in *Zen no kenkyū* and which he went on refuting for the remainder of his life. As one might have anticipated, various Marxist critics have gleefully pounced upon these letters and have held them up as evidence that Nishida did indeed start upon his philosophical quest with the proper attitude; needless to say, however, they see his entire philosophical career as a sad decline from this initial state of wisdom. Some of them, such as Takeuchi Yoshitomo, their dean, do attempt to exonerate Nishida of the major responsibility for this "decline" by placing the blame upon the external circumstances of Japan in the 1890's which made it impossible for Nishida to develop further his materialist and anti-religious views. Takeuchi remarks wistfully that "the materialism and anti-religious attitude which contained the buds of a scientific critique of reality withered and died prematurely, and his reliance on man's intellect was lost."[10] It may be possible to consider that the vehemence—or, more appropriately, the ferocity—of the attacks on Nishida by many of the Marxists (a few, such as Yamada Munemutsu, are much

[10] See Takeuchi Yoshitomo, "Nishida Kitarō," pp. 337-54, in *Nihon no shisōka (Japanese Thinkers)* (Tokyo, 1954).

more objective) stems in part from their deep regret and chagrin that he should have espoused their views in his youth and then have rejected them so conclusively. Yet even Takeuchi recognizes that these early views of Nishida's are not really the result of any profound and creative thinking (would that not, in any event, be expecting too much of a teen-age boy?) but represent, in large measure, borrowings from Nakae Chōmin (1847-1901).[11] Indeed Ueyama Shumpei goes further and makes a detailed comparison of Nishida's statements with passages from Chōmin's works to prove that Nishida drew heavily on the latter.[12] The aforementioned Marxist scholar Yamada Munemutsu also comments on this parallel.[13] Yet even if this is true, and Ueyama is quite convincing, we must try to explain why Nishida at that time should have been so attracted to ideas such as Chōmin's even as we must try to explain why he discarded them later. Here I cannot but feel that the simplest explanation is the correct one, namely that the teen-age Nishida, as he looked out on the exciting and turbulent mid-Meiji world, with all the extraordinary changes that were then taking place in the political, economic, and social structure of Japan, saw what man could do by exercising his intellect, and came to agree with Chōmin that ideas of God, religion, and the immortality of the soul were so much excess intellectual baggage, wholly unnecessary, and even harmful, in the pursuit of tangible goals in what he then considered to be the real world. We must not lose sight of the fact, however, that despite Nishida's materialist and anti-religious views, as expressed in these letters, he did not move so far to the left as to embrace Marxism outright. For Kōsaka tells us[14] that Nishida once spoke to him about a boy (Kōsaka does not name him) at Shikō with whom he was forever having discussions.

[11] Takeuchi, p. 338.

[12] Ueyama Shumpei, "Nishida Kitarō," pp. 151-222, included in *Kindai Nihon no shisōka* (*Thinkers of Modern Japan*) (Tokyo, 1963).

[13] See his *Nihongata shisō no genzō* (*The Basic Image of Japanese-type Thought*) (Tokyo, 1961), pp. 36-39.

[14] Kōsaka, p. 19.

This boy, Nishida stated, was such as we would now characterize as a Marxist but Nishida could simply not accept his ideas. Indeed I think that Ueyama's description of Nishida at this time as a Meiji "liberal" is essentially a correct one. Ueyama points out that Nishida was also attracted to the thought of such enlightenment thinkers as Fukuzawa Yukichi and Tokutomi Sohō. This would moreover be in keeping with Nishida's anti-Satchō attitude, maintained for many years.

Nishida's confidence in the power of the intellect, as well as his youthful enthusiasm and ambition, are even better demonstrated in the third letter to Yamamoto. Since Yamamoto had impaired his health by studying too hard, and had been absent from a meeting, Nishida wrote him to wish him a speedy recovery and to advise him not to overwork in the future. This very ordinary get-well note is quite revealing, however, for he says that even if Yamamoto has the courage of a Napoleon and the intelligence of a Newton (it is interesting that Nishida should mention two Westerners as examples) this will do him no good if he dies an early death. He goes on to say how sad it would be if Yamamoto, with all his talent, were to die in vain and were to be "lost with the spray of the Japan Sea." He exhorts Yamamoto to take care of himself by asking him rhetorically if he does not wish to see the establishment of the Diet, to plan Japan's future, to preserve the freedom of the world. Here we can see clearly the hopes and ambitions of these two youths and how deeply they were involved in the political and social scene of that day. Nishida reveals in his reminiscences of Yamamoto (XII, 248) that he, Yamamoto, and several other Shikō students went so far as to have a photograph taken of themselves on the day of the promulgation of the Constitution in February 1889 as they held aloft a banner proclaiming their undying devotion to freedom.

This latter incident must also be viewed as an expression, by Nishida, Yamamoto, and the other boys, of protest against the changes that had taken place in their school after it had become Shikō. Nishida writes, in the same essay on Yamamoto (XII, 246-48), of how the friendly, "family" (he actually uses the word *kazokuteki*) atmosphere of the old Semmongakkō was replaced by a stiff, bureaucratic, and even "militaristic" (*budanteki*) control. The warm relationship that had existed between teachers and students vanished. Nishida places the blame for this squarely on Mori Arinori, who, as Minister of Education, and as a Satsuma man, was responsible for sending a group of Satsuma administrators, headed by Kashiwada, the newly designated principal, to take charge of the new Shikō. Nishida contends—and, we cannot but feel, correctly so—that their background as Satsuma officials or policemen hardly qualified them as educators. In any event, the closely knit Kanazawa youths and the older teachers were in no mood to accept them. Inevitably tension mounted as the new administrators did not approve of the students' broad academic and literary interests nor of what they considered to be their extremely progressive views. Here it is fascinating to note that these boys from Kanazawa, usually considered to be a redoubt of conservatism, should be cast in the roles of radicals and that the new Meiji leaders should become the reactionaries.[15] In this situation it was natural that Yamamoto, with his aforementioned independent spirit and unwillingness to submit to authority, should have been the first to rebel. Thus he quit the school first and Nishida followed his example shortly thereafter. Here again we have proof of how closely related the two boys were and how deeply influenced Nishida was by Yamamoto. Nishida himself uses the colorful expression: *Watakushi wa tōji Yamamoto-kun no kibi ni fu-shite ita.* (At that time I was playing second fiddle to Yamamoto.) (XII, 247)

In the same essay Nishida is careful to refute the charge that he and Yamamoto had been expelled. Kōsaka states[16] that when he himself was a student at the same Shikō from 1917

[15] Miyajima, pp. 38-41, gives a detailed account of this confrontation and, surprisingly, even shows that Kashiwada was a more substantial individual than Nishida was willing to admit.

[16] Kōsaka, pp. 20-21.

to 1920 there had indeed been a rumor that Nishida and Yama-moto had been expelled because of having started a strike, but Kōsaka goes on to say that he had heard from Yamamoto directly that this was definitely not the case. Thus, since the two principals in the episode have issued vigorous denials, we can consider the matter as settled. And yet we do have evidence from another source, namely a letter[17] from Hōjō Tokiyoshi to Nishida at about this time, May 18, 1890 (Hōjō had already left Shikō in 1888 to take up a position at Ichikō in Tokyo as an instructor of mathematics and physics), to the effect that he is very happy that Nishida has repented of his many absences from class during the previous academic year which had caused his failure, so that we know that Nishida's academic record during the latter part of his stay at Shikō was seriously marred. Kōsaka even speculates[18] whether this failure was the cause for Nishida's leaving Shikō, but this seems unlikely since one would hardly think that the school authorities would wait an entire year before dismissing him, nor would they dismiss him at the precise time when, if we are to believe the implication of Hōjō's letter, Nishida was actually attending classes regularly and working diligently. And yet of course, despite the assurances Nishida gave his old teacher, he did leave Shikō abruptly shortly before graduation. Miyagawa Tōru states[19] that the pretext for Nishida's leaving was illness, but he does not give the source of his information and no other biographer confirms his statement. Here there is a bit of a mystery which needs clarification. Indeed it is rather odd that not one of

---

[17] Quoted extensively in Shimomura, *Wakaki Nishida Kitarō Sensei* (*The Young Nishida Kitarō*) (Tokyo, 1947), pp. 28-29. This work was also useful in providing additional background information on Nishida's youth and early adulthood. I am also indebted to Shimomura personally, for during several visits to his home he spoke to me at considerable length of Nishida, his own revered *sensei*, giving me a better understanding of Nishida's life and work.

[18] Kōsaka, p. 21.

[19] See his *Kindai Nihon no tetsugaku, zōhohen* (*Modern Japanese Philosophy*) (Tokyo, rev. ed., 1962), p. 119.

Nishida's numerous *deshi*, such as Kōsaka Masaaki, Shimomura Toratarō, or Mutai Risaku, should have clarified it by simply asking Nishida himself.

We do know, from an entry in Hōjō's diary, dated August 2, 1889,[20] that Nishida had already appealed to him for help in transferring to Ichikō. Hōjō opposed Nishida's plan as unwise so that it came to nought, but it is reasonable to assume that Nishida's dissatisfaction with Shikō continued throughout the 1889-90 academic year until he finally decided to quit school despite his promises to Hōjō. Yamamoto's example was certainly a factor, as we have already seen, but Nishida too had definite views on how to further his education by himself, unobstructed by the odious Shikō discipline. He states quite bluntly (xii, 170): "At the time I thought it was not necessarily true that one could not achieve anything by studying alone. In fact I thought it would be better to rid myself of the fetters of school and to read freely. Thus I stayed at home all day and read."

Of course this in no way implies that he had not been reading freely prior to leaving Shikō, for in yet another essay of reminiscences, "Shikō no omoide" (Memories of Shikō) (xii, 164-67), he tells us that he would go up to the school library on the second floor and immerse himself in the books there. Here we have the first mention of his reading Western philosophical works, for he states: "I do not know who bought the book or why but I found Wallace's translation of Hegel's *Logic* and Max Müller's translation of Kant's *Critique of Pure Reason*, the latter of which had been given as a memorial for someone. I borrowed these books and tried to read them, but at the time I could not make head or tail of them" (xii, 166).

Nevertheless Nishida obviously felt that he could read even more freely if he did not have to prepare for specific Shikō courses. And in fact he carried out his plan so thoroughly that he ruined his eyes from too much reading before a year had passed. The doctor actually prohibited his reading at all for a

[20] Quoted extensively in Shimomura, p. 27.

time, forcing him to spend several weeks in a dark room in the Kanazawa Hospital. To add to his problems, his family's financial situation deteriorated, verging on bankruptcy. When Nishida had recovered sufficiently from his illness (he never recovered completely, for he suffered from poor eyesight throughout his life) he reluctantly gave up his plan of studying independently. Somehow or other (this poses another riddle in Nishida's biography) his mother coaxed five hundred yen out of his father to enroll both him and his younger brother in school in Tokyo in September 1891. It would seem that his parents did this with the hope that Nishida and his younger brother could later recoup the family's financial losses in their careers as university graduates.[21] Unfortunately the school he was forced to select was the Special Course of Studies (*senka*) of Tokyo University, which Hōjō was quick to point out was the place where only students who had an academic deficiency entered. Hōjō thus reprimanded him rather severely and told him to take the regular entrance examination for the university.[22]

Nishida did not follow his teacher's advice, however, and soon suffered the consequences. These were very real and unpleasant, as Nishida himself said: "A Special Studies student at that time was a truly miserable creature. I somehow felt that I was a failure in life" (XII, 170).

It seems that non-regular students were discriminated against severely and that Nishida, extraordinarily sensitive to such things, suffered greatly as a result. Special students were not even allowed to read in the reading room of the library but had to work at desks lined up in the corridor. And since even regular students could not go into the stacks until their third year, naturally Special Studies students were never allowed to do this. Moreover, when he visited the professors he felt that

[21] See Takeuchi, p. 339.
[22] See yet another of Nishida's reminiscences, "Hōjō Sensei ni hajimete oshie o uketa koro" (When I First Was Taught by Hōjō Sensei), XII, 257-60.

they were very cool and distant in their reception of him. But what seemed to hurt most of all was to see that the former Shikō students, with whom he had associated so closely a short while before and who were now enrolled as regular students, should be treated so utterly differently from him. He says that he "spent his three years there, in a corner, feeling very insignificant." On the other hand he also admits that he had considerable leisure and could pursue his own studies freely. He spent much of his first years, he says, in reading German literature with notes in English, for at Shikō he had barely begun his study of that language. Here we find the beginnings of his turning in on himself, a process of introspection that continued almost without interruption until it bore fruit in the philosophical position which he set forth in *Zen no kenkyū*.

In an essay on Tokyo University life, Nishida indicates that while he learned a great deal as a special student it was not that he was really stimulated by any of the lectures. He tells us that, even though the leading lights of the "first generation" of modern Japanese philosophers, Inoue Tetsujirō, Motora Yūjirō, and Nakajima Rikizō, were all teaching there at the time, philosophy was taught primarily by the young German scholar Ludovic Busse, who had been a student of Lotze in Berlin during Lotze's later years. Even though the course Nishida took from him was supposed to be a general introduction to philosophy, it actually amounted to little more than an outline of Lotze's philosophy. At that time even German instructors at Tokyo University lectured in English, and Nishida makes specific reference to Busse's heavy German accent (for example, pronouncing the word "generation" with a hard "g" and a broad "a"), which was especially in evidence when he warmed up to his subject matter. In Nishida's third year he studied under Raphael von Köber, the much-loved moralist and humanist who taught there for more than two decades, from 1893 to 1914. It was von Köber who introduced him to Schopenhauer and who also urged him to study the classical languages of the West so as to be able to read Greek and medieval philosophy in the original. He is reported to have told Nishida in English: "You must read Latin at least."

Nishida in no way lacked for illustrious schoolmates, but because of the obstacles he did not develop any friendships even remotely resembling those he had formed at Shikō. Among the students in the Philosophy Department at that time were the three so-called "Geniuses of '96": Kuwaki Gen'yoku (1874-1946), Anezaki Masaharu (Chōfū) (1873-1950), and the famed novelist-essayist, Takayama Rinjirō (Chogyū) (1871-1902), all two years behind Nishida. One year ahead of him, in the English Department, was Natsume Sōseki (1867-1916). Nishida gives us the tantalizing bit of information that he and Sōseki were actually in the same class in German literature, reading Goethe's *Hermann und Dorothea* under Florenz, the renowned literary historian. Thus, for a brief moment in their youth the eminent philosopher and novelist, perhaps the two most creative minds of modern Japan, were actually classmates. Although unfortunately this association did not develop any further, Nishida makes several favorable references to Sōseki's work in his journal, and in a post card to Tanabe Ryūji, dated January 10, 1917, one month after Sōseki's death, he says: "I too was filled with sorrow at Natsume's death. Such men as he are truly rare in the modern era and his passing is a tremendous loss to our literary world" (xvii, 190).

Perhaps Nishida was aware that both he and Sōseki were really attempting to achieve the same thing by different means: namely, to probe the nature of reality and define man's place in the cosmos.

Although, as I have indicated, during Nishida's stay at Tokyo University he turned inward, spending most of his time by himself reading and thinking, he maintained his interest in political and social developments to a certain degree. This is amply shown in a letter he wrote to Yamamoto dated May 23, 1892, wherein he waxes eloquent and is exultant over what he hoped might be the beginning of the downfall of the

Satchō clique: "The spring flowers do not last until summer and the bright moon also wanes. Finally might not the desperate measures of interference really be the beginning of the self-destruction of the all-powerful Satsuma-Chōshū forces?" (XVII, 20)

The reference here is to the interference in the second general election of February 1892 on the part of the Satchō-directed government. What really pleased Nishida, however, was the fact that despite this interference the anti-government People's Rights group won an overwhelming majority and that the Minister of Interior of the Matsukata Cabinet, Shinagawa, who had been primarily responsible for the interference, was forced to resign. There can be little doubt that this delight in the government's discomfiture was at least an indirect result of Nishida's earlier bitterness at the government-directed reorganization of Shikō. Be that as it may, Nishida clearly manifested his liberalism at this time, and though his interest in politics lessened during the next two decades it never entirely died. For example, we also find him writing to Tanabe Ryūji on January 22, 1913, expressing the hope that the democratic parties will stand firm and that the bureaucracy and the clan power will be thoroughly destroyed (XVII, 164). Such expressions, and they are numerous, especially after his retirement from Kyoto University in 1928, should go a long way toward proving that Nishida was hardly the apologist for fascism who emerges in the Marxist caricatures of him. And yet these critics appear to have no difficulty in twisting facts and sneering at his philosophy as being that of the petit bourgeois intelligentsia; they consider that whatever good-will (i.e., anti-militarist and anti-nationalist sentiments) he had subjectively, objectively he held views in the same line as fascism and served ideologically to support Japanese imperialism.[23] (Of course there remains the vexed question of some of the writings of Nishida during

[23] See Miyagawa Tōru, *Kindai Nihon shisō no kōzō* (*The Structure of Modern Japanese Thought*) (Tokyo, 1956), p. 123.

World War II which might be interpreted as a partial surrender to Japanese nationalism, and yet surely they must be
viewed in the over-all context of Nishida's work.)

Nishida's loneliness and unhappiness at Tokyo University
seem to have fortified his determination to achieve distinction
in scholarship. Miyajima's interpretation[24] that Nishida wished
to develop his intellectual powers in order to overcome his feelings of inferiority as a non-regular student is an acceptable one.
Indeed, as Miyajima indicates, the truism of depth psychology,
that self-deprecation and a feeling of superiority are but two
sides of the same coin, is amply borne out by several statements
in Nishida's letters to Yamamoto. Be that as it may, however,
Nishida did in fact demonstrate unusual intellectual ability in
a paper entitled "Kanto rinrigaku" (Kant's Ethics) (XIV, 3-20),
believed to have been written as a report for one of his courses
with Nakajima Rikizō toward the end of 1891. Although,
when Nishida allowed this first philosophical work of his to
be published in April 1933, he dismissed it as utterly without
significance other than that of indicating the nature of a student's report in the nineties, it shows us nevertheless that
Nishida could already at this early age grasp basic philosophical concepts clearly and present them concisely. His style, however, is a rather curious one, for he uses English and some
German words (in Roman letters, not *katakana*) for most of
the major nouns and even some of the adjectives and verbs.
This is probably an indication that many of the terms had not
yet been translated into Japanese or at least had not yet been
assimilated. Of course it was Nishida who contributed greatly
to the translating of Western philosophical terms and the creating of new ones throughout his career, and who thereby provided much of the form as well as the content of modern
Japanese philosophy.

In yet another letter to Yamamoto, dated December 18, 1891,
Nishida makes his first reference to Suzuki Daisetu's involvement with Zen meditation (XVII, 16). He even says that at the

[24] Miyajima, p. 47.

end of November he visited Suzuki at a Zen temple, the Enkakuji, in Kamakura, and his brief comment in *kambun* to the effect that he is envious of those who are detached from the world shows that already he was beginning to be attracted to Zen discipline and meditation.

Nishida makes still another reference to Suzuki's study of Zen, this time under the priest Dokuen, in his letter to Yamamoto written on April 14 of the following year, 1892 (XVII, 19). From this we can infer that he had probably maintained contact with Suzuki throughout the winter of 1891-92 and that his own interest in Zen was deepening. Indeed the editors of Nishida's *zenshū* indicate in the *nempu* (XVIII, 470) that he actually did practice meditation at the Chōkonji and Enkakuji in Kamakura at this time, but I have been unable to find any confirmation of this.

Unfortunately we cannot say much about the last two years Nishida spent at Tokyo University, for his major correspondent, Yamamoto, came himself to Tokyo in the fall of 1892 to enter the same Special Studies course that Nishida was taking. (We might well wonder why Yamamoto came after learning of Nishida's many unpleasant experiences, but the riddle is not solved.) Thus there is a hiatus of almost precisely two years between Nishida's last letter from Tokyo to Yamamoto in Kanazawa on September 15, 1892 and his first letter from Kanazawa to Yamamoto in Tokyo on September 19, 1894. Moreover we do not have any other firsthand evidence of his activities at this time other than his reminiscences. We do know, however, that Nishida was graduated from the Tokyo University Special Studies course in July 1894, at the very time that relations between Japan and Ch'ing China became critical and the Sino-Japanese War began.

Nishida laments in his reminiscences (XII, 244) that, although regular university graduates at that time had no difficulty obtaining positions, non-regular graduates such as he were eyed askance by prospective employers. This fact he learned from bitter personal experience, for despite his having been promised

527

a job at the newly established Kanazawa Middle School by the principal, Tomita, it was finally not given to him but to a holder of a regular university degree. We have a full and moving account of this unpleasant affair in the six letters Nishida wrote from Kanazawa to Yamamoto in Tokyo between September and December of 1894. The first, dated September 19, is a long and detailed account of the complexities relating to the competition for the aforementioned post (XVII, 23-24). Nishida's indignation at Tomita's breaking his promise to him is great, for Nishida reports that Tomita did not have enough courage to stand up to the prefectural officials who proposed that another candidate, Miyai, the holder of a regular university degree in English literature, be considered for the same post. His disappointment at Tomita's weakness is even greater because he had always considered him a man of integrity. As an excellent example of this integrity, Nishida refers to Tomita's having strongly opposed Shinagawa's interference in the general election of February 1892. (From this reference, two and a half years later, we can see what a deep impression the event must have made on his mind.) Thus Nishida suffers doubly from Tomita's action. Indeed his disillusionment is so complete that he wonders whether he would be able to work under such a principal even if he were granted the job. Nishida recognizes, however, that Miyai is certainly better qualified than he to fill a position as an English teacher but he is justifiably angry that both the school and prefectural officials should first have promised the position to him and should then have proceeded to change their minds. At the time he wrote the letter he had already been kept waiting over a month for a decision and his resources were fast giving out. Since he had to support himself and his mother (he oddly does not mention his father, who may have been living apart) he even wondered whether he should go back to Tokyo to find some sort of work, however ill-paying.

The other five letters, dated September 20, October 8, October 20, October 24, and December 1 respectively (XVII, 25-32), continue the melancholy tale. His depression at his unemployment deepens, and in his letter of October 8 he expresses his sadness at discovering, upon first leaving what he refers to in English as the "holy" academic life, that the world is such a corrupt place. By October 24 his situation has become almost desperate and he pleads with Yamamoto to help him find some position at a normal school where he might teach psychology, history, or education. Apparently Yamamoto can do nothing for him, for in the letter dated December 1 Nishida states that he might follow the advice various people have given him, that is, gather private students and give them foreign language instruction, presumably in English or German, or perhaps in both. We do not know whether he actually did this since we do not have any direct evidence of the nature of his activities until May of the following year, 1895.

Several Nishida scholars, especially Miyajima,[25] have been quick to observe that Nishida's struggles to obtain employment in the summer and fall of 1894 coincide precisely with the high point of the Sino-Japanese War and that yet there is not a single reference to the conflict in any of the six letters mentioned or indeed in anything that Nishida wrote at the time. Most of the scholars cannot avoid making a harsh value judgment against him at this point, concluding that his concern for his own well-being at that time was so great as to blot out any consideration of the broader national problems. Even if this conclusion is warranted (which is by no means certain since those six letters hardly represent Nishida's entire intellectual life during that period, and moreover he wrote them for the express purpose of explaining his employment difficulties to his close friend), such unconcern with national political matters can only be considered a moral lapse if one makes it a cardinal principle that everyone should be so concerned. It is interesting that at no point do critics such as Miyajima—and of course the full-fledged Marxists such as Takeuchi, Miyagawa, and Yamada—question their own basic premise that

[25] Miyajima, pp. 52-53.

involvement (on the left, naturally) is an absolute
they are so quick to condemn any turning inward to a
consideration of problems transcending the immediate tem-
poral ones—and this even in a philosopher, whose main task it
is to dwell upon the eternal verities and eschew the ephemeral.

And yet, even if we can turn the criticism of the Marxists
back upon themselves, it cannot be denied that Nishida did in
fact move away from his previous involvement with the
national—and even international—political and social scene
and embark upon his broader philosophical quest. In this connection we should admit as well that at this time Nishida still
retained much of the fierce pride which had been nurtured by
the rebuffs at Tokyo University and which now was intensified
by the humiliating experience with Tomita. It is only later, as
we shall see, that he was gradually able to cleanse himself of
the desire for revenge against the world that had not recognized his intellectual eminence and that had treated him so
shabbily; it is only later that he was able to engage in his philosophical pursuits without concern for the reaction of the world
or without concern as to whether he would achieve fame
thereby or not. The fact, however, that his motives at this stage
should still have been impure is not too surprising when we
realize that he was just in his mid-twenties. Indeed, it would
be even more startling if he should have displayed at the age
of twenty-five the serenity and devotion to truth he achieved
only by dint of great effort at the age of forty.

From the same correspondence with Yamamoto in the fall
of 1894 we learn, then, that Nishida was utilizing his time in
writing a study of the British Hegelian philosopher Thomas
Hill Green (1836-1882). As he says in his letter of October 20,
he wants to use his free time to do something "on behalf of the
world," and he would like to introduce to his countrymen
Green's thought, which he had been investigating for some
time. At first he hoped he might bring out a full-length book
on the subject but he subsequently lowered his sights and
intended to prepare only a brief article. He indicates that he

had found Green's thought quite ambiguous and difficult to understand. Nevertheless his determination to present a study of Green, albeit a modest one, may demonstrate that he was attracted to many of Green's ideas on ethics. Moreover, it is clear that Green's basic idea of self-realization exerted a considerable influence on Nishida's system of ethics in *Zen no kenkyū*, where much the same idea of self-realization plays a prominent role. It is interesting to note, however, that by the time Nishida got around to writing this section of *Zen no kenkyū*, some ten years later, he had assimilated Green's ideas so thoroughly that there is not even one direct quotation from Green, or even a reference to him, in the entire volume. In the same letter Nishida asks his friend to help him publish his study, when completed, in the journal, *Kyōiku jiron* (*Educational Topics*), with which Yamamoto apparently had some connection. We know that Yamamoto was able to comply with this request, for in Nishida's letter to him, dated May 20, 1895, he thanks him for his assistance in this matter.[26] Nishida expresses the concern, at the same time, that his article might be too difficult for the general reader. Unfortunately we cannot assess how justifiable Nishida's fears were, for all copies of that particular issue of the journal have been lost,[27] and thus we cannot make any detailed comments on his first published work at all. It is rather surprising that the editors of the *zenshū*, who were otherwise so painstaking, and who are deserving of every praise for their careful work, should have made no special efforts to locate a copy of this particular article, and even more surprising that Shimomura Toratarō, in his Note to Volume xiv (p. 439), where the other early, pre-*Zen no kenkyū*, works are collected, should not have recognized its omission. If this article were extant, it might be fruitful to make a detailed comparison of Nishida's critique of Green's ethics with

[26] xvii, 33-34. We are not absolutely certain that this letter was written in 1895, for only the month and day appear. And yet all the internal evidence points to its having been written in this year.

[27] See Miyajima, p. 66.

his own ethical position as set forth in *Zen no kenkyū*. As it is, however, we can make little more than the general statement I have made above.

Nishida's unemployment finally came to an end in April 1895 when he succeeded in obtaining a position as an instructor at the prefectural-run Nanao Middle School annex (*bunkō*) on the remote Noto Peninsula. This then was the inauspicious beginning of what Nishida termed the second half of his life, his teaching career when he had "his back to a blackboard" (XII, 169). Despite the obvious inferiority of his position, his spirits rose somewhat at his improved economic status. The meager salary from this teaching position was also undoubtedly responsible for allowing him to marry, and one month later, in May, we find him doing so; his wife was his first cousin, Tokuda Kotomi, the eldest daughter of his mother's younger sister. Kotomi's father, and therefore Nishida's uncle-in-law as well, was a Kanazawa saké-brewer. Nishida's eldest daughter, Ueda Yayoi, describes her mother, in the work of reminiscences,[28] which she produced in collaboration with her younger sister, Nishida Shizuko, as an exemplary wife and mother, who not only did not interfere in any way with her husband's academic pursuits but undertook the management of all of the household duties to enable him to devote himself completely to his studies. Yayoi even feels that this selflessness was responsible for her early death at the age of fifty. She died in 1925, having borne Nishida eight children, six daughters and two sons.

Nishida naturally was quick to realize that, if he wished to make a name for himself in the academic world, he could hardly remain buried in a tiny village of the Hokuriku. In his letter to Yamamoto dated September 8, 1895, he is extremely frank in stating his ambitions and in urging his friend to utilize his talents as well.[29] For a brief moment it almost

---

[28] *Waga chichi Nishida Kitarō* (*Our Father, Nishida Kitarō*) (Tokyo, 1949), p. 58.

[29] XVII, 34-35. Here again the year 1895 is not indicated but, from

appears as if his introspective tendencies have been reversed, since he not only advises that Yamamoto advance himself as much as possible but states openly that he has himself recovered from the melancholy which he had indulged in from the previous year. (He undoubtedly refers specifically to his period of unemployment.) Moreover he affirms that his previous retiring and unenterprising attitude (he uses the expressive but not easily translated term *hikkomijian*) had been a great mistake. It is at this point that he makes the statement which, in the light of his previous and subsequent actions, is so startling: "As much as one has obtained [in the way of talents] one should express in the world, and one should [use them to] advance the world. This is our duty." *Onore no etaru dake wa yo ni arawashi yo o susumezaru bekarazu. Kore gojin no gimu nari* (XVII, 35).

A more explicit endorsement of active participation in the world could hardly have been made. He makes his position unmistakable by going on to say, as he had already told Yamamoto earlier during the summer, that he intends to go to Tokyo the following year and study intensively German literature and philosophy, and, casting aside his previous hermit-like attitude, he intends to try to "make his appearance on the stage of the world."

Less than one month later, as shown by his letter of October 2 to Yamamoto, Nishida's mood had changed considerably (XVII, 35-36). He still would like very much to go to Tokyo the following year to pursue his studies, but he now realizes that, with his many dependents, he must find a job to "support" them. (He actually uses the English word.) He laments that he is worrying about this problem day and night. He still is very much involved in his academic work since he indicates that he hopes to complete a history of ethics, treating the major figures of Greek, medieval, and German philosophy, by about

---

the contents of the letter, it must have been written in this year since he spent only one September on the Noto Peninsula.

summer of the following year. He clearly hopes to use this work to further his chances for obtaining a good position in Tokyo. In his letter of November 18 to Yamamoto, he indicates that he is working diligently on the history despite the fact that he has few reference works. And yet it would seem that the work was never completed, for it was not published and there are no further references to such a work in Nishida's letters or journal. Of course it is not impossible that he decided to use his material simply as lecture notes for the course in ethics which he later taught. If this is the case, some of his work at this time found its way, in altered form, into the section on ethics of *Zen no kenkyū*.

But to return to the letter of October 2, we find that Nishida concludes with a paragraph indicating that much of the hopefulness and determination of a month earlier had worn off. He asks Yamamoto to recommend him for any positions that might open up in philosophy or German in Kyoto, where Yamamoto was at that time. It is obvious that Nishida is eager to leave where he is, for he finds teaching middle school students a difficult and unrewarding task, and he ends his letter with the gloomy phrase: "I am indeed spending my days unpleasantly." *Jitsu ni omoshirokarazu shōkō itashi-ori-sōrō* (XVII, 36).

The three remaining letters of 1895 reveal a similarly restless, dissatisfied, unsettled state (XVII, 36-40). In that of October 26 he comments on his straitened circumstances, in that of November 18 he inveighs against the entire educational system of Ishikawa Prefecture, and in that of December 19, regarding various problems of school administration, he makes the rather bitter observation that "nothing can be done at a time when fools possess power." As Ueyama points out,[30] the gap between his high hopes and his miserable actual condition causes him intense dissatisfaction.

The events of the next two years, however, brought about a great change in Nishida's external condition and, more grad-

[30] Ueyama, p. 188.

ually, an equally great one in his internal state as well. We do not know precisely how, for no records remain, but it would seem that it was through the good offices of Nishida's inveterate benefactor, Hōjō Tokiyoshi, that he obtained a new position as instructor in psychology, ethics, and German at his old school, Shikō, which he had left abruptly before graduation six years earlier. This quite naturally represented a substantial betterment of Nishida's staus and automatically meant that he abandoned any plans of studying and teaching in Tokyo or Kyoto. Nevertheless, rather surprisingly, the first letter that refers to this new position, that of March 31, 1896, is in no way a happy one—indeed, quite the contrary (xvii, 41-42). Furthermore, despite the fact that his first child, Yayoi, had been born a scant six days earlier, on March 25, he is not in any way the typical proud father—again, quite the contrary. It would seem that despite this sharp upward turn in his academic career he felt very keenly his greater responsibilities in his home life. This attitude is amply shown by the statements that precede and follow his announcement to his friend of the birth of his daughter. For he clearly states that he now regrets having entered into "family life" and sincerely hopes that his friend will not fall into the same trap (*kikutsu*, literally "devil's lair"). He then laments that he now has many (obviously, too many, as far as he is concerned) links binding him to this "transitory world" (*ukiyo*), and he fears that day by day his energies will be dissipated. Whether this pessimism is entirely the result of his sensing that his responsibilities are too much for him is open to question. It would certainly seem that some other factors are at work, but we have no way of knowing what they are, for in neither this letter nor the following one, written from Kanazawa on April 8 (xvii, 42), does he go into any detail.

And yet the most significant statement in his letter of March 31, which almost every Nishida scholar quotes, is the one which follows immediately in the letter: "When I go to Kanazawa I intend to visit the Zen priest Setsumon and listen to his religious discourses (*myōwa*)." This is the first direct evidence we have that Nishida was moving toward active participation in Zen. It is reasonable to assume that the various religious influences exerted upon him, such as the devoutness of his mother, the example of his revered teacher Hōjō, who had long been deeply involved in Zen meditation and had himself studied under the renowned priest Imakita Kōsen of the Enkakuji in Kamakura, and of course the stimuli from his friendship with Suzuki, had been working within him for quite some time, and now, with a sense of helplessness brought on by the many pressures of his family situation, that they should have impelled him to seek religious solace and enlightenment.

As I have indicated, however, we cannot say much about the process of this movement toward religion or, more specifically, Zen, during the remainder of 1896, since, with the exception of the brief letter of April 8 to Yamamoto, which is almost entirely taken up with Nishida's reporting that certain criticisms had been made against Yamamoto and with his suggestions for dealing with them, we have nothing written by Nishida himself in the way of evidence. Some scholars have speculated that he already visited Setsumon in the spring or summer of 1896, and this is a most reasonable assumption in the light of his expressed desire in the aforementioned letter of March 31. But of course we cannot be certain of it. Indeed the only documents dating from 1896, other than the letters I have mentioned, are two brief studies which Nishida published in the Shikō journal, *Hokushinkai zasshi*, "Hyūmu izen no tetsugaku no hattatsu" (The Development of Philosophy Prior to Hume) (xiv, 21-25) and "Hyūmu no ingahō" (Hume's Law of Causation) (xiv, 26-33). We can agree with Miyajima[31] that these essays, which actually are little more than outlines, are probably sections of reports or theses which Nishida wrote while a student at Tokyo University and that even though they are lucid, careful presentations of the subject matter, they hardly represent any original contribution to philosophy or

[31] Miyajima, p. 66.

even the history of philosophy. Moreover, they certainly do not give us any indication of the trend of Nishida's thought during this important, and perhaps critical, year of his life, 1896.

One of the main reasons for thinking that this year is so significant is that Nishida began keeping a diary from the beginning of the following year, 1897. Apart from the significance of the content of the diary, which is obviously considerable, the very fact that he started writing one is in itself significant. This fact is, rather oddly, overlooked by almost all Nishida scholars. For the diary surely indicates that the process of introspection, which, as we have seen, began with his leaving Shikō precipitately in 1890, had now reached the stage where he felt compelled to record his interior life and chart its progress in a disciplined way. Thus it is especially unfortunate that we should have no letter or random jottings from the latter part of 1896 to give us some clue as to the events which immediately preceded his starting the diary in early January 1897 and which might have been important factors in his deciding to do so.

Although the first entry in the diary is that of January 3, Nishida wrote a series of undated self-hortatory statements on the inside cover and on the front side of the flyleaf of the diary notebook. We may reasonably assume that he wrote these either before beginning the diary proper or at some point in early 1897. At any rate, these statements certainly indicate his mental state at this time and, as such, are quite valuable in assessing the development of his thought. Even though they are written in a terse, dry, semi-*kambun* style, they reveal the depth of his earnestness and the extent of his determination to order his intellectual and spiritual life. And yet, if we did not know that Nishida went on to write *Zen no kenkyū* and build his own philosophical system, we might be tempted to dismiss these exhortations as rather trite and even pompous, excessively sober and utterly humorless, Confucian-type maxims, high-sounding but devoid of any real content.

I translate the Japanese section of them in their entirety:

Non multa sed multum.

He who desires to become an extraordinary person and perform extraordinary deeds must have a will that does not move, even though heaven and earth crumble, and a courageous and heroic spirit such that even the gods give way.

Neither wealth nor rank can dissipate his heart; neither authority nor force can daunt him; by practicing righteousness he need avoid neither water nor fire.

In everything he establishes his own ideas; he puts them into practice himself and does not rely on others.

To excel others one must have greater self-discipline than others.

The great man must have courage to consider himself ignorant and unwise.

It is of first importance to reflect and think deeply oneself rather than to want to read the works of others. One ought not to read greedily many works; one should read carefully the works of outstanding men of past and present.

The first-rank thinker is a man who does not read widely.

Method of study: read, think, write.

If one has not finished thinking through one matter, one ought not to move on to another; if one has not finished reading one book, one ought not to take up another. (xiii, 3)

On the reverse side of the flyleaf he merely lists the names of major Western philosophers in two groups: "Plato, Aristotle, Spinoza, Kant, Hegel, Schopenhauer, Hartmann, Schleiermacher; Locke, Hume, Leibniz, Fichte, Schelling, Lotze" (xiii, 4).

The first indication we have that he actually began to put into practice this ambitious program of moral, spiritual, and intellectual improvement and that he fulfilled his expressed intention of the previous spring to start Zen discipline comes from the entry for January 14 in this diary for the year 1897 (xiii, 5). At this point it should be mentioned that this diary, from the beginning through the entries of mid-October, is written in German, as are several of the November and December entries as well, doubtless as a kind of intellectual exercise to improve his command of that language which he was then teaching at Shikō. Thus, the entry in question, that of January 14, reads as follows: "Ich besuchte Setsumon-Zenji. Selbst-denken."

Thereafter he paid two more visits to Setsumon in February, on the latter of which Setsumon was ill ("er war krank") and presumably could not see him, and he went to listen to the discourses of another Zen priest, Kōshū, in early April and again in early May. Although these five visits to Zen priests over a four-month period surely would not in themselves indicate any very great religious zeal, it is obvious that Nishida was planning much more intensive participation in Zen discipline. He left Kanazawa on June 17 for an extended two-month stay in Kyoto, primarily for the purpose of deepening his spiritual life. He stayed at first with his old friend Fujioka Sakutarō. One week later, on June 24, he had an interview with the Zen priest Kokan at the Myōshinji, one of the most important Zen temples in Kyoto. Doubtless as a result of this meeting, he decided to participate in various Zen practices (*sesshin*), which he did at the Myōshinji from July 1 to July 7 and then again from August 6 to August 12 and also several times at the Taizōin. He returned to Kanazawa on August 20. On August 28 his appointment as professor (*kyōju*) to Yamaguchi Kōtōgakkō was decided upon, for he agreed to follow his benefactor and old *sensei*, Hōjō, who had been newly appointed principal there.

But before examining Nishida's activities during his two years (September 1897-July 1899) in Yamaguchi, we must refer to a serious domestic problem that had arisen in the Nishida household during the early part of 1897 and that continued to present difficulties until it was finally resolved in February 1899. Although the terse German entries in Nishida's diary do not allow us to view this problem in all its complexity, they do provide us with enough material to state that it was a most vexing one and undoubtedly contributed to a sense of spiritual turmoil which he attempted to overcome in some measure by his involvement in Zen meditation. I cannot, however, agree with Miyajima[32] that this problem was the *primary* reason for his deepening interest in Zen. Surely the fact that his interest in Zen was clearly manifested prior to the occurrence of this domestic difficulty and continued long after it was settled is sufficient proof that the two events are only indirectly related.

In substance this problem centered around Nishida's father's interference in Nishida's marriage, the bad feeling that this stirred up, Nishida's wife Kotomi's suddenly leaving her home with the tiny Yayoi, their returning only to be evicted by Nishida's father, and the separation between the young couple which was agreed upon on May 24. I quote the pertinent entries in the 1897 diary:

> January 22 (Friday) [all the dates are written in Japanese]: Herr Mori kam und sprach von unserem Verhältnis mit Vater.
>
> February 17 (Wednesday): Nachts kam Hr Mori. Wir wurden auf den Vater verdächtig.
>
> April 16 (Friday): Am Abend kam der Vater, mit dem wir den Streit gehabt haben.
>
> April 19 (Monday): Der Vater kam und kehrte ein.
>
> May 1 (Saturday): Der Vater kam.
>
> May 5 (Wednesday): Der Vater kam.
>
> May 9 (Sunday): Kotomi ging aus dem Hause ohne Grunde. Wir alle schlafen nicht.
>
> May 10 (Monday): Diesen Tag keine Nachricht von Kotomi und Töchterchen. Ich ging nicht nicht [sic] nach Schule.
>
> May 11 (Tuesday): Ein Brief kam von Tokuda in Uruschisima anmeldend, dass Kotomi in Uruschisima sei. Ich ging nach Schule.

[32] Miyajima, pp. 56-58.

May 13 (Thursday): Heute kam Kotomi. Der Vater wurde darüber sehr zornig.

May 14 (Friday): Der Vater wies Kotomi aus.

May 16 (Sunday): Heute kam Tokuda und sprach mit Vater.

May 24 (Monday): Heute kam meine Tante. Unsere Ehescheidung.

These exceedingly brief and almost staccato entries, then, present us with a stark account of mid-Meiji family discord in a conservative "castle town" where feudal patterns of social behavior still predominated, where a man could evict his daughter-in-law from his son's home for little or no reason, and where a son had to submit to his father's wishes even though he, the son, might be economically independent and even though the father might even be in some degree economically dependent upon that son, as would seem to have been the case in the Nishida family. For it does not require very astute reading between the lines to determine that the cause for the separation (it was not actually a divorce, or "Ehescheidung") does not lie in any misunderstanding or quarrel between Nishida and his wife so much as it does in Nishida's father's interference in their marriage and a serious quarrel between him on the one hand and Nishida, Kotomi, and Nishida's mother Tosa (who was, we must bear in mind, Kotomi's mother's older sister as well) on the other. The "wir" of the February 17 and April 16 entries clearly seems to refer to the latter group. Such an episode as this would certainly be cause for astonishment if it occurred at a later period in a larger city such as Tokyo or Osaka but, as Miyajima wisely points out,[33] similar events take place in Ishikawa Prefecture and other country districts to this very day.

This episode is surely a fascinating one and is fraught with a veritable network of ironies. For here we see the young

[33] Miyajima, p. 58.

Nishida teaching psychology, ethics, and German at a newly established *kōtōgakkō* and delving deep into Western civilization, or, more specifically, Western philosophy, and yet at the same time he is thoroughly enmeshed in a peculiarly Japanese psychology and Japanese ethic to the extent that he cannot stand up to his father on a matter of most intimate concern to himself, his relation with his wife. But perhaps the plight of the Meiji intellectual caught between two cultures is nowhere better epitomized than in the fact that Nishida should write about this feudal or, at any rate, pre-modern, social situation in a Western language, in this case German, the language which perhaps more than any other was the vehicle of modern Western philosophy and indeed of *Wissenschaft* in general. One cannot help wondering whether Nishida himself was aware of the tremendous gulf separating the form and content of this section of his diary.

Although, as I have already indicated, a complete reconciliation between Nishida and Kotomi did not take place until February 1899 (largely, it would seem, through the good offices of Nishida's mother, who was, as we have seen, at once Kotomi's mother-in-law and blood aunt, and even more important perhaps, Kotomi's father's sister-in-law, and therefore ideally qualified to effect such a reconciliation), we learn from the diary entry of August 24, 1897 that "Heute kam Kotomi wieder in mein Haus." We have no way of knowing the precise nature of the relationship between Nishida and Kotomi during the year and a half intervening between August 1897 and February 1899 (in his diary he mentions writing and receiving letters, but these have been lost), but despite any emotional bonds which may have remained between them, they were still physically separated almost the entire period, for Nishida left Kanazawa without Kotomi and Yayoi on September 2, 1897, and after a brief stopover at the Myōshinji on September 4, proceeded on to Yamaguchi, arriving there on September 7. Moreover he lived without his family the entire time he stayed in Yamaguchi, that is, until his departure on July 8, 1899 to take up a position again at Shikō, and thus he and Kotomi were separated, spatially if not emotionally, almost two entire years, except perhaps for a brief visit on Nishida's part to Kanazawa—although we have no actual record of it—in the summer of 1898. Interestingly enough, however, he and Kotomi must have had physical relations during the nine-day period in 1897 between her return to his house and his departure for Yamaguchi, for she bore him their first son, Ken, in June 1898. By a curious coincidence, Nishida's father, the villain of the piece, died in the same month at the age of sixty-three. These two events undoubtedly served to hasten the reconciliation between the young couple. Indeed we may well wonder why another eight months were required for it to be achieved.

Nishida's two-year stay in Yamaguchi represents the period of his deepest involvement with Zen meditation and the time during which he demonstrated his greatest religious concern. Perhaps his freedom from family responsibilities enabled him to engage in the religious life more intensely than had been possible in Kanazawa. (Of course this freedom could not have been complete since he must have provided in some way for Kotomi and Yayoi, and later Ken, in Kanazawa, although we do not know the extent of that support.) Whatever the reason, however, the record is clear: his diary for that period and the few letters that have been preserved show an astonishing zeal in all matters pertaining to religion and the spiritual life. Furthermore, this was definitely not simply an academic, or intellectual, pursuit but one on which he staked his entire being. His sincerity and wholehearted devotion to his spiritual quest cannot possibly be doubted.

Already at the end of 1897, in a letter to Yamamoto dated November 11, Nishida displays a genuine and profound religious mood, quite at variance with his carping and self-pity of two years earlier (XVII, 43-45). I quote extensively from this significant document:

Man's desires are truly deep-rooted, for no sooner is one of them satisfied than he wishes for something further. When desire rears its head it is truly like that of a Hydra. One had better find the happiness which comes from cutting it off at its base. When man is attached to one thing after another, he is forever in a whirl of busyness and cannot be calm even for a moment. If man does not turn back to the very depths of his soul and strike at the root of this delusion, dissatisfaction will cause him to suffer at every point. I too, upon first coming here, was unhappy wherever I turned, but thereafter I pondered the matter carefully and now I can say that somehow my spirit is calm. When I reflect on the various things about which I have been dissatisfied, I am ashamed at my meanness of spirit. Have you pondered deeply the meaning of the verse from the Sixth Chapter of Matthew: "Which of you by taking thought can add one cubit unto his stature?" If we abide by this teaching I think that no discontent can possibly arise.

This body of ours is important but is there any sense in man's unnecessarily preserving it? Indeed man's life does not reside in his body but in his ideals. When man searches deep within his heart and acts contrary to that which he holds to be the good, i.e., when the self is oppressed by another, then that which is the self is already dead. Tokutomi, even though he exists in the flesh, has surely entered his coffin.[34] When man has probed deeply within his soul, and, attaining his true self, has become one with it, then, even if that moment is a mere instant, his life is eternal. Why do we need to make our spirit suffer and preserve this ugly body? For what reason must one desire the survival of this body? If one plans the eternal existence of the body by betraying the spiritual

---

[34] Nishida makes this severe condemnation of Tokutomi Sohō because of his revulsion at what he considers to be Sohō's political betrayal, for Sohō at this time moved from an anti- to a pro-government position. As Ueyama, p. 180, points out, this is a clear indication of how highly Nishida had previously revered Sohō. This passage, moreover, shows us that Nishida had not utterly lost interest in political matters.

self in any way, then, even if the body exists, will not the spirit be dead?

If I now think about dying physically, the first things that come to mind are my parents, wife, and child. I certainly have not been free from worry at this time. And yet upon learning recently of the God of the Sixth Chapter of Matthew who cares even for the fowls of the air, which sow not, neither do they reap, nor gather into barns, I have been able to put my soul at rest somewhat. As you doubtless know, the Bible is truly that which soothes our hearts. I cannot but value it above the Analects—how do you feel on this subject?

These quotations from this important letter show us how far Nishida had departed from the materialist views he expressed in that other letter to Yamamoto written some nine years earlier. We are now, at the end of 1897, clearly in a quite different intellectual atmosphere, much closer to that of *Zen no kenkyū* than to anything that preceded it. Indeed several of the basic ideas of his first major work are to be found here in embryonic form: that man must discover his true self buried under the accretions of desire and a frantic busyness, that man's true life resides in his ideals and not in his biological existence, and, perhaps most significant of all, that by attaining his true self and by uniting with it, man touches the eternal and transcends space and time. This latter idea is surely the nucleus out of which grew his basic concept of "pure experience," which he fully developed in his *Zen no kenkyū*.

Ueyama makes several accurate observations with regard to this letter.[35] He comments on the extent of the change in Nishida's basic outlook from the time of his materialist letters to Yamamoto when they were students at Shikō by stating that "this new set of values was one which, in contradistinction to the scientific world-view which considers 'truth' as a gauge of value and which proceeds from *knowledge concerning matter*, constituted a religious world-view which takes 'happiness' as

[35] Ueyama, pp. 189-91.

a gauge of value and which proceeds from *intuition of life*."
(Ueyama's italics.) This is essentially a correct interpretation
of the process that had taken place in Nishida, one of rejecting,
or gradually discarding, a shallow faith in so-called scientific
truth in favor of an intuitive, religious approach which sought
spiritual enlightenment through attainment of the true self.
I also agree with Ueyama in his statement that Nishida's quotation from the New Testament of a portion of Christ's Sermon
on the Mount is certainly not to be taken as an indication that
Nishida's religious position was a Christian one or even tending in that direction. Rather, his position is one which is neither specifically Christian nor Buddhist (despite his active participation in Zen discipline) but an even more fundamental
one, which goes beyond the distinctions between these two
major religions, to that point from which all religions spring.
Here we have the beginnings of the approach to religion which
Nishida maintained throughout his life: he was profoundly
respectful of all the great world religions in their highest forms,
especially Buddhism, Christianity, and Hinduism, and yet
without adhering to any (he cannot be considered an adherent
of Zen in the sense that Suzuki Daisetsu is, or in the sense that
Kierkegaard is a Christian), he sought to define the nature of
the religious spirit itself and grasp that Ultimate Reality of
which the conventional terms, such as Buddha, God, and
Ātman-Brahman, are but pale reflections. Here we are quite
clearly in the realm of mysticism, and it must be admitted that
Nishida, if not actually a mystic himself, is most certainly a
philosopher of mysticism. A recurring pattern throughout his
work—especially in evidence in *Zen no kenkyū*—is one wherein his thought ascends in spiral rotations, with a careful logic
and a massive and impressive scholarly apparatus, only to end
in quotations from the mystics, often Jacob Boehme, Meister
Eckhart, or Pseudo-Dionysius, and an admission that he has
reached the limits of philosophy. Indeed, his second important
work, *Jikaku ni okeru chokkan to hansei* (*Intuition and Reflec-*

tion in Self-Consciousness) (1917),[36] contains the candid statement in the Preface to the revised edition (1941): "I may not
be able to escape the criticism that I have broken my lance,
exhausted my quiver, and capitulated to the enemy camp of
mysticism" (II, 13). Perhaps the only comment we need to add
to this is that it is highly doubtful that he actually considered
mysticism to be an "enemy" camp.

Religion, and a religious world-view, then, occupy the center
of Nishida's thought from this time on, so that even when he
is treating certain specific problems within philosophy, he is
always doing so within a religious context and he rarely delays
in revealing the basis of his thought. For example, in *Zen no
kenkyū*, he states quite bluntly that there must be religion at
the foundation of learning and morality. And at the very end
of his life, in "Bashoteki ronri to shūkyōteki sekaikan" (The
Logic of Place and the Religious World-View) (XI, 371-464),
published posthumously in 1946, he concludes his life-work on
the same note: "The religious consciousness, as the basic fact
of our lives, must be the foundation of learning and morality."

But, to return again to 1897, it is interesting to note that the
one article which Nishida published in that year, "Senten chishiki no umu o ronzu" (A Discussion of the Existence or Non-
existence of A Priori Knowledge) (XIV, 34-45), published in
Nos. 14, 15, and 16 of the *Hokushinkai zasshi*, does not in any
way reflect this new religious tendency. Instead this brief work
can be viewed as the conclusion of the previous period of his
career when he showed considerable interest in the more formal aspects of philosophy, such as epistemology and logic, outside of any religious framework. Once again, we can agree
with Miyajima[37] that this work adheres quite closely to Kant's
theories on the subject and does not display any startling originality. It is fair to assume that Nishida wrote this article, and

[36] II, 1-350. I have recently finished a complete English translation,
and hope to publish it shortly.

[37] Miyajima, pp. 66-67.

the four earlier ones, including the one on Green's ethics which has been lost, without any very deep involvement in the subject matter. If this is true, we may also say that it was the growing significance of religion in his life which enabled him to express himself creatively in his subsequent works. For the four brief articles prior to *Zen no kenkyū*, which follow the one in question, are devoid of any dryness (unless it be that of the constricting—and, for the Westerner, or at least for this particular Westerner, quite maddening—*bungo* style in the first three) and amply demonstrate that Nishida has something himself to say other than analyzing or reviewing the work of earlier philosophers.

Throughout 1898 and 1899, even after his return to Shikō in the summer of the latter year, his religious zeal continued unabated. Indeed, he began both years by making week-long retreats at the Myōshinji in Kyoto, and it is not surprising that the fervor of these sessions should have persisted after his return to Yamaguchi, so that we find the references to *daza* (Zen meditation) particularly numerous in the late January, February, and March entries of both years. And yet it would be wrong to think that he concentrated on religion to the exclusion of other things. In these same two years there are many references in his diary to his wide reading, not only in philosophy but in literature in general. For example, Goethe, Shakespeare, and Dante are specifically mentioned. Even lesser figures, such as Lessing, Heine, Goldsmith, Shelley, and George Eliot, received his attention, although naturally it would be most difficult to demonstrate what precise effect, if any, these authors had on the development of his thought. (Goethe is an exception since Nishida later wrote a detailed study of his metaphysical background.) The entries in the diary are so terse that virtually the only thing we can say is that he familiarized himself with many of the important literary figures of the West. Concerning his reading in philosophy we can say much more since he quotes extensively in his later works from those philosophers whose thought appealed to him most or most stimulated him to develop his own ideas on the same subjects they treated.

Nevertheless, despite the breadth of Nishida's intellectual interests at this time, religion, as I have indicated, dominated his mind. The first article he wrote which reflects this new tendency is, appropriately enough, entitled "Yamamoto Anno-suke-kun no 'Shūkyō to risei' to iu rombun o yomite shokan o nobu" (A Statement of My Impressions Upon Reading Yama-moto Annosuke's Study Entitled 'Religion and Reason'), which was published in the magazine *Mujintō* (Vol. III, No. 6) in June 1898 (XIV, 46-51). Although it obviously would seem to be primarily a review of another scholar's work, it is actually more a study in which Nishida presents his own views on the subject. Here we can see an amplification of the same views he expressed in the previously quoted letter to his friend Yama-moto. He attacks Yamamoto Annosuke for looking only at the external intellectual aspect of religion and for overlooking its fundamental, internal, emotional aspect. Thus, philosopher though he is, he contends that the definition of religion made by the "cold eye of the philosopher" is not something which has been arrived at by exploring the heart of the actual practi-tioner of religion, and is therefore false. He further makes the ringing assertion that the essence of religion does not reside in any kind of creed or ceremony but in our departing from the finite world and in our entering the realm of the infinite. He goes on to say: "Shall we call this emotion, or shall we call it intuition? . . . In Buddhism it is termed *gedatsu* (deliverance of one's soul, or the Sanskrit *vimokṣa*) and in Christianity it is termed salvation." He contends that the single most impor-tant fact in religion is "the entering, by one leap, into the sublime realm (*myōkyō*) of infinity and acquiring a stand-point of great peace." Therefore, he naturally believes that the essence of religion cannot be expressed intellectually as are the laws of physics or the principles of philosophy. Nevertheless, after contending in this way that religion cannot really be grasped intellectually, he proceeds to present his own *guken* (humble opinion) regarding a philosophical explanation of religion, which, at first glance, seems to be almost a contradiction of some of his earlier statements in the same article. It is at this point that he presents views which are so close to his position as expressed in *Zen no kenkyū* that I am certain most of the many avid readers of that work would quite easily mistake them for passages from it. For example, he states:

> I cannot think that there is infinity apart from finiteness, or that there is the absolute apart from the relative, or that God, apart from this universe, resides transcendent (*chōzai*) outside it. Nay, I think that infinity apart from finiteness is on the contrary finiteness, that the absolute apart from the relative is on the contrary relative, and that God residing transcendent outside the universe is not an omnipotent God. True infinity must be within finiteness; the true absolute must be within the relative. The truly omnipotent God must be within this mutable and fleeting (*ui-tempen*) universe. (XIV, 48-49)

This method of resolving oppositions, such as finiteness and infinity, the absolute and the relative, is basic to *Zen no kenkyū* and all his later work, where he is forever demonstrating that the usual dichotomies of subjectivity-objectivity, activity-passivity, or spirit-matter are more apparent than real and that "true reality" (he particularly favors this redundancy, *makoto no jitsuzai* or *shin-jitsuzai*) is that which includes both terms of the pairs. Thus, this brief review article is significant not only in giving us an outline of some of Nishida's basic ideas but in giving us an indication of his methodology and of the fundamental structure of his thought. He proceeds with his argument:

> However, to enter into the absolute infinity of religion is to enter into true absolute infinity; it is to perceive the reality of the universe (*uchū-jitsuzai*) at the point where it is active in its entirety and it is to attain this in actuality. This cannot

be done with the normal powers of understanding. And yet I am not one who believes that we have a kind of special mystical ability apart from the ordinary functions of the intellect, the emotions, and the will (*chi-jō-i*.) I contend that those things which we term the mind, the emotions, and the will are not separate, individual functions but that there must of necessity be one thing which unifies these three aspects. This unity is directly the absolute and infinity. Must it not be true that at this one point we are able to seize the great source of the universe? (XIV, 49-50)

Here Nishida rejects the view that there is a kind of magical mystical power apart from the ordinary spiritual faculties to unlock the secrets of religion or attain to Ultimate Reality, or that God resides in some far-off nebulous sphere with angels and harps, or with Bodhisattvas and lotus blossoms (choose your imagery). Rather, he maintains, as the great mystics of all faiths have maintained, that God is to be found in the depths of one's soul, that He is there at the very ground of one's being, and that the trinity of the intellect, the emotions, and the will are merely differentiations—and often distortions—of His unity. Surely here we can agree that Nishida is justified in seeing no essential contradiction between Zen and Christianity. For if he arrived at this position through Zen discipline, so too have many Christians arrived at precisely the same position by meditation on and fulfillment of Christ's teaching: "The kingdom of God is within you" (Luke 17:21).

Towards the end of the essay Nishida compares the poet and the philosopher, to the disadvantage of the philosopher, as he quite frequently does in *Zen no kenkyū* and his later works. He rather amusingly states that the poet intuits infinite ideals within finite phenomena and is able to express infinite ideals in finite phenomena but he, Nishida, has not yet heard of anyone becoming a great poet through learning and knowledge. Thus he concludes that the philosopher's manner of looking at the universe is most shallow and incomplete, that the poet's imagination can enter more deeply into the whole than the philosopher's intellectual power, and that the faith of the saint (this is not a precise translation of Nishida's term, *shūkyōka*, but closer to his intent than the simple rendering "religious person") is that which is first able to arrive at the very depths of the entirety of the universe. This section of the essay is a sketch of yet another basic pattern in Nishida's thought, that of setting up a hierarchy of value among philosophy, art, and religion. Throughout his work he very often carries discussion of a particular problem up to a certain point and then terminates it with some reference to the worlds of art and religion as the realms where this problem is fully resolved or where the truth which he is attempting to grasp philosophically is more fully realized. Indeed it may not be an exaggeration to say that Nishida saw his mission in life as one of attempting to discover Reality with his philosophical tools even as do the poet and artist with their pen or brush and as does the saint with his faith and love.

He contends, therefore, further toward the end of the article, that if the philosopher truly wishes to attain his objective of grasping the entirety of reality he must enter into religion, for union (*tōitsu-yūgō*) with reality is not achieved intellectually (*chishikijō*) but in fact (*jijitsujō*). He thus is not one who agrees that we can erect religion on a philosophical foundation, and he here returns to the assertion he made at the beginning of the article. He goes on to say that if religion needs the assistance of learning it is incomplete. Some may boast that Buddhism is a philosophical religion, but for Nishida this is a defect of Buddhism. "We must not say that Christianity is the more precious because of the medieval Scholastics or that Buddhism is the more precious because it is philosophical. Religion is fact (*jijitsu*), and fact does not exist because there is the explanation of knowledge. The value of fact does not depend on the existence or non-existence of an explanation" (xiv, 50).

Nevertheless, at the very end, he makes yet another turn in his thought, qualifying what he has just stated by asserting

552

that he has not meant to imply that knowledge is utterly unnecessary in religion or that religion and knowledge are mutually incompatible. For he believes that true (*shinsei*) religion must naturally fuse with true knowledge. Quite obviously, Nishida saw his role in philosophy as one of hastening that fusion, or, at any rate, as one of contributing to that true knowledge which, far from being at variance with religion, is the gateway to its very essence.

I have dwelt at considerable length on this early brief study because it has intrinsic importance and also because it clearly demonstrates the tremendous changes that were taking place in Nishida's *Weltanschauung* in the closing years of the century.

As I have already indicated, Nishida maintained his interest in Zen even after his return to Kanazawa in the summer of 1899 to take up his duties once again as *kyōju* at Shikō, teaching psychology, logic, ethics, and German. This return to Shikō is yet further proof, if we needed any, of Nishida's intimacy with Hōjō, since Hōjō had been appointed principal at Shikō more than a year earlier,[38] and for the third time Nishida changed jobs to follow his revered *sensei*. From yet another letter (XVII, 48) to Yamamoto (without them the Nishida biographer would be in a sorry plight indeed), dated September 15, 1899, we learn how delighted Nishida is at the prospect of being able once again to practice Zen meditation under the priest Setsumon at the Garyūzan, a Zen temple in Kanazawa. He further reveals the extent of his religious zeal by the following statement: "Recently I have come increasingly to feel that nothing, however precious, is more important than the salvation of one's soul. Even if I should spend many years in vain I still wish to [try to] achieve this one thing."

He goes on to urge his friend to take up the same task and practice Zen during the summer of the following year if he has the opportunity.

---

[38] See letter to Yamamoto, XVII, 46.

In another letter, again to Yamamoto of course, towards the end of the same year, that of December 20 (XVII, 49-51), he is very frank in expressing his devotion to Zen techniques in arriving at so-called intellectual unity, although he indicates that he is not really qualified to instruct Yamamoto in Zen and urges him to consult their mutual friend and old classmate Suzuki Daisetsu instead. I quote from that letter: "I cannot really say anything about Zen. You should, however, consult Daisetsu. And yet what method do you think is best to arrive at a so-called unity of thought (*iwayuru shisō no tōitsu*)? I think that the Zen method is the most expeditious.... Whether I achieve my goal or not I intend to practice it my entire life."

Rather mysteriously we do not have any journal or any letters from the year 1900. Nishida's journal, which breaks off quite abruptly on October 3, 1899, is not resumed until January 1, 1901. And for some unknown reason Yamamoto, who otherwise was so careful in preserving the letters he received from his friend, did not preserve any from that year or else did not receive any from him. The latter possibility is the less likely one, since there was rarely more than a three- or four-month hiatus in their correspondence. Of course it is not impossible that for some reason either the journal or the letters, or both, were suppressed, as was a portion of Sōseki's diary. It is interesting that not one of the many Nishida scholars has speculated on the possible reasons for this gap in our records of his life.

We do, however, have one document from the year 1900 which enables us to assert that even if his diary and letters of that year have been suppressed for some personal or family reasons the development of his thought continued along much the same lines as during the previous three or four years. This document is the extremely brief (a mere two and a half pages in the *zenshū* edition) article "Bi no setsumei" (An Explanation of Beauty) (XIV, 52-54), which appeared in the March 1900 (No. 26) issue of the Shikō journal, *Hokushinkai zasshi*. Despite its brevity, however, it reveals quite well the continuity in Nishida's thought. For in it he treats the aesthetic sense as one of a self-effacement, or ecstasy (*muga*), wherein one has transcended ordinary thought and discrimination (*shiryo-fumbetsu*), and which, at its deepest level, is one with the religious spirit. Beauty, for Nishida, as for Keats, is truth, but an intuitive truth and not a truth attained by the thinking faculty. Here again we have the same hierarchy of value, for he defends this kind of intuitive truth against the criticism that it is merely a poet's fantasy, and asserts that this truth is that wherein we have departed from the self and fused with things (*onore o hanare yoku mono to itchi-shite*) (quite obviously, Nishida uses the term "self" in two wholly different senses, one pejorative, as here, and the other referring to the true, or enlightened, self); thus it is a truth which we have seen with the eyes of God (*kami no me o motte mitaru shinri*) and, since it represents a profound grasping of the secrets of the universe, is indeed far greater than logical truth attained from without by the processes of the intellect. He concludes this particular paragraph with a rhetorical question which is nothing short of prophetic in the light of the present-day low esteem for the great figures of German idealism: "Even if some day the time should come when the great philosophers Kant and Hegel are not paid the least attention, will not the works of Goethe and Shakespeare, as mirrors of the human heart, be transmitted for hundreds of generations?" (XIV, 54)

Surely Nishida's exalting the poets above Kant and Hegel, whom he also deeply respected and from whose works he quotes frequently, is an indication of one of his basic tenets, namely that logical truth must ever be attuned to poetic truth. And of course it can be seen as further confirmation of his belief that the intellect must ultimately bow before the intuition of the artist and the saint.

He ends the essay by stating that although the aesthetic sense is of the same kind as the religious spirit, they differ in extent. For beauty is ecstasy (*muga* again) of the moment whereas religion is eternal ecstasy. Then, almost as an afterthought, and indicating that his organization is somewhat faulty, he adds that morality, although it originates in the same realm as beauty and religion, still belongs to the sphere of discrimination (*sabetsukai*), for it is built on the idea of duty and that of the differentiation between the self and the other, and good and evil. Thus it does not yet reach the sublime realms of religion and art. The essay, then, begins by attempting to define beauty and ends by comparing the depth and scope of religion, art, and morality.

This brief study can also be seen as a very rough sketch of his mature, detailed work *Geijutsu to dōtoku* (*Art and Morality*) (1923) (III, 237-545), in which he presents a comprehensive treatment of the relationships between the realms of art and morality, covering, among other topics, the three possible pairs within the trinity of truth, goodness, and beauty (*shinzembi*). Inevitably there is also a section of the work entitled "Shinzembi no gōitsuten" (The Fusion Point of Truth, Goodness, and Beauty) (III, 350-91), which begins, significantly, with a lengthy quotation from Saint Francis of Assisi's "Hymn to the Sun." Here we have clear proof of the logical course of development from Nishida's ideas in "Bi no setsumei," for once again, almost a quarter of a century later, he sees religion, and the intuition and ecstatic rapture of the saint, as the ultimate state to which both art and morality tend.

Nishida's diary, which, as I have indicated, was resumed on January 1, 1901 after a hiatus of more than a year (that is, if the diary for 1900 has not been either suppressed or lost), further confirms continuation of this religious concern, scarcely diminished from the peak which, by Nishida's own admission,[39] it had attained during his stay in Yamaguchi. A sampling of some of the early entries (XII, 46-57) for the year 1901 tells us quite eloquently (much of the earlier terseness of the diary is gone, together with the German) of the extent to which he was driving himself in his spiritual life and also of his frequent setbacks and periods of aridity:

[39] See Kōsaka, p. 33.

January 6:[40] The purpose of Zen meditation is salvation. Apart from this there is nothing [of value]. I have much to reflect on within myself.

January 10: I have not meditated for some time; my heart somehow is disturbed.

January 15: When I read I frequently have feelings of impatience. Also I have desire for fame, and my heart is not at peace. I must reflect on this deeply.

February 1: My heart is tarnished and it never seems to have a fixed point; I truly feel that I have achieved nothing for all of my efforts of the past several years.

February 2: A new person arrived, whose specialty is philosophy, and I am concerned and unhappy about the number of my courses being reduced.

February 3: Troubled by yesterday's event I called on Hōjō Sensei. He was absent so I could not talk to him, but I meditated and I was deeply ashamed of myself for having so many selfish, petty thoughts. I also realized that this type of problem is not really of any importance.

February 7: One must not forget the source of peace in the pursuit of learning. Fukuzawa Sensei has died. He certainly maintained his independence. A great man must be like that.[41]

February 14: My will to dwell on the Way is slight, and I do not know how many times a day I have forgotten the Way because of trivial desires and fleshly lust. This too is primarily a result of my lacking will power.

February 19: I cannot but be ashamed at the weakness of my religious spirit.

March 17: I received the *gō* of Sunshin from Setsumon.[42]

March 25: Beneath the dim lamp the whole family ate

[40] For brevity I omit reference to the day of the week.

[41] Thus we see that Nishida's respect for Fukuzawa was maintained until the latter's death.

[42] Setsumon selected it from a poem by Tu Fu. See Kōsaka, p. 38. Nishida used this *gō* in all his literary works for the remainder of his life.

their meal with their trays lined up. For some reason I felt this to be sublime. Man's joy does not reside in having mansions and pleasing prospects but simply in the ordinary things and the commonplace.

April 26: These past several days I have been spiritually indolent and have done nothing.

An essay which Nishida wrote later during this year 1901 demonstrates his religious earnestness even more clearly. It is also a brief one, since he seems not to have wanted to write lengthy articles at this time; he was, by his own admission,[43] conserving his energies for the sustained effort of producing *Zen no kenkyū*. This essay, entitled "Genkon no shūkyō ni tsuite" (Concerning Present-day Religion), was published in the December 1901 issue of *Mujintō* (Vol. VI, No. 12) (XIV, 55-58). In it Nishida addresses the Japanese youth of his day, who were seeking new avenues in religion, which he felt to be in a state of stagnation at that time. He asserts that he desires a reform of both Buddhism and Christianity but goes on to say that he does not mean that *both religions themselves* (*Butsu-Ya ryōkyō sono mono*) (Nishida's italics) should be reformed; rather, he maintains that present-day men of religion (here he uses the word *shūkyōka* in its more common sense) should return to the true intent of both the Founders (*ryō-kyōso no shin-i*). He concludes this particular paragraph with a series of statements that prove conclusively how deeply he respected these two major religions. Rather surprisingly, he here shows even greater respect for Christianity. First he poses the rhetorical question: "How can we disparage Buddhism and Christianity, which were both built by the hands of unexampled saints" (here he uses the familiar term *seijin*) "and which have a history of several thousand years?" Then, while disclaiming any profound knowledge of the sacred scriptures of either religion, he exhorts his readers to look at the four gospels of the New Testament. He declares that the depth of Christ's

---

[43] *Waga chichi Nishida Kitarō*, pp. 53-54.

religious insight is such that today, after several millennia, we are still able to grasp only a small portion of His true spirit and that the more we ponder His every word the more profound this spirit seems. He asserts that never again shall we have a book such as the New Testament. His last sentence is in a sense a summation of some of his statements earlier in the essay to the effect that "religion is life" (*shūkyō wa seimei nari*) and not the "fabrication of scholars" (*gakusha no sakui*), for he now declares: "Why then do we need to follow blindly any shallow new religion of scholars?"

The next paragraph consists of a blistering attack on some of the professional purveyors of religion, those who make its propagation an occupation, and who, while having no personal religious experience themselves, cling to dead forms, emphasizing the letter rather than the spirit of the sacred texts. He particularly assails the Christian missionaries who place undue emphasis on the miracles of Christ, using them to prove His divinity. Here Nishida shows his affinity to the most profound Christian thinkers by declaring that Christ's divinity is amply proved in other, deeper senses and that there is nothing baser than appealing to people with this "bribe" (*wairo*) of miracles. He realizes that some may think, by his so arguing, that he opposes Christianity, but he maintains that actually its true significance does not lie in external forms and that Christ Himself, opposing the formalism of the Pharisees, reveals the true spirit of religion.

He ends this brief essay with an appeal to Christian missionaries to develop a pure heart and to merge with the mind of Christ rather than to concentrate on theology, and with an appeal to Buddhist priests to reflect deeply and to give of themselves sacrificially rather than to concentrate on Sanskrit or philosophy.

This essay is a somewhat curious one in that it is the most purely religious, and the least philosophical, of Nishida's entire work. It is, for example, the only one in which he makes detailed references to specific Christian and Buddhist doctrines or criticizes actual religious institutions. Moreover, in several ways this work can even be considered as an attack upon philosophy, or at least as a representation of the view that excessive philosophical speculation can be a hindrance to the attainment of religious insight. And yet of course this essay is, as I have already shown, an excellent indication of the extent of Nishida's earnestness in the spiritual life at that time (late 1901) and of his emphasis upon grasping the essence of religion beneath all of its external forms. Furthermore, we may also view it as the fruition of his religious concern, initiated some five years earlier.

To return to a consideration of his diary, we note that the religious mood, with much self-flagellation and self-exhortation, is maintained throughout 1901 and well into 1902. But from about March or April of the latter year, a very gradual tapering off of religious zeal is perceptible.[44] Perhaps the most reasonable explanation for this change is that Nishida was slowly resolving the basic spiritual problems which had first impelled him toward Zen meditation and discipline. In other words, his zeal was gradually replaced by a calmer, more serene mood, wherein he was able to apply the insights gained by Zen discipline to every area of his life.

I agree with Kōsaka,[45] therefore, that from about the end of the following year, 1903, we see this new mood manifesting itself even more clearly. Now that the sense of urgency concerning his own spiritual state has been largely removed, he comes to *reflect* upon religion more than to *participate* in it, and he begins seriously to consider the relationship between religion and philosophy. He extends much further the scope of his reading in Western philosophy in general and the philosophy of religion in particular.

We might perhaps consider that this broader, more comprehensive view of Nishida's manifests itself already with the last of the pre-*Zen no kenkyū* essays, "Jinshin no giwaku" (The

[44] Miyajima, p. 62, is justified in making this observation.
[45] Kōsaka, pp. 41-42.

Questions of the Human Heart) (xiv, 59-63), begun on May 16, 1903, and published shortly thereafter, in June, in the *Hokushinkai zasshi* (No. 35). Undoubtedly because this brief essay immediately precedes the organizing of his material for *Zen no kenkyū* it is the closest in mood to that work. For, rather than treating exclusively religious problems, in it he discourses freely on science, life, and society in general, dwelling particularly upon man's doubts, fears, and questionings in these areas. (Hence the title.) His style here shifts to the colloquial for the first time. From this change alone we may realize how very close this essay is to *Zen no kenkyū*, also written in the same colloquial style.

Nishida maintains in this work that, no matter how happily and unconcernedly man may lead his life, if he intends truly to grasp its essence, he must grapple with the deepest and greatest questions: where life comes from, where death leads to, why he is living, why he is working, and why he is dying. Unless man can cope with these questions which lie in the depths of his heart, he will never be able to obtain true peace. And yet after posing these difficult problems Nishida comes up with a surprisingly simple solution. For he states that neither research, nor great learning, nor talent is needed to solve them but, rather, a pure heart. He asks the reader to look at Peter, a simple Galilean fisherman. He concludes his presentation at this point, obviously referring to religious faith as the answer to the deepest questions of the human heart, although he does not treat religion directly in this essay.

Thus this work can be seen almost as a manifesto proclaiming that Nishida is thereafter going to treat, from a religious viewpoint, these basic philosophical—or, more precisely, metaphysical—problems.

We are now, in 1903, on the very threshold of the world of *Zen no kenkyū*. Nishida's apprenticeship is ended, and he now begins in earnest to fashion the work which will establish him as the "founder of modern Japanese philosophy." Quite obviously the many important events in his life, such as his encounter with the thought of William James, the death of his younger brother Hyōjirō in the Russo-Japanese War, and his deep empathy with the brilliant young mystic Tsunashima Ryōsen, during the three years before the first section of his famous work was actually published, deserve careful treatment to complete the portrait of the early Nishida, and I hope at some future date to make my own interpretation of them. Nevertheless the major outlines of that portrait are already clear by 1903. For we have seen how he changed from an ambitious, self-confident, extroverted youth at Shikō to a retiring, unhappy, and even bitter young man at Tokyo University, during his period of unemployment, and as a middle school teacher on the Noto Peninsula. Then, with the events of 1896-97 as the turning point, he plunged into Zen meditation and the religious life to effect a complete transformation of his personality and world-view. He changed from a student of philosophy to a philosopher, producing four short essays, in which he adumbrated several of the major themes not only of *Zen no kenkyū* but also of much of his later work. The last of the four, as we have just seen, foreshadows even more startlingly the major works that are to follow. The foundation is laid; he has but to rear the structure.

I hope that in presenting the background to his early years I have also demonstrated that Nishida's thought is not merely of historical interest but has considerable significance for the present day. Indeed I cannot but feel that thinkers of Nishida's stature and type are in extremely short supply, and the world would do well to pay them much greater attention.

CHAPTER XIV

Millenarian Aspects of the
New Religions in Japan

CARMEN BLACKER

IN CERTAIN conditions of rapid and bewildering change a society seems to produce a messiah. This powerful figure promises to lead the world out of its present state of wretchedness into the millennial joys of a new and perfect age. The renewed world is no mere improvement on the present. It implies a total break, a total discontinuity with the relative conditions we now endure. The new age will be one of complete and everlasting perfection, from which evil and fear have been entirely expunged.

Often the messiah seems to appear when the society feels itself impotent to cope with the situation in a rational, human manner. The conditions of change and disrupted tradition have somehow paralysed ordinary human initiative, so that the society resorts, not to rationally considered means of solving its stresses, but to irrational phantasy. To fulfill these expectations the messiah appears bringing his good news of an imminent earthly paradise.

We know from Norman Cohn's important book that the movements of "revolutionary chiliasm" in the middle ages appeared only when the traditional pattern of feudal agricultural life had begun to disintegrate. It was among the new population in the towns, living in conditions of chronic frustration and anxiety, cut adrift from their familiar mode of life and custom, that a charismatic figure would arise, proclaiming himself to be the saviour destined to lead the world into a new age in which history should find its consummation.

In medieval Europe these movements were facilitated by various ancient and powerful prophesies of which they claimed to be a fulfillment. The Book of Revelations and the Sibylline Oracles had both foretold that out of an immense cosmic catastrophe there would arise a new Eden, a paradise regained; that the Tyrant of the Last Days, the prodigious and demonic figure of Antichrist who had plunged the world into evil and horror, would at last be overthrown by the even more prodigious figure of the Saviour, destined to rise up in wrath, vanquish the tyrant and usher in the Kingdom of glory.[1]

Such movements do not however depend on a Jewish or Christian tradition of prophesy or on a medieval world view. During the past hundred years similar figures claiming messianic revelation have appeared in Europe, in Africa, in America, in Melanesia and Indonesia. So conspicuous indeed is the messianic character of these new movements that one authority has described it as "one of the most meaningful chapters of the modern history of religions." The conditions under which they have appeared, however, are always those of the rapid change, invalidated tradition and mass insecurity which gave rise to the chiliastic movements of the middle ages. It is societies whose traditional way of life has been disrupted by the intrusion of Western culture which have produced the most celebrated modern messiahs.[2] Among the North American Indians, for example, to whom the coming of the white man had meant pestilence, disinheritance and humiliation, a number of prophets appeared during the last half of the nineteenth century announcing the imminent advent of a terrestrial paradise. The whole Indian race, alive and dead, would be "reunited upon a regenerated earth, to live a life of aboriginal happiness, forever free from death, disease and misery."

[1] Norman Cohn, *The Pursuit of the Millennium* (1957), especially pp. 1-32 and 307-14. Also by the same author, "Medieval Millenarism: Its Bearing on the Comparative Study of Millenarian Movements," in *Millennial Dreams in Action*, ed. Sylvia Thrupp (The Hague, 1962).

[2] Vittorio Lanternari, *The Religions of the Oppressed: A Study of Modern Messianic Cults* (1963), especially Chap. 8. I must express my grateful thanks to Professor Lanternari for the valuable advice he has given me in the writing of this paper.

Wovoka, for example, the messiah of the Ghost Dance of 1890, was apprised of his mission by a revelation in which he was taken up to the other world. There he was told by God that he must go back and teach his people a dance which would hasten the coming of the spirit hosts, already advancing to the boundaries of the earth to usher in the great cataclysm. This apocalyptic event, variously described as a flood, a wall of fire or an avalanche, would engulf the white nations, leaving the Indians to enjoy the renewed world of perfect bliss.[3]

Among the natives of Melanesia, also oppressed and disinherited by the coming of the white man, a succession of saviours has appeared during the last hundred years, announcing that the time has come when the dead ancestors will return in ships laden with an inexhaustible store of food and wealth. The arrival of the "Cargo" ships will bring about a renewal of the world, in which the white man will be totally vanquished, the natives will become white, and will live forever in complete liberty with such an abundance of food and goods that all work will be unnecessary. In some of these Cargo cults we find an extreme form of eschatological expectation. The believers were commanded by their prophets to destroy all their tools, burn their stores, and abolish all traditional laws and sexual taboos, none of which would be needed in the new world which the arrival of the ships would inaugurate. The repeated disappointments which the natives have suffered from the non-appearance of the ships have not discouraged new and similar movements from constantly appearing in the area.[4]

[3] James Mooney, *The Ghost Dance Religion and the Sioux Outbreak of 1890*, 14th Annual Report of the Bureau of American Ethnology, 1892-93 (Washington, 1896), Chaps. 9 and 10. Mr. Mooney was a sympathetic observer from the Bureau of Ethnology who personally interviewed the Indian Messiah, and both witnessed and took part in the Ghost Dance among the Arapaho Indians.

[4] A recent disappointment was reported in the New York *Times* of August 24, 1966. "Members of the 'cargo cult' had predicted that the white man's world would end today (August 21st) and that all his cargo—cars, food, money and machinery—would shower on to

In Brazil since the latter part of the nineteenth-century messianic movements have appeared in a number of forms. Notable are those of the Sebastianic inspiration, in which the belief that King Sebastian would shortly return to destroy the wicked and establish the terrestrial paradise stimulated chiliastic excitement in many places. Other prophets claim to lead people to the Promised Land, where the miseries brought about by the impact of western culture will disappear and a life of eternal bliss and ease come into being. Among the Guarani people in particular the myth of the Land without Evil lying to the east has stimulated tragic mass migrations across thousands of miles of continent. Other prophets claim to be the reincarnation of Christ or of a popular thaumaturge come to announce the imminent end of the world and the regeneration of mankind.[5]

In the Congo too the prophet of the Kimbangu movement, who claimed to be a reincarnation of Moses and Christ, preached an imminent new Golden Age, in which the dead would return and the white man be destroyed. In China the inspiration behind the Taiping Rebellion of 1851 was the messianic doctrine of Christianity combined in an inflammatory way with certain Chinese ideas of an age of Great Peace, a golden age in the remote past to be recreated in the future.[6]

---

the natives of the Morobe district of New Guinea. Villagers and plantation workers quit their jobs and stopped tending their gardens to await the event."

See also Peter Worsley, *The Trumpet Shall Sound: a Study of the 'Cargo' Cults in Melanesia* (1957); Mircea Eliade, "Cosmic and Eschatological Renewal," Chap. 3 of *The Two and The One* (1962), first published in *Eranos Jahrbuch* 1960, "Dimensions religieuses du renouvellement cosmique"; F. E. Williams, "The Vailala Madness in Retrospect," in *Essays presented to C. G. Seligman* (1934); J. Graham Miller, "The Naked Cult in Central West Santo," *Journal of the Polynesian Society* (Dec., 1948).

[5] Lanternari, pp. 245-46. Rene Ribeiro, "Brazilian Messianic Movements," in *Millennial Dreams in Action*, pp. 55-69.

[6] E. G. Boardman, "Millenary Aspects of the Taiping Rebellion (1851-65)," in *Millennial Dreams in Action*, pp. 70-79.

These are merely a few examples of the more celebrated of the modern messianic movements which have arisen among peoples oppressed, disinherited and humiliated by the intrusion of a foreign culture. They have arisen as a specific solution to these miseries, a solution through myth to a problem which mere human enterprise seems powerless to remedy. The saviour appears in direct response to the yearnings of the people for their traditional way of life, transformed in imagination to an age of perfect bliss such as never at any previous time existed.

Such millenarian movements are not always, however, traceable to the unrest caused by the intrusion of a foreign culture. They can also be "endogenous," arising within a society as a result of baffling internal changes in the traditional way of life. Catastrophes such as famine, plague, or disintegration of an established order which has been taken for granted since the beginning of memory as part of the fixed order of nature—such conditions as these are apparently fertile ground for messianic or chiliastic expectations.

Are we justified in classifying the *shinkō shūkyō*, the new religions of Japan, among the millenarian movements of this kind? Let us first define our terms. What exactly is meant by the phrase *shinkō shūkyō*?

The description "newly arisen religions" usually indicates the new cults which arose in such remarkable profusion at the end of the last war. No sooner were the legal restrictions on religious liberty abolished by General MacArthur's "Shūkyō Hōjinrei" of 1945 than the number of "religious bodies" began to rise in a spectacular manner. In two years it leapt from 43 to 207, and continued to rise until by 1951 it had reached the extraordinary figure of 720. Of these groups, 258 were classified as Shinto; 260 were Buddhist, 46 were Christian while the remaining 156 were simply "unclassified." Among them were several groups which had made their appearance before the war and been suppressed, such as Ōmoto, Seichō-no-Ie and Hito-no-michi Kyōdan, resuscitated under the new name of PL Kyōdan. The great majority however were truly "newly arisen." Among this huge number several were too bizarre to deserve either serious attention or long life. The Denshinkyō, for example, founded by an electrician in Osaka, which worshipped electricity as its principal deity and Thomas Edison as one of its lesser deities, quickly petered out. So did Dai Nippon Fusō Shinjinkai which worshipped the late Dr. Frederick Starr of the University of Chicago. A good many other groups were quickly discovered to be entirely fraudulent, being no more than commercial enterprises exploiting the loose wording of the law of 1945 to masquerade as "religious bodies" in order to avoid paying taxes. After the law was revised in 1951 with the intention of weeding out such bogus concerns, the number of registered groups fell steeply, to reach by 1958 the comparatively modest figure of 171. The latest available figure, given by the *Shūkyō nenkan* of 1964, is 378—145 Shinto groups, 165 Buddhist, 39 Christian and 29 "others."[7]

[7] The "Shūkyō Hōjinrei" or "Religious Bodies Law" of 1945 had stipulated that a "religious body" could enjoy the privilege of exemption from taxation on the income from its "religious activities." But it failed to specify any conditions by which a "body" should call itself a religious one. A good many enterprises were not slow to take advantage of this loophole. Most notorious of these bogus cults was the Kōdōjikyō, which sheltered a number of smaller concerns under its wing, and whose activities were exposed in 1947. A subsequent investigation by the Mombushō revealed a shocking state of affairs. One registered "church" proved to be a hot-spring hotel which claimed as its "religious activity" the promotion of happiness in the lives of men and women. A hairdressing establishment claimed to be a religious body with the religious activity of making life more beautiful. Many diverse concerns—restaurants, old clothes shops—claimed to be religious bodies putting into practice the precept *seikatsu soku shūkyō* (life is religion). Such manifestly fraudulent groups were abolished by the new legislation, the "Shūkyō Hōjinhō" of 1951. See *Sengo shūkyō kaisōroku*, published by the Shinshūren Chōsashitsu (1961), pp. 170-73. This work is translated serially into English under the title of "Reminiscences of Religion in Postwar Japan" in *Contemporary Religions in Japan*, from Vol. vi, 2 (June, 1965) until Vol. vii, 3 (Sept., 1966).

It should be remembered that the figure of 378 as given in the

Such anomalous groups were given sufficient publicity, however, to bring for some time the whole new religious movement into disrepute. It was several years before the *shinkō shūkyō* were considered to be a fit or respectable subject for investigation by educated Japanese. By 1958 however it was obvious that several of the new groups were becoming spectacularly larger and richer every year, and manifestly fulfilling a need in the post-war world which the older religions were for some reason failing to meet. Their large membership, aggressive propaganda, huge cathedrals of startling modern architecture and reinforced concrete, were in marked contrast to the depleted registers and dilapidated structures of many temples of the older religions. The highly successful incursion into politics of Sōka Gakkai in 1959 was the signal for a number of studies of the *shinkō shūkyō*, in both Japanese and Western languages, which sought to survey and classify the new groups into comprehensible categories, and to place them intelligibly in some context of the history of Japanese religion.[8]

Properly speaking, however, the term *shinkō shūkyō* should not be confined to the strange outcrop of postwar cults alone. In the course of the last hundred years there have been two other specific periods when groups of very similar religious movements have emerged. The first of these occurred during the middle years of the last century, at the time when the feudal system was beginning to disintegrate and give way to the new centralised, industrialised society. During this period many new religious movements appeared, though the only ones to survive the restrictions imposed both by the Bakufu and by

---

Shūkyō nenkan of 1964 accounts only for those groups incorporated with the Mombushō. It does not include the substantial number of lesser groups incorporated on the prefectural level.

[8] See, for example, W. Schiffer, "New Religions in Postwar Japan," *Monumenta Nipponica*, xi (1955). C. B. Offner and H. van Straelen, *Modern Japanese Religions* (1963). Harry Thomsen, *The New Religions of Japan* (1963). For a very useful and more recent study see the last chapter of Professor J. Kitagawa's *Religion in Japanese History* (1966).

the Meiji government were the thirteen groups known subsequently and misleadingly as the thirteen "sects of Shinto." The second period of sudden religious growth was the 1920's, when Ōmoto and Hito-no-michi Kyōdan made great headway among the less educated classes, and the more prominent of the earlier groups, Tenrikyō and Konkōkyō, conspicuously increased their membership. There is every indication that many more such cults would have emerged at this time had it not been for the totalitarian restrictions on religious liberty, which savagely suppressed, on charges of lese majesty, the Ōmoto cult in 1935 and Hito-no-michi Kyōdan in 1937.[9]

The cults "newly arising" at all three periods during the last hundred years have been widely recognised to be a response to the "acute anomie" into which the Japanese people were thrown in the course of their rapid modernisation and by their eventual humiliating defeat.[10] To what extent, however, can they be properly classified among the "modern messianic movements"? If they are to fall into this category, as distinct from any other religious movement of a salvationist or consolatory kind, we should expect them to fulfill the following requirements.

First, they should appear at times when long accepted beliefs and customs are in some way threatened and invalidated. Sec-

[9] *The Japan Christian Yearbook* of 1937 reports (p. 77) that more than 200 new religious sects had come to the notice of the authorities in the past few years, but that such "superstitious mushroom cults" were already declining owing either to government pressure or to internal disorders (p. 89).

[10] See for example Hori Ichirō, "Penetration of Shamanic Elements into the History of Japanese Folk Religions," in *Festschrift for Adolf Jensen* (1965), p. 251. J. A. Dator in his "Sōka Gakkai, A Sociopolitical Interpretation," *Contemporary Religions in Japan*, Vol. vi, 3 (1965), p. 213, gives the following examples of Japanese who are likely to fall prey to anomie: persons who have moved from a tightly-knit rural community to a big city; middle-aged housewives whose children are grown up and whose husbands neglect them; students of the "wrong" universities; persons in marginal occupations; persons who, though intelligent, have limited formal education.

ond, they should arise at the inspiration of a charismatic figure claiming, if not personal divinity, at least unique divine revelation. And third, the revelations proclaimed by these figures should point the way out of the present state of chaos to a new paradisal age on this earth, wherein man's nature will be purged of all impulses which lead to misery and disorder, and his surroundings likewise resolve into total beneficence. We should also expect to find these movements in some way claiming to be the fulfillment of a myth or a prophesy deeply embedded in religious tradition.

All three periods in which the new cults made their appearance were, needless to say, ones of especially bewildering upheaval, insecurity and disrupted tradition. During the first period, stretching from the 1830's until the Meiji Restoration in 1868, famine and civil war culminated in the disintegration of the feudal system taken for granted by most people for two centuries as part of the immovable order of nature. The 1920's were a time of economic depression and increasingly oppressive totalitarian militarism. The years immediately after the war saw the collapse and disgrace of the system of State Shinto, which for a generation had sought to persuade the Japanese people that they were uniquely singled out for divine favours, and ineluctably destined to rule the world. This disgrace was succeeded by the catastrophe, unprecedented in Japanese history, of defeat and occupation by a foreign power.

That these conditions of widespread misery and loss of accepted values have had a powerful influence on the growth of the new cults is obvious to the most casual observer. Talks with believers from almost any of the groups will confirm that overwhelmingly the most potent motive for joining them was a desperate *personal* predicament of misery, anxiety and loss of direction. The group, one is told, came as a miraculous escape from the state known as *happō fusagari*, "all eight directions blocked." With strange monotony the believers eagerly recount how they were slowly wasting away with a mysterious and apparently incurable illness, which doctors were powerless to relieve. Or that they were desperately in need of money. Or that they were quarrelling fearfully and compulsively with their husbands or mothers-in-law. Or doing so badly at their work that they lived in daily fear of being dismissed.

And then, just as they had reached the point of hopeless despair, someone from down the road came along and told them about the new cult and the marvellous power it possessed of ending all one's troubles in a shower of miraculous mundane blessings. They decided, as a last resort, to "try" worshipping in the group, and lo, in a week the mysterious illness had quite disappeared. Or money came pouring in from a totally unexpected source. Or unprecedented harmony began suddenly to reign at home. Or the baby, which had been at death's door, suddenly recovered. A taxi driver in Tokyo once told me that a few years ago his wife had suddenly gone blind. Unable to face life after such a calamity, they had decided to commit suicide together. They had actually set out to go to the waterfall over which they intended to fling themselves when someone waylaid them and told them the good news of Sōka Gakkai. They had returned home, joined the local branch, and in a few days his wife had recovered her sight.

The discovery that the cult really seems to "work," to give in return for worship a rain of marvellous worldly blessings, came to them, they all affirmed, as a turning point in their lives. After this they were changed people. Life, which before had been meaningless drudgery, suddenly blossomed into joyful and invigorating purpose. An enormous and exhilarating access of self-confidence had come upon them, so that problems which hitherto seemed insurmountable simply melted away. They realised that they must have been singled out specially for supernatural favours, selected to take part in the momentous task which the cult proclaims for regenerating the world.

In this state of mind, which seems often to be a kind of ecstatic acceptance of the world as it stands, they can attribute every stroke of good fortune which comes to them to the miraculous power of their new faith, and every stroke of bad luck to a "warning" or "punishment" for lack of sufficient effort along the lines dictated by the cult.

Takagi Hiroo's interesting book shows us that although such dramatic conversions are not undergone by all members of the new cults, yet those who form the hard, devoted core have usually gone through such an experience. Without the initial anxiety and despair the good tidings would scarcely have been heard. Hence without the prevailing conditions of insecurity and misery it is doubtful whether the groups could have progressed at all.[11]

The psychological processes involved in this kind of conversion are undoubtedly facilitated by the peculiar personalities of the Founders and Foundresses round whom most of the cults revolve.

Here we come to the second of the features we distinguished as characteristic of the millenarian cult: the presence at the centre, as the original inspiration of the movement, of a charismatic figure claiming unique divine guidance to rescue the world from its present misery and usher in the millennial paradise.

The largest, richest and most successful of the *shinkō shūkyō* all trace their initial inspiration to a Founder, either male or female, to whom the message of the cult has been divinely revealed. Each one of these portentous figures of course claims a unique communication with the supernatural world, yet it is clear that in their personal histories and in the manner of their initiation they conform to a curiously persistent pattern which has its roots deep in the traditions of Japanese folk religion. Here we undoubtedly have a specific type of Japanese saviour or "messiah." Takagi Hiroo showed how remarkably uniform were the personal histories of the Founders up to the moment of their initiation.[12] Hori Ichirō in a recent interesting study has shown this persistent pattern in the lives of the Founders

[11] Takagi Hiroo, *Shinkō shūkyō*, 1958, pp. 64-73, 87-104. Also my "New Religious Cults in Japan," *Hibbert Journal* (July, 1962).

[12] Takagi, pp. 144-64.

and the manner of their initiation to be due to the surviving shamanic elements in Japanese religion.[13]

Almost without exception the Founders come from poor, low-class families, peasants or small shopkeepers. They are often sickly, eccentric, moody and introspective. They suffer unusually bitter tribulations in early life. The women are married to drunken husbands, or bullied unmercifully by tyrannical mothers-in-law. The men are sent away from home as apprentices or adopted sons, where they meet with similarly brutal treatment, varied by illness and worldly failure. As a kind of culmination of a series of scarcely endurable sufferings and anxieties, they have a violent initiation experience, coming usually in the form of possession by a god (*kamigakari*), who announces through their mouth that he has chosen them to be his instrument for regenerating the world.

Let us look at the biographies of a representative few of these Founders, and see how in each of the three periods of religious growth the same pattern tends to persist.

Nakayama Miki, the foundress of Tenrikyō, now the largest and richest of the "old" new religions, was born at the end of the eighteenth century in a village in Nara prefecture. Melancholy and introspective by nature, her early life was dogged by a series of personal misfortunes as well as by widespread social misery. Married at the age of thirteen to a man she disliked and bullied by her mother-in-law, she also lived through the famines of the 1830's and the disturbing phenomena of the *okage mairi*, when huge crowds of ecstatic pilgrims surged through her village on their way to Ise. Her response to these anxieties was to plunge herself even further into suffering. When a neighbour's small boy fell gravely ill while under her care, she petitioned the local deity to take the lives of two of her daughters as substitutes for the boy. In due course the boy recovered, and her two daughters died.

Her next tribulation came in 1837 when her son Shūji was suddenly afflicted with agonising pains in his legs. Doctors and

---

[13] Hori, pp. 251-57.

ointments were powerless to help, and it was not until they called in a *yamabushi* by the name of Ichibei to recite spells over the patient that he felt any relief. Thereafter for more than a year, whenever the mysterious pains came upon the boy, they would always call Ichibei, whose spells would bring infallible, if only temporary, relief. Ichibei's method of treatment was one traditionally practised in his order, known as *yosekaji* or *yorigitō*. In the presence of the patient's family and friends he would recite sutras and mantras designed to force the malevolent spirit causing the sickness to leave the patient and enter into a medium, through whose mouth it would announce its identity and its reason for molesting the patient. Ichibei for this purpose usually employed a professional *miko* from a neighbouring village. One night in September 1838 however the *miko* was unable to come, and Miki took her place as the medium.

As the spells began to get under way Miki's face suddenly changed and she fell into a violent state of trance. To the question as to what deity was possessing her she answered, "I am Ten-no-Shōgun." "What manner of god might Ten-no-Shōgun be?" they asked. "The true god and the original god who has descended from Heaven to save all mankind," the deity answered through Miki's mouth. It then demanded that Miki's body should be given over as a shrine for its own use. Miki's husband, much taken aback, replied that such a request was impossible to grant, since Miki was the mother of four children, the youngest only a few months old. The god thereupon threatened that if its orders were disobeyed it would blast the whole family with curses.

For three days after this exchange Miki is said to have been in an uninterrupted state of possession, sitting bolt upright transmitting the god's answers to questions without touching a drop of water or a grain of rice. Eventually her husband saw no alternative but to capitulate, and formally renounce to the god his responsibility for his wife. At once Miki returned to her normal state of consciousness.

Shortly afterwards she is said to have been wakened suddenly in the middle of the night by a loud thump on the ceiling and a feeling as though a great weight were pressing down on her. Then a small voice, apparently of supernatural origin, made itself heard. This was followed by several more until in all ten different *kami* had announced themselves. Some had names of familiar deities in the *Kojiki*. Some bore the names of animals, while others had names unknown and meaningless except for vaguely sexual associations.[14]

These strange and violent experiences were Miki's initiation into her role of divine vehicle, whereby her body was chosen by the god to be the instrument for transmitting his revelations to the suffering world. From that time she was frequently visited by further fits of possession, and her behaviour became increasingly eccentric. She began to give away to all and sundry, apparently in response to divine commands, all the family possessions and property. If restrained from such prodigal charity she would turn pale, fall into convulsions and refuse to eat until allowed to do as she wished. Her husband, convinced that she must be suffering from fox-possession, beat her, threatened her with a sword, and threw cold water over her, but all to no avail. Eventually she gave away the entire family substance, even to the extent of insisting, with the usual convulsions when thwarted, on the family house being pulled down. She is said to have sung with joy during this operation and to have entertained the workmen with wine and fish.

After some years of the complete destitution and virtual ostracism not unnaturally brought about by such unusual behaviour, she was discovered to possess miraculous healing powers, particularly in the granting of painless childbirth. Her fame spread throughout the district and believers began to flock round. When in 1863 their ranks were joined by one Izō

[14] Inui Tadashi, Oguchi Iichi and others, *Kyōso* (1955), pp. 20-30; Murakami Shigeyoshi, "Bakumatsu ishinki ni okeru minshū shūkyō no sōshō," in *Nihon shūkyōshi kōza*, II (1959), pp. 208-36; *Tenrikyo kōyō*, published by the Tenrikyo headquarters in 1932, pp. 44-73.

Iburi, who proved to be a devoted and entirely efficient and shrewd organiser, her cult began to make rapid headway. In 1869 she started to write the *Ofudesaki*, an enormously long poem in 1,711 verses, apparently divinely inspired and recorded largely in automatic writing. It took her fifteen years to complete. In 1872, again in response to a divine command, she is recorded as having accomplished a seventy-five-day fast without the smallest fatigue or discomfort.[15]

Persecuted by the authorities during the early years of Meiji, and imprisoned several times, Miki died finally in 1887 at the age of ninety. Her cult, with its body of teachings based on her copious revelations, had already a large following, although it was not until the year after her death that it was finally given official recognition, somewhat misleadingly under the title of a "Shinto Sect."

The life of the foundress of the Ōmoto sect followed a remarkably similar pattern. Deguchi Nao was likewise possessed by a god in middle age as the culmination of a series of miseries and calamities. Born in 1837 in the midst of famine and unrest, she was sent out to work at the age of eleven owing to the extreme poverty of her family. Six years later she was married unhappily to a drunken and spendthrift husband, to whom she eventually bore eleven children. Of these, three died in infancy, the eldest son disappeared after attempting suicide, and the second son was killed in the Sino-Japanese War. Her husband died in 1887 after lying for three years paralysed by a stroke, leaving her with her three youngest children to pick up a bare pittance by selling rags and working long hours in a silk mill. In 1890 one of her married daughters suddenly became insane with puerperal mania, and the following year the same fate overtook her eldest daughter. In that year there were apparently many cases of madness in the Ayabe district where the family lived.

A few days after this latest and culminating disaster, in January 1892, Nao had a vivid dream that she was wandering

[15] Inui *et al.*, pp. 31-54.

in the spirit world. A day or two later she fell suddenly into a violent state of trance. Her body almost torn apart with the strain she leapt up and down from a sitting position while loud roars like those of a wild beast burst from the pit of her stomach. In the course of this seizure the following dialogue is said to have taken place between her own voice and the terrible "stomach" voice of the deity inside her.

"I am Ushitora no Konjin."

"You cannot be. You only say such things in order to deceive me."

"I am not a fox or a badger. I am the god come to rebuild and renew the world and make it into the Three Thousand World. The Three Thousand World, the world of Ushitora no Konjin, will open up like a plum blossom in spring. Now that I have appeared I will roll the Three Thousand World into one, and make a divine world which will last for all eternity."

The god's message was in effect that the present hideous condition of the world had been brought about by evil deities. Now that Konjin had made his appearance in Nao's body, these would eventually be vanquished and a new and golden age be brought into being.

After this first initiatory possession she often during the next year or so fell into similar states of violent trance, wandering round the town roaring at the top of her voice. Eventually she was arrested on suspicion of arson, and confined to a room in her house for forty days. During this period she became quieter, and began to scratch with a nail on the pillars of the room rough *hiragana* characters. These words were the beginning of the immense *Ofudesaki*, the transmission of her revelations in automatic writing which continued for the next twenty-seven years of her life and which eventually ran to more than 10,000 fascicules.

On being released from her confinement she was discovered to possess powers of healing. Sick people for whom she prayed seemed to recover. Inevitably, therefore, believers began to flock round her, soon in such numbers as to cause resentment to the authorities of Konkōkyō, of which up till then she had professed herself a believer.[16]

In 1898 her life was transformed by her meeting with the man who later became the "co-founder" of Ōmoto, Deguchi Ōnisaburō, at that time known as Ueda Kisaburō. In his biography too we can find an example of the pattern which seems so persistent in the lives of these Japanese saviours. He was a sickly child, haunted by visions of ghosts. At the age of twenty-eight, in 1898, he suddenly disappeared, to return after a week in an exhausted condition announcing that at the behest of a divine messenger he had climbed up Mt. Takakuma for a period of fasting and ascetic exercises. There his soul had left his body and journeyed into spiritual realms, where he had been apprised of his mission to save the world. He was granted certain occult powers, such as clairvoyance and clairaudience, with which he had seen back into the past as far as the creation of the universe, and into the future as far as the ultimate destiny of mankind. He subsequently wrote a long account of his experiences during this initiatory period under the title of *Reikai monogatari*. He learned too from an ascetic of the Inari cult that the deity which had elected him during his initiatory experience in the mountains was one by the name of Komatsubayashi-no-Mikoto.

Shortly afterwards he happened to hear of Nao and see some of her inspired writings. These he declared to be completely in accordance with the revelations he had himself received on Mt. Takakuma. He thereupon visited her, and was eventually adopted into her family as the husband of one of her daughters. The Ōmoto cult, which came into such prominence during the 1920's and was forcibly dissolved in 1935 on charges of lese majesty against the national polity, was brought into being by the combined efforts of Nao and this remarkable personality.[17]

[16] Inui *et al.*, pp. 60-69; Hori, p. 256.
[17] Inui *et al.*, pp. 70-77. It may be remarked that the period of the first upsurge of new cults, roughly 1830-70, was in fact no more turbulent for the ordinary peasant in Japan, not actively engaged in the

The same pattern can again be traced in the lives of the founders of post-war cults. Let us take two representative examples.

Okada Mokichi, the founder of the now flourishing sect of Sekai Meshiakyō, or "World Messianity" was born in 1882 of poor parents who made a precarious living from a wayside stall. As a young man he was shy, diffident and introspective. He seems to have endured an almost incredible number and variety of illnesses. Among other maladies he suffered from eye trouble, pleurisy, tuberculosis, cerebral anemia, typhoid fever, intestinal disorders, heart disease, rheumatism and nervous collapse. No doctor was able to help him. Every enterprise to which he put his hand failed, until the great earthquake of 1923 reduced him to complete penury. His initiation came in 1926, when for some three months he was almost continuously possessed by the Bodhisattva Kannon, who announced that she had chosen his body to be the vehicle by which all men might be saved and a new age brought about in which all sickness should disappear. He wrote, under divine inspiration, a long account of the origins of Japan in remote antiquity and of the nation's destiny in the future after the new paradisal age had arrived. He was also granted the gift of a new method of healing. This dispensation accounts for the special emphasis on

---

momentous political events of the Bakumatsu and early Meiji periods, than the preceding fifty years. The 1770's and 1780's saw disasters very similar to the famines and rebellions which so disturbed the lives of the early Foundresses. Why then did no messiahs emerge? Some may well have done so, but failed to achieve more than a local and limited following owing to the lack of modern methods of communication. We know, for example, that a number of *kō*, or local religious societies, were organized by ascetics or *gyōja* at this period, notably the Ontake-kō and Fuji-kō. These *kō* bear a number of interesting resemblances to the later *shinkō shūkyō*, but they show no trace whatsoever of messianism. The faithful sought little more from their religious exercises than *gensei riyaku*, local and temporary blessings, accruing here and now.

healing in the cult which subsequently grew up round him and which now boasts a membership of 591,000.[18]

Lastly let us look at the dramatic example of Kitamura Sayo, the foundress of Tenshō Kōtai Jingukyō, more popularly known as the Dancing Religion. Ōgamisama, as everyone now calls her, was married to a weak and colourless man, whose mother was reputed to be the greediest and stingiest woman in the district. She was in the habit of finding a bride for her son just before the busy farming season in spring, using the girl unmercifully as unpaid labour, only to divorce her as soon as the busy season was over. A few months later, when the autumn harvest time approached, she would find another bride for her son, and divorce her once the harvest was safely in. Ōgamisama was the sixth bride to be chosen in this way in the space of three years. She rarely had enough to eat, and was reduced sometimes to eating tangerine peel and rotten pumpkins. Scarcely ever did she have more than three hours sleep a night. When the time for her confinement approached, her mother-in-law was too stingy to pay for a midwife, and refused to give any help herself on the score that she had a cold. Ōgamisama therefore had to give birth to the baby entirely unaided.

A crisis of conscience about her own unworthiness caused her to start various ascetic religious practices, which she continued for a couple of years until in 1944 she became suddenly aware that there was another "being" inside her body which conversed with her and ordered her about. It explained many things to her, of the past and the future and of her previous lives. It also gave correct weather forecasts and lessons in laundering and cooking, together with useful advice on diet and vitamins. Its advice was always good, but if for any reason Ōgamisama were to disobey its commands she was immediately racked with agonising pains. She soon found that she only had to open her mouth for sermons and songs to pour forth

[18] Inui *et al.*, pp. 182-91.

from the being inside her. As she became increasingly governed by its will her character underwent a notable change. Her former modesty and politeness gave way to her celebrated coarseness of speech, in which she would frequently abuse her audience, irrespective of their social standing, as maggot beggars and traitors. The deity inside her announced itself, shortly after the end of the war, to be Tenshō Kōtai Jingū, who had chosen Ōgamisama's body to be the vehicle for the salvation of the world.

So rough and unconventional was apt to be the language of this deity that for all her public appearances and particularly for her sermons, Ōgamisama would always wear a man's suit. It would look incongruous, she once told me, for such language to come from someone in female attire.

Her followers, who now number more than 223,000, worship her as the true messiah, the successor of the Buddha and Jesus. Her divinity, they claim, has been abundantly proved by countless miracles. She has cured sickness, raised people from the dead, diverted the course of storms and arrested the spread of fires. At her headquarters at Tabuse in Yamaguchi Prefecture, which now boasts a gigantic concrete temple designed by Tange Kenzō, she delivered sermons several times a day until the day of her death. Her discourse was frequently punctuated by bursts of extempore song, which her followers, who listened with closed eyes and clasped hands, recognised to be the words of the deity inside her. She taught her followers to perform a dance, known as Muga-no-mai, or the Selfless Dance. The believers glide to and fro with closed eyes, their faces wearing expressions like those of ecstatic sleep walkers. In 1964 she accomplished a world missionary tour of the most taxing nature, visiting something approaching thirty-six countries and giving sermons unfailingly three times a day.[19]

From these examples we may infer that the messiah or

---

[19] Personal communications from Ōgamisama, 1959 and 1961. Also *The Prophet of Tabuse*, published by Tenshō Kōtai Jingūkyō (1954), passim but especially pp. 13-47.

saviour, the bringer of good tidings in Japan, tends to conform to a specific and recognised type. Hori Ichirō has shown that the most marked features of this type can legitimately be described as shamanic. The weak, introspective or eccentric personality of the founder before his initiation is common also among the people of Central Asia who spontaneously become shamans. The possession or election by a personal deity is another feature which the founders have in common with the Siberian shaman. We may note in this connection that the deities which possess the founders are rarely celebrated members of the Shinto or Buddhist pantheon. More often they are virtually unknown, or at least of only minor and local importance. Professor Hori also notes as a shamanic feature the manner in which the founder's personality tends to alter after his initiatory possession. Supernormal powers of various kinds are granted to him, so that his former weakness, diffidence and love of solitude give way to a courageous and often aggressive missionary spirit.[20]

Other examples of successful and flourishing *shinkō shūkyō* which made their beginnings through the shamanic experiences of a founder include Konkōkyō, whose founder, a poor peasant by the name of Kawate Bunjirō, was possessed and elected in 1857 by the deity Konjin. The Reiyūkai, a powerful offshoot of the Nichiren sect of Buddhism, was likewise founded by a poor peasant woman, Kotani Kimi, who was possessed by spirits. The Risshō Kōseikai, another extraordinarily rich and flourishing offshoot of the Nichiren sect with a gigantic pink cathedral on the outskirts of Tokyo, had its beginnings in the possession of another poor peasant woman, Naganuma Myōkō, by various Buddhist deities.[21]

Certainly there are several highly successful cults which do not owe their inception to the shamanic possession of their

[20] Hori, p. 257.
[21] Takagi, pp. 146-47; Hori, p. 254; Oguchi Iichi and Murakami Shigeyoshi, "Minshū shūkyō no ruikei," in *Nihon shūkyōshi kōza*, III, pp. 221-30.

founder. The founder of Sōka Gakkai, for example, a school-teacher named Makiguchi, arrived at the theology which became the basis of his sect without any such dramatic and character-changing experience. Nor did the revelations of the true meaning of the Lotus Sutra, which are now the basis of the flourishing sect of Kōdō Kyōdan on a hill in Yokohama, come to "Bishop" Okano by divine possession. Nor were the revelations of the "true meaning of life," which subsequently formed the basis of the healing sect of Seichō-no-Ie, directly transmitted to Taniguchi Masaharu by a personal deity.

Yet the pattern is sufficiently persistent to warrant our distinguishing a specific type of Japanese "saviour," wherein "there still survive some of the fundamental elements of genuine arctic shamanism." This becomes the more intelligible when we remember that shamanic cults were undoubtedly widespread in Japan in ancient times, and have survived ever since as part of the little tradition of unwritten folk religion.

Let us now turn to our third characteristic of the messianic sect, the revelation proclaimed by the messiah of the imminent coming of the millennial paradise on earth. Can we find any such message in the teaching of the founders?

With almost every successful and growing "new religion" the core of the founder's teaching is the same: if people will conform in absolute faith with the few and simple rules of the cult, the present brutal age can be vanquished and a new age of unprecedented bliss, peace and harmony inaugurated.

One of the central revelations of Nakayama Miki, the foundress of Tenrikyō, was that at some fairly imminent moment a heavenly dew (*kanro*) would descend from the sky and inaugurate a new divine era of perfect bliss (*yōkigurashi*). The present age of misery and strife will disappear and the world at that moment will be born anew, all those who partake of the dew living in effortless and perfect wisdom and virtue for 115 years. The place where in 1875 the foundress experienced this revelation is in fact the spot where the heavenly dew is first expected to fall. It is known as the *jiba* and is marked by a hexagonal pillar known as the *kanrodai*, on top of which is a shallow dish to catch the dew as it falls through a hole in the temple roof immediately above it.

As for the moment when the millennial age can be expected to dawn, this will depend on the efforts men make at present towards changing and purifying their lives on the lines dictated by the cult. The more diligently we all rid our minds of the "eight dusts," as indicated by the foundress in her revelations, the sooner the divine dew will fall and we shall enter the new age.[22]

In the revelations committed to writing by Deguchi Nao, the foundress of Ōmoto, a similarly millenarian note is prominent. The present age is a brutal one of beasts and devils, a *kemono no yo*. But very soon it will end in cataclysms and prodigies of nature and we shall build out of the ruins a divine age, the Three Thousand World, which will endure for all eternity in peace and bliss.

Indeed, the cult went so far as to prophesy that the year 1922 would mark the end of the world as we know it, with a cataclysm in which all should perish save those who took refuge at the cult headquarters at Ayabe. It was this millenarian eschatology which apparently earned the particular disapproval of the authorities of State Shinto—the cult had intimated that the Emperor could, if he wished, take refuge at Ayabe when the destruction occurred in 1922—and later led to the ruthless suppression of the cult.[23]

The millenarian quality of many of the postwar sects is equally marked. Jikōson, for example, the foundress of Jiukyō and the first female *kyōso* to attract public attention in 1947,

[22] *Tenrikyō kōyō*, pp. 208-11. Offner and Van Straelen, pp. 52-53. The "eight dusts" described on pp. 191-94 of *Tenrikyō kōyō* are: *hoshii*, wanting something for nothing; *oshii*, sluggish carelessness; *kawaii*, absorption in oneself and one's family; *nikui*, selfish hate; *urami*, vengeful spite; *haradachi*, bad temper when thwarted; *yoku*, greed; *kōman*, pride.

[23] Saki Akio, *Shinkō shūkyō* (1960), pp. 186-87.

was the mouthpiece for a divine announcement that the present abject condition of Japan would soon end in convulsions of nature, and that out of the ruins a new divine land, replete with bliss and peace, would come into being.[24]

The postwar cult in which the expectation of an imminent paradise on earth is perhaps most insistently stressed is Sekai Meshiakyō, "World Messianity," whose founder, Okada Mokichi, we have seen to number among those divinely possessed and elected. The core of the founder's message is that the time is at last at hand when the divine plan for the creation of a paradise on earth (*chijō tengoku*) can be fulfilled. It is therefore the inestimable privilege of mankind today that we can take part in this momentous revolution. The "motto" of the sect is said to be "Construction of a Paradise on Earth, filled with Truth, Virtue and Beauty." This immense task may be accomplished by eradicating the three great misfortunes— sickness, poverty and strife—which have always plagued men because they have flouted God's original prescription for a harmonious world.

Before the new age can dawn, however, a prodigious cataclysm is to be expected, a final *dies irae* in which disease, famine and war, together with the elemental catastrophes of water, wind and fire will consume all but those who have sufficiently striven to purify themselves through the teachings of the cult.

The sect prepares its faithful for the coming holocaust by giving them amulets, believed to be repositories of divine light and capable of accomplishing miracles of healing. The members are therefore conscious that with divine power working

---

[24] Jikōson proclaimed herself to be an incarnation of Amaterasu, and the present miseries of Japan to be a divine punishment fallen on those who had forgotten this deity. Her cult received wide publicity for a short time, partly because the champion *sumō* wrestler Futabayama and the champion chess player Gō Seigen both became believers. It was finally accused of violating the ordinance forbidding the possession of swords and soon sank into obscurity. *Sengo shūkyō kaisōroku,* pp. 51-53.

through them they are serving humanity in the most momentous manner possible. They realise that in order to qualify for
the new ideal world they must take steps to "pass God's examination," to acquire the three marks of a world free of disease,
poverty and strife, namely health, wealth and love of peace.
The only way properly to acquire these qualities is to join the
cult, where we will be purified in such a way as to gain health,
sufficient wealth and a loathing of strife.[25]

Sekai Meshiakyō has even constructed two prevenient "models" of paradise—a large and sumptuous hall of startling modern architecture on a hill above Atami, and a tastefully laid out
garden near Hakone. These are "patterns," small models of
perfection which in time will radiate outwards until the whole
world is encompassed. The faithful apparently believe that
these places are truly abodes of bliss where all human problems
can be comfortably suspended. We can perhaps regard them
as modern instances of the tendency in Japanese folk religion
to impose on the present world a kind of mythical or eschatological geography; to see in certain geographically accessible
places such as mountains or sulphur springs, such realms as the
abode of the dead, heaven, hell or the dry river bed where dead
children are believed to make their piles of stones.

We may note here the tendency of many of the *shinkō
shūkyō* to visualise the millennial age as making its beginning
in one particular spot of intense sacredness, conceived to be the
centre of the earth, the axis mundi, or the birthplace of the
human race. The Paradise of Sekai Meshiakyō at Atami is
believed to be the centre of the earth, and at the same time the
microcosm of perfection later to be universalised. The spot
known as *jiba* where Nakayama Miki had her revelation about
the millennial dew, is invested for the faithful of Tenrikyō
with great eschatological significance. It is both the beginning
and the culmination of the world; both the birthplace of man-

---

[25] Information taken from two pamphlets issued by the Sekai
Meshiakyō headquarters: "Tengoku no ishizue" (1959) and "World
Messianity and what it means," in English, anonymous and undated.

kind and at the same time the spot where the divine dew will first descend to herald the millennium. The headquarters of the Ōmoto sect at Ayabe, razed to the ground by the authorities of State Shinto in 1935, was again considered to be the centre of the earth, the only spot to escape destruction when *solvet saeclum in favilla.*

Let us look finally at the millenarian tendencies of Sōka Gakkai. We have already noticed that the founder of this celebrated cult, Makiguchi Tsunesaburō, did not number among those directly inspired by a deity. Nevertheless the whole character of this militant sect is strongly millenarian. It looks forward to a new era, a spiritual revolution of the world, by applying to the present age all the prophesies delivered by Nichiren in the thirteenth century.

Nichiren had based most of his teachings on the conviction that Japan in his day had entered the depraved age of *mappō*, the Latter Days of the Law, long predicted in Buddhist doctrine when the Buddha's law would begin to lose its force. The strife, misery and natural calamities which were so abundant in the early thirteenth century Nichiren took to be evidence that the Latter Days were come upon the land. At the beginning of his *Risshō ankokuron* he describes the unmistakable stigmata of a degenerate age. Strange prodigies, famine and sickness convulsed the land. Horses and cattle died in the streets, skeletons filled the roads. The world had turned from good to evil so that the benevolent deities fled and devils approached. Why should this be? Because the people had reviled the true Law and turned to false and evil ways of worship, reciting *nembutsu*, reciting mantras for long life, sitting alone in vacant meditation. The whole root and cause of misery and degradation lay in following false creeds. Likewise the only hope of salvation and peace was to follow the right religion, the creed proclaimed by Nichiren himself.[26]

[26] "Risshō ankokuron," in *Nichiren Shōnin bunshū*, Yūhōdō edition, p. 89. Also Takase Hiroi, *Daisan bummei no shūkyō* (1962), pp. 253-56.

All these warnings have been taken by Sōka Gakkai to apply just as much to the present age as to the time of Nichiren. All the horrors which made the land wretched in Nichiren's day are repeated today, with an extra one which Nichiren did not have to endure—defeat and invasion by a foreign foe: the very *bōkoku*, national ruin, which Nichiren predicted would be the result of following wrong faiths. All these miseries can thus be attributed to *butsubatsu*, a divine punishment to the people for their intransigeance.[27]

It is now seven hundred years since Nichiren died, but ever since that time the followers of the true religion have had engraved on their hearts the words: "Wait for the right time." And now, at last, there is abundant proof that the time is at hand, when right beliefs will spread throughout the world and inaugurate an age of perfect peace and joy. This new age was described by Nichiren in his essay *Nyosetsu shugyōshō* in apocalyptic terms. "The wonderful Law will spread throughout all the peoples of the world, and all will with one voice chant Namu Myōhō Rengekyō. Behold how the world will enter the golden age of the Sages. Disasters and calamities will cease, and the principles of perpetual youth and everlasting life will be revealed to men. Here are the signs of *gensei annon*—peace and joy on this earth."[28]

Before this joyful age can be inaugurated however it is necessary that the *sandai hihō*, or three great secret rites, be completely disseminated throughout the world. These three things are the *daimoku*, or sacred formula *Namu Myōhō Rengekyō*, Hail to the Lotus of the Wonderful Law; the mandala, a perpendicular strip of paper inscribed in the year 1279 in Nichiren's distinctive spidery characters with the mystic formula; and lastly the *kaidan*, or ordination platform. When all three

---

[27] *Shakubuku kyōten*, compiled by Toda Jōsei and published by Sōka Gakkai (1958), pp. 235-40.

[28] *Shakubuku kyōten*, p. 243. "Nyosetsu shugyōshō" is in *Nichiren Shōnin bunshū*, p. 333.

are accepted and worshipped by all mankind we can expect the millennial age to dawn.[29]

Meanwhile, however, it is the manifest duty of all members of the sect to labour unceasingly to bring this moment nearer. To labour, as *kokushi* or knights fighting for their country, to eradicate the false creeds which are the direct cause of calamity, misery and humiliation, and to propagate the true religion which alone can usher in the millennial joys. Here, therefore, is the ultimate motive behind the *shakubuku*, the militant and alarmingly effective propaganda by which the sect has made itself so notorious.[30] Every new convert, whether drawn into the fold by fear and threats of divine punishment, or by the genuine fervour for promoting the new age, brings the longed-for millennium a step nearer. Here too can be discerned the reasons behind the sect's incursion into politics. The Kōmeitō has so far announced only a vague, innocuous and uncontroversial political platform. Peace, clean politics, more education and social security, preservation of the Constitution, opposition to the manufacture of nuclear weapons—such principles argue little that is more inflammatory than sound and decent common sense. There is little doubt, however, that behind these uncontroversial protestations, behind the militantly efficient electoral organisation, behind the unscrupulous disregard of means in the employment of propaganda, lies the teleological pull of the expected millennium.

Finally we must ask whether in the Japanese religious tradition there can be found any myth or prophesy of which these new cults could claim to be the fulfilment. Is there any thing comparable, if not with the prophesies of the Book of Revelations, at least with the common myth of the hero, ancestor or supreme being who promises to return to regenerate his country in time of need?

[29] *Shakubuku kyōten*, p. 236.
[30] Takase, pp. 256-59. See also Noah Brannen, "False Religions, Forced Conversions, Iconoclasm," in *Contemporary Religions in Japan*, Vol. v, 3 (1964).

Such myths exist in both the great and little traditions of Japanese religion, but never before modern times do they seem to have become dynamic social forces.

In Mahayana Buddhism, the doctrine of the "future Buddha," the Bodhisattva Maitreya, reached Japan before the eighth century A.D. Maitreya, or Miroku, is stated in the *Mirokugeshōkyō* and other Mahayana sutras to be at present residing in the Tushita heaven. After the unimaginably long period of 5,670,000,000 years he will reappear on this earth and preach three times. After his first sermon 9,600,000,000 people will be immediately and fully enlightened. After his second sermon 9,400,000,000 will be similarly illumined, and after his third 9,300,000,000 will join the ranks of the Arhats. Thereafter the whole world, now fully emancipated from delusion and passion, will enter into the perfect and paradisal age known in Japanese as *Miroku no yo*.

The cult of Miroku never seems to have been a widespread or popular one before modern times. Perhaps the enormous length of time which must elapse before the expectation of the millennial age could be fulfilled was too daunting to have inspired excitement or enthusiasm. Miroku was never so beloved a Bodhisattva as Kannon or Jizō, and the fact that his cult was so quickly superseded in medieval times by Amidism, with its promise of a pure and spotless paradise in the *next* world rather than in this, indicates that it never stimulated millenarian yearnings to any notable extent. Indeed, the only evidence of the effect of the cult of Miroku on popular religious behaviour is of practices strange and marginal. The odd custom of "burying sutras" in Heian times has been connected with the Miroku cult. The inspiration which prompted those men in the seventeenth and eighteenth centuries to undertake the appalling austerities of self-mummification was apparently the conviction that by this means they could escape death and enter the state of suspended animation known as *nyūjō*. In this condition, purified of defilements, they could await the advent of Miroku on earth in the remote future.[31]

It is significant however that whereas in ordinary times the coming of Miroku was relegated to this inconceivably remote point in the future, in times of special calamity and misery he was urgently expected to descend at once. In his compassion he would postpone his arrival no longer, but descend to redeem so chaotic a world forthwith. In a year of particular calamity, for example, the name of the *nengō* or year period was sometimes unofficially changed to Miroku. After the widespread destruction and misery caused by the Ōnin war, for example, faith in the imminent coming of Miroku suddenly flared up, and unofficial *nengō* called Miroku were found in many places in eastern Japan. 1335 and 1507 were other examples of "Miroku years." In times of unrest too "Miroku songs and dances" were performed in certain districts as late as the 1850's. The words of the Miroku songs were largely talismanic invocations for a reign of plenty. Miroku was expected to arrive in a ship laden with goodly bounty. "The world has reached the end of the kalpa, the end of an age. Miroku's ship has arrived."[32]

A probable connection is relevant between Miroku's boat and the ancient belief in *marebito*, the mysterious visitors from the Other World across the sea who arrive at New Year to fertilise the rice seed and bless the home. To ensure, in short, a renewal of the world in the coming spring. Orikuchi Shinobu links this belief in *marebito* with the southern stream of culture which made its way to Japan in prehistoric times.[33] In the vision of Miroku's ship, therefore, arriving laden with an inexhaustible store of goods and wealth to bring about a

[31] Tsuruoka Shizuo, "Nihon ni okeru Miroku geshō shinkō," in *Shūkyō kenkyū*, No. 144. Also Andō Kōsei, *Nihon no miira*, pp. 1-20.

[32] Yanagita Kunio, "Miroku no fune" in "Kaijō no michi," *Teihon Yanagita Kunio shū*, I, 73-84. Also C. Ouwehand, *Namazu-e and their Themes* (1964), pp. 101-106.

[33] Orikuchi Shinobu, "Tokoyo oyobi marebito," *Minzoku*, Vol. IV, 2, 1-62.

renewal of the world, we may possibly see a dim reflection of the Cargo ships of the returning dead arriving on the shores of the Melanesian islands with wealth enough to ensure an everlasting life of ease and bliss.

There is no evidence, however, of the cult of Miroku stimulating chiliastic excitement in Japan on a scale in any way comparable with the rebellions which took place in China in expectation of the imminent arrival of the Future Buddha. The vision of Miroku's boat does not seem to have inspired any of the numerous peasant revolts which during the last century of Tokugawa rule attested to the growing misery of the peasantry.[34] Only in 1867 on the eve of the Restoration, when already the new cults we are considering had begun to make their appearances, there occurred the strange commotion round Kyoto and Osaka known as the *Ejanaika sōdō*. Supernatural portents were manifested. Divine beings, including Miroku, were seen to fall from the sky into people's houses in a variety of strange forms. People dressed themselves in transvestite clothes and rushed to temples and shrines crying "*Yonaoshi da. Ee ja nai ka.*" It is now thought that this strange and sudden disturbance was due, not, as has been suggested to the instigations of fanatical loyalist samurai, but to a spontaneous reaction to oppression and anxiety in hopes that the promised age had at last arrived.[35]

---

[34] Maitreya rebellions occurred in China during the T'ang, Sung and Yüan periods. Indeed the Future Buddha has figured throughout Chinese history as one of the major "rebel ideologies." See Vincent Shih, "Some Chinese Rebel Ideologies," *T'oung Pao*, XLIV (1956), 188-89; Yuji Muramatsu, "Some Themes in Chinese Rebel Ideologies," in *The Confucian Persuasion*, ed. Arthur F. Wright (1960), pp. 245-47.

[35] Wakamori Tarō, "Kinsei Miroku shinkō no ichimen," in *Shichō*, No. 18 (March, 1953). Hori Ichirō interprets the *Ejanaika sōdō* as one of the "pseudo-messianic dancing orgies" which he sees as occurring during the course of Japanese history in times of crisis. See his "Nihon no minzoku shūkyō ni arawareta futsujō girei to shūdanteki orugii ni tsuite," *Bunka*, Vol. XXX, 1 (June 1967). An interesting longer analysis of the phenomenon is given in Fujitani Toshio's *Okagemairi to Ejanaika* (1968).

Another figure from the folk religion in Japan which conforms to the saviour and regenerator is the *yonaoshigami*, the god who renews the world. The *yonaoshi* is one who out of the ruins of an appalling catastrophe will transform the world anew into a paradise; one who reverses the existing order, causing the mighty to fall and the lowly to rise. A hero or saint who rescues the populace from starvation, from plague, from penury, is often apotheosised after his death as a *yonaoshigami*. A curious example is to be found in Sano Zenzaemon, who assassinated Tanuma Okitomo in 1784. The day after the assassination of Tanuma the price of rice, for some time almost at famine level, fell sharply. Sano was accordingly after his execution worshipped as a *yonaoshigami*, a deliverer from starvation, a restorer of prosperity.[36]

Evidence that a sudden frightful calamity will rouse expectations of the advent of a *yonaoshi* is to be found in Dr. Ouwehand's interesting book on "catfish prints." The terrible earthquake of 1855, which devastated large areas of Edo, was quickly followed by a flood of the anonymous colour prints known as *namazu-e*, catfish prints, the symbols of which revealed unmistakable expectations that out of the ruins would rise a renewed world. The very image of the catfish, believed to be the prime cause of earthquakes, was represented in some of the prints closely associated with various symbols which identified it unequivocally with the *yonaoshigami*. The catfish was thus both destroyer and saviour; one who both convulses the world and who out of the ruins will bring about a new age, a reversal of the existing order.[37]

Other mythical and philosophical doctrines which in China produced millenarian disturbances seem to have roused no such enthusiasm in Japan before modern times. The doctrine of the T'ai P'ing or Great Peace, envisaged by both Taoists and

[36] Miyata Noboru, "Ikigami shinkō no hatsugen," in *Nihon minzokugaku kaihō*, No. 28 (May, 1963).
[37] Ouwehand, pp. 79-83.

Confucianists as a state of ideal harmony which existed in the primordial antiquity of the Sages and was also potentially realisable in the future, was the inspiration, together with eschatological borrowings from Christianity, behind the Taiping Rebellion of 1851. The armies of the prophet Hung Hsiuchüan devastated south and central China from Kwangsi almost to Peking. In Japan there is no evidence that either the messianic teachings of Christianity or the doctrine of the T'ai P'ing ever fermented religious movements, let alone active disturbances.[38]

Such traditions, though potentially productive of millenarian enthusiasm, curiously failed, except locally and temporarily in periods of crises, to become dynamic social myths until modern times. Until a century ago the vision of the renewed world and the paradise on earth seems to have roused little enthusiasm. It was rather the promise of a paradise in the next world which brought comfort and joy. The conditions of misery during the twelfth century—civil war, famine, the elemental catastrophes of earthquake, fire, typhoon and flood—produced not a saviour or messiah promising an imminent shift to perfection on this earth, but the movement which guaranteed an easy rebirth, *after* death, in the Pure Land of Amida. Now, it is interesting to note, it seems to be this very "other worldly" quality in the traditional Buddhist sects which has most earned them disapproval and sent their faithful into the arms of the new cults. Traditional Buddhism, one is told, is *sabishii*, remote, forlorn, otherworldly, utterly uninspiring by comparison with the glowing vision of the paradise on this earth promised by the new religions.

Though the *shinkō shūkyō*, or at any rate the larger and

[38] E. G. Boardman, *op. cit.* Accounts of the potentially revolutionary doctrine of the T'ai P'ing may be found in Joseph Needham, *Time and Eastern Man* (1965), pp. 27-31; Martin Bernal, *Chinese Socialism until 1913*, unpublished Ph.D. thesis for Cambridge University (1966), pp. 20-25.

more successful of them, have conformed with the conditions we suggested as characterising the millenarian cult, they differ in a number of significant ways from most other modern messianic cults which have arisen in response to the intrusion of Western culture.

In the first place, the Founders rarely claim to be the messiah in the strict sense of one who has *returned* to the world, in accordance with a promise made when he died, to redeem it in time of crisis. Many modern saviours claim to be the mythical hero who at the beginning of time taught men the elements of culture and then disappeared promising sometime to return and regenerate the world. Prophets of movements in Dutch Guinea, among the Plains Indians and in Brazil have derived their power from this claim.[39] The prophets of the Cargo cults in Melanesia have gained their following through claiming a revelation of the imminent *return* of the dead ancestors in their ships. The Founders of the new religions in Japan, however, rarely announce a second coming. The rich mine of Japanese folk tales is not lacking in the motif of the undying hero or saint, the figure who, like Barbarossa, Charlemagne, King Arthur or Alexander in Western folklore, was too powerful or too holy to die, but is at present asleep or wandering disguised awaiting the right time to return in all his glory to transform chaos into joy.[40] Yet few of the Founders seem to have identified themselves with any figure, whether historical or mythical, from the past. A notable exception is Deguchi Ōnisaburō, the "co-founder" of Ōmoto, who claimed during the 1920's to be the Bodhisattva Miroku come down to earth, in accordance with the prophesies in the sutras, to inaugurate the new terrestrial paradise.[41] In most cases, however, the Founders' claim

[39] V. Lanternari, "Messianism: its Historical Origin and Morphology," *History of Religions*, Vol. II, 1 (1962), 55-56.

[40] Kōbō Daishi, the eminent founder of the esoteric sect of Shingon Buddhism in Japan, is perhaps the most noted example of such a figure. See U. A. Casal, "Kōbō Daishi in Popular Lore," *Folklore Studies*, XVIII (1959), 139.

[41] Inui *et al.*, pp. 89-90.

to supernatural power rests solely on their divine possession and election to the role of divine instrument.[42]

The general forward-looking character of the Japanese movements is further borne out by their vision of the future earthly paradise. Many modern messianic cults promise that the new age will be a *return* to a golden past which society once enjoyed but long ago lost owing to some primordial catastrophe. The new age will be a kind of rolling up of the process of history, the return of society to its original source. Among the *shinkō shūkyō* there seems to be little evidence of such nostalgia for a past paradise. This is perhaps remarkable in view of the sway exercised by the vision of a golden past in the history of Japanese thought. In the great tradition of both Confucianism and the Shinto Revival, the scholars looked for their inspiration to a time in remote antiquity of simple uncorrupted perfection which they strove not very hopefully to renew. Even allowing for the fact that the *shinkō shūkyō* belong more properly to the little than to the great tradition, it is perhaps strange that none of the Founders should have felt moved to identify the earthly paradise they announce with one which once upon a time existed.

The answer may lie in the fact that their paradise is unequivocally identified with the "image" of the modern world. The golden age in the past, envisaged by the Confucianists as ruled by Sages perfect in wisdom and virtue, and by the Shinto revivalists as a time before men's hearts were corrupted by foreign vice and selfishness, is a picture of innocent simplicity

---

[42] It should be added that the Founders also find a place in the tradition of the *ikigami*, or "living god," in Japanese folk religion. *Ikigami* is a broad term indicating various kinds of persons endowed with powers beyond the ordinary. Heroes, pioneers, people with special skills, particularly benevolent ministers, ascetics who died unpleasant deaths with vows to save humanity on their lips—all these have been acclaimed as *ikigami*. Those gifted with superhuman powers and knowledge as a result of divine possession are therefore one species of this large category. Miyata, *op. cit.*; Yanagita Kunio, "Hito wo kami ni inoru fūshū," *Minzoku*, II, 1; Saki Akio, pp. 191-96.

scarcely compatible with the outward signs of modern progress. These signs are now too widely accepted as symbols of
prestige to be thought dispensable in paradise. The *shinkō
shūkyō*, though professing beliefs of great antiquity, are always
careful to equip their concrete cathedrals with the latest heat-
ing and cooling devices, the latest acoustic equipment, the most
up-to-date networks of closed circuit television. There is no
doubt that the earthly paradise, like these cathedrals which are
often conceived to be its miniature forerunners, will boast a
modern image. It will be no throwback to the age of the gods.[43]

It is relevant perhaps to remember in this connection that the
millenarism of the *shinkō shūkyō* is not directed against any
specific enemy. Again unlike most other modern messianic
cults, which arose in answer to the problems of the wretchedness and humiliation caused by the white man, the *shinkō
shūkyō* feel no hatred towards Western culture. The problem
which these movements arose to answer is not the destruction
of an alien enemy who has brought sickness, slaughter and
degradation to the community. It is the problem of smooth and
happy adjustment to the new conditions. Hence the Enemy or
Tyrant, whose destruction is necessary before the millennium
can come to pass, is neither a specific hated race nor a specific
class. It is simply, and a little undramatically, "wrong thinking." To bring the earthly paradise into being we must simply
learn to think aright. First and foremost, of course, right thinking implies devout faith in the principles and programme of

[43] An interesting exception to this rule is provided by the recently
incorporated sect known as Sekai Mahikari Bummei Kyōdan. The
Founder, Okada Kōgyoku, experienced in 1959 and 1962 a number
of revelations remarkably reminiscent of the beliefs of the Shinto
revivalists: the age of the gods at the beginning of history was a
golden age, an earthly paradise; this paradise can be regained by following the teachings of Mahikari; Japan was the original *place* of
the earthly paradise, and Japanese the first and original language of
the gods. See K. P. Koepping, "Sekai Mahikari Bummei Kyōdan, A
Preliminary Discussion of a Recent Religious Movement in Japan,"
Contemporary Religions in Japan, Vol. VIII, 2 (1967).

the cult. It is right thinking, the faithful are repeatedly told, which will on a local and individual scale rid us of all sickness and anxiety and bathe us in a blissful shower of *gensei riyaku*, mundane blessings. On a magnified and universalised scale it will inaugurate the earthly paradise. We have only to bring about this simple change in ourselves, and the trumpet shall sound.[44]

This aspect of the millenarism of the *shinkō shūkyō* puts them by and large into the category of "active" as opposed to "passive" movements. We do not simply have to wait, as for example in the classical form of messianism in ancient Israel, for supernatural intervention to bring about the Kingdom, unable to hasten its arrival through any effort of our own. There is important, indeed momentous work for us to do without which the new age cannot make its appearance. Eternal bliss will therefore ultimately depend on our own efforts to secure it.

This feature of Salvation by Works is more stressed in Sōka Gakkai than in any other movement and accounts, as we have seen, for the militant aggressiveness of its missionary propaganda. But in other successful movements where millenarism is marked—Tenrikyō, Sekai Meshiakyō and the Dancing Religion, for example—the faithful are exhorted to propagate the cult in order that more people will learn right thinking, in order that the millennium may be hastened. Here incidentally, we find another contrast, not only with those modern messianic movements which restrict human effort to promote the new age to ritual and symbolic preparations, but also with the tenu-

---

[44] In many modern messianic cults, the Cargo Cults and Ghost Dances for example, the hope of the message lies entirely in the promised millennial joys in the future. The faithful are promised no mitigation of present miseries until the final advent of the Kingdom. But in the *shinkō shūkyō* this seems rarely if ever to be the case. No cult, so far as I know, promises the paradise on earth in the future without laying equal if not greater stress on the shower of worldly blessings which will fall on believers here and now, both as the natural outcome of right thinking and also as a foretaste of the millennial bliss to come.

ous strands of the Miroku cult as practised in Japan before modern times. The descent of Miroku was believed to be not only a whole kalpa in the future, but also, in time, divinely predetermined. He would descend only at the moment prescribed by the sutras. In short, *active* millenarism, except for outbursts in the past too shortlived and localised to be noteworthy, is a feature of Japanese religious history peculiar to the modern scene.

This active quality in the millenarism of the *shinkō shūkyō* prevents the drastic leap from reality to phantasy found in other messianic movements. If the earthly paradise is to be modern, belonging to the new order rather than the old, and advanceable by one's own efforts, one will not burn one's store, smash one's tools, cease to work and break all traditional customs in a frenzy of chiliastic expectation. On the contrary, the *shinkō shūkyō* have taken shrewd and energetic steps towards rational adaptation to the new conditions. That they have not allowed millennial phantasies to become a substitute for human action is attested by the schools, the hospitals, the economic opportunities and the programmes of social welfare organised under the auspices of the cults. The divine shower of mundane blessings promised to the faithful is firmly supported, in the largest and richest of the movements, by substantial benefits of an undeniably objective kind. The *hōza* or discussion groups, where one may go to tell of one's troubles, listen to similar cases and receive comforting advice, are merely one among a number of sensible means of allaying the anxieties of the disoriented and the wretched. Indeed, with new friends, new glittering surroundings of which the members feel themselves peculiarly and intimately a part, a new and prodigious aim in life, a new certainty in the midst of flux, the *shinkō shūkyō* have already, even before the coming of the new kingdom, transformed the lives of many unhappy people.

CHAPTER XV

Levels of Speech (*keigo*) and the Japanese Linguistic Response to Modernization

ROY ANDREW MILLER

To speak improperly of one's husband or superior is very bad. It is quite disagreeable when one's servants use such expressions as *oFasuru* "deign to be" or *notamaFu* "deign to say" [with reference to their own husbands]. How often it seems that one hears things said in such a way that one wishes the word *Faberu* "respectfully wait upon" had been used instead. When someone without taste attempts to employ elegant terms, both the person thus addressed and anyone else who hears it will laugh. (Sei Shōnagon,[1] ca. 1000?)

[1] This *Makura no sōshi* passage is a celebrated one, often cited in the Japanese *kokugogaku* literature as one of the earliest references to *keigo* and its difficulties, but unfortunately the text itself is not without its own serious problems. (See Appendix, p. 666.)

Early Middle Japanese (Heian) citations in the present paper are transcribed in a modified historical transcription which helps distinguish them from modern forms; in this writing the symbol *F* for the bilabial (and in intervocalic position sometimes voiced) fricative is the only feature that needs special comment. In the transcriptions in this paper the hyphen has been used somewhat more generously than usual to help indicate *keigo* morpheme boundaries. All books for which no place of publication is indicated are Tokyo.

In its present form this paper has greatly benefited from suggestions made by several colleagues and friends, especially Arthur F. Wright and Samuel E. Martin; at the Puerto Rico meetings other useful criticisms were made by many of the participants, particularly by Edward J. Seidensticker and Donald Keene. Above all, it has benefited from the suggestions and criticisms of Robert H. Brower, who kindly undertook to record and summarize the discussion of the paper at Puerto Rico in my absence; and who in addition later commented upon it at length in correspondence. I am particularly grateful to him for draw-

I am disturbed by the glaring over-use of polite language on the television cooking programs; it is offensive to the ear. I don't so much object to *o-tamago* "egg [with the deferential prefix *o*-]," *o-ninjin* "carrots," and *o-supūn* "spoon," but *o-hanbun* "half" which I recently heard really sets my teeth on edge. I do wish the persons in charge of these programs would be more careful about such things. (Nakamura Tokiko, in a letter to the editor of the radio and television page of the Tokyo *Mainichi Shinbun*, June 7, 1965, evening edition.)

It is a pleasant Sunday morning. My grandchild, who began to go to elementary school this year, is reading his Japanese language textbook. "The pig went *bū, bū bū* (*ippiki no buta ga 'bū, bū, bū' to iimashita*)." My grandchild's friend, sitting near him, was reading from his second-year text: " 'You understand this, don't you,' the teacher said (*yoku wakarimasita nē to sensei ga iimashita*)." Hearing this, I was astonished. *Iimashita* was used both of the pig and the teacher. I wondered if democratic education is something that treats both pigs and teachers alike. I thought that perhaps it had been decided that elementary school pupils had no need for polite language, but when I took the texts away from the children and looked at them myself, this did not appear to be the case. There were plenty of examples using polite language, such as "The teacher was good enough to write on the blackboard (*sensei ga kokuban ni kaite kuremashita*)," or "the teacher was kind enough to post a chart of the *katakana* syllabary (*sensei ga katakana no hyō o hatte kudasaimashita*)," or "getting the teacher to read just that part for us (*soko dake sensei ni yonde itadaite*)"; then,

---

ing my attention to the bibliographical intricacies of the Tanizaki *Genji* translations, most of which had until that time escaped my notice, and for supplying me with a reproduction of the relevant passages from his own copy of the Tanizaki *Shin'yaku*, which was not available to me in either the Yale or Columbia collections.

thinking this unusual, I went on into the third-year text and found that here we were strangely enough back to the *sensei iimashita* level again! Since I have nothing personal against the compilers of these texts I will not give their names here, but it was a text with the official approval of the Ministry of Education. . . . It is perfectly alright, in Japanese language textbooks, to teach "mother said (*o-ḳāsan ga iimashita*)," but I must strongly maintain that I wish the compilers would revise the other passages so as to read "the teacher said (*sensei ga osshaimashita*). (Shiota Ryōhei, Professor of Japanese Literature, St. Paul's University, in the front-page feature *Cha no Ma* in the Tokyo *Mainichi Shinbun*, May 29, 1965, evening edition.)

These three passages cover a span of cultural and social experience almost as great as their gross chronological range, but they clearly share a common and abiding concern—one which might be paraphrased as "not caring nearly as much about what is said as about how it is said"—in particular about how something is said with reference to those formal features of the Japanese language which the grammarians generally call *ḳeigo* "language of respect" or "honorific language." Any cultural phenomenon or element of special concern to a society which remains valid for this impressively long span of time must surely be central to the concerns of that society and its culture; and any changes or developments in such an element of concern would obviously appear to have a direct and significant relationship to other changes and developments within that society. Unfortunately, once having said this, about all we have done is to have brought ourselves squarely face to face with the basic problem of the relationship of language to human behavior; and the exact nature of this relationship probably remains as obscure today as ever despite several decades of rapidly developing and changing linguistic science. It would seem, on the surface of it, that we should know far more about this than we actually do. The agreement seems to be in finding the conclusions of classical Western philosophy on this subject, particularly those of the Greeks, basically unsatisfactory, even though these same conclusions still form the basic approach to the problem of most non-professional discourse, and indeed have perpetuated themselves to large measure in the general folkloristic approach to the issue.

For the Greeks and for Western philosophy following them neither the problem nor its solution offered any particular difficulty. Language was in a direct, a vertical, and above all, a controlling relationship with social behavior. Language provided, in this system of thought, not only a model through which the basic patterns of social behavior might be observed but also a norm in terms of which these patterns of social behavior were and ideally ought to be ordered. The familiar dichotomy which this system established between "name" and "thing" only partially concealed the vertical, controlling relationship in which the philosophers presented these two entities. The proper selection of the "name" determined the "thing," the "thing" itself as well as its nature. Improper names led to improper things, improper terms to improper roles in life, improper functions in society, and improper modes of human behavior.

The great advantage of this system (the resemblance of which to the classical system of Chinese philosophy is too obvious to be elaborated upon here[2]) is of course that it generally provides a rapid and efficient answer to the question of "how" things work, and often indeed to the question of "why." Its greatest drawback is that it almost surely is not true. This too has been apparent in almost every society from early times; in Greece the proposition was challenged by several non-orthodox schools, as it also was in China, but in both of these great classical cultures the early challenges ended unsuccessfully, so

[2] Thus, the title of Liu Hsi's *Shih Ming* (cf. Nicholas C. Bodman, *A linguistic study of the* Shih Ming, *Initials and consonant clusters* [Harvard-Yenching Institute Studies, xi, Cambridge, 1954]) corresponds quite neatly to the *orthótēs onomátōn* of Protagoras; cf. *TP* 44.281 (1956).

that for most subsequent history even to question it was to skate on the thin edge of lunacy.

The issue is an important one for us because without making a few statements, imperfect and tentative though they must necessarily remain, about the nature of the relationship between the formal features of language, any language, and social behavior, the behavior of any society, it will be impossible to make any meaningful statement on the possible role, if any, as an index of social change or modernization which we may discern for those formal features of the Japanese language with which we are particularly concerned here.

The formal features of the language which the Japanese today designate as *keigo* have been variously described in the grammatical literature,[3] and each of these descriptions is of

[3] For an introduction to the Japanese bibliography on the subject, in addition to the chief works on *keigo* cited in this paper, see the bibliographical information in Samuel E. Martin, "Speech levels in Japanese and Korean," in Dell Hymes, ed., *Language in culture and society* (New York, 1964), pp. 407-15; in addition, the Kokusai Bunka Shinkōkai's *Bibliography of standard reference books for Japanese studies with descriptive notes*, Vol. vi (A) (1961), and Joseph K. Yamagiwa, ed., *Japanese language studies in the Shōwa period* (Ann Arbor, 1961) (Center for Japanese studies, Bibliographical series, 9) will be found useful. The May, 1956 issue of the journal *Kokubungaku—kaishaku to kanshō* is subtitled *Keigo—hensen to gendai no kadai*, and the entire issue is devoted to articles on *keigo* and its changes and development; on bibliography see particularly the article in that issue by Ekoyama Tsuneaki, "Keigo kenkyūshi," 55-59. Joseph K. Yamagiwa, "Language and ways of thinking," in John W. Hall and Richard K. Beardsley, *Twelve doors to Japan* (New York, 1956), pp. 213-18, deals with the subject in a somewhat different way, as does also his "Language and modernization," *ibid.*, 218-21; on both see my remarks in "Approaches to Japan," *The Yale Review*, 55.608-14 (1966). Here and in several other summaries of bibliographical data below (see especially notes 11, 27, and 35), it has been impossible for me to take proper cognizance of titles appearing later than the end of 1966, apart from a few exceptional cases. For an introduction to some of the significant work in the field appearing in the period from 1967 on, the reader may wish to consult my review in *Language*, 45.697-701 (1969). Bruno Lewin, ed., *Beiträge zum interpersonalem Bezug im Japanischen*

importance since each is based on a somewhat different set of postulates (generally unverbalized) concerning the nature of the relationship of "word" and "thing." For most Japanese scholars the system of *keigo* appears to be primarily a semantic device by means of which the language makes it possible for a speaker in his dealings with others to honor them, flatter them, treat them badly, treat them as equals, or on occasion treat them without actually committing himself in terms of any of these elements. On occasion it may also be used in much this same fashion with respect to a third person or persons not present, or in special cases by speaker or speakers with reference to him(them)selves. For these students of the phenomenon *keigo* is basically and essentially a tool, and often appears to function only as a means to an end. Their statements about it seem to be far less concerned with *keigo* as a system existing in its own right than they are with the utility which they find in the system. As we shall see below, this approach contrasts sharply with another one, according to which whatever else we may decide about the phenomenon it is clear that one of its most salient characteristics remains its essential non-utilitarianism, since almost all of its operation on the formal level is predicated upon discriminatory choices among already redundant features of the language.

Be that as it may, for most traditional Japanese scholarship the system of *keigo* is essentially utilitarian. It is a device or mechanism by which the society implements, administers, and otherwise carries out non-linguistic decisions which are generally and in the majority of cases consistent with social role

---

(Wiesbaden, 1969) also provides valuable guidance to the recent literature, quite apart from the considerable value of the several papers of which the volume itself consists. The long period of time that has elapsed between the completion of the original version of this chapter and the publication of the present volume also explains certain overlaps between some of the material presented here and in chapter 7 (" 'Special and Notable' Utterances") of my book *The Japanese Language* (Chicago, 1967); the book was completed after the original draft of the present chapter.

and function. Viewed in this way the phenomenon is a mechanism which in theory at least could be replaced by a different mechanism, with perhaps more cumbersome results but with no essential difference in effectiveness. If the *keigo* phenomenon is solely a utilitarian mechanism nothing would change were it to be replaced, for example, by a system of flag signals or even by some less elegant but considerably more striking signaling devices such as wiggling the ears, twitching the nose, arching the eyebrows, or eye winks. If we can imagine the lively scene which would result were such overt physical actions added to the linguistic chain of discourse as replacements for *keigo*, still viewed essentially as a utilitarian tool mechanism, the only thing that would have changed in the sum total of language-with-and-plus-society would presumably be the resulting more lively aspect of everyday life in Japan, together with a good deal less verbal signalling (and perhaps, hopefully, far less noise).[4]

The most important single Japanese monograph on *keigo*, and still the basic source for most traditional treatments of the subject, is the *Keigohō no kenkyū* of Yamada Yoshio (1873-1958), a notable scholar whose shelf of detailed grammars for each of the major periods in the history of Japanese continues to hold the field against most contenders. Originally published in 1924, this study supplemented and brought under a unified approach scattered statements about *keigo* from some of his still earlier work, and in its 1931 revised version it continues

---

[4] Signalling systems with the blessed virtue of silence are not unknown in other cultures; for example, Simon D. Messing, "The Nonverbal language of the Ethiopian Toga," *Anthropos* 55.558-60 (1960) reports on nonverbal communication developed by the Amhara of Ethiopia who use various ways of draping their characteristic toga-like garment: "this has the advantage of [making it possible] to communicate at a distance, beyond the sound of speech, what mood one is in, whether or not one wishes to maintain social distance, what status one has and what role one wishes to assume, [and] what type of function one is about to attend." Messing's article has a bibliography of other work on symbolic behavior systems.

today to dominate the field. A fair idea may be gained of Yamada's approach to the problem in the following extract from his introduction to this volume:

> *Keigo*, as a formal feature of language used in social contacts, is not a phenomenon which is to be found only in our national language, but there is no other language in the world in which such a feature has developed as fully as it has in Japanese. Thus, Chamberlain says, "no Language in the world is more saturated with honorific idioms than is Japanese." This was his fair judgement from the viewpoint of linguistics; and no other conclusion was possible for anyone who like him knew the languages of the world (*sic*), and at the same time had a true understanding of our national language.
>
> In general, *keigo* has its origins in human social dealings. And it is one of the ways in which individuals give expression to their spirit of mutual deference. Even though originally this *keigo* was suited for expressing distinctions between high and low, and noble and base, it is not now necessarily a result of the class system. As individuals deal with each other as individuals, each valuing the personality of each other, and each respecting the abilities, knowledge, virtues and qualities of each other, it is really true human nature (*jitsu ni shizen no ninjō*) for all these to be expressed in language. The existence of such features is only because in our race the laudable custom of mutual deference is practiced; and so their existence, rather [than being something of which to be ashamed] should be an occasion for much rejoicing. (pp. 1-2)

The reference here to Basil Hall Chamberlain's (1850-1935) account of *keigo* in his *Handbook of Colloquial Japanese* (London, Tokyo, Yokohama, etc., 1888) is neither accidental nor trivial; reading Yamada and his followers makes it clear that Chamberlain's attention to and treatment of the phenomenon was an important stimulus in focusing Japanese academic attention upon *keigo*, and especially makes it clear that the note of "uniqueness" which he, perhaps unwittingly, sounded here called forth deep chords of response from the leading figures in late Meiji and early Taishō Japanese language scholarship. Chamberlain's complete introductory statement read:

> No Language in the world is more saturated with honorific idioms than is Japanese. These idioms affect, not only the vocabulary, but the grammar. Therefore, although scattered references have been made to them in former chapters, it seems advisable to gather together under one heading all the leading manifestations of a habit of speech, without a proper mastery of which it is impossible to speak Japanese with any approach to correctness. (p. 219)

It is not difficult to see why this appealed both to the sentiments and to the ambitions of early modern Japanese language scholarship. "Scattered references" to the *keigo* there had been in abundance in the traditional Japanese exegesis of classical literature,[5] for example, but the phenomenon had never been treated as a unified system, and certainly no one had ever considered holding it up as something in which Japanese was not only different from the other languages of the world but in which it was more highly developed and hence, manifestly superior. (Yamada and his followers, either from ignorance of the nuances of the English or from design, concealed Chamberlain's rather disparaging "saturated" by translating it with the elegant *yū suru* "to have," thus completely shifting the sense of the passage for their readers.)

With this background, few surprises await us in the ways in which during the war years *keigo* became one of the favorite themes for those who were most eager to visit the advantages of Japanese culture and society (if not citizenship) upon the

[5] For the scattered references to *keigo* in early Japanese literary scholarship see particularly Ishizaka (correct Martin, *loc. cit.*, who has "Isibasi") Shōzō, *Keigoshi ronkō* (1944), which is largely devoted to this subject.

inhabitants of less favored areas. A typical example is the following, which sets the tone for a volume by a certain Maruyama Rinpei, then a professor at the "Build-the-State" (Kenkoku) University, which he published in 1941 under the title *Nihon keigohō* (even his title was jingoistic, and points up the fact that for him *keigo* related directly to Nihon, not even to Nihongo):

> Japanese is rich in *keigo*; actually, it seems to be over-rich. For this reason even many Japanese do not understand how to use *keigo*, or use it incorrectly. How much more, then, might we expect persons for whom Japanese is not their native language, as for example, people from the continent [of Asia], to feel that the Japanese *keigo* is difficult, and even that it is a nuisance. But the richness of *keigo* is, in one respect, something that has arisen from the special nature of the Japanese race, and hence, it is a rather vital feature of the Japanese language.
>
> The day will probably come in the future when this rich and variegated *keigo* will be simplified, but be that as it may, for the time being, I would like here to cast an eye over the entire *keigo* as it now exists. . . . If as a result of the present volume, the Japanese spoken by people who speak Japanese (sic *Nihongo o hanasu hitobito no Nihongo*) should become even a little bit more refined and beautiful, I am sure that the present author will not be the only one to rejoice. (pp. i-ii)

Ekoyama Tsuneaki's *Keigohō* of 1943 is actually still quite a useful volume, though superficially at least its theme was of a piece with the above, and its preface, from which the following is taken, might easily put off anyone unacquainted with the difficulties under which most scholars in Japan were operating at the time of its publication:

> Now that the construction of Greater East Asia has become the most pressing task of the day for us, it is only to be

expected that the Japanese language should present itself as a much debated issue—to be expected, and to be rejoiced about! . . . The permeation of the Japanese language throughout the Co-prosperity Sphere will require extraordinary exertion and patience, and it goes without saying that as far as *keigo* is concerned, this must be done in terms of exhaustive knowledge and exact measures. But as a matter of fact, some people today complain about the poverty of *keigo*, while others bewail its over-use, and there is agreement only upon one thing—that *keigo* today is in a state of confusion. . . . In order to solve the problem of how to refine *keigo* even further, and to secure the proper appearance of the divinely endowed Yamato language, it is first necessary to realize scientifically what the proper forms for *keigo* actually are; then on the basis of this knowledge, we must effectively grasp and criticize the present state of affairs. . . . What an honor it will be for the author of the present volume if, by some odd chance, he is here able to make some contribution to the purification of our national language. (pp. iii-iv)

Apart from all this flag-waving, Ekoyama's approach shows his great debt to Yamada's work, a feature which it shares with virtually all the Japanese literature in the field.

Even though in the post-war years the overt mode of scholarly expression has changed considerably, it is difficult to find any significant change in the basic approach of Japanese scholarship to the questions posed by *keigo*. The article on *keigo* in the authoritative Kokugo Gakkai's *Kokugogaku jiten* (1955), *s.v.*, still defines it as "a linguistic habit in which different forms are employed for the linguistic expression of the same referent or for similar referents due to reasons (*kankei*) of respect, status, and intimacy obtaining among speaker, hearer, and third person." Or, to quote another brief definition of even greater currency, Kamei Takashi in his *Gaisetsu bungo bunpō* (revised ed., 1962, of 1st ed. of 1955), which is probably the one nonspecialized work on the Japanese language most widely used in Japanese higher education today, introduces the subject as follows:

> Japanese has fixed forms as a social convention (*shakai teki na shūkan to shite*) as a means of expression corresponding to the consciousness of human relationships; these are the *keigo* usages (*keigohō*), and if one does not understand them well, one cannot really expect to achieve correct expression. (p. 180)

The traditional themes which these widely respected contemporary authorities continue to perpetuate in their work were given added emphasis in the Kokuritsu Kokugo Kenkyūjo's well-known but somewhat controversial 1957 report *Keigo to keigo ishiki* (= Kokuritsu kokugo kenkyūjo hōkoku 11); the official English sub-title of this volume is "Socio-psychological survey on Japanese polite expression," which tells us virtually nothing about what was actually intended by the Japanese title but is somewhat informative about the directions in which the authors of the study attempted to direct their work. Chiefly they were concerned with *ishiki* "consciousness," "self-realization" or "self-awareness" on the part of the speaker of his own use of *keigo*; and these were the slippery commodities which they attempted to test and tabulate with a variety of ingenious statistical devices. As an example of the application of fairly sophisticated techniques to what is at least a variety of quasi-linguistic data the study is of considerable interest, but its great drawback was and is its initial decision to attempt to measure the "consciousness" of native speakers to formal features in their own language without first determining whether or not such a factor is actually one that admits of positive detection, much less measurement. The substantive aspects of the report which grew out of this study have been discussed elsewhere;[6] here it is more useful for our purposes to see

[6] On the *Keigo to keigo ishiki* report and some of its many problems, cf. Martin, *loc. cit.*, and my book, *The Japanese Language* (Chicago, 1967), pp. 282-84.

instead a few of the basic assumptions of the workers on this project concerning the nature of *keigo* and something of the ultimate goals of their study, as set forth in the report's introduction:

Keigo is a striking idiosyncrasy (*ichijirushii tokuchō*) of the Japanese language. Before and during the war it was thought that since *keigo* is a unique feature of Japanese it must by all means be preserved. Then, following the war, it was thought that *keigo* was a leftover habit from the feudal period and ought properly to be liquidated (*seisan*) in a democratic world. However, the basis of democracy is predicated upon individuals respecting each other, and since *keigo* is an effective tool (*yūkō na shudan*) for expressing that sentiment of respect, it has turned out that even in the world from now on, a certain amount of *keigo* will continue to be necessary. But upon reflection, must we not conclude that this [necessary minimum] will be as far as possible a simplified *keigo* (*kanso na keigo*)?

Nevertheless, both before and after the war, one has heard of "confusion of *keigo*" (*keigo no konran*). This probably indicates that there have arisen discrepancies in the consciousness of *keigo*, or in the way of thinking about *keigo*, chiefly between the older and younger levels [of the population]. This variety of discrepancy sometimes interferes with communication, and furthermore, has an [adverse] effect on the communal sentiment of regional society (?? *chi'iki shakai no kyōdo no kanjō*).

It is for this reason that we have undertaken to come to grips with the actual conditions of the *keigo* in regional society, and through this to lay bare the factors tending to make *keigo* increasingly complex (*keigo o fukuzatsu ni shite iru gen'in*). In this way, we have felt that it would be possible to obtain a clue to the means (*hōsaku*) by which *keigo* may be simplified. (p. 1)

The more one reads this and similar statements concerning

the purpose and operating principles of such studies the more one is tempted to conclude that they are not about language at all but rather about popular morality—after all, like *keigo*, this too is something that appears always to have been, at any given point in time, as bad as it might ever be supposed to become, but which somehow manages to survive into a following period, when once again, it is generally held to be bad, mixed up, and in a state of confusion—and so forth.

All these are statements by scholars and would-be scholars of the Japanese language; but it is an interesting and significant commentary on cultural continuity to note that the same main themes appear virtually without change in the references to *keigo* in the *Bunshō tokuhon* (1934; references to the 50th printing of 1942) of Tanizaki Jun'ichirō (1886-1965), where the great modern prose master sums up his views on Japanese literary style. The theme of uniqueness receives particularly forceful expression at Tanizaki's hands:

> Our language has one special feature which must not be overlooked. Do you ask what that is? It is that in spite of the defect of its words being few in number, and its vocabulary poor, it is actually surprisingly rich in the variety of its expressions which degrade one's self and honor others; and in this it has been pursuing a complex development that is beyond comparison with that of any other language of any other country (pp. 244-5). . . . No other people in the world sets as high a store on etiquette (*reisetsu*) as do we Japanese; and consequently, our language also reflects this national trait, with which it is intimately bound up. (p. 247)

For Tanizaki too the essence of *keigo* is to be found in its utility; and in explaining precisely how, in his view, this utility operates, he gives overt expression to certain elements of Japanese prose style which many readers and translators have certainly more than once thought must be true, but which it is rather surprising to find set forth with the following candor:

By using *keigo* in verbs and auxiliary verbs, subjects can be omitted without causing subsequent confusion, and it becomes possible to put together long sentences of complicated construction (*kōzō no fukuzatsu na nagai sentensu*) ... (p. 267-8). . . . This variety [i.e., the variety of forms made possible by *keigo*] is a valuable tool (*riki*) which our national language possesses for supplementing the defects and shortcomings of its sentence structure. (p. 270)

For Tanizaki, *keigo* was an important element in Japanese prose style; it was part of the unique resources of the Japanese language, and at the same time one of the ways in which the unique limitations of the Japanese language (the phrase and the concept are his, not the present author's) could be successfully overcome. One way in which these limitations can be overcome is to create more and more complex prose structures, and in this work of complicating the complicated, *keigo* is without question a tool of considerable utility.

However, even if we find the basic orientation of most Japanese scholarship and writing on this problem somewhat unsatisfactory, it still has many elements both of truth and of fact which we must consider carefully, even if this means sifting through an extraordinarily large amount of chaff for an occasional kernel of substance. The assumption which is stressed over and over, for example, that the *keigo* phenomenon is totally unique to Japanese life and culture, and one of the elements which (like the unlamented *kokutai* of an earlier period) distinguish that which is Japanese from other superficially similar phenomena in the world, is apparently a protective covering built up around a tiny but real grain of irritant substance. The initial irritation here goes back to the beginnings of the study of classical Chinese in Japan, and to Japan's initial contacts with foreign language and foreign culture. The gradually evolved school traditions for reading classical Chinese texts as if they were Japanese texts (*kanbun, kundoku*)

615

rigorously avoided all *keigo* forms,[7] but in the early stages of their development, and before these school traditions were completely jelled, many attempts were made to force *keigo* forms into some sort of relationship with Chinese vocabulary and syntax. This happened in two main ways—identifying elements in the original Chinese texts which could without too much forcing or bending be associated with Japanese *keigo* elements, and also gratuitously reading *keigo* elements according to the demands of Japanese grammar into Chinese texts even in cases where nothing overt in the text itself provided any justification for such a *keigo* insertion.

The first variety shows up well in, and was an important factor in the development of, the *senmyō* documentary style; to a Chinese original (composed in Japan by Japanese to be sure, but nevertheless a Chinese original text for our purposes here) involving Chinese *feng* "receive with both hands; offer; serve respectfully" the Japanese *keigo* form *tatematuru* "do worshipfully" would be associated, even when the Chinese morpheme was involved in a construction which did not justify the semantic equation which this process presupposed.[8] In the second variety Chinese morphemes with absolutely no semantic associations that could properly earn them a relationship with the *keigo* system were nevertheless, in certain contexts, associated with the system in the process of turning the texts in which they appeared from Chinese into Japanese; thus Chinese *ch'u* "place" as *mi-moto* with the deferential prefix *mi-*; *chih* "know" as *sirosimesu*, and *yen* "words; speak" as *notamaFu*[9] (one of the forms concerning the proper usage of which we earlier saw Sei Shōnagon being so concerned). In a subclass of this second variety the earlier, less rigidly controlled

[7] Ōno Susumu, Nakada Norio, Doi Tadao, Yoshida Sumio, and Matsumura Akira, *Nihongo no rekishi* (6th ed., 1961, of the new revised ed. of 1958), p. 139.

[8] Tōdō Akiyasu, *Kanbun gaisetsu, Nihongo o sodateta mono* (1960), p. 301.

[9] Tōdō Akiyasu, *Kanbun yōsetsu, Kanbun gakushūsha no tame ni* (1963), pp. 179-80.

stages of the school reading tradition often used Japanese *keigo* equivalents for Chinese morphemes which in the later, more elegant style in which the *kanbun* tradition has by and large come down to us, were rendered by direct loanwords from Chinese. There is some evidence that much of this rigidity set in roughly around 1200; for example, in two different Japanese reading versions of the same original Chinese passage involving *yeh* "have an audience with a superior" in a past-tense context, an early Heian version renders it *tukaFematuriki*, while a later version dated in correspondence with 1116 reads the identical passage as *esseri < etu seri*, with the loan morpheme *etu* for original Middle Chinese $* \cdot j \, vt.$[10] It is clear that as the classical Chinese reading tradition developed toward elegance and precision it became necessary to isolate it more and more completely from its early associations with the Japanese *keigo* phenomenon. It is probably due to experiences of this sort that Japanese scholarship has traditionally tended to combine its essentially utilitarian approach toward *keigo* with an equal emphasis on its unique Japanese-ness; at any rate these two elements continue to be the dominant themes for most Japanese scholarship on the subject.

The traditional Japanese approach to the problem cannot at present be sharply contrasted with any major theme of Western scholarly approach. Western scholarship, when it has viewed the problem at all, has either reproduced (again mechanically and for purely utilitarian ends) the usual Japanese statements, or has made minor adjustments in them in an attempt to conform them to one or the other theories of the relation of language to human behavior current at the moment in Western linguistic scholarship.

These theories at present fall into two major groups:[11] (1)

[10] *Ibid.*, p. 180.
[11] Philip K. Bock, "Social structure and language structure," *Southwestern Journal of Anthropology* 20:4.393-403 (1964), an article to which I am greatly indebted for much of the theoretical portion of the present paper; see it also for much of the relevant non-Japanese

that reflected in the work of Benjamin Whorf and his follow-ers who to us today, from the vantage point gained by the passage of a few years' time, now appear to have been seeking CONGRUENCIES between language and the values, ideals, behav-ior, and customary practices of the society using that lan-guage; and (2) the work of Kenneth Pike and others who more recently have been attempting instead to devise a UNIFIED THEORY embracing the total structure of human behavior, within which system language now simply appears to be a special though always central case of the larger phenomenon. With Pike's approach the problem of congruencies immediately disappears, and with it also much of the superficial appeal of the usual Japanese utilitarian and mechanistic approach to such features as *keigo*. For Pike the "word" is no longer in a direct relationship with the "thing"—it is neither in the vertical rela-tionship of Greek and Chinese philosophy nor in the horizon-tal congruency of Whorf and the other earlier American lin-guists. Language exists and so does the "thing." Just as name and word exist, so do act and behavior pattern, along with the STATUS and ROLE of Linton's social structure,[12] and all of these co-exist as different but communicating areas in a great commonwealth which may be called "human behavior." The task of the linguistic scientist then becomes that of any social scientist: to describe the particular variety of human behavior, in his case language, which he has selected for his particular field of study. But since this object of his study is not, as it turns out, in a congruent or causal relationship with the object of study of any of his neighboring social scientists, he need not unduly concern himself with mechanistic and utilitarian approaches. And as we work in terms of Pike's unified theory, we see that linguistic forms (morphemes, morphological and

---

bibliography. Again, I have not attempted to keep the bibliography in this area up to date later than the end of 1966.

[12] Robert K. Merton, "The Role-Set: Problems in sociological the-ory," *British Journal of Sociology* 8:106-120 (1957).

syntactic structures, sets of formal features such as *keigo*, etc.) merely constitute a subclass of the more general category CUL-TURAL FORMS; but linguistic forms are always and essentially cultural forms par excellence.

Among recent studies Samuel E. Martin's treatment of the *keigo* phenomenon as a set of compulsory categories[13] probably comes closest to freeing itself from the limits of the congruency approach. In Martin's treatment the system is still somewhat mechanical and almost utilitarian—except that actually it now has very little utility. It is still a tool which retains its cutting edge, though it is not clear any longer precisely for what the tool is designed to be used. Martin describes the compulsory categories of *keigo* as a set of choices which the speaker must make before he can initiate or at least before he can complete an utterance: "before they can utter the verb form the Japanese . . . are forced to make a choice alien to us, that of speech levels."[14] The presumption here is that the choice is forced upon society by the language, so we are not after all completely free of a classical, and essentially vertical, cause and effect relationship. But probably this is to do Martin something of an injustice by reading rather more into his definition of "compulsory" than was meant to be found there, and his emphasis on compulsion is probably a worthwhile and enlightening one, even though it is necessary to avoid the question of who or what compels whom. With Pike, Martin finds the *keigo*, apart from these unresolved problems of cause and effect, clearly to be a special and central case of human behavior.

The superiority of this approach to that of other students of the language working in the Yale linguistic tradition is so obvious that it need not be elaborated upon. Eleanor Jorden, for example, despite her painstaking and exhaustive cataloging of Japanese syntax,[15] which perhaps is still the most impressive

---

[13] See Martin, cited in note 3 above.

[14] *Ibid.*, p. 408.

[15] Eleanor H. Jorden, *The syntax of modern colloquial Japanese* (Baltimore, 1955) (*Language* Dissertation 52, supplement, *Language* 31:1[3]).

segment of the "Yale Description of Japanese," dismissed the entire phenomenon simply as a system of "connotations."[16] For her *keigo* seems to be little more than a superstructure of linguistic diacritics which somehow are brought into the chain of discourse as a variety of decoration, reminding us a little of what Donald Keene has called DECORATIVE LANGUAGE (Keene was talking about rather different phenomena but still about styles of language which capitalize on linguistic features having much in common with *keigo*).

Among the many advances which Martin's approach offers over much of the more traditional scholarship on the subject must be counted his emphasis on comparison with a similar system in Korean. Japanese scholars have from time to time attempted somewhat similar comparisons but they have too often contented themselves with noting that somewhat parallel phenomena are "not unknown" in other languages, and they have in general retreated from the comparative field before their findings could successfully challenge their a priori conclusions concerning the unique nature of Japanese language, society, and culture.

Several necessary additions to and refinements of Martin's analysis suggest themselves, however, and one which is of immediate importance for the purposes of the present investigation is further to investigate the possibility that one of the main functions of the *keigo* system is its utility as a linguistic means for the AUTOMATIC (here and below probably to be preferred to COMPULSORY) categorization of behavior into successively halved segments. This is rather as if the linguistic *keigo* system were a knife which first cuts up the real-world pie into two parts, and then sets about cutting up each of these into smaller halves, and so on down to the point where there is about as much knife left as there is pie. This cut-off point is perhaps better illustrated by the process involved in tearing in half a piece of paper, then tearing in half each of the two

[16] Cf. the author in *JAOS* 76.39 (1956).

resulting halves and so on, until eventually one is left with bits too small to fragment by anything short of a nuclear explosion. Viewed in this way *keigo* provides binary "on" and "off," "yes" and "no" demarcations operative in successively reduced linguistic areas.

A few of the labels which can be attached to some of the fragments surviving each bifurcation are "we" as against "non-we"; male as against female; high social status as against low; important social role as against unimportant; and Japanese as against non-Japanese.

Immediately involving the *keigo* system are binary sets of contrasting elements such as, for "we," *mōsu* "say," *haiken suru* "see," *kaku* "write," and *wakai* "is young" against for "non-we," their parallel but contrasting forms *ossharu, goran ni naru, o-kaki-ni naru,* and *o-wakai desu.* What deserves more recognition than it has had to date is that this two-way contrast—which generally has been identified with a division into "polite" and "humble" or "elegant" and "rude"—is a splitting up and sorting out of the forms of the language by means of their membership in sets which then contrast with each other as sets, and that this operation is exactly parallel to other contrasts, some of which involve forms that are commonly considered *keigo,* others of which do not. Thus among the "we" forms there are *koe* "voice" and *kao* "face," but for "non-we" the corresponding members of the binary contrasting set are *o-koe* and *o-kao.* This demarcation intersects with a "male" vs. "female" contrast in a variety of complicated ways, notably involving different sentence-final particles (female *wa,* male *yo, zo,* etc.), as well as *o-mizu* "water (spoken of by a woman)" against male *mizu*; and in addition there are sets of contrasting forms which have no etymological connection with each other (female *oishii* "is delicious," male *umai*).

Japanese and non-Japanese are carefully distinguished in the language in many cases, again by means of a major dividing line which sometimes intersects and sometimes runs along together with a *keigo* isogloss. Japanese ship-names have the suffix *maru*, but non-Japanese ships replace this with *go*. Japanese islands may end in -*shima*, -*jima*, but foreign islands must end in -*tō*, -*dō*. (This is very much parallel to the type of variation that linguists call morphologically determined allomorphs—we might think of these forms as racially determined allomorphs.) Japanese *tennō* is of course unique for Japanese; but foreigners may however have a *kōtei* "emperor." And the division goes farther than this, of course—on a very elementary level, for example, Japanese have Japanese names (Yamamoto, Kobayashi, Tsuneo, Yoshiko) and foreigners have foreign names (Johnson, Smith, Edward, Mary); the two groups remain in fixed and rigid contrast. Even foreign religious systems which place liturgical and theological importance on name-changing have difficulty interfering with this system, so that the man who at Rome is known as Petrus Cardinal Doi, in Tokyo remains Doi Tatsuo. (One is reminded of the Puritans who erected as one of their major defenses against the evils of an idolatrous age their own unique and contrasting set of non-saint's-names names, leaving both old and New England with their heritage of Eliphalets, Ephestions, Peletiahs, Hepzibahs, and the like.)

One important intersection of this dichotomy with the *keigo* system occurs in the kind of Japanese which non-Japanese are represented to speak in modern Japanese newspapers, books and magazines,[17] and on television movies with dubbed in Japanese sound-tracks. This is perfectly intelligible and fluent

[17] The same dichotomy is carried over into the orthography, where non-Japanese (even when their language is otherwise normal, grammatical Japanese) most often "speak" in *katakana*, and almost always without *kanji*—a curious but undeniably consistent orthographic discrimination that can be observed all the way from cartoons in daily newspapers at one end of the literary scale to the speech of the White Russians in *Sasame yuki* at the other. Donald Keene has also pointed out to me that the use of *katakana* in imperial rescripts and other state documents based on imperial authority is another example of the utilization of the two *kana* syllabaries to express a "we-they" dichotomy.

Japanese, but would never for a moment be mistaken for the Japanese spoken by Japanese, from which system it is separated by a significant bundling of isoglosses, even quite apart from those involving the *keigo*.

A concrete example of this variety of language will make clear at least a sample of one of its contrasts with the Japanese of Japanese (which is no doubt quite close to what Maruyama had in mind for his *Nihongo o hanasu hitobito no Nihongo*, already cited). The following specimen of this extremely specialized type of discourse is drawn from the Kyōdō translation of an Associated Press dispatch, datelined Washington, June 7, and printed in the June 8, 1965 evening edition of the Tokyo *Mainichi Shinbun*; it reports the first two lines of a telephone conversation between President Lyndon Johnson and returned astronauts McDavid and White:

> *daitōryō: makudebitto shōsa ka ne.*
> *ma shōsa: sō desu, daitōryō.* (i.e., "*Yes, Mr. President.")

Titles are an important part of the *keigo* system; and in non-Japanese as contrasting with Japanese they generally appear in the position of *daitōryō* in this second sentence above, a syntactic occurrence unknown to the contrasting or non-non-Japanese system. This postponed title structure is a favorite one in the non-Japanese set; on the dubbed-in television dramas it is especially common in the non-Japanese female greeting formula (totally unknown in all its elements, even apart from the displaced title) *o-ai-suru koto ga dekite ureshii x-san* "I'm so happy to meet you, Mr[s.] X." For an example of masterful literary employment of this special feature of the language, the speech of the White Russians in the first chapters of Tanizaki Jun'ichirō's *Sasame yuki* comes to mind as an extremely affecting and touching use of the device; it has already been mentioned above because of its use of the *katakana* orthography in which the White Russians "speak." But the wealth of non-literary materials which modern communications and particularly the dubbed-in films on TV now make available means that any linguist interested in the much-needed description of this feature need no longer limit himself to artificial materials which regardless of their literary value would always be partly suspect.

The same dichotomy extends into other somewhat surprising areas. Japanese may be and sometimes are members of a Christian denomination called the *seikōkai*, historically a continuation in Japan both of the Anglican Communion and of the American Protestant Episcopal Church; but when Luci Nugent née Luci Baines Johnson leaves this latter group to become a Roman Catholic the *Shūkan gendai* (7:29, p. 23, for July 22, 1965) reports that she was originally a member of the *kantokukyōha*, which of course originally translated "episcopalian" but now appears to be for non-Japanese what *seikōkai* is for Japanese, just as *go* for ships is in complimentary racial distribution with *maru*.

Another contrast between two major sets which partly intersects and partly runs parallel to the *keigo* system's contrasts is that between two groups which we may call COMMENDATORY and PEJORATIVE; thus, in the first category, *yakusha* "actor," *seijika* "politician," *keieisha* "entrepreneur," *sensei* "teacher," and *shinbun kisha* "newspaperman," are in parallel as a set with, in the same order, *haiyū*, *seijiya*, *jūyaku*, *kyōshi*, and *jānarisuto*. For assigning these terms to their class membership here I have followed the evaluations of the anonymous "K." writing in the *Yūrakuchō* column of the July 9, 1965 evening edition of the Tokyo *Mainichi shinbun*; there he discussed the plight of a notable TV actor who had earlier that week been quoted as saying *haiyū de naku yakusha ni naritai* "I would like to become a *yakusha* 'actor' rather than a *haiyū* 'actor.'" (Until recently *haiyū* had been by and large specialized to refer to movie and TV actors as against the "legitimate" theater, but this specialization now seems to have shifted in the direction of membership in a larger set of class contrasts.) "K." suggests that membership in each of these two sets can best be tested by determining whether or not the person to whom the

term refers is primarily concerned with making money (*haiyū,
seijiya, kyōshi,* etc.) or not (*yakusha, seijika, sensei,* etc.). The
intersection of this set of contrasts with certain of the *keigo*
lines of demarcation is clearly seen when we consider the fact
that *o-mizu* is, at times and in certain contexts, a commendatory equivalent of pejorative *mizu,* and so also for *koe* against
o-koe, etc.

Another large-scale dichotomy which also involves a special
variety of *keigo* is that between names for the QUICK, i.e., all
the many types of names used in reference to living persons,
and the DEAD, represented in Japanese society particularly by
the *kaimyō* "monastic names" awarded to the dead, identifying them as *koji* "lay (i.e., deceased) Buddhist follower." It is
interesting to note that redundancy and synonymy play their
part here too as they do in virtually every aspect of all known
linguistic systems, and it is possible to document at least one
recent instance where a person has been awarded at least two
competing *kaimyō* designations. Before Tanizaki Jun'ichirō
(1886-1965) died he had selected his own grave site on the
grounds of the Hōnen'in in Kyoto, and had also gone to the
trouble of preparing his own grave marker inscribed with a
kaimyō of his own selection in his own calligraphy, *anraku-
jū'in kōyō monrintoku Jun koji,* roughly "the lay Buddhist
Jun['ichirō], [replete with] honor of accomplishment and the
virtue of the forest of literati, [of] the cloister of the longevity
of peaceful delight." But it turns out that the *kaimyō* is not at
the disposal of the deceased, even in the case of someone as
likely to know his own mind as Tanizaki, and the final official
kaimyō by which he was eventually to be associated with the
set of names for the "dead" as distinguished from the other
set for the "quick" was quite different. Kon Tōkō was responsible for it, and it read in final form, *montoku'indono kyōnen
Junrō daikoji,* again most roughly "the great lay Buddhist
Jun[-ichi]rō, the majestic, my lord of the cloister of literary
virtue."[18] Here as in all portions of linguistic systems, set and

[18] The difficulties with Tanizaki's posthumous designations were

class membership are not only arbitrary elements but they are considerations about which the item being assigned to such membership has very little to say; and the decisions upon which such membership eventually hinges are not for the individual concerned to make.

Still another major bifurcation which involves the *keigo* system to a very important extent is that according to which Japanese morphemes are distributed among two great groups, SECRET and OVERT. A partly fortuitous but striking result of this is that the society is able to maintain a fairly strict condition of formal internal security concerning many of the details of its table of organization, rather after the style of old-fashioned military units in combat. Thus the "secret" term for a given individual—for example, the father of a family engaged in operating a small retail flower shop—would be his given name Matsuo, used only in certain exceptional though well defined contexts, as for example, his own mother as speaker to him; this is paralleled in the contrasting "overt" group by a NONCE SET which can often be extremely large, each constituent item of which could be further identified in terms of the particular speaker for whom it would be the vocative. With Matsuo in the example here cited might go, to give only an incomplete sampling of one such overt nonce set, *shachō* (used by young female employee in shop), *aniki* (by younger brother, partner in and also employed in shop), *danna* (by younger male employee), *otōsan* (by son, to his face), *oyaji* (by son, behind

---

reported in the Tokyo newspapers, as for example the *Mainichi shinbun*, in the evening editions of July 30 and in the morning editions of July 31, 1965. The confusion arose because Tanizaki forgot (or more likely had intended to go counter to) the traditional behavior pattern for posthumous name bestowal. Only someone in orders (and Kon Tōkō is a Buddhist clergyman) can participate in this final age-grade ceremony, in which he and the deceased are the principals; the deceased is by this point also "in orders" by virtue of his *kaimyō*. Cf. Richard K. Beardsley, "Religion and Philosophy," p. 324 in John W. Hall and Richard K. Beardsley, *op. cit.*

his back), *koko no shujin* (by younger sister to third party), *onīsan* (by sister-in-law), *ojisan* (by non-related younger female lodger in home), *anata* (by wife to face), *uchi no hito* (by wife behind back), *Matsuo-san* (by prospective bride to sister), *Matsuo* (by younger sister to prospective bride; also by mother to his face), and *ore* (by self).[19] (All these terms are vocatives except those for which third party or other supplementary information is indicated.)

The extent of these successive bifurcations of the language and the degree of the involvement of the *keigo* system in their resulting dichotomies both find a significant parallel in the fact that many of the *keigo* forms are themselves set aside from the other normal morphological patterns of the language. The morphological contrast of such forms as *nasar-u* but *nasaimasu* and *osshar-u* but *osshaimasu* with *masar-u* but *masarimasu* and *kazar-u* but *kazarimasu* is paralleled in the functional role of these forms in establishing different but parallel contrasting sets throughout the language.

Given this elaborate system of interlocking bifurcations and successive dichotomy, it is almost inconceivable that any element which, like *keigo*, is intimately bound up in it should not provide vital clues to the nature and operation of many varieties of social change, particularly any set of social displacements as major as those generally treated under the rubric of "modernization." Fortunately certain recent work in anthropologically oriented linguistics has begun to point out some of the ways in which it may soon be possible to treat linguistic phenomenon such as *keigo* with maximum effectiveness. One of these investigators is Philip K. Bock, whose work with the

[19] Data recorded during a telecast of the program *Noren taiheiki* on Tokyo Channel 6 on the evening of May 29, 1965; all the terms listed were used to refer to the character played in this series by the popular actor Katō Daisuke. For an analysis of most of these words in relationship to the Japanese system of kin terminology in general, see Harumi Befu and Edward Norbeck, "Japanese usages of terms of relationship," *Southwestern Journal of Anthropology* 14:66-86 (1958).

description of Micmac Indian behavior provides a theoretical framework of considerable value.[20] Of greatest importance is probably his suggestion that cultural forms involving other than verbal behavior may be consistently defined and their relationships stated systematically and economically just as we have long done for phonology and morphology. Here the linguistic analog of the SOCIAL ROLE is to be found in the morpheme with its free or conditioned allomorphs and its membership in descriptive classes.

The kind of systematic and economical description which Bock suggests is predicated upon three types of units: (1) social roles and classes of roles; (2) periods and dimensions of social time; (3) areas and dimensions of social space. The essential similarity of the formal features of language (including but of course not limited to their selection and arrangement) to the structuring of roles in society has been convincingly demonstrated in Bock's description of, for example, a Micmac wake. First of all we must identify what he designates as BEHAVIORAL ATTRIBUTES—among the Micmac these might be abstract, such as mild joking, the exercise of jural authority, or concurrent speaking to the group, or concrete, such as preparing food. Among the Japanese one might suggest a parallel and equally wide variety of still almost unstudied and certainly ill-defined behavioral attributes—for example, a great variety of joking relationships including many sub-types of stylized courting and ritualistic enticement as, for example, at *geisha* parties and other formalized performances. For Bock, it is the distinctive selection and arrangement of such attributes which makes possible the constructive identification of any one role in a particular culture. Just as the inherently meaningless phonemes of a language cluster into utterances—so that meaningless /y/, /a/, and /m/ cluster into the meaningful item *yama*—so also do the inherently meaningless behavioral attributes appear clustered together with each other to result contrastively in a

[20] See Bock, *op. cit.*, particularly pp. 395-97 and pp. 398 ff.

particular social role—company president, *geisha*, wife of salaried employee, foreigner teaching English, etc.

These roles, consisting as they do (on the equivalent of the phonological level) of social attributes, have (again much like morphemes) external distribution in their own right since they can co-occur, and in this process of co-occurrence they result in ROLE-SETS. The role-set has been set forth in considerable detail by Merton. He describes, for example, the role-set of a school teacher in the United States not as a single role but as an array of roles, i.e., a set involving co-occurrence by "pupils, colleagues, the school principal and superintendent, the board of education, professional associations and, on occasion, local patriotic organizations."[21] Merton's discovery that there are several social mechanisms which serve to articulate these role-sets and thus mitigate the impact of diverse expectations upon a status occupant is an important one for us, though admittedly it does also have certain utilitarian implications of the kind we have been trying to avoid. Still it would be difficult to find a more succinct description of one important way in which *keigo* functions (this is different from saying "the functions of *keigo*") than this statement with its emphasis upon the articulation of the role-set and the consequent mitigation of the otherwise potentially disruptive impact of divergent expectations.

Bock finds a parallel between the allomorphs of, for example, the English plural morpheme *-s* and the isomorphism of a given role. Any given social role is therefore made up of several different subsets of behavioral expectations (variants a_1, a_2 . . .

---

[21] Merton, *op. cit.*, especially pp. 110 ff. Most of the specialized varieties of behavior in Japanese society await more rigorous description and analysis; work along the lines of Felix M. Keesing and Marie M. Keesing, *Elite communication in Samoa, a study of leadership* (Stanford, 1956), would help to reveal many important structural principles in Japanese public behavior (most of them with significant linguistic connections). Cf. also J. E. Buse, "Two Samoan ceremonial speeches," *BSOAS* 24.104-115 (1961), for examples of descriptions of formal speech-making and ritualized talk that point the way toward work still badly needed with respect to Japan.

a_n), and which of these variants, which are on the level of the morphologically determined allomorph, will be manifested (or what would be on the phonological level called "realized") depends upon which of the roles in its role-set it occurs together with.

The recurrent social situation may itself be a cultural form with the possibility of description in terms of social space and social time. Such large scale ritualized performances as the various activities of the Japanese New Year (house cleaning, midnight watch, temple or shrine visit, toasts at first meal, visits to friends, indoor and outdoor games, etc., together with a variety of elaborate and specialized greeting liturgies) immediately come to mind here. At each stage of this performance cycle those participating either continue to implement their customary roles with special additions for the particular time and place, or they assume fictitious roles of limited duration as part of the price of their entry here into what Bock calls the SITUATION MATRIX. If we had a description of the Japanese New Year at hand as precise as Bock's situation matrix for the Micmac wake there is little doubt that the associate role of *keigo* in it would be immediately apparent.

Another theoretical framework which is of great importance for the analysis of *keigo* materials as clues to changes in social behaviour is Emeneau's amplification of Bloomfield's postulates on the nature of language, to the effect that linguistic forms are ordered in classes or subclasses corresponding to systems or subsystems within the environment.[22] It is necessary to be on our guard against any temptation to interpret Emeneau's "corresponding" in the traditional "cause and effect" terms of much earlier scholarship. This is ruled out by Emeneau's original presentation of his postulate, and with this caution in mind his formulation may also be of considerable importance for any treatment of *keigo* either on the descriptive level or as grist for an extra-linguistic analytic mill.

[22] M. B. Emeneau, "Language and Non-linguistic patterns," *Language* 26.199-209 (1950).

It would be difficult to find any part of the real world which is segmented into systems and subsystems quite as elegantly or as minutely as is Japanese society. The language "corresponds" to this segmentation by ordering its forms into classes or subclasses corresponding to these systems and subsystems, and this ordering is to be observed chiefly and typically in *keigo*. Numbers are, in Japanese as in other languages, another excellent example of arbitrarily ordered sets ("one" follows "two," "six" follows "five" in a way that is not to be observed within any other set of forms), but numbers lack the "correspondence" with real-world segmentation which gives significance and interest to the parallel phenomenon in *keigo*.

But even with this theoretical and conceptual framework, the utility of *keigo* in an investigation of the nature and processes of change in social behavior is still plagued with several difficulties, the most limiting of which is the fact that we still lack a complete and detailed synchronic description of the operation of the *keigo* phenomenon at each historical stage of the language including, it is embarrassing to add, the modern language. It is a commonplace to say that no comparative linguistic study is possible without multiple and parallel sets of data, and the more complete the date, the more comparison will reveal. The history of the study of comparative Indo-European grammar often shows how much comparison still can reveal even with impartial and fragmentary data, but the temptation to make a virtue of necessity here must be continually resisted. What we have today for the earlier stages of Japanese are the merest fragments of description for *keigo*. With the modern language we are in a somewhat more satisfactory situation, but even if one stage were quite fully described, comparison requires at least two, and ideally more than two, quite complete descriptions before it can produce any really worthwhile data on the processes and operations of change. This means that any answers which are possible today are tentative in the extreme, since they are based on shockingly incomplete evidence and fragmentary descriptions, which may very well later turn out to have been trivial or irrelevant.

Another complication is that we still lack sufficiently sophisticated techniques for distinguishing between the functional, or if one prefers, the productive (in Martin's terms the compulsory) categories of *keigo* and what appear on the surface to be formally identical features but which are rather borrowings of literary forms into the spoken language, and hence actually neither functional nor productive. The literary language at each of its historical stages, including that of the modern literary language, has its own different though parallel systems of *keigo*. Constant borrowings take place back and forth between them and, most importantly, from them into the spoken language. These borrowings do much to explain the historical origins of many complicated problems seen today on the purely synchronic level in the description of *keigo*. A good example is the use of the so-called deferential prefix *o-* with nouns. We must distinguish first of all an inseparable *o-*, which cannot be removed from the nominal element with which it appears without changing the identity of the lexical item (*naka* "middle," *o-naka* "stomach"; *share* "wit, pun," *o-share* "a dandy, fancy dresser"; *tsuri* "fishing, angling," *o-tsuri* "change [small money]"; *ashi* "foot," *o-ashi* "money"), and contrasting with it a second and separable *o-*, whose employment with a following noun is a matter of choice (functional or compulsory) and which therefore is the more important item, perhaps the only important one among the different varieties of *o-*, in any analytic consideration of *keigo* usage. This second variety is found with a wide variety of items (*o-zubon* "trousers," *o-bōshi* "hat," *o-mune* "breast," *o-cha* "tea," *o-biiru* "beer," *o-kashi* "candy") and is far more productive a factor in women's speech than in men's. As we shall see below in somewhat greater detail, it is in this second category of *o-* that the element of choice as well as the factors operative in such choice become issues of considerable importance in any attempt at extra-linguistic analysis.

But in addition to this basic and generally valid dichotomy, further complications are also introduced by sets like *kane* "metal" and sometimes "money," but *o-kane* always and solely "money." Historically we probably have to reckon here with a rather interesting semantic back-formation, with the sense of *kane* in *o-kane* coming to be attached in time to the unprefixed form as well. Of course the problem in this particular case is also further complicated by the fact that "money" was anciently the most highly specialized and socially the most significant form of "metal" known in the Far East; but on the descriptive level at least such items simply form another and third subclass for the description of the deferential prefix *o-*, and must be recognized and treated as such in our analysis.

Another way in which borrowing from the literary language into the spoken language (or among different stages of the literary language) has complicated the resulting description may be cited, also for this same *o-*. From the literary language still another morpheme *o-* (and one best treated as totally different) meaning "of or pertaining to the Imperial person, household, or family" has been borrowed into the modern language as part of a few forms, notably *o-bunko* "the Imperial library," specifically meaning those buildings within the Imperial palace moat in downtown Tokyo in which the Emperor and Empress lived from the fire-bombing of the palace until the recent completion of their postwar personal residence. Of the same origin is *o-kotoba* "Imperial rescript, specifically an Imperial message opening a session of the National Diet," which since the conclusion of World War II has officially replaced *chokugo*.[23]

This list could be extended almost indefinitely if we were to admit to it the hundreds of forms with which *o-* appears in the Imperial Household argot known as *go-sho kotoba* "palace language." Typical examples are *o-suzu* "tin bottle-vase for

---

[23] Togashi Junji, *Kōshitsu jiten* (1965), p. 170. Mr. Togashi's data are the result of his 45-year career as Mainichi reporter assigned to the Imperial Household Agency.

warming *sake* for the Imperial table," *o-mono* "food to be eaten by the Emperor," *o-tōsho* "toilet for use by the Emperor," *o-sumaru* "the Emperor's sleep," etc., etc.[24] Since these terms have no normal linguistic existence outside of the Imperial household they need not be included in a description of the modern colloquial language, but the list does nevertheless contain important suggestions about some of the historical developments underlying the present complex nature of the phenomenon. Thus, in *go-sho kotoba*, the term *o-bon* is found in the sense of "a round, hollowed-out wooden dish or tray for use at the Imperial table"; this is to be considered alongside of and in association with (but not as identical with) *o-bon* "a tray" in the modern colloquial, where the *o-* prefix is of the second general or separable variety. In much the same way the allomorph *gyo-*, as for example in *gyo'en* "the Imperial gardens (of Shinjuku)", a morphologically determined allomorph of *go-*, itself an allomorph of *o-*, is historically a borrowing into the modern colloquial either from the literary language or from *go-sho kotoba*.[25] Also relevant here are the spoken forms *o-kage de* and *o-kage-sama de* "thank goodness," aphaeretic borrowings of literary *shinbutsu no o-kage-sama de* "by the grace of the gods and the Buddha."

Thus, complex linguistic systems arise through equally complex historical processes. Our knowledge of the modern spoken language provides one fairly fixed point for comparison, but for fully satisfactory comparative study we need in addition and beyond this similar knowledge, i.e., descriptions for several other fixed points in the history of the language, and it is these which at present we lack in great measure.

Even admitting this dearth of data, however, it is surely not necessary to adopt uncritically the ethical and essentially mystical approach to be found in the speculations of such writers as Nakamura Hajime. For him the use of this deferential prefix

[24] *Ibid.*, pp. 172-81.
[25] Cf. Bruno Lewin, *Abriss der japanischen Grammatik* (Weisbaden, 1959), p. 49, §61.

634

with everyday words comes from "the tendency in Buddhism to admit the spirituality of grass, trees, and even non-living beings"; boiled rice is called *gohan* out of "respect for labor in vocational life (which) resulted in the high esteem of things produced as the fruits of labor."[26] All of this is very edifying but unfortunately most of it breaks down immediately if we inspect the way the language operates at the only stage for which we have even a fragment of a consistent description, the modern spoken language. It is difficult to see, for example, how we are to fit into such an elevating as well as elevated system of description the following extremely common examples of the prefix *o-*: *o-shikko* "urine (nursery word)," *o-nesho* "bed-wetting," *o-tsuwari* "morning sickness," *o-nara* "breaking wind"; and *o-kara* "husks left over from beans in the process of fermenting bean-curd" and *o-heso* "navel." (All these are inseparable except the last two citations, which involve choice.) It is admittedly always somewhat difficult to rule out the influence of this great world religious system upon any aspect of Japanese behavior, but here at least we may perhaps be forgiven for electing not to follow Professor Nakamura in his view that the use of the deferential prefix arises from any very pronounced recognition of the spirituality of anything, living or non-living. What we have instead is, among other things, a partial subclass of the non-separable prefix, in which it is used with (its occurrence corresponds with, in Emeneau's terms) terms for certain undesirable bodily secretions and physiological functions (the two final separable citations belong to other sub-classes). But perhaps refinement of description must always involve a certain loss of spirituality, whether we seek it out or not.

Such difficulties cannot in the final analysis be overcome by anything short of a number of major new descriptions of the language, none of which appear at the present moment to be

[26] Nakamura Hajime, *Tōyōjin no shi'i hōhō* (1948-49), cited from the 2nd rev. English translation (Honolulu, 1964) in Joseph K. Yamagiwa, "Language as an Expression of Japanese culture," pp. 214-15.

under way, but it is still possible to make a tentative analysis and to reach certain conclusions. This can be done by working on the basis of a few elementary assumptions and applying these to a variety of more or less unsatisfactory and unsophisticated materials, which do however have the great advantage of being close at hand and which can be made to serve our purposes in lieu of complete descriptions.

None of these assumptions are at all theoretically challenging, and hence they need little more than bare statement here. All of them derive from the basic assumption, which we must take as our point of departure even though it is beyond experimental proof, that LANGUAGE HAS MEANING. Since most modern linguists are traditionally (and generally rather unfairly) accused by their colleagues from the other social sciences of denying that language has meaning at all, this assumption probably needs to be verbalized very clearly and very early in our work. All that modern linguistics has ever denied in this connection is the validity as scientific measuring devices of most of the traditional techniques for dealing with meaning—translation, paraphrase, reference to extra-linguistic systems, etc. (It is also forced to deny the possibility of ever proving this basic assumption, though this last is in somewhat less demand.) Language, then, may be assumed to have meaning. It "has" this meaning in its morphemes, in much the same way that we "have" our heredity in our genes, to indulge ourselves in a probably misleading metaphor. Different genes imply different physical characteristics as well as different heredity; different morphemes in somewhat the same way suppose different meanings. In addition, more morphemes represent more meaning, fewer morphemes fewer meanings, or less meaning, whichever one prefers.[27] Once "morpheme" is estab-

[27] There are several theoretical problems remaining in this approach, not all of which have yet been solved even to my own satisfaction. My colleague Samuel E. Martin has pointed out to me that it is also quite common for the utterance with fewer overt morphemes actually to have more semantic marking, e.g., "Wish I could have some too,"

lished on the left-hand side of our equation and "meaning" on the right, our lack of reliable techniques for dealing with the right-hand side becomes less of a handicap in our study thanks to our ability to deal with the left-hand members with a fair amount of precision. More is greater than less; that which is not the same is different;[28] and differences which are beyond our grasp of mensuration on the meaning or right-hand side of our equation can effectively though indirectly be gauged on the left-hand or morpheme side.

In concrete application all this fortunately works out to be rather simpler than it sounds. "Equivalent expressions" such as the following set of four parallel utterances exist in Japa-

---

which is marked for the English CASUAL style by the omission of the otherwise synonymous (and drab) first word in the fuller "I wish I could have some too." The point (along with many others of relevance to the present paper) is made in Martin Joos, *The Five Clocks* (*IJAL* 28:2, Part V, April, 1962), p. 20, a fascinating if somewhat embarrassing essay, especially valuable for its statements about change and redundancy in language. It would be interesting to speculate what form Joos' autopsychoanalysis might have taken if he had been acquainted with the Japanese relatives of his own dear Miss Fidditch. In the several years that have elapsed since the completion of the original draft of this chapter, the field of linguistics has sustained a series of major shifts in theory and method—in particular, the widespread popularization of the "transformational-generative" school—with the result that some of what is said in the text above at this point, while true enough in 1966, is no longer true in 1971. The transformational-generative school no longer denies the validity of translation, paraphrase, or reference to non-linguistic systems as devices for dealing with meaning in language; quite to the contrary, these are now the very techniques with which they chiefly operate on every level of their analysis. Translation and paraphrase in particular have become the major tools of the non-Bloomfieldian linguist. For a recent example of this approach to Japanese *keigo*, the reader may now wish to consult Gary D. Prideaux, *The Syntax of Japanese Honorifics* (The Hague & Paris, 1970).

[28] Leonard Bloomfield, "A set of postulates for the science of language," *Language* 2.155 (1926), or as reprinted in Martin Joos, ed., *Readings in linguistics* (Washington, 1957), p. 27.

nese: *kore kudasaimasen ka* :: *kore kudasai* :: *kore kure* :: *kore*.[29] The right-hand side or "meaning" part of each is, in default of any effective and reliable technique for its identification, notation, or mensuration, in each case best simply tagged (i.e., glossed) as "give me this." Of course, even English translation permits what appear to be further categories, involving for example "please!" or other elements; but if we attempt to use these rigorously to build one-to-one parallels with the Japanese we not only get ourselves into skewing difficulties almost immediately, but by erecting facade-only structures we are really only obscuring in part the essential lack of symmetry which here is our main concern.

If we then assume that language has meaning, and that a morpheme present goes together with meaning while one absent does not (and forgetting for the moment about zero morphemes, which a more formal study would also have to take into account), we end up with the conclusion that *kore kudasaimasen ka* is different in meaning from *kore kudasai* which differs also from *kore kure* which differs from *kore*, and that any one item in the chain also differs from any other one. (The chain could be further expanded to include versions with the direct object particle *o < wo*, which versions would then also differ minimally in meaning from otherwise parallel utterances without this *o*, etc.) These differences in meaning involve *keigo*, and we shall agree to treat that example in any chain of parallels having the most morphemes (in the four-member set above, *kore kudasaimasen ka*) as the most complicated (or, if one prefers, the most polite). Even more complicated (or, more polite) than this would be *kore o kudasaimasen ka*, for the same reasons and following the same assumptions.

The data employed in what follows are drawn from three different types of sources, each with its own strengths and weaknesses, and each representative of a large body of other

---

[29] Cf. the expository employment of this set in *Keigo to keigo ishiki*, p. 2 (where they ignore the possibilities with *o < wo*!).

available materials of the same sort. The first is a published account of an attempt to apply statistical methods to informant sampling; the second is an attempt at an analysis of non-scientific materials for purposes for which they were not originally designed; the third is a different kind of analysis of a specialized variety of modern written materials which contain, *inter alia*, information on actual *keigo* usage.

Indications of Change in the Employment of the Deferential Prefix o- with Nouns and Nominals

Shibata Takeshi has reported[30] on a study which attempted to test the employment of *o-* with 4,830 vocabulary items chosen at random, using 18 informants (a disappointingly small number), all women either married or "having experienced marriage," and currently resident in Tokyo. In addition further testing for *o-* with different semantic categories (roughly here equivalent to "subsystems within the environment") employed a shorter list of 1,100 "basic vocabulary words" developed by Doi Kōchi largely for the purposes of teaching Japanese as a foreign language in the occupied areas of the Co-prosperity Sphere.[31]

In each case subjects were tested for their self-confessed willingness or reticence to use *o-* with a given lexical item, and the results tabulated according to the 39 Doi semantic categories into which this list of "basic" items is divided (they include such rubrics as "man," "body," "dwellings," "drink," "earth's surface," "time," "sound," "organization," "actions," and "emotions," sometimes with fairly surprising membership within each of these categories; for example, under "actions" we find *kō* "filial piety," *matsuri* "religious festival," and *naku* "to cry.") Unfortunately Shibata's study appears to have con-

---

[30] Shibata Takeshi, " 'o' no tsuku go, tsukanai go," *Gengo seikatsu* 70.40-49 (1957). This issue of *Gengo seikatsu* is subtitled *Tokushū—Gendai no keigo*, and contains *inter alia* a good deal of interesting if uneven writing on various aspects of the problem.

[31] Doi Kōchi, *Nihongo no sugata* (1943), pp. 333-37.

tented itself with asking the informants whether or not they used certain forms freely, but it did not attempt actually to inspect their linguistic production to see if they did or not. Reliance on such introspection and "instant analysis" on the part of informants is all but out of the question for any sophisticated study of language, and here detracts greatly from the value of Shibata's findings; it is also one of the major limiting factors for the data reported in the *Keigo to keigo ishiki* study.

Shibata's statistical compilation of this testing with the 1,100 list showed that the Doi semantic categories which appear to present the prefix *o-* with the most marked opposition are those of nature (such items as *sekai* "world," *hoshi* "star," *hi* "fire"), earth's surface (*tsuchi* "earth," *kawa* "river," *tokai* "city"), minerals (*kin* "gold," *dō* "bronze," *tetsu* "iron"), plants (*ki*, "tree," *tane* "seed," *kinoko* "mushrooms"), animals (*tori* "bird," *mushi* "insect," *uma* "horse"), forms (*sugata* "appearance," *dai* "platform," *sumi* "corner"), colors (*ao* "blue, green," *shiro* "white," *kuro* "black"), machinery and industry (*kenchiku* "architecture," *kuruma* "vehicle," *semento* "cement"), and organization (*mura* "village," *shakai* "society," *zoku* "tribe"). Among these the semantic areas of nature, minerals, plants, forms, colors, machinery and industry, and organization were in that order identified as offering maximum resistance to the use of *o-*.

In the same way, a reverse treatment of the data as tabulated by Shibata shows that the categories most favored for use with *o-* were meals (such forms as *ryōri* "cooking," *aji* "taste," *kamu* "to chew"), mental operations (sic; it includes *miru* "to see," *kiku* "to hear," and *negai* "a request"), emotions (*ai* "love," *ikari* "anger," *tanoshimi* "happiness"), and physical operations (*iki* "breath," *tsukare* "fatigue," *nemuri* "sleep"). Also of considerable frequency with *o-* were the categories of furniture (*kagami* "mirror," *kagi* "key," *koppu* "drinking glass") and food (*kome* "uncooked rice," *mame* "beans," *imo* "potatoes").

By extrapolation on the basis of this sampling Shibata estimates that *o-* is potentially available for use with about 40 percent of the total noun and nominal vocabulary of the language; but despite this large potential range of usage only 0.4 percent of the larger vocabulary sample was ALWAYS used with *o-* by all informants tested on all occasions. This segment of the usage spectrum is probably to be traced historically in large measure to borrowings from the literary language, as outlined above, and hence provides an interesting hint of one of the ways in which synchronic description can sometimes identify segments of the language sharing a common layer of historical origin.

The most clear-cut evidence for change and identification of the direction of drift of such change is to be found here in the employment of *o-* with loanwords from European languages, chiefly English, the overwhelming majority of which date of course from the first years of the present century. Shibata's testing showed the following distribution pattern for the 4,830-item random vocabulary sample tested:

No. of informants using *o-*	0	1 to 5	6 to 11	12 to 16	17 or 18
with loanwords from European languages	211	7	1	0	0
with native Japanese words	2578	1559	336	122	16

Here it is clear that while some loanwords do take *o-* (we have already seen *o-supūn* "spoon" in the letter-to-the-editor cited at the beginning of this paper; other common examples include *o-biiru* "beer" and *o-toire* "toilet") certain forms which might be expected apparently never occur, such as for example **o-uisukii* "whiskey," which we might logically expect after the analogy of *o-biiru*, nor does **o-mayonēzu* "mayonnaise" occur, though it might very well be expected after the analogy of *o-su* "vinegar," with the native Japanese morpheme *su* and an example of the inseparable *o-*.

Among the many factors of choice involved in these linguistic decisions formal features apparently loom large. The *o-* is clearly more common with short forms than with longer ones, which is probably the main factor behind the non-occur-rence of both *o-uisukii* and *o-mayonēzu*; this also goes well with its occurrence in the truncated loanword *o-toire*, since no *o-toiretto* is recorded. It is also more favored for forms not otherwise and already beginning with another *o-*, thus *o-heya* "room" is common but *o-ōsetsuma* "parlor" seems not to occur.[32]

The loanwords participate in this scheme despite and totally without regard for their etymological origin; but since they are additions to the system, once they have been taken into it the system as a whole becomes more rather than less compli-cated because of their very existence. (If the loanwords existed in the language but were somehow barred from participation in the *o-* prefixation process their existence would be without significance here.) Thus the *keigo* system, in particular that portion of it constituted by *o-* prefixation to nouns and nomi-nals, is more complex today than it was 100 or 50 or 10 years ago because of and in direct ratio to the increase in the num-ber of loanwords from European languages in that period.[33]

[32] Data largely from Shibata, *loc. cit.*, especially p. 43. An observant student has pointed out to me an additional socio-linguistic factor that surely is concurrently operative in the *o-biiru* / *o-uisukii* matrix: in a Japanese bar, one most usually orders beer simply as "beer," but speci-fies brand-names when ordering whiskey. This means that the lexical item *biiru* enters the chain of discourse, and is available for the litur-gical-repetition as *o-biiru* by the bar "madame" or waitress, in a critical context not available, under ordinary circumstances, to *uisukii*. This factor does not by any means rule out the formal-stylistic considerations suggested in the text; rather, the two must be considered together. The entire problem provides a good example of the bundles of complex factors that are apparently involved in even the "simplest" cases of pre-fixed *o-*.

[33] In 1928 Ichikawa Sanki reported that he had found 1,400 English words "in a few months' reading of Japanese newspapers and maga-zines," but only two years later another "Japanese researcher" claimed to be able to list 5,000 words of what he called "Japanized English." (H. L. Mencken, *The American Language* [New York, 1951], 591.)

Forms of the type *o-supūn*, *o-toire*, and *o-biiru* involve complications in the system unknown before the introduction of these loanwords, and the *keigo* system of which they are now a part is because of this fact more complex than it was before.

Popular Accounts of "Misusage" of Keigo Constructions

There is a large popular literature in modern Japan which attempts to point out and correct what it considers "mistakes" in the use of *keigo*. Much of this material is roughly at the level of the American drug-store paperback books whose covers ask the question, "Do You Make These 87 Common Mistakes in English?," and like these Western books (upon which to a considerable extent they are no doubt modeled) they capitalize upon feelings of social insecurity and the reader's desire to "get on in the world" by ridding himself of what they manage to make him feel are non-standard or non-elegant expressions in his speech and writing. This variety of material may seem to be a rather strange place in which to seek technical information about the developments of the *keigo* system, but in spite of its orientation, which is of course non-linguistic, and much of its exposition and "explanations," which are teleological at best and at worst completely beside the point—and above all, in spite of its basic assumption, which is that "incorrect usage" exists, is a problem, and can be remedied—it still can be made to yield certain valuable types of information.

This is because in the course of pointing out what it considers "errors in usage" this type of source inevitably describes what people actually say and write, as distinguished from what they think they are supposed to say and write, or again as distinguished from what they would like to be able to remember to say and write because they think it is more proper or elegant. Patterns and constructions which are likely to escape the school grammarian may often be found, in the absence of really complete modern descriptions of the language, only in such ephemeral sources, and that is certainly the case with the *keigo* phenomenon. Here they show the currency of several *keigo* patterns and locutions which never appear in the formal reference works, and these are all of particular interest to us because they represent modern developments of and on occasion conflations within the *keigo* system. Hence they help show something of the direction in which its drift[34] has been operating in recent years.

It is difficult to choose among these sources, since they are prolix, repetitious, and if anything in over supply, but the following sampling concerning *keigo* will give a fair idea of the type of materials they contain as well as of their statements about these materials, and some indication of their possible value in more sophisticated linguistic study.[35]

[34] Edward Sapir, *Language, an introduction to the study of speech* (New York, 1939), pp. 157 ff.

[35] My citations derive chiefly from Saigo Hideo, "Keigo no tsukai-kata," in Iwabuchi Etsutarō, ed., *Akubun* (1961, with 8 subsequent printings by 1964!), 181-215, particularly from his "syllabus of errors" on 196 ff. The author, like all those appearing in this volume, is a member of the Kokuritsu Kokugo Kenkyūjo, of which the editor is director. For more of the same under even more impressive official auspices, see the NHK publication *Hōsō bunshō no kakikata* (mimeographed, 1964), pp. 136 ff., especially 150-60 on "errors." The issue of *Gengo seikatsu* cited above also contains similar materials, notably in Miyaji Yutaka's article "Keigo no konran," 26-34. Miyaji, a member of the Kokuritsu Kokugo Kenkyūjo, and also represented in the *Akubun* collection, was one of Tanizaki's three assistants in the period during which he was working on his second *Genji* translation (*shin'yaku* preface, p. 11). It is all but impossible to keep up to date with this literature; the July, 1966 issue of *Kokubungaku* is a special number devoted to *keigo*, especially *keigo* in the earlier stages of the language (hence its subtitle *Keigohō no subete—kotengo to gendaigo*), but it too finds room for several pages on different varieties of "errors" in modern usage, Miyaji Atsuko's *Machigaidarake no keigo*, 194-99. Far more important in this issue are Okada Kazue's comparative table of different approaches to *keigo* description by Japanese scholars (*Keigohō gakusetsu*, 200-209), and the very extensive bibliography of Japanese work on *keigo* by Tahara Yoshiko *et al.*, *Keigohō kenkyū*

1. *o-* . . . *suru* IS SAID NOT TO BE A POLITE *keigo* CONSTRUCTION AND SHOULD NOT BE SO USED (BUT COMMONLY IS IN MODERN JAPANESE).

These sources hold that *o-* . . . *suru*, originally and historically a self-deprecatory formula, still is one and hence cannot be used, as it commonly is today, as a mildly polite locution; in other words, they ignore and attempt to suppress the development in the modern language of a formally identical but quite different *o-* . . . *suru*, historically related to but no longer the same as the only *o-* . . . *suru* they would permit. The customary greeting of the bus-girls in Japan comes under their ban: *kippu o o-mochi shitenai kata wa o-kirase negaimasu* "anyone not holding a ticket please buy one." "But," says one of these books, "she does not realize when she says this that she is actually being rude, not polite, to her customers."[36] Neither do they, and one is left concluding that the only one who really is being rude here is the person who takes these poor over-worked and ill-paid girls to task for using their own language in the only way they have always used it. The sources approve of such sentences as *o-kaban o o-mochi shimashō* "let me help you with that bag"; this preserves the original construction of which the modern (and supposedly incorrect) pat-

---

bunken sōran, 210-25. Again, I have made no attempt to keep up with the countless works in this genre published since late 1966.

[36] *Akubun*, 196. The phenomenon is nothing new in the Japanese language, and examples may be cited from a variety of early texts; but when it happens in Old Japanese the grammarians face up to it with considerably more grace. In older texts it is not considered to be a mistake but rather termed *jishō keigo* "honorific language used by the speaker of himself." See for example the long note with citations of several relevant passages by Tsuchihashi Yutaka in *Kodai kayōshū* (*Nihon koten bungaku taikei* 3) (1957), p. 109; typical examples are to be found in *Kojiki* poem 2, *wa ga tatasereba*, and in *Kojiki* poem 28, *wa ga keseru*; in both cases the *-s-* is an honorific morpheme. When the bus-girl does it, it is a mistake in grammar; when Yachihoko-no-mikoto does it, it is *jishō keigo*.

tern is a later changed form, developed by a conflation of the *keigo* system.

Other examples of this construction, also "in error," are cited from official press-release accounts of the birth of Prince Hiro, showing (oh, shocking, shocking) that such "errors" are by no means the exclusive property of the lower orders:

Michiko-hi wa . . . sasuga ni kōfun no go-yōsu ga nukeki-ranai yō de makura moto ni tsukiso'o haha Fuji-san to o-hana-shi shite iru koto ga ōi "Princess Michiko, as might be expected, appears still to be considerably excited, and often speaks to her mother Fuji who is keeping her company at the bedside."

This, we are told, is erroneously written as if it were a case of an ordinary mother and daughter, in which instance it would be proper to use the deprecatory formula *o-hanashi suru*; but here it should have read *haha Fuji-san to o-hanashi nasatte iru.*

zenkokumin no kango ga kodamasuru uchi ni, utsukushiku seiketsu na minkan no josei to go-kekkon sareta no wa, saku-nen no sakura hiraku shigatsu tōka datta "it was on April 10 of last year, at cherry-blossom time, that (the Crown Prince) married the beautiful, chaste daughter of the people, amidst the adulation of the entire nation."

kōtaishi-sama wa mamonaku kunaichō byōin ni ikare, o-ko-sama to go-taimen sareta "the Crown Prince went immediately to the Imperial Household Agency hospital and met his child."

Michiko-hi no go-shussan yoteibi wa sangatsu tsuitachi datta ga, yotei yori isshūkan mo hayaku jintsū o uttaerare go-nyūin sareta "Princess Michiko's estimated delivery day had been March 1, but her labor pains began a week early and so she has been admitted to hospital."

In the last three examples above, *go-kekkon sareta, go-taimen sareta,* and *go-nyūin sareta* are all held to be errors; the *go-* in each is taken as an allomorph of *o-*, hence they equal *o- . . . *sareru.* Recommended instead are *kekkon sareta, taimen sareta,* and *nyūin sareta,* or *go-ḳeḳḳon ni natta, go-taimen ni natta,* and *go-nyūin ni natta.* When those close to the Imperial House-hold Agency fall into such error, what is a simple bus-girl to do?

Nor is the language of business letters and advertising circu-lars free from error, according to these sources:

ḳisha ga ḳoi ni go-shiyō shite orareru mono to wa ḳangaera-remasen ga "we can hardly believe that your firm has been using this (patent) intentionally, but . . ." The sources demand that *go-* be omitted.

sassoḳu go-sōdan shite ḳudasai "please consult us at once." The sources point out that ("as is well known") *go-sōdan suru* is deprecatory; of course what was intended as was *go-sōdan nasatte* or *go-sōdan ni natte.*

o-benḳyō sureba "if your children study." To win the cus-tomer's affection, use instead the "correct" polite forms *go-benḳyō ni nareba* or *benḳyō nasaru to;* do not insult him with this deprecatory formula.

2. *o-/go- . . . shite itadaḳu* IS A MIXTURE OF *o-/go- . . . suru,* WHICH IS DEPRECATORY, AND *. . . shite itadaḳu,* WHICH IS POLITE; HENCE IT SHOULD BE DECLARED OUT OF BOUNDS AND OFF LIMITS

To be sure, some of the examples cited for this one do seem fairly offensive, but this is probably more a function of their content than of their language: *yoi gyūnyū o yori yasuḳu go-aï'in shite itadaḳeru yō ni narimashita* "we can now supply our customers with fine milk at lower prices." The sources prefer to *go-aï'in* such expressions as *nonde itadaḳeru, o-nomi ni natte itadaḳeru, riyō shite itadaḳu,* or *go-riyō ni natte ita-daḳu;* and one gathers that they in fact prefer virtually any-thing to *go-aï'in.* This variety of locution seems to attract ini-tially unfavorable attention because of its over-use of Chinese loanwords, and so the original sin is probably that of the *aï'in* "lovingly drink," which is stylistic jarring, or *shiḳḳuri shinai,* as one of the sources puts it.

3. *o-* . . . *dekiru* IS "REALLY" THE POTENTIAL OF *o-* . . . *suru* AND
LIKE IT A DEPRECATORY FORMULA; THEREFORE IT IS AN ERROR TO
USE IT IN A POLITE CONTEXT (AND HENCE ALL THAT GOES FOR
o- . . . *suru* OF COURSE GOES ALSO FOR *o-* . . . *dekiru*)

Examples: *go-jiyū ni o-tsumitate dekiru X X tsumitate* "X X
deposit (plan) which you can add to at will." *o-tegara ni
o-motome dekimasu* "you can easily acquire." *o-hitori de
kigaru ni go-sanka dekiru shinryoku no basuryokō* "a bus trip
to view spring verdure in which (even) an unaccompanied
person may feel free to join." For these examples, the recommended substitute forms are *o-tsumitate ni nareru, o-motome
ni naremasu,* and *go-sanka ni nareru.*

4. DOUBLED-UP *keigo* ELEMENTS "WHERE A SINGLE ONE WOULD DO"

Virtually universal disapproval appears to attach to *o-gohan*
"cooked rice," *go-hōmei* "guests' names," and *sensei-sama*
"teacher"; it is difficult not to join in the condemnation of
these forms, but they occur—or if they did not, why would
books have to be printed and articles written demanding that
people stop using them?

Along much the same lines is the difficulty with *o-* . . . *ni
narareru.* By post-war fiat of the Ministry of Education the
most elevated level of *keigo* to be tolerated in the modern language, and hence suitable for descriptions of the activities of
the Imperial family, is to be *o-* . . . *ni naru;*[37] but *o-* . . . *ni
narareru* is still very common, though it comes under the "double *keigo*" ban. It appears to annoy the normative authors particularly when they find it in advertising copy for patent medi-
cines, as for example: *desu kara mainichi o-tsuzuke ni narare-
masu to kenkō ga zōshin sare, o-hada mo taisō utsukushiku
narimasu* "and so, if you use it daily, it will improve your
health and your skin will become very beautiful." Here
o-tsuzuke ni narimasu to would, they plead, have been quite
sufficient.

[37] Monbushō, ed., *Kore kara no keigo* (1952) (cf. Martin, *op. cit.*,
p. 412); Togashi, *op. cit.*, p. 172.

5. THE USE OF A FINAL PLAIN FORM CONCLUDING A SEQUENCE OF POLITE FORMS IS DISAPPROVED

This is rather subtler than any of the rubrics above, since the consideration is on the paragraph rather than on the sentence level; the construction to which it objects nevertheless appears to be gaining rather than losing ground:

Michiko-hi wa nijūninichi gogo jūichiji go-jintsū o uttaera-reta no de Kobayashi go-yōgakari ga nijūsannichi gozen reiji nijippun chinryō no kekka, tadachi ni go-nyūin to kettei, gozen ichiji gojippun kunaichō byōin ni nyūin sareta. chinryō no kekka masumasu go-shussan no hō ni susumarete iru ga genzai wa seiyōshitsu de seigachū de aru "Since Princess Michiko began to complain of labor pains at 11:00 PM on the 22nd, the Official-[physician]-in-charge Kobayashi, as a result of an examination at 20 minutes past midnight on the morning of the 23rd ordered immediate hospitalization, and at 1:50 AM she was admitted to the Imperial Household Agency hospital. Examination showed that delivery is imminent, but at present she is resting quietly in a retiring room." Here the problem is that all verbs are polite except the last *de aru*, which it is suggested should have been made uniform with them—except that in this style of writing, it often is not.

6. OTHER "ERRORS" WHICH THESE SOURCES POINT OUT ARE DIFFICULT TO CLASSIFY BUT ARE OF INTEREST SINCE THEY SHOW OTHER EXPANSIONS AND CONFLATIONS OF THE *keigo* SYSTEM.

From a TV commercial: *o-kosama no yume o ōkiku soda-teru kore ga X X no hoken desu. naze tte sore wa ichinichi hyakuen hodo no kakegane de hyakuman'en mo no hoshō o mōshiageru kara desu* "It's X X insurance makes your children's dreams grow up big and strong. Why? Because it provides the protection of a million yen for premiums of only ¥100 a day." Here if the huckster had wanted a self-deprecatory term for "(our company) provides the protection (*hoshō suru*)" he ought according to the rules to have said **hoshō mōshiageru*, but by inserting the object particle *o* in the middle he has instead made it into the deprecatory equivalent of *hoshō o yū* "to talk about protection," according to these purist sources.

Other miscellaneous examples include the following: *o-chikaku no mise ni mōshikomi kudasai* "please make application at your neighborhood store"; *ichido haiken kudasai* "please view"; and *annaisho okure to mōshikomi kudasai* "please ask us to send the explanatory booklet." In each of these last three cases the sources claim that the expression should instead have been *o-/go . . . kudasai*. The combination *haiken kudasai* is signalled out for particular criticism, and it does indeed seem strange to find it here instead of the expected and conventional *goran kudasai*.

It would be possible to expand these six rubrics and their examples to virtually any length, but further specimens would only reinforce the information provided by those already cited without probably adding anything essentially new. What has happened in the changes which have produced each of these "errors" has been roughly along the following lines: two (or more) originally distinct patterns or formulas involving *keigo* have blended or in some other way conflated to produce a new and different pattern or formula, which now exists as a *keigo* element in its own right, despite the outcries of the compilers of the "syllabi of error" from which these citations come. This expansion and conflation has here made the *keigo* system more complex than it was before it began to undergo this process of change, since by definition more and different patterns involve a greater inventory of meaning differentials than do fewer patterns.

The formula *o- . . . suru* when used in the fashion which these manuals of "correct usage" decry with such energy is more than (if it even is to be counted) an error. The bus-girl knows what she is saying, and she is using the construction in the way in which it exists to be used in her language (and this is true even if, as is likely, she learned the phrase together with the rest of her verbal liturgy only after getting the job—language is still language, even when it results from language learning). The construction is now something different from the original and historical *o- . . . suru* self-deprecatory formula with which these sources insist on identifying it, but that does not mean she is wrong, or that she does not know her own language. It means that the *keigo* system is in this respect and to this admittedly minor extent more complex at the present point in time than it was at that earlier point to which the usage manuals insist on referring as solely correct and valid. The system has changed—indeed, it is probably seen here in the very process of change—and the direction of drift of this change is toward more rather than less complexity.

Essentially the same conclusion may be reached concerning each of the six rubrics of "error" summarized above; for example, a paragraph-length sequence in which all verbs and verbals appear at a uniform level within the *keigo* system would be less complex than the pattern castigated by the usage manuals, in which this uniform (and less complex) formula is broken up, conflated, and rendered more complex by the interpolation of forms on different levels.

An Experiment with More Precise Determination of Direction of Drift in Keigo Change Using a Limited Corpus

A third possibility for an approach to the problem of determining the direction of drift in changes which may be observed in *keigo* usage is that afforded by internal comparison of a limited and rigorously defined corpus of written materials. Mention has already been made of Tanizaki's manual of style, the *Bunshō tokuhon*, and of the evidence it provides for his interest in the problems of *keigo* and *keigo* usage in Japanese prose. Tanizaki chooses to illustrate his concept of *keigo* as an essentially utilitarian device by citing and commenting in detail upon a passage from the *Genji monogatari*, where he shows how the *keigo* of the original indicates (among other things, to be sure) the identity of the speaker and of the person spoken to, without necessity for overt reference or use of personal pronouns or pronoun-like words; hence, his point is, *keigo* is a useful, practical device for avoiding ambiguity and unintelligibility.[38] Tanizaki's interest in the *Genji* was, of course, a profound literary and aesthetic concern which left its traces in almost every part of his work. He translated the entire *Genji* into modern Japanese three different times—first in 1939-41, a second time in 1951-54, and finally in a third version completed shortly before his death in 1965.[39] In the preface to

[38] *Bunshō tokuhon*, §3, pp. 264 ff. The same device is used (but with a different *Genji* passage) by Kamei Takashi, *Gaisetsu bungo bunpō* (see citation in text above), pp. 185 ff.

[39] Tanizaki's first translation of the *Genji* into modern Japanese, under the title *Jun'ichirō yaku Genji monogatari*, was published by the Chūō kōron-sha (which has also published all subsequent versions) between 1939 and 1941 in 26 small volumes; in the 1938 preface to the first of these volumes Tanizaki says that he began work on the translation in September, 1935, and that his manuscript was completed and ready for the printers in September, 1938. He seemed to recall first having been approached by the Chūō kōron-sha in this connection sometime in 1933, but as early as 1938 Tanizaki's memory was already unclear on this point. In this same 1938 preface he predicted, with what turned out to be extremely acute vision, that this was only a "first draft" (*dai ichikō*), and that working and reworking over it would prove to be "the delight of his old age." This was precisely what happened. His second translation, whose full title was [*Yamada Takao kōetsu*] *Tanizaki Jun'ichirō shin'yaku Genji monogatari*, was published in twelve somewhat more substantial volumes between May 1951 and September 1954; and this "new translation" (*shin'yaku*) was soon the point of departure for two secondary versions which predate his third and final complete re-translation. In October 1955 he published a five-volume edition de luxe (*aizōbon*) version of the *shin'yaku*, which incorporated some corrections and revisions (we are not told precisely how many or how important they were) which by this time he had already made in the text of the *shin'yaku*. This 1955 de luxe edition was then, between 1956 and 1958, re-issued in a popularly priced edition (*fukyūban*), which reproduced intact the text of the 1955 version. Finally, in 1965 his third completely new version, *Tanizaki Jun'ichirō shinshin'yaku Genji monogatari*, appeared, its last

his second translation he discusses the three main reasons why he found it necessary completely to re-do his first translation instead of simply revising it (as he had initially thought would be possible). First, with the perspective afforded by the passage of a decade, Tanizaki had come to feel that it would be best to adhere whenever possible somewhat more closely to the sentence structure of the original than he had often done in his first version. Second, he agreed with many of the critics of his first version that it often was too redolent of the language of the university lecture hall and "translationese," and that a new version which would hew more closely to the actual spoken language of the present day was now desirable. Third, "in the first translation," he now felt, "there had been too generous usage of *keigo*, so that sometimes the translation had even more of these expressions than the original, and this had to be judged a real defect; now the *keigo* should be if and when possible (*tekitō ni*) reduced in number." (*Shin'yaku* preface, p. 10). Tanizaki's interest in the problems of *keigo* as a factor in prose style, evidenced by many of the passages in his *Bunshō tokuhon*; his equally well documented concern with the same problem as it was involved in his life-work of rendering the Heian language of the *Genji* into modern Japanese prose; and his own stature in modern Japanese letters all converge to suggest that his different versions of the *Genji* will provide us with

---

volumes published shortly before Tanizaki's death on July 30, 1965. Most libraries, including Yale, have the first 1939-41 translation and the third 1965 translation; as I noted above, Robert H. Brower has shared with me his own copy of the 1955 *shin'yaku*, otherwise unavailable to me; and I have never seen the 1955 *aizōbon*, but Columbia has a copy of the 1956-58 *fukyūban* reprint of this version. This note is based upon inspection of those versions which have been available to me, and their prefaces, particularly the preface to the 1956-58 *fukyūban*. For other aspects of Tanizaki's work on the *Genji monogatari*, there is Niima Shin'ichi, "Tanizaki no Genji," in Kazamaki Keijirō and Yoshida Sei'ichi, eds., *Tanizaki Jun'ichirō no bungaku* (1954), pp. 321-35.

a suitable corpus for an experiment with the possibilities of internal comparison of written materials.

If, in order somewhat to simplify our initial approach to the problem, we focus our attention initially on the two extremes of this corpus, Tanizaki's first and last versions, we find a great many differences between these two texts. Many of these differences, as might be expected, are simply the result of different renderings of the original text into modern Japanese on the basis of the many advances in *Genji* scholarship during the three decades which passed between the first and last versions—passages which Tanizaki understood differently and no doubt usually better the last time around. In many other cases, his last translation differs from his first for stylistic or aesthetic reasons—again resulting in a different and what he surely felt was finally a better translation. But in a surprisingly large number of other cases, the only difference between these two versions is in the *keigo* expressions used to translate the Heian original. This is not at all unexpected, given Tanizaki's already demonstrated interest in *keigo* and particularly in the problems presented by this variety of special linguistic usage when translating Heian language into modern Japanese; but it also reassures us that there may well be value in attempting a controlled experiment based chiefly on the two extremes of this corpus, i.e., Tanizaki's first and last translations.

Such an attempt, of course, also raises many other problems both on the theoretical and on the practical level, which cannot be solved here. All of Tanizaki's *Genji* translations represent a very special and extremely specialized form of discourse—an attempt by a celebrated literary figure to render the sense and sentiment of Heian prose into the modern language of which he was in his own right a notable master. The subject matter itself is very special, involving high-ranking persons close to the Imperial line and hence calling for special *keigo* devices at almost every turn. Tanizaki's decision to keep his version increasingly close to the original may well have caused him to develop almost automatically generated one-to-one translation equivalents for many commonly recurring phrases and forms; the totally unrelated modern Japanese translation by Yosano Akiko (1878-1942), for example, is extremely free and makes no attempt to follow the original line for line and phrase for phrase, nor does its employment of *keigo* forms and patterns fall into any easily discernible relationship with parallel elements in the original. All these unsolved problems are present in what follows, but the opportunity which these materials afford for attempting to observe linguistic change in a limited corpus during three decades—a period of great change in all extra-linguistic aspects of Japanese society and culture—makes it worthwhile to risk the difficulties which these and other similar considerations impose.

The passage selected for this experiment is a short one near the beginning of *Genji monogatari* 6, the book called *Suetsumuhana* (< Heian *suwetumuFana*), Waley's "The Saffron-Flower"; in the edition of the Iwanami *Nihon koten bungaku taikei* 14 (1956) (=*Genji monogatari* 1), ed. Yamagishi Tokuhei, it occupies p. 236 line 5 through to p. 240, line 6; the original text as edited there is hereafter cited as Q. In Tanizaki's first translation, *Jun'ichirō yaku Genji monogatari* 3 (1939) it is found from p. 3 line 6 through to p. 9 line 11, hereafter cited as B. In his second translation, *Tanizaki Jun'ichirō shin'yaku Genji monogatari*, it is found from p. 210 line 8 through p. 213 line 14 of volume 1 of the *fukyūban* (on the relation of this version to the 1951-54 *shin'yaku* see note 39 above), hereafter cited as C. In his third and last translation, *Tanizaki Jun'ichirō shinshin'yaku Genji monogatari* 3 (1965) it is found from p. 4 line 8 through to page 7 line 15, hereafter cited as A. In Arthur Waley's translation, *The Tale of Genji, A Novel in Six Parts by Lady Murasaki*, 2 vol. ed. (n.d.) the passage is that beginning with "Among his old nurses there was one called Sayemon . . ." (p. 109) and concluding with ". . . and blushing made no reply" (p. 111). In Yosano Akiko's translation into modern Japanese, *Genji monogatari* 1 (1936; reprinted as *Sekai bungaku senshū* 4, 1949), it is found on p. 119 line 12 through

p. 122, line 5; the Waley and Yasano translations are cited here only for possible further reference by the reader, and no direct use is made of them in the present study.

In the attempt at a methodical inspection of this limited corpus which follows, the *Genji* passage cited above was compared in Q, A, B, and C, and all differences among A, B, and C noted. Since A and B, as explained above, represent the two extremes of the corpus selected for the experiment, attention was initially focused on how these two versions differ from each other. Differences between A and B which appeared to be solely due to different translations were ignored, as for example Q *aFare no koto*, A *o-kinodoku na koto*, B *o-kawaisō na koto* "a sad thing," or Q *sabeki yoFi*, A *dō ka shita yoi*, B *sarubeki yoi* "such a night." (The tag translations are only for further identification of the citation, and can claim neither literary merit nor always a perfect semantic "fit" with the total context of the extract.) All differences between A and B involving *keigo* were then classified under three main categories: I: cases in which A selected a *keigo* level more complicated or elevated than B; II: cases in which B selected a *keigo* level more complicated or elevated than A; III: cases presenting no clear basis for classification under either category I or category II but involving *keigo* in some way. Differences between A and B involving *keigo* amounted to a total of 48 passages. At this point, each of these passages was then re-checked in C. This re-checking revealed that as far as the usage of *keigo* is concerned, C is very close to A, so close, in fact, that in a total of 38 from among the 48 cases in which A and B differ in *keigo*, A is identical with C. In only four cases was B identical with C; in two additional cases, A, B, and C are all independent of each other; in two additional cases, B and C agree on having the allomorph *yoi* where A has the allomorph *ii*; and in two additional cases A and C are actually identical but appear to differ because a negative verb form in C is written with final *-nu*, the orthographic equivalent of the final *-n* with which the same verb ends in A.

In the summary of the data which follows, readings from C have been included only in the two cases where A, B, and C are all independent; those cases in which B agrees with C have been so marked (six in all), and otherwise the abbreviation A below is to be understood throughout as meaning A = C. The citations are numbered serially under each category; the number in parentheses at the end of each set of citations gives the order of that case in the total corpus compared.

Category I

1. Q samuraFu, B uchi e go-hōkō ni agatte iru no wa, A uchi e go-hōkō ni agatte imasu "she was in service at the palace" (2).

2. Q wakaudo nite arikeru wo, B wakanyōbō de, A waka-nyōbō na no deshita ga "she was a young person" (3).

3. Q mesitukaFi nado sitamaFu, B tokidoki o-meshitsukai ni natte irasshatta, A tokidoki o-meshi ni natte, go-yō o ōsetsuke nado shite irasshaimashita "he used her as a servant etc." (4).

4. Q yuki kayoFu, B go-sho e kayotte iru no de atta ga, A go-sho e kayotte imasu "she frequented the palace" (5).

5. Q [has no precise equivalent], B = C miko ni sakidata-rete, A miko ni sakidataretamōte "she was predeceased by the prince" (6).

6. Q katarikikoekereba, B mōshiageru to, A o-hanashi mōshi-agemasu to "when he said" (7).

7. Q toFikikitamaFu, B o-tazune ni naru, A o-tazune ni narimasu "he asked" (8).

8. Q to kataraFitamaFu, B to ōse ni naru, A to ōse ni nari-masu "he said" (14).

9. Q to iFeba, B to mōshiageru to, A to mōshiagemasu to "saying" (15).

10. Q to no tamaFeba, B to ōse ni naru no de, A to ōse ni narimasu no de "since he said" (16).

11. Q koko ni Fa kuru narikeri, B shijū kochira e ukagō de atta ga, A shijū kochira e ukagō no deshita "she used habitually to frequent this place" (18).

12. Q oFasitari, B o-koshi ni natta no de, A kimi wa o-koshi ni narimashita "he entered (the residence)" (19).

13. Q to notamaFeba, B to ōse ni naru, A to ōse ni narimasu no de "saying" (20).

14. Q sinden ni maFiritareba, B shinden no hō e itte miru to, A shinden no hō e itte mimasu to "upon going to her quarters" (21).

15. Q mesiyosuru mo, B o-toriyose ni naru no ni, A o-toriyose ni narimasu no de "even though she made to play (the musical instrument)" (27).

16. Q nani bakari Fukaki te naranedo, B o-jōzu to yū hodo no koto mo nai keredomo, A jōzu to yū hodo no koto mo arimasen keredomo "though I have no profound skill at all" (29).

17. Q sudi kotonaru mono nareba, B medetai mono da kara, A kakubetsu na mono desu kara "since (the sound of the *koto*) is something in a class apart" (30).

18. Q obosarezu, B o-kanji ni naranai, A o-kanji ni narimasen "he did not feel it" (31).

19. Q to obosedo, B to mo o-omoi ni naru ga, A to mo o-omoi ni naru no desu ga "though he thought" (34).

20. Q mimi narasase tatematurazi, B o-kikase senu hō ga yoi, A o-kikase mōsanai hō ga ii "probably should not play for him" (35).

21. Q [has no precise equivalent], B = C kikashite itadakimasu, A kikasete itadakimasu "have listen" (36).

22. Q to notamaFedo, B to ossharu no de atta ga, A to ossharu no deshita ga "he said" (38).

23. Q kaFeritamaFu, B o-demashi ni naru, A o-kaeri ni narimasu "he departed" (42).

24. Q to kikoyureba, B to mōshiageru to, A to mōshiagemasu to "when he said" (43).

25. Q to notamaFeba, B to ōse ni naru, A to ōse ni naru no deshita ga "he said" (46).

26. Q kau notamaFu wo, B yoku konna fū ni ossharu no de atta ga, A yoku konna fū ni osshaimasu no de "said this" (48).

Category II

1. Q oboitaru ga musume, B oboshimeshite irashitta hito no musume, A omotte irashitta mono no musume "the girl of whom he thought highly" (1).

2. Q kokorobaFe, B o-kokorobae, A kokorobae "her disposition" (9).

3. Q [has no precise equivalent], B hissori to shite irassaimashite, A hissori to shite irashitte "silently" (11).

4. Q kataraFiFaberu, B o-monogatari o mōshiageru no de gozaimasu, A o-aite o itashimasu "I will speak" (12).

5. Q natukasiki kataraFibito, B yoi o-aite, A ii tomodachi "a dear companion" (13).

6. Q to iFeba, B to mōshiageru to, A to iimasu to "saying" (24).

7. Q yukikaFu Fito, B tsukaete iru yō na o-hito, A deiri o suru hito "a person who frequents . . ." (25).

8. Q to te, B to ossharinagara mo, A to iitsutsu "saying" (26).

9. Q ikaga, B dono yō na o-kokoromochi de, A dono yō na kokoromochi de "how" (28).

10. Q omoFituduketemo, B kangaetsuzukerarete, A kangaetsuzukete "he kept thinking" (33).

11. Q [has no precise equivalent], B = C on-arisama, A arisama "appearance" (39).

12. Q tigiri tamaFeru kata ya aramu, B o-yakusoku nasutta tokoro de mo o-ari ni naru no ka, A o-yakusoku nasutta tokoro de mo aru no deshō ka "there must be someone whom she has promised" (41).

13. Q utiwaraFite, B o-warai ni narinagara, A warainagara "laughing" (44).

14. Q [has no precise equivalent], B o-namida ni natte irashitte, A namidatte irashitte "cried" (45).

15. Q obosite, C o-omoinasarete, B oboshimeshite irassharu no de, A omowarete "(Genji) thought" (47).

Before continuing with an inspection of the small number of cases to be found in Category III (which however contains some of the most interesting examples), we may immediately note that of the total of 48 cases turned up in the sample of text tested, Categories I and II contain a total of 41, and that 26 cases or some 65 percent of these are in I, and 15 cases or some 35 percent in II. This is quite remarkable, since it means that in a majority of the instances where Tanizaki's two translations of the *Genji* differ from each other in their use of modern *ƙeigo* equivalents for the Heian language of the original, his 1965 translation makes more complex and more elaborate use of *ƙeigo*, or at least operates on higher *ƙeigo* levels, than did his 1939 translation. The direction of drift which these data indicate, then, is clearly away from, rather than toward, simplification and simplicity of form and expression.

Category III

1. Q katachi, B, A go-kiryō "her appearance" (10).

2. Q Fimegimi no atari wo musubite, B himegimi no o-soba o o-shitai mōshite, A himegimi no on-atari ni shitashinde "she was fond of the princess' company" (17).

3. Q miidasite, C nagamete irassharu no desu, B nagame ni natte irassharu no de, A nagamete irasshaimasu "she was gazing" (23).

4. Q [has no precise equivalent], B chichigimi ga o-ide ni natte, A chichigimi ga o-ide nasarete "father has come" (32).

5. Q obositari, B o-oboe asobashite, A o-oboe ni natta no deshō "he felt" (37).

6. Q kokorogurusige ni monosi tamaFu meru wo, B = C misuborashii kurashi o asobashinagara, A misuborashii kurashi o nasarinagara "since she seems to be suffering" (40).

7. Q mada kausi mo sanagara, B mada kōshi nado mo sono mama ni shite atte, A mada himegimi wa kōshi nado mo ageta mama de "even the shutters were still open" (22).

Each of these seven cases is instructive of certain directions and tendencies of change, though a full consideration of any one of the developments which they indicate would exceed the limits of this chapter. In 1 both A and B have chosen a *keigo* equivalent for the non-*keigo* of the original; it would be easy to locate many other similar examples by further comparison of a larger corpus (there is, for example, the case of the two different translations, both with *o-*, for Q *aFare no koto*, already cited). Such a study if pursued would shift the chronological range of the investigation into an enormous time span—the entire period stretching from Heian times down to the present day—and would itself be of interest quite apart from the more limited scope of this chapter. In 2 we are presented with something rather similar, since both A and B equate forms with *o-* with the non-*keigo* form *atari* of Q, no doubt in order to bring it up to the level of *himegimi* < *Fimegimi*. Otherwise A and B differ in different ways so that rather than attempt a ranking on uncertain grounds the case has been put in III. But we should note that using equivalents with *o- / on-* for a non-*keigo* form in Q means an increase in meaning differentials as well as in net linguistic complexity over the language of the original. Case 3 is an example where all three versions differ slightly; but it is difficult to evaluate the differentials involved except to note that all three texts are constructed from the same *keigo* elements, even though they are all different. Case 4 has been put under III because it seems to afford no clear basis for ranking A and B; since the translation here (untypically) does not correspond to any single item in Q the parallel with 2 and 3 breaks down. In 5 the problem is that A and B once more present no ground for ranking; here they do not represent an increase in *keigo* level and complexity over Q; and the same is true of 6. In 7, there is no basis for ranking A and B, nor for that matter, does either involve formal *keigo* features, and hence the case might perhaps just as well have been omitted from the total data inventory. It is included here because the interpolation of *himegimi* in A, missing in B and corresponding directly to nothing in Q, shows still another variety of increase in complexity which, while otherwise ignored in this study, merits further investigation. Q is a clear and sufficient text without this element, as was B; the insertion of *himegimi* in A, no doubt for greater clarity and to facilitate understanding of the passage on the part of the reader, is (no matter how well intentioned) nevertheless a redundant feature which involves an increase in the complexity of formal expression. The same phenomenon may be observed under I above, for example, in citation 12, where A interpolates a *kimi* into the text which was not present in B and which directly corresponds to nothing in Q. It would not be difficult to collect many other examples of this same advance in complexity and redundancy of expression in A as against not only Q, which is not particularly surprising or significant, but also as against B.

Each of these three attempts at analysis of *keigo* forms in order to determine something of the overall pattern of their development in recent years turns up data which help us understand why the authors of *Keigo to keigo ishiki,* already cited, felt that their essential mission was to discover "the factors tending to make *keigo* increasingly complex (*keigo o fuku-zatsu ni shite iru gen'in*)." Increasing complexity is the only general pattern of drift which we can discern in the developments of *keigo* in the modern period, and for that matter, probably in earlier periods of Japanese history as well. It must be pointed out again that the significance, if any, of this conclusion, if true, depends entirely upon the particular variety of conceptual structuring which we prefer for the relation of language to reality—and several alternatives have been proposed above, in a very loaded fashion to be sure. The non-linguist has the privilege, which cannot be extended quite as freely to the linguist, of paying his money and taking his choice.

But if, as these data seem to indicate, the direction toward which this linguistic system is moving is one of increasing complexity, what then is the relation of this to other aspects of modernization in Japan; and indeed, is it possible to relate it to modernization at all? If we are to be bound to Weberian rationality, and if the distinguishing feature of modernization is to be the "purposeful, systematic, and sustained application of human energies to rational control of man's environment,"[40] then in this development in the linguistic system we are faced with the exact opposite of what otherwise we might expect. What evidence of change we have been able to identify and what data we have been able to isolate from admittedly sketchy and unsatisfactory materials both indicate the development of patterns of greater and greater complexity. Surely this is not purposeful or systematic (though it may very well be a sustained application of human energies); and it seems to have very little to do with the rational control of man's environment, though this last is not as distressing a conclusion as it might at first glance appear to be. After all, since we are dealing with language and only indirectly with environment, we are not actually entitled to expect that whatever change we might discern would be directly related to environmental control. Perhaps rather than control we again have here something more of the order of coordination. But in a process like this one—historical change resulting in later patterns of a greater degree of complexity than the earlier ones from which they originate—it is difficult to identify any elements either of rationality or efficiency.

Finally, if we can accept the conclusion that this linguistic system appears to be moving in the direction of greater complexity, is it possible to go a step further and speculate on how long such movement may reasonably be expected to continue? Are we to expect it to go on and on, toward greater and greater complexity, or are we to expect that other factors will intervene, perhaps shifting the direction of change, or otherwise altering its development, to result eventually in a kind of equilibrium? The work of the American anthropologist Anthony F. C. Wallace seems to indicate that the latter is the more likely possibility—to borrow the title of one of his papers on the subject, such systems appear to develop toward a point where they

---

[40] John Whitney Hall in Marius B. Jansen, ed., *Changing Japanese Attitudes toward Modernization* (Princeton, 1965), p. 21.

become "just complicated enough,"[41] at which point equilibrium sets in, at a degree of complexity which can be measured through componential analysis methods, and which he sets as 2^6.

It is clear from what has been said here that the Japanese *keigo* system is today in a state of transition and change; at the same time, the system itself is probably a transition phenomenon, in the sense that it is now half-way between what Wallace calls a "folk taxonomy" on the one hand and one of his "new [i.e., non-folk]" taxonomies on the other. A "folk taxonomy" is one that is "used by all normal members of a human society and which does not require specialized training for successful use"[42]—and certainly one important point which we may learn from the manuals of usage and their syllabi of errors is the fact that the *keigo* system in modern Japan does indeed appear to require specialized training for its effective and successful use. This puts it well along the way to becoming one of Wallace's "new" taxonomies; and the significant factor here is that in his system of analysis, these "new" taxonomies are precisely the media by which complex industrial cultures (he cites the U.S. and Japan as his two specific examples; in both cases his argument is limited to kin terminology) grow more and more complex. The "new" taxonomies characteristically include some training in "specialized literary and technical skills," through which we escape the otherwise iron-clad limits of the "2^6 Rule," that perimeter of complexity outside of which human beings appear to be virtually unable to operate. Learning to conform to the norms set up for the use of *keigo* by the manuals of style, and indeed, learning to operate within the system at all, is "specialized literary training" of the most practical and immediate sort.

Changes in linguistic systems are micro-innovations, and it is hardly to be expected that they would demonstrate visible

[41] Anthony F. C. Wallace, "On Being Just Complicated Enough," *Proceedings of the National Academy of Sciences* 47.458-64 (1961).

[42] *Ibid.*, 462.

elements of rational evaluation;[43] nor, as we have seen, do they show such elements in the case of the Japanese *keigo* system. But at the same time that the system is tending toward increasing complexity, it is confined within rigid outer limits which finally act to prevent its expanding indefinitely and infinitely:

> [The] Principle of Maximal Organization . . . asserts that an organism acts in such a way as to maximize, under existing conditions, and to the extent of its capacity, the amount of organization in the dynamic system represented in its mazeway; that is to say, it works to increase both the complexity and the orderliness of its experience.[44]

[43] Anthony F. C. Wallace, *Culture and Personality* (New York, 1961), p. 128.

[44] Anthony F. C. Wallace, "The Psychic Unity of Human Groups," in Bert Kaplan, ed., *Studying Personality Cross-culturally* (Evanston, 1961), cited in *Culture and Personality*, p. 125.

Appendix to Footnote 1

The pericope in question is §262 in the arrangement of the Sankan-bon tradition of the *Makura no sōshi* text as it appears in the edition of Ikeda Kikan and Kishigami Shinji in the Iwanami *Nihon koten bungaku taikei* (1958), XIX, 273; this corresponds to §246 in the arrangement and edition of the same Sankan-bon text tradition by Tanaka Shigetarō in the *Nihon koten zensho* (1947; 6th ed., 1956), XXIX, 344-45, and to §24-b in the edition and arrangement (essentially Kitamura Kigin's *Shunsho-shō* text) in Kaneko Motoomi, *Makura no sōshi tsūkai* (1929; 59th ed., 1955), 79. The translation above is based on the version of the passage in the Den Nōin shoji-bon text tradition as reflected in the *Shunsho-shō* and the Edo vulgates (*rufu-bon*), using the edition of that text tradition in Kurihara Takeichirō, *Makura no sōshi zenshaku* (1927), where it is §24 on p. 136; cf. André Beaujard, *Les notes de chevet de Séi Shōnagon', Dame d'honneur au Palais de Kyōto (Essai de traduction)* (Paris, 1934), p. 32. One of the important difficulties of the passage is found in the last sentence translated above, following the Den Nōin shoji-bon and *Shunsho-shō* tradition. In the Sankan-bon tradition this sentence has been badly conflated to read: "when one says to those persons who speak in such a manner, "how unseemly, how tasteless! why is your language so rude?" both those who are listening and the person spoken to laugh." There can be little doubt that the vulgate here is superior (and elsewhere even in this short passage it betrays other obvious signs of secondary conflation). The Sankan-bon conflation of the final sentence in this extract was apparently due to a scribal confusion between a cursive *kana* graph for *si* (= *kokorozasi*) and a cursive writing of *Fa* (= *mono*), with ... *Fa nameki* thus resulting from an original ... *sinameki*, and the remainder of the passage then altered and rewritten to accommodate the new (and incorrect) reading. The sentence which follows, not translated here, involves other even more involved problems in all the texts. Essentially the same pericope appears ultimately to underlie the translation in Ivan Morris, *The Pillow Book of Sei Shōnagon* (New York, 1967), 1.28, appearing as part of §27 in his arrangement of the text, beginning with the phrase in his translation "when servants fail to use honorific forms of speech in referring to their masters." But it is impossible to reconcile Morris's translation with either of the two text traditions noted above. In particular, there is nothing in any of the texts to correspond to the phrase "honorific forms of speech" in Morris's translation; for this the Edo vulgates have simply *waroku iFu ito warosi* "it is very bad to speak badly"; Kurihara's 1927 edition of this text tradition emended this reading, which is a fairly obvious case of dittography, on the basis of the general testimony of the Sankan-bon tradition, to read instead *nameku iFu ito warosi* "it is very bad to speak impolitely." The author of the original peri-cope was not concerned with any general or far-reaching breakdown in the usage of the honorific verbs but only (and as usual in the *Makura no sōshi*) with a very limited and extremely specialized vio-lation of the mores of her peer-group—in this case, the completely understandable tendency of female servants or attendants to slip into the habit of using, in reference to their own husbands, the same honorific verbs that they would habitually and correctly use for exalted male persons at court. This is the problem to which the pericope refers, and *pace* both Beaujard and Morris (*op. cit.*, 2.31, note 129), the refer-ence to *Faberu* is not irony but a factual statement of preference in linguistic usage. The textual difficulties of the passage are particularly unfortunate since they mean that only the original pericope, which now can be recovered only in part, can with any confidence be assigned to Heian time; nor are we able to determine whether that original pericope is to be assigned to the *Makura no sōshi* Urtext, i.e., the Heian nuclear text which was completed by 996, or to its primary Heian conflation (through the addition of *zuihitsu* and *nikki*-pericopes to a nuclear *uta makura* Urtext), which was completed by 1000. The resulting uncertainty in dating somewhat reduces the value of the extract for the linguist, though it remains of considerable interest for the general history of the language.

LIST OF CONTRIBUTORS

CARMEN BLACKER is Lecturer in Japanese at Cambridge University. She is the author of *The Japanese Enlightenment* (1964) and is at present engaged on a book on shamanism in Japan.

ROBERT H. BROWER, formerly of Stanford University, is Professor of Japanese Literature at the University of Michigan. He is co-author of *Japanese Court Poetry* (1961) and of *Fujiwara Teika's Superior Poems of Our Time* (1967), and has published a number of articles and translations in the field of Japanese classical poetry and poetics.

TŌRU HAGA is Associate Professor of Comparative Literature and Culture at Tokyo University and has been Visiting Research Associate at Princeton University. He is co-translator of George Sansom's *Western World and Japan* (1966) and translator of Donald Keene's *Japanese Discovery of Europe* (1968). He is the author of *Taikun no shisetsu* (1968), a book on the Tycoon's embassy to Europe, and *Meiji hyakunen no jomaku* (1969), on the Meiji centenary.

HOWARD S. HIBBETT, Professor of Japanese Literature at Harvard University, is the author of The *Floating World in Japanese Fiction* (1959), co-author (with Gen Itasaka) of *Modern Japanese: A Basic Reader* (1965), and translator of several novels by Tanizaki Jun'ichirō.

DONALD KEENE, Professor of Japanese at Columbia University, is the author of various books on Japanese literature and theater. He has translated works of both classical and modern literature, and edited the anthologies *Anthology of Japanese Literature* and *Modern Japanese Literature*. He is currently writing a history of Japanese literature.

WILLIAM P. MALM is Professor of Musicology and Director of the Japanese Music Study Group at the University of Michigan. He is the author of *Japanese Music and Musical Instruments* (1959), *Nagauta: The Heart of Kabuki Music* (1963), *Music Cultures of the Pacific, the Near East, and Asia* (1967), and articles on Japanese music.

EDWIN MCCLELLAN, Professor of Japanese Literature at the University of Chicago, is the author of *Two Japanese Novelists: Sōseki and Tōson* (1969) and translator of Natsume Sōseki's *Kokoro* (1957) and *Grass on the Wayside* (1969).

ROY ANDREW MILLER, formerly Professor of Far Eastern Languages and Director of the Institute of Far Eastern Languages at Yale University, is now Professor of Asian Languages at the University of Washington. Most of his publications have been concerned with Tibetan studies, and with Tibeto-Burman comparative linguistics; in the Japanese field he is the author of *The Japanese Language* (1967) and *Japanese and the Other Altaic Languages* (forthcoming).

MICHIO NAGAI, who was previously Professor of Sociology at Tokyo Institute of Technology, has recently become an editorial writer of the Asahi Press. He has taught at Columbia University, Hong Kong University, Stanford University, and El Colegio de Mexico. Among his books on Japanese education are *Nihon no daigaku* (1965), *Daigaku no kanōsei* (1969), and *Kindaika to kyōiku* (1969).

BENITO ORTOLANI, is Professor of Comparative Literature at Brooklyn College. He has taught at Sophia University, the University of Hawaii, and in the School of Arts at Columbia University. He is the author of *Das Kabukitheater: Kulturgeschichte der Angaenge* (1964), *The History of the Japanese Theater* (forthcoming), and of several other studies on the Japanese theater and its cultural background.

JOHN M. ROSENFIELD is Professor of Art at Harvard University, and has taught at the University of California, Los Angeles. A student primarily of Buddhist arts, he has also worked in the general history of Japanese art. He is author of *Japanese Arts of the Heian Period* (1967), co-author of *Traditions of Japanese Art* (1970), and translator of Noma Seiroku's *The Arts of Japan—Ancient and Medieval* (1965).

EDWARD SEIDENSTICKER is professor of Japanese at the University of Michigan. He is the author of *Kafū the Scribbler* and the *Japan* volume in the Life World Library and of numbers of articles on Japanese literature and culture. He has translated *The Gossamer Years* and novels by Tanizaki Jun'ichirō and Kawabata Yasunari.

DONALD H. SHIVELY, Professor of Japanese History and Literature at Harvard University, is the author of studies on the theater, law, and cultural history of the Tokugawa period. He has also written on traditional thinkers of the late nineteenth century.

EUGENE SOVIAK, formerly of the University of Chicago, is Associate Professor of Japanese History at Washington University. He is preparing studies of the early Meiji political thinker Baba Tatsui and the historian Kume Kunitake.

VALDO HUMBERT VIGLIELMO, Professor of Japanese Literature at the University of Hawaii, translated *Zen no kenkyū* (A Study of Good) by Nishida Kitarō (1960) and has written articles on modern Japanese literature and philosophy in both Japanese and English. His complete English translation of the novel *Meian* (Light and Darkness) by Natsume Sōseki was published in 1971.

Index

Abe Jirō, 337
Abosch, David, 117n, 167n
Adams, Henry, 206
Aikoku-kōtō, 62
Akaki Kakudō, 414
Akiba Tarō, 156n
Akita Ranga (*Akita Dutch Painting*), 190, 190n
Akutagawa Hiroshi, 476
Akutagawa Ryūnosuke, 377n, 422, 428-29, 431-33, 435, 437, 443, 444, 453, 467, 469n, 476
Alcock, Rutherford, 233n
Allan, James, 140-41n
Amada Guan, 388, 413, 414
"Amaririsu," 272
Amida, 591, 595
Anderson, Maxwell, 496n
Andō Kōsei, 592n
Anezaki Masaharu, 524
Anjōke no kyōdai, 430-31
Anya kōro, 427-28
Aōdō Denzen, 225, 229, 230, 236
Ara Masahito, 311n
Araragi School, 403, 407-08
Aristotle, 306, 460, 472, 538
Arnold, Edwin, 147-49, 149n, 150, 173-74
art, Edo Period, 224-25; education, 115-17; Japanese revival, 115-16; during the Sino-Japanese War, 130, 135-38, 141, 145, 161-66; schools, 115, 116, 182, 195-96, 199-200, 207, 222, 226n, 249, 253; Western style, 165-66. *See also* Bunjin-ga, *namazue*, Nihon-ga, *nishikie*, painting, *ukiyoe*
Asahi shimbun, 322, 327, 329, 332
Asai Chū, 223, 255
Asaka Society, 382
Asukai, 381
Atsumi Seitarō, 289n
Austen, Jane, 377
Ayukai Kaien, 387

Baelz, Erwin, 81, 81n, 94, 98, 98n, 118n

Bairin, Keene Plate II
Balzac, Honoré de, 306, 424, 425
banki goshinsai, 64
Bansho Shirabesho, 193-94, 225, 228n, 229, 236
Barbizon School, 218, 249, 251
Bashō, 117, 242, 309-10, 353, 353n, 395, 457
"Bashoteki ronri to shūkyōteki sekaikan," 547
"Battō-tai," 134, 284, 285-86
Beardsley, Richard K., 605n, 626n
Beaujard, André, 666-67
Bergson, Henri, 448, 458, 459, 460
Bernal, Martin, 595n
Bi no setsumei, 554-56
Bigelow, William Sturgis, 206, 208, 211, 212
Bismarck, Otto von, 84, 141
biwa, 258, 259, 271
Blacker, Carmen, 111n, 504
Blake, William, 466
Bloomfield, Leonard, 630, 637n
Boardman, E. G., 566n, 595n
Bock, Philip K., 617-18n, 627-30, 628n
Bodman, Nicholas C., 604n
Boehme, Jacob, 546
Boissonade, Émile, 97, 118n
Bōkoku no on, 382-83, 385, 388
Bokujū itteki, 405-07, 408, 409, 411, 414-15, 416, 417
Boston Museum of Fine Arts, 212, 215, 216
Botchan, 310n, 312, 325, 327
Boulger, Demetrius C., 132n
Boxer Rebellion, 162
Brannen, Noah, 590n
Brooks, Van Wyck, 206n
Brower, Robert H., 304, 401n, 402n, 413n, 601-02n, 653n
Bulwer-Lytton, Edward, 114, 354
bummei kaika ("Civilization and Enlightenment"), 34, 47, 69, 81, 100, 110
Bungakkai, 367, 367n, 368-69, 374

Bungakuron, 319-20
Bungei Kyōkai, 484-85, 487, 488, 489, 499
Bunjin-ga (Wenjen-hua), 188-89, 191-92, 210, 216n, 224, 226, 252
bunraku, 160
Bunshō tokuhon, 614-15, 651-52, 652n, 653
Burn, Robert Scott, 184, 194n, 198
Buse, J. E., 629n
Byōshō rokushaku, 410-11

Casal, U. A., 596n
Chamberlain, Basil Hall, 94, 94n, 608-09
Chateaubriand, François de, 342, 342n
Chekhov, Anton, 308, 472, 477, 489n
Chikafusa (Kitabatake), 444-45
Chikamatsu Monzaemon, 117, 144, 494
China, Japanese attitudes toward, 121-26; war with France, 122; cultural influence, 121-22; Sino-Japanese War, 121-76; music, 287-88, 293, 296; millennial religions, 566, 593, 593n, 594-95; and *keigo*, 615-17. *See also* Sino-Japanese War
Chiossone, Edoardo, 115, 187, 187n, 197-98
Chisolm, Lawrence, 204n, 251n, 253, 253n
Chitani Shichirō, 310-12
chōka, 409
Ch'ü Yüan, 182, 182n, 202-03, 208; Rosenfield Plate II
"Civilization and Enlightenment," see *bummei kaika*
Cohn, Norman, 563-64, 564n
colonialism, Western, 19
commerce, Western, 18-20
Confucianism, in education, 78, 81
conservative societies, 102-13
Council of State, see Dajōkan
court music, see *gagaku*
Craig, Albert M., 111n
criticism, literary, 419-61; Kobayashi

Hideo's definition, 421-25, 440-41; of "psychologism," 425, 428, 432, 433, 466, 467; of history and war, 441-54; of classical Japanese literature, 454-57; and Fukuda Tsuneari, 465-73. *See also* individual critics and authors
Curie, Eve, 469n

Daidō Danketsu, 99-100, 109
Daidō sōshi, 107
Dai Nihon shi, 444
Dai Nippon Fusō Shinjinkai, 568
Dajōkan (Council of State), 53-54, 86
Dante, 548
Dator, J. A., 570
Deguchi Nao, 577-79, 585
Deguchi Ōnisaburō, 579, 596
Denshinkyō, 568
De Vos, George, 310n
Disraeli, Benjamin, 114, 354
Doi Kōchi, 639-42, 639n
Doi Tadao, 616n
Doi Takeo, 310n
Doi Tatsuo, 622
Dokuen, 527
Dore, Ronald P., vii, viii
Dōshisha University, 108, 109
Dostoevsky, Fyodor, 328, 328n, 355, 356, 431-32, 435, 445-47, 458, 465, 469
Dramatic Arts, Institute of, 477, 484, 494n, 499, 499n
Du Gard, Martin, 496n
Dusenbury, Jerry K., 35n
Dutch learning, see Rangaku

Eastlake, F. Warrington, 151n, 152, 152n
Ebina Danjō, 108
Eckert, Franz, 263
economics, and the school system, 57-59
Edison, Thomas, 568
education, East and West compared, 30-31; in Meiji Japan, 35-75; French influence, 38, 48-50, 52,

54, 75; American influence, 38-39, 61, 62, 68, 76, 81, 82, 87, 101; Prussian influence, 39, 69, 73-75; and Japanese tradition, 40-41; Emperor's role, 44-47; for women, 45, 47; and art, 115. *See also Gakusei*, Education Ordinance, *Kyōgaku taishi*

Education Ordinance, 38, 39, 42, 61-76; system organization, 65-66, 68

Ekoyama Tsuneaki, 605n, 610-11

Eliade, Mircea, 566n

Eliot, George, 548

Eliot, T. S., 472, 473, 476n

Ejanaika sōdō, 593, *see also Yoi ja nai ka*

Ekawa Yogorō, 262

Emeneau, M. B., 630, 630n, 635

Emerson, Ralph Waldo, 205, 422, 459, 461

Emi Suiin, 131, 131n, 144

Engeki hyōron, 365

England, 78, 81, 82, 83, 87, 90, 104, 111, 132

Erikson, Erik H., 309n

Etō Jun, 311n, 312n

Etō Shimpei, 8

Exhibition, National Industrial, 198-99, 238-39

"Expel the Barbarians," *see jōi*

Fe, Alessandro, 249

Fenollosa, Ernest, 115-16, 118n, 191, 198, 201, 203, 204-19, 217n, 248, 250-55, 251n

Fenton, William, 260, 262, 263

Flaubert, Gustave, 355, 435, 436, 468

Florenz, Karl, 524

Fontanesi, Antonio, 115, 199-200, 229, 238, 249, 250

Foster, Stephen, 272, 275

France, 78, 81, 82; French Revolution, 20, 49; educational system, 49-51; Guizot Law, 49; Civil Code, 90; War with China, 122

Frazer, James, 472

French, Calvin, 190

Friedländer, Max J., 242n

Fujikawa Hideo, 230n

Fuji-kō, 580n

Fujioka Sakutarō, 221n, 226n, 228n, 513, 514, 539

Fujisawa Morihiko, 278n

Fujitani Toshio, 593n

Fujiwara Kamatari, 487

Fujiwara Kiyozō, 87

Fujiwara Shunzei, 460-61

Fujiwara Teika, 390, 390n, 461

Fukada Tsuneari, 463-99; life and work, 463-78; literary criticism, 465-73; cultural criticism, 477-78; concept of modernization, 478-83; interpretation of shingeki, 483-99. *See also* criticism, literary; individual works

Fukuchi Gen'ichirō, 236, 236n

Fukuchi Shigetaka, 135n

Fukumoto Nichinan, 388

Fukuoka Takachika, 87-88, 210, 210n

Fukuzawa Yukichi, 9, 40, 40n, 54, 88, 88n, 110-12, 110n, 111n, 112n, 127, 127n, 189, 210, 224, 231, 232, 232n, 244, 518, 557, 557n

Fundamental Code of Education, *see Gakusei*

Futabatei Shimei, 114, 167, 247, 303, 305, 308, 354n, 356n, 364n, 375-76, 375n, 382

Ga Noriyuki, 12

gagaku, 257, 263, 267, 268, 274, 290, 293, 294, 295

Gakusei, 36, 38, 42, 47-76, 80, 86; foreign influence, 48; system organization, 48, 52-53, 59; reaction against, 54-57; financial difficulties, 57-59; cultural difficulties, 59-61

Garasudo no naka, 312, 342-43

Gardner, Isabella Stewart, 206

Garnett, David, 472

Geijutsu to dōtoku, 556

Gendai bungaku no fuan, 428-29

Genji monogatari, 306, 460, 602n, 644, 652-60, 652-53n
"Genkon no shūkyō ni tsuite," 558-60
Genroku, 117, 378
Gen'yōsha, 119
Germany, 78, 79, 81, 84, 85, 86, 90, 97. *See also* education
Gide, André, 437
Glazer, Nathan, ix, 446n
Gō Seigen, 586n
Goethe, Johann Wolfgang von, 489n, 524, 548, 555
Gorki, Maxim, 486, 488
Goseda Hōryū, 234
Gotō Shōjirō, 8n, 99
Gray, Thomas, 250
Greater East Asian Co-Prosperity Sphere, 610-11
"Great Principles of Education," *see Kyōgaku taishi*
Green, Thomas Hill, 530-31, 548
Grundmann, Emil Otto, 251
Gundry, R. S., 133n
gunka, 275
Guthrie, Woody, 282
Gyakusetsu ni tsuite, 429

Haga Tōru, 9n, 179, 194n, 199n, 221n, 228n, 230n, 245n
Hagino Yoshiyuki, 115, 116, 382n
Hagoromo, 292
haiku (haikai), 115, 242, 306, 312, 318, 319, 381n, 384, 385, 386, 387, 389, 391, 394, 395-96, 398, 400, 418; during the Sino-Japanese War, 146-54, 155, 168
Haiyūza, 495
Hakai, 347, 348, 356n, 356-57, 361-64, 365-66, 367, 369, 370, 371, 374
Hakubakai, 166
Hall, John W., vii, viii, ix, 231n, 605n, 626n, 663n
Hamao Arata, 212
Han no hanzai, 426
happō fusagari, 571
Hara Kei, 171
Harada Jūkichi, 151-52, 159

Harada Naojirō, 247, 255
Haru, 348, 365, 368, 369-74, 378
Harunobu, 190
Hashimoto Gahō, 116, 206-07, 208, 216, 234
Hauptmann, Gerhart, 486, 488, 489n
Hawkes, David, 182n
Hawks, Francis, 260n
hayariuta, 277, 277n
Hayashi Hiromori, 263
Hayashi Motoi, 231n
Hayashi Razan, 13
Hayashi Shihei, 122, 220
Hearn, Lafcadio, 135, 135n, 146, 147n, 154n, 166, 166n, 322
Hegel, Georg Wilhelm, 205, 251-52, 521, 538, 555
Heike monogatari, 259, 409, 454
Hibbett, Howard S., ix, 304, 353-54, 354n
Higeki kigeki, 465
Higuchi Ichiyō, 126, 367n, 376n
Hijikata Teiichi, 221n
Hino Ashihei, 448, 449, 451-52
Hiraga Gennai, 190, 230, 232
Hiraga Motoyoshi, 414-17
Hiraizumi Toyohiko, 134n
Hirata Takuboku, 166-67, 167n
Hiroshige, 225
Hishida Shunsō, 204, 207, 213n, 216n
Hitler, Adolf, 449
Hitomaro, 390, 390n, 415
Hito-no-michi Kyōdan, 567, 570
Hoff, Frank, 221n
Hōjō Tokiyoshi, 510, 511, 520, 521, 522, 522n, 535, 536, 539, 553, 557
Hokusai, 192-93, 225, 229, 244
Homma Hisao, 146n
Honda Isei, 510
Honda Toshiaki, 230
Hori Ichirō, 570n, 573-74, 574n, 583, 583n, 593n
Horioka Yasuko, 208n
Hoshu Chūsei Tō, 107
Hoshu shinron, 107
Hotta Masahira, 224

Huang Tsun-hsien, 125
Hung Hsiu-chüan, 595
Huxley, Aldous, 445-46n
Hyakuchū jisshu, 394, 397
Hyakunin isshu, 60
Hymes, Dell, 605n

Ibsen, Henrik, 486, 487, 488, 489n, 494
Ichikawa Sadanji, 485, 486, 488
Ichikawa Sanki, 642n
Ichikawa Wataru, 246, 246n
Ie, 348, 361n
Ikeda Kikan, 666
Ike no Taiga, 191-92, 192n, 252
Ikuta Kengyō, 258
Illustrated London News, 132n, 162-63, 173, 233
Imakita Kōsen, 536
Imperial Rescript on Education, 36, 37, 41, 44, 45, 46, 71, 75, 77, 88, 108, 119, 214
improvement societies, *see kairyōkai*
industrialization, in the West, 17-18, 20
Inokuchi Mōtoku, 510
Inoue Enryō, 102, 104
Inoue Kaoru, 90, 91, 91n, 96, 100
Inoue Kazuo, 229n
Inoue Tetsujirō, 119, 504, 523
"I-novel," *see watakushi shōsetsu*
Inui Tadashi, 576n, 577n, 579n, 581n, 596n
Ishii Hakutei, 221n
Ishimura Kengyō, 293
Ishizaka Shōzō, 609n
Issa, 353, 353n
Itagaki Taisuke, 7, 8, 8n, 62, 97, 156
Itō Hirobumi, 7, 11, 12, 41, 64, 65, 66, 67, 69-70, 71, 72, 74, 75, 84-86, 86n, 88, 95, 100, 101, 110, 184, 199, 215, 235, 249
Itō Miyoji, 85
Itō Sachio, 398, 418
Itō Sei, ix, 128n, 473
Iwabuchi Etsutarō, 644n
Iwaki Heijirō, 292n
Iwakura Embassy, 4, 7-34, 49-50, 81,

89, 179, 199, 245; objectives, 10-11; composition, 11; itinerary, 12. *See also Tokumei zenken taishi Bei-Ō kairan jikki*
Iwakura Tomomi, 7, 10, 11, 12, 13, 84
Iwasa Jun, 51
Iwata Toyō, 495
Izawa Shūji, 265, 267, 268, 268n, 269, 270n, 277, 300
Izō Iburi, 576-77
Izumi Kyōka, 130, 167

James, Henry, 458, 471
James, William, 562
Jansen, Marius B., vii, viii, ix, 14, 14n, 91n, 98n, 663n
Japan Christian Yearbook, 570n
Japanization, 3-6; in education, 35-76; in middle Meiji, 77-119; the intellectual protest against Westernization after 1887, 100-13; as a stage in modernization, 117-19; of painting, 210-19, 250-56
Japan Weekly Mail, 96n, 110n
Jihen no atarashisa, 442
Jikaku ni okeru chokkan to hansei, 546-47
Jikōson, 585-86, 586n
Jinnō shōtōki, 444-45
"Jinshin no giwaku," 560-61
Jiukyō, 585-86
Jiyū Gekijō, 485, 499
Jiyū minken undo, 60, 62-63, 64, 65, 67, 71, 97, 114, 156, 278, 279, 525
Jiyūtō, 107
jōi, 78, 89, 100
Joos, Martin, 637n
Jorden, Eleanor, 619-20, 619n
Journal of the Envoy Extraordinary Ambassador Plenipotentiary's Travels through America and Europe, see Tokumei zenken taishi Bei-Ō kairan jikki
journalism, 6; Meiji periodicals, 103-10, 113-17 *et passim*; during the Sino-Japanese War, 130-33,

journalism (*cont.*)
168. *See also* individual authors
and periodicals
Jun'ichirō yaku Genji monogatari,
652, 652n, 653-60

kabuki, 158-60, 476, 477, 485, 486,
487, 497-98. *See also* Chikamatsu
Monzaemon
Kagawa Kageki, 381
Kaigo Tokiomi, 35n, 45, 61, 64, 69,
71
kairyōkai, 93
Kaishintō, 107
Kaizō, 423
Kakegawa Tomiko, 77
"Kakurembo," 273
Kamei Takashi, 611-12, 652n
Kamiyama Sōjin, 488
Kamo no Mabuchi, 382, 388, 390-91,
413, 414, 415, 417, 418, 456
Kamura Isota, 467
Kanagaki Robun, 375, 375n
Kaneko Motoomi, 666
Kangaeru hinto, 458
Kangakai, 116, 211, 212
Kangaku, 43-44, 51, 70
Kannagara, 108
Kannagara Gakkai, 107-08
Kanō Hōgai, 116, 206, 211, 211n,
212, 234, 255
Kan Sazan, 230
kanshi, 306
Kant, Immanuel, 464, 521, 526, 538,
547, 555
Kantō Takanori, 466
Kanzaburō, 477
Kaplan, Bert, 665n
Karasawa Tomitarō, 151n
Kashiwada, 519
Katō Daisuke, 627n
Katō Hiroyuki, 236
Katō Shūichi, 9n
Katō Yoshikiyo, 146-47
Katori Hotsuma, 248n, 398
Katsu Kaishū, 124-25
Kawabata Yasunari, 307, 422, 429-30,
466
Kawaguchi Ichirō, 496

Kawai Kiyomaru, 107
Kawakami Otojirō, 142, 156-58, 282
Kawakami Tōgai, 181-82, 184-95,
199-201, 202, 209, 211, 219, 226,
226n, 229, 235, 244; Rosenfield
Plates I ànd III; biography,
187-88, 188n, 197-99; Bunjin-ga
influence, 188-89; education in
Western art, 193-96
Kawakita Michiaki, 184n, 190n
Kawase Hideharu, 116, 211, 211n
Kawatake Shigetoshi, 159-60, 159n,
160n
Kawate Bunjirō, 583
Kawazoe Kunimoto, 356n
"Kayabemine District," 185;
Rosenfield Plate III
Kazamaki Keijirō, 653n
Keats, John, 555
Keene, Donald, ix, 5, 192n, 231n,
257n, 357n, 367n, 375n, 601n,
620, 622n
Keesing, Felix M., 629n
Keesing, Marie M., 629n
Keien School, 381, 381n
keigo, 504-05, 601-67; utilitarian
level, 606-07, 615, 617, 618, 619,
620, 632, 651 *et passim*; as a
reflection of "Japanese uniqueness,"
608-11, 614-15, 617; Chinese
influences, 615-17; Western
approaches, 617-20; binary
demarcations, 620-27; case studies,
639-65
Kido Takayoshi (Kōin), 7, 11-12,
58, 63, 64, 85
Kierkegaard, Søren, 546
Kiguchi Kohei, 150-51
Kikkawa Eiji, 296
Kikuchi Kan (Hiroshi), 422, 438-40,
448, 449, 452, 458, 460
Kikuchi Yōsai, 224, 224n, 229
Kikutaka Kengyō, 296, 297
Kimata Osamu, 383n, 399n, 401n,
408n, 409n
"Kimi ga yo," 262-65, 290
Kimura Sakae, 512
Kineya, 271n

Ki no Tsurayuki, 390, 390n, 391, 394, 417
Kishida Ginkō, 232, 234n, 235
Kishida Kunio, 495, 496
Kishigami Shinji, 666
Kishimoto Saisei, 126n
Kitabatake, see Chikafusa
"Kitaeru ashi," 276
Kitagawa, J., 569n
Kitamura Kigen, 666
Kitamura Sayo, 581, 582n
Kitamura Suehara, 292
Kitamura Tōkoku, 309, 367, 367n, 368, 369, 374, 421
Kitayama Takashi, 311n
Kitazumi Toshio, 130n
Kiyochika, see Kobayashi Kiyochika
Kiyomoto, 257
Klages, Ludwig, 311
"Kōbai," 295
Kobatake, K., 286
Kobayashi Hideo, 304, 419-61; and the "China Incident," 448-53; and the Pacific War, 453-54; postwar, 457-58; Western influences, 458-61. See also individual works
Kobayashi Kiyochika, 136, 137, 138, 162-65, 192, 192n, 236, 244; Keene Plate III
Köber, Raphael von, 523-24
Kōbō Daishi, 596n
Kōbu Bijutsu Gakkō, 115, 199-200, 249, 253
Kōda Nobu, 292
Kōda Rohan, 114, 436
Kōdōjikyō, 568n
Kōdōkai zasshi, 102
Kōdō Kyōdan, 584
Koepping, K. P., 598n
Koizumi Tōzō, 381n, 383n, 397n, 414n
Kojiki, 576, 645n
Kōjin, 310, 312, 328, 329-37, 338, 340, 353
"Kōjō no tsuki," 291
Kokan, 539
Kokinshū, 262, 306, 387, 388, 391, 392, 402, 408, 412, 415, 416

Kokka, 116, 212
Kokkyō, 70
Kokoro, 308, 328, 332-33, 337-42, 343, 346, 353, 361n, 376
Kokoro no hana, 398
Kokugaku (Japanese Learning), 43-44, 51, 106, 121, 382, 388, 413, 418
Kokugo Gakkai, 611
Kokumin no tomo, 109
kokumin shugi, 106
Kokuritsu Kokugo Kenkyūjo, 612-14, 644n
Kokuryūkai, 119
Kokusai Bunka Shinkōkai, 605n
kokyū, 267, 268, 269, 270
Kōmeitō, 590
Komiya Toyotaka, 257n, 312n, 342
Konakamura (Ikebe) Yoshikata, 382n
Konjiki yasha, 359-61
Konkōkyō, 570, 579, 583
Kon Tōkō, 625, 626n
Korea, invasion of, 7, 8, 58, 64; during the Sino-Japanese War, 126, 127, 128, 131, 133, 154; language, 170, 620
Kōsaka Masaaki, 509-10n, 512, 512n, 515, 515n, 517, 517n, 519, 519n, 520n, 521, 556n, 560, 560n
Kōshū, 539
Kotani Kimi, 583
koto, 258, 267, 268, 269, 270, 274, 293, 294, 295, 296, 297, 298
Koyama Shōtarō, 181-82, 184-89, 198, 200, 209-10, 211; Rosenfield Plate I
Koyama Yūshi, 496
"Kuang-i," Keene Plate III
Kubota Beisen, 130, 162
Kubota Mantarō, 495, 496
Kuga Katsunan, 106-07, 109-10, 388, 397
Kuki Ryūichi, 60, 208
Kumamoto Kenjirō, 184n, 185n, 187n, 196, 196n, 221n, 226n, 228n, 235n, 237n, 238n, 244n, 249n
Kume Keiichirō, 256n

Kume Kunitake, 13-14, 244-45, 245n, 246, 256n
Kune Masao, 435
Kunikida Doppo, 122n, 128-29, 129n, 309, 436
Kunisawa Shinkurō, 229, 244
Kuniyoshi, 225, 233, 244
Kurihara Takeichirō, 666-67
Kurimoto Joun, 246
Kuroda Seiki, 165-66, 202n, 222, 223, 239n, 256, 256n
Kusamakura, 312, 327
Kusumoto Kenkichi, 385n, 400n, 404n
Kutsugen, *see* Ch'ü Yüan
Kuwabara Takeo, 379, 379n
Kuwaki Gen'yoku, 524
Kyōgaku taishi, 40-41, 61-62, 69-76, 87n; summary, 69; elementary education, 71-72; revisions, 72
Kyōgoku-Reizei Court poets, 401-02, 401n, 408, 410
Kyōgoku Tamekane, 402
Kyōiku chokugo, *see* Imperial Rescript on Education

La Farge, John, 206
Lane, Richard, 184n
language, reform of, 167-72; *keigo*, 601-67
Lanman, Charles, 11n
Lanternari, Vittorio, 564, 566n, 596n
Lawrence, D. H., 466, 468, 471, 472, 473, 474
Leroux, Charles, 284
Lewin, Bruno, 605-06n, 634n
Li Hung-chang, 134, 141-42, 157-58; Keene Plate II
"Li sao," 182
literature, traditional revival, 116-17, 168; reactions to the Sino-Japanese War, 126-33, 144; impact of the Sino-Japanese War on, 154-56, 166-72; proletarian, 424, 430-31, 435, 439, 440, 465. *See also* criticism, literary; individual titles; novels; poetry; theater; *watakushi shōsetsu*
Liu Hsi, 604n

Lockwood, William W., vii, viii
Loti, Pierre, 282
Lotus Sutra, 584
Lotze, Rudolf, 523, 538

MacArthur, Douglas, 567
Machida Kashō, 258n
Maeno Ranka, 230
Mainichi Shimbun, 229n, 623, 624, 626n
Maitreya, *see* Miroku
Makiguchi Tsunesaburō, 584, 588
Makino Nobuaki, 8, 8n
Makura no sōshi, 601n, 666-67
Malm, William P., 179, 263n, 274n
Mamiya Michio, 300
"Manshū no inshō," 420, 450-51
Manyōshū, 304, 380, 388-91, 392, 402-18, 428, 434, 456, 457
mappō, 588
marebito, 592-93
Martin, Samuel E., 601n, 605n, 609n, 612n, 619, 619n, 620, 632, 636-37n, 648n
Maruyama Ōkyo, 188, 191, 191n, 212, 217n, 230
Maruyama Rinpei, 610, 623
Maruyama Sakura, 388
Marx, Karl, 424, 425
Marxism, 419, 423, 466
Marxist, 422, 432, 446, 465n, 469, 470-71, 475, 479, 481, 493, 507, 508n, 516-17, 518, 525, 529, 530
Masamune Hakuchō, 347, 421, 446, 459
Masanobu, 192
Masaoka Shiki, 115, 129-30, 171, 223, 247-48, 248n, 304, 318-19, 379-418; biography, 384-87
Mason, Luther W., 259n, 265, 267, 268, 277
Masuko Tokuzō, 262n
Mathy, Francis, 367n
Matsui Sumako, 488
Matsui Toshihiko, 129n
Matsukata Masayoshi, 525
Matsumoto Bunzaburō, 512-13, 514
Matsumoto Kōshirō, 476

Matsumura Akira, 616n
Matsuzaki Naoomi, 144-45
May, Elizabeth, 265n
Mayazumi Toshirō, 300
Mayo, M. J., 10n
McClellan, Edwin, 303, 308n, 333n, 337n, 339n, 340n, 341n, 342n, 356n, 362n
McKinnon, Richard N., ix
Meian, 329, 337, 346, 671
Meiji Constitution, 14, 44, 85, 86, 214
"Meiji setsu," 260, 261
Meiji Taishō ryūkōka-shi, 277n
Meirokusha, 33, 81, 92, 93, 101, 189. *See also* individual members
Meiroku zasshi, 109
Mekata Tanetarō, 265
Mencken, H. L., 642n
Mendelism, 338
Merton, Robert K., 618n, 629, 629n
Messing, Simon D., 605n
Meyer, Adolph E., 49n, 74n
Michikusa, 310, 310n, 312, 329, 336, 337, 342, 343-46, 348-51, 353, 361n, 376
Michio Kitahara, 294n
Migita Toshihide, 138; Keene Plate I
Miki Company, 286-89
"Mikuni no homare," 296, 297
Miller, J. Graham, 566n
Miller, Roy Andrew, 504-05, 605n, 606n, 612n, 620n
Minamoto Sanetomo, 388, 389, 390, 413, 416, 417, 454, 456-57
Minamoto Yoriie, 413
Minamoto Yoritomo, 413
Miner, Earl, 401n, 402n, 413n
Mingei, 495
Ministry of Education, 72n, 74n, 648, 648n
Minkentō, 8n
Min'yūsha, 109
Miroku, 591-93, 596, 600
Mishima Tsūyō, 255
Mishima Yukio, 347, 348, 471
Mitsukuri Rinshō, 51
"Mitsu no Keshiki," 297

Miyagawa Tōru, 520, 520n, 525n, 529
Miyagi Michio, 298
Miyaji Atsuko, 644n
Miyaji, T., 290n
Miyaji Yutaka, 644n
Miyajima Hajime, 508, 508n, 519n, 526, 526n, 529, 529n, 531n, 536, 536n, 540, 540n, 541n, 547, 547n, 560n
Miyakawa Torao, 204, 208n, 209n
Miyake Setsurei (Yūjirō), 102-04, 106, 169-70, 214
Miyake Tomonobu, 225n
Miyamoto Kenji, 423
Miyamoto Musashi, 457, 459-60
Miyao Shigeo, 255n
Miyata Noburo, 594n, 597n
Mon, 337
Mooney, James, 565n
Mori Arinori, 72, 74, 88, 93, 170, 189, 227n, 519
Mori Ōgai, 128, 128n, 171, 223, 226n, 247-48, 247n, 255, 303, 347, 376, 376n, 437, 471, 487
Mori Tetsuzan, 229
Moriguchi Tari, 221n
Morimoto Kaoru, 496
Morley, James W., vii, viii
Morris, Ivan, 471, 666-67
Morris, William, 218
Morse, Edward Sylvester, 205-06
Motoda Nagazane (Eifu), 45, 64, 69-71, 75, 87, 88
Motoori Norinaga, 224, 224n, 230, 457, 460
Motora Yūjirō, 523
Motoyama Yukihiko, 77, 97n
Mozart, Wolfgang, 453-54
Mujō to iu koto, 454
Müller, Max, 521
Murakami Shigeyoshi, 576n, 583n
Muramatsu Yuji, 593n
Muraoka Tsunetsugu, 229, 229n
Murasaki Shikibu, 306. *See also Genji monogatari*
Murray, David, 65, 66, 67, 68, 118n
Musakōji Saneatsu, 433
Musashino, 358-59

Museum of Fine Arts, Boston, 212, 215, 216
Museum, Tokyo Imperial, 103, 182, 212
music, 179, 257-300; in the mid-nineteenth century, 257-59; Western music, 259-300; church, 259-60; military, 260-65; public school, 265-77, 299-300; popular music, 277-92, 299-300; Chinese, 287-88, 293, 296; composition, 292-98. *See also* individual instruments, songs
Music School, Tokyo, 267, 269, 270, 270n, 292, 293
Mutai Risaku, 514n, 521
Mutsu Munemitsu, 92
Myōjō, 383-84, 410, 418

Nagai Kafu, 354, 356, 356n, 364n, 377n, 433, 453
Nagai Michio, 4, 44n, 72n, 74n
Nagai, Y., 286
Naganuma Myōkō, 583
Nagasaki, 13, 52, 190, 217n, 225
Nagatsuka Takashi, 398, 418
nagauta, 257, 258, 269, 289
Naikoku Kaiga Kyōshinkai, 115, 211
Nakada Norio, 616n
Nakae Chōmin, 223, 517
Nakai Sōtarō, 227n
Nakajima Rikizō, 523, 526
Nakamura Fusetsu, 129n, 385
Nakamura Ganjirō, 144-45
Nakamura Hajime, 634-35, 635n
Nakamura Mitsuo, 468
Nakamura Tokiko, 602
Nakano Shigeharu, 241, 242-43, 243n, 245n, 248n, 440
Nakauchi Chōji, 290n
Nakayama Miki, 574-77, 584-85, 587
namazue, 594
Naruse Masakatsu, 306n
Natsume Kyōko, 318, 320-21, 322, 322n, 323, 323n, 325, 325n, 343
Natsume Sōseki, 171, 172, 303-04, 305-46, 437, 471, 504, 524, 554;

influences, 305-07; individualism, 307-08, 317, 337-38, 339-40, 346; illness, 310-13, 319-29, 343; early biography, 313-17; London experiences, 321-22; and Shimazaki Tōson, 347, 348-51, 353, 354, 356, 356n, 360, 361n, 376, 376n; and Masaoka Shiki, 384-86, 397, 410. *See also* individual works
Nazarenes, 217
Needham, Joseph, 595n
Negishi Tanka Society, 214, 386, 397-98, 414
New York *Times*, 565-66n
Nichinan, 413
Nichiren, 583, 588-90
Nihon, 106-07, 109, 115, 385, 387, 388, 389, 394, 397, 398, 409
Nihon Bijutsu-in, 208, 214, 215-16
Nihon bungaku zensho, 116
Nihon dōtoku ron, 101
Nihon-ga, 202-08, 210-19
Nihongo, 469
Nihonjin, 102-03, 104, 106, 214
Nihon Kōdōkai, 102
Nihon Kokkyō Daidō Sha, 107, 109
Nihon oyobi Nihonjin, 107, 477-78
Nihon zokkyoku shū, 286; Malm Plate I
Niima Shin'ichi, 653n
Nijō, 381
Nishi, Amane, 92-93, 244
Nishida Kitarō, 503-04, 507-62; years preceding first employment, 509-32; illness, 521-22; diary, 537-43, 554, 556-58, 560; religious development, 516-17, 536-62; domestic problems, 539-43. *See also* individual titles
Nishida Shizuko, 532, 532n, 558n
nishikie, 135-38, 141, 144, 145, 152, 161-65
Nishimura Shigeki, 60, 101-02
Nishio Minoru, 467
Nishizawa Yōtarō, 465
Nisshin kōsenroku, 135n, 139n, 140n, 144n, 161n

Nisshin sensō jikki, 127n, 140n, 146n
nō, 160-61, 258, 259, 271, 292,
　453-55, 486. *See also* Zeami
"No Church" movement, 108
Nogi Maresuke, 332, 340, 429, 453
Nomura Kōishi, 265n, 267n
Norbeck, Edward, 627n
"Normanton," 97, 284, 287
Norumanton-gō chimbotsu no uta,
　284, 287
Nose Sakae, 108
novels, autobiographical, 347-78; Edo
　revival, 114-15; modern, 303-79,
　382; naturalistic, 347-49, 367-78,
　429, 434, 435-37, 446, 461, 464,
　488, 494; political, 112, 114,
　303, 354; psychological, 305-46,
　353; realistic, 114, 356, 359,
　361-64, 374; translations, 113-14,
　303. *See also* literature, individual
　titles, *watakushi shōsetsu*
Nowaki, 327, 356

Oath of Five Articles, 77
Ochiai Naobumi, 116, 382, 404
Odakane Tarō, 251n
Oda Nobunaga, 442
Odano Naotake, 230
Offner, C. B., 569n, 585n
Ofudesaki, 577, 578
Ogata Hiroyasu, 35n, 47, 48, 52, 58
Ogata Tomio, 232
Oguchi Iichi, 576n, 577n, 579n,
　581n, 583n, 596n
Ōi Kentarō, 278
Oiran-zu, 241, 243, 244; Haga
　Plate II
Okada Kazue, 644n
Okada Kōgyoku, 598n
Okada Masayoshi, 169
Okada Mokichi, 580-81, 586-87
Oka Fumoto, 398
Oka Senjin, 125n, 126n, 155n
Oka Yasuo, 129n
Okakura Kakuzō (Tenshin), 115-16,
　172, 174, 174n, 181-82, 191,
　195, 198, 200, 201-19, 203n,
　209n, 211n, 216n, 222, 253, 487
Ōkawa Shūmei, 441, 442

Ōki Takatō, 52
Ōkubo Toshiaki, 227n
Ōkubo Toshimichi, 7, 8, 11, 63, 64,
　199
Ōkuma Shigenobu, 7, 8n, 83, 100
Ōmoto, 567, 570, 577, 579, 585,
　588, 596
O'Neill, Eugene, 477, 491
Ōnin War, 592
Ōnishi Chinnen, 188
Ōno Susumu, 616n
Ontake-kō, 580n
Ōoka Shōhei, 471
Opium War, 122
"Oppekepē-bushi," 282, 283-84
"Oranda manzai," 293, 294
Origas, Jean-Jacques, 247, 247n
Orikuchi Shinobu, 592, 592n
Ortolani, Benito, 304, 463n
Osanai Kaoru, 485, 486, 487, 488,
　491, 493, 494
Ouwehand C., 592n, 594, 594n
Ozaki, Kōyō, 114, 359-61, 364, 366,
　367, 436
Ozaki Shūdō, 192n, 193n
ozashiki, 257

pacifism, 127, 450
painting, Western style, 179,
　181-256; portraiture, 181-82,
　184-204, 237; principles and
　materials, 186, 196-97, 237; Edo
　Period, 189-93; Meiji Period,
　197-219; government patronage,
　198-201; offensive against, 210-19,
　250-56; realistic, 239-49. *See also*
　art, Bunjin-ga, Nihon-ga
parties, political, *see* individual
　names
Peace Preservation Law, 100
Pearl Harbor, 449, 453
peerage system, 85-86
Peers School for Boys, 45
Peers School for Girls, 45, 101
Perry, Matthew, 260, 279, 280
"Peruri torai no uta," 279, 280
Pevsner, Nikolaus, 198n
Pike, Kenneth, 618, 619
Pirandello, Luigi, 477, 488, 491

Poe, Edgar Allan, 458
poetry, 114-15, 214, 367, 434. *See also* chōka, haiku, Kyōgoku-Reizei Court poets, *Manyōshū*, tanka
Poetry, Imperial Bureau of, 381, 381n, 397
Port Arthur, 141; Keene Plate II
Pre-Raphaelites, 217-18
Prideaux, Gary D., 637n
Privy Council (Sūmitsu-in), 86
Protagoras, 604n
Proust, Marcel, 311, 437
Pyle, Kenneth B., 110n

Ragusa, Vincenzo, 115
rakugo, 282, 384
"Rakuyō no odori," 298, 299
Rangaku, 121, 192, 231
"Rappa-bushi," 284, 288
Reiyūkai, 583
Reizei, 381
religion, millenarian, 563-600; Brazilian, 566, 596; Congolese, 566; Chinese, 566, 593, 593n, 594-95; European, 563-64; Japanese, 571-600; Melanesian, 564, 565, 565-66n, 593, 596, 599n; North American Indian, 564-65; definition of "modern messianic movements," 570-71. *See also shinkō shūkyō* (new religions), Zen
Revelations, Book of, 564, 590
Ribeiro, Rene, 566n
Rice, Elmer, 496n
Risshō Kōseikai, 583
Rogers, Minor L., 227n
Rokumeikan, 94-95, 113, 163, 215, 260
Rolland, Romain, 491
Rosenfield, John, 116n, 179, 226n
Rousseau, Jean Jacques, 218, 312, 342
Ruskin, John, 218
Russo-Japanese War, 138, 143, 162, 284, 292, 309, 562
Ryan, Marleigh Grayer, 354n
Ryūchi-kai, 211, 212, 251
ryūkōka, 277, 277n

Saigō Takamori, 7, 8, 8n, 63, 64, 83
"Saigyō," 454, 455-56
Saikaku, 114, 117, 353
Sainte-Beuve, Charles, 420, 458
Saionji Kimmochi, 170, 171
Saitō Mokichi, 248n, 393, 407-408, 418
Sakanishi Shio, 469
Sake, 239-40, 243, 244, 250, 255; Haga Plate I
Saki Akio, 585n, 597n
Sakuma Yoshisaburō, 510
Samazama naru ishō, 423-25, 434
Sanetō Keishū, 125n, 139
"Sanetomo," 454, 456-57
Sanjō Sanetomi, 10, 10n, 66, 84, 184
Sano Tsunetami, 210, 210n
Sano Zenzaemon, 594
Sansom, G. B., 82n, 95n, 112n, 113n, 192n, 244, 244n, 246, 252n
Santeuil, Jean, 311n
Sapir, Edward, 644n
Sapporo Agricultural School, 104, 108
Sartre, J. P., 472
Sasaki Nobutsuna, 153-54, 398
Sasaki Seiichi, 221n, 239n
Sasaki Takamori, 11
Satake Shozan, 230
Satō Haruo, 377n
Satomi Ton, 430-31, 496
Satsuma Rebellion, 58, 63, 64, 83, 138, 199, 250
Sawamura Sentarō, 226n, 234n
Sazawa Tarō, 52
Schiffer, W., 569n
Schopenhauer, Arthur, 523, 538
Scott, Walter, 309
Security Treaty, 478
Seichō-no-Ie, 567, 584
Seidensticker, Edward, 257n, 304, 356n, 367n, 601
Seikōkai, 624
Seki Akiko, 277
seikyō bunri, 70
seikyō itchi, 41, 70
Seikyōsha, 102, 214
Sei Shōnagon, 353, 601, 616, 666-67

Sekai Mahikari Bummei Kyōdan,
    598n
Sekai Meshiakyō, 580, 586-87, 587n,
    599
Seki Akiko, 277
Sekiguchi Kai, 510
Senda Koreya, 494, 495
Sensō ni tsuite, 442-43, 449-50
"Senten chishiki no umu o ronzu,"
    547
Setsumon, 535-36, 539, 553, 557,
    557n
Shakespeare, William, 459, 466, 467,
    472, 473, 475, 476, 477, 484n,
    485, 486, 488, 489n, 491, 492,
    548, 555
shakuhachi, 258, 268, 271, 274
shamisen, 257, 267, 268, 269, 279,
    282, 290, 293
shasei, 380, 385, 386, 401, 410, 418
Shaw, George Bernard, 489n
Shiba Kōkan, 189-91, 225, 227-32
Shibata Takeshi, 639-42, 639n, 642n
Shiga Naoya, 425-28, 430, 438,
    439, 441, 448, 452
Shiga Shigetaka, 102, 104, 214-15
Shih chi, 444
Shih, Vincent, 593n
Shijō School, 188, 217n, 252
Shimamura Hōgetsu, 203, 488
Shimazaki Tōson, 117, 117n, 137,
    137n, 246, 303, 309, 347-78, 385
Shimbun shūsei Meiji hennen shi,
    144n, 153n, 170n, 173n
Shimomura Eiji, 210n, 211n
Shimomura Kanzan, 207
Shimomura Toratarō, 507n, 520n,
    521, 521n, 531
Shimooka Renjō, 236
Shimpa, 156-60, 282
Shinagawa, 525, 528
Shinchō, 467
shingeki, see Fukuda Tsuneari,
    theater, Tsukijiza
shinkō shūkyō (new religions),
    567-600; definition, 567-70;
    messianic characteristics, 571-600.
    See also individual sects, religions
Shinsei, 348, 351-53

Shinshisha, 383-84
Shinshū Sect, 54
Shintai shishō, 114, 379n, 380,
    380-81n
Shiobara Shōnosuke, 315, 316
Shiota Ryōhei, 603
Shiozaki Yoshio, 310n
Shirakami Genjirō, 145-51
Shiryō Hensanjo, 117
shishōsetsu, see watakushi shōsetsu
Shishōsetsu ron, 434, 435
Shitsuki Tadao, 230
Shively, Donald H., vii, viii, ix, 5,
    87n, 88n, 101n, 215n, 271n
Shizugaki pattern, 295
Shōgaku shokashi shōden, 263, 268
Shōheikō, 13
"Shūkyō hōjinrei," 567, 567-68n
Sibylline Oracles, 564
Sino-Japanese War, 5, 119, 121-76,
    214, 382, 386, 413, 527, 529,
    577; outbreak and reaction,
    126-33; creation of hostility
    against China, 133-43; Japanese
    heroes, 143-54; literary and artistic
    importance, 154-72; foreign
    reactions, 172-75
Smith, Adam, 59
Smith, Henry D., 104n
Soeda Tomomichi, 133n, 152n
Soejima Taneomi, 8n
Sōka Gakkai, 277, 569, 570n, 572,
    584, 588-90, 589n, 599
songs, war, 133-35, 142-43, 152,
    153-54, 157, 166. See also music
Sonobe Saburō, 284n
Soviak, Eugene, 4, 199n, 245n
Spectator, 132n, 174n
Spencer, Herbert, 94, 94n, 104, 205
Stanislavsky, 491
Starr, Frederick, 568
Stein, Lorenz von, 12, 73
Strindberg, August, 489n, 494
Suehiro Tetchō, 112-13, 355n
Sugawara no Michizane, 203
Sugita Gempaku, 230, 231
Sugiura Jūgō, 102, 104-05, 106
Sugiura Mimpei, 356n
"Sutoraiki-bushi," 279, 281-82

Suzuki Daisetsu, 513, 514, 526-27, 536, 546, 554
Suzuki Jūzō, 229n
"Suzuki method," 276n
Suzuki Teruo, 295, 295n

Tachihara Kyōsho, 229
Tagore, Rabindranath, 214, 217
Taguchi Ukichi, 9
Tahara Yoshiko, 644-45n
"Taima," 453-55
T'ai P'ing, 594-95
Taiping Rebellion, 566, 595
Taiwan, 58
Takada Tamotsu, 489
Takagi Hiroo, 573, 573n, 583n
Takagi Taku, 466
Takahama Kyoshi, 129n
Takahashi Yoshio, 94
Takahashi Yoshitaka, 464, 466
Takahashi Yuichi, 187, 193, 194, 195, 196, 198, 200, 211, 221-56; Haga Plates I and II; early years, 223-27; encounter with Shiba Kōkan, 227-32. *See also* individual works
Takasaki Masakaze, 381n
Takase Hiroi, 588n, 590n
Takashina Shūji, 222n, 239n
Takayama Chogyū, 119, 126-27, 155
Takayama Rinjirō, 524
Takemitsu Tōru, 300
Takeuchi Minoru, 125n, 126n
Takeuchi Yoshitomo, 516, 516n, 517, 517n, 522n, 529
Takeyama Michio, 221n
Taki Rentarō, 291, 292
Takumi Hideo, 184n, 209n, 221n
Tamura Akiko, 495
Tanabe Hisao, 277n, 295n
Tanabe Ryūji, 524, 525
Tanaka Chikao, 496
Tanaka Fujimaro, 11, 12, 50, 51, 65, 66, 67
Tanaka Shigetarō, 666
Tange Kenzō, 582
Tani Bunchō, 188, 192, 224, 229
Tani Kanjō, 45, 97, 106
Taniguchi, Masaharu, 584

Tanizaki Jun'ichirō, 137, 137n, 347, 348, 434, 435, 602n, 614-15, 623, 625, 625-26n, 644n, 651-60, 652-53n
Tanizaki Jun'ichirō shinshin'yaku Genji monogatari, 652, 652-53n, 653-60
Tanizaki Jun'ichirō shin'yaku Genji monogatari, 602n, 644n, 652, 652-53n, 653-60
tanka, 105, 115, 247-48, 379-419, 507
Tanuma Okitomo, 594
Tanuma Okitsugu, 230, 231
Tayama Katai, 347, 435-36
Tayasu Munetake, 413
Tekukin dokukeiko, 290; Malm Plate II
Tenkai Gakusha, 251, 255
Tenkairō, 238
Tenrikyō, 570, 574, 576n, 577, 584-85, 587-88, 599
Tenshō Kōtai Jingukyō, 581-82, 582n, 599
terakoya, 60, 68
Terashima Munenori, 89-90
theater, during the Sino-Japanese War, 142, 144-45, 153, 154, 156-61; shingeki, 203, 463 *et passim*, 463n, 476, 477, 479; shingeki periodized by Fukuda, 483-99. *See also* bunraku, kabuki, nō
Thomsen, Harry, 569n
Ting Ju-ch'ang, 138; Keene Plate I
Ting-yüan, 122-25
Toda Jōsei, 589n
Tōdō Akiyasu, 616n, 617n
Togashi Junji, 633n, 634n, 648n
Togashi Yasushi, 292n
Toita Yasuji, 484
Tōkai Sanshi (Shiba Shirō), 112, 335n, 375
Tokio Times, 82n
Tokuda Kotomi, 532, 540-43
Tokuda Shūsei, 347
Tokumei zenken taishi Bei-Ō kairan jikki, 8-9, 12-13, 14-34; basic theme, 14; national studies, 15-17;

industry, 17-18; commerce, 18-20; "social technology," 20-21; management and labor, 22; natural resources, 22-24; tradition, 24-27; Eastern vs. Western world views, 27-29; religion, 28-30; education, 30-31; international relations, 31-32. *See also* Iwakura Embassy

Tokutomi Roka, 130

Tokutomi Sohō Iichirō, 87, 109-10, 518, 544, 544n

Tokyo Bijutsu Gakkō, 116, 182, 195, 196, 207. *See also* Tokyo Geijutsu Daigaku

Tokyo Geijutsu Daigaku, 116, 222, 226n. *See also* Tokyo Bijutsu Gakkō

Tokyo Imperial University, 319, 322, 384, 385, 423, 465, 466, 522-24, 526, 527, 530, 536, 562

Tokyo Shūshin Gakusha, 102

Tolstoy, Leo, 435, 446, 459

Tomoda Kyōsuke, 495-96

Toon-kai, 271n

Torio Koyata, 107

Tōsei shosei katagi, 357-58

Toyama Masakazu (Shōichi), 91-92, 122-24, 134-35, 135n, 149-50, 169, 170, 381n

Toyonobu, 192

Toyota Saburō, 466

Toyotomi Hideyoshi, 442

Tōzai namboku, 383

treaty revision, *see* unequal treaties

Tsubouchi Shōyō, 114, 126, 168n, 246-47, 357-58, 359, 364, 367, 382, 485, 486, 487, 488, 489, 491

Tsuchihashi Yutaka, 645n

Tsuchiya Tadao, 35n, 48, 49, 52, 53, 53n, 55, 56n, 59, 67, 72, 72n, 73

Tsuda Seifū, 337

Tsuda Sōkichi, 230n, 238n

Tsuji Zennosuke, 95n

Tsukijiza, 465, 465n, 490-94, 495, 496

Tsunashima Ryōsen, 562

"Tsurezuregusa," 454

Tsurumi Shunsuke, 125n

Tsuruoka Shizuo, 592n

Tu Fu, 557n

Uchida Masao, 51, 234

Uchimura Kanzō, 108-09, 127-28, 171, 172

Uchimura Naoya, 496

Ueda Akinari, 230

Ueda Kisaburō, see Deguchi Ōnisaburō

Ueda Yayoi, 532, 532n, 540-43, 558n

Ueyama Shōsaburō, 510, 512, 534, 534n, 545-46, 545n

Ueyama Shumpei, 517, 517n

ukiyoe, 161-65, 191, 192-93, 217n, 224, 225, 236, 241, 242, 244

Umezawa Waken, 201n

unequal treaties, 7, 11, 89-100, 118

Uno Kōji, 377n, 495

Usui Yoshimi, 387n

utagoe, 277, 277n

Utamaro, 192

Utayomi ni atauru sho, 389-93, 395, 397, 400-01, 414

Uyeno Naoteru, 184n

van Straelen, H., 569n, 585n

Vienna, International Exhibition of, 12, 210n

Viglielmo, Valdo H., 503, 507n, 547n

Wagahai wa neko de aru, 312, 324, 325, 327

Wagatsuma, Hiroshi, 310n

waka, *see* tanka

Wakai, 427

Wakamori Tarō, 593n

Wakanashū, 368-69, 385

Waley, Arthur, 190n, 306n, 655-56

Wallace, Anthony F. C., 663-65, 664n, 665n

Wang T'ao, 125

Ward, Robert E., vii, viii, ix

Waseda Bungaku, 131n, 134n, 136, 136n, 143n, 154, 155n, 156, 160n, 166, 169n, 170n, 172n, 485

Washburn, Stanley, 429, 432-33, 443, 453
Watakushi no jinseikan, 460
Watakushi no kojinshugi, 308-09, 320, 342
watakushi shōsetsu, 307, 312, 343, 347, 348-49, 354, 356, 365-78, 377n, 425, 434, 435, 436-37, 438, 439, 453, 464, 467, 468. *See also* individual authors, titles
Watanabe Ikujirō, 84n, 92n, 93n, 94n, 103n, 105n, 107n, 108n
Watanabe Kazan, 192, 192n, 224-25, 232, 237
Weber, Max, 662
Wedekind, Frank, 486, 488
Wei-hai-wei, 138; Keene Plate I
Weld, Charles G., 206
West, attitudes toward, 14-16, 32-34
Westernization, xiv, 3-6, 32-33; in Japanese education, 35-76; in Middle Meiji, 77-119; in the seventies, 80-84; and treaty revision, 89-100; and the arts, 113-17
Whorf, Benjamin, 618
Wilde, Oscar, 458, 473, 476n, 489n
Williams, F. E., 566n
Wirgman, Charles, 162-63, 195-96, 200, 229, 232-33, 233n, 235n, 237
women, in education, 45, 47; social relations with, 92; Kōdōkai auxiliary, 102
Wordsworth, William, 436
Worsley, Peter, 566n
Wright, Arthur, 593n, 601n

Yachihoko-no-mikoto, 645n
Yakamochi, 461
Yamabe Akahito, 390, 390n
yamabushi, 575
Yamada Akiyoshi, 11
Yamada Bimyō, 114, 358-59, 367, 375-76
Yamada Kengyō, 258
Yamada Koscak (Kōsaku), 292
Yamada Munemutsu, 516-17, 529
Yamada Yoshiaki, 151n, 152, 152n
Yamada Yoshio, 607-09

Yamagata Aritomo, 88, 95, 134, 171, 185
Yamagishi Tokuhei, 655
Yamagiwa, Joseph K., 605n, 611, 635n
Yamaguchi Naoyoshi, 11
Yamamoto Annosuke, 549
"Yamamoto Annosuke-kun no 'Shūkyō to risei' to iu ronbun o yomite shokan o nobu," 549-53
Yamamoto Ryōkichi, 513, 514, 515, 518, 519, 520, 524, 526, 527, 528, 529, 530, 531, 532, 533, 534, 536, 545, 553, 553n, 554
Yamaoka Tetsutarō, 107
Yamauchi Yōdō, 236
Yamazaki Shoichi, 464
Yanagi Genkichi, 224n
Yanagita Kunio, 592, 597n
Yasuda Rōzan, 189
Yi In-jik, 133n
Yoakemae, 348, 361n
Yoi ja naika, 278. *See also Ejanaika sōdō*
"yoking" (Zeugma), 401, 402
Yokoi Tadanao, 142-43
Yokomitsu Riichi, 466
Yokoyama Matsusaburō, 229
Yokoyama Taikan, 182, 195, 202-04, 207, 213, 216, 256; Rosenfield Plate II
yonaoshigami, 594
Yosa Buson, 192, 230, 242, 252, 385
Yosano Akiko, 384, 410, 655-56
Yosano Tekkan (Hiroshi), 127, 382-84, 385, 387, 388, 389
Yoshida Kumaji, 53n
Yoshida Rokurō, 311n
Yoshida Seiichi, 357n, 653n
Yoshida Sumio, 616n
Yoshida Susugu, 163n, 164n, 165, 165n, 192n
Yoshikawa Kōjirō, 171n
Yoshizawa Chū (Tadashi), 207n, 225n
Yoshizumi, 271n
"Yūkan naru suihei," 265, 266

Zeami, 454-55

Zen, 503-04, 514, 526-27, 535-36, 538-39, 540, 543, 546, 548, 553, 554, 557, 560, 562

Zen no kenkyū, 507-08, 509, 513, 515, 516, 523, 531, 532, 534, 537, 545, 546, 547, 548, 550, 551, 558, 560, 561, 562

Zola, Émile, 355, 436, 458